The Relay Race of Virtue

SUNY series in Ancient Greek Philosophy

Anthony Preus, editor

The Relay Race of Virtue
Plato's Debts to Xenophon

William H. F. Altman

SUNY PRESS

Published by State University of New York Press, Albany

© 2022 State University of New York

All rights reserved

Printed in the United States of America

No part of this book may be used or reproduced in any manner whatsoever without written permission. No part of this book may be stored in a retrieval system or transmitted in any form or by any means including electronic, electrostatic, magnetic tape, mechanical, photocopying, recording, or otherwise without the prior permission in writing of the publisher.

For information, contact State University of New York Press, Albany, NY
www.sunypress.edu

Library of Congress Cataloging-in-Publication Data

Name: Altman, William H. F., author.
Title: The relay race of virtue : Plato's debts to Xenophon / William H. F. Altman.
Description: Albany : State University of New York Press, [2022] | Series: SUNY series in Ancient Greek Philosophy | Includes bibliographical references and index.
Identifiers: ISBN 9781438490915 (hardcover : alk. paper) | ISBN 9781438490939 (ebook) | ISBN 9781438490922 (pbk. : alk. paper)
Further information is available at the Library of Congress.

10 9 8 7 6 5 4 3 2 1

Socrates was confident that those of his companions who adopted his principles of conduct would throughout life be good friends to him and to one another.

—Xenophon, *Memorabilia* 1.2.8
Translation by E. C. Marchant (1864–1960)

In memoriam
Leslie Victoria Altman
(1945–2020)

Contents

Preface: How Xenophon led Chion of Heraclea to the Academy   xi

Introduction: Standing on the Shoulders of Giants   1

Chapter 1   Xenophon in Plato's Dialogues   7

Chapter 2   Xenophon's Debts to Plato   67

Chapter 3   Ordering Xenophon's Writings   131

Chapter 4   Plato's Debts to Xenophon   195

Chapter 5   A Socratic Relay Race   255

Notes   295

Bibliography   341

Index   357

Preface

How Xenophon led Chion of Heraclea to the Academy

At a 2014 conference in Israel on "Plato and Xenophon: Comparative Studies," I read a paper that contained this book's nucleus.[1] Immediately afterward, Katarzyna Jażdżewska asked me in the friendliest way if I was familiar with Chion of Heraclea. I confessed ignorance, and after remarking that my approach had reminded her of this text, Kasia was kind enough to send me Ingmar Düring's edition of these apocryphal but nevertheless ancient letters a few days later. If I were given the opportunity to manufacture apparently ancient evidence to support my own views about the relationship between Xenophon and Plato—and much else[2]—I could never have imagined anything that does so more effectively, and I am deeply grateful to Kasia as a result. The simplest point must be emphasized from the start: Plato can be indebted to Xenophon only if Xenophon is in some sense prior to Plato, and it is ancient testimony about Xenophon's *pedagogical* priority that *Chion of Heraclea* provides.

In the words of Patricia Rosenmeyer, *Chion of Heraclea* is "our only surviving example of the ancient epistolary novel."[3] At the center of its "single unified story" is Chion himself, a student of Plato's who leaves the Academy and returns to his native Heraclea in order to liberate it from tyranny, and who dies in his failed attempt to do so. This act of "tyrant-killing [τυραννοκτονία]"[4] is historical: Chion of Heraclea *did* kill the tyrant Clearchus in around 352 BC, when Plato was in his seventies and Xenophon was already dead.[5] Naturally, nobody believes that those we have are his actual letters—they are clearly a unified and innovative work of art written hundreds of years later—but no consensus has been reached even as regards the century of their composition, let alone the identity of their author.⁶ In any case, Xenophon enters the epistolary narrative before Chion reaches Athens; indeed, the literary purpose of his entrance is to show that the youth may never have reached the Academy at all without the heroic example of "Xenophon the companion of Socrates [ὁ Σωκράτους γνώριμος]."⁷ It is Chion's admiration for Xenophon that overcomes his initial reluctance to devote himself to philosophy, as his father wants him to do. This fictional encounter illustrates "Xenophon's pedagogical priority."

Given its context in the novel as a whole, the third letter—from Chion to his father—must be counted as a narrative masterpiece, skillfully and creatively mixing the historical Xenophon's actions as described in *Anabasis* with a fictional incident in Byzantium,⁸ where Chion sees him for the first time rallying his dispirited soldiers:

> While this was going on and the Greeks were in disorder, I saw a man wearing long hair, a person of beautiful and mild aspect, striding in their midst and stilling their passions. That was Xenophon.⁹

Beautiful in appearance, Xenophon is also brave, and Chion's narrative demonstrates its author's familiarity with both *Anabasis* and *Cyropaedia*.¹⁰ Next comes a Cicero-inspired tribute to Xenophon's eloquence,¹¹ captured not by his words—for Chion cannot hear them—but by the effect or end (τὸ τέλος) they have on his auditors: "And as in this thing at least they feared to disobey him, Xenophon—having taken his stand in their midst [εἰς μέσον]—was setting forth wondrous words [θαυμαστοὶ λόγοι] as the result [τὸ τέλος] of them made clear, for they were not distinctly audible to us."¹²

It is a nice touch: the man of action is also a man of words.¹³ But it is the actions of others that constitute the proof: his words speak more eloquently as a result. "This sight was a demonstration [ἐπιδείξις] of Xenophon's soul [ψυχή]; also how he was able both to think clearly [φρονεῖν] and to speak [λέγειν]."¹⁴ It is therefore the invisible content of Xenophon's soul¹⁵—rendered visible by his effect on others, and that includes Chion himself—that is not only expressed in his inaudible words but more importantly in the kind of man he is.¹⁶

The author of Chion's letters probably expected them to be a similar kind of ἐπιδείξις for us, and the encounter with Xenophon therefore introduces the novel's philosophical theme. Until Chion, the future tyrant-killer and would-be liberator, actually sees a philosopher in action, he had been justifiably worried that philosophy would divorce tranquil contemplation from heroic deeds.[17] Xenophon's inaudible words not only inspire his soldiers to fight some Thracians but persuade Chion to study with Plato:

"I introduced myself to him [sc. Xenophon], and he remembered your friendship with Socrates and encouraged me to study philosophy and, for the rest, did not talk at all like a soldier but like a very educated man."[18] As a result, Xenophon is responsible for the youngster's change of mind, and he therefore tells his father: "Know then that I am now much more eager to sail on to Athens as a philosopher."[19] Although expressed in fictional terms, this third letter nicely captures what I regard as an important and ancient response to Plato's debts to Xenophon. It also suggests a modern response.

Thanks primarily to the work of Louis-André Dorion, the study of Xenophon has recently emerged from the shadow of "the Socratic Question," that is, the question of which of the two Socratics preserved a more accurate portrait of Socrates. This has allowed us to see Xenophon more clearly, and on his own terms. Although this book's purpose is to illustrate the back-and-forth nature of his relationship with Plato, it follows *The Letters of Chion* on a crucial point: as the scholars of tomorrow embark on the great adventure that is the study of Ancient Philosophy, they can once again come to Plato and Aristotle through Xenophon. Xenophon's Greek is famously sweet and instructive; his writing delights both on the surface and at a deeper level. Although he has suffered from neglect, he is currently the darling of the Straussians. Most importantly, at a time when our civic fabric is fraying, Chion's dissatisfaction with armchair philosophy should resonate, and the student who brings to Plato's dialogues a respect for Xenophon's virtues will find in them something very different from what earlier generations have found in them. This book offers an alternative to a modern conception of the relationship between Plato and Xenophon that has become so dominant that those who were brought up under its influence can perhaps no longer follow in Chion's footsteps. But for those who can, *The Letters of Chion* may conveniently serve as much the same kind of preface to this book that Xenophon's writings so often do to Plato's.[20]

Introduction

Standing on the Shoulders of Giants

Classicists might regard Aristophanes as having preserved a more lifelike picture of Athens as she was during the Peloponnesian War than Plato did but there's an important difference between them that has nothing to do with the quarrel between philosophy and poetry. Aristophanes' comedies belong to the moment for which he wrote them, and were literally intended to be prizewinners for the day. Plato managed to capture the reality of Athena's πόλις so well that he makes it easy to forget that by the time he wrote his dialogues, the Athens of his youth was only a distant memory, and he would open his Academy at around the time when the violet-crowned city, for the sake of preserving the rump of her former empire, would bargain away the freedom of the Ionian Greeks of Asia to the Persians, thereby abandoning the cause for which she had fought at Marathon. Apart from the glaring anachronism in *Menexenus*, you'd never realize that it was to this terrible moment to which his dialogues belong, and without Xenophon's *Hellenica*, we'd know very little about the King's Peace of 387.

Plato's achievement required him to stand on the shoulders of giants. By this I mean not only that he couldn't have achieved greatness without the example of Homer;[21] rather, he depended so heavily on his predecessors that he needed their works to survive along with his, for his could not be understood without theirs. To take Aristophanes, for example, it is not just that the poet himself appears in *Symposium* or that *Clouds* plays a prominent role in *Apology of Socrates*: there are at least three passages in Plato's *Republic*, none of which mention Aristophanes by name, that require the reader's familiarity with *Frogs*, *Congresswomen*, and *Knights* if they are to be appreciated. In fact, Plato's relationship with the Greek literature available in his day creates *the single most important question* that must be answered by anyone who sets about interpreting his dialogues in a serious way, and that means anyone who attempts to do what the myriad mysteries in Plato's dialogues will require his readers to do until the end of time.

The question is: Was Plato writing for his contemporaries, as we can be sure Aristophanes did, or was he creating what Thucydides called a κτῆμα εἰς ἀεί when he wrote (*History* 1.22.4): "Perhaps for some listeners, this non-mythic account of events will seem unpleasant. It is enough for me if it is judged to be useful, for such things—or very similar ones—will come to be again. I have not written this book to be a prizewinner for the day but as a possession into eternity." Plato never tells us that he too intended his dialogues to be a κτῆμα εἰς ἀεί, and it has naturally been doubted that he intended them to be, and that not only by those who regard discussions of an author's intentions with suspicion or contempt. But as deadly to any great author as is the rejection of "authorial intent," the view that Plato was writing only for a contemporary audience is particularly deadly for him, and that precisely because of the point with which I began: Plato was writing about a city whose past had already been recorded by three great historians.

Thucydides the son of Olorus is clearly by far and away the greatest of these. Unlike the case with Aristophanes, it is not a question of whether a passage or two cannot be fully appreciated without him: there are entire dialogues, *Laches* and *Symposium* prominent among them, that are unintelligible without the reader's knowledge of the events, speeches, and people he described. Any reader can appreciate the image of the rolling human ancestors, cleft in twain by Zeus, in Aristophanes' speech at Agathon's victory party. But any reader who is not aware that Plato set his *Symposium* on the eve of the departure of the Sicilian Expedition, that the drunkenness of Alcibiades was going to play just as important a role in the aftermath of its departure as he was in causing it to depart, and that the result of it all would be a catastrophe—and indeed the greatest of Attic Tragedies, played out in the Great Harbor of Syracuse—any reader unaware of this will be in no position to understand Socrates' claim at the end of the dialogue that a poet who could create a comedy could write a tragedy as well, let alone see that its truth is the key to interpreting it.

It is more economical to introduce "the shoulders of giants" with a humbler example. In *Laches*, a dialogue between Socrates and two famous generals, Plato illuminated his dependence on Thucydides. To begin with, it is Thucydides' *History* that made Laches and Nicias "two famous generals." But the dependence goes deeper, as when Laches makes the following reply to Socrates:

> *Socrates*: But a man enduring in war, and willing to fight, calculating reasonably, knowing, on the one hand, that others will come to his aid, and, on the other, that he is fighting against fewer and feebler men than those with whom he is, and further that he holds stronger positions [χωρία κρείττω]; would you then say that this man, enduring with this reasoning and preparation, would be braver than the one in the opposing army who is willing both to remain and to endure?
> *Laches*: Rather the one in the opposite position, as it seems to me, Socrates.[22]

Although one must also know in advance that it is "holding the high ground" that creates what Socrates calls χωρία κρείττω,[23] it is only the reader who encounters this passage with Thucydides in mind who is in a strong position to appreciate the irony of Laches' noble answer. It is because of Thucydides that we know that Laches, whose army was larger, and was being daily augmented by the arrival of allied troops, himself led his army down from the high ground before it was routed at Mantinea, where he was killed: "The generals, half-stunned for the moment, afterwards led them down from the hill [ἀπὸ τοῦ λόφου], and went forward and encamped in the plain, with the intention of attacking the enemy."[24] Since every reader of Thucydides knows that Laches made a strategic blunder by coming down off of that ridge, Laches' response to Socrates' question must be examined in that light.[25]

Nicias, the other famous general, fares no better when he reaches the intersection of Plato and Thucydides. Nicias considerably understates the case by saying that it is only one's past and present that Socrates will test (*La.* 187e10–188a2): like Laches, he will also be measured against a future that he cannot see. As many scholars have noted,[26] the conversation in *Laches* unfolds in the shadow of Nicias' disastrous overreliance on the soothsayers in Syracuse (cf. Thucydides 7.50.4, and *La.* 195e3–196d6). Immortalized by Thucydides, Nicias repeatedly shows himself to be useful to Plato, especially after Alcibiades has spoken his last word in *Symposium*, and no matter how ineptly he may have handled the army in Sicily, it would not have been there at all if it were not for his young and power-drunk opponent.

Although the relationship between Plato and Xenophon is the subject of this book, it begins with Thucydides in order to make a larger point. Although his value to Plato—like his status as a giant—has been vastly underestimated, Xenophon is by no means the only author on whose shoulders Plato stood. There are many others who deserve this kind of recognition but whose contributions to Plato's achievement will inevitably recede into the background as this book progresses. Because Xenophon, among other things, wrote histories, Thucydides is particularly useful for illuminating one of the ways in which Plato depended on both. But Xenophon was also a Socratic and an educator, and there were other Socratics as well, and in Isocrates, there was another great schoolteacher. The focus on Xenophon should not obscure the extent to which Plato was also in dialogue with other contemporary authors such as Isocrates, Aeschines Socraticus, or Antisthenes. What makes Xenophon a good place to begin recovering such dialogues is that all his Socratic writings survive; what makes Thucydides a good place to begin reconsidering Plato's dialogue with Xenophon is that he too provided the readers of the future with the knowledge of history upon which Plato's dialogues so frequently depend.

At this point, a reader might plausibly object: "What about the alternative possibility that Plato was basing his account on something like an oral tradition about the relevant historical events? Not everything a contemporary reader knew about Laches et al. came from Thucydides." The theoretical answer to this objection is that this book has been written by someone who regards Plato's dialogues as having been intended to be "a possession into eternity," and who has thus answered the crucial interpretive question raised above *in the affirmative*. I will be assuming throughout that Plato intended his dialogues to be what they have become and will forever remain, and thus that, along with Thucydides, Xenophon helped him to secure this amazing effect. But given Xenophon's universally recognized inferiority to Thucydides as a historian, and his rarely questioned inferiority to Plato as a writer of Socratic dialogue—and perhaps to many others including Aeschines and Antiphon—the question arises: "Why did Xenophon's writings survive?" I will be offering an answer this question, but the important point for now is not only the brute fact that Xenophon has survived, or the even more surprising fact that he was the first Greek philosopher whose writings have done so. He is also the only Athenian other than Thucydides to record the fact that he expected his work to survive forever (*Cyn.* 13.7). The closest Plato came to stating that this was his intention as well was by building on both.

And then there is the practical answer to the objector's claim that "something like an oral tradition about the relevant historical events" is sufficient to prove that "not everything a contemporary reader knew about Laches et al. came from Thucydides." My response is that what the objector means by "a contemporary reader" has no more practical value than "an oral tradition" of which no actual evidence remains. Yes, there may well have been fourth-century readers who knew about Laches (d. 418) independently of Thucydides or about Critias or Charmides—neither of whom Thucydides mentions—without Xenophon; clearly Plato, for one, did not need to rely on Xenophon's *Memorabilia* and *Hellenica* for knowledge about his own relatives.[27] But Plato was not writing for himself, and without Xenophon's *Hellenica*, no reader who actually exists—or of whom any historical record remains—could have recognized that there is an anachronism in Plato's *Menexenus*, without which recognition Plato's purpose in writing it cannot be understood. Finally, the objector's "a contemporary reader" is a chimera of whom we can prove no more than we can prove about a lost "oral tradition" or about "lost Socratic works" to which Plato or Xenophon may have been responding rather than to each other. Such objections rest on an appeal to a plausible but spurious realism: they appear to be empirical and skeptically critical regarding the importance of the sources we have but in fact achieve their plausibility by hypothesizing the existence of sources that we don't. As interpreters of his κτῆμα εἰς ἀεί, we are the readers for whom Plato wrote, not the unrecoverable "contemporary reader" hypothesized by the objector, and we should not deny that Plato stood on the shoulders of giants because the interpretation of his dialogues might more plausibly have depended on the existence of ghosts.

Chapter One

Xenophon in Plato's Dialogues

Xenophon Unnamed

The name "Xenophon" never appears in Plato's writings: that much is certainly true. Those for whom this fact is sufficient to prove that a study of Plato's debts to Xenophon is a waste of paper are therefore advised to put this book aside immediately. For the rest, the Introduction has demonstrated that even though Thucydides of Olorus is never mentioned in Plato's writings either, his presence is ubiquitous. The signs of Xenophon's presence are similarly ubiquitous, and this study is intended to persuade the open-minded that his presence is far more pervasive and philosophically significant than Thucydides'. But no attempt to overturn or even to question critically long-established and settled patterns of thought can afford to address itself to the open-minded alone: the goal is to open minds, not to presuppose them. Consider two other names that never appear in Plato's writings: Democritus and Sophron. Aristotle informs us that the mimes of Sophron provided the literary precedent for Plato's Socratic dialogues,[1] and no reader of the *Timaeus* can reasonably doubt that its author was familiar with the atomic theory of Democritus. Xenophon's presence in Plato's dialogues combines the three ways that Thucydides, Sophron, and Democritus are present in them as well: he offered historical background like Thucydides, he created literary precedents like Sophron, and provided useful philosophical friction or inspiration like Democritus.

Xenophon does, however, mention Plato. In *Memorabilia* 3.6, he explains Socrates' attempt to dissuade Glaucon from mounting the podium and haranguing the democratic assembly that ruled Athens. There was no law that prevented Glaucon from doing so, not even an age restriction that would have prohibited a nineteen-year-old from beginning an active political career. Xenophon tells us that others had tried to prevent the youngster from making himself ridiculous unsuccessfully; the dialogue between Socrates and Glaucon narrated in 3.6 alone would do the trick. Although Xenophon does not tell us so, Glaucon was Plato's brother; he does tell us that Socrates undertook the task of dissuading Glaucon out of his affection for Plato and Charmides, and the opening words of 3.6 are worth quoting as a whole:

> Glaucon, son of Ariston [ὁ Ἀρίστωνος], when he was attempting to address the people [δημαγορεῖν] and striving [ἐπιθυμῶν] to lead [προστατεύειν] the city [ἡ πόλις], being not yet twenty years of age, nobody among either his relations or friends was able to prevent [παύειν] him getting dragged off the podium [τὸ βῆμα] and being made ridiculous [καταγέλαστον]. But Socrates, being well disposed [εὔνους] to him on account of both Charmides the son of Glaucon and on account of Plato [διὰ Πλάτωνα], alone put a stop to it [παύειν].[2]

Among many others, the single most important word here is εὔνους, and what makes it so important are the persistent rumors—irrefragable external evidence of Xenophon's implicit presence in Plato's dialogues—that the two were rivals. If Xenophon wanted to diminish Plato's Socratic authority, he never would have told us that Socrates was εὔνους to Glaucon διὰ Πλάτωνα, because this explanation indicates that Socrates was even more εὔνους to Plato.

Both because it already needed to be challenged by Aulus Gellius and because it resurfaced as fact after him in Marcellinus, Athenaeus, and Diogenes Laertius, the rivalry between Plato and Xenophon was a literary axiom in antiquity.[3] Not only was the notion of a literary contest titillating, interesting, and inevitable in the case of two roughly contemporary Athenians, each of whom had written an *Apology of Socrates* and a *Symposium*, but there was well-established literary precedent for such an ἀγών in the legendary case of Homer's contest with Hesiod and the historical reality of yearly contests in comic and tragic poetry, a fundamental fact of Athenian cultural life. There had been a contest between Athena and Poseidon for naming the ivy-crowned city, and Socrates himself was no stranger to such contests, as the ἀγών with the famous sophist Plato allows "him" to describe in *Protagoras* tends to prove.[4] To reiterate, then, if—as so many ancient authorities believed—there was an ongoing rivalry between Xenophon and Plato, that should in some measure diminish the force of the objection that since Plato never names Xenophon, there is no basis for detecting his presence in his dialogues. If the two really were rivals, that presence would be implicit throughout, and especially obvious in *Symposium* or *Apology of Socrates*.

But what has kept and still keeps modern minds closed on this point is not the ancient axiom of literary rivalry between the two great Socratics but the modern axiom of Plato's priority. In many ways, the rise of this axiom—the elevation of a critical hypothesis to the status of virtually unquestioned dogma—is emblematic of the kind of modernity that emerged in Germany during the nineteenth century. Since no ancient author had suggested that Xenophon was copying Plato from one end of the corpus to the other, the view that he was could only be a modern one, and it supplanted the obvious hypothesis that Xenophon's writings had preceded Plato's precisely because they were simpler, less brilliant, and more apt to capture the pedestrian historical reality of "the true Socrates." It was a new critical spirit that swept away the merely implicit prejudice that the simpler must generally precede the more highly developed, and the aftershocks of that spirit are still with us. There would be far less resistance to a book whose subtitle was "Xenophon's debts to Plato" than there will be to this one. It is the distinctively modern view that Plato wrote first where the two overlap and that Xenophon was (ineptly) copying Plato—what I am calling "[the modern axiom of] Plato's Priority"—that creates an apparently insuperable barrier to the project I am undertaking in this book, namely, to demonstrate the extent of Plato's debts to Xenophon.

Implicitly opposed to Plato's Priority, my project is equally opposed to "[the ancient axiom of] Literary Rivalry," and I therefore have emphasized the word εὔνους. Although it is the most important word in the passage with respect to the actual state of relations between the two Socratics, it is not the only one that bears on their relationship. Plato's *Republic* begins with Socrates telling how he went down to the Piraeus with Glaucon ὁ Ἀρίστωνος, and how he gave him—along with all the rest of us who have read Plato's masterpiece—a thorough education in politics and ἡ πόλις. Since *Republic* soars in its middle books to the Idea of the Good and the outer reaches of Platonism, it was inevitable that whatever education Xenophon's Socrates had provided or would provide to Xenophon's Glaucon in politics and ἡ πόλις would necessarily be less elevated and more down-to-earth than what Plato's Socrates had provided or would provide to Plato's Glaucon. I hammer the phrase "had provided or would provide" so as not to beg the question of Plato's Priority in this particular case; it is best to reserve judgment for the time being. The crucial point for now is that if Xenophon was, for example, criticizing Plato's soaring Platonism by countering with a more pedestrian training in practical politics as administered to Glaucon by his Socrates in 3.6, he would not have framed that dialogue in terms presupposing that Socrates was at least as εὔνους to Plato as he was to his brother Glaucon, and indeed was obviously more so.

It will be noticed that the example I just gave of Xenophon attacking Plato's *Republic* in *Memorabilia* 3.6 combines the ancient with the modern axiom, and it is against this combination to which my response throughout this book will be polemical. Coincident with the decline in the status of Platonism and more specifically in the wake of ultramodern attempts to divorce, insulate, or even to protect Plato from the taint of his Platonism, a new synthesis has arisen that combines Literary Rivalry with Plato's Priority. The nature of my polemical response must be made clear: it is ultramodernity that rejects Plato's Platonism, not Xenophon. But precisely because Xenophon is less of a Platonist than Plato—who isn't?—he can be deployed to create an ancient attack on Plato. There are crucial elements of both Literary Rivalry and Plato's Priority that will be preserved here: after all, chapter 2 is called "Xenophon's Debts to Plato," and I will be trying to show throughout that they were responding to each other. It is against an un-nuanced ultramodern synthesis of these two prejudices—one modern and one ancient—against which the polemical aspect of what follows will be directed,[5] and even though I will also be rejecting both of them individually in their most extreme forms, the gentle art of persuasion will there be the only appropriate weapon.

The talk of weapons and polemics is required by the necessity of the case, and the best example of what makes it necessary is the relationship between 3.6 and Plato's *Republic*, and more specifically, with the way I have argued in *Plato the Teacher* that his *Republic* should be read.[6] By locating the Allegory of the Cave at the center of Plato's concerns throughout the corpus, my reading of *Republic* makes it an exhortation to philosophers to return voluntarily to the Cave of political life. Moreover, I am maintaining throughout that the Academy's original purpose was to persuade the young men who attended it to mount the βῆμα and, moreover, that in tandem with Plato's other dialogues, it provided them with the tools—above all, a thorough education in politics guided by the idealism of the Platonic Idea—to do so in a way that will not render them καταγέλαστον.[7] When Socrates tells the rebellious guardians: "Just as in a beehive, we have engendered you to be both leaders and kings" (*R.* 520b5-7), there is reason to think that he is telling Glaucon and the rest the very opposite of what Xenophon's Socrates—who alone among Glaucon's friends and relations, persuaded him to παύειν—is telling his Glaucon. Were this case to be generalized, it would create a problem for my reading of Plato: if Xenophon's Socrates is telling Glaucon *not* to enter politics, how can it be that Plato's Socrates is trying to persuade *his* Glaucon to return to the Cave, and indeed to προστατεύειν in ἡ πόλις, which, as long as it is a democratic city, may even require the philosopher to δημαγορεῖν in the sense of learning how to speak persuasively to the Assembly from τὸ βῆμα?

If it were the purpose of Xenophon's Socrates to deter his followers from learning how to δημαγορεῖν and προστατεύειν, Xenophon's own case proves that he failed miserably. Throughout the narrative of how he responded to a dream in *Anabasis* (*An.* 3.1.12–45), Xenophon emphasizes his youth, so much so, indeed, that a sensitive nineteenth-century reader argued that he was less than twenty when he rose to address the dispirited officers and men after Cunaxa.[8] So effective was Xenophon's own ability to δημαγορεῖν that the army elected him to προστατεύειν. But there is evidence much closer to home that indicates that Socrates' purpose was not to deter Glaucon from mounting τὸ βῆμα because, for instance, Xenophon is accurately portraying his low regard for the political as opposed to the philosophical life, but because the youngster was woefully ignorant of what any leader of ἡ πόλις needs to know. Leaving aside the question of whether Plato's Socrates is doing the same thing with his Glaucon, that is, *preparing* him for the political life rather than putting a permanent stop (hence παύειν) to his ambition to enter politics,[9] there is evidence in *Memorabilia* that it was not even the purpose of Xenophon's Socrates to accomplish this result.

As Xenophon tells us, Socrates was εὔνους to Glaucon not only διὰ Πλάτωνα but also because of Charmides. In a clear indication that 3.6 and 3.7 were intended to be a matched set,[10] *Memorabilia* 3.7 recounts a conversation in which Socrates is trying to persuade the younger Charmides to do just the opposite, that is, enter politics and, thus, as it were, to mount τὸ βῆμα and prove to the people of Athens (δῆμος at *Mem.* 3.7.1) that he is fully capable to both δημαγορεῖν and προστατεύειν.[11] These words do not reappear in 3.7, and for those who seek to reveal a more subversive Xenophon than will be on offer here,[12] it has become convenient to forget that they are implied; indeed *Memorabilia* 3.1–7 is united by Socrates' concern to illuminate the qualifications and obligations of *elected* leaders.[13] So before turning to Charmides' later career, the important thing for now is that Xenophon's Socrates is not opposed in principle to encouraging young men to serve ἡ πόλις, and therefore his determination to prevent Glaucon from entering politics had no programmatic aspect. His purpose in 3.6 was to stop him from making a fool of himself by doing so prematurely and ignorantly, and we need only ask ourselves the following question to reach this conclusion: "Was it the purpose of Xenophon's Socrates to wean Plato's brother from whatever had attracted him to a political career, or was he indicating the kinds of questions Glaucon would need to be able to answer if he were to pursue such a career in a manner creditable to himself and his family, and serviceable to Athens?"[14] The proper answer to this question is confirmed in the case of Charmides, whom he clearly does not regard as ignorant and therefore encourages. It is equally telling that Socrates felt it necessary to provide this encouragement as it is that he was unable to overcome the young man's reticence. It is as an advisor to the Athenian people that Charmides could have been useful, and that is something he never became.

Plato enters this story because he wrote a dialogue called *Charmides* in which Socrates is introduced to a much younger version of the younger Charmides, already in the company of Critias, the future leader of the Thirty Tyrants. Since Xenophon's *Hellenica* is our primary source for the Thirty, for Critias' leadership role among them, and for the intelligence that Charmides supported this murderous regime (*Hell.* 2.4.19), *Charmides* is a paradigmatic example of Xenophon's presence, albeit unnamed as such, in Plato's dialogues. But *Hellenica* is so important for Plato that a comprehensive overview of the philosophical basis of its importance will be delayed until chapter 4, and since Plato's *Menexenus*—the subject of the next section of this chapter—is an even more obvious example of Plato's debt to Xenophon's *Hellenica* than *Charmides*, the phenomenon in question will not be discussed here. Suffice it to say for now that any reading of *Charmides* that would consciously bracket out the information about both Charmides and Critias that Xenophon's *Hellenica* uniquely provides would be every bit as inadequate of a reading of Plato's *Laches* that consciously bracketed out what Thucydides tells us about Laches and Nicias.

For now, the relevant question is rather a political than a literary one, and it implicates the problem of whether Xenophon's and Plato's Socrates are at odds with respect to Athenian politics, a problem that bears directly on the relationship between Xenophon and Plato themselves. Since we know that Charmides supported the Thirty, and since Xenophon's Socrates encourages him to take an active political role in *Memorabilia*, the friends of a tyrant-friendly Xenophon—and there is good reason why such friends exist, as we shall see, even if Xenophon should prove not to be tyrant-friendly—will be inclined to link what happens in 3.7 to the murderous activities of the Thirty as described in *Hellenica*. The obvious objections to doing so must be stated clearly: (1) Xenophon attacks Critias vigorously in *Memorabilia* 1.2, (2) his *Hellenica* is solely responsible for the murderous image of the Thirty that has come down to us and of Critias' leadership role in the regime, (3) the details of 3.7 prove that by entering politics, Socrates was not referring to conspiring with a small clique of disgruntled oligarchs but rather to mounting τὸ βῆμα in order to δημαγορεῖν, (4) the details of 3.6 prove that Socrates' attempt to dissuade Glaucon from entering politics in no way denigrated the people, the polis, or democracy, but rather illuminated the youngster's inability to be of any assistance to ἡ πόλις, and (5) the whole thrust of 3.1–7 implicates Socrates' desire to make his associates *more useful to the city in its democratic form* (beginning with αἱρεθῆναι at *Mem.* 3.1.3), not to prepare for the day when a cabal of oligarchs—disdainful of the democracy, and therefore inactive in the Assembly—might overthrow it and institute, for example, the Thirty.

A sensitive reader of Plato's *Charmides* must recognize that Charmides is already under the influence of Critias but also that Socrates manages to cause a rupture in their relationship.[15] If it was his objective to do so, then, he failed in the long term, just as Xenophon's Socrates did with *his* Charmides. Of the previous five points, the fifth is the most important when supported by the third: Socrates fails to persuade Charmides to practice the art of persuasion on the Athenians for their benefit. And thanks to Xenophon's *Hellenica*, we know that Plato's Socrates failed as well: he did not detach Charmides from Critias even though the drubbing he administered to Critias clearly had the effect—and was intended to have that effect—of diminishing him in Charmides' eyes. To be clearer about *Charmides*: Charmides offers an account of temperance that Socrates suspects from the start that the youngster has learned from Critias. When

Socrates undermines that account, Critias becomes angry at Charmides in a manner that confirms Socrates' initial suspicion (*Chrm.* 162c4–6), while Charmides himself expresses no regret about revealing his source or incurring his wrath. As the foregoing account should be sufficient to indicate, no reader who compares *Charmides* with *Memorabilia* 3.7 could have the slightest doubt that Plato's literary gifts operate on a very different level from Xenophon's.

On the other hand, no reader of the *Anabasis* could imagine that even if Plato had had Xenophon's dream after the murder of the generals, he could have so effectively swung into action for the benefit of the Ten Thousand, thanks to his capacity to δημαγορεῖν and προστατεύειν, that is, to λέγειν τε καὶ πράττειν (cf. *An.* 3.1.45 and *Mem.* 4.2.1). Plato's inferiority to Xenophon in this regard looms all the larger for a reading of his *Republic* that—however incompatible it may appear to be with an antipolitical reading of 3.6 when considered in isolation—is consistent with *Memorabilia* 3.1–7 when considered as a whole. In the matched set of 3.6 and 3.7, we see the necessity—at once Platonic and Xenophontic[16]—of acquiring a comprehensive training in politics before entering it, not a programmatic message about, say, the radical insufficiency of the political as opposed to "the philosophical life."[17] If Plato's purpose is to persuade his readers to Return to the Cave, then they can learn at least as much from Xenophon about how to effectively operate down there as they can from him.[18] In fact, their excellences complement and indeed compliment each other, and it is a pity that some of the ink spilled in attempting to reconcile Plato and Aristotle was not devoted to making the far stronger case for reconciling Plato and Xenophon. Naturally, nobody should believe that this reconciliation has now been anything more than proposed, not proved.

What has been proved is the existence of a complex dance between Plato and Xenophon. More specifically, and less metaphorically, the fact that while Xenophon mentions Plato, Plato never mentions Xenophon, by no means proves that either can be fully understood without the other. A section on *Menexenus* follows this one because the clearest evidence for Plato's debt to Xenophon in his *Charmides* is its dependence on *Hellenica*. But the fact that Xenophon chose to mention Plato in the context of Glaucon and Charmides not only demonstrates that his goal was not to criticize him, but that he had either understood or anticipated the message of Plato's *Republic*. Thanks to the fact that 3.6 is the only time that either Xenophon or Plato mentions the other, neither of them will ever suggest that the other was anything but a genuine follower and sincere admirer of their respective versions of Socrates. For example, even though neither Plato nor Xenophon was present when the historical Socrates drank the hemlock, Plato names Hermogenes—Xenophon's source for his indirect knowledge of that event (*Ap.* 2 and *Mem.* 4.8.4)—in his list of those who did witness this event (*Phd.* 59b6-10). Had Plato wished to undermine Xenophon's Socratic credentials, he would not have emphasized Hermogenes; had Xenophon wished to do the same to Plato, he would not have told us that Socrates was εὔνους to Glaucon "on account of Plato." Although by no means the only evidence that the ancient axiom of Literary Rivalry is misconceived—this book as a whole will gather only part of that evidence—it is sufficient to raise doubts about it.

The modern axiom is another matter, and expressions such as "either understood or anticipated" in the previous paragraph should be taken as evidence that no substantial criticism of Plato's Priority has yet been offered with respect to the relationship between *Memorabilia* 3.1-7 and Plato's *Republic*. Instead, the evidence that has been offered undermines the capacity of the ultramodern synthesis of the two axioms to use 3.6 as evidence to make *its* point, and it has done so by indicating the way in which the goals of Socrates in both 3.1-7 and *Republic* are consistent with and not opposed to each other. Just as we must imagine *Charmides* taking place before 3.7, so too should we imagine 3.6 as taking place before *Republic*. And quite apart from the dependence of *Charmides* on *Hellenica*, this interplay of before and after is sufficient to indicate what it means to claim that each of the two Socratics is present in the writings of the other even when they are unnamed. By showing how Socrates persuaded Glaucon to cease and desist in 3.6, Xenophon gives the backstory as to why Glaucon will subsequently accompany Plato's Socrates on the way down to the Piraeus. But since 3.7 does not mention Charmides' relationship with Critias, it is now rather *Charmides* that supplies the backstory. As brilliantly brought to life by Plato, it is that unhealthy relationship—in tandem with its disastrous consequences that Xenophon described in *Hellenica*—that explains why Socrates was so intent on persuading Charmides to participate in the democratic politics of Athens.

As already mentioned, one of the good reasons not to read 3.7 as tyrant-friendly is that Xenophon carefully distinguishes Socrates from Critias at the very beginning of *Memorabilia*: although he consorted with Socrates for a time, Xenophon insists that Critias did so without understanding and for the wrong reasons, and that they ended up as enemies. I will conclude this section by showing that whatever may be the great complexities clouding the literary relationship between 3.1–7 and *Charmides*, Plato depicts the relationship between Socrates and Critias in that dialogue in a way that presupposes the reader's familiarity with *Memorabilia* 1.2. In *Charmides*, Critias attempts to regain the argumentative high ground lost, as he believes, through Charmides' argumentative incapacity, by repeating something he has heard from Socrates. Leaving aside the details, here we have another clear example of Xenophon having supplied the backstory for *Charmides*—this time the nature of Critias' prior relationship with Socrates as opposed to the tyrant's subsequent activities as described in *Hellenica*—and we can see once again that Plato depends on the reader knowing that backstory.

Memorabilia 1.2 is primarily devoted to showing why Socrates should not be held responsible for the subsequent actions of either Critias or Alcibiades. Although he joins them inseparably in the text, Xenophon never suggests that the two were friends or even that they knew each other; they are joined by their ignorant apostasy, not by ties of intimacy. Note that the same is true of Critias and Charmides: the latter is not mentioned in 1.2 nor the former in 3.7, while in Xenophon's *Symposium*, where Charmides' character is far more artfully depicted than in 3.7, Critias is likewise not mentioned. It is Plato, then, who joins Charmides and Critias in the Socratic context, and since it is Xenophon who joins Critias and Alcibiades—albeit not personally—it is remarkable that one of the two clearest analogues to the way Socrates tries to dissuade Glaucon from entering politics in 3.6 is the first conversation between Socrates and Alcibiades in Plato's *Alcibiades Major*.[19] Although the ignorance of Xenophon's Glaucon might anachronistically be said to be practical whereas that of Plato's Alcibiades is theoretical—Socrates proves that he does not know what justice is—the fact that he too is nineteen is striking enough in the context of an identical plot structure.

Although his portrait of Alcibiades in *Protagoras*, the *Alcibiades* dyad, and *Symposium* revolves around and riffs throughout on the precedence and consequence of Socrates' failure to do for him what Xenophon's Socrates did for Glaucon, Plato never actually tells us that his Socrates failed, that is, he never tells us that Alcibiades mounted τὸ βῆμα prematurely, and began to δημαγορεῖν and προστατεύειν before he was in any position to do the πόλις any good. He does not need to do so, for Plato stands on the shoulders of giants. Even if Alcibiades was not already a central figure in Athenian drama before Thucydides recorded his early career in his *History*,[20] Xenophon's continuation of that story—the early sections of *Hellenica* are our oldest source for the return of Alcibiades to Athens after his treason along with his death—meant that Plato did not need to retell it. He could rather presuppose it, and that means more specifically that he could presuppose his reader's familiarity with it. And just as important as the existence of a historical record of Alcibiades' misadventures was the fact that Xenophon, in the earliest sections of the *Memorabilia*, had paired the pseudo-Socraticism of Alcibiades and Critias with a condensed retelling of the subsequent careers of both. As a result, when Critias and Alcibiades arrive together at the home of Callias just after Socrates and Hippocrates arrive in *Protagoras* (*Prt.* 316a4–5), Plato has dramatized the pairing that Xenophon deployed for the better defense of Socrates in *Memorabilia* 1.2, and, at least for readers like us,[21] has found a way to mention Xenophon in everything but name.

Menexenus

Confronted by Plato's *Menexenus*, it is Xenophon who both reveals and resolves this curious little dialogue's greatest curiosity. That curiosity, dwarfing in strangeness the already amazing facts that Socrates is studying rhetoric and moreover that it is Aspasia who is teaching him ῥητορική, is the monstrous anachronism that allows Socrates, channeling his teacher, to pronounce a Funeral Oration for Athenian soldiers who died long after Socrates himself was already dead. Ending with the ignominious "King's Peace," the Corinthian War ended in 387 while Socrates died in 399. It was by swearing to this Treaty that Athens, joining Thebes and Sparta, bartered away to the Persians the freedom of the Greek cities in Asia—for the sake of which she had risked everything at Marathon in the Persian War the century before—in order to restore the rump of the empire she had lost in the Peloponnesian. Since Socrates will tell the story of the Persian and the Peloponnesian Wars as described in Aspasia's speech en route to this ignominious conclusion, the anachronism it implicates is anything but arbitrary: as the foregoing thumbnail sketch makes evident, the ignominy in question depends on a backstory, and it is obvious to everyone that Plato is referring throughout to events more accurately described by Herodotus and Thucydides.

But since the *History* of Thucydides breaks off before the great sea battle Aspasia describes before discussing, in a highly misleading way, the defeat of Athens in the Peloponnesian War, he can contribute nothing to our knowledge of those events. With respect to the Peloponnesian War, Thucydides' account is therefore incomplete, and it is in the same early portions of *Hellenica* that include the return of Alcibiades, his death, the Thirty, and the death of Critias which make Xenophon solely responsible for completing it. The fact that Xenophon chose to continue the *History* of Thucydides deserves careful consideration in the context of the modern axiom of Plato's Priority. As the previous section has demonstrated in the case of *Charmides*, *Republic*, and *Memorabilia* 3.6–7, there is evidence that admits of opposed conclusions. Such is by no means the case with respect to what might be called "Thucydides' Priority." By beginning his *Hellenica* without any introduction and at a point in the story of the Peloponnesian War that can be considered a sensible place to begin only in the context of where Thucydides' *History* ends, Xenophon proves beyond a shadow of a doubt that when he is building on someone else's work, he is willing to make it obvious that he is doing so. The fact that he does nothing similar in the case of Plato demands more careful consideration than it has received.

Because Plato wrote dialogues and studiously eliminated or at least concealed his authorial voice in all of them, he can never do what Xenophon does repeatedly: mention the works of his literary predecessors. It is true that Plato's Socrates purports to channel Aspasia and Diotima, that he builds his *Phaedrus* on a speech, possibly authentic, by Lysias, and that he might or might not be accurately repeating the written words of Protagoras in both *Protagoras* and *Theaetetus*. But in none of these cases are we warranted in assuming that Plato is acknowledging to these predecessors the kind of literary precedence that Xenophon is clearly so willing to acknowledge in the case of Thucydides. Even when Xenophon depicts Socrates doing the kind of thing that Plato does in the case of Lysias and Protagoras, he does so far more convincingly: as a result, no reader of *Memorabilia* 2.1 can doubt that Prodicus had written or recited "The Choice of Heracles" and that Xenophon is crediting him unequivocally with having done so. In other words, not only is Xenophon himself prepared to acknowledge his literary predecessors when he is following them but his Socrates is prepared to do so as well. Of neither Plato nor his Socrates can the same thing be said.

As indicated in the Introduction, I am by no means claiming that Xenophon's shoulders are the only ones on which Plato stood and is still standing, and the purpose of the previous paragraph is not to demonstrate that while Xenophon is forthright in revealing his literary sources, Plato ungenerously conceals them. On the contrary: Plato is revealing his dependence on a vast panoply of sources—considerably more numerous, in fact, than those on whom Xenophon depends—but he does so indirectly. And it is because he routinely does so indirectly that it will eventually become possible to show that Xenophon is one of the most important sources on whom Plato depends. Plato never names Herodotus or Thucydides either, but no reader of *Menexenus* can seriously doubt that he had read them. And although the theoretical basis of the corollary claim will not be provided until chapter 4, he likewise expected his readers to have read them, because if they had not, they would not realize how ignominiously Athens had betrayed her heritage by swearing to the King's Peace, nor how misleadingly Aspasia had suffused that heritage with flattering embellishment to reveal that betrayal as all the more shameful.

The punchline should by now have become obvious: until 1906,[22] Xenophon's *Hellenica* has been our only primary source for the King's Peace. But before using that fact to offer further proof that Xenophon, despite being unnamed in them, is present in Plato's dialogues, I want to return to Xenophon's willingness to announce the existence and even to provide the names of his literary predecessors. In *Apology of Socrates*, his first Socratic essay,[23] he tells us that there were other accounts of what Socrates said to the jury—and among them I don't include Plato's, for reasons to be considered in chapter 2—that missed a crucial point; he also names Hermogenes as his source of information (*Ap.* 1.1-2). Throughout *Memorabilia* 1.2, he is responding to a writer he calls "the accuser [ὁ κατήγορος]" (*Mem.* 1.2.9), and who has traditionally been identified as Polycrates, composing an attack on Socrates years after his death preserved by Libanius as if spoken at the trial by the no longer living Anytus (more on this below). And he begins *On Horsemanship* by acknowledging an earlier book of the same name by Simon to which he will be adding but will by no means be universally condemning (*Eq.* 1.1). In short: beginning with a decision to continue the *History* of Thucydides, Xenophon repeatedly draws attention to his literary predecessors whether he is correcting, attacking, or supplementing their views. Plato does not.[24] And since his only mention of Plato emphasizes Socrates' active affection for him—something he would hardly have done if he wanted to discredit Plato as a rival Socratic—it is *prima facie* unlikely that he is correcting Plato.

But the most famous instance of Xenophon citing a literary predecessor is best understood as a joke. At the beginning of the third book

20 | The Relay Race of Virtue

of *Hellenica*, he refers the reader to the writings of Themistogenes the Syracusan:

> As for how Cyrus both collected an army and having it went up against his brother. And how the battle happened, and how he [sc. Cyrus] died, and how out of this [ἐκ τούτου; predicament understood?] the Greeks preserved themselves [all the way] to [the] sea [ἐπὶ θάλατταν], it has been written by Themistogenes the Syracusan.[25]

The joke, of course, is that "Themistogenes of Syracuse" was the *nom de plume* Xenophon used while describing his own role in getting the Greek army safely ἐκ τούτου and—and thanks to his ability to δημαγορεῖν and προστατεύειν, that role was considerable and probably decisive—leading the Ten Thousand ἐπὶ θάλατταν. This famous passage raises an interpretive issue crucial to the approach I will be taking in this book.

Although it is only in chapter 3 that the knotty questions concerning the order in which Xenophon wrote his books will be considered, it deserves mention that eminent scholars have used *Memorabilia* 3.5,[26] a chapter that is no less deeply embedded in 3.1–7 than 3.6–7, to establish a date for these chapters—and indeed for *Memorabilia* as a whole—that would place their composition well after *Charmides* and probably *Republic* as well. Although the evidence that 3.5 could not refer to the situation that provides the backdrop for the advice Socrates gives to the young Pericles is far from conclusive,[27] it is necessary at this point to alert the reader to the existence of a chronological as opposed to a literary solution to the priority problem raised in the previous section. Postulating late dates for the composition of Xenophon's various writings is inseparable from the modern axiom of Plato's Priority, and doing so depends on the assumption that the composition of Xenophon's longer works can be dated to the latest event mentioned in them.

What makes the reference to Themistogenes of Syracuse at the start of *Hellenica* 3 so important is that if we place the composition of Xenophon's *Hellenica* after the latest date mentioned in it, we can "prove" that Plato must have composed *Charmides* before he knew that posterity would have access to the historical record of the Thirty preserved by Xenophon. The same applies to a unitary *Anabasis*: if we date its composition to the latest date our version of it mentions, it can plausibly be made unavailable to Plato at the time he composed *Meno*, a dialogue between Socrates and a blackguard vividly described as such in *Anabasis* 2.6. The text I have just quoted is important because it indicates that the version of *Anabasis* to which Xenophon refers in *Hellenica* ended with the Ten Thousand reaching the Sea in *Anabasis* 4, and I regard this four-book version as the original form in which it became available not to us but to "a contemporary reader," Plato in particular. In the same way, I will follow the lead of many nineteenth-century philologists in maintaining that the first two books of *Hellenica*—ending with the reconciliation that followed the death of Critias—belong to its earliest version, and were thus available to "a contemporary reader" before the new beginning, explicitly dependent on *Anabasis* 1–4, made in *Hellenica* 3. In the course of this chapter, I intend to show that Xenophon's longer works—*Hellenica*, *Anabasis*, and *Memorabilia*—were not composed as wholes but were composed by their author and made available to Xenophon's contemporaries over time and in installments.

Since Xenophon's *Hellenica* is going to reach the King's Peace at the beginning of what is now book five, I can anticipate the complexities to which I just referred by suggesting that beginning immediately before the reference to the march ἐπὶ θάλατταν in *Hellenica* 3.1 and ending with the ignominy of the King's Peace in 5.1, we have left behind the earliest version of the *Hellenica*, namely, books one and two. This section will consider with care the case for a three-stage *Hellenica*, and use the evidence of Plato's *Menexenus* to support that case. But for now, the important thing is to make the easier case for a two-part *Anabasis*, the first part of which ended with book four, where the most famous words Xenophon ever wrote appear at 4.7.24: Θάλαττα θάλαττα. Although uniformly translated as "the Sea, the Sea," the article is missing, just as it is in ἐπὶ θάλατταν. By referring in this way to the most famous words in *Anabasis*, shouted out by the weeping and joyful Greeks at the end of its fourth book, Xenophon is informing us that in its original form, *Anabasis* ended with the Ten Thousand reaching the Sea.

By the end of the nineteenth century, Plato scholars felt themselves free to posit the existence of *Republic* 1 as having originally been a separate dialogue; Ferdinand Dümmler christened it *Thrasymachus*.[28] On close examination, this hypothesis does not hold up: there is too much evidence that *Republic* 1 is an integral and artfully integrated part of the whole,[29] to which could be added the rather more controversial claim that if Plato wrote an independent introduction to *Republic*, its name is *Clitophon*.[30] In Xenophon's case, it is perfectly true that the so-called Parabasis that begins in *Anabasis* 5—and 5.3.7–13 in particular—must have been written long after the events he described in *Anabasis* took place either as a whole or in part. And if we are to imagine that it must have been as a whole that he wrote and published his *Anabasis*—whatever "publication" may have meant at that time, a subject about which we know next to nothing—then this must have happened well after the King's Peace, when Xenophon was settled in Skillus.[31] Quite apart from the possibility that the Parabasis might have been added later, the decisive evidence for a two-part *Anabasis* is not the work's lack of artistic integrity—although there have been throughout the ages far more readers who have read no farther than book 4[32]—but the synopsis of what "Themistogenes the Syracusan" had written, as described in *Hellenica* 3.

As one of the most gripping true-life adventure stories ever written, and both the first and best of such stories written by a Greek, the "publication" of Xenophon's *Anabasis* under the pseudonym "Themistogenes" could be compared with the early writings of Winston Churchill, another cavalry officer and historian. A series of field reports he had previously published anonymously in newspapers became the basis for his first book, *The Story of the Malakand Field Force* (1898). As a relentless self-promoter, Churchill, unlike Xenophon, wrote that book under his own name; in fairness, he had little reason not to do so in comparison with Xenophon's far more impressive achievements. Since the siege of Malakand was lifted in August 1897, Churchill's literary speed was remarkable, and was no doubt made possible by the synthesizing into a whole the field reports he had written contemporaneously. Without claiming that Xenophon was in any position to "publish" his "field reports," no reader of the *Anabasis* who puts any trust in the veracity of its author could possibly doubt that Xenophon was making written memoranda of the Ten Thousand's march, if not on a daily basis, then whenever he had a moment to write. The slower pace of activity after arriving ἐπὶ θάλατταν would have allowed him to synthesize those memoranda into a whole, and since reaching the sea meant contact with the larger Greek world, it also opened the possibility of "publishing" *Anabasis* 1–4 under a pseudonym even before Socrates was killed in 399.[33]

The consequences of rejecting this kind of sequence can be illustrated in connection with the attempt to date the composition of *Meno*. As is also the case with *Menexenus*, it is primarily on the basis of anachronisms that we can determine or rather approximate the date that one of Plato's dialogues was written. In other words, even scholars who give no serious thought as to *why*, for instance, Plato refers to the King's Peace in *Menexenus* can find value in the fact that he did so because it allows them to assert with confidence that Plato wrote it after 387–86, as indeed he must have done. It is likewise an anachronism that allows us to date *Meno*: when Anytus enters, Socrates compares the way his father acquired his wealth favorably to the way a Theban named Ismenias acquired his (*Men.* 90a3–5). On the basis of these references, scholars have dated *Meno* to around 386 as well, when Ismenias—although he had been bribed by the Persians to rouse Thebes against Sparta some years before—was put on trial, in the course of which, one can reasonably assume, the treachery behind his wealth was revealed. But if Plato wrote *Meno* in 386, and if Xenophon wrote his *Anabasis* as a whole only long after he was settled in Skillus, then Plato's portrait of "Meno the Thessalian," although certainly referring to the same person, cannot be based on the villain Xenophon describes in *Anabasis* 2.6.

The consequences of insisting that Plato could not have read the obituary for Meno in Xenophon's *Anabasis* 2.6—and thus that he could not have expected us, his readers, to have read it either—are far-reaching. As was the case with the charming Critias in *Charmides* (as well as *Protagoras* and *Timaeus-Critias*), the literary priority of Xenophon is charitable to both, making it possible for us to gain a greater appreciation for Plato's artistry while recognizing Xenophon's indispensable contribution to it. Although just this kind of hermeneutic charity will be exercised throughout this book, it may already have become evident that it was the preexistence of Xenophon's harshly negative portraits that allowed Plato to depict both Meno and Critias in ways that might suggest to the unwary that they are, as it were, "not so bad after all." What has been overlooked is that what makes Plato's literary mastery so obvious in both *Meno* and *Charmides* is that he can offer us characters who effectively present themselves as good who are really bad, just as bad characters in real life always manage to do, and the worst of them, the better. Plato gives a façade that it is necessary for us to learn how to see through, but he can only match the deceptiveness of those who have created that façade because he knows that Xenophon has made it possible for us to see through it no matter how artfully deceptive it may be. In this case, Xenophon's are the giant's shoulders upon which Plato stands and on which his artistry depends.

Moreover, since Xenophon has already ably defended Socrates against ὁ κατήγορος in *Memorabilia* 1.2, Plato can afford to be just as artful in depicting his hero as Xenophon has allowed him to be in depicting villains such as Critias and Meno. Milton can make Satan so compellingly persuasive because we already know from Scripture that Satan is evil; Plato can allow Socrates to make such slippery and fallacious arguments in *Protagoras* because Xenophon has already taught us that he is good. If *Protagoras* begins at dawn by depicting an eager schoolboy "with shiny morning face" rushing willingly to school *because* Plato made this delightful dialogue his introduction to the Academy, then the nonexistent sign over its equally nonexistent doorway should have prevented not the un-geometrical but the un-Xenophontic from entering, and it is because a young Xenophon had already written his *Cynegeticus* that Plato could begin *Protagoras* with the observation that Socrates has just arrived from a hunt.[34] This is one more variant of a theme that runs through this book, of which the simplest example is that it is Herodotus, Thucydides, and Xenophon who allow us to recognize the distortions of Athenian history that Plato allows Aspasia to teach Socrates in *Menexenus*.

Insistence that Plato could not possibly have read *Anabasis* 2.6 before writing *Meno* is not only uncharitable but the evidence proving it is weak; the reference to Themistogenes in *Hellenica* 3 makes it easy to see how he might plausibly have done so. But there is even more to the story. It is not just that the defenders of Plato's Priority, in the case of *Meno* and *Anabasis* 2.6 at least, have not proved it "beyond a reasonable doubt," but their case for dating both of these texts depends entirely on Xenophon. In addition to an assumption about the composition of his *Anabasis* that makes it a unitary work, no part of which could have been known to Plato until the latest date mentioned in or associated with it, the basis of our knowledge about the bribery (*Hell.* 3.5.1) and trial of Ismenias (*Hell.* 5.2.25)—indeed, about Ismenias himself, who is only mentioned in those two passages—is Xenophon's *Hellenica*. To summarize the paradox: since assessing the extent of Plato's debts to Xenophon immediately runs headlong into the modern axiom of Plato's Priority, and since establishing it as such has depended on a chain of claims to the effect that Plato's dialogues were written before Xenophon's writings had been, it is remarkable that the nineteenth-century champions of this interpretive paradigm—itself no longer in fashion—depended on Xenophon's *Hellenica* for establishing dates for Plato's *Symposium*, *Menexenus*, and *Meno*.

It is likewise remarkable that the dates of composition proposed for all three of these dialogues places them around 386. And if the scholarly consensus is correct that Plato founded the Academy in 387, then this offers some support for the hypothesis that some subset of Plato's dialogues constituted the curriculum of his Academy from the start. Note that this subset would not have included *Menexenus*, *Symposium*, and *Meno*, all written after, albeit only shortly after, the Academy opened. Nor should this surprise us. Quite apart from the fact that those who concern themselves with the order in which Plato composed his dialogues regard both *Meno* and *Symposium* as products of his "middle," or at the earliest of his "transitional" or "latest early" periods, there were also some number of other dialogues that he had written before. As a proponent of the view that Plato's dialogues were the Academy's curriculum,[35] I regard it as certain that he had already written several of them before he opened it, because nobody would open a school before they had something to teach in it. Rather than imagining Plato writing his dialogues in the Academy, it is more plausible to imagine him writing only some of them *in*, and all of them *for* the Academy. Finally, since *Menexenus* is closely linked to *Symposium* by the prominent roles assigned to the Peloponnesian War, rhetoric, altruism versus selfishness, and the dazzling brilliance of didactic women in both dialogues,[36] it belongs in the company of *Meno* as well, with all three datable thanks to Xenophon's *Hellenica*.

But not necessarily thanks to *Hellenica* as a whole, which covers Greek history down to 362, the terminus reached at the end of its seventh and final book. By contrast, the evidence that allows us to date all three of these Platonic dialogues is found in book five. The significance of this fact should by now be clear: if Xenophon's *Anabasis* was written in two parts, it is equally plausible that his *Hellenica* was written in three. At the very least, it was probably written in two: even scholars who doubt the possibility of a three-part *Hellenica* acknowledge the probability of the continuation of Thucydides in its first two books. Supplementing this independence, I would suggest that the first two books of the *Hellenica* were finished before Xenophon left Athens in 401 to take part in the Great Adventure that he would then chronicle in *Anabasis*, and were begun whenever it became obvious to him that Thucydides' *History* was going to progress no farther than it did.[37] In fact, it would have been from Thucydides, who expected the Peloponnesian War to be an event of unparalleled magnitude from the start, that Xenophon would have learned the value of keeping contemporaneous notes of his adventures, and of course it was not from Plato that he had learned how to δημαγορεῖν and προστατεύειν with the skill he demonstrates repeatedly in *Anabasis* 1–4 and beyond. The question is, then, whether we are going to follow John Dillery in upholding a two-part *Hellenica* or restore the older three-part conception paradigmatically although by no means originally upheld by H. G. Dakyns.[38]

In upholding the claims of the latter, three points deserve emphasis: (1) Dillery himself, by revealing that the moral purpose of books 5–7 is to reveal the inevitable consequences that followed and recompensed Sparta justly for her arrogance, has provided a far better argument than Dakyns does in support of Dakyns's position. In other words, he has made an indirect argument for separating books 3–5 from books 5–7, and that argument is both compelling and brilliant.[39] (2) Although Dakyns makes a compelling case for seeing books 3–5 as a coherent and integrated sequel to books 1–2 as well as being separate from books 5–7, he does not use the curious repetition between 5.1.34 and the last sentence of 5.1.36 to do so. With this observation, please note that I have been using the word *books* loosely, and thus as nothing more than approximations for convenience; henceforward, I will use *Hellenica* I, II, and III to designate its three parts. (3) Dakyns did not use Plato's *Menexenus* as corroborating evidence that *Hellenica* II ended with the King's Peace. Leaving further discussion of (1) and (2) for chapter 3, it is this third point that will receive attention here.

But before turning to the relationship between *Menexenus* and *Hellenica* II, a more general point must be made. Over the course of a multivolume study of Plato, I have taken up a pointedly agnostic position on the chronology of the composition of his writings and a resolute opposition to an image of "Plato's Development" that depends on determining the chronological order in which Plato wrote his dialogues as way of showing how his thought changed and evolved over time. As a result, a whole series of methods associated with "Order of Composition" were ignored when not overtly criticized, and a pedagogical triad of preparation, instruction, and test—to speak very loosely of the interplay of proleptic, visionary, and basanistic elements as implemented in *Plato the Teacher*—replaced the chronological typology of early, middle, and late dialogues, a typology that informs and supports an approach to reading and interpreting Plato that continues to dominate the field despite rising criticism. As a "separatist" division of Xenophon's *Hellenica* into three parts should now have made crystal clear, I will be applying one of the principal tools others have used for interpreting Plato to the interpretation of Xenophon, and it is around that tripartite division that I will build a case for characterizing and classifying his writing as "early," "middle," and "late." In other words, *Hellenica* I, written under the continuing influence of Thucydides, will be considered as paradigmatic of Xenophon's early writings, *Hellenica* II will be taken as introducing the first stage of his middle period, and *Hellenica* III, will be considered as emblematic of his late works.

Although this typology may eventually be used to support some general claims about what might be called, by analogy with Plato, "Xenophon's Development," pegging its origin to a three-stage *Hellenica* reflects a far more modest conception. Xenophon's *Hellenica* covers more than forty years of Greek history, and if only because of the historical necessity of maintaining written memoranda in order to tell such a story accurately, it was necessarily written over a long period of time. The reason that the typology of early, middle, and late applies paradigmatically to it follows from the necessity of the case: it is an account of events unfolding in time, of how things came to be, of generation and corruption, and more broadly of what Plato called "Becoming." Not only did Plato produce no book like Xenophon's *Hellenica*: he was philosophically opposed not only to writing such a book, but even to devoting thoughtful attention to the kind of objects that would allow him to write one. The proof that Xenophon was not so opposed is *Hellenica* itself, and regardless of whether his way of thinking changed over the course of writing it—which hardly seems unlikely *prima facie*, for Athens engrosses his attention only in *Hellenica* I, and criticism of Sparta becomes thematic in *Hellenica* III—it is his concern with historical events in general that makes a typology that I regard as inapplicable to Plato both consistently and perfectly applicable to Xenophon.

There are other considerations that distinguish the two Socratics, quite apart from the fact that only one of them is one of the two giants of ancient thought and unquestionably one of the greatest and most influential philosophers that any period of time has produced. Plato was a teacher, and his students constituted a built-in audience. If students came to the Academy to study the dialogues, it would have defeated Plato's purpose to publish them, and aside from a single late anecdote that reading *Gorgias* led a farmer to enter the Academy,[40] there is no evidence that he did so. Even a story to the effect that it was reading "almost the first two books" of *Republic* that prompted Xenophon to write *Cyropaedia*—a story that I believe and will defend in chapter 5, section 1—does not entail publication but rather the kind of friendship and mutual admiration, at once personal and Socratic, that I am claiming existed between Xenophon and Plato as long as the former remained alive. But unlike Plato, Xenophon had no school, no built-in audience for his writings. In order to be read, he needed to "publish" in something like our sense, and the fact that he can refer his readers to *Anabasis* at the beginning of *Hellenica* II proves what the *Gorgias* anecdote merely suggests: that he published his writings and intended them for the reading public in general. In other words, there is more reason to think that Xenophon wrote for "a contemporary reader" than that Plato did. It was Plato who first, last, and always—so I am claiming—wrote for us, and therefore depended on the survival of Thucydides and Xenophon, for the readers of the future would not understand, for example, *Menexenus*, if they did not survive.

Insofar as my approach to Plato has received enough attention to be criticized, an ongoing criticism, albeit only expressed in private, has been that it denies "Plato's Development," and seems to make him uniquely impervious to any changes of mind. It is true that I regard Plato's concern with unchanging Being as opposed to the vicissitudes of Becoming as the lodestar of his thought, and that he opened his Academy only after catching sight of the Platonic Idea and never thereafter abandoned it, instead choosing to test whether *we* would abandon it under the pressure of authoritative critics he had created to do so. For critics, my approach has unacceptably configured Plato as somehow superhuman, exempt from intellectual modification and changing ideas. As already indicated, Xenophon will not be exempted from such vicissitudes, and on the basis of his concern with historical events, that exemption would indeed be particularly inappropriate. But there is more: beginning with *Anabasis*, Xenophon is revealing himself in a way that Plato never did, and the human-all-too-human element is everywhere emphasized in his writings. This is not criticism: Xenophon reveals himself to be an exemplary human being, and I believe his friend Plato continued to regard him and ultimately mourned him as such. But the crucial point is that it was precisely because he stood on the shoulders of giants that my Plato too is human-all-too-human, and illuminating the ongoing stimulation and support that Xenophon provided him throughout his life will justify employing a more chronological approach to interpreting Plato's dialogues than the one that guided me in writing the five volumes of *Plato the Teacher*, albeit an approach that leaves intact his ongoing and unwavering commitment to his unchanging Ideas.

In turning at last to *Menexenus*, it is obvious that Plato did not include in it an anachronistic reference to the King's Peace so that nineteenth-century German philologists could use it to determine a *terminus a quo* for this dialogue's composition. Why did he include it then? My answer is that he did so in order to test whether his students knew enough about the history of Athens to recognize it as an anachronism. Recall the ambitions of Xenophon's Glaucon in *Memorabilia* 3.6, he who desired to mount τὸ βῆμα, to lead ἡ πόλις, to δημαγορεῖν and προστατεύειν. In order to teach the nineteen-year-old that he was unprepared to do so, Socrates tested him on his knowledge of Athens, of her finances and resources, of her weaknesses and strengths. Reappearing as Socrates' student in Plato's masterpiece, Glaucon will receive a higher education in *Republic*, and every attempt to imagine what Plato taught in the Academy has depended more on what happens in his *Republic* than on any other dialogue. But it is easy to see that a young student might more easily identify with Xenophon's Glaucon than with the decorated war hero who accompanies Socrates down to the Piraeus. The point, then, is that Plato's *Menexenus* performs the same kind of intellectual jujitsu on Plato's students in the Academy that Socrates performed on the young Glaucon in *Memorabilia* 3.6.

And *Menexenus* uses both Xenophon's *Hellenica* I and II to do so; such is this section's principal claim. Aspasia's Funeral Oration does more, of course, than test whether Plato's students have read Xenophon's *Hellenica*, and his very first students uniquely had no need to have done so anyway, since for them, the events of 387–86 were contemporaneous. But such was not the case for other events that Aspasia describes, and while it is not anachronism that Plato uses to test the student's knowledge of Herodotus and Thucydides but rather deletion and distortion, the methodology of the exam remains the same. By asking his students to read and thus respond to a deliberately deceptive account of Athenian history, a history that has now been illuminated and preserved by Thucydides and Herodotus, Plato is already imitating Xenophon's Socrates in 3.6, but by allowing Aspasia to offer a Funeral Oration for Athenian soldiers killed in the Corinthian War, a war that only Xenophon has described, he honors him in a second way. Beginning in the Introduction, I have made it axiomatic to my approach that Plato intended his dialogues to constitute "a possession into eternity," and it is on this basis that I am arguing for his dependence on Xenophon; the fact that, for instance, Diodorus Siculus (first century BC), also described the King's Peace (14.110.3) is irrelevant because Plato, at the time of his death, could have had no knowledge of this source. *Hellenica* 5 is the oldest evidence we have—and the only evidence that we know had been recorded before Plato's death—that would allow the readers of the future to realize what was already obvious to Plato's contemporaries: that the entire basis of Aspasia's Funeral Oration, crowned by the presence in it of the King's Peace, rests on an anachronism, as glaring as it is amazing.

This anachronism is not a case of carelessness nor is the choice of the King's Peace adventitious or arbitrary: it is not a case, that is, of Plato including in his *Menexenus* a mere factoid, perfectly well known to "a reader," that just happens to have been preserved for us only in Xenophon's *Hellenica*. Quite apart from the defining and culminating role that the King's Peace plays in *Hellenica* II, consider the no less culminating and defining role it plays in Plato's *Menexenus*. In an illuminating chapter on *Menexenus* in her 2004 study *Lessons of the Past*, Frances Anne Pownall shows that throughout the speech, Aspasia has emphasized (1) peace treaties, (2) the implacable hostility between Athens and the (Persian) barbarians, and (3) Athens' defense of the freedom of her fellow Greeks, the very freedom that she now bargains away to Persia in the King's Peace.[41] Of course, there is more to Aspasia's speech than a history lesson on Athenian hypocrisy, and whatever we may think we know about Plato's antipathy to rhetoric from *Gorgias*, he shows himself to be a master orator in *Menexenus*.[42] Particularly striking both for rhetorical and ethical excellence is the address of these honored dead—no matter vain may be the cause for which they died—to their children as Aspasia reports it, giving voice to the silent.[43] Only if their children defeat them in a contest for virtue will the dead achieve happiness; their victory in this contest will bring shame (*Mx.* 247a4-6). The conceit that the winners have lost and that the losers have won will reappear in Demosthenes' most famous speech, where he swears by the heroes of Marathon that he would have supported fighting Philip at Chaeronea even if had known in advance that Athens would lose.[44]

In the darkling light of later and apolitical forms of Platonism, we have lost sight of the reason the ancients believed that Demosthenes was Plato's student. The possibility that Plato's goal was merely to replace Glaucon's youthful desire (he was ἐπιθυμῶν) to δημαγορεῖν and προστατεύειν, with a mature sense that it was rather his onerous duty to do so (*R.* 520e1–521a2), would have been perfectly unintelligible to Plotinus,[45] and it remains for the most part equally so today. It is that same desire that explains why it was Xenophon alone who could persuade Chion to study with Plato, why the youthful Euthydemus has the twinned goals of λέγειν τε καὶ πράττειν ("both to speak and to do") in *Memorabilia* 4, and why Plato's most student-friendly dialogues are built around Alcibiades. Even though nineteenth-century scholarship has succeeded in making it impossible to cite the example of Demosthenes, nobody has yet had the temerity to deny that Phocion, Lycurgus, and Hyperides were Plato's students.[46] But it is an undefended and implicit axiom that Aristotle was a far better example of what it meant to be a student of Plato than any number of Attic orators, minor or otherwise. As son to the court physician of Philip of Macedon, Aristotle was the opposite of paradigmatic for two good reasons: he was not Athenian and he was not opposed to Philip.

The kind of students for whom Plato wrote *Menexenus* were both, and those whose image of the Academy is not mediated by either Aristotle or a long line of later Platonists—the most intellectually gifted of whom imagined that the views of Plato and Aristotle could be reconciled, for it takes considerable gifts to make such a thing plausible—can detect its influence on both Demosthenes and Hyperides. Nobody could claim that Plato stood on Aristotle's shoulders but when it comes to interpreting his dialogues or imagining his school, we have allowed the Stagirite, not Xenophon, to do the heavy lifting. This book constitutes an attempt to counteract that tendency, claiming as it does for the most part merely implicitly that we can learn more about Plato from Xenophon than we can from Aristotle, not least of all because Plato himself learned far more from one than from the other. Aristotle was seventeen when he entered the Academy, and Plato was already sixty. And when Plato died in 347, Xenophon had already been dead for some eight years. Finally, all forty-odd years of Plato's Academy in the strict sense—the Academy as it was while Plato was its head and guardian—were before the Battle of Chaeronea, a crushing defeat for Athenian independence and the cause of an equally profound transformation of the Academy.[47]

As indicated by *Menexenus* and *Hellenica* II, both Xenophon and Plato were equally aware of the kind of betrayal the King's Peace constituted and thus of the kind of restoration it demanded. In *Memorabilia* 3.5, Socrates instructs young Pericles in how to bring about this kind of restoration, to make Athenians mindful once again of what the newly elected general calls ἡ ἀρχαία ἀρετή: "'What can they do now, then,' he said, 'that they take up once again their ancient virtue [ἡ ἀρχαία ἀρετή]'"? (*Mem.* 3.5.14). Those who regard Xenophon's Socrates as inferior to Plato's will scarcely be surprised that this question does not reduce him or anyone else to a state of dialectical ἀπορία, and he duly points Pericles to "the institutions of their ancestors [τὰ τῶν προγόνων ἐπιτηδεύματα]," much as Socrates while channeling Aspasia will point Plato's readers. The King's Peace looms large in *Menexenus* not because Athens is evil, but because Athens has become degenerate: it is an indictment only insofar as it is an exhortation to her sons to defeat their fathers in a contest for virtue. Since the problems associated with 3.6 have been emphasized from the start, the solution to those problems becomes invisible if we ignore the fact that Socrates persuades Glaucon that he is unfit to enter politics in between a conversation with one who is fit but has deployed his considerable gifts to the city's detriment and another with a newly elected leader who learns from Socrates how to make Athens great once again.

And only someone who is familiar with the information that Xenophon preserved—either from reading him or from reading someone else who has—will know why, where, and when the Athenians soldiers whom Aspasia is celebrating in *Menexenus* have died, or will recognize that in channeling her words, Socrates will need to refer to events that took place a dozen years after his death. We are welcome to create a ghostly image of "Plato's audience" that would know these things without needing Xenophon's testimony, but such speculations ignore two obvious facts: *your* dependence on Xenophon, and Plato's determination, at once ambitious, natural to an Athenian, and realized in fact—to address the likes of you into eternity. So no, Xenophon is not mentioned in *Menexenus*. But without his *Hellenica*, we would have no check on Aspasia's hymn to Athenian greatness and unselfish generosity beginning with the Battle of Arginusae—or something resembling it (*Mx.* 243a7–d1)—continuing through the defeat of Athens in the Peloponnesian War (*Mx.* 243d1–7), the Civil War (*Mx.* 243d7–244b3), the origins and consequences of the King's Peace (*Mx.* 244b3–245e6), and the battles around Corinth (*Mx.* 245e7–246a4), which explain the immediate context of the speech. A skeptic would need to maintain that Plato likewise did not intend his readers to use Herodotus (*Mx.* 238e1–241d1) and Thucydides (*Mx.* 241d1–243a7) as a similar check in order to prove that this could not possibly be the way Plato is using Xenophon in what follows. There is, however, another expedient: one might insist that Xenophon could only have published his *Hellenica* as a whole after the death of his son Gryllus in 362.

In conclusion, it is interesting to note that Xenophon creates the precedent for the way I am claiming that Plato is using him in *Menexenus* by the way he uses himself in *Memorabilia*. In 3.5, there is no hint that young Pericles, so open to learning from Xenophon's Socrates about restoring ἡ ἀρχαία ἀρετή, is one of the generals that the Athenians are about to put on trial en masse over the objections of Socrates after the Battle of Arginusae (*Hell.* 1.7.15); for this incident—which will reappear in Plato's *Apology of Socrates* (*Ap.* 32b1–c3) without so much as his naming Arginusae—Xenophon is once again our primary source. In this case, it is *Hellenica* I that we are required to remember if we are to appreciate the full pathos of 3.5. Better than any others, both Plato and Xenophon realized the implications of Socrates' death: there was with his failure to steer the likes of Charmides, Alcibiades, and Critias into better channels, along with his parallel failure to see men such as Menexenus, young Pericles, or even a well-educated Glaucon at the head of the state. Both of these two great Socratics are determined to prove that Socrates has not failed nor has he died in vain, and indeed they prove themselves to be the greatest Socratics as a result. As recorded in this book's epigraph, Socrates expected his associates to be friends to him *as well as to each other* (*Mem.* 1.2.8), and both Xenophon and Plato know that he would not be happy unless his spiritual sons surpassed him in teaching others how to win a contest in virtue. And they would do so in the same way. By keeping Socrates alive—for all of their writings constitute his Funeral Oration—they were standing on the shoulders of a giant, a thing that both of them thereby proved themselves to be ready, able, and willing to do.

Meno

Among the ancients who regarded Plato and Xenophon as rivals, Athenaeus was the most hostile to Plato, and this explains why he believed that an emulous and nasty Plato had written *Meno* in polemical response to Xenophon (*Sophists at Dinner* 11.114). Meanwhile, the only example of rivalry that all three of our ancient sources mention as proof is that Plato criticized Xenophon's *Cyropaedia* in *Laws* 3.[48] We have no record that the proponents of either—Aulus Gellius regards these proponents as completely responsible for their alleged rivalry (*Attic Nights* 14.3)— attributed an across-the-board priority to their favorite, and as the example of Athenaeus proves, there is no reason to think that it would have been the partisans of Plato who would have insisted on his priority. In modernity, all is altered; even without recourse to the ancient prejudice regarding literary rivalry, our modern prejudice has awarded the crown to Plato without a contest, for now Xenophon must either become both emulous *and* tasteless or else the down-to-earth and laudably skeptical critic of Plato's "hifalutin' theories."[49] Instead, the recognition that Plato constructed his *Meno* on the foundations Xenophon had given him is the best place to begin replacing both the ancient and modern prejudices—and of course their combination—with a more charitable model of cooperation that fully justifies Socrates' confidence that those who had embraced the things he esteemed would thereby become good friends to one another (*Mem.* 1.2.8).

The number four is dominant in Plato's *Meno*. Meno's opening question admits of four possible answers, the square Socrates draws for Meno's slave is a four-sided figure, and there are four characters in *Meno*. Nobody doubts that *Meno* is one of Plato's greatest dialogues, and some might regard it as his pedagogical masterpiece. Without denying that it is both of these things, the purpose of this section is to show that it is also something else that others have not seen: Plato's homage to Xenophon. The four characters in this brilliant dialogue have one thing in common: all of them are based on the foundations that Xenophon provided Plato. If I can demonstrate that it is not only "Meno the Thessalian"—revealed as a scoundrel in *Anabasis*—but his slave, Anytus, and Socrates himself, who are based on Xenophon's writings, then for the first time in this book I will be illustrating its principal thesis: that Plato's ability to create such masterpieces depended on the fact that he was standing on Xenophon's shoulders. In fact, the more readily we are prepared to regard *Meno* as a pedagogical, literary, and philosophical masterpiece among Plato's dialogues, the greater will be our appreciation for the extent of his debts to Xenophon.

The connection between *Meno* and *Hellenica* II has already been mentioned, but now it must be considered in greater detail. By referring to Ismenias the Theban, Plato once again did more than provide nineteenth-century German philologists with the information they needed to determine a *terminus a quo* for the composition of his *Meno*. But he also is doing less than he did in *Menexenus*: the reference to Xenophon's *Hellenica* in this case is more like the icing than the cake itself; naturally, the heavy lifting will be done, in the first place, by the portrait of "Meno the Thessalian" in *Anabasis* 2.6. Nevertheless, the Ismenias passage must be quoted: "*Socrates*: Anytus, in the first place, is the son of a wise and wealthy father, Anthemion, who became rich not by a fluke or a gift—like that man the other day, Ismenias the Theban, who has come into the fortune of a Polycrates [τὰ Πολυκράτους χρήματα]—but as the product of his own skill and industry" (*Men.* 90a1–5 (W. R. M. Lamb). Along with Anytus himself (*Hell.* 2.3.42 and 44), Ismenias of Thebes enters the historical record when Xenophon tells us that he was bribed by the Persians to stir up a war between Thebes and Sparta in 395 (*Hell.* 3.5.1). Because the sum in question scarcely made Ismenias "as rich as Croesus," some scholars have found here a reference to Polycrates of Samos;[50] others have used Xenophon's report that the money was paid by a man named Timocrates to correct Plato on the basis of *Hellenica*.[51]

Of course, the obvious point is that since Socrates died in 399, and since Meno could only have been in Athens before 401, the reference to Ismenias' wealth creates an obvious anachronism. For those who fail to realize that it is primarily on the basis of Xenophon's *Hellenica* that Plato's anachronisms are detectible, it is worth consulting a paper by J. S. Morrison,[52] who argues that the Polycrates in question was Xenophon's ὁ κατήγορος, that is, the author of a later attack (c. 393) on Socrates—already mentioned—that its author placed in the mouth of Anytus,[53] and to which it is generally agreed that *Memorabilia* 1.1 and 2 are a response.[54] But even if Morrison is wrong—and there is much in his article with which it would be easy to disagree—the close connection between Anytus and *a* Polycrates cannot be doubted. The fact that we cannot get to the truth behind this enigma is no obstacle to what I regard as the important claim: that Plato was forcing anyone who tried to get to this mystery's bottom to begin the search with Xenophon's *Hellenica*. For one thing about this enigmatic and otherwise unnecessary reference is certain: thanks to *Meno* 90a1-5, no scholar who makes an effort to explain τὰ Πολυκράτους χρήματα—as the most frequently cited contemporary authority can no longer be bothered to do[55]—will be able to avoid citing *Hellenica* 3.5.1 and 5.2.25.

Next, there is Anytus. Granted that Plato clearly intended to anticipate the trial of death of Socrates in *Meno*, why did he decide to use Anytus to establish that link rather than Meletus, who figures so prominently in his *Apology* and other dialogues?[56] In addition to his presence in *Hellenica* 2, it is Anytus, not Meletus, who figures most prominently in Xenophon's *Apology of Socrates* (*Ap.* 29-31). Although it has been plausibly doubted that Xenophon is responding to Polycrates in *this* work,[57] he certainly goes out of his way to attack Anytus in it—to such an extent, indeed, that Polycrates may very well have been responding to it—and he does so through reporting Socrates' prophetic remarks about his son (*Ap.* 30).[58] Xenophon does not tell us the name of this besotted youngster, but since Plato tells us the name of Anytus' father (*Men.* 90a2)—he is the only source who does so—the suggestion is that whatever χρήματα Anytus inherited from one Anthemius (his father) would be misspent by another. This bears directly on the argument about the sons of prominent Athenians between Anytus and Socrates in *Meno* (*Men.* 92e3-95a1).[59] And since Xenophon tells us what Plato does not—i.e., that Anytus failed to give a proper education to his son, who came to a bad end as a result—anyone who has read Xenophon's *Apology of Socrates* before reading *Meno* will not only more clearly recognize the hollowness of Anytus' views on education (*Men.* 92e3-93a4) but will also laugh when Plato's Socrates tells Meno that Anytus does not yet know what slander really is (*Men.* 95a4-6), for it is Xenophon's Socrates who will administer it to him by prophesizing about his son.

As already mentioned, the ancient scholars who linked Xenophon and Plato on the basis of *Meno* in antiquity were not yet guided by the axiom of Plato's Priority. Modern scholarship has progressed only to the extent that the position of Athenaeus has been rejected, and unfortunately not for the cogent reason that Plato's portrait of Meno is by no means unambiguously sympathetic. Instead, it has been rejected because the assumption that Xenophon's *Anabasis* was only available to "a reader" after the latest date mentioned in our version of it has been taken "to prove" that Plato could not possibly have been responding to Xenophon. Why not? Since the Parabasis in *Anabasis* 5—and thus *Anabasis* as a whole[60]— was clearly written after the trial of Ismenias the Theban, and since the reference to him in *Meno* allegedly fixes the moment when Plato wrote it, he cannot be. Instead of being one more reference to Xenophon in a dialogue filled with them,[61] the reference to Ismenias proves that Plato did not refer to him there at all. As unlikely as Wilamowitz's claim that the two portraits of Meno were created independently of each other is,[62] it is preferable to the only acceptable modern alternative, dependent as it is on Plato's Priority.

It is now easy for us to see that an uncritical acceptance of Literary Rivalry led to absurdities, for the notion that Plato admired Meno so much that he thought it worth his time to counteract Xenophon's negative portrait of him in *Anabasis* 2.6 is even more absurd than the notion that Xenophon had Plato's *Meno* in mind when he revealed that scoundrel's resolute commitment to malefaction.[63] Both positions presuppose the view that Plato's portrait of Meno is a sympathetic one, but to show that supposition's absurdity to those who can't already see it would probably require a full commentary on the dialogue. Suffice it to say that if it were still possible for a modern scholar to overlook Socrates' irony and Meno's merely apparent interest in virtue,[64] there had already been indications that doing so would be interpretive malpractice,[65] for to find a positive portrait of Meno in Plato's dialogue requires selective reading, if not outright misreading,[66] and Callicles (*Grg.* 482c5-483a2) might easily explain why

Plato's Meno proves to be less forthright than Xenophon's. It is because Xenophon has already told us what "was clear [δῆλος ἦν]" about Meno (*An.* 2.6.21) that Plato can show us how an even more complete villain would try, albeit not altogether successfully, to make it less obvious, for as Xenophon also tells us, Meno "was delighting in being able to deceive" (*An.* 2.6.26).

But it is not only his literary skill that Xenophon's Priority allows Plato to demonstrate through Meno. The reason that the Socratic Paradox that nobody does wrong willingly reappears in *Meno* is because Meno has already refuted any moral implications of that claim in Xenophon: "Honored [τιμᾶσθαι] and served he deserved to be by demonstrating [ἐνδείκνυσθαι] that most of all he would be able [δυνάσθαι] and wishing [ἐθέλειν] to do injustice [ἀδικεῖν]" (*An.* 2.6.27). This is why Plato's Meno, at least at first, will insist that there are some men—and he naturally has himself in mind—who desire bad things, that is to say, to *do* bad things (*Men.* 77b7–c7). And this is the most interesting aspect of the argument, precisely because the most obvious way to refute the Socratic Paradox is to make the confession that Protagoras claims, not entirely without cause, that nobody is willing to make (cf. *Prt.* 323b2–7): "I do injustice willingly, have done it before, am doing it now, and will do it again." And of course the people who could admit, if only privately, that this is what they do are doing injustice not because they regard doing bad things as bad *for them*, but rather because doing it conduces to their own good. Plato therefore borrows Xenophon's Meno because Xenophon has created a character who is itching to say openly (δῆλος ἦν) what others conceal: he is ready, able, and willing to do injustice, and he does it well. Hence this crucial exchange:

> SOCRATES: But there are some [who are desirous] of bad things [τὰ κακά]? MENO: Yes. SOCRATES: Thinking the bad things [τὰ κακά] are good, do you say, or even knowing that they are bad but all the same they desire them: MENO: Both, they seem to me [to desire]. SOCRATES: Then there is someone [τις] who seems to you, O Meno, while knowing [γιγνώσκων] that the bad things [τὰ κακά] are bad, all the same desires them? MENO: Most of all.[67]

At the risk of beating a dead Thessalian horse (cf. *Men.* 70a6), Meno is resisting Socrates because he is thinking of τὰ κακά as things that are bad *for others* but good for him,[68] that is, things that are bad, base, and ignoble to desire by the conventional standards used by fools,[69] but which he, "knowing" (γιγνώσκων) that he is able and willing to do injustice, has made it clear (thanks to Xenophon) that he was doing "knowingly [γιγνώσκων]." In short, Meno is ignorant only to the extent that Socrates can successfully demonstrate that he would never do things that he knew were bad *for him*:

> SOCRATES: Then is there anyone who wants to be [βούλεσθαι εἶναι] miserable and unhappy [κακαδαίμων]? MENO: It does not seem so to me, Socrates. SOCRATES: No one, then, Meno, wants bad things, if no one wants to be such a one: for what is being miserable but both to desire bad things and to obtain them [ἐπιθυμεῖν τε τῶν κακῶν καὶ κτᾶσθαι]? MENO: You are quite possibly speaking the truth, Socrates, and nobody wants bad things [οὐδεὶς βούλεσθαι τὰ κακά].[70]

Only the reader who has rejected the axiom of Plato's Priority can fully appreciate the truly hollow implications of Meno's "conversion" to "the Socratic Paradox."[71]

If *Anabasis* reveals that Plato's "Meno the Thessalian" is Xenophon's, and if "Anytus the son of Anthemius" can be recognized as coming to us straight from Xenophon's *Apology of Socrates* by way of *Hellenica* 2, 3, and 5, it is *Oeconomicus* that explains the Xenophontic provenance of the dialogue's other two characters. I might as well say at the outset that despite the trailblazing character of his *Apology*, the literary innovations introduced in *Memorabilia*, and the literary charm of his *Symposium*, I regard *Oeconomicus* as Xenophon's Socratic masterpiece, and *Meno* indicates that Plato was the first to regard it as such. One indication of its excellence is that Xenophon's depiction of the dialogue between Socrates and Ischomachus has persuaded most of his readers that Ischomachus is a real person,[72] and more importantly—since he could ostensibly be just as "real" as Diotima—someone with whom Socrates is at odds.[73] In fact, Ischomachus is a character that Xenophon's Socrates uses to teach Critobulus, and as a result, too many have been persuaded that the dialogue Socrates narrates—the schooling in agriculture he received from Ischomachus in the portico of Zeus the Liberator[74]—is on an entirely different level from the schooling in love Plato's Socrates receives from Diotima. In fact, the two are parallel. In order to educate Agathon, Socrates describes a conversation in which *he* was the neophyte (*Smp.* 201d1-e7); Xenophon's Socrates does the exact same thing through Ischomachus in *Oeconomicus*, and, given the dialogue's concern with τὰ φυτά, "neophyte" is the right word. As a result, when Socrates says to Critobulus: "Concerning the ploughed field [ἡ νεός] you see, O Socrates, that the same things seem so to both of us" (*Oec.* 17.1), we are already being told one joke—for "both of us" are Socrates[75]—even before the gentleman's merely apparent interlocutor, but in fact his creator,[76] confirms this to be the case.

Since Robin Waterfield regards Plato's Priority as axiomatic,[77] he must also revive the ancient axiom of Literary Rivalry when he comes to describing the most important connection between *Oeconomicus* and *Meno*: "In *Oeconomicus*, while making himself out to be Socrates' teacher and using question and answer to this effect, Ischomachus pointedly and repeatedly alludes to Plato's doctrine of recollection."[78] To begin with, by making Ischomachus the relevant agent, Waterfield runs afoul of the misconception mentioned above: it would therefore be better to say that it is by making himself out to be Ischomachus' student that *Socrates* makes the allusion in question, placing it in the mouth of his character. Waterfield knows this,[79] but misses the kind of pedagogical humor that Xenophon brings into play by depicting Socrates as both student and teacher.[80] Instead, he is concerned with another kind of humor that exists only in relation to Plato's Priority:

> The irony of having Socrates comment, as the interlocutor, on the method of questioning he himself puts interlocutors through in both Xenophon's and Plato's works, is exquisite. It is not going too far to say that in this case Xenophon seems to want to correct Plato.[81]

The correction in question will render the most significant passage in Plato's *Meno* ridiculous: Waterfield's reconstruction of "Xenophon's Mission" proves that "Socrates has no need of hifalutin' theories of reincarnation and prenatal knowledge."[82]

In turning from Waterfield's revealing comments to *Oeconomicus* itself, it is useful to make an artificial distinction between what Socrates says as Ischomachus and what Socrates says in response to "him." Starting with the latter, most relevant are the two times that Socrates praises Ischomachus, once for using an illustrative image as a pedagogical device—the image involves bees, as it happens (*Oec.* 17.15; cf. 7.32-38)—and the second for teaching him through the use of questions (*Oec.* 19.15; cf. 16.8–17.1). Although the bee-image in *Oeconomicus* has more in common with the reference to drones in *Republic* 8 (*R.* 552c2–554c2), Socrates promptly introduces bees in *Meno* (*Men.* 72a6–b9). But let's not miss the forest for the trees: throughout *Oeconomicus*, Socrates is teaching Critobulus by using the image of a prosperous and effective gentleman farmer, namely, Ischomachus "himself." It is not so much Xenophon's irony that is "exquisite" here but rather his sense of humor: in addition to the fact that Socrates is really praising *himself* for using images to teach, he constructs a situation in which the image he has created appears to be the one who is creating images.[83] The fact that his Socrates teaches Critobulus by means of Ischomachus—a character who presents "himself" as teaching his wife what he learned from a Phoenician steward (*Oec.* 8.15–16)[84]—suggests that Xenophon learned as much from Plato's *Symposium* as Plato did from Xenophon's *Oeconomicus*, for the cooperative model I will be defending in this book necessarily works both ways (see chapter 2, section 3).

The passage where Socrates praises Ischomachus for teaching him through questions creates the dialogue's most important connection to *Meno*, for it is this kind of pedagogy that Socrates will practice there on the unnamed slave. Indeed, it is *by casting himself as the slave* in relation to a Socratic Ischomachus that this new and neophyte "Socrates" can praise the image-making Socrates in a way that Meno's slave cannot. Starting from the naive question " 'Is then, Ischomachus,' said I, 'this interrogation [ἡ ἐρώτησις] (a kind of) teaching [διδασκαλία]?' " (*Oec.* 19.15), Xenophon was opening the door to a kind of pedagogy that depends as much on the teacher's ability to ask the right questions as on the student's ability to answer them properly.

The fiction of Ischomachus the Teacher allows Socrates to say many other important things through him. For example, Socrates presents himself as misunderstanding the limits of a διδασκαλία that proceeds through ἐρώτησις (*Oec.* 19.16) and Ischomachus promptly points this out to "him." He also remarks Socrates' use of what looks like insincere flattery (*Oec.* 11.6), playful error (*Oec.* 17.9), and willful misconstruction (*Oec.* 20.27–28). More specifically, he accuses Socrates three times of playing around, and since Xenophon's Socrates is speaking through Ischomachus, this claim is as humorous as it is true: "but you're playing [σὺ μὲν παίζεις]" (*Oec.* 11.7 and 20.29; cf. 17.10) points to the same kind of humor that runs throughout the dialogue.

Thanks to the fiction that it is Socrates who is being taught, Socrates can make teaching look easy, but we should keep in mind that it is only when the teacher knows which questions to ask and in what order to ask them—and just as importantly asks them about a subject that has an inner logic of its own—that those questions can disclose illuminating answers. It should surprise no one that attempts have been made to deflate the value of the διδασκαλία through ἐρώτησις concerning farming as being based explicitly on nothing more than what Socrates already knows and has seen about farming (*Oec.* 15.10).[85] But it is not the student's dependence on "merely" empirical knowledge that is relevant here—after all, it is Plato, not Xenophon, who will emancipate recollection, at least partially, from sense experience through geometry in *Meno*—but rather the kind of dialogic διδασκαλία that proceeds through ἐρώτησις.[86] This is, at any rate, the aspect of Xenophon's *Oeconomicus* that Plato saw fit to imitate, and this is why Plato's Socrates can reenact Ischomachus in his questioning of the slave boy.

The prior knowledge of farming that Socrates possesses is based on what he has heard and seen;[87] it is manifestly, repeatedly, and explicitly rooted in nature or φύσις.[88] When attempts are made to deflate the kind of instruction Socrates receives in *Oeconomicus*, the aspect of φύσις that is responsible for farming's "inner logic" is ignored, but this is precisely the important point disclosed by an effective διδασκαλία through ἐρώτησις. When Plato's Socrates predicates recollection on "the whole of nature [φύσις] being kindred" (*Men.* 81c9–d1), he can count on Xenophon to have already illustrated the kind of διδασκαλία that depends on this kind of kinship on the most literal and observable level of φύσις. But even when attention is diverted from the common method to its apparently heterogeneous objects, we will be confronted with the fact that it is geometry (γεωμετρία) that Plato's Socrates uses to illustrate recollection in *Meno*: less obvious in translation, both γεωμετρία and γεωργία are equally dependent on the earth, and the kind of φύσις that makes Socratic διδασκαλία possible is no less dependent on what Meno's slave can see or hear than it is on what Ischomachus' pupil has already heard and seen. It is, after all, the only diagram preserved in the Platonic *scholia* that makes the lesson in geometry intelligible.[89]

To conclude: like the square in that diagram and the alternatives about virtue that Meno offers Socrates at the start (*Men.* 70a1–4), there are four persons in Plato's dialogue; the remarkable thing is that Xenophon's influence can be seen in all four of them. Regardless of priority, Socrates uses the same kind of pedagogical method in both *Meno* and *Oeconomicus*; that is the most obvious example of the latter's influence.[90] But thanks to linking Anytus to his father so emphatically at the start,[91] and thanks to contrasting that father with Ismenias of Thebes, the light that Xenophon's *Apology of Socrates* has shed on his drunken son has made Anytus almost as recognizable as one of Xenophon's characters as Meno the Thessalian. The reference to Ismenias is the seemingly insignificant clue that binds the whole together, for it is Xenophon's influence that provides the kind of shared φύσις that unites all of the characters in Plato's *Meno*. But the most beautiful connection is the one that illuminates Xenophon's Socrates not only as the master of instruction through questioning as implemented by Ischomachus but also, thanks to the parallel, as the voice of Meno's slave. By showing Socrates teaching while describing himself in the process of being taught, Xenophon prepared the way for the most striking aspect of Plato's *Meno*, for the direct dialogue between Socrates and the slave about γεωμετρία is the spiritual and literary descendent of the narrated dialogue between Ischomachus and Socrates about γεωργία. It was with gratitude and admiration that Plato wrote *Meno*, a veritable *tombeau de Xénophon*.[92]

Alcibiades

In 1906, a German philologist summarized as follows a critical aspect of his argument that *Alcibiades Major* could not possibly be a genuine Platonic dialogue:

> I believe I have collected all the passages in Xenophon that were models for the author. What can be concluded? First it can now be concluded with even more certainly that Plato was not that author. Not only was Plato too great to be forced to imitate another so obviously, but Xenophon—whom the best authors of that age never mention—he would in no case have imitated. Therefore, since the author of *Alcibiades Major* reproduced Xenophon, it is for that reason manifest that he was not a great author.[93]

Here is the new position: Plato is too great to have imitated a mental midget like Xenophon. By contrast, my ongoing claim that Plato is standing on the shoulders of giants is not meant to preclude the possibility—indeed, my equally axiomatic certainty—that Plato himself is a giant, and that *in contrast* with him, Xenophon may well be a midget. But even if he were so, he would still be a necessary and indispensable midget, upon whom Plato's giant stature depends. By this point it should be obvious that the Xenophon on offer here is a giant even if the literary and philosophical brilliance of Plato's *Symposium* and *Meno* dwarfs the degree of brilliance of Xenophon's *Symposium* and *Oeconomicus*. To be sure Xenophon isn't as great a writer as Plato, but then again, who is?

However great Plato is, Arbs is wrong: he was not "too great to be forced to imitate another so obviously." Note here that the previous section is not claiming that Plato was imitating Xenophon, he was, rather, building on his foundations, playfully, and delightedly paying tribute to the debts he had incurred by doing so. But the subject of this section is not *Meno*, but *Alcibiades Major* and, to a lesser extent, *Alcibiades Minor* as well. Although the former is making a comeback in the sense that an increasing number of scholars are now willing to read it as authentic, the same cannot be said for its literary twin, and there is an advantage in this. For example: there are even more connections between the allegedly pseudo-Platonic *Lovers* and *Oeconomicus* than there are between the latter and *Meno*.[94] Even if Plato wrote these dialogues, along with *Theages* and *Clitophon*,[95] there is a silver lining to the cloud that obscures their authenticity. Since the author (G. der *Verfasser*) of inauthentic or pseudo-Platonic dialogues is necessarily copying Plato, he at least is not too great to be copying Xenophon as well. Indeed, Athenaeus tells us that some believed that Xenophon was the actual author of *Alcibiades Minor*.[96] Less drastically, modern scholars have shown themselves to be willing in the case of a dialogue such as *Alcibiades Major* to assert what they would never be willing to admit about, for example, *Meno*: that its *Verfasser* was relying on or responding to Xenophon.

This is already visible in Schleiermacher, the first scholar to deny the authenticity of *Alcibiades Major*, a dialogue revered in antiquity as the proper place to begin the study of Plato. Consider how he describes the long speech of Socrates (*Alc.1* 121a3–124b6) that divides *Alcibiades* into two sections of dialogue: "The second [sc. of those features that constitute the inadequacy of dialogue, i.e., its long speeches] glories *ad nauseam* in amazing statistical evidences of Persian and Spartan virtues and treasure, of which even the virtues are already more Xenophontic [*Xenophontisch*] than Platonic, whereas the treasure with its effeminate luxury [*die weichliche Pracht*] is thoroughly un-Socratic [*unsokratisch*]."[97]

Since Alcibiades will eventually prove himself to be famously susceptible to this *weichliche Pracht,* the critical question is not whether it is Socratic but rather Platonic, for the speech serves to address itself to Alcibiades' dreams and aspirations, not to Socrates' conceptions of what constitutes true treasure. And to the extent that Xenophon might be considered an important source for Alcibiades' susceptibility to luxury—and is in any case the Athenian who knows the most about both Sparta and Persian—the speech is certainly what Schleiermacher calls *Xenophontisch.*

It is important to understand what Schleiermacher means by *Xenophontisch* in the context of his claim that *der Verfasser* of *Alcibiades Major* cannot be Plato because he is both un-Platonic and *unsokratisch.* To begin with, he is suggesting that it is possible to be at once *Xenophontisch* and *unsokratisch,* and it is easy to forget that linking these two shows that Schleiermacher was de-authenticating Xenophon as a Socratic as well as de-authenticating *Alcibiades Major* as Platonic. It would be difficult to say which move was more revolutionary;[98] what is easy to see is that for Schleiermacher they are inseparably linked. Secondly, even if Schleiermacher is willing to posit some other author, he is essentially echoing the position of those who regarded *Alcibiades Minor* as *Xenophontisch*: he is claiming that whoever wrote the long speech was writing at the very least as if he were Xenophon. In short, Schleiermacher's postulated author is not paying homage to Xenophon, alluding to his writings, or even simply copying him; what makes "him" *Xenophontisch* is that he is channeling Xenophon and has assimilated his conceptions to the degree that his Socrates is just as *unsokratisch* as Xenophon's is.

Reaching an apogee in Karl Joël's brilliant book *The True and the Xenophontic Socrates,* at its end,[99] the nineteenth century produced so many German philologists who would embrace, strengthen, and extend the radical position that Schleiermacher was taking here, that it would be safe to say that it was *German philology* that embraced it, nor should anyone imagine that this movement ended with Joël or even that it is today a thing of the past.[100] This is all the more striking because it overturned the earlier consensus of German scholarship that Xenophon's writings were particularly useful for distinguished characteristically *Platonic*—and thus *unsokratisch*—elements in what would later be called his "middle" and "late" dialogues.[101] Combining Aristotle's claims about (the historical) Socrates with Xenophon's more down-to-earth and above all Idea-less Socrates, it became a commonplace that Plato is leaving Socrates behind with, for instance, the so-called higher mysteries in *Symposium.*[102] Although further discussion of the truly radical character of Schleiermacher's position is not germane to the project in hand,[103] it must be recognized as remarkably consistent and integrated: he rejected Aristotle's testimony that Plato, but not Socrates, had separated the Forms—a position that the *xenophontische* Socrates tends to support—not on the grounds that Socrates had but on the amazing position that Plato had not.[104]

What is eminently germane to that project is to determine whether the following passage from Socrates' long speech in *Alcibiades Major* is *Xenophontisch* in Schleiermacher's sense, which I am claiming it is not:

> SOCRATES: I [ἐγώ] once heard from a trustworthy man [ἀνὴρ ἀξιόπιστος] among those who had gone up [ἀναβεβηκότες] to the King, who said he traversed a region very ample and good in a journey of nearly a day which the inhabitants call "the belt of the King's woman," and there is also another which again is called "veil," and others, many places beautiful and good, chosen out for the ornamentation of the woman, and each of the places having names from each part of her ornaments.[105]

The author of this passage is not copying Xenophon but rather citing his *Anabasis*, and the participle ἀναβεβηκότες conveys the fact of this citation just as unmistakably as *Anabasis* 1.4.9, where "Xenophon claims that he camped in a place allocated to a Persian Queen in order to provide her belt."[106] The quotation is from Nicholas Denyer's 2001 green-and-yellow edition of *Alcibiades Major*—the principal text in the ongoing rehabilitation of the dialogue as Platonic—as is this comment on ἀναβεβηκότες: "[I]t is hard not to catch in this word an allusion to Xenophon, the author of the *Anabasis*."[107]

Since Schleiermacher made it inevitable that all further discussion of *Alcibiades Major* would be enmeshed with the problem of its authenticity that he had created, it became unnecessary for later scholars to point out the anachronism involved in having Socrates claim to have heard before 431 what only Xenophon could have told him some thirty years later. But it is important to observe that unlike the anachronisms of the King's Peace or Ismenias the Theban, this allusion to Xenophon—for it is even more obviously an allusion to him than the other two are—proves nothing about when *Alcibiades Major* could, let alone must, have been written. If *Anabasis* 1-4 was published under the name Themistogenes the Syracusan, if, that is, we don't need to insist that "a reader" could not have heard the story of the Queen's Sash until, say, 380 or even later, then it is not necessarily anachronistic for Plato to write as if Socrates had heard the story and retold it, but only that he is writing as if he could have told it Alcibiades. Whoever wrote *Alcibiades Major*, the allusion to Xenophon tells us nothing about when he did so except on the basis of the late publication of a unitary *Anabasis* that emphasizes the latest part of the Parabasis (*An.* 5.3.6–13) at the expense of a previously published narrative by one of the ἀναβεβηκότες that ended with the Ten Thousand arriving ἐπὶ θάλατταν (*Hell.* 3.1.2).

To deploy the typology applied previously to *Hellenica* for the first time, although I regard it as likely that *Anabasis* I reached Athens before Socrates died—this explains why Xenophon tells the story of Socrates and the oracle (*An.* 3.1.5–7)—I regard the ἐγώ in the passage just quoted as Plato, not Socrates: it is Plato who has heard the story from Xenophon. And since I subscribe to the pre-Schleiermacher view that *Alcibiades Major* is an authentic Platonic dialogue, and more importantly to the view of many ancient Platonists that its purpose was to introduce his readers to Platonism, this passage suggests that those young readers were familiar with Xenophon as well, just as they were already aware of who Alcibiades was and what he had done.[108] In short, this passage indicates that the long speech of Socrates is *Xenophontisch*, but not in Schleiermacher's sense of that word: it is Xenophontic because Plato is alluding to Xenophon and indeed assuming that his readers will recognize him as doing so. It is not because Xenophon is absent from his dialogues that Plato does not name him in them; he expects his readers to bring Xenophon along with them, just as—in a metaphorical sense—Chion of Heraclea had done. In other words, those apocryphal letters capture an important truth: a prior affection for Xenophon inspired students to come to the Academy, and beginning with *Alcibiades Major* if not before, Plato capitalizes on that inspiration.

As already indicated, my position toward the order in which Plato composed his dialogues is agnostic throughout *Plato the Teacher*. Moreover, this agnosticism was applied there to *Alcibiades Major* in particular: though childishly simple and pedagogically elementary, it is a dialogue that Plato need not have written while he was young, and indeed I surmised that only an experienced teacher could have written such an effective introduction. Because the subject of this book is the back-and-forth between Plato and Xenophon, the chronological element necessarily plays a much greater and indeed a decisive role. In the specific case under consideration, I have shown that Plato could have written *Alcibiades Major* before he opened the Academy in 387; on the other hand, even if there was never an *Anabasis* I, it might already have been part of the Academy's curriculum in the 380s, when Xenophon presumably had the time to write his memoirs, including the Parabasis, in the gentlemanly leisure that Skillus provided him.[109] It is especially important to emphasize these possibilities before considering the most important evidence that not only Socrates' speech about the kings of Sparta and Persia,[110] but *Alcibiades Major* as a whole is *Xenophontisch*.

On the first page of his commentary, Denyer attaches the following comment to θαυμάζειν ("to wonder"), the sixth word in the dialogue:

> Cf. the wonder that Euthydemus felt, and was attempting to suppress, at the outset of Socrates' attempts to turn him to philosophy (Xen. *Mem.* 4.2.3; cf. 4.2.6). "All of Socrates' dealings with Euthydemus, as represented at Xen., *Mem.*, 4.2, 3, 5 and 6, make instructive reading: for comparisons on points of detail, see the notes on 104a5, 104b7, 104c2, 104d7–9, 104e5, 105a7 ἐὰν θᾶττον, 106d6 ἐλπίδας, 112b1, 116e3–4, 117e4, 118b6–7, 118c3–4, 120c1, 124b1, 130d6 and 135c8.[111]

To state the obvious point first: there are a large number of parallels between *Alcibiades Major* and *Memorabilia* 4, especially to 4.2, most of them to 4.2.1; in what follows I will discuss the passages Denyer mentions in the order in which they appear in Xenophon, not, as here, in the order in which they appear in Plato. But since this book began with 3.6, it is worth remarking that Arbs begins with the parallels to that chapter, and discovers and discusses four of them before finding and discussing five in 4.2, two in 4.4, and one in 3.7.[112] And given the multiple references to mounting τὸ βῆμα in this chapter's first section, *Alcibiades Major* 106c6 should be added to the list:

> SOCRATES: Bear up, then. For you are planning, as I assert, to come forward so as to counsel the Athenians, and at no distant time. If, then, with you about to mount the podium [τὸ βῆμα], having taken you aside I were to ask: "O Alcibiades, since the Athenians are planning to take counsel concerning something [περὶ τίνος], it is for the purpose of counseling them that you're mounting? Is this since it is concerning things you understand better than they?" What would you reply?[113]

By dramatizing Socrates' intervention in the life of an ambitious young man, Plato seems to be taking a characteristic step beyond 3.6: he is bringing to life a nonexistent moment to create an imaginary conversation. Plato's Socrates clearly aims to bring about the exact same goal as Xenophon's, and the Platonic germ of the way in which he will try to prevent (παύειν) Alcibiades from doing something ridiculous (καταγέλαστον) is already visible in περὶ τίνος. As soon as the young man declares what it is "concerning which" he claims to know more than they do, Socrates will find a way to ask Alcibiades: τί ἐστι; ("What is it?"). We have four choices, as always in the case of such parallels. One possibility is that both Xenophon and Socrates are describing a phenomenon we call "Socrates" whose actual practices were such that both are describing, and doing so independently of each other, the common basis of those phenomena: the historical Socrates. The next possibility is that they are not independent of each other, but that it is impossible to say who is imitating, criticizing, or building on whom. Only then do we reach the dilemma that divides Plato's from Xenophon's priority.

Denyer discovers five passages, all of them early in the dialogue (*Alc.1* 104a5–106d5), that echo or anticipate *Memorabilia* 4.2.1 among the sixteen that do the same in 4.2 as a whole. Although not enough has yet been said about the composition of the *Memorabilia*—a difficult subject that will not receive anything like systematic consideration until the following chapter—and although what has been said earlier in the first section of this chapter about 3.5–7 has taken a similarly open-minded stance, the clear reference to *Anabasis* considered above, like the dramatic intervention of Socrates while Alcibiades is actually mounting τὸ βῆμα, inclines me to think that "echo" has by now become the appropriate word. In any case, it is worth remarking that Socrates' conversations with an ambitious young man named Euthydemus, introduced in 4.2.1, make up most of the last of the four books of *Memorabilia*, and that tips the scales back toward "anticipate," since Xenophon's Socrates more nearly resembles Plato's version here than elsewhere.[114] Again and again he refutes the claims of the youngster, reducing him to a particularly painful admission of despairing ἀπορία (4.2.23), and it is worth remarking that Euthydemus seems considerably more shaken by this process than Alcibiades is, as is the major reason that he is so: it is not on his body, his soul, his wealth, and naturally not on his connection with Pericles (cf. *Alc.1* 104a3–c1) that Euthydemus take pride but rather on his library and wide reading in it

(*Mem.* 4.2.1). Since Socrates needs to teach the word *music* (μουσική) to Alcibiades (*Alc.1* 108c7-d4), the contrast between whatever Alcibiades is and the proudly intellectual Euthydemus could not be clearer. Indeed, this makes the parallels all the more striking.

> I will now show his method of dealing with [προσφέρεσθαι] those thinking they had received the best education [παιδεία] and priding themselves [μέγα φρονεῖν] on wisdom [ἐπὶ σοφίᾳ]. He was informed that Euthydemus, the handsome [ὁ καλός], had formed a large collection of the works of celebrated poets and sophists [ποιῆταί τε καὶ σοφισταί], and therefore was supposing himself to excel his age-mates in wisdom [ἐν σοφίᾳ] and having great expectations [μεγάλαι ἐλπίδες] that he would surpass everyone [πάντες] in the capacity [τὸ δύνασθαι] both to speak and to do [λέγειν τε καὶ πράττειν].[115]

Here then are the opening words of 4.2, which, along with 1.2 (where Xenophon tries to distance Socrates from Alcibiades and Critias) and 2.1 (where Socrates retells Prodicus' tale of "The Choice of Heracles"), are the three longest "chapters" in the *Memorabilia*. Since it is not because of his παιδεία, his knowledge of the ποιῆταί τε καὶ σοφισταί, or even for his wisdom (ἐπὶ σοφίᾳ and ἐν σοφίᾳ) that Alcibiades prides himself, we are left with the following parallels, none of which prove that Plato is once again dramatizing—this time by creating a dramatic historical setting for it—what he had already found in Xenophon: both young men must be said to μέγα φρονεῖν, both are described as ὁ καλός (*Alc.1* 113b9; cf. 104a5), both have μεγάλαι ἐλπίδες (*Alc.1* 105a7, 105c6, 105d7), and both are confident in their "capacity" (δύναμις at *Alc.1* 105c4). But Denyer cites 4.2.1 not only in his comments on 104a5, 105c6, and 105a7, but also on 104c2, where he contrasts the two with respect to the causes of their pride albeit only after pointing out on the basis of 4.2.9 that no more than Alcibiades did Euthydemus pride himself on his wealth, and 104e5, where Plato too uses the verb προσφέρεσθαι to describe how Socrates approached Alcibiades. Although striking in quantity, these parallels suggest that both Xenophon and Plato are describing phenomena that existed independently of either's text.

But consider the following as a basis for seeing a closer connection, not only between Alcibiades and Euthydemus, but also between Xenophon and Plato:

SOCRATES: I believe you would be equally loath to live on those sole conditions either—if you are not to fill, one may say, the whole world with your name and your power [δύναμις]; and I fancy that, except Cyrus and Xerxes, you think there has never existed a single man who was of any account. So then that this is your hope [ἐλπίς], I know well enough; I am not merely guessing.[116]

Between parallels based on Xenophon's use of τὸ δύνασθαι and his reference to μεγάλαι ἐλπίδες in 4.2.1, Plato places a passage that makes Alcibiades look more like Euthydemus with respect to books, for where else has he derived his knowledge of Cyrus the Great and Xerxes? While Denyer observes that the two are "the worst models for a citizen of the Athenian democracy,"[117] he does not mention Herodotus, Antisthenes,[118] or Xenophon. He does, however, comment on an interesting peculiarity of the pairing: "The aspect of imperial power that particularly attracts Alcibiades is therefore, it seems, the opportunity to command large armies at war, *regardless of success or failure*, and regardless of the good or harm he might do."[119]

For much the same reason that it is strange that Callicles will reference both Xerxes and Darius (*Grg.* 483d6–7), it is strange that Alcibiades will refer to Xerxes, ignominiously defeated in the Persian Wars and reduced to a tragic figure by Aeschylus. This suggests that Plato is making no attempt at historical accuracy here: Xerxes was not Alcibiades' role model, and indeed not even in Sparta does Alcibiades suggest that Athens did anything wrong by defeating Xerxes' navy at Salamis or by helping the Spartans defeat his army at Plataea. But if the reference to Xerxes is strange, the reference to Cyrus is stranger, especially in a passage that already teems with parallels to Xenophon. One point is clear: if it is not only to Herodotus' account of Cyrus but also to Xenophon's *Cyropaedia* that *der Verfasser* refers, then we really must consider *Alcibiades Major*, whether written by Plato or somebody else, a "late" work. In addition to the story of the Queen's Belt from *Anabasis*, Denyer finds allusions to Xenophon's *Agesilaus* in *Alcibiades*;[120] the reference to Cyrus here at least suggests the possible presence of a third Xenophontic work. And there is another parallel to be considered, this time between Plato's Alcibiades and Xenophon himself, for both would "cross over into Asia" (*Alc.1* 105c1), both would admire Cyrus, and both would gain experience of both Persia and Sparta.

While not exactly collapsing the difference between Alcibiades and Euthydemus with respect to literature, Denyer finds a connection to the latter's collection of ποιήται τε καὶ σοφισταί: "*Alcibiades*: It is said, O Socrates, they say he [sc. Pericles] did not become wise [σοφός] on his own [ἀπὸ τοῦ αὐτομάτου], but having consorted with many and wise men [σοφοί], and with Pythocleides and Anaxagoras; and even now [καὶ νῦν ἔτι], old as he is, he still confers with Damon concerning that very thing."[121] Here, of course, the parallel is between how Pericles is said to have become σοφός and how Euthydemus hoped to surpass others ἐν σοφίᾳ: by intercourse, whether in person or through books, with those who were σοφοί. But this parallel seems to accentuate the difference between Euthydemus and Alcibiades once again: it is not through books or even consort with the wise that the latter hopes to realize his μεγάλαι ἐλπίδες but rather ἀπὸ τοῦ αὐτομάτου, and even when Socrates proves that Alcibiades could not have discovered justice for himself—since there never was a time when he thought himself ignorant of it (*Alc.1* 109e1-110a4)—he falls back on naming the same people who taught him how to speak Greek as his teachers (*Alc.1* 111a1-4), which must count as closer to acquiring that knowledge ἀπὸ τοῦ αὐτομάτου than from the ministrations of the wise, or from the books of the ποιήται τε καὶ σοφισταί. And although the words ἔτι καὶ νῦν will become a *Leitmotiv* in *Cyropaedia*, it would be silly to see this as yet another allusion to Xenophon.

One of the passages that Denyer cites in connection with *Alcibiades* 118c3-4 also contains parallels to several other parts of 4.2:

> "How strange it is," he [sc. Socrates] said, "that those who want to play the harp or the flute, or to ride or to get skill in any similar accomplishment, work hard at whatever it is of which they plan to become capable [δυνατοί], and not by themselves [καθ' ἑαυτούς] but from those seeming to be best, doing and enduring all things so as to do nothing without their guidance, as if they could not otherwise become eminent [ἀξιόλογοι]. But of those wishing to become capable [δυνατοί] both to speak and to do [λέγειν τε καὶ πράττειν] the city's affairs [τὰ πολιτικά], some think that without preparation and care [ἐπιμελείᾳ], on their own [αὐτόματοι], suddenly, they will be capable [δυνατοί] to do these things."[122]

If *Alcibiades Major* could be said to have a single *Leitmotiv*, Socrates' repeated use of the word ἐπιμελεία would a plausible candidate for that honor. In the long central speech on Sparta and Persia, Socrates so skillfully describes the kind of ἀγών or contest[123] that awaits the ambitious

Alcibiades that the youngster, whose prior inclination had been to rely on his natural gifts (*Alc.1* 119b9–10), responds by asking what kind of ἐπιμελεία (*Alc.1* 124b7–8) will be necessary to make him competitive with his true antagonists [ἀνταγωνισταῖς] (*Alc.1* 119d7), and along with the verb ἐπιμελεῖσθαι,[124] ἐπιμέλεια is thereafter used repeatedly.

But let's not miss the forest for the trees: whether in *Alcibiades* or *Memorablia* 3.6 and 4.2, it is Socrates' purpose to persuade ambitious youngsters—who, for whatever reasons they may consider themselves to be already δυνατοί—that they require the kind of preparation and ἐπιμέλεια that only Socrates can provide them. And although the goal of becoming ἀξιόλογοι, of learning how to λέγειν τε καὶ πράττειν, and more specifically to πράττειν τὰ πολιτικά (or τὰ τῆς πόλεως) appears to have been the widely shared goals of ambitious young Athenians,[125] Socrates directs the attention both Euthydemus and Alcibiades to the need for self-knowledge, citing γνῶθι σεαυτόν in both 4.2 and *Alcibiades*, as of course Denyer points out.[126] All of this tends to support the independence of these two accounts, or at least their shared foundation in the methods of the historical Socrates. The same is also true of the young men on whom he practiced those methods, and despite the fact Alcibiades seems more inclined than Euthydemus to imagine that he can achieve his goals ἀπὸ τοῦ αὐτομάτου, he nevertheless accompanies Critias to the home of Callias in *Protagoras* so as to hear the sophist discourse on, among other things, the poetry of Simonides; it is therefore not only Euthydemus, it seems, who is determined to become wise through intercourse with ποιῆται τε καὶ σοφισταί.

On the other hand, of the four possibilities mentioned above—i.e., a nonliterary basis for parallels in the historical Socrates, indeterminate literary influence, Plato's priority, or Xenophon's—it is the third that seems most unlikely, not only because Schleiermacher was right about the speech being *Xenophontisch*, but for many other reasons as well, and the most important of these will be considered in this chapter's last section. But since the parallels between Euthydemus and Alcibiades extend to *Protagoras*, where of course it is the latter who is prominently identified as ὁ καλός (*Prt.* 316a4; cf. 309c9–10), another argument against Plato's Priority can be offered now, one that suggests the literary priority of 4.2 with respect to both *Alcibiades Major* and *Protagoras*, or rather, to the literary conceit that joins the two. The basis of that conceit is the fact that Socrates has never even spoken directly to Euthydemus—i.e., has only spoken in his presence, and with the express purpose of being heard by him—when he says what he has just been quoted as having said in 4.2.6.

As already mentioned, many ancient Platonists placed *Alcibiades* at the beginning of their Platonic reading lists, and of course none of them had any doubts about its authenticity. They also paid little attention to the historical concerns that had already led Thrasyllus to place *Euthyphro* in the first position of his edition; it was a natural concern with chronological order that explains his First Tetralogy. Of course there were limits to Thrasyllus' attention to such matters as well, as is proved by the fact that *Euthyphro* really belongs between *Theaetetus* and *Sophist*, dialogues he placed in his Second Tetralogy. The decision to begin with *Alcibiades Major* creates the same kind of dramatic problem that beginning with *Euthyphro* does: just as the latter clearly follows *Theaetetus* in a dramatic sense—his awareness of this explains why Thrasyllus placed the difficult dialogues of the Second immediately after the more accessible ones of the First Tetralogy—so too does *Alcibiades Major* follow *Protagoras*. When Alcibiades says he learned justice (the answer to the περὶ τίνος of *Alc.1* 106c7) from the many the same way he learned to speak Greek from them (τὸ ἑλληνίζειν at *Alc.1* 111a1) he is echoing an argument Protagoras had used (*Prt.* 327e1-328a1) in the course of his ἀγών with Socrates, and with Alcibiades made prominent there as an active auditor.

The best basis for denying that *Protagoras* precedes *Alcibiades Major* in a dramatic sense is that the latter purports to be the first conversation between Socrates and Alcibiades, just as 4.2 contains the first conversation between Socrates and Euthydemus.[127] Since Alcibiades proves himself to be familiar with Socrates' antics in *Protagoras* (*Prt.* 336d2-4), the fact that the two never actually speak to each other in the dialogue is easy to miss;[128] in any case, Xenophon uses a similar device in 4.2. At the start of *Protagoras*, Socrates' unnamed comrade—Denyer notes that the only literary precedent for his opening question of is found in Xenophon[129]—is already well aware that Socrates has been hunting Alcibiades; just as Xenophon tells us that Socrates has been stalking Euthydemus long before they actually speak to each other for the first time at 4.2.8. By revealing the kinds of things Socrates said in the presence of Euthydemus for the express purpose of securing his attention and interest (4.2.2-7), Xenophon employs the same conceit that joins a prior *Protagoras*, replete with its hunting theme, to the first one-on-one conversation between Socrates and Alcibiades in *Alcibiades Major*. Because of the additional complexity created by splitting between two of his dialogues what Xenophon accomplishes in a single integrated chapter in *Memorabilia*, the pendulum here swings a tad farther away from the historical Socrates—for the conceit is literary, even if, as seems likely, Socrates employed such tactics—and farther away from either literary indeterminacy or Plato's Priority. Of course those who are uncomfortable with this result can leverage the inauthenticity of *Alcibiades Major* against the plausibility of Xenophon's Priority as Arbs did.

Finally, a few remarks about *Alcibiades Minor* are in order. Leaving aside the fact that its opening moves revisit a remarkably weak argument that Socrates uses in *Protagoras* (cf. *Prt.* 332b3–333a5 and *Alc.2* 139a10–d4), and the more obvious circumstance that Xenophon's Socrates likewise reduces Euthydemus to a condition in which he no longer knows what he should pray for (4.2.36)—the core subject of *Alcibiades Minor*—it is the following passage that bears most directly on the unnamed presence of Xenophon in Plato's dialogues:

> SOCRATES: Perchance however, Alcibiades, a certain thoughtful man [φρόνιμός τις] that poet [ἐκεῖνος ὁ ποιητής] was [the whole phrase, difficult to translate, is φρόνιμός τις εἶναι ἐκεῖνος ὁ ποιητής], who making use of certain foolish friends it seems to me, seeing them both doing and praying for things that were not better [for them], but which were seeming so to them, on behalf of all of them in common, poetically crafted a prayer: "King Zeus, the things that are noble [τὰ ἐσθλά]," he says, "both prayed for and un-prayed for, give to us, while the ignoble ones [τὰ δειλά], even those prayed for, from us ward off," he enjoins. And to me, at least, he seems to speak [λέγειν] beautifully [καλῶς] and impeccably [ἀσφαλῶς]; but as for you, if you have anything in mind about these words, don't keep silent.[130]

Although this prayer is preserved in the *Greek Anthology*,[131] it should surprise no reader who can discern that Plato is *der Verfasser* of *Alcibiades Minor* that Socrates himself is this φρόνιμός τις, and thus he is ἐκεῖνος ὁ ποιητής. In case we missed the joke the first time, Socrates will mention the possibility that the Spartans may have been emulating "the poet" (*Alc.2* 148c1) in composing a similar one, "enjoining the gods to give the beautiful things [τὰ καλά] to the good" (*Alc.2* 148c3–4). Nor will it surprise any reader who is prepared to recognize the extent of Plato's debts to Xenophon that it is Xenophon's Socrates who has introduced this prayer in *Memorabilia* 1.3:

> And again, when he prayed he asked simply for good things [τἀγαθά], "for the gods know best what things are good." To pray for gold or silver or sovereignty or any other such thing, was just like praying for a gamble or a fight or anything of which the result is obviously uncertain.¹³²

It is easy to see why some thought Xenophon himself had written *Alcibiades Minor*. But it should even easier to see that if it was written by Plato, he wrote it for those who had read Xenophon's *Memorabilia*, at least whatever version of it already contained 1.3. In fact, Socrates is no more unnamed in the case of the words φρόνιμός τις εἶναι ἐκεῖνος ὁ ποιητής than Xenophon is unnamed in Plato's *Alcibiades* dyad. The only safe way to reject Xenophon's Priority in this case is to preserve the inauthenticity of *Alcibiades Minor*, and to secure Plato's Priority, it may well be necessary to follow Schleiermacher's lead and do the same for *Alcibiades Major*.

Euthydemus

Just as it is possible to find Xenophon the Writer in Plato's *Second Alcibiades*, it is possible to find Xenophon the General in the kind of παιδεία that Socrates offers Euthydemus: "But if a certain general [τις στρατηγός], seeing his troops to be despondent [ἀθύμως ἔχειν], were to invent a tale to the effect that reinforcements were coming, and by means of this false statement should put a stop to [παύειν] his soldiers' despondency [ἡ ἀθυμία], to which of the two accounts shall we place that act of fraud?"¹³³ In his translation of *Memorabilia*, H. G. Dakyns appends a note to this passage citing *Hellenica* 4.3.10 and *Cyropaedia* 1.6.31 as parallels;¹³⁴ he might also have mentioned Agesilaus or added the whole of *Cavalry Officer* 5. But there is another στρατηγός τις to be found in Xenophon's *Anabasis*, who begins his first speech to the soldiers—and that means the first time he allows us to see him mounting τὸ βῆμα and commencing to δημαγορεῖν and προστατεύειν—as follows:

> "The perjury and faithlessness of the barbarians has been spoken of by Cleanor and is understood, I imagine, by the rest of you.

If, then, it is our desire to be again on terms of friendship with them, we must needs feel great despondency [πολλὴν ἀθυμίαν ἔχειν] when we see the fate of our generals, who trustingly put themselves in their hands; but if our intention is to rely upon our arms, and not only to inflict punishment upon them for their past deeds, but henceforth to wage implacable war with them, we have—the gods willing—many fair hopes of deliverance [σὺν τοῖς θεοῖς πολλαὶ ἡμῖν καὶ καλαὶ ἐλπίδες εἰσὶ σωτηρίας]." And while he's saying this, somebody [τις] sneezes.[135]

Xenophon never tells us that he had planted this sneezing τις in the audience, although he does tell us that he had prepared himself carefully to look his best (*An.* 3.2.7). More importantly, he has emphasized the despondency of both officers and men in the previous chapter: so much are the soldiers said to ἀθύμως ἔχειν that few of them can eat (*An.* 3.1.3), if they see you to be ἄθυμοι, he tells the officers, the soldiers will be worthless (*An.* 3.1.36) and by way of proof he emphasizes how despondently they are presently performing their duties by using ἀθύμως twice (*An.* 3.1.40). So this particular στρατηγός τις—although he has not yet been elected general, he proves that he deserves to be by already demonstrating the skills of one—is fully aware that he is addressing despondent men, and he knows full well that the source of their ἀθυμία is not the demonstrated perfidy of the Persians but the fear they will never return to Greece. And that is why, after honoring the gods for the good omen of the sneeze (*An.* 3.2.9), he repeats the comforting promise that he knows is completely beyond his own control when he begins to speak again: "I happened to be saying that many and beautiful were our hopes of deliverance [πολλαὶ και καλαὶ ἐλπίδες ἡμιν σωτηρίας]" (*An.* 3.2.10). Even without the planted sneezer, it is by encouraging his soldiers' ἐλπίδες that Xenophon shows us that he is the τις στρατηγός Socrates used to teach Euthydemus.

In order to reconstruct what he calls "the Life of Xenophon," Éduard Delebecque (1910–1990) is forced to find Xenophon within his writings even when he has not mentioned himself. A well-known example is the supposition that Ischomachus the gentleman farmer of *Oeconomicus* is really a self-portrait, and that we can use "him" to reconstruct Xenophon's agricultural and housekeeping activities in Skillus.[136] As a result, the most insightful passage in Delebecque's *La vie de Xénophon*—he has just mentioned the fiction that led Xenophon to create "Themistogenes of Syracuse"—deserves both to be quoted at length and given an English translation:

He uses the same artifice differently when he inserts himself into the story under a false name. The Theopompus of Athens who responds proudly to the ambassadors of the Persian King after the Battle of Cunaxa just before the entrance of Xenophon (*An.* 2.1.12) and is called "young man" when he emphasizes precisely his youth (*An.* 2.1.13; cf. 2.1.19), has every reason to be confused with the author. In the last two books of the *Hellenica*, in the full domain of pure history, Xenophon attributes two great speeches to a certain Procles of Phlion who—while he may have lived—he now uses as an interpreter in order to express his own political views: "Procles" is merely an assumed name. In a book far closer to fantasy like *Symposium*, the author assumes for a moment the characteristics of Charmides, but even more so those of Hermogenes, son of Hipponicus and half-brother of Callias. In book four of the *Memorabilia*, long after the first time he introduced himself as present impersonally [*Mem.* 1.3.8] as a third party named "Xenophon," he now takes the characteristics of a new personage, who is no longer Hermogenes but Euthydemus.[137]

Although it is Xenophon's use of Euthydemus that is of present concern, Delebecque is right on the money in the other cases as well, and the general phenomenon in play is so important that it will be discussed in the central section of chapter 3. Suffice it to say for now that many of those who do not recognize the name Martin Handford have found delight in *Where's Waldo*;[138] my claim is that Xenophon invented the game, since he challenges you repeatedly to find *him* in his texts.

First consider merely what Socrates says to Euthydemus in 4.2 about the τις στρατηγός who deceives his soldiers for their own good. We could claim that Xenophon is reporting something that the historical Socrates actually said, and this would explain why Plato's Socrates defends a similar use of deception in *Republic* 1 (*R.* 331c1–d3) as well as giving a lengthy primer on deliberate falsehood in *Hippias Minor* with many parallels to *Memorabilia* 4.2.18–20. In the light of those parallels, we can debate literary priority, with three possible outcomes as aforesaid. But we can also step out of the priority paradigm completely and debate the following dilemma: is Xenophon channeling Socrates and Plato, or: is he placing his own concerns and opinions in the mouth of his Socrates? Although this game can be also be played with Plato—and Aristotle famously invented it—on matters such as the tripartite soul and the Platonic Idea, scholars have found it irresistible in Xenophon's case, all based on the premise, whether defended explicitly or merely implied, that Xenophon's Socrates is a rather boring pedant because Xenophon was a rather boring pedant himself. On that model, Socrates' lesson to Euthydemus in 4.2.17 is profoundly ahistorical: Socrates already knows what Xenophon would discover years later. But there is also another possibility, and its autobiographical basis is this section's theme. In a word, it synthesizes Xenophon the Writer and Xenophon the General in Xenophon the *Socratic*, and by showing what Socrates taught Euthydemus, he is revealing the Socratic source of what he accomplished on the long march home to the Sea.

If not the scribe who long ago replaced "Theompompus" with "Xenophon" (*An.* 2.1.12, see the OCT *apparatus criticus* on line 19), Francis Bacon (1561-1626) appears to be the first to have recognized that in Theopompus the Athenian Xenophon created a self-portrait,[139] but the freshness of Hartmann's account leaves little doubt that he could still regard himself as original in 1887.[140] Certainly I was under the false impression that I was original for making the same "discovery" in 1978, as so many others probably have been and had already had been even before Bacon. This is what makes Xenophon's version of "Where's Waldo" so much fun: he gives the reader who can find him the illusion that the two of you alone are "in on" the secret, and this creates or in the present case created a lifelong bond of friendship and admiration. But since it was only *Anabasis* that I read for the first time in Greek, the pair became a trio in the case of Euthydemus. If H. G. Dakyns no more discovered Xenophon in Euthydemus than Hartman discovered him in Theopompus, he nevertheless distinguished himself by including in the Introduction to his translation a section called: "On the Personal Note in the Ἀπομνημονεύματα: Who is Euthydemus? (in Bk. IV)."[141] Many is the time I've counted myself fortunate that the first writer I read for pleasure in Greek was Xenophon, and that the first translation of Xenophon's *Memorabilia* that I read was by Henry Graham Dakyns (1838-1911), and it is worth mentioning that Dakyns too was very fortunate to pass away before the Great War. A disaster for untold millions, the war was a personal disaster for Xenophon.

Before turning to Dakyns, a few words on the impact of World War I on Xenophon are in order. In Jean Renoir's classic *La Grande Illusion* (1937), two cavalry officers, one French and one German, have a conversation in English during which the German says: "I don't know who will win this war, but whatever the outcome, it will mean the end of the Rauffensteins and the Boeldieus." It also meant the end of Xenophon's political ideal, and it is truly amazing that it only received its death sentence in 1914.[142] Moreover, given that Winston Churchill was a cavalry officer before leading Britain in World War II,[143] there might be a sense in which the ideal survived a bit longer. At least as late as 1914, almost every European knew the difference between Hussars, Uhlans, Dragoons, and Cuirassiers, and it is worth remembering that every member of St. Cyr's graduating class of 1914 was killed in the Great War. Many of these had read Xenophon's *Cavalry Officer* in Greek, as had young cadets in military schools all over Europe and the Americas. From the machine gun, Xenophon has not yet recovered. And while she raises the right question—"[T]his lack of interest in Xenophon puzzles the present writer too"—Bodil Due does not mention World War I while wondering about it.[144]

Dakyns begins this section not with Euthydemus but with what he calls "the personal note." Beginning with "I have often wondered [πολλάκις ἐθαύμασα]," the first two words of *Memorabilia*, Dakyns defends his sense that the book as a whole is "an honest attempt, on the part of one who knew, to explain the character and position of Socrates who seemed to misconceive him."[145] For textual support, he then quotes five passages—three of them from book 2, the others from books 1 and 4—in which Xenophon as narrator claims to have been present, and in the last of these, he presents himself as having witnessed a conversation between Socrates and Euthydemus (*Mem.* 4.3.2). Since this is the first reference to 4.3, it is worth remarking that the role of Euthydemus in book 4 is unique: although Socrates has, for instance, two conversations with Aristippus (2.1 and 3.8), four chapters (4.2, 4.3, 4.5, and 4.6) describe the Socratic education of Euthydemus. But Dakyns does not for the present pause over 4.3 or reveal the humor of the narrator's claim in the light of his section's purpose. Instead he provides a comprehensive list of the *dramatis personae* in *Memorabilia*,[146] noting where appropriate evidence of that he calls "the personal note," but likewise emphasizing the likely external sources of Xenophon's information, namely, Hermogenes.

When he comes to book 4, he inserts the following general and virtually shorthand note about 4.1 before turning to specific comments about the characters in it and likely sources for it: "Author's introduction to final book—which I take to be of later date in composition and written on a somewhat different plane of thought, less literally 'apomnemoneumatic.'" Turning next to 4.2, he exploits the distinction between the first conversation between Socrates and Euthydemus that begins at 4.2.8 and to which there were no witnesses, and the provocative remarks Socrates make in public to catch the young man's attention before speaking to him one-on-one. Concerning the source of 4.2.1–7, Dakyns observes: "Xen. might have been there; *if* Euthydemus is a real person or a *nom de plume*." In other words, it is plausible that Xenophon may have been an eyewitness to this public and preliminary stage even if he was not Euthydemus. But when he comes to 4.2.8–40—"S. and Euthydemus, a *tête-à-tête*; §8, μόνος ἦλθεν"—his observation is remarkable: "Xen. might have heard it from the real Euthydemus, or invented it, or experienced it, or divined it. Xen artistic to the nth."[147] It is a comprehensive and revealing range of possibilities.

The numerous parallels between 4.2, 3.6, and *Alcibiades Major* stand athwart the possibility that Xenophon invented it out of whole cloth; if we are willing to admit what only the most vigorous Xenophon-haters deny—i.e., that Xenophon knew Socrates—the most plausible alternatives are: (1) Xenophon was generalizing from his own experience (hence Dakyns's "experienced it") or (2) he "heard it from the real Euthydemus." Although there is some basis for considering *this* Euthydemus to be a real person—Cobet had long before distinguished him from both the eristic in *Euthydemus* or the brother of Lysias mentioned in *Republic*[148]—it is by no means dispositive, and will in any case be considered later. Naturally, the possibility that Euthydemus is Xenophon—as Delebecque believed and Hartmut Erbse suggests[149]—unites the two possibilities: he is remembering his own lived experience with Socrates and presenting it to the reader the way he does for the same reason that he will describe the words and actions of "Xenophon" in the third person while writing his *Anabasis*. The revealing joke of 4.3 has already been mentioned, Xenophon as narrator tells that he was present, and as such collapses the distinction between (1) and (2).

Dakyns raises an interesting question here. The conversation with Euthydemus about σωφροσύνη in relation to the gods at 4.3.2–18 echoes what Xenophon has already said on the same subject as Socrates' defender in 1.4.1–8. Naturally, there is no difficulty about this if Xenophon was reporting in 1.4 the kinds of things he had personally witnessed Socrates saying to Euthydemus in 4.3, and in opposition to a revealing joke, there is the possibility that the statement of autopsy was necessary in order to give a factual basis to the things Socrates says in 1.4. The question of whether Xenophon is a jokester or a scrupulous authenticator of information is now enmeshed with whether or not Xenophon is Euthydemus. In the context of both dilemmas, it deserves mention that Xenophon introduces Euthydemus in 1.2, as the love-object of the reprehensible Critias (1.2.29). And in response to these facts and possibilities—predicated as they are on the recognition that the resulting dilemmas are unresolved—Dakyns concludes: "[O]ne is forced to ask oneself, who is Euthydemus?"[150]

Dakyns never states that Euthydemus is Xenophon, who "might have heard it from the real Euthydemus, or invented it, or experienced it, or divined it." Why does he include this last and palpably improbable alternative? Because it is the *reader* who must be the diviner here, and find Xenophon where he has hidden himself. It is an artful but open-ended concealment,[151] pervious only to the reader who is prepared to divine the author's intention, and to assert it in the full knowledge that it could never be known to be true, for to have made his identity simply knowable, Xenophon would have defeated his purpose. And what was that? The question, "Who is Euthydemus?" is merely one example of an ongoing pattern, a subspecies of the question that Xenophon raises throughout his writings: "Where's Xenophon?" When Dakyns comments on 4.2.8–30 that Xenophon is being "artistic to the nth," he could mean either that he is inventing it out of whole cloth, with no experience of his own on which it is based, or that he is artfully concealing himself. It is therefore that other question, far more personal, that Xenophon is forcing us to ask: is Xenophon a reliable reporter—e.g., "I heard it from Euthydemus"—or an artist, and if the latter, is he a whole-cloth inventor or a subtle Socratic who makes his readers sift his words in order to discover the truth, knowing that with that discovery, they will be making the acquaintance of a lifelong friend?

Nothing has been said so far about Leo Strauss, influential creator of a new and far subtler Xenophon, and self-styled defender of his greatness. Since Strauss began writing about Xenophon in 1939,[152] Strauss's own defenders would naturally reject out of hand my earlier suggestion that Xenophon—along with Uhlans and Cuirassiers—was a casualty of World War I, apparently believing that, thanks to Strauss, he rose again like a phoenix on the eve of World War II. Although those who think they know what "Straussians" do or think might be inclined to find Strauss's influence behind the words "subtle Socratic" in the last paragraph, they are in error: nothing could be more foreign to Strauss's own reading of Xenophon than finding him between the lines of 4.2, or rather, to avoid any possible ambiguity, than identifying Xenophon with Euthydemus. After mentioning the fact that Euthydemus "had great hopes that he could surpass all others in power of speaking and acting," Strauss wrote: "Being a youth of this kind, Euthydemos had no longer a desire for learning and had had at all times a rather perverse desire for learning: he was not a good nature."[153] The library of Euthydemus proves he would not be susceptible to Socrates; a previous desire to learn from books is presumably—according to Strauss here—incompatible with a subsequent willingness to learn anything more.[154] If this were true, Xenophon would not be writing books, and Strauss would never have gained an influential following by reading and interpreting them.

Xenophon naturally never asserts that Euthydemus "was not a good nature," or that he was "a quite unpromising youth."[155] At the conclusion of 4.2, the narrator observes that many of those who received from Socrates the kind of intellectual drubbing he has just administered to Euthydemus—a humiliating revelation of his or rather their intellectual incapacity—avoided him thereafter. If any, it was these who lacked "a good nature," although Xenophon does not even say that, calling them "rather stolidly squishy [βλακότεροι]." Here is what he does say:

> And so he [sc. Euthydemus] went away very dejected, disgusted with himself and convinced that he was indeed a slave. Now many of those who were brought to this pass by Socrates, never went near him again and were regarded by him as mere blockheads [βλακότεροι]. But Euthydemus guessed that he would never be a man worthy of account [ἀνὴρ ἀξιόλογος] unless he spent as much time as possible with Socrates. Henceforward, unless obliged to absent himself, he never left him, and even began to imitate some of his practices. Socrates, for his part, seeing how it was with him, avoided worrying him, and began to expound very plainly and clearly the knowledge that he thought most needful and the practices that he held to be the strongest.[156]

In response to this distinction, Strauss commented: "We have to add here this remark: the fact that Euthydemos was a better man than those who avoided Socrates because he had deflated them does not prove he was a good nature."[157] And we have to add here another remark: Strauss has proved himself in this instance to be an unreliable interpreter of Xenophon, and if behind "Euthydemus" we can find Xenophon, he has done so in a particularly revealing manner.

Nor is this an isolated case. When Delebecque included Hermogenes on the list that included Theompompus and Euthydemus, he was not referring to Hermogenes in his evidentiary role as Xenophon's source of information about Socrates' last days but as the character in Xenophon's *Symposium*. The conceit that allows the banqueters to make speeches in Xenophon is not that all of them offer an encomium to love or ἔρως as in Plato's, but rather all explain what each takes pride in, as proposed by their host Callias: "I am therefore telling you that upon which I set greatest stock [μέγιστον φρονῶ]" (*Smp.* 3.4). Hermogenes, of whom Socrates will remark that he is melting away with ἔρως for excellence (καλοκἀγαθία at 8.3), and who displays an exquisite sense of Socratic pedagogy a few moments later (8.12), makes a speech (4.46–49) about his powerful friends, who turn out to be the gods. After attributing to them omniscience including the power to know a man's thoughts (4.47),[158] he describes how the gods guide him through voices, dreams, and birds (φῆμαι καὶ ἐνύπνια καὶ οἰωνοί at 4.48).[159] Socrates confirms that this is possible (4.49). In response to Socrates' question about how he serves the gods, Hermogenes replies that he praises them; this in turn leads Socrates to link the gods to καλοκἀγαθία (4.40).

Although Strauss is aware that dreams (ἐνύπνια) are the central item in Hermogenes' list of three sources, he fails to comment on it, and this is remarkable because Xenophon's dream about "a great light from Zeus [φῶς μέγα ἐκ Διός]" (*An.* 3.1.12) was a turning point for the Ten Thousand and, of course, for Xenophon himself. Like a good Straussian, Strauss is determined to find Xenophon in his *Symposium*, since he tells us at the start that he was present (*Smp.* 1.1). In doing so, Strauss is doing what Xenophon wanted him to do: he is playing the ancient version of "Where's Waldo?" But he is not playing it well. Thanks to the fact that Strauss would provide two different answers to this excellent question over the course of his career,[160] it is evident that he did not know. But another thing is just as evident: his pronounced, vituperative, and consistent hostility to Hermogenes: "His deplorable heavy-handedness (consider the contrast with *Memorabilia* III.524 [sic])—his complete lack of understanding of what irony is or requires—confirms everything that the *Symposium* had suggested regarding him before."[161] As before with Euthydemus, the same conclusion stands in the case of Hermogenes: Strauss is an unreliable interpreter of Xenophon. To take a step farther, Strauss is every bit as hostile to the pious Socratic cavalry officer who had earned Schleiermacher's contempt, German philology's marginalization, and execution by machine gun in the Great War, as Xenophon's open enemies are.

To return to more important matters at the end, the many parallels between 4.2 and *Alcibiades Major* discussed in the previous section suggests that it is Plato, not Xenophon, who was being "artistic to the nth." As the passage just quoted indicates, what Socrates did to Euthydemus he did to many others, and among those we should probably include both Plato and Xenophon. In that sense, both were drawing on their own experiences with "the historical Socrates" while writing up two initial conversations *tête-à-tête*, both of which followed a preliminary "softening up" that avoided direct address. Xenophon is either transcribing what he learned from "the historical Socrates" or what he himself experienced, merely renaming the youth he then was. Plato, whether on the basis of his own experience or on the basis of what he learned from "the fictional Euthydemus," transferred into the historical past the kind of conversation he needed to imagine that Socrates had had with Alcibiades. Independent of each other 4.2 and *Alcibiades Major* might be, with both derived from similar experiences with Socrates, but two things are not the case: (1) that Xenophon is the one being "artistic to the nth," and (2) that Xenophon modeled the conversations with Euthydemus on *Alcibiades Major*. Those who regard the latter as inauthentic have nothing to lose by admitting this; those who do not are in a good position to see how Plato went beyond Xenophon while standing on his shoulders.

There is, of course, the possibility of the historical Euthydemus, and this is the last matter Dakyns addresses in "Who is Euthydemus?" He lists five instances of that name in Greek literature, and excludes the possibility that Xenophon's Euthydemus is either the eristic or Lysias' brother; this leaves three: Two of them have already been mentioned, Xenophon's Euthydemus in book 4 and Xenophon's Euthydemus in book 1. Since the former is called ὁ καλός and the latter is being pursued erotically by Critias (4.2.1 and 1.2.29), they are clearly the same. Plato mentions the third, and unlike Xenophon, provides him with a patronymic: "'And indeed it is not to me only that he has done such things, but also to Charmides, son of Glaucon, Euthydemus, son of Diocles [ὁ Διοκλέους], and a great many others, whom he deceives as a lover [ἐξαπατῶν ὡς ἐραστῆς], establishing himself more as a boyfriend than as a lover'" (*Smp.* 222a8–b4). The speaker, of course, is Alcibiades. Since Apollodorus is telling his story to a Glaucon that cannot be Charmides' father (*Smp.* 172c3), Plato has managed to refer to three passages in Xenophon's *Memorabilia*: 3.6,[162] 3.7, and the greater part of book 4. Given the possibility that he wrote *Alcibiades Major* with 4.2 in mind, it was a nice touch on Plato's part to entrust the only mention of Euthydemus outside of Xenophon to Alcibiades. And if Euthydemus exists only at the point of literary intersection between Plato and Xenophon, ὁ Διοκλέους was a particularly thoughtful and respectful choice of patronymic for a young man who would name his second son "Diodorus," who began to δημαγορεῖν and προστατεύειν only after seeing a φῶς μέγα ἐκ Διός, and who achieved an eternal and undying fame or κλέος (cf. κλέος ἐς τὸν ἀεὶ χρόνον ἀθάνατον at *Smp.* 208c5-6) as a result. It is in this way that Plato may have found a way to mention Xenophon after all.

Chapter Two

Xenophon's Debts to Plato

Memorabilia

Diogenes Laertius is an important witness for the ancient axiom of a Literary Rivalry between Plato and Xenophon, and his testimony regarding Plato's Priority likewise makes him distinctly and distinctively premodern. The opening words of his chapter on Xenophon make this crystal clear and are well worth quoting:

> Xenophon was the son of Gryllus; he was an Athenian of the Deme of Erchia. He was modest and extraordinarily handsome [αἰδήμων δὲ καὶ εὐειδέστατος εἰς ὑπερβολήν]. It is said that Socrates met him in a narrow lane, extended his staff and blocked his way, inquiring where [ποῦ] each kind of food was being sold; on receiving an answer, he then asked, "Where [ποῦ] do men [ἄνθρωποι] become good and honorable [καλοὶ κἀγαθοί]?" Xenophon was perplexed [participle from ἀπορεῖν], and Socrates he said, "Follow me, then, and learn [ἕπου τοίνυν καὶ μάνθανε]." And from then on he was a student [ἀκροατής] of Socrates. He was the first [πρῶτος] to note down [ὑποσημειοῦσθαι] Socrates' words [τὰ λεγόμενα], which he published [εἰς ἀνθρώπους ἄγειν] under the title *Memorabilia* [Ἀπομνημονεύματα].[1]

As indicated by the brackets, there is a great deal to be discussed here. But first it is worth noting the most amazing aspect of Diogenes' impact on the reception of Xenophon and Plato: while a report about what "some say" about Plato's *Laws* and *Epinomis* has become the interpretive bedrock for the modern interpretation of Plato,[2] this clear statement in the author's own apodictic voice about the priority of Xenophon's *Memorabilia* has been completely ignored.

Diogenes clearly does not recognize Euthydemus in *Memorabilia* 4 as Xenophon, and this simpler alternative version of his first encounter with Socrates has considerable charm. On the essential points, however, the two versions are the same: like Euthydemus ὁ καλός, Xenophon is notably handsome [εὐειδέστατος εἰς ὑπερβολήν], Socrates asks him a series of questions that reduce the youth to ἀπορία, and instead of turning away from Socrates in frustrated disgust (cf. *Mem.* 4.2.40), Xenophon follows the Socratic directive ἕπου τοίνυν καὶ μάνθανε, and thereafter becomes his ἀκροατής, just as Euthydemus did. There are other elements, however, suggesting that Diogenes or rather his source has oversimplified matters: the desire to become one of the καλοὶ κἀγαθοί plays no explicit part in the conversion of Euthydemus—his desire is rather to become an ἀνὴρ ἀξιόλογος as Socrates knows full well (cf. *Mem.* 4.2.40 and 4.2.6)—and recalls the pious Hermogenes of Xenophon's *Symposium* instead. And in response to Socrates' first attempt to draw him out, Euthydemus keeps silent because he wishes to surround himself with a *reputation* (δόξα at *Mem.* 4.2.6) for σωφροσύνη—which seems to mean something like "modest stillness and humility"—a considerably less self-serving description than Diogenes' αἰδήμων εἰς ὑπερβολήν. With respect to Xenophon's honesty, it is interesting to compare Euthydemus' desire to become an ἀνὴρ ἀξιόλογος with Plato's use of "a trustworthy man [ἀνὴρ ἀξιόπιστος]" to describe the source of the Queen's Sash (*Alc.1* 123b4).

The crucial matter, however, are Diogenes' claims about Xenophon's *Memorabilia*, beginning with his use of the word πρῶτος. Note first that this unequivocal statement of Xenophon's Priority has been disregarded because it clashes with the modern prejudice, not because Diogenes' version of the first meeting between Xenophon and Socrates is less accurate than the one I am claiming that Xenophon the ἀξιόπιστος provided in 4.2. The second claim is implicit in the verb ὑποσημειοῦσθαι (LSJ, "note down"), coupled with the sentence that immediately follows the passage just quoted: "He was also the first [πρῶτος] philosopher to write a work of history [ἱστορία]."[3] This suggests an inner connection between the author of *Anabasis* and *Hellenica*—making written memoranda as he went—and the "auditor [ἀκροατής]" of Socrates, and perhaps what made Xenophon Plato's ἀνὴρ ἀξιόπιστος was precisely that his Ἀπομνημονεύματα were based on the written notes of a philosopher who also studied with care a historian who had written a great ἱστορία and would write several more himself. The use of ὑποσημειοῦσθαι in this passage suggests that he wrote three: *Hellenica*, *Anabasis*, and *Memorabilia*. Meanwhile, Xenophon's affection for the written word is suggested not only by ὑποσημειοῦσθαι but also by the book collection of Euthydemus (*Mem.* 4.2.1 and 4.2.10) and the way Socrates teaches him by writing (4.2.13). Finally, it is not clear that these two uses of πρῶτος are separable: Diogenes may be suggesting that what made Xenophon πρῶτος with respect to Literary Priority is intimately linked to what made it possible for him to be "first of philosophers" to write ἱστορίαι.

Any ancient justification or explanation of the literary priority of Xenophon's *Memorabilia* must be considerably less important to moderns like ourselves than whatever it is that has persuaded us to disregard Diogenes' testimony entirely. It really has been a sea change, because even though Diogenes gives voice to the ancient prejudice that Xenophon and Plato were rivals in his biographies of both, the way he does so is once again rather more consistent with Xenophon's Priority than with Plato's. Having noted first that the chapter on Xenophon directly follows the chapter on Socrates in *Lives of the Eminent Philosophers*, consider what Diogenes writes there: "For the sweetness of his style [γλυκύτης τῆς ἑρμηνείας] he [sc. Xenophon] was called the Attic Muse [Ἀττικὴ Μοῦσα]; hence he and Plato were jealous [ζηλοτύπως ἔχειν] of each other [πρὸς ἀλλήλους], as will be mentioned in the chapter on Plato."[4] Here is the relevant passage from the latter:

> And it seems that Xenophon was not on good terms with Plato. They have written similar works, at any rate, as if out of rivalry [ὥσπερ διαφιλονεικοῦντες] with each other [πρὸς ἀλλήλους]—a *Symposium*, and *Apology*, and memoirs [ἀπομνημονεύματα] that deal with ethical matters. And one of them wrote a *Republic*, the other an *Education of Cyrus*. In his *Laws* Plato says that Xenophon's account of Cyrus's education is a fiction, for the real Cyrus did not resemble the man portrayed by Xenophon. They both make mention of Socrates, but nowhere do they refer to each other except for Xenophon's mention of Plato in the third book of his *Memorabilia*.[5]

Although Diogenes presents the rivalry as mutual—hence the use of πρὸς ἀλλήλους in both places—the facts that (1) he mentions that rivalry for the first time after referring to Xenophon as Ἀττικὴ Μοῦσα in the context of his γλυκύτης τῆς ἑρμηνείας, praise that would suggest why Plato might desire to surpass him, (2) the longer account of that rivalry is in the life of Plato, and (3) the only concrete example in that account depends on the priority of Xenophon's *Cyropaedia* to Plato's *Laws*, make the implication clear: the ancient axiom in no way implied the modern one.

It is obviously no secret that I regard Plato's Priority as a merely modern *prejudice*, and since the clearest ancient evidence for Xenophon's Priority is Diogenes' unequivocal πρῶτος in the context of the Ἀπομνημονεύματα, it must seem strange that the first section of a chapter on "Xenophon's Debts to Plato" should begin with his *Memorabilia* given my own evident prejudice. The explanation for this apparent anomaly is that even though I regard Diogenes' πρῶτος as containing an important, overlooked, and unjustly despised element of truth, I no more regard Xenophon's *Memorabilia* as a unitary work—i.e., as having been written once and for all as a unified whole, and made available all at one time—than I do *Hellenica* or *Anabasis*. And I may as well admit at the start that even though I will be making some assertions as to when and where its various portions were written, I regard the problem with which Franz Hornstein struggled in "Komposition und Herausgabe der Xenophontischen *Memorabililien*"[6] as a problem with which I too will continue to struggle throughout this book. The new element I propose to bring to the old and unsolved problem of "the composition and publication of Xenophon's *Memorabilia*" is the light Plato's dialogues might shed on the chronological order of its various parts. So even though I regard the first and oldest part of *Memorabilia* to be older than any of Plato's dialogues with the possible exception of his *Apology of Socrates*, I also regard its later parts as repeatedly or at least potentially demonstrating "Xenophon's debts to Plato."

In short: what makes the addition of "potentially" necessary is that "the composition" of Xenophon's *Memorabilia* is and will remain a problem. A far stronger case can be made for a two-part *Anabasis* or a three-part *Hellenica*;[7] the maintenance of a resolutely tentative tone is therefore unnecessary in those cases despite the by no means unproblematic speculations that undergird them. The case of *Memorabilia* is infinitely more complicated since it may well consist of more than three separate parts, with the possibility of multiple additions or accretions not to be ruled out. Only two expedients will be ruled out in what follows: an all-at-once "publication" of *Memorabilia* and a posthumous editor or "redactor."[8] It is therefore between these two extremes that a hunt for the truth will take place, and the new aspect of that hunting expedition is the hypothesis that traces of Plato will be used to articulate its parts or strands. The latter may be the better word choice, not least of all because it cannot be assumed that even chapters, let alone entire books, are the best basis for articulating the whole into parts. Since Xenophon himself will occupy here the role nineteenth-century scholarship often assigned to an anonymous redactor, there will be no reason to suppress or devalue the strong indications of the work's unity.[9] As for the rejection of the latter, it suffices to suggest at the outset that it was Xenophon's way not only to build on the foundations of others—of Thucydides in particular—as well as on his own.

Given the tentative character of the initial stance taken to the problem, some other methodological observations might aptly precede the following attempt to grapple with it. The tools of nineteenth-century philology can be applied both usefully and destructively; the comparative worth of their application to Xenophon and Plato illustrates the difference. When applied to a teacher such as Plato—using his texts in a paradigmatically academic context and tinkering with the details with which they so delightfully abound until the end of his life[10]—the tools requisite for analysis of compositional order prove to be blunt instruments indeed. But when to this bluntness are added the facts that Plato was a dramatist of extraordinary gifts as well as the philosopher of the unchanging and eternal Idea, the resulting analysis becomes farrago if not farce. The peculiarities of speech with which he endows his Athenian Stranger tell us next to nothing about his own "mature style," while it is the crude and possibly erroneous identification of his own views with those of his characters—including, in the allegedly terminal case of the Athenian Stranger—on which depends the merely "likely story" of his Socratic tutelage, his middle period, and his modification or abandonment of "the Theory of Ideas."

The tools in question are better applied to Xenophon. First of all, as a historian, he was primarily concerned with vicissitude and change; this point has already been made. And when we consider the objects of his concern, it is in the nature of the case that his views and valuations of those objects should likewise change over time. Even while arguing against *Hellenica* III, Dillery has illuminated the overarching theme of Spartan crime and punishment that informs the work's structure beginning in book 5; changing views of both Sparta and Athens might plausibly be used to date the composition of a number of Xenophon's other writings. Without for the present examining the complexities associated with Xenophon's narrative voice,[11] his lack of Plato's dramatic gifts make it far more plausible that, for example, the complete absence of the particle μήν in *Cynegeticus* is sufficient evidence that it is Xenophon's earliest work.[12] And the crown jewel of nineteenth-century *Kritik*, the analytic tools forged by Wolf for the dismemberment of Homer, and then applied with equally devastating effect to the Pentateuch, are far more applicable to Xenophon's *Memorabilia* than to, for instance, Plato's *Republic*, or indeed to a "developmentalist" approach to his writings as whole. It is striking, for example, that so many more scholars have taken a unitarian approach to Xenophon's *Memorabilia* than to Plato's dialogues, which are conventionally articulated into three parts. Finally, there is the easily overlooked fact that it was Xenophon, not Plato, whose lack of a school made it necessary for him to *publish* his writings, which is what I take Diogenes Laertius to mean by the words εἰς ἀνθρώπους ἄγειν. In approaching *Memorabilia*, then, and without claiming anything like the ability to use them as well as the German scholars who invented them, all the tools of nineteenth-century philology are in play, for no matter how misapplied they may have been in the case of Plato, they can be usefully applied to the "Komposition und Herausgabe der Xenophontischen *Memorabililien*."[13] As a general matter, I will be applying to Xenophon's writings "developmentalist" philological methods that have been inappropriately applied to Plato's, while applying to Plato's a "unitarian" approach that has been equally misapplied to Xenophon's.

But if something like the chronological order of Xenophon's writings can be established on the basis of repurposing these philological tools, and if that order implicates the writings of Plato to which Xenophon responds (and vice versa), this result creates something unmistakably strange, and for that an explanatory palinode is required. In a word, the assiduous agnosticism regarding Order of Composition that presided over the investigation of Reading Order in *Plato the Teacher* will here be dropped. It was always even more obvious that Plato had not written all of his dialogues at one time than that Xenophon wrote *Memorabilia* in installments; it was the destructive impact of using the alleged order of their composition in order to *interpret* the dialogues against which this assiduous agnosticism was deployed. My palinode's justification is that using a dialogue with Xenophon as a basis for reopening the chronological question is to put that ordering on a literary basis that is more respectful than the one that misinterprets the relationship between Plato and his characters, ignores his dramatic capacity to speak and write in other voices and styles, and which presupposes changing views about the unchanging Platonic Idea. A literary dialogue with a fellow-Socratic who blazed his trail and was then enriched in turn—a pattern that repeats itself again and again—is a better basis for thinking about Plato's progress *as a writer*,[14] and because it does not, this dialogue will not be used here to shed light on his thought, already discussed at length in *Plato the Teacher*.

Moreover, "the tools of nineteenth-century German philology" is not the best term of art even where my approach to Xenophon is concerned. To take a single example, the present consensus among contemporary German philologists continues to uphold the nineteenth-century view that Xenophon did not write the *Cynegeticus*,[15] and in origin as well as in application, *Echtheitskritik* cannot be easily separated from philological *Kritik* in general.[16] Having already gratefully acknowledged Dakyns's influence, it is worth pointing out that he was MA, that is, he neither earned nor sought to earn a PhD, the academic badge of *Wissenschaft* and *Kritik*. And neither did E. C. Marchant (1864–1960). Mere gentleman-scholars by German standards, both Marchant and Dakyns rather take for granted than defend at length the authenticity of Xenophon's *Cynegeticus*,[17] and an interesting case could be made that the philological roots of the Great War—if indeed there were any—are more obvious in this case than in others; to put it simply and provocatively, Xenophon was too much the English country gentlemen to be taken seriously by the proponents of *Alterthumswissenschaft*.[18] But even if this is unfair to German philologists, it is considerably less so to, for example, Marchant. Consider these excerpts from his obituary in the *Times*:

> Mr. E. C. Marchant, for many years Sub-Rector of Lincoln College, Oxford, and a well-known classical scholar, died yesterday at his home at Oxford at the age of 95. He was a man of vigorous mind, unmethodical as an administrator (though with a gift for rapid improvisation), with a lively humor, a shrewd appreciation of human nature, and a devotion to the classics which made him in his day a notable Oxford personality. His keenness of mind remained with him well after his ninetieth birthday. . . . He was an assistant master at St. Paul's School from 1887 to 1891, in the great days of Dr. Walker's High Mastership, and after a brief return to Peterhouse with a fellowship he took over in 1894 part of the classical work of the upper eighth at St. Paul's. . . . In 1914 he married Miss Ethel Winifred Mallet, and moving out of college he began to develop the interest in gardening that was to become his chief

hobby in later life. . . . His temperament was mercurial, but company infallibly revived him and he had a buoyancy and vivacity which made him an entertaining companion. And beneath his gaiety there was a true human understanding and a practical sympathy to which his pupils owed much.[19]

I don't mean to suggest that there were no nineteenth-century German scholars who produced high quality academic work while teaching in a *gymnasium*, who were beloved by their students, married at fifty, and cultivated their gardens, but none of them failed or rather never sought to earn a PhD. Marchant's career is nothing but English, and redolent of an England that was already long gone in 1960; in addition, his "mercurial temperament," his "buoyancy and vivacity," and his combination of humor and "a shrewd appreciation of human nature" explain his sympathy for Xenophon.

On the other hand, the scholar who will preside over this section (and over everything else in this book where Xenophon's *Memorabilia* is concerned) is Hans von Arnim,[20] who was born in Brandenburg in 1859 and died in Vienna in 1931. For context, it may be remarked that he earned his PhD under Wilamowitz with a dissertation on Euripides in 1882,[21] taught in a *Gymnasium* between 1881 and 1888, and habilitated in 1888 writing on Philo of Alexandria. For present purposes, his most significant accomplishment was his 1923 book *Xenophons Memorabilien und Apologie des Sokrates*. As a pioneer in the stylometric analysis of Plato,[22] he possesses the requisite philological skills, but von Arnim also brings to the study of Xenophon a sympathy that is very unusual in German scholarship, thus combining all that is best in Anglo-German friendship, itself definitively destroyed only on August 4, 1914. Nothing in the foregoing remarks should indicate that there is anything like academic parity between the editor of the four-volume *Stoicorum Veterum Fragmenta* and the likes of Dakyns and Marchant, which of course is not meant to detract from the amiable contributions of the English pair. And quite apart from von Arnim's approach to *Phaedrus*, his famous debate with Max Pohlenz—of whom more in due course—on *Lysis* leaves no doubt which of the two was a more sensitive reader of Plato's playful dialogues.[23]

After arguing for the authenticity of Xenophon's *Apology of Socrates*, von Arnim establishes its chronological priority to the reprise of similar material at the end of the fourth book of *Memorabilia*. In turning to the later work, he makes his most valuable contribution to "die Entstehungsgeschichte von Xenophons *Memorabilien*"[24] by taking a broader and more inclusive view of the so-called *Schutzschrift* of 1.2. First, he joins it to 4.8, which he has already shown to follow and indeed to modify the earlier but similar *Apology of Socrates*.[25] Crucial for the present book is von Arnim's claim that what caused Xenophon to rewrite the material in the *Apology* in *Memorabilia* 4.8 was not only the need to respond to the pamphlet of Polycrates,[26] but also the intervening appearance of Plato's *Apology of Socrates*.[27] Here, then, is the first example in this chapter of its actual theme: Xenophon's debts to Plato:

> It seems certain to me that Xenophon, through studying the Platonic *Apology*—which shows itself to have influenced the revision of the transferred section—came to the conclusion that in his own *Apology*, because of insufficient information, he had not given an entirely accurate report of Socrates' trial.[28]

This first debt is characteristic of the man Xenophon was: he was indebted to Plato for revealing the inadequacy of the information he had received from Hermogenes,[29] and instead of digging in his heels to defend what he had written—as so many so-called academics are wont to do—he decided instead to revise and resubmit accordingly; the oldest version of his *Memorabilia* was the result.

It is certainly true that both *Apologies* contain what Diogenes Laertius calls τὰ λεγόμενα of Socrates, and to that extent, Xenophon's *Apology* alone might entitle him to that easily ignored πρῶτος. But it is specifically to Xenophon's *Memorabilia* that Diogenes accords Socratic priority, and if we are willing to see beyond the most famous speech of Socrates to his conversations—clearly the subject of published discussion before Xenophon (*Ap.* 1)[30]—the revised version of his *Apology* in *Memorablia* 4.8 may be able to maintain conversational or dialogic priority to Plato's dialogues if not to his *Apology* depending on how much more of *Memorabilia* 4 the original *Schutzschrift* included. And it is precisely here that von Arnim breaks with earlier conceptions of the *Schutzschrift* by adding to 4.2 to 1.2.[31] With German certainty, von Arnim announces the stunning conclusion:

> I therefore see it as proved that in book 1, chapters 1–4.1 + book 4 we read the oldest part of the *Memorabilia*, the Defense [*Schutzschrift*] against the accusation of Polycrates, with which Xenophon wanted to replace his earlier published *Apology*

after he had become aware of its shortcomings through the publication of the Platonic *Apology*.³²

The fact that von Arnim is rather too liberal in including all of *Memorabilia* 4 in the *Schutzschrift* cannot diminish the enormous significance of this expansion.³³ As the discussion of 4.2 in the previous chapter indicates, its addition to what von Arnim calls the *Urmemorabilien*³⁴ has the potential of making the dialogues with Euthydemus the first of Socrates' τὰ λεγόμενα to be written down, a result that justifies the use of the words ὑποσημειοῦσθαι and ἱστορία in Diogenes and combines that justification with Dakyns's and Delebecque's answer to the question "Who is Euthydemus?" All the more remarkable, then, is the fact that von Arnim never considers the possibility that Euthydemus is Xenophon himself. Throughout his third chapter ("Die *Memorabilien* als geschichtliche Quelle"),³⁵ von Arnim labors under the traditional burden of "the Socratic Question,"³⁶ and is forced to postulate Xenophon's return to Athens if only to give him the chance to interview Euthydemus³⁷ and, even more humorlessly, to gain access to the memoranda that "he" had made.³⁸ Naturally there is a far simpler hypothesis at hand: Xenophon had no need for "Euthydemus' papers" even if had failed to make any memoranda of his own.³⁹

The fact that von Arnim's *Urmemorabilien* combines the greater part of book 1 with the whole of book 4 makes it easier for him to imagine only two more versions of the *Memorabilia*, the second adding 1.4.2 thru 2.1, the third the rest of book 2 and the whole of book 3.⁴⁰ He will also avail himself—primarily for the purpose of adding the conversation between Alcibiades and Pericles in 1.2.40–46—of a posthumous redactor, who can fuse the three editions while adding "einiger Paralipomena aus seinem Nachlaß."⁴¹ And having allowed von Arnim to introduce that characteristically German conception, it is time to bid him a fond farewell, remarking only that he has laid the foundation for what follows, and despite his heavy-handed approach to Euthydemus, he has made it possible to combine the fruits of his philological precision—and throughout, his discussion of parallel texts is magisterial—with the playful hypothesis that discovers in Xenophon the inventor of "Where's Waldo?"

The need to leave von Arnim behind at this point arises from the fact that he leaves the most difficult problems unsolved, and although a solution for all of them cannot be promised, their broad outlines must now be sketched. Of these, the most difficult is the relationship between *Memorabilia* 3.8 and *Hippias Major*, and, more generally, the unity of book

3. As indicated in the first chapter, there is good reason to regard 3.1–7 as a whole; this leaves the unresolved problem of whether it anticipates Plato's *Republic* or builds on it,[42] especially by providing the backstory for Glaucon while showing Socrates preparing his auditors for "doing the things of the city." Although neither 3.8 nor 3.9 appears to be connected with this project,[43] the relationship between the latter and both *Euthydemus* and *Protagoras* is just as striking as the former's to *Hippias Major*. As for 3.10–12, it is difficult to determine how or even if these three chapters are connected to either of the other two parts of book 3, nor do Plato's dialogues shed much light on the question.[44] But 3.8–9 do have important connections of a dialectical nature to both 4.6 and 4.4,[45] with the latter standing in opposition to the problematic dialogue between Alcibiades and Pericles in 1.2.40–46.[46] By way of making some further progress, this group of "dialectical" passages will be treated provisionally as a unit,[47] and the hypothesis that it constitutes the last section added to the *Memorabilia* will hereafter be explored.

At this point, a brief digression is required. The use of "dialectical" must be clearly understood since it will come to function as a technical term in what follows. The textual basis for its use is 4.6, where Xenophon writes the following about Socrates: "How he was also making his companions more dialectical [διαλεκτικώτεροι], I will try to explain this as well [πειράσομαι καὶ τοῦτο λέγειν]."[48] My use of "dialectical" starts from the use of πειράσομαι: what makes Xenophon diffident about his ability to explain how Socrates made his companions διαλεκτικώτεροι is that it is difficult to do so. It is one thing to explain to someone how to build a house (*Mem.* 3.8.8–10) or to ride a horse (*Eq.*); my use of "dialectical" rests on the idea that it is not by telling someone the truth and telling it to them "straight" that you can accomplish καὶ τοῦτο, that is to say, making them διαλεκτικώτεροι as well. Xenophon can only *try* to show how Socrates did so, and in another place I have argued that the simplistic definitions Socrates will go on to offer in 4.6 have received criticism not only for being simplistic but also wrong-headed and sometimes at odds with what Socrates has said elsewhere is that this is precisely the reaction they were created to provoke.[49] Only when students can recognize bad arguments do they become "dialectical," and the best way to make them more "dialectical" is for their teacher to use such arguments herself, and use them deliberately.

To return to the thread of discourse, in many respects 2.1—and, if von Arnim is to be trusted, the last three chapters of book 1 to which he

78 | The Relay Race of Virtue

connects it—creates the same problem as 3.1–7, and once again in relation to *Republic*. By showing Heracles making a decision between an easier and a more difficult path, is Xenophon merely channeling Prodicus, or anticipating the Longer and Shorter Ways in Plato's *Republic*? Complicating this dilemma is that one of the few positions for which I feel ready to argue is the philosophical coherence of at least the remainder of book 2, and perhaps the whole of it. And for this unit, I also will propose a time and place of origin: after the King's Peace, and with Xenophon married with children in Skillus, and that means in what I will call his "middle period." Inclined to identify the dialectical chapters as "late," this typology provides a skeleton for a three-phase *Memorabilia* without claiming any adequate solution as yet for the place of 1.4–2.1, 3.1–7, or 3.10–12 within that framework. But even if presently unprepared to speculate on the exact nature of the debts, I regard it as clear that there are debts to Plato to be discovered among the dialectical chapters, as well as in 3.1–7 and book 2.

But being presently unable to identify them, this section's title must be justified not on the promise of coming attractions but only on the basis of von Arnim's expanded conception of the *Urmemorabilien*. Having begun with his *Apology of Socrates*, the dual impetus of Polycrates and Plato's *Apology* led Xenophon to write the oldest strand of his *Memorabilia*,[50] and by deciding to preserve for posterity his own early conversations with Socrates by calling himself "Euthydemus," he not only used the same kind of trick he had already used in publishing *Anabasis* I—albeit in reverse—but also showed that he truly deserved the πρῶτος that Diogenes would accord him. His oldest debt to Plato is, to repeat an important claim, characteristic of the man: Xenophon recognized the superiority of Plato's *Apology of Socrates* to his own and modified his approach to defending his hero accordingly, creating in the process a literary precedent of great originality with even greater ramifications. The principal flaw with Plato's Priority is that it makes Xenophon both unoriginal and tasteless; on offer here is a more nuanced alternative to both ancient and modern prejudices, one that preserves Xenophon's Priority without ignoring his debts to Plato.

Symposium

Cited in antiquity as evidence of Literary Rivalry, the two *Symposia* are the prime example of the more cooperative model—equally charitable to both Plato and Xenophon—which I am proposing. To begin with, every sensitive reader of Plato's *Symposium* must realize that Socrates' claim about comedy and tragedy in the wee hours of the morning (Plat. *Smp.* 223c2-d6) is the key to the interpretation of this brilliant dialogue, and that Plato himself is the poet who reveals himself to have mastered both comic and tragic poetry, the proof of that dual mastery being *Symposium* itself.[51] Unlike Plato's, Xenophon's *Symposium* is explicitly comic from beginning to end: his narrator narrates the victory party Callias gave for his beloved in order to show Socrates at play (Xen. *Smp.* 1.1), and since the party ends with a sexually titillating pantomime (Xen. *Smp.* 9.2-6) that puts most everyone in the mood to have sex (Xen. *Smp.* 9.7), Xenophon gives us the classic comic ending. By replacing a soon to be sexually consummated pantomime about Ariadne and Dionysus with the equally comic story of Alcibiades' failure to consummate a sexual relationship with Socrates (Plat. *Smp.* 218b8-219d2), Plato went beyond Xenophon while standing on his shoulders. By staging his *Symposium* only a few years after Xenophon's, and thus by displacing the hopeful days that followed the Peace of Nicias in 421 with the impending disaster of 415 arising inevitably from Alcibiades' ambition to conquer Sicily,[52] Plato added tragedy to his masterpiece while at the same time preserving the comic structure he inherited from Xenophon. While acknowledging Plato's literary superiority, the cooperative model that allows for the literary priority of Xenophon's *Symposium* thus makes him indispensable for fully appreciating Plato's achievement.[53]

Current thinking on the relationship between Plato's *Symposium* and Xenophon's is, of course, dominated by the modern axiom of Plato's priority, and the results of this domination are devastating for Xenophon without in any way enhancing our appreciation for Plato. Given that Plato's *Symposium* is one of the crown jewels of World Literature, the notion that Xenophon wrote his after Plato's convicts Xenophon, to begin with, with the poor taste of not recognizing unsurpassable literary excellence when he saw it. In addition to a copyist's poor taste, Xenophon also presently stands convicted of being an inept and careless copyist, attributing to Pausanias what Plato attributes to Phaedrus (cf. Plat. *Smp.* 178e3-179a2 and Xen. *Smp.* 8.32-34). In Xenophon's *Symposium*, only Socrates delivers a speech on ἔρως—the sole topic of all the speeches in Plato's until the comic disruption caused by the arrival of Alcibiades—in which he is only prepared to bless the relationship between his host Callias and the recently crowned youth Autolycus on the grounds that their relationship will not be sexual but will rather have as its laudatory goal the youngster's acquisition of virtue (Xen. *Smp.* 8.11). In the course of rejecting sexualized pederasty, Xenophon's Socrates invokes a distinction between two aspects of Aphrodite (Xen. *Smp.* 8.9–18), while associating Pausanias with the sexualized form of ἔρως he rejects with contempt (Xen. *Smp.* 8.32). It is here that Xenophon's Socrates attributes to Pausanias the view that an army based on sexualized pederasty—where every soldier is either the lover or the beloved of another soldier in the army—would be unbeatable. Since it is Phaedrus and not Pausanias who cites this army of lovers in Plato's *Symposium*, and since Plato wrote first—as we presently all seem to think that we know—Xenophon shows himself to be Plato's probably tasteless, but in any case, careless imitator.

What this interpretive model fails to explain is why it should be the speech of Plato's Pausanias that Xenophon took as his model while composing the speech of Socrates.[54] Despite the fact that the two speeches are diametrically opposed on the basic question—Plato's Pausanias endorses sexualized pederasty even under the worst conditions—there are equally obvious similarities, for here it is Pausanias who invokes the two different aspects of Aphrodite (Plat. *Smp.* 180d3–181c6) and uses the acquisition of virtue to justify the sexualized version of boy-love ἔρως he is defending (Plat. *Smp.* 184b6–e4). The priority of Xenophon's *Symposium* makes better sense of what Plato is doing here: by allowing Pausanias to borrow two persuasive elements in the speech of Xenophon's Socrates—education in virtue and the heavenly Aphrodite—while employing them in defense of precisely the same position for which Socrates attacks him, savagely, in Xenophon's *Symposium*, Plato created a highly deceptive speech against what we still call "Platonic Love" despite the fact that, thanks to Xenophon, it is more proper to recognize such asexual love as "Socratic." So important is deception to Plato's Pausanias that he defends the boy's decision to sexually gratify his lover even if that lover's claim to teach the boy virtue is fraudulent (Plat. *Smp.* 185a5–c3). Thus, although Pausanias defends sexualized pederasty in both *Symposia*, Plato's Pausanias is far more deceptive, not only because he explicitly defends the lover's use of deception—note καλὴ ἡ ἀπάτη at 185b1—but because what allows his own speech on ἔρως to be a masterpiece of deception is that it imitates the speech of Xenophon's Socrates while arguing for a position that Socrates' speech opposed diametrically, and does so, moreover, in a brilliant dialogue that has immortalized the opposing and Socratic conception of "Platonic Love."[55]

It is because Xenophon has already depicted Pausanias as an intemperate defender of sexualized pederasty that Plato can present him as dangerously deceptive as well, that is, not as better or more benign, but as worse and all the more dangerous precisely because he appears to be better or even "Socratic." In the previous chapter, both Critias and Meno were cited as examples of this phenomenon and thus of how the hypothesis of Xenophon's literary priority enables us to better understand and appreciate Plato's artistry in just this way; here I will suggest that the first time Plato illustrated his debts to Xenophon in what would become this characteristic manner arose from his decision to model the speech of Pausanias on Xenophon's Socrates. And to further implement the previous section's palinode on compositional agnosticism, I am claiming that all of the following Platonic dialogues would not only be written with his own *Symposium* in mind, but were all composed after it: *Protagoras, Alcibiades Minor, Lovers, Hippias Major, Menexenus, Lysis, Euthydemus*, and of course *Republic*. Of these eight, the last three are dialogues for which *Symposium* itself prepares; for the other five, *Symposium* is their τέλος, and thus the "end" for which they prepare. If Xenophon's *Symposium* prepared the way for Plato's, and if Plato then brought into being a whole series of supporting dialogues, this would constitute a crucially important and indeed paradigmatic case of Plato's debts to Xenophon, and it will be considered as such in chapter 5. But since the subject of this chapter is rather "Xenophon's debts to Plato," it is another question that will primarily concern us here: to what extent did Xenophon's decision to write his *Symposium* in the first place demonstrate another example of those debts?

The stated purpose of Xenophon's *Symposium* is to preserve as worthy of remembering (ἀξιομνημόνευτα) not only the deeds (ἔργα) of καλοὶ κἀγαθοὶ ἄνδρες "done with seriousness . . . but also those [deeds done] in play [ἐν ταῖς παιδιαῖς]" (*Smp.* 1.1). Since Xenophon begins the next sentence by claiming himself to have been present—the claim that initiates another round of "Where's Waldo" until we find him in Hermogenes—the play begins immediately: from beginning to end, we find ourselves ἐν ταῖς παιδιαῖς. At this point, it might be useful to recall Marchant's "lively humor" and the "vivacity which made him an entertaining companion" as qualities that well suited him to be a Xenophon scholar. But it is once again German philology that proves its importance where Plato's own impact on Xenophon's *Symposium* is concerned, and above all on his unmistakable turn to the playfully comic in it.

Born in Louisiana in 1928, Charles H. Kahn is of course not German himself,[56] but his teacher Ernst Kapp (1888–1978) was, and it was on the basis of what he learned from Kapp that Kahn challenged the orthodox view that Plato had written *Gorgias* before *Protagoras*.[57] Before getting into the intricacies that are the subject of this section, note the relevance of this claim to what has already been said: Kapp and Kahn claim that the delightfully comic and puzzling *Protagoras* with its playfully deceptive Socrates was written after the darkly serious *Gorgias*. With the tragedy of Athens already in full view, *Gorgias* has traditionally been read as a product of Plato's disappointment with the results of his own "Sicilian Expedition."[58] But if Kapp and Kahn are right that *Gorgias* is the older work, and if I am right that Xenophon wrote his playful *Symposium* as a comic corrective to it, then that would explain why not only Plato's *Symposium* but also his *Protagoras* represented his own Janus-like response to Xenophon, and thus a further instance of Plato's debts to Xenophon. But what is relevant here is rather to recover and strengthen the case for an early *Gorgias*—on the basis of Xenophon's *Apology* and the *Urmemorabilien*—and then to show how and why *Gorgias* prompted Xenophon's response in his delightful and amazingly productive *Symposium*.

Kapp was a student of Eduard Schwartz (1858–1940), who, along with von Arnim, was a student of Ulrich von Wilamowitz-Moellendorff (1848–1931). Whether or not it had its roots in the methods or temper of the great Wilamowitz, both Kapp and von Arnim displayed a highly developed sense of Plato's playfulness: just as von Arnim regarded the argument in *Lysis* to the effect that good men cannot be friends as deliberately fallacious,[59] so too Kapp—and after him Kahn—used the chronological priority of *Gorgias* to show that Plato had never accepted as either Socratic or true the equation of the Good and the Pleasant in the final argument of *Protagoras*. Instead of what is now and had already become the orthodox position, then, Kahn argued for an early *Gorgias*, placing it in the same group that contained *Apology* and *Crito* rather than the one including *Protagoras*, *Laches*, and *Charmides*.[60] In a 1988 article called "On the Relative Date of the *Gorgias* and the *Protagoras*," and again in his 1996 book *Plato and the Socratic Dialogue*, Kahn defended claims that Kapp had made long before.[61] Naturally, he did so without recourse to Xenophon; that oversight will be remedied here.

If von Arnim is right that Xenophon lost confidence in his own *Apology* after reading Plato's, Plato did not share his assessment. To begin with, he discovered in Xenophon's *Apology* the roots of his *Crito*, and by building an entire dialogue around a single incident in that early essay (*Ap.* 23), he marked out a path that made it possible for him both to follow Xenophon and to surpass him. If Diogenes is wrong, and Xenophon's *Memorabilia* was not the first record of Socrates' conversations, then Plato's *Crito* has as good a claim as any to be considered πρῶτος instead. But since Kahn has no difficulty showing the connection between *Gorgias* and *Crito*—above all, based on the critical claim that it is preferable to suffer an injustice than to do one (*Cri.* 49a4-b11)—it seems at least equally plausible that both were Plato's responses to Xenophon's *Urmemorabilien*, and, more specifically, that Plato's Callicles was his response to Xenophon's *Euthydemus*.[62] In addition to what I will be claiming is an autobiographical element in both *Gorgias* and *Memorabilia* 4.2, I will also use the references to the historical Gorgias in both apologies—and to his "Defense of Palamedes" in particular[63]—and of course *Gorgias* itself to strengthen the kind of compositional connections on offer here.

But a more strictly philological case for an early *Gorgias* is based on reading it as a response to Polycrates, a case that depends on Pindar. We know from the *Schutzschrift* that one of the charges "Anytus" leveled against Socrates was that he selected the most morally objectionable passages from the poets and used them to lead his followers astray.[64] Although Xenophon does not mention Pindar in this context, Libanius does so in his reply to Polycrates, and he makes the interesting point that Anytus misquoted the poet, heightening its lawless message.[65] The same misquotation also appears in *Gorgias*,[66] and there Plato places it in the mouth of Callicles (*Grg.* 484b6) who relies on its subversive message while confessing that his grasp of the poem is incomplete—a clear indication that Plato is fully aware that his character is misquoting it.[67] Jean Humbert examined these connections in 1930 and argued that by conflating Callicles and Polycrates—implicating both in the same erroneous misquotation—Plato was likewise responding to Xenophon's ὁ κατήγορος in *Gorgias*, allowing Socrates to rebut the latter's charges in opposition to the independently corrupted Callicles.[68] Peerless in his response to earlier attempts to explain the Pindar connection,[69] Humbert could have strengthened his case by recognizing in "the enigmatic Callicles"[70] something more familiar to Plato than "the historical Polycrates."

With this in mind, consider the following sequence: Xenophon writes his *Apology*, relying on information from Hermogenes as well as literary tropes from Gorgias; the earlier authors to whom Xenophon refers (*Ap.* 1.1) are lost, and do not include Plato.[71] The latter then writes his

Apology, correcting Xenophon where necessary. Under the dual influence of it and the speech for Anytus penned by Polycrates in 393, Xenophon then produces the earliest version of his *Memorabilia*, which creates an important literary precedent thanks to the dialogues with Euthydemus, based on his personal experience—especially 4.2—that he attached to the opening *Schutzschrift*.[72] In response to both Xenophon and Polycrates, Plato then writes his *Gorgias*,[73] either before or more likely after having written *Crito*, itself under the inspiration of Xenophon's *Apology*. In response to the unsurpassable brilliance of the darkly tragic *Gorgias*—where both the tragedy of Athens and the trial of Socrates are always plainly in view— Xenophon displays another aspect of his character: instead of attempting to challenge Plato on the plane of high politics and Socratic seriousness, he hits on the happy idea of bringing out his hero's playful side in his *Symposium*. Plato's response, although not strictly relevant here, will be Janus-like: while reasserting the tragic element already on display in *Gorgias*, he realizes the tremendous power of Xenophon's latest precedent, and will never thereafter fail to remember how much value can be found ἐν ταῖς παιδιαῖς. Both his *Symposium* and *Protagoras*—as but one example of this connection, note the presence of Pausanias and Agathon at *Protagoras* 315d7-e3—will follow this realization.

Next there is Palamedes. He appears first in Xenophon's *Apology*, where Socrates compares their fates:

> But further, my spirit need not be less exalted because I am dying unjustly [ἀδίκως ἀποθνῄσκω]; for the ignominy of that attaches not to me but to those who condemned me. And I get comfort from the case of Palamedes also, who died in circumstances similar to mine; for even yet now [ἔτι καὶ νῦν] he lends himself to much more beautiful songs [πολὺ καλλίονες ὕμνοι] than does Odysseus, the man who unjustly put him to death [ὁ ἀδίκως ἀποκτείνας]. And I know that time to come as well as time past will attest that I not only never did injustice to anyone [ἠδίκησα μὲν οὐδένα πώποτε] nor rendered anyone more wicked, but have rather profited those who conversed with me by teaching them, without reward, every good thing that lay in my power.[74]

Without denying that both *Crito* and *Gorgias* are πολὺ καλλίονες ὕμνοι to the proposition that it is better to suffer an injustice than to do one, the basis for that statement is already present here. There is no doubt that Xenophon's Socrates finds it preferable to be able to say "ἀδίκως ἀποθνῄσκω" than be ὁ ἀδικῶς ἀποκτείνας, and if this way of putting it is considerably less general than what we will later find in Plato, there is both a moral and rhetorical sublimity in the words ἠδίκησα μὲν οὐδένα πώποτε. Despite the presence of one of Xenophon's most characteristic phrases here (ἔτι καὶ νῦν), it seems likely that the root of these connections might have been found in the historical Socrates, along with the revealing comparison with Palamedes.

It is that comparison that allows us to repair to the strictly literary plane. In 1926, Josef Morr, a student of von Armin's, called attention to the passage that immediately follows this one in an article entitled "Das Gorgias *Palamedes* und Xenophons *Apology*," the purpose of which was to demonstrate Xenophon's literary reliance on "The Defense of Palamedes."[75] Here is the relevant question asked by Xenophon's Socrates: "Have you not known all along that from whenever I was born [γίγνεσθαι], death [ὁ θάνατος] had been decreed [κατα-ψηφίζεσθαι] for me by nature [φύσις]?"[76] Morr then quotes the following words of Gorgias' Palamedes, found at the beginning of his speech: "For nature [ἡ φύσις], by a manifest decree [ὁ ψῆφος], has condemned to death [θάνατος] all mortals on the day that they were born [γίγνεσθαι]."[77] Morr need not argue at length for the echo; it would speak for itself even if it didn't immediately follow the mention of Palamedes. After citing all the passages where Xenophon cites Gorgias by name,[78] he goes on to make another point: the reference to πολὺ καλλίονες ὕμνοι as literal songs not only suggests a reference to Euripides' lost *Palamedes* but also makes sense out of the following passage in Diogenes Laertius' biography of Socrates: "And Euripides reproached them [sc. the Athenians] in his *Palamedes*, saying, 'You have slain, have slain, the all-wise, the harmless nightingale of the Muses.'"[79] And Morr is not done, finding another reference to ὕμνοι about Palamedes in the following exchange between Socrates and Euthydemus in 4.2:

> "But wisdom [σοφία] now, Socrates,—that at any rate is indisputably a good thing; for what is there that a wise man would not do better than a fool?" "Indeed! have you not heard how Daedalus was seized by Minos because of his wisdom, and was forced to be his slave, and was robbed of his country and his liberty, and essaying to escape with his son, lost the boy and could not save himself, but was carried off to the barbarians

and again lived as a slave there?" "That is the story, of course." "And have you not heard the story of Palamedes? Surely, for all the poets sing of him, how that he was envied for his wisdom and done to death by Odysseus [πάντες ὑμνοῦσιν ὡς διὰ σοφίαν φθονηθεὶς ὑπὸ τοῦ Ὀδυσσέως ἀπόλλυται]." "Another well-known tale!"[80]

Concerning this passage there is a great deal that might be said, and the most important has nothing whatsoever to do with either Palamedes or Gorgias. Just as Socrates makes it clear that σοφία is not an unqualified good here at 4.2.33, he will do something similar with happiness or εὐδαιμονία in the passage that follows (*Mem.* 4.2.34). These observations, attributed by Xenophon to Socrates in what may well be the oldest or rather earliest Socratic dialogue, cannot easily be brought into harmony with what Plato's Socrates says in the First Protreptic of his *Euthydemus*.[81] A comparison of what Plato's Socrates says about "good luck" (εὐτυχία) and εὖ πράττειν there (*Euthd.* 279d6–280b3) cannot be squared with *Memorabilia* 3.9.14–15,[82] and as a result, Xenophon casts doubt on what is often uncritically taken to be a foundational statement of Socratic intellectualism and "the philosophy of Socrates."[83] The second point, more important in the immediate context of the previous chapter, bears on the identity of Xenophon and Euthydemus. If the two are the same, the fact that Xenophon is echoing Gorgias while writing his *Apology of Socrates* finds a firm foundation in the library of Euthydemus, filled with the writings of ποιῆται τε καὶ σοφισταί (*Mem.* 4.2.1). If it is primarily to preserve verisimilitude that Euthydemus is demonstrably familiar with, for instance, the *Palamedes* of Euripides and those who hymn his wisdom, Xenophon's own familiarity with Gorgias points to the same identity from the opposite side: both Euthydemus and Xenophon demonstrate familiarity with ποιῆται τε καὶ σοφισταί for the same reason.

But in the immediate context of this section, the more important point is Morr's: the use of φθονηθείς in the context of σοφία—i.e., Odysseus envies Palamedes for his wisdom—finds another echo of Gorgias' *Defense of Palamedes*: "But if he [sc. Odysseus] fashioned this accusation out of jealousy [φθόνος], subterfuge, or wickedness, just as for those reasons he would be the most excellent {κράτιστος} of men, so too he would be the most evil {κάκιστος} of men."[84] To present oneself as a good man accused by bad ones is naturally a commonplace but the influence of Gorgias on the early writings of both Xenophon and Plato is extraordinary. And it is all the more so because Morr wrote another article on the relationship between the *Defense of Palamedes* and Plato's *Apology*.[85] In doing so, he was scarcely unique; originally deployed by Heinrich Gomperz to demonstrate the authenticity of Gorgias' *Defense of Palamedes*,[86] its impact on Plato's *Apology* has subsequently received considerable attention.[87] It is in the context of Gorgias' presence in Xenophon's *Apology*, *Memorabilia* 4.2, and Plato's *Apology* that it is possible to strengthen the case Kapp and Kahn made for an early *Gorgias*.

As already mentioned, Xenophon's Euthydemus appears not only in *Memorabilia* but in Plato as well. No other author mentions Plato's Callicles, and he appears only in his *Gorgias*. His brilliance is obvious to all of Plato's readers but he seems to have entirely escaped the attention of his contemporaries.[88] Attempts have been made to discover a historical person in Callicles, but a more sensitive approach has discovered in him a self-portrait.[89] Articulating with even greater power and perception the same point of view the Athenians espouse Thucydides' Melian Dialogue—a point of view strongly supported by his "Pindar" (*Grg.* 484b1–8)—this kind of "Callicles" would embody Plato's response to Xenophon as well. It is characteristic that he would rewrite *Memorabilia* 4.2 not once but twice, both times with less emphasis on what Dakyns called "the personal note." In *Alcibiades Major*, he will transform Xenophon's account of a young man's first conversation with Socrates to an altogether more significant historical plane. And his invention of Callicles illustrates the origins of that phenomenon, for "he" is the analogue of Xenophon's Euthydemus. Xenophon could construct Euthydemus entirely out of his own memories and experiences; in creating his Callicles, Plato goes a step farther on the same path.

In Callicles, Plato created a synthesis of personal experience and imagination, and placed it in the historical past, already enlivened by Thucydides. It is easy to forget that the powerful, self-confident, and hubristic Athens that forms the dialogue's vivid backdrop was already long gone when Plato wrote his *Gorgias*. There, Socrates can deplore the Long Walls as if they were a permanent feature of Athenian power and misplaced values, but it is only because they had first been torn down that it is possible to identify the date of Polycrates' speech, since the Athenians began to rebuild them in 394.[90] It is often said that Plato was a critic of Athens, and his *Gorgias* has just as often been used as a proof-text for his critical attitude or even his hatred for her; this is a shortsighted approach. When Plato decided to do something similar to what Xenophon had already done with

Euthydemus, it is only himself that he will need to reimagine creatively; his memories will recapture Athens as she was. Xenophon will chronicle the Athenian present in his *Hellenica*; Plato lives in her past. By allowing his Callicles to channel Alcibiades—for it was his spirit that created the nakedly self-interested basis for the Melian Dialogue—and by placing him imaginatively in his city's past, Plato is already demonstrating the same characteristic habits of mind that will cause him to place Alcibiades in his *Symposium*, and thus to replace the comic ending of Xenophon's with something far more tragic and complex.

Arnim placed the composition of Plato's *Gorgias* before the speech of Polycrates, configuring the latter as a response to it.[91] E. R. Dodds, who is prepared to acknowledge both possibilities, seems rather more inclined to the same view, quoting Olof Gigon's observation that "Plato shows himself astonishingly indifferent to the charges of Polycrates."[92] What gets missed is that it was Xenophon's *Schutzschrift* that allowed Plato to appear indifferent; his predecessor had already delivered a *Vernichtungskritik* of "Anytus." Thanks to the dialogue with Callicles, Plato's *Gorgias* is an even more effective response to the charge that Socrates was responsible for the later misdeeds of Alcibiades than Xenophon's more direct approach in *Memorabilia* I—to use that nomenclature for the first time—but only because he could count on the prior existence of that approach. And even though common sense would suggest that a shorter *Crito* inspired by Xenophon's *Apology* must certainly precede a longer *Gorgias* inspired by *Memorabilia* I, the claim that it is preferable to suffer an injustice than to do one is defended at length in one and taken for granted in the other: insofar as the critique of Athens in *Gorgias* may have given too much ground to the charges of Polycrates, *Crito* recaptured that ground thanks to Socrates' respect for established law (cf. *Mem.* 4.4). As a matter of chronology, then, Plato's *Gorgias* was *published* in response to Xenophon's response to Polycrates, and combined a creative mix of autobiography and history with an ongoing concern with Gorgias, whose influence had already united the *Apologies* of Xenophon and Plato, to which Polycrates had then felt it necessary to respond.

The word *published* is italicized because an early *Gorgias* would predate the creation of the Academy in 387. As already mentioned, *Gorgias* is the only Platonic dialogue for which we have anecdotal evidence that it was published, that is to say, available to readers outside of the Academy. In addition to the story of the farmer, there is another anecdote to the effect that Gorgias read and responded to Plato's *Gorgias*.[93] Both stories are consistent not only with publication but with publication in the 390s. To spell out the hypothesis: *Apology*, *Gorgias*, and *Crito* were unique among Plato's dialogues for being published, and the rest of them, beginning with *Symposium*, were for intra-Academic use only. His three earliest dialogues were enticement enough to attract students; publishing *Symposium* would have destroyed an important aspect of Platonic pedagogy: piquing adolescent interest in the by no means philosophically insignificant but in any case salaciously enticing problem, introduced in *Protagoras*, of whether Socrates and Alcibiades are having sex.[94] Naturally, it is on the prior publication of Xenophon's *Symposium* that this pedagogical device depends, for there is no mystery whatsoever about Socrates' attitude toward sexualized pederasty in that delightful dialogue.

Aside from the governing prejudice of Plato's Priority, there are two ancillary considerations that tend to make it impossible that Xenophon wrote his *Symposium* before the King's Peace. When considered as published unities, all of his longer works can be dated in the last few years of his long life, and even those that weren't written until the very end must have been composed in the peaceful retirement of Skillus. Against these conceptions and the prejudice that grounds them, a youthful *Cynegeticus*, along with the continuation or completion of Thucydides in *Hellenica* I, indicate that Xenophon—fully consistent with the bookish Euthydemus—was already an accomplished writer before he left for Asia and Cyrus. His ability to write *Anabasis* I on the march and to complete it shortly after having reached "the Sea" has already been mentioned. But a pre-Polycrates publication of his *Apology* along with a post-Polycrates publication of *Memorabilia* I indicates that it was not only *Anabasis* that he wrote, as it were, in a tent. With no need to return to Athens to sift through the nonexistent notes of von Arnim's Euthydemus, Xenophon might just as easily have not returned to Athens as returned to it although his express statement of dependence on Hermogenes supports the latter. But there is no reason that he couldn't have written his *Symposium* "on the road" before 390—as opposed to writing it in the peaceful leisure of Skillus—and indeed what makes this work both innovative and characteristic is most easily appreciated the hypothesis that he did.

At the beginning of the chapter called "Xenophon: The Ordinary Athenian Gentleman" in *The Greek Way*, Edith Hamilton juxtaposed Xenophon and Thucydides in a characteristically insightful manner:

> Thucydides' world was a place racked and ruined and disintegrated by war, where hope was gone and happiness was

unimaginable. Xenophon's was a cheerful place with many nice people in it and many agreeable ways of passing the time.[95]

Of his *Symposium* specifically, she writes the following about the modest Autolycus, whose victory in the games is the occasion for the celebration at the house of Callias: "It is an attractive picture of Athenian boyhood in the brilliant, corrupt city where Thucydides could find nothing good." Thanks in no small part to the fact that Plato is channeling Thucydides in *Gorgias*, what Hamilton writes here applies to the relationship between him and Xenophon as well. Xenophon's "attractive picture" of "a cheerful place" was his response to Plato's "corrupt city." And herein lies his debt: without the searing accuracy of Plato's *Gorgias*, Xenophon would not have needed to revolutionize the Socratic dialogue in his *Symposium*.

It was not to Thucydides that Xenophon's *Symposium* served as anodyne, and his debt to Plato was less direct than dialectical. Nor was it exclusively literary, although the explosive energy of *Gorgias* made it not so much a difficult act for Xenophon to follow as an impossible one. There is also a psychological dimension to consider, played out in the domain of geography. In imagining "the Life of Xenophon" on the basis of his writings, Delebecque repeatedly makes the same mistake: since Ischomachus is an Athenian farmer, Xenophon must have written the second part of *Oeconomicus* in Athens; he wrote his *Symposium* after his return to Athens because it is set there.[96] This demonstrates no awareness of nostalgia: whether or not he had already been exiled, it was natural for Xenophon to dream of Athens while far from home. Xenophon had included no historical dimension to the conversations in *Memorabilia* 4.2, and as the object of Critias' lust, the beautiful Euthydemus of 1.2 belongs to an ugly time (*Mem.* 1.2.29–30). It is likewise difficult to see that Plato's portrait of Athens in *Gorgias* is rooted in nostalgia, but it is impossible to miss it in Xenophon's *Symposium*. Xenophon could rely on his personal yearning for the distant Athens of his youth but he made her visible only with Plato's prompting. Writing in postwar Athens, Plato captures the heat of battle in his *Gorgias*; writing his *Symposium* as a soldier far from home, Xenophon dreamt of a bygone time of peace.

In accordance with the modern prejudice, it is Xenophon who is indebted to Plato's *Symposium*, and he wrote his in imitation of Plato's. The results are obvious: since both works belong to the same genre, Xenophon is competing with or at least offering an alternative to Plato on Plato's chosen ground, exactly what Xenophon does not do if *Sym-*

posium, as I am proposing, was his ground-shifting response to *Gorgias*. In addition to showing a lack of invention with respect to genre and a lack of taste in failing to recognize Plato's excellence, the traditional Xenophon is, as already indicated, a careless copyist. We are left with a conception of Xenophon's debts that teaches us nothing about Plato and which slanders Xenophon. In fact, it begins to look as if the axiom of Plato's Priority would not so much replace as merely assimilate Literary Rivalry to Plato's superiority, regardless of whether its modern proponents are intent on reducing Xenophon to the level of dunce or elevating him as a down-to-earth critic of Platonic idealism.

Compare all that with an account of Xenophon's debts that begins not with Plato's *Symposium* but with his *Gorgias*. To begin with, it leaves the genius of Plato intact: even though he will follow Xenophon with respect to genre, he finds a way to surpass him in it. In place of an innocuous Pausanias and a dull copyist, we have an innovative trailblazer and a master of both pedagogical deception and its detection (cf. *Phdr.* 261d10–e4). Seldom has there been a case that better illustrates the value of interpretive charity, especially since the latter has frequently been invoked and misapplied to palliate or even to conceal Plato's deliberate use of fallacy and deception.[97] As he did in the case of Plato's *Apology*, Xenophon will once again recognize the excellence of Plato's *Gorgias*: able to lead, he is likewise content to follow, and—proving that he can do both at the same time—he finds a beautiful and productive way to honor that excellence. If imitation is the highest form of flattery, then Plato pays this compliment to Xenophon in his *Symposium*. But Xenophon's conception of what it meant to be καλὸς κἀγαθός seems to have made him uncomfortable with receiving greater benefits than he was able to bestow (e.g., *Mem.* 2.6.35). While recognizing and appreciating the nature of the compliment Plato was paying and would continue to pay him, Xenophon paid Plato an even higher compliment by not imitating him where he had proved himself inimitable. He shifted ground instead, blazing a new trail. And having already seen Plato respond to his *Apology* and *Memorabilia* I, it is difficult to believe he was much surprised by how Plato responded to his *Symposium*, for he responded in the same way to all three.

In considering the shift of ground that led Xenophon to write his *Symposium* after Plato's *Gorgias*, it is not enough to note his literary debt to Plato: it is necessary to consider the character of the man who realized that he had incurred this debt, and who chose to respond to it in the way he did. The ethical character of that response has already been indicated; to the pettiness of Literary Rivalry there is Xenophon's ongoing commitment to καλοκάγαθία that must be and has been mentioned (cf. Socrates on Hermogenes at *Smp.* 4.49). But it is also necessary to see the human being who merely strove to be καλὸς κἀγαθός, a brave but lonely young man of considerable literary gifts, schooled by Socrates, though deserting him too soon, filled with regret and homesickness, who—despite finding his own voice in the darkest of Persian nights—would nevertheless be forever after a stranger in a strange land, far from home, bereft of his teacher and the scenes of his youth, and driven to find solace in writing, at once the loneliest and the most other-directed life imaginable. It is pleasant to imagine Xenophon with a loving wife and two fine sons riding and writing, hunting and farming, in Elis. But the Peloponnese is a long way from Attica,[98] and before he managed to get even that close to home, he had spent many a night in the field, writing whenever he could, as so many other soldiers have done. It was reading Plato's bitter *Gorgias* in a tent that made Xenophon remember the home of his dreams, and he was indebted to Plato for having been inspired to preserve it in his delightful *Symposium*, without which Plato's own would never have been conceived or even imagined.

Oeconomicus and Memorabilia 2.2

Admittedly "in a tent" is over the top with respect to speculation, but as any reader of Delebecque or J. K. Anderson knows, the life of Xenophon must be reconstructed from his works, and that requires informed speculation throughout. The best an informed speculator can do is to be at least an *informing* speculator, keeping the reader abreast of whatever basis those speculations may have. The textual basis for the friendship between Xenophon and Plato—presupposed throughout—is, to begin with, their writings. Naturally there is circularity here, because by "their writings," I mean their writings when composed in the order I am proposing here, an order that in turn presupposes their friendship. Perhaps not entirely, however: what Xenophon says about Socrates' affection for Glaucon, his concern that his followers be friends with each other (*Mem.* 1.2.8), and the reference to Euthydemus, son of Diocles in Plato's *Symposium*, may be of some corroborating value. Ancient tales of their rivalry presuppose their familiarity with each other, and they were of course not only contemporaries but also fellow Athenians, fellow Socratics, and occupied an elevated status in society that makes it difficult to doubt their acquaintance if not their intimate friendship. It is the latter that I am presupposing on the basis of the former, and since I have already made the suggestion that Plato did not publish his *Symposium* as he had his earlier works, that intimacy must now for the first time be addressed directly, since this section depends on Xenophon's familiarity with and appreciation for Plato's *Symposium*. Note that this is simply taken for granted on the traditional view, since Xenophon is conceived of as having both read and copied it, and thus that Plato had published it.

Unlike Delebecque, who divides *Oeconomicus* into two parts, and argues at length for the late composition of its second, and at tedious length for its having been composed in Athens,[99] Anderson accepts the traditional view that Xenophon wrote all of it in Skillus, where his own concerns turned toward married life, housekeeping—since at long last he owned a house in which he lived—and farming.[100] This seems plausible enough on its face, and Anderson does well to begin his chapter on "Domestic Life" with the Skillus passage in the Parabasis,[101] that is, the clearest evidence for both *Anabasis* II—and therefore also *Anabasis* I—and for his settlement in Elis. He does what he can, writing the following about Xenophon's wife, named for us only by Diogenes:[102] "Philesia is far more likely to have resembled Ischomachus' wife in the *Oeconomicus*, though, as has been suggested already, this work seems to contain memories of Xenophon's childhood and youth."[103] This apparently innocuous sentence deserves careful attention. To begin with, the previous section has suggested why Xenophon was inclined to record such memories in both *Oeconomicus* and *Symposium*. As for Anderson, he is merely justifying the role *Oeconomicus* played in his prior account of "Xenophon's childhood and youth,"[104] and his "far more likely" depends on comparing Philesia to the kind of hunting woman for whom he wrote *Cynegeticus*. This seems less likely to me than it does to Anderson.

Since we know that Philesius the Achaean appears as an officer in *Anabasis*, that it was not uncommon to name daughters after their fathers, and that there were women among the Ten Thousand, Xenophon's Philesia might well have more closely resembled an outdoorswoman than the closeted and completely inexperienced wife of Ischomachus. It deserves mention, but only in passing, that so intent have Xenophon's modern defenders been to shield their proto-Machiavellian hero from a contaminating concern with agriculture that they have latched upon a tenuous string of inferences based on Andocides to prove that Socrates and Xenophon are attacking Ischomachus through the alleged promiscuity of his chaste and charming wife.[105] What seems more relevant is that Ischomachus never mentions any children while describing for Socrates how he educated his wife, and this is one of two indications that Xenophon wrote *Oeconomicus* during his earliest years in Skillus, before Gryllus—his eldest boy who was killed near Mantinaea in 362—was born and perhaps even conceived. The second reason, more revealing, will be considered in a moment.

First, it is necessary to reconsider a highly objectionable clause in the previous paragraph, which, if was not instantly recognized as such by the reader, points to the principal problem of interpreting Xenophon's *Oeconomicus* in anything resembling a Xenophontic manner: "Ischomachus never mentions any children while describing for Socrates how he educated his wife." This should be rewritten as follows: "While using Ischomachus to educate Critobulus, Socrates never allows 'him' to mention any children while describing how he educated his wife in the process of allegedly educating Socrates." Even with all the additional information, the word *allegedly* is still required. Ischomachus is no more or less real that Diotima: like her, "he" is a character Socrates introduces, describes, and speaks through for the purpose of educating an internal audience—Critobulus in this case, Agathon in the other—as well as an external one, namely, the reader. The evidence of Andocides is useful to those who want to drive a wedge between Socrates and Ischomachus, a misguided project that assumes Ischomachus was ever real enough to be inimical to Socrates, who has introduced him and is in the process of using him entirely for reasons of his own. In short: it is the way Xenophon's Socrates uses Ischomachus in *Oeconomicus* that reveals Xenophon's debt to Plato's *Symposium*.

Diogenes Laertius tells us that Xenophon began following Socrates around and learning from him in accordance with his opening words to the young man: ἕπου τοίνυν καὶ μάνθανε. Rather than sift through Xenophon's Socratic writings in order to decide what things the historical Socrates might really have said to Xenophon and taught him—a list that naturally never includes agriculture as taught in *Oeconomicus* or, for instance, how to be an effective cavalry commander (*Mem.* 3.3)—and what things he didn't and couldn't have, it shows a better understanding of Xenophon to imagine that by teaching him how to learn (μανθάνειν) Socrates never left his side, and that he continued to follow (ἕπεσθαι) his teacher every step of the way through the mountains of Asia Minor and beyond. Whatever else it teaches us, *Oeconomicus* is obviously also about a method of learning, and that is why the verb "to teach" (διδάσκειν) appears with greater frequency in it than in, say, *The Education of Cyrus* or *Memorabilia*. What it meant for Xenophon to be Socrates' follower is that he approached all the problems he faced in what he took to be a Socratic manner. Rather than seek for a reductive definition of what that manner or method may have been, we would do better to imagine that it was exemplified and embodied in Xenophon himself, in everything he wrote and, more generally, in everything he did.

As already indicated, Anderson first uses *Oeconomicus* to reconstruct his youth, presumably on a prosperous farm in Attica with his father Gryllus imagined as very much like Ischomachus, the householder whom Socrates describes instructing him in householding.[106] Aside from the likelihood that he learned to ride and hunt at an early age, there is no evidence that he already had considerable interest in agriculture before he settled in Skillus. In a word, the only evidence of Xenophon's interest in and knowledge of γεωργία is his *Oeconomicus*. Now the literary conceit in that dialogue—for which Xenophon is indebted to Plato on my account—is that Socrates teaches an art by showing how he learned it. The reason *Oeconomicus* should be considered an early work of Xenophon's "middle period" is that he only now needed to learn how to farm, and that this dialogue is the written record of that learning process. The questions Ischomachus asked his wife about housekeeping are the kind of questions Xenophon needed to ask himself, for approaching problems by coming up with clear answers to a series of simple questions was—in lieu of some richer conception—Xenophon's Socratic method. Practical problems must have a practical solution; farming can be no different. Xenophon needed to learn how to farm and so he naturally used what he had learned from Socrates—not about farming, but about learning and teaching—to teach himself.

To be sure it is not the most obvious or natural response to Plato's *Symposium*, and although there is reason to believe that Xenophon would continue to add new chapters to his *Memorabilia*, *Oeconomicus* would be his last new book about Socrates. Understood in the context of Plato—and thus as mediating the distance between Plato's *Symposium* and *Meno*—and with full appreciation of the humor that arises just as much from its central literary conceit as from his apparent awareness that most readers won't get the joke, Xenophon's *Oeconomicus* is his Socratic masterpiece. By depicting Socrates as ignorant of γεωργία in the process of teaching it, as much as by teaching it through the vehicle of his own ignorance,

Xenophon offered his own solution to a problem that Plato's Socrates raises but never resolves: How are we to reconcile Socratic Ignorance with the claim that Virtue is Knowledge?[107] It is often said that Xenophon's overly didactic Socrates is un-Socratic precisely because he's a preachy know-it-all who never admits his ignorance; to this image, *Oeconomicus* stands opposed. By locating the subject's inherent intelligibility *within the subject itself* rather than in the knower, and by depicting the learner as fully aware of her initial ignorance of what is nevertheless learnable—as long as the right questions are being asked in the right order—Xenophon's Socrates was never more Socratic than he is in *Oeconomicus*.

There are, of course, examples of Socrates teaching other practical arts in *Memorabilia*, and one might profitably consider *Oeconomicus* in the light of the architecture lesson in 3.8.8–10, and of the various τέχναι Socrates manages to teach in 3.10. But the section of *Memorabilia* that seems most likely to be a product of his years in Skillus is book 2, especially the chapters about motherhood (*Mem.* 2.2) and fraternal relations (*Mem.* 2.3). To be sure *Memorabilia* 2 has a coherence of its own that transcends the plausible occasion of its composition, and since a claim has just been made to the effect that *Oeconomicus* is Xenophon's Socratic masterpiece, the rival claim of 2.2–10 to that honor deserves consideration now that we have arrived in Skillus. Moreover, the problem with which Xenophon is struggling in this part of *Memorabilia* is a problem that confronted Plato as well, one for which he offered a deliberately inadequate answer by means of the equivocal words εὖ πράττειν, which colloquially means "to fare well" and thus to be happy (*Euthd.* 280b6) but which literally means "to do well," with some object implied.[108] The notion that if we do things well then we will be happy lends itself to a utilitarian conception of virtue, and since Xenophon's justification for doing the right things in *Memorabilia* 2.2–10 appears to be that you will reap rewards for doing them, we are touching here on a central ethical problem of great and perhaps paramount concern to the Socratics.

Consider first Xenophon's own treatment of εὖ πράττειν in *Memorabilia* 3.9:

> When someone asked him [sc. Socrates] what seemed to him the best pursuit [ἐπιτήδευμα] for a man, he answered: "Doing well [εὐπραξία]." Questioned further, whether he thought good luck [ἡ εὐτυχία] a pursuit, he said: "On the contrary, I think luck and doing are opposite poles. To hit on something right

by luck [ἐπιτυχεῖν] without search I call good luck [εὐτυχία], to do something well [τι εὖ ποιεῖν] after study and practice I call doing well [εὐπραξία]; and those who pursue this seem to me to do well [εὖ πράττειν]."[109]

It is certainly possible to construe this concluding εὖ πράττειν colloquially, as if to say that it is thanks to εὐπραξία that we fare well, prosper, flourish, and succeed. But Socrates may also be stating what looks like a clarification of terms that reduces itself to a tautology, that is, that εὐπραξία—as to do or make *something* well (note the τι in τι εὖ ποιεῖν)—is the same thing as to εὖ πράττειν. Consider then what Socrates says next:

"And the best men and dearest to the gods in agriculture," he added, "are those who do the agricultural things well [οἱ τὰ γεωργικὰ εὖ πράττοντες]; in medicine, the medical things; in politics, those [who do well] the political things [τὰ πολιτικά]. He who does nothing well [ὁ μηδὲν εὖ πράττων] is neither useful in any way nor dear to the gods."[110]

This passage makes it clear: Xenophon's Socrates is not sliding from "to do well" to "to fare well" or from εὐπραξία to the colloquial sense of εὖ πράττειν.

Compare this with the way Plato's Socrates shamelessly exploits the equivocal εὖ πράττειν as he slides from "doing things well" to "to be happy" at the end of one of the most amazing passages in *Gorgias*, where Socrates has been forced to enact both himself and his interlocutor:

SOCRATES: "As a result it is fully necessary, Callicles, for the temperate man [ὁ σώφρων], as we have described him—being just and brave and pious—to be a completely good man, and for the good man to do both beautifully and well [εὖ τε καὶ καλῶς πράττειν] whatever he does [πράττειν; i.e., ἃ ἂν πράττῃ]; and for the man doing well [participial form of εὖ πράττειν] to be both blessed and happy [εὐδαίμων] and for the wicked—even while doing badly [participial form of κακῶς πράττειν]—[to be] wretched."[111]

As long as πράττειν takes a direct object as in "the things he does," there is no problem here: it is only when Plato's Socrates slides from what

Xenophon's will call εὐπραξία to the colloquial sense of εὖ πράττειν that is identical with being happy (i.e., εὐδαίμων) that a deceptive use of equivocation is in play.[112]

With this shortcut to an instrumental and utilitarian defense of "doing things well" in mind, consider the *Leitmotiv* of *Memorabilia* 2: if you want be benefited by someone, benefit them first. It is on the basis of this formula that Socrates attempts to reconcile the quarrelling brothers (2.3.11), explains friendship (2.4.7 and 2.5.1), and teaches Critobulus yet again (2.6.28; cf. 2.6.16). Not only does Socrates make this theme conspicuous at the end of the book (2.10.6) but he refers to it as a magic potion or φίλτρον at *Memorabilia* 2.3.11 and 2.3.14, a term that will reappear at 2.6.10 when Critobulus asks:

> "But how do they become friends [φίλοι]?" "There are certain enchantments [ἐπῳδαί], they say, which those who are understanding enchant [ἐπᾴδοντες] those whom they wish to make their friends [φίλους ποιεῖν], and magic potions [φίλτρα] which those who are understanding use on those by whom they wish to be loved [φιλεῖσθαι]."[113]

In a world where "do unto others as you would have them do unto you" is virtually proverbial, it is easy to imagine that Xenophon is exaggerating the importance of the φίλτρον in question; this would be an error. To begin with, the scriptural analogue merely *implies* the temporal element, making Xenophon's φίλτρον closer to Vince Lombardi's "do unto others *before* they do unto you" albeit in the benign sense of benefiting them first rather than harming them.

The next point is that although the clear implication of Socrates' advice is that if you make yourself lovable you *will* be loved, or if you benefit your brother first, he *will* reciprocate by benefiting you, there is in fact no guarantee that one will necessarily end up benefiting oneself by benefiting others. For that reason, we might well wonder to whom Xenophon's Socrates is offering his ἐπῳδαί: cloaked in the language of utilitarianism, the necessity to do the right thing *first* inevitably involves both risk and moral excellence. In other words, an opaque future (cf. *An.* 6.1.21 and *Hipp.* 9.1) makes Socrates' magic potion for securing benefits from others an ethical idealism in disguise. It merely appears to be utilitarian, but can only do so if we are enchanted by it, as any decent person will find it very easy to be. No less importantly, the ethical priority of benefiting others to the enchanting anticipation of being benefited by them in return is at the dead center of Xenophon's *Memorabilia*: famously put to death by the citizens he was so intent on benefiting, it is precisely, consistently, and ultimately as beneficial (ὠφέλιμος) that Xenophon praises Socrates at the beginning of *Memorabilia* 4:

> Socrates was so beneficial [ὠφέλιμος] in all circumstances and in all ways, that any observer gifted with ordinary perception can see that nothing was more beneficial [ὠφελιμώτερον] than the companionship of Socrates, and time spent with him in any place and in any circumstances. The very recollection of him in absence benefits [ὠφελεῖν] in no small way his constant companions and followers; for even in his light moods they were profiting [λυσιτελεῖν] no less from his society than when he was serious.[114]

Nor does Xenophon's Socrates place the happiness of his students as being of greater value than their capacity to make *others* happy, once again, as it were, *first*:

> Thus he would often say he was "in love"; but clearly his heart was set not on those who were fair to outward view, but on those whose souls were naturally suited to virtue [ἀρετή]. He recognized these good natures [αἱ ἀγαθαί φύσεις] by their quickness to learn [μανθάνειν] whatever subject they studied, ability to remember [μνημονεύειν] what they learned, and desire for all kinds of knowledge [τὰ μαθήματα πάντα] through which to manage well [καλῶς οἰκεῖν] both an estate [οἶκος] and a city, and generally to handle well both human beings and human concerns. For he believed that those having thus been educated [παιδεύεσθαι] would not only themselves be happy [εὐδαίμονες], and would manage well [καλῶς οἰκεῖν] the members of their own estates [οἶκοι], but would also be able to make other people and cities happy [εὐδαίμονες].[115]

Arnim's claims about 4.1 belonging to the *Urmemorabilien* notwithstanding, it is not difficult to imagine that Xenophon only added this passage to *Memorabilia* after he had already written *Oeconomicus*, and it is in its light that those who require their Socrates to be opposed to Ischomachus in order to be able to maintain their respect for him should reread Xenophon's Socratic masterpiece.

But let's not get ahead of ourselves, for it is on the basis of 2.2, where Socrates instructs his son about motherhood, that the rival claim of 2.2-10 to be that masterpiece entirely depends. The chapter builds on Xenophon's *Symposium*, where we learn that Socrates' wife Xanthippe was notoriously difficult (*Smp.* 2.10); in 2.2, Socrates' son Lamprocles can no longer endure her tongue lashings (*Mem.* 2.2.8). His son's ingratitude for the benefits he has received from his mother makes this one of the most important chapters in Socratic literature. Xenophon's defense of motherhood—and above all of its moral sublimity—probably needs to be situated in relation to both the modest wife of Ischomachus and the didactic Diotima, but for all the latter's eloquence, and despite the fact that Xenophon is not defending motherhood in a woman's voice, that defense soars beyond Diotima's claim that heroes die on behalf of others for the sake of their immortal fame (*Smp.* 208d2-e1). Above all, it is in juxtaposition with Socrates' claims about a mother's love for her children that "the Temporality of Virtue" in the chapters that follow 2.2 (this term will be used hereafter to describe Xenophon's anticipatory and apparently utilitarian φίλτρον as described above) must be reconsidered:

> Having been impregnated, the woman then carries this load, being both burdened down and endangering her own life—sharing the nourishment by which she too is nourished—and with great labor bearing through and giving birth, she both nourishes and takes cares of [the child], and having neither received in advance [προπάσχειν] anything good, nor the babe knowing from whom it is receiving benefit [εὖ πάσχειν] nor yet able to signify what it needs, she, by contrast, both conjecturing what things are to its advantage [τὰ συμφέροντα] as having been gratifying [κεχαρισμένα] to it, tries to supply them in full, and nourishes it for a long time, steadfastly enduring to toil for days and nights, never knowing if she will receive in return for these things any gratitude [χάρις].[116]

In the chapters of *Memorabilia* 2 that follow, the opacity of the future—and thus the epistemological uncertainty of whether any return will in fact follow from a prior benefit—is merely implied. Here, this uncertainty is made explicit, and is indivisibly connected to the nature of the case. The significance of its placement must be emphasized: by placing 2.2 before the passages that promote the Temporality of Virtue, Xenophon unmasks the utilitarian basis for right action (cf. εὐπραξία in 3.9.14) that his Socrates will repeatedly deploy in what follows. In other words, this passage in 2.2 reveals what the other dialogues in book 2 will disclose only to those who have been prepared by it to see through the kind of ἐπῳδαί Socrates will be using. The self-sacrificing truth precedes the benignly self-interested deception.

First, there is the truth. Xenophon's Socrates emphasizes that the Temporality of Virtue does not guide a mother: without having received any prior benefit—she cannot be said to προ-πάσχειν—she nevertheless bestows one; hence, the babe is said to εὖ πάσχειν in express contrast. Having called attention to this already selfless devotion by emphasizing not only the benefits she bestows—and the use of τὰ συμφέροντα proves to be particularly revealing[117]—but also the pains she endures and will long continue to endure, Xenophon hammers the crucial point: she does not know if she will receive any χάρις in return.[118] Not only is the future opaque in general; it is intrinsically so in this case given the mental state of the infant. In short, this is not like inviting some friends to dinner in order to secure an invitation from them in return (*Mem.* 2.3.11). Since the baby cannot speak, the mother must conjecture on the basis of what has already been κεχαρισμένα to it, and the baby is completely unaware of the source of these gratifications. The Temporality of Virtue does not guide motherhood, and it is no accident that Ischomachus never teaches his new wife anything about childbearing, because it was probably Philesia who taught Xenophon about it.

And now for the deception that follows the truth: beginning with the φίλτρον of 2.3.10-11, quickly followed by two uses of "prior [πρότερος]" (2.3.12-13), Xenophon invites us to imagine that he has discovered a magic potion for obtaining the things we desire. It is, of course, sane and practical advice: "Bestowing benefits is generally the best policy." But it is repeatedly presented as a *policy*, as a strategy that conduces to our own benefit; even the necessity of this "generally" is concealed. It works. And because it is easy to see why it usually works, we are invited to imagine that Socrates is recommending it because it *always does so*. In isolation from 2.2, we might be tempted to believe that even if his utilitarian defense of benefiting others fails, his defense of it is unquestionably intended to be utilitarian. And thus we get the Xenophon we seem to prefer: an incompetent defender of a morally bankrupt pragmatism. In any case,

Xenophon's Socrates never calls attention to the need for "usually" or "generally," he never mentions the opacity of the future, he praises highly and repeatedly the φίλτρον he has discovered, and completely conceals the ethical idealism that "doing good first" requires from one who knows what they don't know.

Except that he doesn't. He conceals it only beginning with 2.3; he has revealed it, indeed hymned it—connecting it to the most intimate aspect of our humanity—in 2.2. And it is Xenophon, not Socrates, who has done this. It may well be the case that the historical Socrates deliberately created the illusion that virtue would always be rewarded, that benefiting others brought self-benefit, and that doing well led inevitably to faring well; certainly, both Xenophon's and Plato's Socrates appeared to defend justice, ἀρετή generally, and εὐπραξία on this basis. But in *Memorabilia*, Xenophon did something far more important than simply throw together a random potpourri of Socratic discourses: he arranged them in order. Given the many echoes or anticipations of 2.6 and *Oeconomicus*,[119] it may be difficult to determine in what order Xenophon wrote them or intended them to be read; the advent of motherhood in the latter is the best evidence that "echoes" is the right word. But that Xenophon expected and indeed required us to experience the advent of motherhood in 2.2 before reading 2.3, this we cannot doubt, and the implications of that certainty are profound and far-reaching (see chapter 4, section 3). For the present, the salient implication is that although Xenophon has good reason to praise Socrates' φίλτρον, Philesia had already taught Xenophon its inadequacy.

It is no accident that even a chapter devoted to Xenophon's debts to Plato must inevitably and repeatedly disclose just as much, as here, about Plato's debts to Xenophon. But it would be a serious mistake to underestimate the debt that Xenophon owed to Diotima. Xenophon never mentions Philesia by name, the wife of Ischomachus is only a girl, the defense of Xanthippe in 2.2 is a defense of motherhood in general, and when Socrates defends his marriage in *Symposium* 2.10, that defense is self-interested: since he sought to get along with everyone, he married the most difficult person he could find. Diotima is unquestionably a force to be reckoned with, and it is possible that she made it easier for Xenophon to find a more substantial place for women in his Socratic dialogues. It is also possible that what might be called "womanly humanism"[120] had emerged with Diotima before receiving a much fuller defense in 2.2. Mother animals will sacrifice their lives for their offspring even if Admetus' mother did not (cf. *Smp.* 207a6–b6 and 179b8–c3); in dying on behalf of her husband

(*Smp.* 179b5-d2), Alcestis had more in mind than her own fame (*Smp.* 208c1-e1).[121] Although it is uncertain that Xenophon learned from Plato's *Symposium* how to undermine a selfish defense of excellence by means of a prior account of a selfless one, it was there to be found. What isn't uncertain is the astonishing parallel between Diotima and Ischomachus, and the remainder of this section will be devoted to enlivening it.

If what will eventually allow Plato to find a place for the slave in *Meno* (see chapter 1, section 3) is the student-Socrates of Xenophon's *Oeconomicus*, it is the student-Socrates of Plato's *Symposium* that starts the ball rolling. He's a hopeless student; continuously praising his teacher while failing to answer three of her questions (*Smp.* 204d8-9, 206b1-6, and 207c2-6). Although Diotima treats Socrates as an idiot (*Smp.* 201e10-202a3, 204b1-2, and 210a2-4), the gentlemanly Ischomachus will not do so, merely claiming that Socrates is playing around three times (*Oec.* 11.7, 17.10, and 20.28), the first after Socrates has made himself look like the idiot (*Oec.* 11.3-6). The common conceit has already been mentioned: Socrates is teaching by describing himself being taught. There is humor in the self-presentation of Plato's Socrates, to be sure, although not as broad as the kind he will use in *Hippias Major*, where he will show himself being schooled by the nonexistent housemate who is really himself (*Hp. Ma.* 286c5-d2, 288d4-5, 298b7-c2, and 304d1-e3). But while staying firmly in the orbit of Plato's *Symposium*, Xenophon's use of Ischomachus is more humorous than Plato's, apart, that is, from the fact that a contemporary audience might well have found a man being taught by a woman as intrinsically humorous.

But this is not the only shared conceit, and among the three most important of these, the subtlest and most complex is the following: because both Diotima and Ischomachus are merely enacted by Socrates, neither is really an active agent, and thus no more real—even within the already fictional world of the ongoing mimesis (cf. *R.* 395b4-8) that is a Socratic dialogue—than the housemate in *Hippias Major*. We are asked to imagine a dialogue between Ischomachus and Socrates, but the only real dialogue is between Socrates and Critobulus. The fact that there are only two characters and a narrator in Xenophon's *Oeconomicus* invites us to assume that it is far simpler than Plato's *Symposium* from a narrative standpoint, where Apollodorus tells us what he learned from Aristodemus about what Socrates told Agathon and the rest about what Diotima said to him. But for all that complexity, Diotima never tells Socrates what anyone else ever said to her, let alone taught her. Ischomachus, by contrast, not only describes the way he taught his wife but the way he was taught by his father. As a result, when he uses what a Phoenician steward taught him to teach his wife how to organize her household (*Oec.* 8.10–17), we are hearing Socrates teach Critobulus by describing how Ischomachus—in the process of teaching him—taught his wife how to store their goods on the basis of what he, Ischomachus, had been told by a Phoenician steward.

Albeit only on the basis of the first two shared conceits, it is with the third that Xenophon stands alone, and in any case surpasses Plato in humorous effect. In a sense, it is Xenophon's comparative clumsiness as a writer that allows him to surpass Plato as a humorist: because Socrates' speech in *Symposium* is imbedded in a dialogue with multiple speakers, we never lose sight of the fact that Diotima appears only in a speech, and when Socrates comes to the end of her speech to him, he resumes his own by addressing Agathon and the rest (*Smp.* 212b1–c3). Albeit as merely represented by Socrates, Ischomachus speaks the last word in Xenophon's dialogue (*Oec.* 21.12). There is not even any concluding statement to the effect that "this is what Ischomachus taught me," nor is Critobulus so much as mentioned after Socrates brings Ischomachus onto the stage. Not altogether unfairly, this failure to return to the dialogue's frame—and note that this way of speaking likewise makes the error of treating the conversation with Ischomachus as "the dialogue"—could be taken as proof of Xenophon's literary clumsiness, and in any case made it possible for Delebecque to distinguish an older "*Oeconomicus* I" containing a dialogue with Critobulus from the dialogue with Ischomachus in "*Oeconomicus* II."

It is Xenophon's humor that allows us to see past this apparent clumsiness, or rather, it is that clumsiness that makes his best joke possible. Ischomachus seems more real than Diotima, and this is due to Xenophon's apparently clumsy failure to return to Critobulus, a return that would have revealed the "dialogue with Ischomachus" for what it was. But it is that failure, and the merely apparent reality that results from it, that creates the funniest joke in the dialogue, and perhaps because Xenophon realized that so few of his readers would get it if he only told it to them once, he tells it three times. In the course of using Ischomachus to teach Critobulus how to farm, Socrates tells us that Ischomachus told him three times—on the basis of the fact that γεωργία is so easy to learn that Socrates will be able to assure himself that he already knows how to farm simply by answering Ischomachus' questions—that Socrates himself, should he ever wish to do so, will soon enough be able to teach someone else to master it (*Oec.* 15.10, 18.9, and 20.24). And this, of course, is perfectly true, for teaching Critobulus how to farm is exactly what Socrates is presently doing. It is also hilarious. So even if Xenophon was not indebted to Plato for his sense of humor, he was nevertheless in his debt for making possible the most delightful joke in his Socratic masterpiece. As to whether 2.2 has a better claim to that title, our mothers must judge.

Cyropaedia

Before introducing Ischomachus, Socrates uses the Kings of Persia for a similar purpose. In order to persuade Critobulus to lead the demanding but rewarding life of an Athenian gentleman-farmer, Socrates shows that war and agriculture are the chief concerns of "the Great King," and in the course of this demonstration, he mentions both Cyrus the Great—the central character in what will become Xenophon's *Cyropaedia*—and Cyrus the Younger, whose march up-country against his brother creates the basis for the *Anabasis*. Containing as it does the nucleus of both *Cyropaedia* and *Anabasis* II, *Oeconomicus* 4.16–25 will be discussed in a moment. But first it is important to understand the strategy Socrates is using to convert Critobulus: since the youngster clearly admires Cyrus—as Plato's Socrates was aware young Alcibiades did as well (*Alc.1* 105c5)—the binding theme of *Oeconomicus* is not agriculture but leadership, and the argumentative conceit at its philosophical center is the claim that the skill that makes it possible to manage well (εὖ οἰκεῖν) a country estate (οἶκος) is the same one (i.e., οἰκονομική) that makes it possible to rule a kingdom. All of the major interpretive questions about Xenophon coalesce in the problem of how we should understand the vector of this parallel.

To introduce this problem, consider the relationship between Xenophon and the following trio of the thinker-politicians: Marcus Tullius Cicero, Thomas Jefferson, and Niccolò Machiavelli.[122] Cicero translated Xenophon's *Oeconomicus* as a young man, and the question is: Why? Whatever we may ultimately decide about Xenophon's purpose in writing this dialogue, it is impossible to misconstrue the sincere interest in agriculture demonstrated by the intellectuals of Rome, indeed "scratch a Roman, find a peasant" is a useful maxim in approaching writers as diverse as Cato the Elder, Lucretius, Varro, Tibullus, and Vergil. Quite apart from Columella, Cicero proves that this list is incomplete. It is obvious that Cicero's interests were political, not agricultural, but it is equally obvious that he was a Roman *eques*, "a knight." As anyone who has taught the fall of the Roman Republic knows, the decline of the Italian family farm was a political disaster for Roman liberty, and even under Augustus—who had assassinated both it and Cicero—the agricultural mystique was strong enough to produce Vergil's post-republican *Georgics*. At the turning point of the Battle of Pharsalus, itself the turning point of Rome's Civil War, the older Caesar instructs his battle-hardened legionaries to aim their blows at the faces of the young cavalryman coming against them.[123] If there had been more of those horsemen, and if they had been more inured to hardship and less concerned with appearances than Pompey's volunteer cavalry, flushed with patriotism but short of experience, Pharsalus might have turned out differently. For the purpose of rejuvenating the Italian countryside, of swelling the ranks of the *equites*, and thus providing the Roman Republic with a capable and patriotic cavalry force, Cicero could have picked no better book to translate into Latin than Xenophon's *Oeconomicus*.

Anyone who has taught the foundations of the American Republic knows that Jefferson's ideal citizen was a farmer but it is easy to forget that this agriculturalist would be a soldier and a horseman as well as a patriot. And since Jefferson's Louisiana-based ideal remained a practical and political reality at least until July 4, 1863, and survived as a soul-stirring dream to millions in William Jennings Bryan's "Cross of Gold" in 1896, the mowing down of Germany's cavalrymen in August 1914 demonstrates how long Xenophon's hymn to the gentleman-farmer maintained its appeal. The ironic reading of Xenophon's *Oeconomicus*—where Socrates cannot be serious in an encomium of agriculture that anticipates Bryan's (*Oec.* 5.17)—is a post-1914 phenomenon with its roots in the nineteenth century's growing idealization of the machine as opposed to the horse and the engineer as opposed to the gentleman-farmer. A living reality for Jefferson and the ideal citizen of the American West, the capable horseman, soldier, and citizen embodied in Ischomachus has only recently became an embarrassment which a serious and Machiavellian Xenophon could never have taken seriously, and from which he must therefore be absolved.

The two faces of Machiavelli bring the problem to a head. The dilemma confronting the reader of Xenophon's *Cyropaedia* is whether it is best understood in relation to Machiavelli's *Prince* or to his own *Oeconomicus*.[124] Understood as "a mirror of princes" by which Xenophon communicated his royal ideal of a perfect and all-powerful monarch—describing as a pattern for imitation the means and methods by which Cyrus gained that power—*Cyropaedia* is Xenophon's *Il Principe*, and the more immoral but expedient are Cyrus's methods, the wiser and less embarrassing does his creator become. On the other side, there stands not only Xenophon's *Oeconomicus*—where Socrates' goal is to tame Critobulus' imperial ambitions by showing how every effective farmer's home is a palace and its fields a kingdom—but the pre-Medici Machiavelli, organizing the citizen-soldiers of the Florentine Republic. From *Oeconomicus* through *Ways and Means*, and with important way-stations in *Cynegeticus*, *Memorabilia* book 3, *Concerning Horsemanship*, *The Cavalry Officer*, and *Cyropaedia* itself—Xenophon gives abundant evidence that it is the republican Machiavelli who resembles him, not the tyrant-friendly author of *The Prince*.[125]

The last chapter of Xenophon's *Oeconomicus* includes his clearest statement about tyranny, his most powerful and effective image, and he identifies with the word τὸ ἀρχικόν or "leadership" the thread that connects all of his writings. Having demonstrated the ease with which γεωργία can be taught, Ischomachus makes it clear that the same is by no means true of leadership:

"But I am considering, Ischomachus," I said, "how well you have presented the whole argument in support of your hypothesis. For you hypothesized that agriculture is the easiest of all arts [τέχναι] to learn, and now I [sc. Socrates], from everything you have said, hold this to be the case, and I have been completely persuaded by you." "It is, by Zeus," Ischomachus said, "but note this as well, Socrates: the common thing for all these practices [πράξεις], both for agriculture, politics, estate management [οἰκονομική], and warfare is leadership [τὸ ἀρχικόν]. And in this I would agree with you that some people differ greatly from others with respect to their intelligent capacity [γνώμη] shown by different classes of men varies greatly. As it is also on a trireme," he said [οἷον καὶ ἐν τριήρει ἔφη], "when it's on the open sea, and it is necessary to drive on with day-long rowing, some boatswains are able to say and do [λέγειν καὶ ποιεῖν] the things that sharpen the spirits [ψυχαί] of their people, making them want to work, while others are so intellectually incompetent [ἀγνώμονες] that in more than twice the time they complete the same voyage. And the first crew disembarks, drenched with sweat and praising each other—both the boatswain and those who obeyed him—while the others, arriving with no sweat, hate their boss and are hated too."[126]

Beginning with the words οἷον καὶ ἐν τριήρει ἔφη, Xenophon uses an image of Socrates using an image of a καλὸς κἀγαθός using an image of τὸ ἀρχικόν. There appears to be nothing royal about this vivid image of the sweating rowers; it sings "not deeds of heroes or of kings."[127] Yet the simile is Xenophon's most Homeric moment, and introduces the theme with which his *Oeconomicus* ends: the difference between the voluntary obedience secured by one who has "something of a kingly ethos [τι ἤθους βασιλικοῦ]" (*Oec.* 21.10) and the involuntary obedience on which a tyrant must rely. Despite the words γνώμη and ἀγνώμονες, a capacity for τὸ ἀρχικόν is not called a τέχνη; indeed, this passage's purpose is to demonstrate that unlike agriculture, leadership is by no means easy to learn. But teaching it is best understood as Xenophon's purpose throughout his writings,[128] and the ongoing problem that confronts the reader who would understand him is as follows: given that both boatswains and kings share the same kingly ethos, is Xenophon's purpose to inflame the ambition of those young men who admire kings and who desire to become one—roughly speaking, this amounts to the view that Xenophon is a corrupter of the Athenian youth—or is he trying to persuade ambitious young men like Critobulus that a thrifty and hardworking estate manager may possess more of the *je ne sais quoi* that Socrates calls τι ἤθους βασιλικοῦ than the absolute monarch of a vast domain?

A similar problem confronts the reader of Plato's *Republic*. Is his purpose to inflame the desire of his readers to become the Philosopher-Kings of Kallipolis, or does the Allegory of the Cave simply promote the view that until Kallipolis comes into being, the philosophers "who are born in the other cities" (*R.* 520b1–2) have no responsibility to participate in politics?[129] Of course, there is another alternative that aligns *Republic* more closely with *Oeconomicus*: just as it will not be as the King of Persia that Critobulus takes up the duties of managing his estate—albeit with τι ἤθους βασιλικοῦ if he is to do so well—along with serving his city as mounted soldier and practiced speaker, so too Plato's purpose could be to practice justice on a more modest scale, as nurses or fireman, for example, as teachers, mothers, citizen-soldiers, and public servants; as good citizens, in short.[130] The common qualities that make τὸ ἀρχικόν everywhere the same creates the problem of vector: would it be because Glaucon can now manage his uncle's estate that he can now realize his ambition to mount τὸ βῆμα (*Mem.* 3.6.14–15) or was Socrates' purpose to persuade him that imitating a man such as Ischomachus—whether in Attica, Umbria, or Louisiana—is a noble course, quite apart from achieving any greater ambition than to combine self-sufficiency with civic responsibility, and to serve the city as a leader (note βοηθεῖν τε καὶ σῴζειν at *Mem.* 3.6.13) when required? Even after 1914, those whom Plato's *Republic* has persuaded to return to the cave can still learn from Xenophon's *Oeconomicus* how to operate there effectively, pending, that is, the coming of Kallipolis or the chance to be born a third Cyrus.

After a review of the *Anabasis* beginning with the younger Cyrus's revolt against his brother and ending with his death (*Oec.* 4.18-19), Socrates tells a charming story—Cicero retold it[131]—about a conversation between Cyrus and the Spartan general Lysander (*Oec.* 4.19-25), and from the way Xenophon links the two in *Hellenica* I (*Hell.* 1.5.1-7), we can discover the circumstances of their talk. Quite apart from the story's lesson, then— roughly that Cyrus was an accomplished agriculturalist, and had planted the trees Lysander admires himself, sweating appropriately in the process (*Oec.* 4.24)—Xenophon is referring to his own earlier works, much as he has already done or is about to do with the reference to Themistogenes at the beginning of *Hellenica* II. While it is remarkable that Xenophon is asking us to believe that Socrates has read *Anabasis* I—for he could not otherwise know the details about Cyrus's death[132]—it is within those details that Xenophon finds a way to use another literary trick. In addition, then, to the fact that his Socrates is implausibly if not impossibly referring to one of his own earlier books, the trick in question is that he misstates or rather contradicts some information in that book, thereby forcing the reader to compare the two passages. Moreover, the context of that discrepancy is significant, because it is relevant to the question of Cyrus's virtue, and thus of how much Xenophon actually admires him:

> "And I [sc. Socrates] believe this too to be a great proof [μέγα τεκμήριον] of a leader's virtue [ἀρετή], whereby those who willingly obey wish to remain alongside even in dire straits [ἐν τοῖς δεινοῖς]. And in the case of that man [sc. Cyrus], his friends were both fighting for him while he was alive, and when he was dead, they all died fighting for his corpse, except Ariaeus; Ariaeus happened to be stationed on the left wing."[133]

As Xenophon (or Themistogenes) tells us the first time this name appears in the earlier book, Cyrus had assigned the left wing to his principal lieutenant Ariaeus in the Battle of Cunaxa (*An.* 1.8.5; note ὕπαρχος), and the words "happened to be stationed on the left wing" appear there as well (*An.* 1.9.31). But immediately after those words, Xenophon writes: "And as he [sc. Ariaeus] was perceiving Cyrus to have fallen, he fled, taking also the whole army, of which he was in command." Quite apart from this man's subsequent service to Cyrus's brother and his duplicity toward the Greeks (see especially *An.* 2.5.37–42), the fact that his most trusted lieutenant fled and thereby failed to provide proof of Cyrus's virtue, would create a revealing contradiction even without the rest of the relevant passage in *Anabasis*, which already contained the same contradiction for which *Oeconomicus* itself provides an even greater τεκμήριον:

> Furthermore, what happened to Cyrus at the end of his life is a strong indication [μέγα τεκμήριον] that he was good himself [αὐτὸς ἦν ἀγαθός] and was able to judge correctly those who were faithful, devoted, and constant [οἱ πιστοὶ καὶ εὖνοι καὶ βέβαιοι]. When he died, namely, all his bodyguard of friends and table companions died fighting in his defense, with the exception of Ariaeus; he, it chanced, was stationed on the left wing at the head of the cavalry, and when he learned that Cyrus had fallen, he took to flight with the whole army that he commanded.[134]

I might as well admit that I regard the whole of *Anabasis* 1.9 to have been rewritten contemporaneously with the publication of *Anabasis* II, citing as proof the anticipations of *Cyropaedia* at the chapter's start (*An.* 1.9.1–6),[135] the proof of Cyrus's cruelty (*An.* 1.9.13), the repeated use of the stylistically "late" μήν (1.9.16–20), along with the heavy-handed contradiction here (1.9.30–31). If the chapter wasn't rewritten in Skillus, then *Oeconomicus* was likely the first work he wrote there; if it was, *Oeconomicus* was likely the second, following *Anabasis* II. But what is in any case clear is that Xenophon is giving us a μέγα τεκμήριον in *Oeconomicus* of his capacity *to contradict himself deliberately* not only by referring to an earlier works but also internally. Second in excellence only to "[the Simile of] the Sweating Rowers" (for so *Oec.* 21.3 will hereafter be called), the image of the divided Athenian assembly gives proof of this kind of internal self-contradiction. In response to the invasion of Attica, the craftsmen of the city vote to huddle behind the city's walls; the patriotic citizen-soldiers of the countryside are ready, willing, and able to ride out against the invaders (*Oec.* 6.6–7). To prove that the latter decision embodies Xenophon's political ideal, the evidence of what happens in *Oeconomicus* after the arrival of Ischomachus (*Oec.* 7.1) can join *Memorabilia* 3.5, *The Cavalry Officer*, and *Ways and Means* once again. But when Socrates claims that he has already told the story of "the Patriotic Division" (another piece of shorthand)—he prefaces it with "the clearest proof [τεκμήριον] of this we've said" (*Oec.* 6.6)—Xenophon expects us to realize that Socrates has done no such thing, a device that emphasizes his story's importance for those who don't regard it as indicating its teller's incompetence.

And then there is the entrance of Cyrus the Great. As part of Socrates' ongoing attempt to valorize agriculture by claiming that it is one of the Great King's two chief pursuits, he mentions the gifts (δῶρα) they bestow, first on the soldiers who add more territory to their empire, and then on the skilled farmers who make that territory profitable (*Oec.* 4.15). He then tells the following story, and although the point Critobulus takes from it is clearly the one Socrates wants him to take, Xenophon expects us to take from it another:

> "It is said that once upon a time Cyrus, he who has become the most famous King, said to those who had been summoned to receive his gifts [τὰ δῶρα], that he himself might justly receive the gifts [τὰ δῶρα] of both kinds, for he said that he was best both at stocking land and the best at protecting the stock." "Cyrus, then, O Socrates," said Critobulus, "was taking no less pride, if he said these things, in making his territory productive and stocking it than to be warlike [πολεμικός] in getting it."[136]

Although Cyrus is continuously bestowing gifts on others in *Cyropaedia*, Xenophon (or rather its narrator)[137] will never make as clear there what his Socrates indicates here: that in bestowing τὰ δῶρα, he always regarded *himself* as the one who rightly ought to be rewarded (cf. *Cyr.* 5.5.25–27). Socrates' Cyrus is tactless here but honest; Xenophon's will differ in appearance but not in substance, for the reader will research *Cyropaedia* in vain to discover a single example of Cyrus's generosity that does not benefit, and was not intended to benefit himself.[138]

By this point, it is high time to begin considering how Xenophon's *Cyropaedia* demonstrates his debts to Plato, and the first point to be made is that the μέγα τεκμήριον that those debts exist does not depend exclusively or even primarily on the comparison of parallel texts. It is Aulus Gellius, at once the oldest source for Literary Rivalry and that story's earliest critic, who records the following: "This also they [sc. the proponents of Literary Rivalry] believed to be an indication of no sincere or friendly volition: that Xenophon, with almost two of its books having been read [*lectis ex eo duobus fere libris*] which first had gone forth among the public, reacted against that famous work of Plato's which he wrote about the best state of the polity and about the administration of the state, and described a different kind of royal administration, which has been entitled *The Education of Cyrus*" (Aulus Gellius, *Attic Nights*, 14.3). Here then, for the first time, is ancient, external, and credible evidence of Xenophon's debt to Plato, and more specifically, that it was Plato's *Republic*—or rather "almost its first two books"—that led him to write his *Cyropaedia*. In the rest of this section, I will cite parallel themes and texts to support the substance of Aulus Gellius' testimony.[139]

Working backward from almost the end of *Republic* 2, the first text to be considered indicates the problem that makes it necessary to devote so much attention to the education of the city's soldiers: "'How then, O Glaucon,' this was I, 'that they will not be savage to one another and to the other citizens, being of this sort in their natures?' 'By Zeus,' was he, 'not easily'" (*R.* 375b10–13). By "of this sort" he means, of course, that unless someone is high-spirited—and this applies to horses, dogs, and any other animal—he will not wish to be courageous, will not be impossible to frighten, and unbeatable (*R.* 375a11–b3). This quickly leads to a clear statement of the difficulty of achieving this self-contradictory combination: "What then,' was I, 'are we to do? Where will we find an ethos [ἦθος] at once gentle and great-spirited? For it seems the gentle nature is opposite somehow to the high-spirited one" (*R.* 375c6–8). Although this formulation already looks forward to the Law of Non-Contradiction (*R.* 436b9–c2), the problem was long since introduced by Polemarchus (*R.* 332a9–b8), for how is it that the one who is so effectively terrible to his enemies will not prove to be equally dangerous to his friends (φίλοι)? Coming to Socrates' aid at this point is the analogy to hunting dogs (*R.* 375d10–376a10), the subject to which Xenophon had already devoted his youthful *Cynegeticus*. And by introducing philosophy at this point—a conception that naturally will make dogs philosophical because they love what they know and not what they don't (*R.* 376a5–7)—Socrates demonstrates that although difficult, philosophy proves that such a combination is possible, and asks (*R.* 376c4–6). At this point, almost three-quarters of the way through book 2,[140] Adeimantus replaces Glaucon, and a conversation about literature begins.

If Plato's answer to this problem is "the Education of the Guardians," Xenophon's answer to it is "the Education of Cyrus," and the first step toward clarity is to recognize that Xenophon's answer is no more practical, sensible, and plausible than Plato's. It is because most of us don't recognize the problem as virtually insoluble except on the basis of voluntary selflessness that we regard the solutions Socrates will proceed to unfold in conversation with Adeimantus—based on literary censorship, multiple lies, and strictly supervised regimentation—as delightfully problematic. Xenophon's response, embodied in Cyrus, puts a clearer focus on the problem by offering what appears to be a more attractive solution to it. The most obvious debt to this passage is found in the homily clad in a retrospectively conversational form that Cambyses imparts to his son Cyrus immediately before the young man is set free from supervision entirely (*Cyr.* 1.6). In defending the principles of a Persian education—in which doing harm to others is confined to lessons in hunting animals (*Cyr.* 1.6.28–29)—Cambyses contrasts it with another kind. There, instead of discouraging deception, wrongdoing, and taking advantage unfairly altogether (*Cyr.* 1.6.31–32), the only way to avoid its misuse was to uphold as absolute the difference between friend and foe (*Cyr.* 1.6.31) so as never to practice against a friend the skills that ensure success against enemies. Cambyses defends the choice to exclude this two-sided education on the sensible grounds that makes the problem of the fierce but gentle Guardians of *Republic* 2 more palpable: "There thus arose some who were naturally well-suited both to deceive effectively [τὸ εὖ ἐξαπατᾶν] and to take advantage well [τὸ εὖ πλεονεκτεῖν], and perhaps also being not naturally ill-suited toward greed [τὸ φιλοκερδεῖν], did not abstain from trying to take advantage [πλεονεκτεῖν] even of their friends [φίλοι]" (*Cyr.* 1.6.32).

Not surprisingly, Cyrus wants his father to teach him how to do both (*Cyr.* 1.6.30), which is not to say that by this point he needs any such lessons: he has already whetted his officer corps that has committed itself to πλεονεκτεῖν in open opposition to traditional Persian austerity and self-denial (*Cyr.* 1.5.9). The question that confronts the reader of Xenophon's *Cyropaedia* is whether he practices his remarkably capacity for τὸ εὖ ἐξαπατᾶν, τὸ εὖ πλεονεκτεῖν, and τὸ φιλοκερδεῖν only on his enemies, or on his friends as well.[141] But perhaps it would be better to say that this is the question that confronts someone who rereads *The Education of Cyrus*,[142] for so effectively, obligingly, and even obsequiously does the narrator present Cyrus's actions that virtually nobody could realize from the start that he is anything other than Xenophon's hero and a role model of ἀρετή. It is only at the very end of the book (*Cyr.* 8.8)—when despite the homily the dying Cyrus gives to his sons (*Cyr.* 8.7), this time without even the appearance of dialogue, we discover that the quarreled and Persia descended into lawless and amoral chaos—that the narrator retrospectively casts unmistakable doubt on the effectiveness of Cyrus's imperial arrangements, so much so that the last chapter has not infrequently been regarded as inauthentic.[143] But beginning with the conquest of Babylon,[144] the signs of his willingness to practice τὸ εὖ ἐξαπατᾶν, τὸ εὖ πλεονεκτεῖν, and τὸ φιλοκερδεῖν on his friends become so obvious that it requires a resolute resistance to deny them, at least when reexamined on the basis of Persia's subsequent degeneration.

The second book of Plato's *Republic* begins with the great speech of Glaucon in which he prepares, as if with chisel and polish, the statues of two men, challenging Socrates to prove that the life of one is more choice-worthy than the second (*R.* 360d8–361a2; cf. 361d4–7). As is so often the case, a discussion of Xenophon's debts to Plato's can hardly avoid referring in the process to Plato's debts to Xenophon, and in the case of Glaucon's choice of lives, to "The Choice of Heracles" in *Memorabilia* 2.1. Remarking only that it seems likely that the publication of *Memorabilia* II, including the "Choice," precedes both Plato's *Republic* and Xenophon's *Cyropaedia*, the superiority of the choice Plato uses Glaucon to create resides in the fact that it is no longer a question of Pleasure's capacity to deceive but of the unjust man's complete success with respect to what Xenophon will call τὸ εὖ ἐξαπατᾶν:

> In this way also the unjust man [ὁ ἄδικος] who tries to do unjust actions rightly [ἐπιχειρῶν ὀρθῶς τοῖς ἀδικήμασιν], let him escape notice if will be altogether unjust [σφόδρα ἄδικος]; the one who's caught must be thought incompetent. For extreme injustice [ἐσχάτη ἀδικία] is to seem be just without being so. It is therefore necessary to give to the perfectly unjust man [ὁ τελέως ἄδικος] the most perfect injustice [ἡ τελεωτάτη ἀδικία] and necessary to detract nothing from it but to allow him, while doing injustice in the greatest things [τὰ μέγιστα] to have secured for himself the greatest reputation [ἡ μεγίστη δόξα] for justice.[145]

In quoting this passage in the context of Xenophon's *Cyropaedia*, and in order to illustrate his debts to "almost the first two books" of

Plato's *Republic*, it is really the reader of this book who must make a choice. Up to this point, emphasis has fallen on literary debts, and in any case not on readings of either Xenophon's or Plato's texts that break so profoundly with interpretive orthodoxy.[146] To suggest that Xenophon's Cyrus is his version of Glaucon's ὁ τελέως ἄδικος, and that he practices throughout *The Education of Cyrus* ἡ τελεωτάτη ἀδικία is so far removed from the traditional "mirror of princes" reading of the book as not so much to strain credulity as to abandon any relation with what presently seems credible.[147] In response, it is precisely because it seems completely incredible that Cyrus is anything but Xenophon's hero that we can see how great an artist his dialogue with Plato had made him by this point. As Socrates says of Cyrus in *Oeconomicus*, he was εὐδοκιμώτατος; the "most well-reputed" βασιλεύς of all; Xenophon's *Cyropaedia* polishes away all of the flaws Herodotus had revealed, allowing him in the process to secure ἡ μεγίστη δόξα. In other words, if Cyrus were widely recognized to be ὁ τελέως ἄδικος, he would not have achieved ἡ τελεωτάτη ἀδικία. Xenophon's artistry is only apparent if most readers will see Cyrus as just, benevolent, and generous. As for discovering that he merely *appears* to possess these admirable qualities, Socrates' story of who really deserved τὰ δῶρα has prepared us.

This is not to say that Xenophon's Cyrus has fooled everyone, and the interpretation of *Cyropaedia* is contested as a result. The defenders of a "sunny" reading of Xenophon's book as "a mirror of princes" regard Strauss and his followers as responsible for a "dark" reading;[148] in due course, Plato will be shown to deserve that honor.[149] In fact, the Straussian reception of Xenophon's *Cyropaedia* is complicated by a number of factors that are best explored elsewhere, one of them being that Strauss's own published reading takes a "sunny" approach to things that others, some Straussians included, have rightly found to be "dark."[150] As a result, then, of the presently contested interpretation of *The Education of Cyrus*, the proposal that Cyrus is not what he appears to be and even that he is a master of τὸ εὖ ἐξαπατᾶν is not so great an exception after all. But what does make the reading implied by Xenophon's debt to Glaucon's speech exceptional is that it radicalizes more typical "dark" readings in a number of important ways: (1) it is based on the view that Xenophon is advancing a Platonic project visible, in accordance with the testimony of Aulus Gellius, at the very beginning of the second book of his *Republic*; (2) it interprets *Cyropaedia* on the basis of that project, thus configuring Cyrus not only as flawed, self-serving, and overly ambitious, etc., but as ὁ τελέως ἄδικος; and (3) it regards the proponents of the traditional "sunny" reading as a μέγα τεκμήριον that Xenophon has been successful in illuminating ἡ τελεωτάτη ἀδικία, for if the Persian Empire did not belong to the realm of τὰ μέγιστα, if Cyrus the Great were not εὐδοκιμώτατος, and if he had not achieved ἡ μεγίστη δόξα, Xenophon could not have used him to test the reader's ability to recognize ἐσχάτη ἀδικία when they see it, or rather, when they take a second look at a book whose shocking ending has forced them to reread it.[151]

Viewed in this light, Xenophon's *Cyropaedia* filled up a lacuna in Plato's masterpiece. Beginning with its opening word (κατέβην), Plato is preparing the reader to recognize Socrates as the perfectly just man who nevertheless appears to be unjust; if his judicial murder by hemlock is considerably less unpleasant than the whipping, blinding, and crucifixion Glaucon so vividly describes (*R*. 361e4–362a1), it is nevertheless his failure *to appear to be just* that is responsible for his later conviction, a fate already made to haunt *Republic* itself (*R*. 496c3–e3). But seen in this light, Socrates is only one of Glaucon's two statues, and if the reader is going to be offered the kind of choice that will really test their mettle, the Socratic appeal of the misunderstood just man's life must be placed next to another life for comparison. Just as Glaucon describes the fate of the just man who appears to be unjust in a manner that leaves Socrates far behind, so too we need to examine an equally enhanced image of the unjust man who appears to be just in order to balance it. This is what Xenophon supplied in *Cyropaedia*: the life of a famous king, presented in a manner that has made it natural to consider Cyrus as one of Xenophon's heroes,[152] an effective ruler who never errs in pursuing his goals, and dies peacefully in his bed. As great as Plato's *Republic* undoubtedly is, Xenophon has managed to show that it remains one-sided. Of course he can only do so by building on Plato, and he does so in a way that reveals his debts.

Apart from the mythical Gyges, Thrasymachus is the closest thing to ὁ τελέως ἄδικος in Plato's *Republic*, not the tyrant of book 9. By describing the psychological origins of the latter in prior forms and characters, Socrates brings him on the stage already freighted with misery and ignorance. But Plato scarcely makes Thrasymachus an appealing alternative to the just man. To begin with, he is merely a sophist, and a foreigner as well, things that an ambitious Athenian youngster would never wish to be (*Prt*. 312a1–2). By comparing him to a wild animal (*R*. 335b5–6), by describing his threat to depart (*R*. 344d1–7), and by making visible his embarrassed and telltale blush (*R*. 350d3), Socrates ensures that no reader is going to choose the life of Thrasymachus in preference to his own. The closest Thrasymachus comes to offering the reader the kind of unjust man that might actually appeal to an ambitious youngster is in the following passage:

> You think that the shepherds and the cowherds [οἱ βουκόλοι] are considering the good of their sheep [τὰ πρόβατα] and cattle and fatten and tend them [θεραπεύειν] with anything else in view than the good of their masters [οἱ δεσπόται] and themselves; and by the same token you seem to suppose that the rulers in our cities, I mean those who truly rule [ἀληθῶς ἄρχειν], differ at all in their thoughts of the governed from a man's attitude towards his sheep or that they think of anything else night and day than how they themselves may be benefitted [ὠφελεῖσθαι]. And you are so far out concerning the just and justice and the unjust and injustice that you don't know that justice and the just are literally the other fellow's good—the advantage of the stronger and the ruler, but a detriment that is all his own of the subject who obeys and serves.[153]

Throughout *Cyropaedia*, Xenophon leaves no doubt that Cyrus knows how to ἀληθῶς ἄρχειν, and in the process he is also shown to ὠφελεῖσθαι, that is, to be benefited. And from the very beginning, the problem of securing the kind dominion over men that will not cause those being dominated to rebel has been expressed in terms of ruling animals; as a result, both οἱ δεσπόται and οἱ βουκόλοι enter early (*Cyr.* 1.1.1–2). Although he will make it clear to his officers in book 2 that he regards the leaders as those whom the lead are to θεραπεύειν (*Cyr.* 2.1.23), it is not until the last book that he compares those whom he leads—both officers and men, both foes and friends—to πρόβατα:

> And an argument of his is remembered that says the functions of a good shepherd [νομεύς] and a good king are similar, for he said that just as the shepherd ought to make use of his flocks while making them happy (in the happiness of sheep [πρόβατα], of course), so a king similarly ought to make use of cities and human beings while making them happy. So it is not to be wondered at, if in fact he was of this judgment, that he competed to be superior to all human beings in service [θεραπεία].[154]

These parallels should be allowed to speak for themselves about Xenophon's debt to Plato. But even Thrasymachus' image of the well-served herdsman falls well short of the image of the skilled νομεύς in *Cyropaedia*. In explaining the image, Thrasymachus merely emphasizes the ruler's happiness: "[I]njustice is the contrary and rules those who are simple in every sense of the word and just, and they being thus ruled do what is for his advantage who is the stronger and make him happy in serving him, but themselves by no manner of means [οἱ δ' ἀρχόμενοι . . . εὐδαίμονα ἐκεῖνον ποιοῦσιν ὑπηρετοῦντες αὐτῷ, ἑαυτοὺς δὲ οὐδ' ὁπωστιοῦν]" (R. 343c1–d1). Xenophon's Cyrus, by ruling men as shepherds rule sheep, is able to make οἱ ἀρχόμενοι *happy* in making him happy, albeit merely in "the happiness of sheep [ἡ προβάτων εὐδαιμονία]." This difference—at two removes from Thrasymachus—shows that Xenophon really did respond to "almost the first two books" of Plato's *Republic* and it explains how he did so. It also explains why Plato would need to write both *Statesman* and *Laws* in order to pay back his debt to Xenophon having made the right choice of lives as difficult in a written text as it is life itself.

Hiero

A late date has been assigned to the composition of *The Education of Cyrus* on the basis of its last chapter; in partial agreement with those who regard 8.8 as inauthentic, I would suggest it was added only to the last edition of Xenophon's longest work. Given its later reception, it seems that *Cyropaedia* was too deceptive in the version that did not include 8.8; the deception was transparent only to a reader such as Plato.[155] An indication of how early Xenophon's *Cyropaedia* might have been published can be found in *Alcibiades Major*, where the youngsters Plato is addressing there can be assumed to share Alcibiades' admiration for Cyrus the Great, possibly on the basis of Xenophon, and whose familiarity with *Anabasis* is in any case presumed (see chapter 1, section 4). A second edition of *Cyropaedia* that included 8.8 could be considered a palinode but it would be better to imagine it as a simpler and more reader-friendly version—or rather re-reader-friendly—of the first, which could have been written considerably earlier than the last chapter proves, with its date plausibly pegged to whenever Plato is presumed to have "published" or at least finished his *Republic*.

But whenever Xenophon published the first edition of *Cyropaedia*, it is probably best to think of it as already "*Cyropaedia* II," with the final edition including 8.8 imagined as "*Cyropaedia* III." Delebecque's *Vie de Xénophon* has inspired this hypothesis with the parallel suggestion that Xenophon's *Memorablia* was written in Skillus, and was originally intended only for the oral instruction of his young sons.[156] This hypothesis is far more applicable to the oral *Urkyropädie* that I will be calling "*Cyropaedia* I." If Xenophon's *Education of Cyrus* did not contain a large number of instructive and entertaining episodes, it could not achieve its remarkable effect, and it is easy to imagine that the various stories that constituted the oral version were told to Philesia, Gryllus, and Diodorus "straight," that is to say, with no intention to make them anything other than what they appeared to be: entertaining and instructive. It is plausible to add Philesia because of the remarkable element that the wise, courageous, and loyal Panthea adds to the story, and Bodil Due usefully speculated that women and girls constituted part of Xenophon's intended audience.[157] Although useless for demonstrating Xenophon's debts to Plato, the hypothesis that the oldest version of *Cyropaedia* was oral, and conceived with two little boys in mind, helps to explain the remarkable appeal of the written book when read "straight."

In turning to *Hiero*, the first point to make is that if Xenophon had wanted to criticize Plato, a dialogue about a wise man paying court to a Syracusan tyrant was the right place to do it. In many ways, Plato's decision to become directly involved in Sicilian affairs was the analogue of Xenophon's earlier decision to involve himself in Asian ones: one travels east, the other west, and since both men wrote extensively about Alcibiades, it is interesting that he had already combined both vectors, setting off for Sicily before dying within sight of Asia. It is difficult to escape the conclusion that Plato's "Sicilian Expeditions" damaged his reputation for sagacity almost as much as Xenophon's earlier decision to follow the young Cyrus had damaged his with respect to loyalty,[158] and if Xenophon had wished to "score" against his fellow Athenian, it would have been wisest to attack him at his weakest point. Considered as a whole, Plato's *Letters* are particularly damning, ranging from petulant self-importance in the first to obsequious solicitude in the first, with the bookeneds of the collection arranged in reverse chronological order. If *Letters* is genuine, it is difficult to imagine how anyone could have made Plato look worse than its author did.[159]

If Xenophon intended to attack Plato by making him visible behind Simonides, his choice of this particular "wise man" was a curious and ill-advised one. Given the poet's role in *Republic*—where Polemarchus uses him to introduce the distinction between harming enemies and benefiting friends (*R.* 331d4–332c1)—he might seem to some rather more Xenophontic than Platonic. But the more important text is *Protagoras*, where the motives behind Simonides' willingness to praise powerful men such as Hiero are discussed (*Prt.* 346b5–8). In comparison with Xenophon's *Hiero*, Plato's version of Simonides in *Protagoras*, while clearly no great moral paragon, is still defensible on the grounds that he had often been forced to praise, for example, tyrants, and had only done so unwillingly (*Prt.* 346b7–8). In *Hiero*, Simonides "did make love to this employment," coming to the defense of tyranny when the tyrant himself was attacking it. If Xenophon is criticizing Plato, there is better evidence that he is criticizing his comparative sympathy for Simonides, and that seems about as likely as the view that Plato wrote his *Meno* to counteract the negative portrait in *Anabasis*. If Xenophon's *Hiero* demonstrates another example of his debts to Plato, it is almost certainly not because it is an artifact of their Literary Rivalry, for if it were, it would be a clumsy one.

A more promising line of inquiry might be thought to begin from tyranny, a subject that joins *Hiero* to both *Oeconomicus* and *Cyropaedia*. Xenophon's Cyrus is not and could not be presented as a tyrant; the Athenian Stranger in Plato's *Laws* was the first to identify him as such (*Lg.* 696a1). *Oeconomicus* ends with an image of the tyrant in hell, tortured by a fear from which all the other dead are spared, and from which Socrates was free even while alive (cf. *Ap.* 1 and *Ap.* 38e4–5): the fear of dying (*Oec.* 21.12). There Ischomachus distinguishes the king from the tyrant on the basis of voluntary as opposed to involuntary obedience; if only by granting his followers ἡ προβάτων εὐδαιμονία (*Cyr.* 8.2.14), Xenophon's Cyrus is either no tyrant at all—for they willingly follow him—or a uniquely effective one.[160] Xenophon's *Hiero* might easily be imagined as standing between these two alternatives, with Hiero himself giving voice to fears unknown to other men, and Simonides trying to persuade him to be more like Cyrus. But the inescapable fact is that the significance of this mediation will only become clear to a reader who decides on the basis of solid evidence as opposed to prejudice where Xenophon's own sympathies lie in this short but enigmatic dialogue. And it can do no harm to name the four logical possibilities: he either endorses the position of Simonides, of Hiero, of neither, or of both. And in gaining any clarity on this—and it is only on the basis of gaining it that any judgment can be made as to Xenophon's debts—one fact is indisputable: Hiero makes his case first, and that means if Xenophon's sympathies are with his position, then the structure of the dialogue indicates that it is a test, that is, that the reader must be able to resist the temptation of believing Simonides.

A more natural interpretation of this ordering is that by allowing Simonides to speak second and thus to address Hiero's position—and that means roughly to defend tyranny from an attack made on it by a tyrant—Xenophon was indicating his sympathy for the poet's position. The dialogue would then constitute progress, with something like enlightened despotism triumphing in the end. This reading will obviously tend to align Xenophon more with a "sunny" attitude toward Cyrus than with the Plato-inspired depiction of ὁ τελέως ἄδικος and ἐσχάτη ἀδικία described in the previous section. As for the other two logical possibilities, only "a curse on both your houses" account has much prospect of being true since it's much harder to see how both could be right than to see how both represent flawed positions.[161] It therefore seems most economical, if only to test the hypothesis advanced in the previous section—to determine whether or not it is possible that Xenophon's own views are plausibly assigned to Simonides. If they are, the case is closed, for choosing it will exclude the other three, and in addition to a literary convention that puts the stronger case last, it avoids the unlikely possibility that Xenophon is endorsing the views of a tyrant attacking tyranny.

For settling this question, a 2005 article by Stephan Schorn deserves notice. To begin with, Schorn takes a balanced approach to Strauss's *On Tyranny*, acknowledging as an indisputable fact this 1948 book's impact on the interpretation of *Hiero*.[162] Schorn's core claim is that Xenophon expects the reader to encounter *Hiero* only after reading his Socratic writings, and that for the reader who does so, it becomes obvious that both Simonides and Hiero make Socrates' position conspicuous by its absence. As opposed to Vivienne Gray and Louis-André Dorion,[163] Schorn therefore refuses to collapse the difference between Simonides and Socrates; in opposition to Strauss, he makes the simple point that it is not Xenophon but only Hiero who identifies Simonides as wise.[164] By suggesting the existence of something like a Xenophontic "reading order," he breaks ground in a manner that suggests a debt to Plato that will be explored in later chapters. And by making the ongoing claim that Socrates is present in the dialogue only insofar as his readers, prompted by both of the dialogue's equally un-Socratic characters, bring him along with them, he could be said to be either anticipating or responding to Platonic dialogues in which other characters—Timaeus, the Eleatic, and the Athenian Strangers—replace

Socrates. Without claiming that Hiero speaks for Xenophon, Schorn makes a compelling case that Simonides doesn't.

Despite his article's merits, there is one simple observation that Schorn fails to make with crystal clarity. The passage in which he comes closest immediately follows discussion of *Memorabilia* 2.6, where Socrates persuades Critobulus that friendship is only possible if both people possess ἐγκράτεια or self-control:

> For the reader who knows *Memorabilia*, Hiero's lack of friends—like his relations with the unjust {ἄδικοι}, the un-self-controlled {ἀκρατεῖς} (!) and slavish people {ἀνδραποδώδεις, [5.2]}—can be explained through his deficits in character. Hiero himself indeed recognizes the effects of the problem of lacking friends, but cannot get to the bottom of it [*nicht auf den Grund gehen*]. Xenophon never allows the two interlocutors to speak the tyrant's character in the first half of the dialogue. He will be *described* as ἀκρατής but not named as such. But when his personal environment will be characterized in this way, this is a reference to the tyrant himself as well as to a fundamental solution to the problem [*eine grundsätzliche Lösung des Problems*] with which an analysis of the presuppositions of his actions must begin.[165]

What Schorn does not say is that it is the tyrant's desire *for tyranny itself* that makes him ἀκρατής; he is content to show that he was already ἀκρατής—and thus incapable of Socratic friendship—before he became a tyrant. This, of course, is true, but likewise does not *auf den Grund gehen*: the burdens of tyranny as described by *Hiero* have their ineradicable roots in the tyrant's desire to become one in the first place.

There is a simpler explanation for Xenophon's refusal to illuminate the flaws in Hiero's character, and this becomes clear once it is recognized that the tyrant's need to acquire Socratic ἐγκράτεια does not constitute *eine grundsätzliche Lösung des Problems*, since this acquisition would be *ipso facto* impossible for a tyrant, especially as described by Plato in *Republic* 9. But if Hiero cannot recognize his own character flaws, he clearly recognizes the deficits of being a tyrant, and once we have disposed of a "wise" or "Socratic" Simonides, attention must shift to the truth of what Hiero says in the first part of the dialogue, and the impossibility of having any friends is an easy and characteristic example of such truths. As opposed to "a curse on both your houses" reading, the line of Shakespeare that becomes more apt is: "I am a king that finds thee and I know." Only if we are intent in finding a truthful Simonides and a tyrant-friendly Xenophon does it become possible to miss the fact that whatever might be Hiero's deficits of character, he speaks the truth about tyranny, already expressed in the last words of *Oeconomicus*. And for assessing the truth of Simonides' response in the dialogue's second half, another line from the same speech in *Henry the Fifth* (Act IV, scene 1, 255-56) comes to mind: "What drinks thou oft instead of homage sweet but poisoned flattery?"

In order to sustain a reading along these lines, it will be necessary to document both Simonides' "poisoned flattery" and Hiero's right to that "I know." The most economical approach to doing so begins with Simonides:

> And Simonides said: "but if in the matter of spectacles you are at a disadvantage [μειωνεκτεῖν], with respect to hearing you get the advantage [πλεονεκτεῖν]. Never are you in want of the sweetest sound: praise [τὸ ἥδιστον ἀκρόαμα ἔπαινος]. For all those who are around you are praising everything whatsoever you say and whatsoever you do. But the harshest sound, abuse, you don't hear, for nobody wishes to criticize the tyrant *ad oculos* [κατ' ὀφθαλμούς]."[166]

It is not difficult to see how these words instantiate rather than refute Hiero's inevitable response. The reader will instantly see the problem with "praise" of this kind quite apart from Simonides' endorsement of the tyrant's characteristic desire to πλεονεκτεῖν[167]—the elimination of which would really be what Schorn calls *eine grundsätzliche Lösung des Problems*. The self-contradiction is recognizable by using κατ' ὀφθαλμούς in the explicit context not of what the tyrant sees but what he hears. The truth is not only what the tyrant never hears, but it is also equally what Simonides is presently concealing, and it is the offstage reader who has already refuted the poet even before Hiero responds:

> And Hiero spoke: "And why do you suppose," he said, "him to take delight in [εὐφραίνειν] those who are not speaking evilly when somebody knows clearly [σαφῶς] that all those keeping silent are thinking bad things against the tyrant? And why do

you consider him to take delight in [εὐφραίνειν] those praising him since those offering praises would be suspected [ὕποπτοι] of doing so because of flattery [τὸ κολακεύειν]?"[168]

It is with these two unanswered questions ringing in our ears that we should consider everything else Simonides has the effrontery to say in the dialogue. In short, the relevant question here is: Will we, as readers, be ὕποπτοι of Simonides, recognizing σαφῶς not just the hollowness of his previous attempt to employ τὸ κολακεύειν, but the inner necessity that will lead him to continue doing so hereafter? If we do, it is Xenophon's readers who will be prepared to εὐφραίνειν on account of his delightful *Hiero*.

Consider Simonides' use of εὐφροσύνη (*Hier.* 7.4), the noun that describes the mental state associated with εὐφραίνειν. Consistent with the flatterer the dialogue shows him to be, Simonides constructs a theory of human nature that creates a necessary and important place for the praise-singer, the one who can sing hymns of praise in honor of those rare men, so far above the vulgar crowd, whose ἔρως is directed to what is nearest the divine:

> "For indeed it seems to me, Hiero, that in this man differs from other animals—I mean, in this craving for honor [τιμή]. In meat and drink and sleep and sex all creatures alike seem to take pleasure [ἥδεσθαι]; but the love of honor [ἡ φιλοτιμία] is rooted neither in the brute beasts nor in every human being. But they in whom is implanted a passion for honor and praise [τιμῆς τε καὶ ἐπαίνου ἔρως], these are they who differ most from the beasts of the field [τὰ βοσκήματα], these are accounted men [ἄνδρες] and not mere human beings [ἄνθρωποι]. And so, in my opinion, you have good reason for bearing all those burdens that despotism lays on you, in that you are honored [τιμᾶσθαι] above all other men. For no human pleasure [ἀνθρωπίνη ἡδονή] seems to be nearer the divine [τὸ θεῖον] than the delight concerning honors [ἡ περὶ τὰς τιμὰς εὐφροσύνη]."[169]

It is easy to see how Simonides' distinction between ἄνδρες and mere ἄνθρωποι might well appeal to an admirer of Nietzsche,[170] for the gulf between τὰ βοσκήματα and τὸ θεῖον anticipates the one dividing "the vulgar herd" of "the Last Men" from the *Übermensch*. But it was already possible to recognize not only the self-contradiction that endows Simonides' so-called ἄνδρες with merely ἀνθρωπίνη ἡδονή, but also how this conception of "the divine" makes the tyrant's pleasure dependent on those who sing his praises.

At this point, it should be easy for Xenophon's readers to anticipate Hiero's reply, since it reprises both the worthlessness of "poisoned flattery" and the impossibility of a rich man being loved as if he were poor, that is, sincerely, and by those who give their love without fear, force, or favor (cf. *Hier.* 7.5-6 and 1.34-37). Thanks to these repetitions, Hiero will begin by speaking for us, since we have already recognized and assimilated the truths he has spoken. In vividly describing sincere praise offered willingly to the one who is loved not feared (*Hier.* 7.9-10), the same vector-reversal visible in *Oeconomicus* reappears: being honored is by no means the exclusive domain of the tyrant. Eager to derail Hiero's attack on tyranny, Simonides demands to know why—if tyranny is so terrible—he does not simply give it up; Hiero's arresting reply to this question is a brilliant one as well (*Hier.* 7.12-13). In response to this, no mere question will provide sufficient derailment, and this is why Simonides interrupts him again (*Hier.* 8.1; cf. 6.9).[171] The basis of his defense of tyranny will be the tyrant's greater ability to bestow gifts (δώρημα at *Hier.* 8.4). It is not difficult to see this move's comic implications: "'Whenever then [γε], for sure [μήν], from equal services you [ὑμεῖς] receive greater gratitude, *how can it not be* [γε] that you [ὑμεῖς], obtaining many times more things [πολλαπλάσια], are *able* to bring benefit [ὠφελεῖν], and also you have many times more things [πολλαπλάσια] to bestow as gifts [δωρεῖσθαι], that it would not befit you [ὑμεῖς] also to be loved [φιλεῖσθαι] much more than private men?'" (*Hier.* 8.7). How can we regard this mixture of overemphasis and falsehood as a "word from the wise" when it is so easy to see in δωρεῖσθαι and the doubled πολλαπλάσια the sugarplums already dancing in Simonides' imagination?

But Xenophon does not make things too easy, although considerably easier than he made them in *The Education of Cyrus* apart from 8.8. Following Hiero's interruption (*Hier.* 8.8), Simonides' advice to let others bear the onus of punishing while reserving the right to reward to himself (*Hier.* 9.3-11) undoubtedly increases the reader's confidence in his wisdom. In *Cyropaedia* itself, Cyrus's ability to create competition among his underlings (*Hier.* 9.6 and *Cyr.* 8.2.26-28; cf. 8.1.47) is at once the engine of his empire's success and, through the deadly rivalry between his sons, the cause of its subsequent collapse. The image of the tyrant presiding over competitions also recalls the anticipation of *Cyropaedia* in *Oeconomicus* (note γεωργία at *Hier.* 9.7), where Socrates has already informed us that instead of giving τὰ δῶρα to others, Cyrus the Great would have preferred to award them to himself. Simonides will more perfectly illuminate the indirect route to self-benefit through rewarding others: "And to speak concisely, if it also is obvious in all matters that the one suggesting any good thing [ἀγαθόν τι] will not be without honor, it will incentivize many to do this work: to search for something good [τι ἀγαθόν]."[172] Here, there is no need to inquire about *cui bono*; the tyrant's generosity rewards himself.

Hiero responds to this speech with praise, and his "beautifully [καλῶς] to me you seem to speak" (*Hier.* 10.1) might suggest that the tyrant has now become the flatterer. To speak concisely, the dialogue turns on the sincerity of praise, and Hiero's praise for Simonides is just as insincere as Simonides' is self-interested. The proof of this is that by having Hiero follow up this praise by asking Simonides whether he can dispense with mercenaries (*Hier.* 10.1)—that is, with those who serve the tyrant for pay—Xenophon is forcing the poet to reveal his flattery's hidden source. He does so with three words in his last speech's peroration: "Take heart then, Hiero! Enrich your friends [πλουτίζε τοὺς φίλους], for you will be enriching yourself; grow the city, for you will be attaching power to yourself (*Hier.* 11.13). Three themes come together here: the essence of Simonides' advice insofar as it is wise, its deceptive nature insofar as it is poisoned flattery, and synthesizing both is its self-interested motivation, for Simonides' advice for Hiero is to enrich Simonides. With πλουτίζε τοὺς φίλους, the wisdom of Simonides is his skill in advantaging himself, and it is therefore no accident that the lesson he imparts to Hiero has the exact same kind of self-interest as its essence.

As a result, although Xenophon doesn't make it too easy, he likewise refuses to make it too difficult. With respect to degree of difficulty, Xenophon's strategy in *Hiero* places it between *Cyropaedia* II and III, and this may suggest its time of composition as well. By expressly identifying Hiero as a tyrant, and by creating parallels between what Simonides advises a tyrant to do and what Cyrus has presumably already done—above all, by repeatedly making the selfishness of generosity transparent—Xenophon makes *Hiero* easier than *Cyropaedia* II, where the noble king dies peacefully in his bed, surrounded by friends and family. By contrast, Simonides will end his last speech and thus the dialogue with another self-contradiction (*Hier.* 11.15), for as long as men desire to become tyrants, the happy tyrant will be an object of envy, and tyranny is necessarily short-lived (*Cyr.* 1.1). To the extent that Xenophon had made Cyrus too attractive in *Cyropaedia* II, it would eventually become necessary to add the final chapter to *Cyropaedia* III; *Hiero* accomplishes a similar result in a less obvious way, forcing the reader, as it does, to compare two different texts rather than reexamine one in the light of its jarring conclusion. As for *Hiero*, placing the words πλουτίζε τοὺς φίλους only two sentences from the end makes its conclusion rather hilarious than jarring.

It is now possible to begin considering to what extent Xenophon's *Hiero* indicates any debts to Plato. The first, identified by Schorn, might well be the most important if also the simplest and easiest to overlook. What made Xenophon's *Memorabilia* so innovative was its composite nature; regardless of the skill with which he joined its various parts, the fact that those parts were part of a greater whole meant that we would read them in the order in which he arranged them, clearly and unmistakably. By arguing that *Hiero* presumes the reader's prior familiarity with Xenophon's Socratic writings—and curiously enough, with emphasis on the dialogues with Critobulus in both *Oeconomicus* and *Memorabilia* 2.6—Schorn suggests that there had begun to take shape in Xenophon's mind something like an inter-dialogue reading order (see chapter 3, section 2), and for this conception, he had Plato to thank. It was already implicit in Plato's decision to add a separate *Crito* to an already self-standing *Apology of Socrates*; if *Hippias Minor* and *Ion* are likewise early and were available to Xenophon, this pair too could have planted the seed. But as already indicated, it was Plato's *Symposium* that spawned a whole series of related dialogues, some of which were intended to prepare the reader for it; if Xenophon recognized why Plato expected the reader of *Symposium* to have already read *Hippias Major* or *Menexenus*, he himself had been prepared to write *Hiero* as he did.

Insofar as Schorn's purpose is polemical, it is to discredit the view that Simonides plays Socrates in *Hiero*. The result is that Xenophon has given us a recognizably "Socratic" dialogue not only without a character named "Socrates" but without his substance as well. If Xenophon's *Hiero* predates Plato's *Timaeus-Critias*, his *Sophist-Statesman*, and his *Laws-Epinomis*, then the debt will be Plato's, since Xenophon will once again be the pioneer. But the chronological priorities here make it by no means certain that *Hiero* was earlier than all three, and if it could be shown to be later than even one of the three pairs—as hardly seems impossible—then Xenophon would once again be in Plato's debt. Schorn would not need to be polemical if it were not easy to mistake "Simonides als Sokratesfigur,"[173] and on that basis to identify his views with Xenophon's, not least of all because the Socrates-Ischomachus figure in *Oeconomicus* appeared to many to be Xenophon himself. This is the same kind of identification that caused Aristotle to write the fatal words in *Physics*: "As Plato says in *Timaeus*."[174]

And here it is useful to revisit the hypothesis mentioned at the start of this section that a dialogue between a wise man and a tyrant would have created a convenient basis for attacking Plato. If only because the dialogue's setting called Plato to mind, it also created the possibility that just as *Meno* was Plato's homage to Xenophon, so too was *Hiero* Xenophon's to Plato. Although it has been suggested that 4.6 belongs to the latest or "dialectical" stage of *Memorabilia*, it has also been claimed by others that the method of division applied there depends on Xenophon's knowledge or rather misunderstanding of Plato's *Sophist*.[175] If the composition of *Hiero* likewise postdates *Sophist*, then Xenophon's creation of Simonides would indicate a far more advanced appreciation for what Plato is doing with the Eleatic Stranger than Andreas Patzer suspects. But whether as blazing Plato's trail or letting his friend know that he had gotten the joke, Xenophon's Simonides needs to be recognized as belonging to the same company as Plato's Strangers and Timaeus: close enough to be mistaken for representing both Socrates' and their author's own views and yet sufficiently un-Socratic to reveal a very different lesson to those, like Hiero, who are willing to prove themselves to be ὕποπτοι, that is, suspicious.

Less susceptible to chronological complications is the debt to Plato indicated by the internal structure of *Hiero*. The foregoing analysis has located more veracity in Hiero than in Simonides, and that means that the truth about tyranny precedes the self-interested and flattering lies the praise-singer is willing to tell about it. Lest there be any misunderstanding along the lines indicated by Schorn, it is not because Hiero is a good man, let alone a philosophic or wise one, that he speaks the truth about tyranny: it is, rather, because tyranny itself is bad that he can do so. Plato had made this point in *Republic*, and had defended democracy on the compelling basis that it's better than tyranny. Xenophon apparently thought Plato had let his readers off too easily, and he made tyranny look far more attractive in *Cyropaedia*, so much more attractive than Plato had made it in either the first book of his *Republic* or in its ninth, indeed, that he managed to make Cyrus appear to be something other than a tyrant. Xenophon's *Hiero* follows *Cyropaedia* for the opposite reason that Simonides defends tyranny after the tyrant has told the truth about it.

At this point, it is useful to recall the Kapp-Kahn hypothesis mentioned in the first section of this chapter, that Plato had written *Gorgias* before *Protagoras*. Armed in advance by the attack on pleasure in the dialogue with Gorgias, Plato's readers would not be taken in by Socrates' apparent endorsement of hedonism in *Protagoras*. Here, then, is a chronologically early example of the truth preceding deception, demanding from the reader the ability to withstand the sequel on the basis of what they have already learned. Did Xenophon invent this pedagogical structure? The priority of *Memorabilia* 2.2 with respect to the Temporality of Virtue might suggest that he did. But it also seems unlikely, if only because he merely implements but never describes it. Albeit not in its first two books, Plato does describe it later in in his masterpiece: in *Republic* 4, Socrates twice applies the verb "to test [βασαανίζειν]" to the training of the Guardians (*R.* 412e4–414a7), and more specifically to the kind of tests that would tempt them to abandon or betray a prior true opinion by means of theft, force, or enchantment:

> "By those who have their opinions stolen from them I mean those who are over-persuaded and those who forget, because in the one case time, in the other argument strips them unawares of their beliefs. Now I presume you understand, do you not?" "Yes." "Well, then, by those who are constrained or forced I mean those whom some pain or suffering compels to change their minds." "That too I understand and you are right." "And the victims of sorcery I am sure you too would say are they who alter their opinions under the spell of pleasure or terrified by some fear." "Yes," he said: "everything that deceives appears to cast a spell upon the mind." "Well then, as I was just saying, we must look for those who are the best guardians of the indwelling conviction that what they have to do is what they at any time believe to be best for the state [ἡ πόλις]."[176]

With respect to the kind of test administered to the reader in *Hiero*, it is the lure of pleasure that seems most pertinent, and here Strauss's *On Tyranny* proves its value. At the core of the chapter "Pleasure and Virtue" is the following insightful claim about Simonides: "[H]is praise of honor would imply that not virtue, but the reward or result of virtue, is intrinsically pleasant."[177] The two paragraphs that follow situate Simonides in relation to hedonism by means of the dialogue with Aristippus in *Memorabilia* 2.1, leading Strauss to make a useful suggestion: "It is not impossible that the historical Aristippus has served to some extent as a model for Xenophon's Simonides."[178] As for Xenophon's Aristippus, Strauss does what he can to make Socrates' use of "the Choice of Heracles" compatible with Simonides, attempting in the process to distinguish a higher form of pleasure from the kind to which Xenophon's Socrates is so obviously opposed. Since "the Choice" takes the form of a contest between Happiness and Virtue (cf. *Mem.* 2.1.26 and 2.1.30), the instrumental view of virtue that Strauss is attempting to ascribe to Xenophon through the mediation of Simonides, Aristippus, and Prodicus is a quixotic project—apart from the absence of any nobility about it—but also a revealing one. The clearest parallel to *Hiero* in *Memorabilia* 2.1 is where Virtue speaks of praise: "But of the sweetest sound of all, praise of oneself [τὸ δὲ πάντων ἥδιστον ἀκρόαμα ἔπαινος ἑαυτῆς], you are unhearing; and of the sweetest sight of all are you unseeing, for never have you beheld a noble work [ἔργον καλόν] of yours" (*Mem.* 2.1.31). Unfortunately, Schorn does not mention this passage, but the parallel with Simonides τὸ ἥδιστον ἀκρόαμα ἔπαινος (*Hier.* 1.14) is deliberate, and in his *Hiero*, Xenophon has showed us exactly how much Simonides praise is worth. Revealingly, not even Simonides dares to praise Hiero for any ἔργον καλόν he has performed,[179] not only because there are none to praise but more importantly because what Simonides clearly would find praiseworthy—putting πλουτίζε τοὺς φίλους into practice for his own personal benefit—Hiero has not yet done. Perhaps the synergy created by forcing the reader to remember Heracles and Virtue from *Memorabilia* while reading *Hiero* marks the extent of Xenophon's debt to Plato where this dialogue is concerned. But if only because Virtue speaks second in "the Choice," the parallel indicates that his debts are more substantial. Even if Xenophon didn't know why Plato had followed his *Republic* with *Timaeus-Critias* in a clearly delineated example of the order in which Plato wished his dialogues to be read, he had clearly learned the power of the kind of pedagogy that tests the reader's determination to uphold Socratic virtue in the face of theft, force, and bewitchment, for he demonstrated that he had done so not only by following *Memorabilia* with *Hiero* but by letting his pseudo-Socratic Simonides make his case last.

Chapter Three

Ordering Xenophon's Writings

The Traditional Order

In this section, attention will be focused on how the traditional order in which Xenophon's writings have come down to us indicates the role Plato played in their survival,[1] and thus to answer the question raised in the Introduction: "Why did Xenophon's writings survive?" As every student of Ancient Greek Philosophy knows, this is a remarkable achievement. Far greater philosophers survive only in fragments, including giants such as Parmenides, Heraclitus, Empedocles, Anaxagoras, and Democritus. In this context, the question is not simply "Why did Xenophon survive?" but "Why was he the first philosopher to do so?" The place to begin, then, is with the recognition that the survival of the entire *corpus Xenophonteum* is a problem, one that requires an answer to this question: Why do we have all of Xenophon when so much of apparently greater importance was lost?

And the place to begin answering this question is with the second philosopher whose writings survive complete: Plato the son of Ariston. We might then ask the parallel question: "Why did Plato's dialogues survive?" And this question is far easier to answer quite apart from their towering literary excellence and philosophical significance. Plato created and endowed a school that survived his own death by hundreds of years, and his dialogues were in some way or other that school's inheritance or legacy if not its foundation. Plato's dialogues would survive because the Academy survived, and its library along with it. But this formula begs the question: it would be better to say that the Academy would survive because Plato wanted it to do so and that he ensured that it could. And to complete the circle, it was his dialogues whose survival the Academy would in turn ensure and was intended to ensure, for there is more of Plato in each one of them than in all of the buildings that once stood in the grove of Academus.

This section's purpose is to show how the traditional ordering of his writings indicates or proves that Xenophon survived because Plato wanted him to do so, and it is by no means clear that "wanted" is a strong enough verb in this case. Plato clearly *wanted* his own dialogues to survive, and therefore took steps to ensure they would do so. But with their survival ensured, there were a whole host of ancillary writings, housed in the Academy's library no doubt, that Plato now *needed* to survive if his precious, brilliant, but also decidedly complex and enigmatic dialogues—replete with allusions, references, misquotations, and anachronisms—were to be fully understood. The cost of writing in this way was that he needed a vast store of literature to survive along with him, and indeed a vast store of literature, much of it written by authors he names in his dialogues, has survived.

In the decisive respect, the traditional order of Xenophon's writings differs from the order in which Plato's writings have come down to us: we can place the date of *that* ordering almost four hundred years after Plato's death. Not only is there is no good reason to believe that Thrasyllus, who edited them in the first century of the Christian era, preserved the order in which the dialogues had come down to him, but there is a decisive indication that he didn't: if he had, we wouldn't know his name. Although the traces of that earlier order may still be detected in various remarks preserved by Diogenes Laertius as well as in Thrasyllus' edition itself, "the traditional" or in any case pre-Thrasyllan order of Plato's dialogues is unrecoverable. But even if we cannot say what that order was, we can be certain that there was one and that Thrasyllus' order is not it.[2] It is therefore possible to posit an older order, which, in distinction to the ordering of Thrasyllus—who was not working in Athens, and was neither the head of the Academy nor even an Academic—will be called "the Academic ordering." There must have been such an order, for Plato's dialogues were the Academy's most important possession, and proved to be what I am claiming throughout he intended them to be: a κτῆμα εἰς ἀεί.[3]

Here, then, is once again my explicit and unequivocal answer to that "single most important question" (see Introduction). In reading and interpreting Plato's dialogues, we are doing exactly what Plato intended *us* to be doing; the dialogues were written to be studied, and so far from being surprised would Plato be to discover that they are still being studied and debated "in states unborn, in accents yet unknown" more than two thousand years after he wrote them, he would be both disappointed and surprised to discover that they weren't. And even though Xenophon is the only Athenian other than Thucydides to record the fact that he expected his work to survive forever (*Cyn.* 13.7), the exquisite care with which Plato wrote them should make the answer obvious, especially since the dialogue form prevented him from stepping out from behind his characters to express his intent—at once wildly ambitious and completely successful—to create a κτῆμα εἰς ἀεί.

The point is foundational, because if Plato wrote only for his contemporaries, Xenophon's survival would have been a matter of no consequence to him. But even if the most important question has received an answer, the problem of Xenophon's survival has not. And it is a problem: Why do we have Xenophon's treatise on hunting rabbits but not Homer's *Margites*, Protagoras' *Truth*, or any one of a huge number of far more significant works? To be even more specific, given Xenophon's universally recognized inferiority to Thucydides as a historian, and his rarely questioned inferiority to Plato as a writer of Socratic dialogue—and perhaps his inferiority to many other such writers including Aeschines, Aristippus, and Antiphon—the question remains: "Why did all of Xenophon's writings survive?" And the answer begins with the fact that there is no equivalent of Thrasyllus in Xenophon's case. In other words, not only is there no good reason to think that there was ever an older ordering of Xenophon's writings but there is a compelling reason to think that there was not. My purpose in this section is to show why the traditional ordering of Xenophon's writings is best understood as "Academic," that is to say, as a product of the Academy.

Hellenica stands first in this traditional order, an indication that the survival of Xenophon was intimately connected to the survival of Thucydides. Following the seven books of *Hellenica* are the seven books of Xenophon's Socratic writings: the four-book *Memorabilia* followed by *Oeconomicus*, *Symposium*, and *Apology of Socrates*. It is important to emphasize that the first two parts of the *corpus Xenophonteum* consist of seven books each not only because *Anabasis*, the third and central part, does so as well, but because the last two parts do not: there are eight books of *The Education of Cyrus* and eight discrete members of the so-called *opuscula*, *scripta minora*, or "minor works." The numerical parallels are elegant, the central place of *Anabasis* is insightful, and following *Anabasis* with *Cyropaedia* is logical; each of these decisions indicates that the traditional order was the product of design, and taken in the aggregate, even more so. But there is no reason to believe that Xenophon would have wanted his writings to survive in this order, and although the question will be taken up in detail only in the next section, it is sufficient to mention that he would have placed *Anabasis* before *Hellenica*, since the latter refers to the former. What we have, then, is an elegant, methodical, and mathematically pleasing—but distinctly non-Xenophontic—arrangement of Xenophon's writings. It is their traditional order—I will be calling it "the Academic Order"—that best explains why they have survived. To put it another way, the solution to the problem of their survival is inextricably linked to the order in which they have survived.

The principal evidence for this claim is the arrangement of the eight members of *scripta minora*, the elegance of which surpasses the already elegant arrangement of the collection's four other major parts. It begins with *Hiero*, and given that the set of *opuscula* immediately follows *Cyropaedia*, this connection looks Xenophontic for reasons indicated in the last section of the previous chapter. *Hiero* is followed by *Agesilaus*, the only other member of the minor writings that is named for a person. And here two things are striking: the first is that once an editorial decision had been made to group the *scripta minora* as a set—a by no means obvious or even consistently implemented decision given the brevity of *Apology of Socrates*, which our nameless editor placed elsewhere—the subsequent decision to join *Agesilaus* and *Hiero* was characteristically elegant and logical. The second makes it less likely that following *Cyropaedia* with *Hiero* was as Xenophontic as it first appeared, for by that kind of logic, *Agesilaus* belonged in even closer proximity to *Hellenica* than *Hiero* did to *The Education of Cyrus*.

The work that follows *Agesilaus* settles the point: the reason *Hiero* precedes Xenophon's encomium of a Spartan King is not because of its possible connection to *Cyropaedia*, the work that precedes it, but because that encomium is logically and elegantly followed by *The Constitution of the Spartans*. Remarkably, then, and solely because of the thought that went into ordering the *opuscula*, the elegance of the link between *Hiero* and *Agesilaus* is at least equaled and possibly surpassed by the link between Xenophon's only two writings devoted to Sparta. But this link once again calls into question whether Xenophon would have separated *Agesilaus* and *The Constitution of the Spartans*, so obviously a mutually supporting pair, from *Hellenica*, to which both are obviously ancillary. But whatever this arrangement loses with respect to Xenophon's probable conceptions—and here it is necessary to recall that he would not have been inclined to place *Hellenica* first—it more than gains with respect to logical elegance in the context of a decision for an eight-part collection of the minor writings.

In taking the next step, caution is necessary. In the last of the five volumes of Marchant's Oxford edition, *The Constitution of the Athenians* is placed last. But in the first sentence of his introduction to that curious work, Marchant writes: "It has seemed more convenient to relegate this rough and unpolished oration [*oratio*] of a certain Athenian Cato to the last place even though in the manuscripts it follows *The Constitution of the Spartans*."[4] By this "Athenian Cato," Marchant was referring to "the Old Oligarch," a moniker first attached to the alleged but in any case merely pseudo-Xenophontic author of *The Constitution of the Athenians* in 1897.[5] Marchant also notes the fact that this work is best understood as a speech or *oratio*, not a treatise, an insightful assessment that will be revisited in this chapter's fourth section. But the most important fact for now is that this *oratio* should not stand last among Xenophon's *scripta minora* but rather fourth, directly after *The Constitution of the Spartans* with which it forms yet another natural and obvious pair. It is possible to conclude from this arrangement that whoever made it regarded *The Constitution of the Athenians* as either an authentic work of Xenophon or at least as an indispensable part not merely of the editor's arrangement of the *opuscula* but of the collection as a whole. This second point deserves discussion before moving on to *Ways and Means*.

Recall in this context that within the five major parts of the collection, the three seven-book works preceded the two that consisted of eight books or parts. Without *The Constitution of the Athenians*, the *scripta minora* would have had only seven parts, thus causing *Cyropaedia* to destroy the reigning mathematical pattern. To preserve that pattern, it would either have been necessary to invent an eighth member of the fifth part or to believe that Xenophon was responsible for all eight. It was probably the fact that there were eight that made it possible to decide to place *Cyropaedia* and the minor writings next to each other in the first place. In other words, the editor did not doubt that Xenophon had written *The Constitution of the Athenians*, and the fact that Diogenes Laertius mentions that Demetrius of Magnesia—a friend of Cicero's Atticus—doubted the authenticity of either *The Constitution of the Spartans* or more likely of the pair of *Constitutions* in the century before Thrasyllus,[6] confirms the view that the doubts that lead to "the old Oligarch" and thus the displacement of this *oratio* from fourth place to either last place or oblivion, arose only long after the traditional or "Academic Order of Xenophon's Writings" had been established. Naturally it is on the basis of the various symmetries governing the collection as whole, not the authenticity of this despised albeit elegantly placed member of it, that the moniker "Academic," albeit without validating it, is explained.

It is a stroke of good fortune that the publication of David Whitehead's commentary on *Poroi* coincided with the coming together of the ideas presented in this book.[7] Generally considered Xenophon's last work, *Ways and Means* blocks the interpretive highroad that finds an ancient Machiavelli in the son of Gryllus, and before expecting to be taken seriously in the field, every Xenophon scholar should commit themself in print to an assessment of this product of its author's abiding love for Athens. En route to reducing the treatise's civic proposals to an ugly dilemma at the end,[8] the introduction to *Ways and Means* in the recently published Strauss-inspired volume on *The Shorter Writings*—another stroke of good fortune, by the way—must include the following, better understood as an admission than as the accurate observation it also is: "By posing the problem as one of finding an alternative source of revenue, Xenophon accepts not only Athenian democracy, but its particular reliance on public funding to enable the common man to participate in public affairs on a frequent basis."[9] If there is anything of Machiavelli in *Poroi*, it is the pre-*Prince* servant of the Florentine Republic, not the one who can be aligned with the apostle of "tyranny at its best" that emerges from Strauss's Simonides-friendly reading of *Hiero*. Every Straussian student of Xenophon needs to exit the echo chamber and ponder their way through Whitehead's learned commentary.

The link between *Poroi* and *The Constitution of the Athenians* is every bit as strong as the one that joins *The Constitution of the Spartans* to *Agesilaus*. Together, the two pairs constitute another chapter—and probably the most important one—in "the tale of two cities" that trained several generations of Athenians to think about politics in a manner that would cause "ancient political philosophy" to become the inescapable repository of insight that it still remains today (cf. ἔτι καὶ νῦν).[10] This "tale" plays so important a role in Xenophon's life and thought that it will receive treatment in a separate section later in this chapter. But the odd mixture of contempt and respect for imperial Athens in the *oratio* of the Old Oligarch is no more antithetical to Xenophon's postimperial proposals in *Poroi* than is the uncritical encomium of Agesilaus with the amazing account of degeneration found in the fourteenth chapter of *The*

Constitution of the Spartans. For the present, the important point is that the turn to Athens embodied in Xenophon's *Poroi* is mediated perfectly by *The Constitution of the Athenians*, and thus more would be lost than another collection of eight to match *Cyropaedia* if it were dropped from the perfectly integrated structure that the Academic Order of the *corpus Xenophonteum* proves itself to be.

The connection between *The Cavalry Officer* and *Ways and Means* is far more obvious than the one that joins the latter to "the Old Oligarch." But first it is necessary to say *ave atque vale* to Xenophon's son Gryllus, the gallant cavalryman whose death explains the end of *Hellenica* (cf. *Hell.* 7.5.16 and 7.5.27) and for whose instruction this treatise on the demands of command was most plausibly written. By dying for Athens, Gryllus could easily be recognized as what it was far more difficult to recognize that his father had always been: an Athenian patriot. By "having laid so costly a sacrifice on the altar of Freedom," Xenophon would eventually secure the restoration that eluded Themistocles, the naval strategist and trickster whose role in the creation of imperial Athens makes him a useful counterpoint to the author of *Ways and Means*. Although fully consistent with the political program detailed in that later work, *The Cavalry Officer* appears to belong to an earlier and happier time, and apart from the gallant Gryllus, its most salient feature is that although it offers precepts of command of universal applicability, it is written thoroughly and self-consciously for Athens. Written earlier than *Poroi*, it would illustrate the continuity of Xenophon's patriotism even without its role in the education of Gryllus, whose death was that patriotism's highest expression.

Linked to *The Cavalry Officer* in an obvious manner, *On Horsemanship* departs from the Athens-centricity that indissolubly binds the three previous members of the *scripta minora*. The logic of the connection is therefore only the horse, and all four of Xenophon's multibook works likewise contain unmistakable signs of his interest in and abiding love for this noble creature. But even though the continuity created by joining *On Horsemanship* to *The Cavalry Officer* requires no justification, it is important to understand why they appear in the order they do. Thanks to the fact that it is a distinctively Athenian officer Xenophon has described, it must precede the perfectly general account of horsemanship. It is important to emphasize this because another explanation is possible: in the last sentence of *On Horsemanship* (*Eq.* 12.14) Xenophon refers to *The Cavalry Officer* as having already been written. Given the opacity implicit in the reference to Themistogenes in *Hellenica* 3, this is the clearest indication of literary order in the corpus. But if it clearly indicates that Xenophon had already written *The Cavalry Officer* when he wrote *On Horsemanship*—if the former precedes latter in order of composition—it is impossible to miss the logical priority of the apparently later work: one must know how to ride and train a horse before commanding a troop of horsemen. While it is possible that the editor was respecting the order of composition implied by Xenophon himself, the dilemma created by the clash of fact with logic deserves further consideration and will receive it in the next section. For now, it suffices to remark that for the Academic editor, the order in which the two appear among the *opuscula* was the only logical, symmetrical, and elegant one.

The culminating place of *Cynegeticus* leaves no doubt about this: a general account of hunting with dogs must follow an equally general account of how to buy, train, and ride a horse. So far from being Athens-centric, *Cynegeticus* contains sufficiently exotic information that Delebecque insisted it could not have been an early work because its author's concerns are so clearly inconsistent and incompatible with the fauna of Attica.[11] On the other hand, there were clearly rabbits in Attica, and hunting hares is the treatise's principal subject, although the attack on sophists with which it concludes is and was clearly intended to be its most striking feature. And having now reached the last member of the collection, the salient facts are clear: we have four pairs of closely related works with the second of each pair bound almost as closely to the first of the next one as are the four pairs themselves. Its editor had, in short, an exquisite sense for placing things in their proper and natural order, and the collection is organized in a coherent, logical, and elegant manner from start to finish.

But thanks precisely to the logical connections that so pleasingly bind its parts into an interconnected whole, there is one feature of the collection that seems arbitrary: it might just as easily have begun with *Cynegeticus* and ended with *Hiero*. To be clear: the same connections that justify its present order are equally applicable to the reverse order, and for the exact same reasons. The priority of *The Cavalry Officer* to *On Horsemanship* in order of composition is the best internal justification for the present order, and there are three objections to regarding this as plausible let alone sufficient. First, precisely because Delebecque finds himself in the minority, *Cynegeticus* has a far better claim to be prior in order of composition not only to *Hiero* but quite possibly to all of Xenophon's writings; thus, if order of composition had been a factor, *Cynegeticus* would not have been last. And then there is *The Constitution of Athens*:

it has been attributed to "the Old Oligarch" because it describes an old Athens that no longer existed during Xenophon's years of maturity and possibly of discretion; the work that stands before it describes a Sparta that has only recently degenerated from its illustrious past. Finally, the connection between *Cyropaedia* and *Hiero* depends on either a warped reading or an eccentric one—Strauss's and mine respectively—whereas references to hunting not only abound in *Cyropaedia*, but the lessons of the hunt are a particularly important aspect of "the education of Cyrus."

The hypothesis that an "Academic Editor" created the Traditional Order is useful for justifying the layout of the *scripta minora*, for explaining, that is, why a quite possibly youthful *Cynegeticus* stands last in the collection and not first in it. And the place to begin that justification is at the collection's other end, with *Hellenica*. Although it stands first in the *corpus Xenophonteum*, *Hellenica* is obviously a sequel to Thucydides, and this is what justifies its primary position. In other words, the same Academic Editor who arranged the writings of Xenophon placed them immediately after Thucydides' *History* in the arrangement of an even larger and more comprehensive collection of the texts a student would need to read before being able to read Plato's dialogues with the store of historical and literary information that an intelligent reading of them presupposes and demands. No matter how anachronistic in detail a statement such as "[T]he works of Xenophon were located right after Herodotus and Thucydides on the bookshelf of the Academy's library," it is not the supposition that there was a library in the Academy within which scrolls were necessarily arranged in some kind of order that makes it so. The purpose of the Introduction was to prove the indispensability of Thucydides for interpreting Plato's dialogues; this book's purpose as a whole is to do the same for Xenophon. The initial position of *Hellenica* creates an unmistakable material link between these two necessities.

In the same way, it is what follows *Cynegeticus* that justifies placing it last in the collection. But before attempting to show why it is Plato's dialogues themselves that do so—and thus why Xenophon mediates the distance between Xenophon and Plato in the same way that, for instance, *The Cavalry Officer* mediates the distance between *Poroi* and *On Horsemanship*—this chapter's structure must first be understood. It will end with an attempt to establish what I regard as the most important way of ordering Xenophon's writings, and that means to reconstruct the order in which he wrote them. As already indicated by the introduction of *Hellenica* I, II, and III, this is a complex and difficult task. It is, however, a necessary one if Plato's debts to Xenophon are to be assessed accurately or even, given the modern prejudice, if the existence of any such debts is to be acknowledged. Between this section and that one, another way of ordering the writings of Xenophon will be considered, one that takes seriously the possibility that he might have intended them *to be read* in a certain order, as, for example, the way he indicates that he may have done at the end of *The Cavalry Officer*.

In summary, then, this chapter offers three different ways of ordering Xenophon's writings: (1-X) the order in which they have come down to us, probably with no input from Xenophon whatsoever apart from the works themselves, (2-X) the order in which Xenophon himself might have intended them to be read ("the Reading Order"), and (3-X) the order in which he wrote them, namely, "the Order of Composition." And since this book's subject is necessarily the writings of Plato as well as those of Xenophon, the same three types of ordering can also be applied to the dialogues, and as well as identifying them, the following list will include some critical comments: (1-P) the ordering of Thrasyllus, that is, the order in which they have come down to us, and once again with no direct input from Plato himself apart from the works themselves, and by way of critical comment, I will add that Thrasyllus achieved far less elegant results in 1-P than the Academic Editor did in 1-X; (2-P) "the Reading Order of Plato's Dialogues" (understood throughout only as I have tried to reconstruct it), which I will be claiming is far more significant for interpreting Plato than 2-X is for interpreting Xenophon; and (3-P) the order in which Plato wrote his dialogues, which, however important it may be for explaining his debts to Xenophon and Xenophon's debts to him, is as much less useful for interpreting Plato as 3-X is useful and indeed indispensable for interpreting Xenophon.

The following section will consider 2-X, and in order to justify the comparative unimportance of this kind of order in Xenophon's case, it will also contain a fuller discussion of 2-P. The fact that this discussion will be postponed until the following section will create an insuperable but unavoidable obstacle to the logical coherence of the rest of this one, where one important result of a more substantial consideration of 2-P to follow—indeed, a far more substantial one than what will follow in the next section—will be presupposed with no supporting argument to justify it for the present. And this result, merely presupposed here, is the priority of *Protagoras* in the Reading Order of Plato's Dialogues.[12] Postponing, then, any discussion of how and why the other Platonic dialogues justify the initial placement of *Protagoras*, the remainder of this section will show why Xenophon's *Cynegeticus* makes an effective introduction to this brilliant dialogue and how the two works reveal a number of mutually illuminating and unmistakably deliberate connections. In short, although the claim that *Protagoras* belongs in the first place among Plato's dialogues depends on a chain of argumentation only offered elsewhere, the connections between it and *Cynegeticus* will explain why an Academic Editor who shared my notions about the Reading Order or the 2-P priority of *Protagoras* was responsible for 1-X.

As already mentioned, the most striking feature of Xenophon's *Cynegeticus* is that it ends with an attack on the sophists. Although he intends it to be striking—for it elevates a treatise about hunting rabbits onto a higher plane of serious concern—Xenophon does not regard the transition from hunting to sophistry to be any more ridiculous or adventitious than his claims about the character-building virtues of hunting. In addition to the fact that sophists themselves are hunters, the lessons they teach are properly counteracted by an education in which hunting plays the most prominent role. Although the importance of sophists in both works is sufficient to begin grounding the connection between them, it is more specifically the role of pleasure in both that is decisive, and here they must appear to be opposite: so far from regarding pleasure as simply good—as Socrates appears to do in the final argument of *Protagoras*, pace Kapp-Kahn—Xenophon singles out the pleasure derived from hunting as the only form of it that isn't bad. And this contrast only touches the surface: the real opposition arises over the phrase "to be overcome by pleasure [ὑπὸ τῶν ἡδονῶν ἡττᾶσθαι]" (*Prt.* 352e6–353a1; cf. *Cyn.* 12.12–13), a phrase that appears prominently in both. In *Protagoras*, Socrates will argue that pleasure is simply good and that "to be overcome by pleasure" is impossible; the three sophists will agree with him. In *Cynegeticus*, by contrast, "to be overcome by pleasure" is a reality against which hunting, which derives virtue from the ability to overcome pain and thus to give no ground to bad pleasures, is the antidote, and more specifically the antidote to the enticements offered by that other kind of hunters, namely, the sophists.

Since Xenophon's sophists offer no antidote to being overcome with pleasure, since they teach a flattering and deceptive doctrine that eliminates the painful path to virtue embodied in hunting, the principal difference between *Cynegeticus* and *Protagoras* has nothing to do with the position of the sophists—who are shown to be effective if dangerous hunters of the idle youth and likewise unprepared to uphold the distinction between good pleasures and bad ones in both works—only with respect to Socrates' own position on "the pleasant" and *his* views on the impossibility of "to be overcome by pleasure." Moreover, Xenophon describes in some detail the sophistic practice of literary criticism, an art that he predicts will be practiced on his own book, whereby the sophists attempt to show what has been written beautifully has not been (*Cyn.* 13.6–7); it is here that he makes his statement about its eternal relevance (*Cyn.* 13.7). Protagoras will do this very thing to Simonides' poem in Plato's dialogue (*Prt.* 339b7–d9). In summary, both works are consistent with respect to the sophists, and each of them can plausibly be regarded—and that's really too weak a way of putting it—as an attack on sophistic education. Although this makes a decent start, the real synergy is found elsewhere.[13]

As already mentioned, his friend assumes at the beginning of *Protagoras* that Socrates has arrived fresh from a hunt; Xenophon's *Cynegeticus* validates this suspicion and explains it. On the literal level of the dialogue's frame, Socrates is hunting Alcibiades, and as subsequent dialogues prove, he succeeded, at least in the short term—i.e., up to and including *Symposium*—in capturing the young man's attention. The Xenophontic provenance of this kind of capture has been mentioned; in *Protagoras*, he speaks in the young man's presence in the same way Xenophon's Socrates captured the attention of Euthydemus in *Memorabilia* 4.2. But Plato's Socrates does so differently in *Protagoras*, and far more brilliantly: using Hippocrates as bait, Socrates traps Protagoras in argument, and so effective is he in hunting down the hunter that the prey lies prostrate before him at the end (*Prt.* 360e4–5). Although Xenophon's treatise is principally devoted to hunting hares—and his memorably attractive picture of the rabbit on the run (*Cyn.* 5.33) should explain why so many have found a sympathetic portrait of the Protagoras in Plato's dialogue—he also explains how to take bigger game, and for the biggest, he recommends the use of poison, made attractive by the use of tasty bait (*Cyn.* 11.2).

If Hippocrates is the bait in *Protagoras* with which Socrates hunts the hunter, the equation of pleasure with the good—initially resisted by Protagoras (*Prt.* 351c1–e7)—is the poison that leads to the sophist's overthrow in the final argument. If one's good intentions can be overcome by pleasure—and here we might recall the testing of the guardians in *Republic* 3 in the last section of the previous chapter—and if pleasure is the good, then the good has been overcome by . . . the good (*Prt.* 355c1–8)! Since this is nonsensical, claims Socrates, there can therefore be no such thing as "to be overcome by pleasure." Finally, since going to war is noble (*Prt.*

359e3-5)—and of course hunting's preparation for "rainy marching in the painful field" plays a prominent role in *Cynegeticus* (*Cyn.* 12.2-11)—and since the noble is the good (*Prt.* 358b3-6 and 359e5-6) and the good is the pleasant, then going to war is pleasant (*Prt.* 360a3), and the coward who avoids it is simply ignorant of his own good (*Prt.* 360c6-7). Made visible by the preposterous equation of the noble and the pleasant—standing in direct opposition as it does to the proverbial "noble things are difficult [χαλεπὰ τὰ καλά]," the pivot around which the alleged contradiction in Simonides' poem turns[14]—the final argument's weak point is the admission that what's pleasant is simply good, and it is by swallowing this poisoned pill that Protagoras is himself "overcome by pleasure" even while being compelled by Socrates to admit that there is no such thing. Finally, it is only the reader who comes to *Protagoras* with *Cynegeticus* in mind who will get this particular joke, but there will be no shortage of other ones for those who haven't and therefore don't.

Reading Order

It is a good rule of thumb in interpreting Plato that whenever you discover two reasons why he does something, you should immediately begin looking for a third. If Plato's Socrates is hunting Alcibiades in the same way that Xenophon's hunted Euthydemus, and if Plato imagined that he could best catch his attention by hunting Protagoras and bringing him down publicly, then we should consider if there is a third κυνηγέσιον—apart from Xenophon's *Cynegeticus*, of course—along with another hunter lurking somewhere in the textual shadows. And having posed the question, it is easy to find the answer. By creating this brilliant dialogue, built to be staged as a play-within-a-play and equipped with a chorus (*Prt.* 314e3-315b2),[15] replete with puzzles, paradox, sophistry, and all built around a fascinating ἀγών or contest (*Prt.* 335a4), it is Plato *who is hunting us*, his readers, and he has been completely successful in capturing our attention for more than two thousand years. If Plato created the *Alcibiades Major* as the first dialogue he intended his students to study, and therefore regarded it as the best place to begin our instruction in philosophy—as so many ancient Platonists thought it was—then he created *Protagoras* to make us want to begin our studies, and he did so not by means of pedagogical clarity but through puzzles and paradox. Nobody who encounters *Protagoras* for the first time could find it either intelligible or boring, and this is why it is the best place to enter the Academy. If philosophy is born from wonder, Plato and Xenophon both knew that Socratic philosophy was born from wondering about Socrates.

The dramatic priority of *Protagoras* to *Alcibiades Major* illuminates in miniature the value of the Reading Order hypothesis.[16] By beginning *Protagoras* with a reference to Socrates' hunt for Alcibiades, he was preparing the path that leads to *Symposium*. Having shown how Socrates captured Alcibiades' attention, Plato would go on to construct two dialogues between the two, the larger preceding the smaller. In addition to connecting the two in various ways, he would find ingenious means to connect both back to *Protagoras*. Beginning with the provocatively erotic language at the beginning of *Protagoras*, Plato would clarify nothing about the nature of their relationship—and more specifically, whether or not it was sexual—until *Symposium*. By the time Plato was finished writing, he had created a chain of seven dialogues between *Protagoras* and *Symposium* that disclose themselves as such by means of much the same blend of logic, symmetry, and elegance at work in the Academic arrangement of Xenophon's *scripta minora*. Indeed, it was considerably more elegant and symmetrical, beginning with the fact that the chain of nine now had a center in *Hippias Major*.[17] Joined to *Protagoras* by Hippias himself and the patently deceptive Socrates who pretends there to have a troublesome kinsman, *Hippias Major* is joined to *Symposium* by "the Beautiful itself." To balance the *Alcibiades* pair, Plato would eventually write two *Hippias* dialogues; to mediate between the two pairs, he would write *Lovers*. And at this point, let's repair to Xenophon.

To start with the simplest and most important point: there is no evidence that Xenophon himself arranged his own works in the way that I am claiming that Plato organized the first of his. The word *first*, of course, here does not mean "oldest," "earliest," or the first *to be written*; the subject of this section is Reading Order, not Order of Composition. The purpose of sketching the interconnections between Plato's initiatory or elementary dialogues is to draw attention to what the *corpus Xenophonteum* is not. Nor should this surprise us: Plato was a teacher, a pedant, an instructor of youth, and a schoolmaster; Xenophon, although just as literary as the self-portrait of the bibliophile Euthydemus suggests, was an exiled intellectual, historian, and philosopher who for many years could only return to Athens through his books. Indications in several of them suggest that they were published; there are also indications that several of the longer works grew with time and may have gone through several editions. Although these hypotheses have also been applied to Plato, I regard them as having been as useless in one case as they are useful in the other. In short, one purpose of discussing the Platonic Reading Order—confined here to the order of only the first nine dialogues, for simplicity's sake—is to demonstrate that Xenophon did not organize his own writings on the same basis.

But in addition to simplicity, there is another justification for considering the first nine Platonic dialogues, one that directly implicates Xenophon. Any reader who can shake off the modern prejudice that Plato's *Symposium* necessarily preceded Xenophon's can easily detect, if only on the basis of the fact that both dialogues are set in the house of Callias, that the latter inspired Plato to create *Protagoras* as well. In the earlier discussion of the *Alcibiades* dyad (chapter 1, section 4) Xenophon's influence, primarily through *Memorabilia* 4.2, was already sketched; by the end of this section, I will extend this result to include the *Hippias* dyad and *Ion*; the impact of Xenophon on *Menexenus* has received separate treatment (chapter 1, section 2). While illustrating the kind of order Xenophon did not create for his own writings, this approach will simultaneously draw attention to the way he helped Plato to do so; this will ensure that the dialogue between the two Socratics continues even in a section devoted to illuminating the kind of order that only one of them used.

The last point to be emphasized before returning to Plato's first nine dialogues recurs to the previous section. The best evidence that Xenophon *did* arrange his writings along the same lines that Plato arranged his is the arrangement of the *opuscula* in the fifth part of the *corpus Xenophonteum*, and more generally, in the way in which that *corpus* as a whole has come down to us. As the last section showed, these eight works in particular are arranged in a carefully interconnected chain. To be sure, that chain is considerably less complex than the one that connects the first nine Platonic dialogues, let alone all thirty-five of them. But it makes a recognizable use of the same kinds of connections, guided by a strong sense of logical order, that can be found in—or which at any rate has been applied to—the reconstruction of the Reading Order of Plato's Dialogues in *Plato the Teacher* as a whole. Once the discussion of Plato is out of the way, this section will conclude with more evidence that Xenophon was not responsible for the careful arrangement of his works in the order in which they have come down to us, and this will strengthen the claim implicit in the hypothesis of the Academic Editor that its order is better understood as Platonic than Xenophontic in provenance.

Although generally regarded as spurious, Plato's *Lovers* (or *Erastai*) plays an important role in the logical coherence of the first nine, and without it, the coherence vanishes in much the same way the excision of

The Constitution of the Athenians would create a logical disconnect between *The Constitution of the Spartans* and *Ways and Means*. Built around a pair of lovers, one musical and the other gymnastic (*Am.* 132d1-2), one called wise, the other ignorant (*Am.* 139a6-7), *Lovers* mediates the difference between the polymath Hippias and the beautiful but scarcely learned Alcibiades (cf. *Alc.1* 108c6-d4). *Lovers* also helps to mediate the greater distance between *Protagoras* and *Symposium*. Like the first, it is a dialogue narrated by Socrates, the only other among the first nine that is so. More importantly it configures philosophy, the object of its search, as a kind of knowledge or τέχνη (*Am.* 135c5-6), reminiscent of Socrates' attempt to create a "measuring art" (*Prt.* 356d4-357b4) to assess the balance of pleasure and pain that his final argument suggests is the basis of virtue.

At the center of *Lovers* is a failed attempt to discover what philosophy is (*Am.* 133c3) and the attempt fails precisely because it configures philosophy as a kind of knowledge, or better, as the composite of a large number of different kinds of knowledge (*Am.* 137d10-138c10). This failure anticipates the success recorded in *Symposium* thanks to the fiction of Diotima: there, philosophy will be situated between wisdom and ignorance (*Smp.* 204a1-b5; cf. *Ly.* 218a2-b5). The first step toward defending *Lovers* as authentic therefore depends on recognizing that by showing how Socrates enlisted the aid of a σοφός and an ἀμαθής in the failed hunt for philosophy, Plato prepared his students for its discovery between ἀμαθία and σοφία in *Symposium*. *Lovers* also prepares for *Hippias Major*, which, it has already indicated, will introduce "the Beautiful itself [αὐτὸ τὸ καλόν]" (*Hp. Ma.* 286d8) and thus plays an even more significant role in preparing the reader for Diotima. The way Plato creates this connection is elegant: the ignorant or gymnastic lover regards philosophy as a waste of time; the wise or musical love regards it as καλόν (*Am.* 133b5-6). Socrates makes the characteristic point that it is only when we know what *philosophy* is that we will know enough to determine whether or not it is καλόν (*Am.* 133b7-c1). The equally valid and obvious point, which Plato leaves for his readers to recognize, is that we also cannot know whether or not philosophy is καλόν until we know what τὸ καλόν is, the question that will be at the center of *Hippias Major* in the sequel.

Naturally, there is no more need to explain why *Hippias Minor* follows *Hippias Major* than there is to explain why *The Constitution of Sparta* and *The Constitution of Athens*, or why Plato's *Alcibiades* dyad creates a matched set. But a connection not much less obvious and even more elegant joins *Hippias Minor* to *Ion*, and that is Homer. Following up Socrates' hilarious use of gross deception in creating his double in *Hippias Major*, Socrates illustrates the claim that the man who deceives deliberately is more knowledgeable than the one who does so involuntarily.[18] In addition to placing knowledge in a morally dubious light—for it cannot be knowledge itself that prevents the misuse that knowledge itself is shown to make possible—Socrates gives an interpretation of book nine of Homer's *Iliad* that ignores precisely the kind of textual expertise that Ion the rhapsode, whatever his other limitations may be, possesses in abundance thanks to his ability to recite all of Homer by heart. In fact, Socrates never allows Ion to practice his art of interpretation, an art that even if practiced on the most elementary level imaginable, would have been capable of refuting the interpretation Socrates has just given of *Iliad* 9.[19] And when Socrates proves by an inspired and inspiring speech about inspiration (*Ion* 533c9–535a5) that it is not by τέχνη that Ion can speak well about Homer—the thing Socrates never allows him to do—but only by "divine dispensation [θεία μοῖρα]" (*Ion* 534c1, 536d3, and 542a4), this looks less like a critique in the light of the moral neutrality of knowledge he has just revealed in *Lesser Hippias*.[20]

Although Ion claims that his knowledge of Homer could make him a successful general (*Ion* 540d1–5; cf. Xenophon's *Smp.* 4.6)—as Pericles had been when he delivered his famous funeral oration in Thucydides—the most important connection between *Ion* and *Menexenus* is rhetoric. The famous speech about the magnet in *Ion* is one of the most compelling and poetic speeches in Plato, and the amazing fact revealed in *Menexenus*—i.e., that Socrates has been studying rhetoric with Aspasia—will come as no great surprise to the reader who has already been captivated by Socrates' eloquence in *Ion*. And it is obviously a concern for speeches that causes Glaucon to ask Apollodorus concerning the λόγοι about ἔρως at the beginning of *Symposium* (*Smp.* 172b2–c3). In addition, then, to the link between *Menexenus* and *Symposium* based on the reader's required knowledge of Athenian History (see chapter 1, section 2), there is a rhetorical connection as well, obvious because Aspasia's rhetorically impressive but historically inaccurate Funeral Oration combines two of the three major links between the two dialogues. The fact that both Diotima and Aspasia are women is the third.

This brief summary should suffice to show that the connections between Plato's nine are even more elegant and far subtler than the ones connecting Xenophon's eight. In the latter case, the mere titles of the *opuscula* are sufficient to create clearly identifiable connections between most of them; only the link between *Poroi* and *The Cavalry Officer* demands deeper insight as to their shared content. In Plato's case, although the names *Alcibiades* and *Hippias* are sufficient to indicate two pairs, the remaining titles tell us nothing useful about how they might be arranged in a logically interconnected manner. But the more closely one looks *inside* the dialogues, the more interconnections will come to light. In fact, the connections emphasized above, going from one dialogue to the one that follows it, tell only one-third of the story: in addition to the fact that the three dialogues between *Protagoras* and *Hippias Major* all connect in important ways to *Protagoras* while the three on the other side of *Hippias Major* do the same to *Symposium*, there is also what looks very much like ring-composition connecting *Alcibiades Major* to *Menexenus* through death in battle (*Alc.1* 115b1–10 and 116a6–8), *Alcibiades Minor* and *Ion* through the divine (cf. *Ion* 530b10 and 533d3 with *Alc.2* 147c6 and 150d9), and *Lovers* to *Hippias Minor* through the limitations of knowledge (cf. *Alc.2* 143b6–c3). In anticipation of this section's conclusion, there is nothing even vaguely resembling this level of concern with Reading Order in the case of Xenophon, and with the foregoing synopsis in place, this statement now remains true even if it was Xenophon who arranged the *scripta minora* in their present order. But the synopsis's purpose is to strengthen the case that he didn't, and that whoever created 1-X was using Plato's methods and sense for order as reconstructed in 2-P.

In turning to Xenophon's influence on the dialogues summarized above, it is convenient to work backward, beginning with the two wherein that influence is least significant. It is true that there is mention of ignorant rhapsodes in Xenophon's *Symposium*, and that the substitution of Ion's ability to discern Homer's "intention [διάνοια]" (*Ion* 530b10–c1) looks like a Platonic improvement on the merely allegorical interpretations that Xenophon's use of ὑπόνοια suggests (*Smp.* 3.6). And there is a more substantive connection between the discussion of knowledge-based deception in *Hippias Minor* and *Memorabilia* 4.2. But although not presently germane, there are indications that it is rather Antisthenes than Xenophon to whom Plato is indebted in the *Lesser Hippias–Ion* pair, not least of all because it is Antisthenes who brings up the rhapsodes in Xenophon (*Smp.* 3.6).[21] It is worth mentioning, however, that Kahn—chief living proponent of a pre-*Protagoras Gorgias*—placed the composition of *Ion–Lesser Hippias* even earlier. This must seem unlikely to anyone who believes the *Hippias* dyad was conceived as a pair and that the purpose of *Ion* was to smooth the transition between that pair and *Symposium*.

Ordering Xenophon's Writings | 149

In turning to *Hippias Major*, it is a completely different story, and so close and important is the relationship between it and *Memorabilia* 3.8 that the reader should not expect any final conclusions about the priorities involved until the final chapter. But the most natural hypothesis is that it was 3.8 that inspired Plato to write *Hippias Major*, and to construct this pedagogical masterpiece around the failure at its center to identify τὸ καλόν with "the useful [τὸ χρήσιμον]" (*Hp. Ma.* 295c1-296d3).[22] In the passage that relativizes τὸ καλόν as χρήσιμον, Plato's Socrates deploys the same examples that Xenophon's Socrates had, and uses the formula "in relation to x" (i.e., πρὸς τι) to do so (cf. *Mem.* 3.8.4-5 and *Hp. Ma.* 295c8-e1). It is precisely the relativized Beautiful that Diotima will teach Socrates to reject at the high point of the *Symposium* (*Smp.* 211a3-4), and the propaedeutic role of *Hippias Major* in preparing for that mountaintop is obvious. But here's the problem: there are two strands of Xenophontic influence in play, and sorting out the priorities involved is difficult. The first is easy once over the hurdle posed by the modern axiom: just as it was in the wake of Xenophon's *Symposium* that Plato wrote his, it was in the wake of his own that Plato wrote *Hippias Major*, that is, it was written later and was intended to be preparatory. But it also appears to respond to 3.8, and it is unclear when it, along with the rest of *Memorabilia* 3, was written.[23] Indeed, it has already been suggested that 3.8-9, 4.4, and 4.6 may have been the final additions Xenophon annexed to his *Memorabilia*. In short, although it may be difficult to determine how long after writing his *Symposium* Plato wrote *Hippias Major*, it is Xenophon who might ultimately provide the key.

And the close connection between Plato's *Lovers* and Xenophon's *Oeconomicus* perhaps provides it. The previous summary has already suggested some reasons why *Lovers* introduces *Hippias Major* and the path that leads from it to *Symposium* through philosophy and the Beautiful. To supplement the foregoing, it is worth mentioning that the subject of philosophy arises there because the boys who are the love-interests of the two rival lovers are discussing physics, a subject already associated with the polymath Hippias in *Protagoras* (*Prt.* 315b9-c7). With this Platonic basis in place, consider the following: the word *philosopher* appears only once in Xenophon's dialogue, where Socrates explains the fact that he will "gladly learn [ἡδέως μανθάνειν]" on the grounds that doing so "is especially [characteristic] of a wisdom loving [φιλοσόφου] man" (*Oec.* 16.9). Since the musician's first definition of τὸ φιλοσοφεῖν (*Am.* 133c1) hearkens back to Solon's apothegm "I grow old always being taught [διδασκόμενος] many things" (*Am.* 133c6), it is easy for Socrates to get him to confirm that φιλοσοφία is πολυμαθία (*Am.* 133c10–d1), that is, much learning. If there is a structural connection between the two dialogues, then, it involves the constant interplay of teaching and learning in *Oeconomicus*, and the discussion of πολυμαθία in *Lovers* should probably be recognized as thematically connected to all the teaching and learning that occurs in *Oeconomicus*.

There are far more specific connections as well. The questions that lead the musician to exclude the illiberal or handicraft arts from the purview of a philosophical πολυμαθία (*Am.* 135b1–7) point to a distinction likewise found in Xenophon's dialogue (*Oec.* 4.1–3). There are also the three references in *Lovers* to οἰκονομική and the οἰκονόμος (*Am.* 138c2–10). The philosopher who does not know how "to manage well [εὖ οἰκεῖσθαι]" his own οἰκία or household at the end of *Lovers* (*Am.* 138e4–7) recalls Ischomachus, who does. And both dialogues feature prominently a kingly kind of rule, practiced equally by an actual king (βασιλεύς) *and* the overseer of an οἰκία (cf. *Oec.* 21.10 and *Am.* 138c7–10). But the most important connection is revealingly disjunctive: in *Lovers* (*Am.* 138c7–10), Socrates—en route to the failed attempt to explain philosophy in terms of knowledge—makes no distinction between "a kingly art [βασιλικὴ τέχνη]" as practiced by a βασιλεύς and its tyrannical counterpart (τυραννική). In *Oeconomicus*, by contrast, Xenophon concludes the dialogue by drawing a sharp contrast between those who secure willing obedience—whether as king, general, or overseer of an οἰκία (*Oec.* 21.2–11)—and the tyrant who rules the unwilling. This suggests multiple waves of Xenophontic influence on the dialogues between *Protagoras* and *Symposium*, one following his *Symposium* and leading to the great bookends of the series, another following *Hellenica* II and leading to *Menexenus*, and a later one following *Oeconomicus*, and responsible for *Lovers*, itself made necessary by the two dyads it was designed to mediate. There is also the impact of *Memorabilia* 4.2 on the *Alcibiades* dyad and of 3.8 on *Hippias Major* to be considered.

The suggestion that Plato wrote *Lovers* for the express purpose of linking two pairs of previously written dialogues creates a revealing contrast with the methods the Academic Editor used to organize Xenophon's *opuscula* as well as the similar methods Thrasyllus used to arrange the Platonic dialogues in his edition. In both of those cases, an editor encountered a number of works that were either completely disordered or encountered in an order he either failed to appreciate or desired to supplant. He then set about applying tools for their logical arrangement, groupings by pairs in the case of the *scripta minora* and by groups of four in the case of Thrasyllus. The latter's decision to place the four short dialogues *Theages, Charmides, Laches,* and *Lysis* in the Fifth Tetralogy and *Euthydemus, Protagoras, Gorgias,* and *Meno* in the Sixth, indicates the kind of tools Thrasyllus used to organize the *disjecta membra* of someone else's production. The Reading Order paradigm imagines Plato as having done something very different: with the bookends of much broader structures already written—in this case, *Symposium* and *Protagoras*—he then created dialogues to connect them more closely. This explains why arranging Plato's dialogues by Order of Composition often leads to mistakes and frequently leads to the excision of entire dialogues, the purpose of which becomes unintelligible without an awareness of Reading Order. To provide but two examples, the best justification for an authentic *Clitophon* is that its purpose is to introduce *Republic*—and this Thrasyllus realized (see the Eighth Tetralogy)—while recurring doubts about the authenticity of *Hippias Major* emphasize that it is an "early" dialogue in form that nevertheless presupposes "the middle period Forms."[24]

Since Xenophon's Socratic writings offer the most obvious parallel to the Platonic dialogues, consider first the connection between *Memorabilia* and the three shorter works that are included with it in the second part of the *corpus Xenophonteum*, beginning with Galen's claim that *Oeconomicus* was intended to be its fifth book.[25] Apart from Galen, there is no compelling reason to think that this was Xenophon's intention, and modern scholars have for the most part rejected it. Nor is this remarkable: not only did Xenophon embed no clues in either *Symposium* or *Oeconomicus* about their intended sequence, but the presence of Critobulus in all three works would have made it very easy for him to have done so had he thought it important. And then there is the monkey wrench that gets thrown into the works by the plausible hypothesis that Xenophon added to *Memorabilia* gradually over time; consider it in relation to the following sentence by Marchant: "Certain linguistic indications point to a date [sc. for *Oec.*] earlier than the *Memorabilia*; but the tone of the work, calm and detached from controversy, strongly suggests that it was at least put into its final shape after the so-called Fourth Book of that work was written."[26]

The reader may recognize that this assessment is consistent with views already expressed here *in letter* but not in spirit. Marchant sees *Memorabilia* 4 as its latest part, and thus *Oeconomicus* as even later. If von Arnim is right that the reprise of Socrates' trial and death at the end of *Memorabilia* was designed to replace his own *Apology of Socrates*, there is no sense in asking in what order Xenophon intended them to be read, and if *Memorablia* was written over a long period of time, a far more nuanced approach to "linguistic indications" of the kind Marchant has in mind is required. And even if it were granted that Xenophon intended us to read *Symposium* after *Memorabilia*—with the philosopher's playful side revealed only after explaining his serious views—nothing in it sheds much light on whether he wanted to it to follow or precede *Oeconomicus*. If there were a Reading Order of Xenophon's Socratic writings, the following seems most plausible, with *Oeconomicus* standing last because in it, Socrates is being at once serious and playful: *Apology of Socrates, Memorabilia, Symposium,* and *Oeconomicus*. After all, if we knew that Critobulus was persuaded by Socrates-Ischomachus, we could plausibly chart his progress to that point through *Memorabilia* 1.3.8–13, 2.6, and *Symposium*.[27]

But even if we were to do so, when would we imagine that Xenophon intended his Socratic writings as a whole to be read? Schorn has usefully suggested that we need to have read them before reading *Hiero* (see chapter 2, section 5), and this seems right. And regardless of whether we should read *Cyropaedia* as perfectly or only apparently consistent with Xenophon's Socratic ideals, it makes sense that we should read it after them as well. But what of the other minor writings? With the exception of the attack on the sophists at the end of *Cynegeticus*, none of them seems to have much connection with Socrates except insofar as their author is a Socratic. And perhaps Xenophon expects us to recognize this from the start, and refers to Socrates in *Anabasis* as a result, expecting us to recognize his decision to mount τὸ βῆμα and lift the spirits of the demoralized army as paradigmatically embodying what Socrates had merely begun to teach Glaucon in 3.6, and had tried to teach Charmides in *Memorabilia* 3.7. In any case, we could not recognize Xenophon as the pious Hermogenes in *Symposium* without having already read *Anabasis*, and the same is probably true of *Oeconomicus* as well, for it is only in the Parabasis that he can situate himself in the countryside.

One of the two clearest examples of Reading Order in the corpus is the reference to Themistogenes in *Hellenica* 3; Xenophon clearly expects the reader of *Hellenica* to have already read *Anabasis*. If Xenophon expects us to recognize the influence of Socrates in *Anabasis* by reading the Socratic works before it, and to read *Hellenica* only *after* reading "Themistogenes," then we can discern the broad contours of a plausibly Xenophontic Reading Order based on three of his four longest works as follows: *Memorabilia, Anabasis,* and *Hellenica*. And with the other three Socratic writings made ancillary to the first, it might just be possible to find among the *scripta minora* works that are equally ancillary to *Hellenica*. Among these, the two *Constitutions* might seem to be properly preparatory; *Agesilaus* might more plausibly be read afterward. There are thus a number of works that enhance our appreciation for *Hellenica* even without considering in this section the important role that the cavalry plays in it. Meanwhile, the reference to *On Horsemanship* at the end of *The Cavalry Officer* is the only other example of Xenophon pointing back to another of his works aside from what we find in *Hellenica*.

But the more important point is that even this brief sketch brings into high relief the difference between anything resembling the kind of Reading Order that Xenophon might possibly have intended and the order in which his writings have come down to us. By placing *Hellenica* first, that order suggests the Academy's priorities, not Xenophon's. It also suggests a way of reading *Hellenica*, and of course regarding it as a historical work that continues Thucydides is a perfectly plausible way of doing so. But it is not clear that this is the way Xenophon intended us to read it, or at least not the only or even the most important way. The goal of the next section is to prove that Xenophon *wants* us to play "Where's Waldo," wants us, that is, to search for him in his works, and in *Hellenica* especially. The sequence *Memorabilia*, *Anabasis*, *Hellenica* suggests this intention; the Academic Order is incompatible with it.

Since *The Education of Cyrus* is Xenophon's longest work, there is a natural temptation to see it as his culminating, latest, and somehow most significant work as well, especially since such considerations have influenced the way Plato's *Laws* has been received. Albeit followed by *Epinomis*, which it either really is or merely masquerades as its sequel, *Laws* is the last of the dialogues in the edition of Thrasyllus, and *Cyropaedia* is the last of Xenophon's major works in the traditional order of his writings. Did Xenophon really expect it to be read last? It's possible but not certain. As already indicated, there are large swaths of the book that can be appreciated by a youngster, but this fact has been ignored in the literature. There, a great deal of attention has been given to the book's genre, and how its innovative mixture of history and myth has arguably made it recognizable as an ancient forerunner of the novel, whether historical, romance, or fantasy. Starting from the παιδεία in its title, the action-packed story line, the battle scenes, the dashing hero, all combined with simple sentence structures and fantastic distortions of historical truth, suggest that it really is child's play. In short, Xenophon may have thought that a novice should read *Cyropaedia* first, albeit one who was already familiar with Herodotus.

But let's see what a more serious reading (or rereading) can make of *The Education of Cyrus* in relation to Reading Order. The modification of the Schorn-hypothesis has already been mentioned: we must bring Socrates along with us to appreciate any number of incidents, and especially the Persian decision to reject the methods used by the teacher of deception, expressly linked to Greek methods by Cambyses (*Cyr.* 1.6.32), and for much the same reason the Armenian sophist killed by Tigranes' father (*Cyr.* 3.1.14–15). A case might be made that *Cyropaedia* cannot be understood unless the reader recognizes Socrates here or rather the significance of something resembling the rejection of his methods and even his murder.[28] Is the reader's familiarity with *Anabasis* likewise presupposed? It certainly looks as if the younger Cyrus's obituary (*An.* 1.9) was intended to anticipate *Cyropaedia* in much the same way *Oeconomicus* seems to do. More importantly, the reference to Cyrus the Great's war against Astyages (*An.* 3.4.11–12) surely disarms any reader's certainty that the narrator of *The Education of Cyrus* is a reliable one; this obviously has a significant bearing on how we should read this book. As for *Hellenica*, one might think that a prior acquaintance with Persian duplicity might have made the last chapter of *Cyropaedia* unnecessary, for clearly the idealized Persia of the one is very different from what we find in the other. On balance, then, it seems plausible to imagine that the Academic Order might have preserved Xenophon's intentions by placing *The Education of Cyrus* last among his major works.

Assuming, of course, that he *had* any intentions with regard to Reading Order. Although the foregoing may indicate that there is a logical order in which one might most profitably read his works, there have been no clear indications—not even of the kind that can be found in Plato—that he had that logic in mind. In point of fact, the preceding exercise is more reminiscent of what a later editor might do. It is one thing to arrange the *disjecta membra* into the most logically coherent order possible; it is quite another to persuade oneself that by doing so, one is disclosing the author's intentions. It is worth pausing over this distinction between imposing order *ab extra* and the detection of an order that originated in the author's mind: it discloses what I regard as the inadequacy of attempting to interpret Plato's dialogues on the basis of the order of their composition. Instead of treating Plato as a teacher who arranged his dialogues in a coherent manner built around sound pedagogical practices—e.g., that whenever Plato may have written *Hippias Major*, he intended it *to be read* early—the dominant paradigm attempts to reconstruct, on the basis of what are not always adequate readings, how Plato's thinking developed and changed. This is an *external* approach: it treats the dialogues as historical objects and presumes that the most important question to ask about them is when they were written. A more respectful approach considers the order in which Plato has sometimes managed to tell us that his dialogues should be read.

Nothing could be more obvious, for example, than that Plato placed *Sophist* between *Euthyphro* and *Statesman* in a dramatic sense, or that—for the same reason—*Theaetetus* precedes the one and that *Apology of Socrates* follows the other, there being no dialogue that stands between *Statesman* and Socrates' trial. But since two of these dialogues have been interpreted as paradigmatically early, and the other three as late, the dramatic order, clearly indicated by Plato, has been ignored. This kind of order should not be confused with any system that makes the patently ridiculous claim that the beginner should begin by studying *Parmenides* because Socrates is a young man it; one form of chronological overdetermination should not be traded for another,[29] that is to say, arranging the dialogues by dramatic dates should not be substituted for the date of composition. But there are many cases in which Plato has used dramatic order in a clear and natural way: *Critias* follows *Timaeus*, and *Timaeus* follows *Republic*, for example. Thanks to Socrates' indirect courtship of Euthydemus, Xenophon plays his part in helping us see that *Protagoras* precedes *Alcibiades Major*; hence, this connection has already been mentioned. But neither Xenophon nor Thucydides is necessary to see that Plato expects us to read *Hippias Minor* after *Hippias Major*. These are all readily obvious examples of *internal* ordering, and the obvious order of the following would revolutionize the study of Plato if only we were willing to respect it: *Theaetetus*, *Euthyphro*, *Sophist*, *Statesman*, and *Apology of Socrates*, the latter occupying the place of the missing Philosopher.

Having spent a long period time studying the dialogues of Plato on the basis of internal considerations alone, and having maintained throughout that study an agnostic position regarding the order in which he might have composed them, I have persuaded myself that "the Reading Order of Plato's Dialogues" exists. And for what little it may be worth: I am equally convinced that there is nothing equivalent in the case of Xenophon's works. The clues with which Plato's dialogues abound, the techniques he used to indicate anticipations and references, and the methods that have brought larger structures into view; none of these appear to have been of any concern to Xenophon in connecting his works to one another. I suspect this had something to do with the fact that it was *within* his longer works that Xenophon was continually doing something similar, not only adding new material but also rewriting the old. As a historian, Xenophon was not committed to the unchanging; whether it demonstrates weakness of mind or a strength, Plato famously was.

Where's Xenophon?

It is in *Hellenica* that we must hunt for Xenophon, and some aspects and results of that hunting expedition will be this section's primary focus. But it is best to begin with *Anabasis* and *Memorabilia*, the only two works where Xenophon mentions himself by name. It is therefore revealing that in both of these cases, where no hunting would seem to be required, Xenophon has also concealed himself under another name. In the passage quoted in chapter 1 section 5, the estimable Delebecque—and another passage by the unrivaled champion of "Where's Xenophon" will be translated in this one—correctly finds Xenophon in both Theopompus and Euthydemus. Of the first, little need be said except that Xenophon uses him to make three points about himself: he is young, he is eloquent, and he is a philosopher (*An.* 2.1.13).[30] It is true that Phalinus says that he only *seems* to be a philosopher, but it is important to realize that Xenophon *is* a φιλόσοφος, and that when he is not recognized as such,[31] he will face the kind of dismissive erasure that Schleiermacher imposed on his reputation at the beginning of the nineteenth century. Note that although the man named "Xenophon" in *Anabasis* is eloquent, emphasizes his possibly disqualifying youth (*An.* 3.1.25), and naturally remains the φιλόσοφος that he is—the meaning of which is perhaps best expressed by Chaucer's description of the equally bibliophile Oxford Clerk[32]—he never tells us directly that he was any of these things.[33]

The relationship between "Xenophon" and Euthydemus is more complicated, and implicates or rather emphasizes the question of sex. Part of what makes *Cyropaedia* an innovative work is its romantic aspect, and although Cyrus himself is only described as kissing a man (*Cyr.* 1.4.27–28), the tale of Panthea and Abradatas is an early hymn to heterosexual love (cf. *Cyr.* 3.1.41), and the same affinity for the physical love between a man and a woman is visible in *Oeconomicus* and justified in *Memorabilia* 2.2.

As a writer, then, Xenophon emphasizes, in a way that Plato does not, that he loved women and, albeit discreetly, he makes it obvious that he loved making love to Philesia. The point of these preliminary remarks is that Xenophon appears in *Memorabilia* only as the defender of a harmless kiss from a beautiful boy (*Mem.* 1.3.8–10); Socrates rebukes him for thinking that such a kiss could ever be harmless (*Mem.* 1.3.11–13). Although the distinction between male and female requires no clarification, the sexual relationship at the center of Greek pederasty is based on the distinction between ἐραστής and ἐρώμενος, that is, between the older "lover" and the younger "beloved," also frequently called "a boy-friend" (although τὰ παιδικά is considerably less intimate a word, and in any case the "boy" in the typical translation should be understood as emphasizing the love-object's age rather than his gender). The first point, then, is that the Xenophon whom Socrates rebukes by name is imagining himself as an ἐραστής, not an ἐρώμενος: he imagines himself as the kisser Critobulus has just been (*Mem.* 1.3.8), not the youthful and beautiful, thus, καλός, *recipient* of a kiss.

Recognizing Xenophon in Euthydemus will give us a very different impression about his youthful sexual experiences. In a word, "Euthydemus the beautiful [ὁ καλός]" (*Mem.* 4.2.1) is pictured as an ἐρώμενος, not an ἐραστής. One of Socrates' quarrels with Critias arises because the latter is lusting, as an ἐραστής, after Euthydemus (*Mem.* 1.2.29); it is here that the young man is first named, and that means that Xenophon introduces himself as Euthydemus before he mentions "Xenophon." Socrates attempts to prevent Critias from pursuing Euthydemus sexually by using much the same arguments he will later use about the deadly kiss, namely, that the ἐραστής will become enslaved to the ἐρώμενος and behave in a manner unworthy of a καλὸς κἀγαθός; Xenophon does not tell us that he succeeded: "And with Critias paying no heed to these arguments, it is said [λέγεται] that Socrates—with many others present, and Euthydemus as well—asseverated that Critias seemed to him to share a pig's experience in desiring to rub himself against [προσκνῆσθαι] Euthydemus, as piglets do to stones" (*Mem.* 1.2.30). It is important to note the devices Xenophon takes here to preserve his chastity. The verb προσκνῆσθαι suggests "dry-humping" rather than actual penetration, and stones of course cannot be penetrated. At this point, however, Xenophon has not yet given us any reason to think that "Euthydemus" is himself; thus not only the use of λέγεται—since if Xenophon is Euthydemus and Euthydemus was present, there would be no reason to rely on what Socrates *is said* to have said—but also the later appearance of "Xenophon" in the next chapter as (nothing but) an ἐραστής.

But we should recognize that Xenophon is telling us something here, and that it is in the domain of confession. It is no great honor to have made out with Critias the Pig,[34] but Xenophon has found a way to tell us not only that he did so, but that he is ashamed of it. To be sure there is a much more straightforward way of defanging the synthesis of these three incidents—Euthydemus the ἐρώμενος (*Mem.* 1.2.29–30), Xenophon the ἐραστής (*Mem.* 1.3.8–13), and Xenophon as Euthydemus (*Mem.* 4.2.1–4.3.2)—just as there is a way to equate the only unequivocal Xenophon among the three with Cyrus the Great. Unlike the younger Cyrus who clearly likes women (*An.* 1.2.12), the elder refuses even to look at the beautiful Panthea (*Cyr.* 5.1.1–8), and offers a homily against the dangers of beauty that might seem Socratic if it were not for Theodote (*Mem.* 3.11).[35] But the Socrates who chastises Critias for lusting after Euthydemus, Euthydemus for allowing him to προσκνῆσθαι, and Xenophon for welcoming a kiss from the beautiful is taking the same position throughout. Though notably erotic and habitually posing as an ἐραστής (*Mem.* 4.1.2), Xenophon's Socrates rejects sexualized pederasty in no uncertain terms,[36] especially in the benediction he is willing to pronounce in *Symposium* on the union of Callias and Autolycon *provided* their love is not sexual (*Smp.* 8.18–24). Between his regrettable experience as an ἐρώμενος in his youth, and his mature love for Philesia, the noble mother of his sons, Xenophon has undergone a conversion, and he wants us to know it. But it is not a conversion that has reduced him to the anti-erotic level of Cyrus.

In turning to *Hellenica*, the first point is that Xenophon never mentions himself there, and with the reference to Themistogenes, he makes it clear that he will conceal himself as well. But when he ends his book shortly after the death of Gryllus—we can recognize both father and son because of Diogenes Laertius, who also emphasizes Xenophon's physical beauty[37]—it would be a hard-hearted reader who could not recognize the historian who laid aside his mighty pen as Homer's Priam, weeping with Achilles for his lost son. Thanks to Diogenes, the loss of Gryllus repeats the same pattern of confession and concealment: in place of the concealing λέγεται and the impenetrable stone, there is the anecdote that Xenophon bore his son's death with proto-Stoic equanimity: "Once having been born, mortal I knew him to be," a translation that if somewhat more literal than "I knew my son was mortal" still cannot preserve the odd blend of Laconic brevity and disjointed obscurity of the Greek. The anecdote conceals his grief; the last words of *Hellenica* tell a different story: "Indecision and confusion was even greater after the battle [sc. Mantinaea] than earlier in Hellas. Up until this point, then, let it be written by me; for the things that came afterwards [τὰ μετὰ ταῦτα], perhaps it will be of concern to another."[38] The general point, then, is that Xenophon's *Hellenica* is not only the story of "Hellenic Affairs," but also Xenophon's own story, written between the lines, and thereby forcing the reader to play "Where's Waldo?"

The possibility that this use of "forcing" is too strong must be confronted promptly. It is perfectly true that Xenophon's *Hellenica* is an indispensable source of information about the years it covers; its principal value *for us* is not in dispute, and if we make ourselves his book's measure, the information it sheds on Xenophon's life is merely peripheral, and seeking it looks like the kind of author-externalizing dissection *ab extra* that the order of composition paradigm has practiced on Plato to his detriment. And not even the practitioners of this art have claimed that they are reading Xenophon *the way he wished to be read*, that is, that he wanted, let alone required, us to seek for him and reconstruct his life on the basis of what he refuses to say openly about himself. Although neither Delebecque nor Anderson—these two will represent a larger class in this section—seem in any way embarrassed by the methods they are *forced* to use, they don't claim they are doing what Xenophon wanted, let alone what he forced them to do. As we will see, Delebecque justifies his own method of disinterring valid bibliographical information from Xenophon's texts almost as if he were outsmarting his author by seeing through him, extorting the truth from a witness who has been made to confess the truth despite his efforts to conceal it.

Without denying that this conception is plausible, I want to offer three reasons why it is inapplicable to Xenophon's *Hellenica*. In the first place, it presupposes the value of an objective and scientific historical account; with this presupposition in place, the critic can then proceed to find Xenophon, who obviously is no Thucydides, wanting. But if Xenophon *wants us to look for him*, knows that we will see through the fiction of Themistogenes and therefore expects that we will bring the Xenophon we know from *Anabasis* along with us, then the bad versus objective history polarity that has been used to dismiss him vanishes. In searching for an objective account that would only be of value if its author left his own conceptions and prejudices out of it, we gain the circularly devalued work to which our own initial prejudice entitles us. While it is plausible to imagine that we are finding nuggets of biographical fact hidden away in an inferior work of history whose author never comes close to attaining the objectivity we demand from a superior or even an adequate one, it is a profoundly disrespectful manner of preceding.

Second, there is Xenophon's life-altering relationship with Socrates to be considered, and the central role that confession plays in anyone's Socratic conversion. On the most obvious level, there is "the confession of ignorance," and it is easy to imagine that all that is required from the student is to admit reaching an ἀπορία. If reaching such a dialectical impasse were sufficient to make one into a Socratic, Meno and Alcibiades would both qualify.[39] More is required, and *Memorabilia* 4.2 gives us firsthand information about what a true confession—and thus a true conversion—looked like:

> And Euthydemus said: "These things as well compel me to agree, and my own worthlessness [ἡ ἐμὴ φαυλότης] is clear. And I am pondering whether it might be my strongest move to keep silent, for I am in danger of simply knowing nothing." And being very despondent [ἀθυμῶς ἔχειν], he departed, both having despised himself [καταφρονήσας ἑαυτοῦ] and having believed himself to be a slave [ἀνδράποδον] in fact.[40]

In examining this crucial text, we are apt to make the same kind of mistake that results from expecting Xenophon to have attempted, unsuccessfully, to provide a scientifically objective and impersonal account of events in *Hellenica*. But in this case, the mistake is far more profound and touches on a fundamental issue: the degree to which our own Judeo-Christian prejudices have made it difficult to see Socratic conversion for what it really was.

Having allowed this statement to elicit a godless "Amen" from the disciples of Nietzsche, let me clarify: it is, rather, the steps we have taken to counter the "infection" of antiquity by Judeo-Christian conceptions that has created the prejudices I have in mind. The disciples of Nietzsche have been so determined to preserve antiquity as *Judenfrei* that it would seem completely prejudiced and unscientific to recognize Socratic conversion for what it was: the Athenian equivalent of confession, repentance, and conversion. In Plato's *Gorgias*, the only legitimate use of rhetoric identified by Socrates is self-accusation, predicated on a clear-eyed awareness of one's own injustices, along with those of your kinsman and your city

(*Grg.* 480b7–d6). A mere confession of ignorance means next to nothing; what Xenophon as Euthydemus realized is ἡ ἐμὴ φαυλότης. He confesses his worthlessness, not only his ignorance, and despises himself as a result. It's considerably easier to confess a lacuna in your knowledge-base than to experience what καταφρονήσας ἑαυτοῦ feels like; Euthydemus does not simply consider himself as uninformed, but as a slave (cf. *Alc.1* 135c10–13), to wit, an ἀνδράποδον.

There are in fact two ways that a prejudice against examining Socratic conversion in the light of Judeo-Christian conceptions distorts what is happening in this passage and more generally in both Plato and Xenophon. These ambitious young Athenians, in full possession of a panoply of goods universally admired by their contemporaries as well as themselves—including wealth, good looks, intelligence, and the ineradicable pride that comes from being a citizen of the greatest and most powerful city on earth—had no tincture of Judeo-Christian humility to counteract their "proper pride" or μεγαλοψυχία. Until they met Socrates,[41] they could say with Moliére's Acaste: "By Jove when I survey myself I find / no cause whatever for distress of mind."[42] An awareness that their milieu did not even know how to pay lip service to the virtue of humility is what makes a Judeo-Christian conception of their conversion not so much possible as necessary. We can now only recognize the phenomenon on the basis of our Judeo-Christianity, and we will misunderstand it if we are determined to try not to do so.

But to really understand it, we need to go farther, and experience an even more shattering awareness of ἡ ἐμὴ φαυλότης than the one "that saved a wretch like me." Augustine already had mother Monnica, and every Jew knew the meaning of *teshuvah* before Jesus. But when anyone of us goes down to the river to be baptized these days, there is a deeply comforting sense of finally coming home, of acknowledging what we always and already somehow knew to be true. There was no such homecoming available to Plato and Xenophon. The Socratic conversion left them isolated and lonely even before Socrates was murdered, for they had said goodbye not only to the values that had informed their youth and which were enshrined in their city, but to a self-conception that made them both outstanding exemplars of those values, in full possession of a self-esteem against which no "revaluation of values" or "slave revolt in morality" had yet given them any reason whatsoever to despise, equipping them instead with an unshakeable self-certainty borne of a pre-Judeo-Christian μεγαλοψυχία that no modern, apart from a Nazi, can even imagine. The attempt to understand Socratic conversion without Judeo-Christian conceptions is to cover up its harrowing nature not once but twice.

These general observations are relevant because the new ground that will be broken in the remainder of this section relates to some passages in *Hellenica* that I will try to show constitute a confession. Socratic conversion, any more than the Christian kind, hardly guarantees the kind of future for which no further apology or repentance will be necessary. To take a famous example, Xenophon expressly acknowledges his departure from Socratic advice in *Anabasis* (*An.* 3.1.5–7): he makes no effort to defend his question to the oracle, and if his motive for telling the story of how he came to ask it was to exculpate Socrates, he can only do so by taking the blame on himself. More relevant to *Hellenica* is the question of how Xenophon came to be banished. About this, three things are clear: he was in fact banished, any search for that banishment's cause must rely primarily on what can be found in *Hellenica*, and Xenophon never says or even implies that his banishment was unjust. In this section, I will be suggesting that Xenophon confesses at least the consequence and perhaps even the cause of his exile, revealing it in the characteristic way. If successful, this example of "Where's Xenophon" will show that its cause was an action of which he was not proud. Naturally, he is not seeking absolution; instead, he is revealing the kind of Socratic self-knowledge that came within his reach when Socrates himself helped him to recognize ἡ ἐμὴ φαυλότης.

Finally, there is what must appear to be a countervailing aspect if the foregoing has gone or been taken too far. It is on the ruins of ἡ ἐμὴ φαυλότης that a Socratic was compelled to rebuild a new structure, and it didn't require an Aristotle to discover that the opportunity to exercise virtue in a situation commensurate with one's abilities is a recipe for happiness. It is this opportunity that Xenophon describes in *Anabasis*, and with the moment of despondency left behind him in Athens, he was now in a position to counteract the state of being ἀθυμῶς ἔχειν in others. The fact that Xenophon is fully aware of his own Socratic excellence as commander of the Ten Thousand's rearguard explains and justifies his decision to publish *Anabasis* I under another name. As should already be clear, the view that Cyrus the Great was not Xenophon's role model and hero is central to this book's argument;[43] in the next section, Agesilaus and Sparta generally are going to be exposed to a similar kind of analysis whereby what looks like encomium will be unmasked as critique.[44] And part of the reason that no effort has been made to conceal the problems created by 3.8-9, 4.4, and 4.6 is because the possibility should remain open that the only hero of Xenophon's corpus as a whole is Xenophon the Socratic.

Xenophon is not Plato: he is not pointing to ἡ τοῦ ἀγαθοῦ ἰδέα as the unchanging and impersonal standard of excellence. It's not that he's rejecting this external standard—this is the poisonous fruit of the ultramodern appropriation of Literary Rivalry—it is simply no part of his experience: at the risk of oversimplification, he was too busy living to devote himself to contemplating the transcendent. Thanks to Socrates, he built a life on firm foundations, and we will misunderstand him radically if we imagine that he regarded either of what a post-Socratic student of Plato's would call "the active" or "the contemplative life" as superior to the other. For Xenophon, this distinction no more exists than does the problem of the separate Forms, and probably for the same reason. He regards his life as a pattern for his readers, and anyone who has not been inspired to become the boatswain of the Sweating Rowers described in *Oeconomicus* should leave Xenophon aside and turn elsewhere for inspiration.

The lack of any distinction between the active and contemplative lives where Xenophon is concerned indicates the necessity of making one last point before actually playing "Where's Xenophon." It was not only by writing books about ἀρετή in action that Xenophon made the application of this distinction anachronistic and unsympathetic; it was by making the experience of *reading* those books—probably the *collective* experience of reading them *aloud*—a deliberately constructed exercise that would implant virtue in the reader who understood them. When someone says: "I love Xenophon," that doesn't mean, "I like the way he writes," or, "I am grateful for the useful information he supplies about Antisthenes, the King's Peace, growing grapes, training dogs, or even leading men" (although the latter comes closest); it means "I love and admire the man who could do all these things." And yet how are we to know him? He wrote the world's earliest biography but never wrote clearly about his own life,[45] and that's why we must turn to *Hellenica* if we are to find him. And this is exactly what I'm claiming he wanted us to do, and that he was fully justified in this desire. The man is instructive, but he can only instruct *because he is so*, not simply because he instructs.

The clearest and most accessible introduction to the game "Where's Xenophon" is Anderson's chapter "The Counter-Revolution at Athens."[46] Having used the Old Oligarch to establish Xenophon's oligarchic views in the previous chapter,[47] Anderson imagines his service to the Thirty as a cavalryman with a conscience.⁴⁸ The game depends entirely on the view—by no means inaccurate—that "Xenophon's account reads like that of an eyewitness."⁴⁹ But most telling is the following passage in which Anderson recognizes both the vivid detail of a firsthand account and a confession:

> Lysimachus was responsible for one more outrage when he butchered some farmers, taken on their land, searching for provisions, "though they made many entreaties for mercy, and many of the cavalry took it hard." If Xenophon was one of these, our own age has seen enough men pleading the orders of higher authority as a reason for acting against their moral convictions to understand, if not to excuse his conduct.⁵⁰

As the allusion to, for example, the Nuremberg Trials indicates, the lessons Anderson disinters from this exercise are of what must count as being of "timeless value." It should go without saying that I don't believe Anderson is finding anything here that Xenophon didn't want us to find.

Delebecque supplies the theoretical basis for the game in the Introduction to his *Vie de Xénophon*. Emphasizing the role of *Hellenica* in distinguishing the broad contours of his life,⁵¹ Delebecque is intent on going farther:

> Is it necessary to be satisfied only with *les grandes étapes*? We can strive to discover a more precise image of the author among his writings, a portrait *dans la fresque*. But it will be necessary to redouble our caution in this case, and to make use always of strict guidelines: we are in effect penetrating into a field sown with pitfalls, and with pitfalls even more dangerous than those that Xenophon has at his own disposal. There are two mysteries in the work: the natural mystery that arises from our distance in space and time and the artificial mystery that Xenophon has produced; we will try to unravel [*débrouiller*] it.⁵²

Although Delebecque sees Xenophon's concealments as rather more self-servingly apologetic than revealingly self-critical,⁵³ he is in hot pursuit throughout of the necessary hints and signs.⁵⁴ Here is how he prepares the way for Anderson:

In some cases, however, the account is so precise and detailed that it could not come from any other witness other than the author; is it possible to doubt, for example, whether it is Xenophon—always the horse's friend—who counts the cavalrymen from the city beaten by the soldiers of Thrasybulus before Phyle, when he applies to the retelling of this defeat the most minute precision, giving the names, the numbers, and that he still hears in memory the sound of the servants currying the horses at daybreak (*Hell.* 2.4.5–7)?[55]

Finally, he concludes his Introduction on almost exactly the right note: "Perhaps we will disentangle thanks to him, and if necessary in spite of him [*malgré lui*], the thread of a new Odyssey."[56] Only *malgré lui* is out of place.

Thanks in large measure to the prominence that Xenophon's *Agesilaus* gave to his brother, Teleutias of Sparta tends to get overlooked, and the remainder of this section is an attempt to redress that error. Although *Hellenica* 5 makes a hard turn toward Teleutias that should have made it easy to recognize his importance, Xenophon has already prepared us in book 4 for this recognition, not only by introducing him as Agesilaus' brother (*Hell.* 4.4.19) but by mentioning how the command of the so-called Κυρεῖοι or "Cyreans"—the remains of the Ten Thousand, Xenophon among them—passed to him from Herippidas (*Hell.* 4.8.11), who had taken command of them in book 3 (*Hell.* 3.4.20; see also 4.3.15–17). Xenophon uses his usual tricks to reveal himself as intimately familiar with the words and deeds of Herippidas (see especially *Hell.* 4.1.11–14), and he will do the same—and to an infinitely greater extent—in the case of Teleutias, whose story he will continue through his death. And since the willingness of a leader's men to die with him has been made the mark of ἀρετή in *Oeconomicus*, thereby revealing the limitations of the younger Cyrus's virtue in a surprising manner (see chapter 2, section 3),[57] it is economical to keep in mind Teleutias' ignominious end before considering the combination of praise and confession that makes the opening chapters of book 5 among the most significant in *Hellenica*.

Teleutias is killed at Olynthus, and Xenophon moralizes on his death with a discussion of the ill effects of anger on a commander. Angered by the successful sortie of the Olynthian cavalry—Xenophon ensures that we already know that a Spartan officer was in command of Teleutias' own

(*Hell.* 5.2.41)—he first rashly orders his peltasts to pursue (*Hell.* 5.4.3), and then, when they are slaughtered (*Hell.* 5.4.4), he orders his remaining peltasts, along with his cavalry and hoplites to avenge them, once again doing so in anger (*Hell.* 5.4.5).[58] After pointing out the strategic error in pursuing an enemy back to its city walls, Xenophon tells how Teleutias' decision to do so resulted in a disaster for his army and his own death, promptly making the crucial point: "And when this happened, the troops about him at once gave way, and in fact no one stood his ground any longer, but all fled" (*Hell.* 5.4.6). The homily follows:

> From such disasters, however, I hold that men are taught the lesson, chiefly, indeed, that they ought not to chastise anyone, even slaves, in anger—for masters in anger have often suffered greater harm than they have inflicted; but especially that, in dealing with enemies, to attack under the influence of anger and not with judgment is an absolute mistake. For anger is a thing which does not look ahead, while judgment aims no less to escape harm than to inflict it upon the enemy.[59]

In its immediate context, this can only be construed as a criticism of Teleutius; in a broader and retrospective context, it begins to look more like self-criticism, as we will see.

The criticism that follows his death is in marked contrast with the oath-certified praise that Xenophon showers on Teleutias at the beginning of book 5. After describing in vivid detail the joyous welcome his troops gave him on his arrival—"[T]here was no one among the soldiers who did not grasp his hand, and one decked him with a garland, another with a fillet, and others who came too late, nevertheless, even though he was now under way, threw garlands into the sea and prayed for many blessings upon him" (*Hell.* 5.1.18)—Xenophon comments as follows:

> I know, of course, that [the μέν will not be answered by the usual δέ] in these matters I am describing neither expenditure nor danger, nor a stratagem worthy of record [μηχάνημα ἀξιόλογον], but by Zeus [ἀλλὰ ναὶ μὰ Δία; this ἀλλά may take the place of δέ], it seems to me that it is worthy for a man [ἀνήρ] to ponder whatever Teleutias was doing that thus affected his followers. For this is the most account-worthy deed [ἀξιολογώτατον ἔργον] of a man [ἀνήρ], prior to great wealth and many dangers.[60]

We are dealing here with three kinds of contradiction: (1) there is the absence of a counteracting δέ, which emphasizes the apparent lack of countervailing considerations, (2) then the self-contradiction that arises from the fact that after claiming (μέν) that he is not describing any μηχάνημα ἀξιόλογον, he then swears that what he is describing is really an ἀξιολογώτατον ἔργον, and (3) the long-term contradiction between this unusual authorial praise for Teleutias in the contradictory context of his equally unusual authorial criticism of him a few chapters later. It is also worthy of note that the repetition of ἀνήρ situates this praise in the context of Simonides' equally "manly" morality.

To say that the passage that follows is one of the most important passages in *Hellenica* is to depreciate its significance, for it is the single most important moment in the game "Where's Xenophon," constituting as it does his most searing confession, and simultaneously creates the moral dilemma on which the interpretation of *Cyropaedia* turns. The passage consists of three parts: first, Teleutius gives his men a rousing speech (*Hell.* 5.1.13-18); this constitutes the ἀξιολογώτατον ἔργον. Next follows the sneak attack on Piraeus (*Hell.* 5.1.19-23), the success of which depended entirely on Teleutias' prior familiarity with Athenian practices that only a citizen of Athens would know (*Hell.* 5.1.20) and which is described—and by this point, this should hardly surprise anyone—in vivid detail:

> When he was distant from the harbor five or six stadia, he remained quiet and let his men rest. Then, as day was dawning, he led on and they followed. Now he forbade them to sink or harm any merchant vessel with their own ships; but if they saw a trireme at anchor anywhere, he ordered them to try to make her unseaworthy, and furthermore, to bring out in tow the merchant ships which were loaded, and to board the larger ones wherever they could and take off their people. Indeed, there were some of his men who even leaped ashore on to the Deigma, seized merchants and owners of trading vessels, and carried them aboard the ships.[61]

Finally, he describes the rewards he offered his men (*Hell.* 5.1.24); naturally, Xenophon makes no reference here to his own personal reward.

Apart from finding Xenophon's betrayal of Athens in this passage, the matter of transpersonal significance is the speech of Teleutias. But since the point of this section is to call into question the legitimacy of this "apart," it is first necessary to spell out what is happening here: through the transfer of the Κυρεῖοι from Herippidas to Teleutias (*Hell.* 4.8.11), we know where Xenophon is; his interest in Teleutias, his ability to record his speech, and the vivid detail of the night raid confirm his presence. His treason is implied by the following: "[I]n the case of ships that were abroad he knew that the sailors would be quartered on board their several ships, while with ships at Athens he was aware that the captains would be sleeping at home and the sailors quartered here and there" (*Hell.* 5.1.20). Although supplying this information to the Spartan admiral would amply justify both Xenophon's banishment and the reward of Skillus in return, the wider context—and specifically the critique of acting in anger with which Xenophon will subject to potential erasure his earlier praise for Teleutias—indicates that this betrayal was rather his angry response to his prior banishment. Without denying, then, that it gave him Skillus, Xenophon is confessing as it were twice: not only for an ἔργον that was far from ἀξιολογώτατον, but also for his equally shameful and sub-Socratic failure to recognize that in fact the μηχάνημα that Teleutias used to secure his treason really was nothing ἀξιόλογον. The two become one when he tells us the audience's reaction to his speech: "[T]hey all set up a shout, bidding him give whatever order was needful, in the assurance that they would obey [οἱ δὲ πάντες ἀνεβόησαν παραγγέλλειν ὅ τι ἂν δέῃ, ὡς σφῶν ὑπηρετησόντων]" (*Hell.* 5.1.18).

The speech is an eloquent appeal to naked self-interest that offers material rewards for what would certainly look like Socratic virtue if the end in view were not wealth. But it's a compelling speech, superior to those of Simonides and at least the equal of Cyrus's address to his officers in *Cyropaedia* 1.5, especially at 1.5.9. Until we reach the death of Teleutias, Xenophon gives us no reason—except the moral turpitude implicit in the speech itself—that he has anything other than respect or even veneration for the speaker. And this holds true quite apart—and this time "apart" is justified—from locating Xenophon among those who shouted the Hellenic equivalent of *zur Befehl!* The address is equally appropriate to a king and a criminal, and we will hear it again from Sallust's Catiline.[62] But in context, and before any of that, it must not only be recognized as persuasive, but as a plausible basis for assessing Xenophon's ethics, especially if all men naturally, inevitably, and therefore blamelessly pursue what they think is most advantageous for them (*Mem.* 3.9.4; cf. *Ath. pol.* 2.20). Until they desert him before the walls of Olynthus, Teleutias' men give every indication that he is Xenophon's ideal leader.

But even if Teleutias resembles the younger Cyrus in this ultimately revealing deficit, the soldiers of Cyrus the Great will never desert *him*, and there is no interpretive dilemma in reading Xenophon that surpasses in significance how we assess the relationship between Xenophon—as opposed to the obviously star-struck narrator of the *Cyropaedia*[63]—and Cyrus. Xenophon tells us that he regards it as worthy of a man to ponder or ἐννοιεῖν how Teleutias did what he did (*Hell*. 5.1.4); "A thought [ἔννοιά] once came to me," are the first words of *The Education of Cyrus* (*Cyr*. 1.1.1). Conceived in full awareness that many will reject a Cyrus-unfriendly reading of his longest book, this section will have reached a more achievable goal if it has situated the problem at the heart of *Cyropaedia* in the context of Teleutias, who says: "I do not bid you do any of these things that you may suffer discomfort, but that from them you may gain something good [ἀγαθόν τι]" (*Hell*. 5.1.15). But it will only have achieved its true goal when the reader recognizes that Xenophon's betrayal of Athens made the words of Teleutias both inapplicable and a cause of repentance to him:

> "For what greater gladness can there be than to have to flatter no one in the world, Greek or barbarian, for the sake of pay, but to be able to provide supplies for oneself, and what is more, from the most honorable source? For be well assured that abundance gained in war from the enemy yields not merely sustenance, but at the same time fair fame [εὔκλεια] among all men."[64]

Xenophon has just confessed that εὔκλεια was not the reward he received by following Teleutias.

Sparta and Athens

As "the Tale of Teleutias" indicates, there is some solid basis for the traditional oversimplification that Xenophon admired Sparta and despised Athenian democracy. Indeed, the assumption—found in Anderson above—that he shared the hostile views of the Old Oligarch has contributed, paradoxically, to making modern scholars so certain that he *didn't* write it. But before considering Xenophon's actual relationship to Athens, it is preferable to begin with Sparta, the city he seems to have preferred, and for whose sake—as we have been told so often that it seems like the truth—he sacrificed his objectivity.⁶⁵ There can be no question that this appears to be his preference, and although John Dillery has rejected the possibility of *Hellenica* III, he has carefully and compellingly documented its theme as introduced at *Hellenica* 5.4.1: the retribution visited on Sparta at Leuctra for her arrogance.⁶⁶ In both *Hellenica* III and the penultimate chapter of *The Constitution of the Spartans*, Xenophon anticipates Shakespeare's John of Gaunt, whose famous lament applies to Sparta as well: "that England that was wont to conquer others hath made a shameful conquest of itself." It is therefore a considerably subtler picture of Xenophon that must emerge from an adequate search for his own position in this "Tale of Two Cities."

And in prosecuting that search, it comes as a great relief to finally set aside a polemical stance toward Strauss. Whatever might be the shortcomings of his interpretations of *Hiero* and the Socratic writings, he demonstrates his characteristic acumen and subtlety in a much better cause when it comes to Xenophon on Sparta. And since Strauss is a preeminent figure in the post–Great War reception of Xenophon, a brief explanation of his greater accuracy in this case than in the others may not be entirely out of place. The highpoint of Strauss's encounter with Xenophon immediately followed his emigration to the United States, and his first article published in the States dealt with *The Constitution of the Spartans* (1939);⁶⁷ *On Tyranny*—which already adumbrates his mature reading of *Cyropaedia*, and therefore refers frequently to "tyranny at its best"⁶⁸—is almost a decade later, while the two other books were published more than twenty years after it. In defense of a "developmentalist" reading of Strauss himself, consider the perfectly sane observation he made about *The Education of Cyrus* in 1938: "The apparent praise of Cyrus' apparently marvelous achievement actually is a most stringent censure of a thoroughly bad management of public affairs: the whole *Education of Cyrus* is thoroughly ironical."⁶⁹ In comparison with the postwar *On Tyranny*, this early insight indicates that what ensued was degeneration, not development.

As he explained to his friend Jacob Klein in a 1938 letter, Strauss's original plan was to write *On the Study of Greek Political Philosophy*, which would show "that Herodotus, Thucydides and Xenophon are certainly no historians [*keine* Historiker—of course not—sind]."⁷⁰ The fragment on *Cyropaedia* was part of this never executed project. Most useful for recovering what seems likely to have been the spirit of that project is a 1968 review called "Greek Historians,"⁷¹ and it is this piece, not his more famous books, that makes Strauss of great value in sorting out the truth about Xenophon's "Tale of Two Cities." Here, he builds on the theme of his first article, which had shown that like Xenophon's "apparent praise" of Cyrus, his praise in *The Constitution of the Spartans* merely apparent.[72] In "Greek Historians," he usefully applies this interpretive principle to *Agesilaus*, beginning with the following:

> But it is necessary to pursue this theme much further, i.e., Xenophon's concealed and serious judgment on Agesilaus. I would not hesitate to say that Agesilaus was not a man after Xenophon's heart. How could a man with Xenophon's lack of pomposity and even gravity have unqualifiedly liked a man as absurd, as pompous, as theatrical as the Agesilaus of Xenophon's description (as distinguished from his explicit judgments)?[73]

With this question as the point of entry, what follows shows Strauss at his characteristic best, that is, it shows him using his characteristic methods in what closely resembles a good cause. After all, if Xenophon is not really praising Agesilaus, Sparta, or Cyrus the Great, will that not point us in the end to the author of *Ways and Means*?

Leaving the answer to that that question for later, here are Strauss's conclusions, which deserve to be quoted at length:

> Xenophon's posture toward Agesilaus, which at first glance seems to be one of the keys to the understanding of his mind, becomes more and more a riddle the more one understands Xenophon. Agesilaus seems to have thought highly of Xenophon (Plutarch, *Agesilaus* 20.2); he, the king and the descendant of a long line of kings, may have been Xenophon's *praesidium et dulce decus*. Thus it would not be surprising if Xenophon was grateful and loyal to him. But Xenophon knew that there are duties higher than those imposed by gratitude and loyalty, that the duties imposed by gratitude and loyalty may sometimes have to be superseded by the duty to see things as they are and to communicate one's insights to those who are by nature and training fit for them. The proof of this is the difference between his obtrusive and his unobtrusive judgments on Agesilaus.[74]

Robert C. Bartlett has recently provided a useful analysis of the relationship between *Agesilaus* and *Hellenica*.[75] While building on "Greek Historians" and *Xenophon's Socratic Discourse*,[76] all the while upholding the spirit of Strauss's reading—and this, of course, is what Straussians must do—Bartlett draws detailed attention to the revealing repetitions of *Hellenica* in *Agesilaus* that suppress Xenophon's criticisms in the prior work.[77] In the process, Bartlett creates a companion piece to Strauss's first article that might be called: "The Virtues of Agesilaus and the Admiration of Xenophon."[78] And in defense of Bartlett's method, it deserves mention that since Agesilaus died in 359, his encomium is necessarily a late work, and follows the king's story after *Hellenica*.

There is much of value here, and since so much else remains to be done, it is economical to consider as proved in substance the Straussian case that Xenophon merely appears to be praising Agesilaus,[79] albeit with the countervailing caveat that he was likewise merely appearing to praise tyranny through Simonides. As for Sparta generally, Strauss unfortunately had his own motives for unmasking an immigrant's apparent praise for his adopted country as esoteric censure in 1939. But whatever his personal motives, they were only ancillary to the political convictions Strauss brought with him from Germany—in 1932 he already was writing about the pressing need for "a radical critique of liberalism"[80]—and which were already responsible for making it necessary for him to deny an obvious truth in his article about *The Constitution of the Spartans*:

> A censure of Sparta, moreover, was liable to be misunderstood by uncritical readers as a praise of Athens; for at the time when Xenophon wrote the uncritical reader scarcely saw an alternative to the choice between the Spartan and the Athenian spirit. And Xenophon did not wish to praise Athens.[81]

Pretty certain about "the uncritical reader" of Xenophon's day, Strauss doesn't attempt to prove this last statement; it is interpretive bedrock for him, and this explains why he never devoted an essay to *Ways and Means*.[82]

In fact, the freedom to combine appreciation for Sparta with criticism of Athens was a distinctively Athenian prerogative. Like Xenophon, Plato appears to be an opponent of the democratic city but his Socrates points out that only here is a meaningful discussion about justice and the right choice of lives possible (R. 557c11–d8). One need not be an oligarch or an authoritarian to recognize the fact that in addition to being a repository of practical wisdom, the laws of Lycurgus constitute an elegant and thought-provoking example of the legislative art. Befitting his name, Lycurgus had applied the same practices and training methods that turn wolves into dogs—and more importantly, had turned dogs into loyal, useful, and obedient servants to human beings—to human beings themselves. Admirable in execution, amazing in operation, logically pleasing, and flawed only to the extent that no freedom-loving person would want to be treated like a dog, Spartan ways could only excite interest and wonder in any thoughtful Athenian, and Xenophon made it easier than ever to enter an amazing world that would spawn for perfectly obvious reasons a multitude of science fictions in the aftertime. It was as an Athenian that Xenophon admired Lycurgus, and in was Athens that gave him the ability to freely admire as well as to criticize Spartan ways.

It is therefore Xenophon's relationship with Athens that is the bedrock phenomenon: after all, no Spartan ever wrote a book about Athens or indeed about anything else. In the Funeral Oration of Pericles, Thucydides wrote, "In short, I say that the city as a whole is the education [παίδευσις] of Greece, and that individually, one and the same man from among us seems to me, in the midst of the most varied circumstances, most gracefully [μετὰ χαρίτων] and dexterously [εὐτραπέλως] to provide for himself, self-sufficient in his own skin."[83] No Athenian better embodies Pericles' description than Xenophon.[84] First by preserving the *History*,[85] and then by illustrating in his own person the most quoted sentence in its most famous speech, Xenophon obviously built on Thucydides in subtler ways as well. But what Thucydides teaches us about him is of equally great importance. With the Funeral Oration in mind, it is easy to see that the *corpus Xenophonteum* as a whole, and the "minor writings" in particular, provide abundant evidence that he deserved Thucydides' "gracefully" (μετὰ χαρίτων) no less than his "dexterously" (εὐτραπέλως), and as an exile, he was unquestionably "on his own." It is tempting to identify Xenophon himself as "the παίδευσις of Hellas," not least of all because he traveled widely throughout the Greek world and beyond, and, like Odysseus, "saw the towns and knew the mind of many men." But it was his experiences in Athens and Sparta that prove decisive, and it was as Athenian that he experienced both.

It will be impossible to get to the bottom of this "Tale of Two Cities" without first confronting the problem of Alcibiades. The parallels between two Athenian exiles, both of whom offered their services to Sparta to the detriment of Athens, have been mentioned, but the spiritual basis of these parallels is a mystery and must remain one. It is therefore *as a problem* that the uncanny connection between the two will be considered here. Nor will the most important *symptom* of that underlying problem be resolved: the degree of sympathy that Xenophon had for a man about whom he wrote a great deal. When Xenophon offers advice to the Athenian generals before the disaster at Aegospotomi (*Hell*. 2.1.25-26), it is easy to see what looks like sympathy and vindication, and since Thucydides had already described the advice Alcibiades had given the Athenians that led to the disaster at Syracuse, a distinctly Alcibiades-friendly reading of *Hellenica* has become possible.[86] On the other hand, the brevity of the anonymous rebuttal to the belabored defense (*Hell*. 1.4.13-17) must point in the opposite direction, and it seems best to leave the matter unresolved. The only contribution to its resolution on offer here is the observation that this interpretive dilemma should be recognized as merely a symptom of the larger problem, and lest that seems too cryptic, I am suggesting the possibility that it is not because of his objectivity that Xenophon's account of Alcibiades is indeterminately "balanced" in this way. A more substantive contribution will perhaps demonstrate the uncanny aspect of the underlying problem.

In 1861, Wolfgang Helbig published an article entitled "Alkibiades als politischer Schriftsteller."[87] He argued on the basis of *The Constitution of the Athenians* 3.5 that its author was familiar with the smashing of the Herms in 415. Using evidence from Aristophanes as well as Thucydides, he reached the conclusion that this *oratio* was written between 415 and 413.[88] It did not occur to Helbig that the relevant verb is not "composed" but rather "set," which is to say that he has only discovered when we were to imagine it was spoken, not when it was written.[89] The structure of the article reveals the prejudices and blind spots of his article's own time of composition: only after a detailed historical account does Helbig reveal his remarkable conjecture that Alcibiades was the *Constitution*'s author.[90] In making this remarkabe claim, Helbig commits only the errors he shares with all of the scholars who took part in a long-running controversy. Having joined Johann Gottlob Schneider in claiming that Xenophon was not the *Constitution*'s author, the immediate problem for Wilhelm Roscher and those who followed him was to determine who was.[91]

Gradually this problem gave way to another and ostensibly more tractable question: *When* was it written? and it was with this question that a long series of German philologists would struggle. Since the proof that Xenophon wasn't its author depended on the alleged author's alleged ignorance of some combination of later historical developments—Schneider himself had used Xenophon's own testimony about the Thirty to get the ball rolling—the identity of *der Verfasser* could in any case only be determined by first determining who *could* have written it, and that required determining its *Abfassungszeit* or "time of composition." Both of these elements vitiate Helbig's otherwise brilliant conjecture: Alcibiades must have *written* the speech, and must have *composed* it c. 414, while he was explaining his betrayal of Athens in Sparta along with his previous loyalty to her. A simple paradigm shift is all that's required to separate the grain from the chaff where Helbig is concerned: Xenophon *set* the speech in Sparta, supplied enough information to date the speech's *delivery* to c. 414, and supplied sufficient information to allow a reader of Thucydides who was not blinded by the assumption that any given speech's author and its speaker are necessarily one and the same to recognize its *speaker* as Alcibiades. Nor should "his" purpose be concealed: it is because Athens cannot be praised that Alcibiades can justify betraying her; it is on the basis of the universal rationality of self-preservation that he can justify both that betrayal *and* his former loyalty (*Ath. pol.* 2.20). The remarkable combination of praise and blame for Athens is evident;[92] what has been overlooked is the possibility that its speaker's only consistent interest is justifying his own pursuit of self-preservation.

Outside the *Constitution of the Athenians*, there are three passages that are most relevant to the hypothesis that Xenophon has written a speech for Alcibiades to supplement the one Thucydides had already written. The first of these is the speech of Alcibiades in Thucydides: "As for democracy, the men of sense among us knew what it was, and I perhaps as well as any, as I have the more cause to complain of it; but there is nothing new [οὐδὲν καινόν] to be said of a patent absurdity—meanwhile we did not think it safe to alter it under the pressure of your hostility."[93]

Considered as a reconstruction of what Thucydides did not allow us to hear—i.e., the *oratio* Alcibiades gave in private to persuade a single influential Spartan to allow him to make his public speech[94]—Xenophon's artful *Constitution of the Athenians* gives the lie, gracefully and respectfully, to his predecessor's οὐδὲν καινόν. Xenophon's Alcibiades will now demonstrate—albeit in an equally self-serving way—something new: that there is method in Athenian madness, and that what appears to the other Greeks to be thoughtless or ἄνοια, they do with forethought (*Ath. pol.* 1.11 and 3.10). In private, Xenophon's Alcibiades justifies his support of Athens more honestly: there, he readily admits that having chosen to live in Athens, he prepared himself to do injustice (*Ath. pol.* 2.20). But he also saves face by saying nothing to the effect that he cooperated with preserving Athens, only that Athens behaved rationally in preserving itself.

This creates a link to the second relevant passage in *Hellenica*, where Xenophon summarizes the views of those who supported Alcibiades' return to power (*Hell.* 1.4.13–16). Crucial to that defense is the claim that Alcibiades had never been in favor of revolutionary change (*Hell.* 1.4.16); it is, rather, his *inability* to do so that Alcibiades will emphasize in Sparta. The most outrageous claim made by his Athenian apologists is that Alcibiades was compelled, like a slave, to serve the enemies of Athens (*Hell.* 1.4.15), and despite the mendacity and necessary wordiness of the prior defense in comparison with the succinct condemnation that follows it (*Hell.* 1.4.17), it has remained possible to imagine that Xenophon too is apologizing for Alcibiades. If it were not for the uncanny personal connection between Xenophon's future—for if he was the author of this fictionalized *oratio*, he probably wrote it in tandem with *Hellenica* I—and Alcibiades' past, it might be thought to counteract this view. In any case, it seems likely that he wrote his *Constitution of the Athenians* not only to demonstrate his own skill as a rhetor and historian but more importantly to reveal the man himself, illuminating as morally bankrupt the self-preserving and allegedly blameless wellspring of all his actions. And here again, we touch on a problem and a mystery, not a clear-cut solution.

An indication that Xenophon's *Constitution of the Athenians* was designed to complement his *Hellenica* is the curious fact that Alcibiades is never given the chance to deliver a speech in the latter. But this scarcely proves that Xenophon was incapable of putting words into the mouth of Alcibiades. The third relevant passage is the dialogue between Alcibiades and Pericles in *Memorabilia* 1.2.40–46. Here there can be no doubt: Xenophon has depicted Alcibiades making a first-person address in private to a single auditor, and he has done so in the context of exculpating Socrates for the subsequent misdeeds of Alcibiades. For his interlocutor Pericles, obedience to Athenian law is justice; he takes the intrinsic excellence of the democratic regime for granted. Alcibiades does not. Athenian democracy can, of course, be justified on the same basis that any regime can be justified: it serves itself well. It is therefore noteworthy that Hartvig Frisch, an able defender of an early date for pseudo-Xenophon—and who would thereby make it impossible for Alcibiades to be its speaker—ably illustrates the continuity between what Alcibiades says in the dialogue with Pericles and what pseudo-Xenophon says in *Constitution of the Athenians*.[95] Frisch's goal is to demonstrate the influence of Protagoras on pseudo-Xenophon;[96] Plato had long since demonstrated that Alcibiades sought out the sophist, attended to his discourses, and imitated him.[97]

Frisch provides convincing evidence for the modified form of Helbig's thesis on offer here, all the more remarkable since he can offer no support for the chronology demanded by what I will call "the Alcibiades Conjecture"; this makes the evidence he does provide for it all the more valuable. His comment on Helbig sets the stage: "Wolfgang Helbig, on the basis of a very complicated argumentation, according to which there was no oligarchic party in Athens before the year 415, has tried to prove that the treatise must have been written after 415, but before 413, and in Alcibiades finds the man who may have been the author, the double tendency of the treatise being explained by Alcibiades' sudden change from one extreme to the other."[98] "In the same section of his book ("Sophistic and Sociology") where Frisch connects the author to Protagorean influence, that he pens his most penetrating observation about "the double tendency of the treatise."

> Thus two souls seem to be fighting in the author's breast, the one which is idealistic and ethical, is seated in his emotional life and finds vent in all the terms of abuse directed against the Athenians and the people, the other, seated in his reason, is realistic and materialistic, and from that all the arguments originate.[99]

This brilliant analysis lends more support to the Alcibiades Conjecture that the aggregate of Frisch's many arguments for a pre-431 date of composition detracts from it. For if Frisch is right, to whom do these words apply more fittingly than to Alcibiades? It is to the drunken speech of Plato's Alcibiades in *Symposium* that these words most obviously apply; the fact that Frisch has disinterred the same findings from what he continues to regard as a treatise and not a speech testifies to Xenophon's artistry. It is by no means easy to capture someone else's "double tendency" or to place in another's mouth the evidence that "two souls seem to be fighting" in the *speaker's* breast. Frisch thinks he is uncovering the psychological cross-purposes of which the *author* is unaware, but that lack of personal awareness becomes artistic mastery when the necessary substitution is made in the following: "[T]he alteration between the absolute and the relative appears by close examination of the treatise to be fundamental to the author's psyche."[100]

As a result, the simplest substitution of all should be applied to the section of Frisch's brilliant book called "The Author's Person,"[101] for here, all that is necessary is to replace "person" with "persona." He begins with an observation that would otherwise seem banal: "[A] striking feature of Pseudo-Xenophon is his self-confidence."[102] But in tandem with his "double tendency" and "two souls," this observation points again to the author's artistry, for to depict the same persona as both self-assured and confused is difficult, and once again it is the creator of Callicles who comes to mind as capable of doing so in Attic prose, not the "Old Oligarch."[103] But Frisch's most insightful observation about the author's person (or persona) places him "between two extremes, the wise reasoner and the traitor to his country."[104] If not to Xenophon in the fourth century, then to whom does this amazing combination apply better than to Alcibiades in the fifth? Instead of conjuring up "a third person" of whom we know nothing, would it not be more reasonable to synthesize the two in a person we know all too well? The renegade follower of Socrates accounts for Frisch's "wise reasoner," Thucydides has immortalized the traitor, but Xenophon has shown how Alcibiades was both. But the mystery remains: If it is impossible that Xenophon was already defending his future actions, how are we to understand the uncanny parallels between the two?

However mysterious on a spiritual level, the recovery of Xenophon's *Constitution of the Athenians* helps to clear up the dilemma at the center of his "Tale of Two Cities." It was the tradition's misplaced certainty that Xenophon was himself an oligarch that is at least partly responsible for the exclusive attention that has been given to the *author* of the *oratio*, not its speaker. Frisch, for example, has no doubts that the author is "a sincere oligarch,"[105] and when we assume that Xenophon was an oligarch himself, that is sufficient to explain why *Constitution of the Athenians* was erroneously preserved among his works. Nothing could more effectively prevent making a distinction between an author and his merely literary persona than the misplaced certainty that Xenophon shared the views of its author: there would have been no "Old Oligarch" if earlier scholars had been less certain that Xenophon was a young one. The tradition's principal error was not to ascribe *Constitution of the Athenians* to Xenophon erroneously but its ongoing failure to discriminate its first-person speaker from Xenophon the author. Long before historians began to grapple with the authenticity question, the damage had already been done: there was already a critical mass of unselfconscious certainty concerning the Sparta-loving Xenophon that the tradition thought it knew. This certainty was sufficient to ensure that they would begin by asking the wrong question, and therefore would get the wrong answers. And at the risk of resolving the unresolvable, it would be better to recognize that while Alcibiades was the real traitor to Athens, Xenophon's *Constitution of the Athenians* not only illuminated the moral rot that justified his treason but would later explain his own.

Constitution of the Athenians may perhaps have been Xenophon's earliest work but *Ways and Means* was certainly his last,[106] and it was here that he showed his love and perhaps his repentance.[107] Because of Xenophon's detailed proposals for Athenian fiscal reforms, Whitehead must repeatedly cite parallel passages in Demosthenes, and indeed the short text bridges the distance between Thucydides and Demosthenes, just as *Hellenica* might be said to do. But it is another Athenian orator who plays the most important supporting role in *Poroi*: in the section of the Introduction devoted to "Delayed Impact," Whitehead shows that it was Lycurgus upon whom Xenophon's proposals would have the greatest impact.[108] Our primary source for Lycurgus' fiscal reforms is [Plutarch], *Lives of the Ten Orators*, and it is there we learn that Lycurgus was Plato's student at the Academy.[109] The link between Xenophon and Lycurgus suggests the need to make a sharp distinction within the so-called Old Academy between Plato's own Academy and its post-Chaeronea descendent. To state clearly an underlying theme of this work: we would understand Plato better if we paid more regard to what we can learn about him from Xenophon rather than from Aristotle. For the Stagirite, the victory of Philip of Macedon represented something entirely different from what it would have meant to Plato and Xenophon, for both of them, along with Athens herself, were defeated with Demosthenes.[110]

Order of Composition

The tripartite division of Plato's literary activity, no matter how detrimental to a pedagogical interpretation of his dialogues, is appropriately applied to Xenophon. Since the last section ended with *Ways and Means*, this one will work its way backward from there (as an aid, see "Table: Order of Composition"). As befits the latest stage of an author's life, the revision and completion of his longest works belongs to his third or "late" period. As already mentioned, by dating the *composition* of his longest works to the latest identifiable date mentioned in them has tended to make the last decade of Xenophon's long life the busiest, and implausibly so. As anyone who has written a multivolume work knows, especially when that work has appeared in discrete installments, there is an imperious necessity to revise if not rewrite, to polish individual passages, and to smooth away the rough edges of any transitions. It was this kind of care that Xenophon will here be presumed to have given all of his longer works in his last years, whether in Corinth or Athens, whether in the early 350s or in the previous decade. In short, it was the completion, but not the composition, of *Memorabilia*, *Anabasis*, *Hellenica*, and *Cyropaedia* that constituted his principal literary activity during this period.

This is not to say that there were no fresh compositions in his late period. Even in the case of his longer works, it was now that he wrote *Cyropaedia* 8.8,[111] finished *Hellenica* III, and possibly wrote and integrated *Memorabilia* 3; he might also have added the obituary of Cyrus to the *Anabasis* here as well. As for entirely fresh composition, it is clear that *Agesilaus* and *Ways and Means* were written in the very last years of his life; it may well be the case that *Hiero* was conceived and executed here as well, probably just before writing the last chapter of *The Education of Cyrus*. The reason I am tentatively inclined to place the dialectical sections of the *Memorabilia* in this latest period is because of the likewise highly dialectical approach visible in "the merely apparent" praise for Cyrus the Great, *Agesilaus*, and tyranny in *Hiero*. But the dating of *Memorabila* 3.8–9 must remain a mystery until the end. So much, then, for what can plausibly be suggested about the last phase of Xenophon's "late" period.

But since it is convenient to consider the years at Skillus as his middle period, the late period was not confined to the foregoing activities of his last years, and it may therefore be convenient to divide the third phase into two parts, of which only the second has now been sketched. And it is in consideration of this longer and earlier part of Xenophon's "late" activities that an olive branch can be extended to the proponents of those who want to fill to the brim his last seven years (362–355). It is rather between 371 and 362 that we can plausibly imagine Xenophon writing in this concentrated way. Although I have suggested that there was an *Ur-Kyrupädie* conceived for oral delivery already germinating in Skillus, the writing of at least the last six books probably belongs to the late period. And although he might have begun *Hellenica* III in Skillus, it was only after the Spartan defeat at Leuctra that the retributive contours of a story about Sparta's self-caused overthrow could have taken shape. As a result, it seems likely that the composition of a considerable part

Table 3.1. Order of Composition

Birth of Xenophon
Birth of Plato
415: Sicilian Expedition
"First Literary Period"
Cynegeticus
Death of Thucydides
Constitution of the Athenians
Hellenica I (bks. 1-2)
401: Xenophon leaves Athens
Memoranda for *Anabasis* I
400: "The Sea! The Sea!"
Anabasis I (bks. 1-4)
399: Death of Socrates
Xenophon's *Apology*
Plato's *Apology*
Memoranda for *Anabasis* II
393: Polycrates
Crito
Memorabilia I (c. bks. 1 and 4)
Gorgias
Xenophon's *Symposium*
Memoranda for *Hellenica* II
Anabasis II (bks. 5-7, not including Skillus)
Plato's First Sicilian Expedition
c. 387: Foundation of the Academy
Alcibiades Major
"Second" or "Middle Literary Period"
Birth of Gryllus and Diodorus
387: Xenophon in Skillus
386: King's Peace
384: Birth of Aristotle and Demosthenes
Hellenica II (bks. 2-5.1)
Plato's *Symposium, Menexenus,* and *Protagoras*
Oeconomicus
Meno
Cyropaedia I (oral stories)
Memorabilia II (c. bk. 2)
Anabasis III (Skillus and Cyrus Obituary added)
Republic 1-2
Cyropaedia II

continued on next page

182 | The Relay Race of Virtue

Table 3.1. Continued

Republic 3–10
Cyropaedia II
371: Leuctra; Xenophon leaves Skillus
"Third Literary Period"
Constitution of the Spartans I
Memoranda for *Hellenica* III
367: Plato's Second Sicilian Expedition
Hiero
Sophist-Statesman
362: Mantinaea
The Cavalry Officer
Memorabilia III (c. bk. 3)
Hippias Major
Hellenica III
Laws
Cyropaedia III
Constitution of the Spartans II
Epinomis
On Horsemanship
Agesilaus
Ways and Means
355: Death of Xenophon
347: Death of Plato

of *Hellenica* 5 and all of 6–7 belong to the first part of his later period, along with at least *Cyropaedia* 3–8.

Nor should we imagine that Xenophon composed no "minor writings" at this time, and although he might only have added the critical penultimate chapter of *The Constitution of the Spartans* after Leuctra, it may well be the case that the whole of it was written later, especially since Delebecque's approach to the problem fails to persuade. Incidentally, Delebecque appended a useful chronology to his *Vie de Xénophon* to which the skeptical reader may be referred,[112] and with reference to it I will only say that his conclusions are no less speculative than mine. In fact, the principal difference is that only his are presented as "conclusions," and mine as what I can only hope is informed speculation. In other words, if I have failed to make it crystal clear that the mood of this section—and its "Table" in particular—is self-consciously tentative, now is a good place to do so. Years of studying Plato has filled me with doubts about not only the interpretive value of the periodization of his dialogues but also about its accuracy; it is only with Xenophon's help that we can establish a few actual dates, as for example in the case of *Meno* or *Menexenus*. The fact that we are in a far better position in Xenophon's case, and yet *even here* are almost entirely in the realm of speculation, should hurl a backdraft of fiery uncertainty onto the elaborate structures built on the periodization of Plato's works.

But speculative though the periodization of Xenophon's writings may be, it creates the possibility for a more natural and respectful approach to imagining the order in which Plato's may have been written. Consider but one example from the forgoing: if all but the last chapter of Xenophon's *Cyropaedia* was written before 362, that gave Plato a full fifteen years in which to have written *Laws*, allegedly his last work. Among the two facts about the *Abfassungszeit* of *Laws* that we actually know—we have merely assumed that we know something about it on the basis of the "some say" in Diogenes Laertius—is that *Laws* 3 was written after *The Education of Cyrus* had become available and that with respect to *Republic* Aristotle was right to refer to "the later-written *Laws*."[113] Neither of those facts entitles us to certainty that *Laws* was his *last*-written work, and with the evaporation of that certainty the scientific claim of stylometric analysis is put at risk. In Plato's case, indeed, we have the testimony of Dionysius of Halicarnassus to the effect that it was Plato's dialogues as a whole on which he was working until the end, not on the longest, least dramatic, and downright ponderous of them. But if written in reply to *Cyropaedia*—as we know for a fact *Laws* 3 was—and in the same spirit as the work to which it responded, it not only looks less "last," but more dramatic and less ponderous as well.

This, of course, is only one example. Throughout this book, an effort is being made to illuminate the dialogue between Xenophon and Plato, and although its principal purpose—to illuminate the underappreciated extent of Plato's debts to Xenophon—will only be essayed in the following chapter, it should already be obvious that a side effect of this project is to peg, however cautiously, the periodization of Plato's writings onto this dialogue. It is not only a more natural and respectful approach, it is a more human and Socratic one as well, or so at least I hope to show. But it is also an almost completely unintended consequence of the Socratic and human aim at the project's heart: the claim that the two greatest Socratics cooperated in a fruitful, playful, and utterly respectful manner—respectful, that is, both to Socrates and to each other as per the epigraph—to keep him alive, in all his dialectical and ironic complexity. It is this complexity that the conventional approach to periodization ignores, configuring it as changes of mind, best explained by order of composition and intellectual development. When the writings of both are reconsidered as elements of an ongoing conversation, the dialectical complexity suggests dialogue without denying development, yet highlights inspiring provocations rather than changes of mind. In a word, perhaps we are looking for "the historical Socrates" in the wrong place, and would do better to seek him within the living dialogue between his two most prolific and impressive followers, indeed as the leaven of dialectical playfulness that lightens their ongoing conversation.

Before turning to Xenophon's "middle period," some remarks about *On Horsemanship* and *The Cavalry Officer* will serve to better indicate the boundary ostensibly dividing his "late" from "middle period" writings. As equestrians know, Xenophon's *On Horsemanship* has aged remarkably well; as a result, it stands out among his writings for maintaining its practical purpose far longer than any of his other books. Naturally Xenophon, like any author worth her salt, wanted to survive and to attain what we would call "classic" status. But what explains the actual attainment? Is it, for example, merely chance that has created the practical longevity of *On Horsemanship* or are there any authorial intentions at work? The back-reference to *The Cavalry Officer* is telling here. Clearly, Xenophon taught his boys to ride, and thus the original form of the treatise was oral, and doubtless delivered at Skillus if not before. Logically prior to *The Cavalry Officer*, the treatise on riding would seem—except for that back-reference, which one might claim could easily have been added later—to be prior in composition as well. Instead of placing rustic writings in a rustic setting, I would suggest that *On Horsemanship* was indeed one of Xenophon's latest writings, designed by him to attain the status it has attained: not only to surpass the efforts of Simon (*Eq.* 1.1) but to be the definitive work in the field into eternity.

And this touches on a deeper matter. As indicated by the remark in his early *Cynegeticus*, Xenophon strove for literary immortality from the beginning, and as the last phase of this section will try to demonstrate, his youthful works were both precocious and impressive. Although his lack of arrogance was already implied by his relationship with Thucydides, it was a real test of character that Plato was about to give him: despite his own numerous innovations and excellences as a writer of Socratic dialogue, it cannot have been easy to see himself repeatedly surpassed not only by the greatest literary master of Attic prose among his contemporaries, but by one of the greatest thinkers and writers of all times. Although a defense of this "cannot have been easy"—which implies, of course, that Xenophon was ultimately able "to do the difficult"—must necessarily form the denouement of this book as a whole, it is already sufficient to justify a late date for *On Horsemanship*. Xenophon remained true to his ambition to survive, and the decision to record for eternity things what many of his contemporaries already knew, makes him the equivalent of one of us writing a book today about, say, driving a car, that makes no assumption that its readers—dwelling in a future that had made this mode of transportation obsolete and even unimaginable—would have any clear notion of what "speedometer," "changing lanes," or "downshift" mean. *On Horsemanship* is a classic because Xenophon, in his twilight years, intended it to be one, and here there was certainty: neither Plato nor anyone else was going to surpass him in this area. This can explain why Xenophon looks back on *The Cavalry Officer* at the end of *On Horsemanship*.

It would likewise be easy to imagine that Xenophon wrote *The Cavalry Officer* to prepare Gryllus for command, a hypothesis that would place its time of composition close to the imaginary dividing line between "late middle" or "early late." Diogenes Laertius preserved the anecdote that made Xenophon appear indifferent to his son's death, but what if *The Cavalry Officer* were written later, with Gryllus' death in mind? This would explain why a book dedicated to hardheaded military science and stratagem ends with the gods. What else could explain to a grieving father, himself the survivor of so many battles, why his beloved son had been killed in his first? Promising material for an officer though he was, there is no evidence that Gryllus was one at the time of his death, and he certainly was not in command of the Athenian cavalry. If he had been, *The Cavalry Officer* could not have been a memorial, for then its message would have been: "If my son had known all this, he'd still be alive." Rather, "If my son's commander had known all this, then not only would *he* would have been successful, but Gryllus would have lived to give me another little Xenophon, so I could teach *him* how to ride." Along with *Memoribilia* 3.5 and *Ways and Means*, *The Cavalry Officer* contains the most practical and patriotic advice Xenophon would give to Athens, having already given her something far more precious. Weak though the standard arguments for a late 3.5 may be,[114] considered in tandem with a post-Mantinaea *Cavalry Officer* and a necessarily late *Ways and Means*, stronger ones can be imagined. Service to the fatherland and the sacrifice of his son may have become inextricably linked for the father of Gryllus, and even though *On Horsemanship* contains no chronological evidence of the usual kind, there is some reason to imagine it as Xenophon's last work, and thus indeed (cf. ἐπειδή below) as later than the latest:

> Since [ἐπειδή is the first word of the treatise] we suppose that we have become experienced in horsemanship because we happened to have been in the cavalry for a long time, we also wished to clarify for the younger of our friends [καὶ τοῖς νεωτέροις τῶν φίλων] how we believe they would behave most correctly with horses.[115]

In this light, *we* are Xenophon's friends, and he wrote *for our children*. My father recommended "The Retreat of the Ten Thousand" to me as a boy; I imagined at the time I had something better to read.

Delebecque devotes three chapters to the years in Skillus, and this creates a tripartite division *within* the middle part of my own. His central chapter locates the composition of *Hellenica* II in the middle of this middle period (379-78); the two flanking chapters describe respectively an "early middle" (388-379) and a "late middle" period (377-71). What makes this tripartite division useful is that it can be better applied to Xenophon's "early" period, with which this section will conclude, it being the most complex. Delebecque, by contrast, regards only two works as having been written pre-Skillus: *Hellenica* I before he left Athens, and *Cynegeticus* while he was, as it were, "on the road" (394-388); this notion will likewise prove useful. In general, Delebecque's "early middle" period becomes very busy, and to it he assigns the composition of *The Constitution of the Spartans*, *Anabasis* as a unity (excepting only the Skillus passage), and the following among the Socratic writings: the redaction of the *Apology of Socrates*, *Memorabilia* I-II, and *Oeconomicus* I (up to the entrance of Ischomachus). He places the composition of *On Horsemanship* here as well. Guiding and vitiating his account is an ongoing reliance on the axiom of Literary Rivalry, and he notes without refuting the position of von Arnim with regard to the priority of Xenophon's *Apology*.[116] An examination of Delebecque's text should in any case satisfy the reader that anyone who attempts to reconstruct Xenophon's life on the basis of his writings—and that means anyone who tries to reconstruct his life—will necessarily incur a critic's contempt, thanks to the curious mixture of informed insight and pure speculation that such a project inevitably entails.[117]

Despite a huge difference with regard to *Symposium*—Delebecque places it in Xenophon's "late" period while I regard it as either "late early" or "early middle"—there is also considerable overlap. Xenophon very probably did compose *Hellenica* II in Skillus, and if not *Anabasis* I, it was at least *Anabasis* II that he did write here. Since I don't divide *Oeconomicus* in two—locating the composition of its second part in Athens since it is so conspicuously set there—the whole of it can be assigned to this period on the basis of Xenophon's contemporaneous agricultural activities. The fact that he was now raising children justifies dating the composition of *Memorabilia* II to this period, especially on the basis of the immortal 2.2. And the need to educate his sons (and entertain Philesia) connects at the very least the oral origins of *Cyropaedia* to this happy and tranquil interlude. It is easy to imagine Xenophon, finally possessed of ample leisure, now finally able to indulge his literary pursuits.

But such an image obscures some basic facts. To begin with, Greek warfare was largely a seasonal affair, leaving the writer-warrior ample time for reflection and composition quite apart from the well-documented periods of bored inactivity that mark and indeed dominate any professional soldier's life. In other words, the literary activities of the "middle" and "late" periods can be lessened considerably by imagining a scribbling soldier, dreaming of happier times at home, as responsible for Xenophon's delightful *Symposium*. But it is equally misguided to connect long stretches of leisure to feverish literary activity. Despite what was probably by our standards the unconscionably small role the typical Greek father played in his children's upbringing, there was still plenty of actual *living* that needed to be done in Skillus, and Xenophon's pedagogical bent tends to suggest that as a father he was anything but typical. Less controversially, however, he was happy and at peace, and this kind of leisurely tranquility is less suitable to literary activity than those who are not writers may imagine. The best writing is often snatched from life, and it is revealing that so many writers have had unsatisfactory personal lives. Anyone who doubts that Xenophon was a good father, showering his sons with playful instruction and rigorous practice, has missed something basic about him.

Rather than Delebecque's tripartite division of the middle period, I would divide it in two, allowing Xenophon's encounter with "almost the first two books" of Plato's *Republic* to make the division. After it, he went to work on *Cyropaedia*; before it, he wrote the rest, most likely in harmony with the equally dispositive seasons of a farmer's life. With the memoranda for *Memorabilia* II and *Anabasis* II already written, they could have been finished quickly and easily. With *Oeconomicus* as a whole conceived as contemporaneous with Xenophon's self-education in farming and therefore early middle, it was primarily the second book of *Memorabilia* that broke new ground thereafter in a literary sense. But Plato entered the story once again, and as a result, much depends on the date he composed *Republic*.

Unfortunately, this is a subject of which we know next door to nothing. While remarking that it "took a long time to write," and that the prevailing view at present is that it was finished c. 374, the ever-judicious Guthrie quoted Auguste Diés (1875–1958): "All of these dates are conjectural and are offered as such."[118] Taking into consideration both this "long time to write" and Gellius' "almost two books," we can plausibly place the fateful encounter that caused Xenophon to begin recasting his bedtime stories into the form of a Plato-rivaling *magnum opus* in the neighborhood of 380, and that would leave nine more years in Skillus for Xenophon to plough ahead with a project that operated on several different levels ranging from delighting his family with a straightforward adventure story that combined action and romance, with the creation of an unreliable narrator showering with the gilding of heroism a technician of injustice who made Thrasymachus' shepherd look like a tyro. As for how long it took him to do so, there is no compelling reason to think it required substantially more time to complete the eight books of *The Education of Cyrus* than it took Plato to write the last eight books of his *Republic*. It does, however, seem a bit too neat to imagine Xenophon as having completed it before being uprooted from Skillus in 371.

In 371, Xenophon still had around sixteen years of life left; Plato had some twenty-four. But both were already old, closer to sixty than fifty. The great adventure of Plato's life lay before him; he would travel to Sicily a second time around 367;[119] Xenophon's adventures belonged to his past. If we are looking for rivalry, it would be sensible to imagine Plato and Isocrates as rival schoolmasters; if we want to find someone with the audacity, acumen, or poor taste of trying to rival Plato as a philosopher and writer, we will need to wait for Aristotle to grow up. Aristotle would enter the Academy at seventeen in 367; the future orator and statesman Lycurgus had probably left it by the time Xenophon removed from Skillus. If Gryllus was twenty in 362, he was eleven in 371; Aristotle was only two years his senior, and thus in his early twenties when he wrote his *Gryllus*, in memory of his teacher's friend and possibly his own.[120] To imagine a lively dialogue between Plato and Aristotle at that time requires one to imagine an Athenian of sixty-five on intimate terms with a Stagirite of twenty-two; this seems trebly unlikely given their age difference, the Athenian pride of the one, the provincial parochialism of the other, and the fact that Plato had many promising Athenian students, all better suited in the decisive respect for doing some good to their πόλις πατρία.[121]

Naturally, very few would dare to speak seriously of Plato's debts to Aristotle, although I've met more than one scholar who has suggested as much after a beer or two. But even those who would never go so far in print are members of a much larger legion of scholars who have paid Aristotle the compliment of reading Plato through his eyes, especially on the basis of his description of Socrates. If we think we know that Socrates sought to *define* the virtues, configured those virtues (incorrectly) as so many forms of knowledge, regarded knowledge as impervious to being "overcome by pleasure," and while seeking "the universal," yet did not separate the Forms, we are reading Plato through Aristotle's eyes while cutting his dialogues in two. It is by no means clear that Plato's Socrates did any of things, unless, that is, we are willing to follow Aristotle in granting the status of an imperiously unquestionable canonicity to what Socrates might seem to be claiming in *Protagoras*.[122] In Xenophon's case, there is at least the chronological possibility of Plato's debts to him, and since *Memorabilia* 3.9.4–5 provides a sounder basis for Aristotle's Socrates than does anything in *Protagoras*, Aristotle's debts to Xenophon deserve more consideration than our understanding of Plato's "early" Socrates should be willing to accord Aristotle's testimony.[123]

To return to the subject at hand, it is not Xenophon's "middle" but rather his "early" period that most deserves a tripartite division. The first of these ended with his departure for Asia, the second followed his reaching the Sea and extended until he got ahold of Polycrates' Anytus-borne slander, most likely published in 393, and the third lasted until he settled in Skillus. Since Delebecque is everywhere the most provocative pioneer, the salient differences can be indicated economically by his competing claims that *Cynegeticus* belongs in the third of these three "early" periods and the oldest part of *Memorabilia* was written in Skillus. By contrast, and following von Arnim, I am placing *Memorabilia* I in that third phase of the "early" period and, in accordance with stylometric analysis, placing *Cynegeticus* in the first. As for the middle "early" period, the characteristic work is *Apology of Socrates*, written (1) after a series of attacks on

Socrates that emphasized his own responsibility for his condemnation had appeared, (2) after Xenophon had gotten firsthand information from Hermogenes, whether in Athens or elsewhere, (3) before Plato had written his *Apology*, and (4) before Polycrates had written his speech "for Anytus." This middle period—the Socratic phase of which extends from 399 to 393—is completely devoid of production for Delebecque. And since this phase as whole begins shortly after θάλαττα θάλαττα, it is particularly important because it was here that the *Anabasis* I appeared under its famous pseudonym.

The "late early" period laid the foundation for the Socratic relay race that will increasingly become this book's focus in its last two chapters. That race had begun with Plato's *Apology* as a response to Xenophon's, but it took its characteristic form only thereafter. In *Memorabilia* I, and especially in 4.2, Xenophon poured his personal experience into the shape of a thorough and multidimensional defense of Socrates. In one fell swoop, Xenophon revolutionized Socratic literature, and if any written dialogues preceded those he stitched together in *Memorabilia* I—and especially in 4.2—they have been lost and forgotten. Defying current orthodoxy while relying on Diogenes Laertius, I see no reason to doubt that Xenophon was πρῶτος. But even if he wasn't—even if Antisthenes or Aristippus or someone else deserves the credit for writing the first and lost Socratic dialogues—he was still prior to Plato; to deny this is simply to shred Diogenes' testimony when it suits current caprice. Xenophon ran the first leg of the Socratic relay race but Plato was about to run his so beautifully that we would eventually forget that he stood on the shoulders of a giant, or rather, to avoid mixing metaphors, that—thanks to Xenophon—he had already been given a very comfortable lead over the Socrates-haters when he took the baton.

Plato's *Crito* could be considered with equal merit Plato's response to Xenophon's *Apology* or to Polycrates' *Speech of Anytus*, so why not both? Any Socratic had to respond to Polycrates, and Plato didn't need to wait for Xenophon's response to offer his. While the Kapp-Kahn school thought that *Gorgias* was his response, I would once again point to a double purpose: just as *Crito* was his response to both Xenophon's *Apology* and Polycrates, so too was his *Gorgias* a response to Polycrates and *Memorabilia* I. Grounding this configuration is Plato's awareness, later indicated by his reference to Euthydemus in his *Symposium*, that Xenophon had drawn on his own personal experience with Socrates in order to defend him in *Memorabilia* 4.2. This was something new, especially since Xenophon made it crystal clear in his *Apology* that he was not relying on his personal experience there. In *Gorgias*, Plato responded in kind, and with characteristically explosive and unsurpassable effect. Hence the following proposed order: Xenophon's *Apology*, Plato's *Apology*, Polycrates' *Anytus*, *Crito*, *Memorabilia* I, and *Gorgias*. And in response to the grimly polemical and utterly serious *ne plus ultra* of *Gorgias*, Xenophon gave one more completely original new direction to the Socratic dialogue—rivaling, but in any case, replicating, the originality that had created the genre in the first place—by mixing sex and humor in *Symposium*. By the time Plato had managed to create his characteristically brilliant response, his future seemed to be set, for *Symposium* pointed him back to *Protagoras* and forward to *Republic*. By this point, of course, Xenophon had moved from "late early" to "early middle," for it is doubtful that Plato would have written *Symposium* as he did unless he knew that *Hellenica* II was, at the very least, in the works.[124]

This leaves the first and earliest stage of Xenophon's "early period" for last, and that's how it should be. Consider first a parallel to the other book—besides Xenophon's *Anabasis*, that is—that seems to have been predestined for use in teaching Victorian and Edwardian Britons how to acquire an ancient tongue before World War I: Caesar's *De Bello Gallico*.[125] On the eve of World War II, Hermann Strasburger published *Caesars Eintritt in der Geschichte*, a slim monograph that would exercise a decisive influence on Ronald Syme, perhaps the greatest English historian of Rome since Edward Gibbon.[126] Strasburger used a razor if not wrecking ball to destroy the credibility of all the early stories about Caesar, and especially those that marked him out as a dangerous and subversive fellow from an early age; it was only when Caesar started writing his own story in Gaul, Strasburger dared to suggest, that he made his "entrance into history."[127] Albeit with no correspondingly ugly political intent—for a harmless Caesar is a danger to republics everywhere—it is easy to imagine Xenophon made his "entrance into history" in *Anabasis*, and of course in some sense this is true: only now, one might well think, did Xenophon himself begin saying and doing things that were worthy of historical record. But just as Strasburger tried to suppress the traces of an earlier Caesar, so too has the literary young man who was already an accomplished author before he wrote his immortal *Anabasis* tended to vanish from sight, not with the bang of a wrecking ball but simply from neglect masquerading as level-headed objectivity and appropriate distrust of historical legends and later tales.

Second only to the tradition's refusal to accord any respect to Diogenes' πρῶτος with respect to Xenophon's relationship to Socratic literature is its parallel neglect of his other claim about Xenophon's relationship to

Thucydides: "It is said that he also made famous the works of Thucydides, which remained unknown until then, and which he could have appropriated for his own purposes."[128] Despite a series of books and articles by Luciano Canfora,[129] the tremendous impact of Xenophon on Thucydides still tends to be ignored, and even the great Niebuhr (1776–1831), who took Diogenes' testimony seriously, dismissed Xenophon as "this old fool" even while claiming that publishing Thucydides "was the best action of his life."[130] It certainly was one of them. But Thucydides' greatness is obvious; it was, rather, Xenophon's willingness to facilitate his publication, uphold his legacy, and to continue his work, that demonstrates the kind of moral greatness Niebuhr failed to see. That he did this as a youngster is even more impressive, especially since his own ambitions were already visible in *Cynegeticus*.

Socrates famously wrote nothing, at least in the way of books, and the examples of him writing anything are few and far between, as in the case of the geometrical diagram in *Meno*. But in teaching Euthydemus about justice and injustice in *Memorabilia* 4.2, Socrates uses a moral diagram, divided into two columns. To begin with, the moral calculus by division will also figure prominently in 4.5, where the phrase "discoursing by kinds [διαλέγειν κατὰ γένη] (4.5.11) has been taken to indicate Xenophon's imperfect understand of "division [διαίρεσις]" as practiced by Plato's Eleatic Stranger.[131] But unlike the Stranger's, it is a method of division both practical—hence καὶ λόγῳ καὶ ἔργῳ—and moral, leading his companions "to prefer the good things and abstain from the bad ones." But the important point for now is that Socrates teaches Euthydemus, atypically, by the written word (*Mem.* 4.2.13–19). After all, the beautiful young man's most distinctive intellectual feature was his collection of books.[132]

Of the two, it is natural to imagine Plato as the more intellectual of the pair, and Xenophon as the horsy man of action—and indeed Socrates hunts for the book-loving Euthydemus in a rein-maker's shop (*Mem.* 4.2.1)—a bit slow, if sometimes well intentioned, and always susceptible, even in youth, to dismissal as "this old fool." It is therefore odd that when Plato recalls his own schooldays in *Lovers*, he makes the wrestler look like the dimwit.[133] Socrates goes easy on the athlete but humiliates his intellectual rival when the bright young man cannot sustain his view that philosophy is much-learning or πολυμαθία. It is near the intersection of *Lovers* and 4.2 that we should look for the young Xenophon, and discern in his high regard for Thucydides corroborating evidence for finding him in Euthydemus. It was as Thucydides' admirer that he both published and edited the great historian's literary remains;[134] it was as a budding literary talent in his own right that he exploited a gap in Thucydides' narrative in order to compose a fictional *oratio* for Alcibiades. It required a remarkable blend of imagination and historical knowledge to write *The Constitution of Athens*, and it was this blend that would resurface in *The Education of Cyrus*. There it would be Herodotus, not Thucydides, who would enable Xenophon to create the unreliable narrator of the *Cyropaedia*, and it should be obvious that the youngster had acquired the historian of Halicarnassus—standing as he does at the intersection of the poets and the sophists, or better, as the eighth of the seven σοφοί—as soon as his books became available.

But Xenophon's πολυμαθία cannot be ignored, and between *Cynegeticus* and *On Horsemanship*, he created a literary image of a distinctively Athenian εὐτράπηλος, the word enshrined in the Funeral Oration of Pericles meaning at once "*easily turning or changing,*" capable of acting "*dexterously, readily, without awkwardness,*" and "*ready with an answer or repartee, witty*" (LSJ). Even the less savory dimension of the word applies, since Xenophon could never have spoken for Alcibiades or Critias (*Hell.* 2.3.24–34), never have created his Cyrus or Simonides, and never have merely *appeared* to praise Agesilaus and Sparta, if he had not also been "*tricky, dishonest.*" The business of ordering his works chronologically, a project beset by the constant need for speculation and psychologizing, is nevertheless a better basis for ordering his works than finding in them a Reading Order, as the Academic Editor did and as I failed to do. At the end of the process, one discovers that it is not so much that Xenophon changed or that his thought "developed" but rather that—like a good Athenian—he continuously adapted dexterously to changed circumstances. But whether as an Athenian, a man, a soldier, a writer, a historian, or a philosopher, the best place to find him is *Memorabilia* 4.2, and it is not his fault if few have looked for him where he disclosed himself for what he really was: a Socratic.

Chapter Four

Plato's Debts to Xenophon

The Preserved Past

In considering the order in which Xenophon's writings have come down to us (see chapter 3, section 1), I claimed that Xenophon survived because Plato wanted him to do so. Hegel provided the beginning of an answer as to *why* Plato did so when he wrote: "When philosophy paints its gray in gray [*Grau in Grau*], then a configuration of life has grown old [*Gestalt des Lebens*], and cannot be rejuvenated by this gray in gray [*mit Grau in Grau*], but only understood; the Owl of Minerva takes flight only as the dusk begins to fall."[1] This famous statement applies well to Plato's philosophy once the Hellenic wheat has been separated from German chaff. To begin with the latter, it is obviously not "the Owl of Minerva" that is taking wing where Plato is concerned: his is the city sacred to γλαυκῶπις Ἀθήνη. And if "Minerva" is too Roman, then even one *Grau in Grau* is too German, let alone two of them. If Goethe's Mephisto was right to say: "Gray, dear friend, is every theory; green is life's golden tree [*Grau, teurer Freund, ist alle Theorie; Und grün des Lebens goldner Baum*],"[2] then Plato's dialogues are unquestionably on the green, not the gray side, and what makes them immortal is rather "life" than "theory."

But Hegel has hit on the truth despite those errors: Plato was writing in the Athenian twilight, and the Athens of his youth—the *Gestalt des Lebens* he so lovingly imitated and preserved—had not only grown old but was already dying, and with the Macedonian victory at Chaeronea just nine years after his own death, that *Gestalt des Lebens* would be dead. So much of Athens survives in Plato because Hegel was characteristically right: a way of life *had* grown old, and philosophy's ability to capture and preserve it depended on that fact. But Hegel was also characteristically wrong: since Plato was not painting *mit Grau in Grau* but with the verdant green of life itself, his philosophy did what Hegel denied that it could: his dialogues rejuvenated Athens, made her young and beautiful once again, as she had been, *and would now forever remain*, thanks to the immortal dialogues written by the Athenian who was best able to hear the wing-beats of Athena's owl.

Plato seems to have recognized from the start how useful to him Xenophon could be. Consider the following passage from his *Apology of Socrates*, arguably his first contribution to Socratic literature:

> My Antiochian tribe happened to be presiding over you when you decided to judge in a group the ten generals—they who had not picked up those from the naval battle [ἡ ναυμαχία]— illegally, as at a later time it seemed to all of you. At that time [τότε] I alone among the presidents opposed you, and voted in opposition to do nothing against the laws.[3]

Thanks to Xenophon, there was no need for Plato to mention "the Battle of Arginusae," for into eternity every reader would know that this is what ἡ ναυμαχία really means here. But the even more important word in this passage is τότε. Unlike Xenophon, who narrates his own personal opinions and explains his own indirect access to the speech in his *Apology of Socrates*, Plato makes us believe that we are there, actually hearing it. In a broader sense, the operative τότε for the reader is the putative "then" of Socrates' speech itself: we are looking back to an ancient past, made vivid by Plato's artistry, and imagining how things were *then*.

But when this literary Socrates himself uses the word τότε, he too is recalling a scene from the past, and he too will make a bygone "then" seem vivid, and indeed just as *present* as Plato is presently in the process of making Socrates "himself." It is this use of τότε that causes us to entirely forget the broader sense of that word described in the last paragraph: we take Socrates to be real because he is so believably talking about what happened way back *then*, at the time of Arginusae. On a literary level, it is a trick: by describing a past event vividly, a fictional character—himself merely a past event—becomes more real, for just as he is making real what happened to him τότε, so also do we accept uncritically the concealed τότε of the speech itself. But the trick can only work effectively if there is already a vividly described τότε for Plato's Socrates to describe, and thanks to Xenophon, there is one. Picking up Thucydides' self-consciously and explicitly immortal narrative shortly before the Battle of Arginusae, Xenophon has preserved the τότε to which Plato's Socrates now refers. In the two-and-a-half pages that John Burnet devoted to this passage in his classic commentary, he cites or mentions Xenophon eight times, beginning with the obvious and inevitable: "Xenophon gives a long account of the trial of the generals after the battle of Arginusae (406 B. C.) in the *Hellenica* (1.7.4 sqq.) but he is rather vague, as usual."[4]

Vague compared to what and to whom? Certainly not in comparison to Plato, who gives us only enough information to send us scurrying back to Xenophon for details. Now, it is perfectly fine for a modern historian to express discontent with the vagueness of those details, but when Burnet does so, he obscures the more important point: without Xenophon, this passage has no historical basis whatsoever, for it is *Hellenica* alone that makes Plato's τότε possible. In order to short-circuit this "alone," an objector must either posit Plato's reliance on the ghostly knowledge of "a contemporary reader," or—when it is acknowledged that he was writing for eternity—must imagine the existence of another but lost continuation of Thucydides. But thanks to the presence of Socrates in the only account that we can read rather than imagine (*Hell.* 1.7.15), written by a fellow Socratic and thus an actual rather than a merely posited "contemporary," it is impossible to imagine that anyone could have done so more effectively from Plato's perspective: Xenophon's account of Arginusae in *Hellenica* places Socrates exactly where Plato's *Apology* requires him to be in order to sustain the historicity of that τότε.

What is easier to imagine is what scholars would have done if instead of Xenophon we had either another source for the trial of the generals that did not mention Socrates or no source at all; in one case it would be Plato's opacity, in the other his veracity, that would have furnished a theme for scholarly criticism. Clearly, what interests Burnet is the historical accuracy of Xenophon's account, and Plato—whose account is far more than simply "rather vague"—is quickly lost to sight amid a discussion of Xenophon's other accounts of the trial in *Memorabilia* 1.1.18 and 4.4.2. In the first of these, Xenophon changes Plato's "ten" to "nine," and in both, he describes Socrates' role as "overseer [ἐπιστάτης]" of the presidency; since Socrates will refer to his role as ἐπιστάτης in *Gorgias* (*Grg.* 473e6), there is plenty of scope for source criticism here. But Burnet does not address the question of whether Plato could have consulted *Hellenica*, preferring to locate the source of Xenophon's erroneous claim that Socrates was an ἐπιστάτης to his misunderstanding of *Gorgias*, yet another example of the modern Priority axiom.

But neither Burnet nor anyone else can cite Xenophon's *Apology of Socrates* in this context because there is no mention in it of Arginusae and the subsequent trial. It is Plato who makes use of a vividly historical τότε, not Xenophon, and the irony is, of course, that it is Xenophon who is allowing Plato to do so. Thanks to the histories of Thucydides and Xenophon, Plato can make his portrait of Socrates' trial, and of Athens generally, immeasurably more vivid than Xenophon did. It is fair to say that Plato found more of value in Xenophon than Xenophon himself did; after all, Plato's *Crito* turns one moment in Xenophon's *Apology* into a fully self-contained and dramatically brilliant dialogue.[5] In any case, the reconstruction of the order in which Xenophon composed his writings makes good sense of what is happening here. Plato could make his *Apology* more vivid than Xenophon's because he incorporated historical information from *Hellenica* I; subsequently, Xenophon responded to Plato's "ten generals" in *Memorabilia* I upon which Plato humorously riffed in *Gorgias*; *Voilà la course de relais*.

Although this demonstration that Plato was already depending on Xenophon's preservation of the historical past in his *Apology* has been confined to his introductory reference to ἡ ναυμαχία, several other passages that follow it likewise refer to events described in *Hellenica* I, including the threat to prosecute Socrates (cf. *Ap*. 32b7–8 and *Hell*. 1.7.13), the shouts of the crowd (cf. *Ap*. 32b9 and *Hell*. 1.7.12), the possibility of imprisonment or death (cf. *Ap*. 32c2 and *Hell*. 1.7.13), and more generally the Thirty's later attempt to implicate Socrates in its crimes (*Ap*. 32c3–e1 and *Hell*. 2.3.39).[6] As a result, it is here that the single most important interpretive question confronting Plato's serious interpreters takes a more specific form: "At the time of writing his *Apology*, did Plato *already* intend to make it a possession for eternity?" Despite all the connections between Plato's *Apology* and *Hellenica* I, the thesis that Plato required Xenophon to survive in order to ensure that the historical background of his dialogues would remain forever intelligible is here at its most questionable and vulnerable point, and that for three good reasons. To be clear: although there are excellent reasons to think that Plato depended on both Thucydides and Xenophon to preserve the memory of the amazing τότε that formed the backdrop for Socrates' last thirty-odd years, it is by no means clear that the connections between *Apology* and *Hellenica* prove that *Plato was already aware* that he depended on Xenophon in this way when he wrote his *Apology*.

To begin with, if Plato's *Apology* was written between 399 and 393, (1) the memory of Arginusae was still green, and he could plausibly count on his readers to have no need for Xenophon's account in order to remind themselves of what had happened only ten years earlier. Hence, the modified question: Was Plato writing only for his contemporaries but *also already* for us? A good reason to think that he wasn't is (2) his age: he had only just begun to write about Socrates, and no matter how highly he may have thought of himself or anything else he may have written on other subjects, he was still a fledging and thus unlikely to have entertained any such grandiose thoughts as would have led him to conclude that it was because Xenophon's *Hellenica* was going to survive along with Thucydides that it was safe for him to fill his *Apology* with references to historical events that would soon be forgotten were they not already part of "the recorded past." It is therefore easy to see why it is far more plausible to think that he was not thinking along these lines. But it's not certain even if common sense assures us that it's likely. After all, it was already in *Cynegeticus* that Xenophon expressed *his* intent to offer instruction that would remain "irrefutable into eternity [ἀνεξέλεγκτα εἰς ἀεί]" (*Cyn.* 13.7) and there is no reason to imagine that Plato was any less ambitious, arrogant, or at any rate righteously self-assured of his literary value in his mid-thirties than Xenophon had already been some years before.

More important than his own youth is that (3) his Socratic project was unquestionably only in its infancy. It is only with the writing of *Symposium* that it can plausibly be claimed that a whole edifice built around it came clearly into view, while the Kapp-Kahn construction sets *Gorgias*, *Crito*, and *Apology* (along with *Ion* and *Hippias Minor*) apart because Plato has not yet conceived the project that will lead, through *Protagoras*, to "the dialogues of definition." It can plausibly be urged against any conception of an integrated Platonic Reading Order, especially when that conception is juxtaposed with "Plato's Development" and takes an agnostic position toward "Order of Composition," that it would have been impossible for Plato to realize at the start where he was already going to go. In the case of his *Apology*, the difference between these two positions comes into focus on ground least favorable to the notion that Plato was intent on creating a pedagogical κτῆμα εἰς ἀεί—indeed, a literary memorial of Pericles' "school of Hellas [τῆς Ἑλλάδος παίδευσις]"⁷—from the beginning. After all, the Academy did not yet exist, so even if Plato actually did come to consider his dialogues to be its "eternal curriculum," he is unlikely to have had that conception so early.

This plausible conclusion may be allowed to stand provided that the skeptic is equally prepared to acknowledge that if not already here, then at some later point, Plato arrived at a far grander conception. At this early stage, his dreams of literary immortality might well have been merely inchoate, but one fact blocks the view that they were not even that: the intersection of Plato's *Apology* and Xenophon's *Hellenica* I, and thus the whole question really comes back to Socrates' use of τότε. The purpose of this section is to demonstrate that Plato depended on Xenophon for contributing to the preservation of the recorded past, and the first of the two examples of that phenomenon it contains has now been described. But in defending the earlier example, another of Plato's debts to Xenophon comes into view, bringing to light the condition of the other's possibility. It is an indirect debt, however, and therefore not suitable for independent treatment. To put it simply: if Plato already imagined that he was creating a κτῆμα εἰς ἀεί, and that he already realized he needed Xenophon's *Hellenica* to make it so, it was Thucydides who was ultimately responsible for allowing him to do so.

The connection between Xenophon's early work in and around Thucydides and his own intent to offer observations—whether about sophists or hunting rabbits—that would be ἀνεξέλεγκτα εἰς ἀεί indicates that he was the first to realize that Thucydides had in fact created a κτῆμα εἰς ἀεί. Anyone who read both Thucydides' *History* and its Xenophontic continuation could console themselves for Athens' defeat with the certainty that the memory of Athenian greatness would never grow old, and that these historians had created, in Horace's phrase, a "memorial more permanent than bronze [*monumentum aere perennius*]." It was to the spirit of this creation that Plato was indebted, and the fact that this spirit affected and inspired him is simply the intersection of his *Apology* with *Hellenica* I. Xenophon must have been aware that if Thucydides was right, he too was assuring his own literary immortality by continuing the *History*. With that in mind, and in full view of the differences in literary quality and philosophical significance between Plato's *Apology* and Xenophon's, consider the following question: Did Plato refer to the τότε of Xenophon's *Hellenica* in order to likewise piggyback on Thucydides' κτῆμα εἰς ἀεί, or did the ambition to which Thucydides had already given classic expression inspire him to strive for literary immortality as well, subordinating the information now preserved by the two historians to an equally ambitious but vastly more important goal? That goal, of course, was to keep Socrates alive in a literary form.

The second example gains strength from the fact that it postdates the opening of the Academy, and thus can safely presuppose that Plato was by this point unquestionably aware that he had something valuable to teach and was now prepared to teach it. There is a sense in which each of Plato's dialogues might be described as "a school text,"[8] but as the ancient commentators seem to have realized, that phrase applies particularly well to *Alcibiades Major*. So deceptively elementary is Plato's *Alcibiades* that Delebecque dates its composition to before 396, making it earlier than his *Apology of Socrates* and *Crito*.[9] Quite apart from his unusual and refreshing certainty that *Alcibiades* is genuine, it is a particularly odd position for a Xenophon scholar to take given its reference to the reliable source of the story about the Queen's Sash (*Alc.1* 123b3–7), especially for Delebecque, who postpones the composition of *Anabasis* until Skillus. Since he is committed to Literary Rivalry, Delebecque cuts off the possibility that Plato's source was an oral communication from his friend Xenophon; he likewise does not embarrass himself by any defense of the chronology he proposes.

A more respectable chronology will place the composition of *Alcibiades Major* after *Anabasis* I, *Hellenica* I, and *Memorabilia* I, finding some historical details from the first two cited to give a historical turn to the first conversation between Socrates and Euthydemus in *Memorabilia* 4.2. As to a *terminus a quo*, one might propose the opening of the Academy, since only after writing this masterpiece of elementary pedagogy can Plato be easily imagined as having a text to teach beginners. It is somewhat painful to write this since throughout the five volumes of *Plato the Teacher*, I have taken an agnostic position on the composition of *Alcibiades Major* in particular.[10] For the present, however, it suffices to emphasize the difference between *Alcibiades Major* and Plato's *Apology* in relation to the information from Xenophon that we encounter in both. In the earlier case of Arginusae, it is plausible that Plato was writing only for his contemporaries while engaging in the same literary controversy that had already led to Xenophon's *Apology* (and its antecedents) and would soon lead to Polycrates. Here, if anywhere, Plato can be imagined as nothing more than a controversialist, with no pretensions to immortality, and dependent not on Xenophon but on the memories of his intended audience.

But whether or not it was written between 393 and 387, *Alcibiades Major* is not vulnerable to the foregoing analysis, and perhaps that in part explains why it continues to be regarded as inauthentic. It would be difficult to decide whether there is greater opposition to the authenticity of *Alcibiades*, to the notion that Plato used his dialogues to teach in the Academy, or that he intended them to survive forever and thus to teach us rather than only his contemporaries. The important point is that a positive answer to the first implicates a positive answer to the second: an authentic *Alcibiades* proves, by its protreptic, pedagogical, and elementary character, that Plato used his dialogues to teach in the Academy. As for the third, both the endowment of the Academy and the pedagogical brilliance of his most elementary dialogue go some way toward suggesting the intent to create "an eternal curriculum." Fortunately, it is not this section's purpose to prove that Plato did have this goal but rather to prove that if he had it, or ever came to have it, he required Xenophon's help to get it. More specifically, this section's purpose is to prove that he needed Xenophon's *Hellenica*—at least its first two parts (i.e., *Hellenica* I and II)—to survive along with Herodotus and Thucydides in order to be able to set his dialogues in what was already, thanks to all three, *the preserved past*.

Plato's dependence on the recorded past touches on a fundamental aspect of his philosophy. No philosopher has so fully committed himself—at least in the great works of his "middle period"—to the otherworldly, unchanging, and eternal existence of what truly is, in distinction to the flux of what comes into being and passes away. As such, it must seem strange that he expresses these ideas and abstractions, and the Platonic Idea above all, in these dialogues of his, filled as they are with individuals long since dead in a city that has decidedly passed away. Unlike Aristotle and so many other philosophers who "have writ the style of gods and made a pish at chance and sufferance," the merely adventitious is ubiquitous in the dialogues, always set as they are at a particular time and place. If the recognition that Plato was a teacher helps us to realize that the lively dialogue form made his teaching more entertaining and thus more accessible to his students, it still does not explain how unnecessarily *embodied* those conversations are,[11] always conjuring up a lifelike image of Athens even when they are, most exceptionally, set on Crete. The fact that Plato is dependent on Thucydides and Xenophon will suggest to some that his thinking must be considerably less otherworldly than the traditional view of Platonism has construed it.

The solution is complex, and ultimately requires a return to the image at the center of Plato's thought: the Allegory of the Cave. But even if this Allegory creates the Platonic bedrock on which all things

Platonic depend, it is still possible to solve the immediate problem solely in relation to "the preserved past." So even if it is true that Plato was preparing his students to return to the Cave of political life, and even if they would need a thorough knowledge of history—and of Thucydides in particular—to do so effectively, and even if the embodied character of his dialogues replicated the relationship between the vision of what is outside the Cave and the necessity to act justly within it, the justification for setting his dialogues in Athens need not rely on such considerations. It is, rather, the following paradox that is in play: it was by setting his dialogues in what was already the preserved past that he could ensure their immortality. So even if it has not been proved that securing immortality was his goal, it can still be shown that it was by locating his dialogues in a context that had already been explained, illuminated, and preserved by others, the κτῆμα εἰς ἀεί he might have hoped to create became a possibility. Obviously, I take it as certain that this was in fact his aim, but to understand his debt to Xenophon's preservation of the past, it need not be presupposed, even though without that preservation, any hope along these lines could not be realized.

In comparing *Memorabilia* 4.2 to *Alcibiades Major*, one must be equally struck by their differences and their similarities. Both depict the first conversation between Socrates and an ambitious young man, both illuminate the interplay of questioning, humiliation, and conversion that forms the bedrock of the Socratic's personal experience, and finally there is considerable and obvious overlap with respect to subjects discussed, the Delphic "Know Thyself" being prominent among them. But it is their differences that are more important here, and by far the most important of these relates to this section's purpose: Plato has given his version of "the Socratic experience" a historical dimension that is entirely lacking in Xenophon's. Drawing on his own personal experience, Xenophon made the bookish Euthydemus—frequenting a shop of value to an equestrian—more or less transparently himself. He doesn't create any additional historical superstructure, not even a patronymic, to make "him" a recognizable person, nor does he expend any effort to make him seem real. Why would he? Apart from the name, he *is* real, and Xenophon need only record his memories of Socrates and his own initial experiences with him, both before they spoke to one another, during their first conversation, and in that humiliating experience's aftermath. There may well be fictional elements in Xenophon's account, he might have conflated several conversations, made himself seem less or more able than he was, and any number of other departures from truth quite apart from the fiction of "Euthydemus." But when it comes to fiction, Plato's *Alcibiades* leaves him in the dust.

And yet it seems more real. Euthydemus is an abstraction quite apart from his name, but we already "know" Alcibiades. The name of one youngster conceals reality; the other causes reality to jump right off the page. In short, Alcibiades, thanks to Thucydides and Xenophon, belongs to the preserved past, and is knowable, recognizable, and lifelike as a result. All Plato need do is give both Socrates and Alcibiades things to say that are consistent with what we already know about the most memorable and thus widely reported Athenian of the age. It is true that Plutarch, who clearly recognized Plato's literary genius as well as his philosophical excellence, will supply other even more memorable and revealing anecdotes about the young man, but in doing so, he will be replicating Plato in a double sense: first of all, he will say nothing that contradicts Plato's portrait, drawn as it is from Thucydides and Xenophon. But he will also do—under the guise of writing history—what Plato had already done: he will create a lifelike image of a man that enlivens him beyond his "most illustrious deeds," etc.[12] In a word, Plato is laying the foundations for what would become the historical novel,[13] enlivening the interstices of the historical record with what seems to be a real person, just as Plutarch would do centuries later.

It's hard to count the jokes in play here, but it's easy to identify two of them. First of all, it's funny that Alcibiades seems to be more real than Euthydemus. In describing his first conversation with Socrates, Xenophon had reality on his side: he knew what had happened, and he preserved it. Along comes Plato, who proceeds to invent out of whole cloth—or very nearly so—a *tête-à-tête* of which he could have had no firsthand knowledge whatsoever. The conversation's apparent realism is an illusion; it only seems real. How does Plato achieve this amazing effect? Let's just say that he couldn't have pulled it off without the historians. Quite apart from the additional realism that numerous details from Xenophon make possible—the Queen's Sash may stand in place of all the rest—Alcibiades seems real because he *is* real, a well-known historical person, and Plato recreates him plausibly in the gaping interstices left by Thucydides and Xenophon, who were describing Alcibiades as part of a much larger story.

Consider again the way Socrates refers to Arginusae in Plato's *Apology*. He can speak in shorthand about ἡ ναυμαχία because he knows we will recognize what he is talking about. How much less natural would it have seemed if Socrates had been less vague, adding names and dates? We believe that we are listening to a historical document, and Plato has indeed fooled venerable scholars into debating the worth of his *Apology* as if there were any possibility that it was something like a transcript. Xenophon is completely candid: "I wasn't there, Hermogenes is my source, and here's my assessment about what occurred." Plato's "testimony" merely seems more candid, and his principal trick—essential to his debt to Xenophon with respect to "the Socratic dialogue"—will be considered only in the following section. For now, the issue returns to that seemingly innocent little τότε. Because of Xenophon, that word is sufficient to make us think that Plato's Socrates is real. Since we know exactly to what that word refers, we find nothing odd about the fact he refers to it elliptically. And "nothing odd" is insufficient: we find it completely natural, for natural is what it seems to be, a perfectly believable way for Socrates to have referred to an event only seven years before, with which, he realistically assumes, his audience is perfectly familiar. And so we are.

The next joke is that it is the information that Xenophon provides, and thus the information that Plato can assume we know, that makes it possible for Plato's Socrates to seem more natural, more realistic, and more properly embedded in the past than Xenophon's. But it is really only that past, carefully recorded and preserved, that is real, and *it* lends the patina of reality to this wondrous fiction. Even the fact that there will be resistance to the claim that Plato was addressing us and not simply his contemporaries—relying entirely on them, their memories, what they knew and we don't—all of this testifies to the brilliance of his mimetic art. In the name of realism, he makes us imagine into existence something about which we know nothing, as in: "Plato's contemporaries were aware." It's not just that they weren't, it's that there's no "they" there at all. It's not easy to find an allusion so elliptical in Plato that we cannot find out precisely what he wants us to know about it, and when we do, it's safe to assume that he wanted us to know that the reason we couldn't is because we can't. When we go scurrying back to Thucydides and Xenophon to find more information about Apollodorus of Cyzicus (*Ion* 541c7–8), we can be sure that the fact that we can find none is exactly what Plato wants us to discover, in this case, that Ion has caught Socrates flat-footed with his words about the Athenian Empire (*Ion* 541c3–6). What generally remains undiscovered is how small is the number of such passages. Their paucity is no accident: Thucydides and Xenophon supply all of the historical background Plato requires us to know.

The crowning joke is that Plato can exceed Xenophon only because of the tools Xenophon gave him. The example of τότε need not be revisited, for it is merely the tip of an iceberg. Nor must more be said about

Alcibiades: he is "so famous," Plato invites us to assume, that we won't bother to ask ourselves who made him so. Alcibiades dominates the first book of *Hellenica*, and there Xenophon provides all the information we need to see the good and bad that was so wondrously mixed in the man. This is no accident: even if Xenophon didn't write *The Constitution of the Athenians*—and that now means if we decide that the speech it contains could not be the kind of thing that Xenophon might have imagined, on the basis of Thucydides, that Alcibiades might have said in 414—*Hellenica* I alone reveals a remarkable determination and capacity to make Alcibiades both complex and lifelike. And since Euryptolemus enters *Hellenica* as an ally of Alcibiades (*Hell.* 1.3.12), and since he makes the eloquent speech in defense of the position that Socrates will take at the trial of the generals immediately after he takes it (*Hell.* 1.7.16–33), and since outside of Xenophon we know nothing about him, we might be inclined to play another round of "Where's Wally."[14] To put it baldly: Plato could not have substituted Alcibiades for Euthydemus without Xenophon, at that not once only but twice.[15]

But the classic cases are the two dialogues Plato built around characters that Xenophon had already revealed as perfectly and irredeemably villainous. As just indicated, Xenophon's portrait of Alcibiades might be said in the aggregate to be complex; there is no such complexity in the case of Critias and Meno. The point was made in the first chapter but the principle involved belongs to the present section. It is because Xenophon the Historian, first in *Hellenica* I and then in *Anabasis* I, has made the wickedness of these two blackguards so obvious that Plato can come along and reveal himself to be the great mimetic artist that he is—unless, that is, we humorously and erroneously assume he is opposed to μίμησις in principle.[16] He has succeeded in making numerous scholars believe that he is sympathetic to "Meno the Thessalian" and the son of Callaischrus, or, at the very least, that he is far more sympathetic to them than "the old fool" Xenophon was. You've got to laugh at this: Plato's artistry—his ability to show how villains are in fact very skillful at making themselves seem virtuous and even Socratic—here depends entirely on Xenophon's portraits. Cassius says of Caesar: "He were no wolf were not the Romans lambs." Thanks to Xenophon, Plato can present as lambs two men who were really wolves, making them that much more dangerous and believable.

In conclusion, although Plato's dialogues were not painted with history's *Grau in Grau*, he needed someone else to have described Athens in order to write them as he did, rendering them verdant with life, as fresh as if they all took place yesterday. Indirectly through Thucydides, directly through his own books, no one man had done more than Xenophon to preserve Athens, making it forever after possible to see it as it was "then." It would be in that frozen τότε, preserved into eternity, that Plato could afford to embed, embody, and even to materialize his bodiless, eternal, and transcendent teaching, securing in the process "both beauty and utility." And so far from hating Plato for having used his own weapons to surpass him, Xenophon demonstrated what it means for a man to both lead and to follow, recognizing excellence when he saw it, and fully aware—as we are not—that he could be even more proud of Plato than Plato was of himself. Although it belongs to a later section of this chapter, let's not forget that *Charmides* and *Meno* didn't cause Xenophon to throw up his hands in despair because Plato had been so successful in making his villains more villainous: he wrote *The Education of Cyrus* instead.

The Socratic Dialogue

In a 2015 article that emerged from the same conference in Israel where Katarzyna Jażdżewska introduced me to *Chion of Heraclea* (see Preface), Boris Hogenmüller argues that Xenophon's *Apology* depends not only on Plato's *Apology*, but on *Crito* and *Phaedo* as well. Although Hogenmüller goes too far here, he does so in a revealing manner.[17] Since Xenophon's thesis in his *Apology* is that the explanation for Socrates' μεγαληγορία during the trial was his belief that the time was ripe for him to die (*Ap.* 1), it is remarkable that the passages Hogenmüller uses to show Xenophon's dependence on Plato's *Crito* and *Phaedo* both involve Socrates making witty remarks that perfectly illustrate his contempt for death. When his friends proposed that he escape from prison, Socrates asked them "if perhaps they knew some place outside of Attica which is off-limits for death" (*Ap.* 23). And when the emotional Apollodorus lamented that Socrates was being put to death unjustly, Socrates asked: "And you, dearest Apollodorus, would you have rather wished to see me die justly than unjustly?" (*Ap.* 28). Since Hogenmüller's purpose is to disjoin narratives relating to post-trial events from Xenophon's account of the trial, and thereby to prove that he is inserting Platonic material where it scarcely belongs, he mentions these high-minded yet comic Socratic responses only in passing, emphasizing instead the dramatic setting of the *Crito*, and the role of the weeping Apollodorus in the context of Phaedo's soon-to-be-shorn hair in *Phaedo*.[18]

What Hogenmüller fails to consider is that it is only for the sake of Socrates' responses that Xenophon narrates these post-trial events: they are best understood as memorable "punch lines" to well-told jokes,[19] and both of them illustrate perfectly—and thereby prove—Xenophon's principal thesis: Socrates "believed that death was preferable to life." And it is this thesis that points to the Achilles heel of Hogenmüller's argument. Announced in the opening words of his *Apology*, Xenophon's thesis is that although others have written about Socrates' μεγαληγορία during the trial, "that he already believed death to be preferable to life for him, this they have not made plain [διεσαφήνισε]" (*Ap*. 1). But as Nietzsche realized so clearly,[20] it would not be easy for someone who had read Plato's *Phaedo* to make this claim: by his advice to Evenus (*Phd*. 61b8-0), his definition of philosophy (*Phd*. 67e5-7), and his last words (*Phd*. 118a7-8)—to name but the most salient examples—Plato's Socrates made it diaphanously plain (διεσαφήνισε) in *Phaedo* why he regarded death to be preferable to life.

Leaving aside, then, the strictly chronological problems that arise from making what is presumably the earliest of Xenophon's Socratic writings dependent on one of Plato's middle-period dialogues, it is unlikely that Xenophon could have written his *Apology* after reading *Phaedo*. On the other hand, the connection between *Crito* and Xenophon's *Apology* suggests that Plato was advancing beyond Xenophon here by building a discrete and stand-alone conversation around one dramatic incident. In short: where Hogenmüller finds evidence that Xenophon synthesized what he found in *Phaedo* and *Crito* in his *Apology*, it is not only unlikely that Xenophon could have claimed that no other author had depicted Socrates as having come to prefer death to life if he had already read *Phaedo*, but it is easy to see that the skill Plato showed in *Crito* by building an entire direct dialogue around an incident of which Xenophon was fully aware, but whose dramatic potential he clearly failed to tap, suggests instead that Plato had found in Xenophon's pioneering *Apology* a negative example, one that pointed toward the necessity of employing skillful dramatic *division*.

The little direct dialogue *Second Alcibiades* provides ancient evidence for the kind of process I have in mind. In his account of their Literary Rivalry, Athenaeus records the fact that there were some who believed that Xenophon, not Plato, was its author.[21] As already noted, there certainly are some echoes of Xenophon in the dialogue: in addition to Socrates' valorization of "the Spartan prayer" (*Alc.2* 150c7-8)—the probable origin of the ascription—there is a more compelling basis: the unidentified and thoughtful poet who turns out to be Xenophon's Socrates (on *Alc.2* 142e1–2, see chapter 1, section 4) and the plaintive lament of the beautiful Euthydemus that he no longer knows what he should pray for (*Mem.* 4.2.36). This is the very conclusion toward which Socrates is leading Alcibiades in *Second Alcibiades*: the youngster is on his way to prayers at the start of the dialogue, and decides not to proceed there at the end (cf. *Alc.2* 138a1–3 and 150c3–7). On the other hand, the same passage in *Memorabilia* 4.2 that contains the embryo of *Second Alcibiades*, also contains the embryo of *Alcibiades Major*: Xenophon's Socrates traces Euthydemus' newly discovered hesitation about prayer to the fact that the young man had previously failed to examine his goals because he firmly believed that he already *knew* them (cf. *Mem.* 4.2.36 and *Alc.1* 109e1–7).

Within the foregoing paragraph, there are to be found three good reasons why Xenophon did not write and could not have written *Second Alcibiades*, all of which suggest that Xenophon lacked Plato's capacity for dramatic division. The first involves the connection between Critias and Alcibiades in *Memorabilia*: Xenophon is at considerable pains to show that Socrates was not responsible for the subsequent misdeeds of either, and it would have defeated the work's underlying apologetic purpose to depict Socrates persuading Alcibiades not to pray (cf. *Mem.* 1.2.12–28). The writer of *Second Alcibiades* therefore presupposes the success of Xenophon's *Memorabilia* I in distancing Socrates from Alcibiades to such an extent that it is no longer necessary to deny, but sufficient merely to depict, and to do so artfully. The entrance of Critias and Alcibiades in *Protagoras* (*Prt.* 316a4–5) is therefore best understood as "post-apologetic," that is, as no longer requiring from Plato any explicit apologetic claims, and thus opening up a safe space for the far more subtle critiques of both men that can easily be found in both *Alcibiades Major* and *Charmides*.

The next point follows from the first: what makes it possible for Xenophon's Socratic writings to achieve a frankly apologetic end is that Xenophon speaks to the reader in his own voice throughout all of them. But like *Crito*, *Second Alcibiades* is a direct dialogue between Socrates and Alcibiades with no authorial introduction, that is to say, exactly the kind of thing that Xenophon himself never wrote (cf. *Hier.* 1). Thanks precisely to the elimination of a narrator, Plato's narrative skill is on an entirely higher level than Xenophon's, and his ability to write self-concealing dialogues with no author-introducing frames is best understood as a dramatic improvement on Xenophon's considerably more natural approach to telling in his own name the story of Socrates, a story he will base on personal experience.

Finally, and most importantly, the very existence of *Second Alcibiades* points to its author's willingness to divide Socrates' story into discrete parts in a manner demonstrably foreign to Xenophon's methods. Once again, the embryo of both *Alcibiades* dialogues can be found in a single chapter in *Memorabilia* 4.2. The author of *Second Alcibiades* clearly possessed the same literary gift that made it possible to conceal himself while allowing his characters to supply all necessary background information and contributed to his ability to delineate and separate pivotal actions such as Socrates speaking to Alcibiades for the first time, as in *Alcibiades Major*, or stopping him on the way to prayers: "*Socrates*: Alcibiades, are you on your way, then, to the god so as to make some prayerful request? *Alcibiades*: Very much so, Socrates" (*Alc.2* 138a1–3). This opening makes it appear to be considerably simpler than it is: a dramatist's eye for a discrete and unifying action is required in order to achieve so natural an affect. Xenophon did not have this gift, and thus could never have written *Second Alcibiades*.

Although Xenophon didn't write *Second Alcibiades*, he helps us to identify who did. While Xenophon did not employ Plato's principle of dramatic division in either his *Apology* or *Memorabilia*, the latter work in particular points the way toward Platonic dyads such as *Alcibiades Major–Second Alcibiades* or, less controversially, *Hippias Major–Hippias Minor*. To say nothing of Xenophon's own depiction of a dialogue between Socrates and Hippias (*Mem.* 4.4), there are, in addition to the series of conversations with Euthydemus in *Memorabilia* 4, three separate dialogues with Antiphon collected in *Memorabilia* 1.6 (*Mem.* 1.6.1–10, 1.6.11–14, and 1.6.15), and two dialogues with Aristippus (*Mem.* 2.1 and 3.8). By collecting many short dialogues into one unified work, Xenophon avoided the danger of any partial transmission: if *Memorabilia* survived, so too, presumably, would its parts. This would not be the case with Plato: by writing a series of discrete works—the result of division—there was always the danger that one or even several of them would be lost or, as was the case with *Second Alcibiades*, deemed spurious. And since he was the first to cast doubt on its authenticity—the only one in antiquity to do so[22]—it is Athenaeus who bears the primary responsibility for the dialogue's present status. But the suggestion of Xenophontic authorship that gave rise to that status proves to be a red herring, and those who originally made it ignored the obvious differences between Plato and Xenophon outlined above. While it is too much to say that Plato wrote *Second Alcibiades* because Xenophon didn't, it is revealing that the only ancient evidence that he didn't write it depends on the false claim of "some" that Xenophon did; the only ancient evidence, that is, aside from *Second Alcibiades* itself.²³

The foregoing should make it obvious that Xenophon did not invent "the Socratic dialogue" as we have come to understand that genre thanks to Plato: a direct dialogue of which the paradigmatic example is *Crito* and which reaches the zenith of artistry in the sizzling *Gorgias*. It is therefore easy to claim that Xenophon could not have written *Second Alcibiades* because he never wrote a direct dialogue without including an (apparently) authorial voice. But the more thought-provoking and revealing corollary is that at least part of the reason that Plato *did* write such dialogues is that by doing so he was drawing a deliberate contrast with Xenophon, indeed going beyond him, perhaps for the first time and in the principal manner. Whatever the impact the mimes of Sophron exercised on Plato, they could not touch the Socratic concerns that led him to the direct dialogue form. Xenophon clearly did not discover the Socratic dialogue in the form that *Euthyphro* first led us to expect—first, that is, thanks to the edition of Thrasyllus—i.e., the direct dialogue form that appears in *Hippias Minor*, *Ion*, *Laches*, *Hippias Major*, *Cratylus*, *Timaeus*, *Critias*, *Phaedrus*, *Sophist*, *Statesman*, *Philebus*, and *Laws*, to say nothing of *Minos*, *Hipparchus*, *Theages*, *Clitophon*, and *Epinomis*. This would be Plato's most basic improvement on Xenophon with respect to "the Socratic dialogue."

There's no concealing the fact that the argument that follows must ultimately depend on that amazing πρῶτος in Diogenes Laertius, and since this text has been so effectively sidelined—for it has been ignored rather than refuted—the arguments that will supplement it may well encounter ridicule or contempt. So before introducing them, some additional support for this πρῶτος, synthesizing a few points made earlier, is necessary. Insofar, then, as this claim has been refuted, that refutation is chronological, and must place the composition of *Memorabilia*—which is the work Diogenes cites in defense of his "first"—*after* earlier Platonic direct dialogues like the ones just listed. The strongest argument for doing so depends on (1) regarding *Memorabilia* as a unified work, (2) postponing its publication and perhaps composition to the latest date implied within it, and (3) finding that date in *Memorabilia* 3.5 where Socrates, in the midst of the Peloponnesian War, identifies the threat the Thebans, not the Spartans, pose to Attica. None of those premises are strong, and certainly not strong enough to dismiss Diogenes' unequivocal claim. More specifically, there is plenty of evidence—and a considerable body of nineteenth-century philology—that *Memorabilia* was composed over a long period of time and might well have been published in ever-expanding stages. In addition, there is evidence that there was in fact a Theban threat to Attica at precisely the moment that Xenophon staged 3.5. Incidentally, a better argument for a late 3.5 is that in this instance, it is Xenophon who is now relying on "the preserved past" relating to Arginusae.

In offering the foregoing, one feels a bit like the lead character in Plato's *Apology*, for the three numbered premises conceal the true identity of "the old accuser." It is, rather, that a chronological and properly historicized case has been made for the real charge: that Xenophon is a mediocrity, and therefore that whenever he and Plato are found to be saying the same or similar things, Xenophon is copying Plato when those things are the same and misunderstanding him when they are merely similar. There is no need to identify any specific names in making this essentially ad hominem argument, for the names of those against whom it is directed are legion. Only the most committed Xenophon-hater could deny that it is contempt for Xenophon—not the details of *Memorabilia* 3.5—that has led to the rejection of Diogenes' testimony. There is, of course, no shortage of these, and by far the most amiable minority among them are those who see themselves as defending Plato by upholding his priority with respect to the invention of the Socratic dialogue.²⁴ But they are a vanishing if not an already vanished breed, and it doesn't require a weatherman to see that the wind is blowing us toward the conclusion that neither Plato nor Xenophon was πρῶτος in this regard but that the honor belongs to some ghostly avatar of Antisthenes, be it Aeschines, Aristippus, Phaedo, or any of the other eleven who follow Socrates and Xenophon in book 2 of Diogenes' *Lives of the Eminent Philosophers*.²⁵

Now for the supplementary arguments, one based on the absence of the direct dialogue form in Xenophon, the other based on the fact that both his *Apology of Socrates* and his *Memorabilia* 4.2 contain within them the germs of several discrete direct dialogues by Plato. Naturally, the historicizing element that unites these arguments is that it posits an early date for both of these texts, and in Hans von Arnim, the reader will discover the philological basis for this posit. Given the author's stature, surprisingly little has been written about von Arnim's 1923 study;²⁶ perhaps the war had something to do with this odd silence; more likely was the fact that it was published not in Germany but in Denmark. In any case, von Arnim's conclusions have not been generally accepted, and if they have never brought down upon his head a scathing *Vernichtungskritik*, that doesn't mean one cannot be imagined. Erbse's unitarian approach is at once a partial exception and the principal cause of the parallel sidelining of von Arnim, and in order to dismiss my own appropriation of his conclusions, the most vulnerable point is neither his early dating of Xenophon's *Apology* nor the bare existence of an early and independent *Schutzschrift*, but the claim that the bulk of *Memorabilia* 4, and all of 4.2, belonged to that original edition. So much, then, for a candid statement about the *locus minoris resistantiae* for what follows; naturally, I've already tried to explain why he is right.

With respect to Xenophon's *Apology*, the argument has already been made in the context of Hogenmüller above, and relies on *Crito*. Plato saw what Xenophon had not seen in the joke Socrates made in response to the suggestion that he escape: here was single moment, embodying what later critics would call the three unities, that nevertheless isolated and emphasized the soul of Socratic ethics, namely, that it is better to suffer an injustice than to do one. The fact that Plato would go on to write *Gorgias* leaves little doubt that he regarded this as the claim that turned the world upside down, and it was as both a Socratic and a gifted literary artist that Plato invented not "the Socratic dialogue" but the Socratic dialogue in one of its most compelling forms, the "one of the most" being required in order to leave plenty of room for indirect Platonic masterpieces such as *Protagoras*, *Symposium*, *Republic*, and *Phaedo*. The argument, then, is a variation on the characteristically Athenian claim that competition in the arts leads to progress and specialization.[27] And since "the old accusers" have been identified in a polemical vein, the parallel "traditional defense" of Xenophon's priority likewise deserves mention: that since the less highly developed precedes the acme, Plato can't be prior.

But this is not the basis for Diogenes' πρῶτος, and he says nothing about Xenophon's *Apology*. Nor should he have: it certainly contains Socratic statements, responses, and two witty examples of repartee, but if this were sufficient to entitle Xenophon to priority with respect to the Socratic dialogue, one might almost just as easily cite the statements Socrates makes or is said to make in *Hellenica* (*Hell.* 1.7.15) and *Anabasis* (*An.* 3.1.5–7). Moreover, *Memorabilia* 4.2 is a much better example of the same two phenomena observable in the transition between Xenophon's *Apology* and *Crito*. In fact, the two supplementary arguments are one: it was the presence of multiple moments that called out for dramatic isolation and emphasis that called into existence the Socratic dialogue in its distinctively early Platonic form, a genre combining direct dialogue with dramatic unity. In the case of 4.2, Plato could find the roots of at least three of his direct dialogues: *Alcibiades Major*, *Alcibiades Minor*, and *Lesser Hippias* (*Mem.* 4.2.14–17). Encountering a veritable hodgepodge of Socratic cross-questioning in Xenophon, Plato came, saw, and divided.

The core claim, of course, is that there was already something worth finding in Xenophon, and "the Socratic dialogue" is what Plato found there. In the case of the *Alcibiades* dyad, it is not only because the direct dialogue was a dramatic improvement on what Plato found in 4.2 that reveals Xenophon's priority. In this case, there is also the historical dimension described in the previous section. Any given Socratic's firsthand experience of Socratic refutation necessarily preceded their ability to give that experience a literary form. The implication is obvious: even if Euthydemus was a real person that Xenophon knew and whose experiences he had in part witnessed directly and had learned about the rest from "Euthydemus himself," this is infinitely closer to reality than Plato's decision to impose upon Alcibiades either his own direct experiences with Socrates or those of Xenophon, regardless of whether it was orally or through a literary medium that he learned of the latter. I'm not claiming that Plato relied on Xenophon's account of, for example, Critias for his own knowledge of his notorious kinsman any more than I am claiming he needed to have read 4.2 to learn what it felt like to be refuted by Socrates. In the first case, it was *our* knowledge of Critias that *would* depend on Xenophon; in the second, Xenophon didn't provide Plato with information but only with inspiration.

This inspiration was at once literary and personal. Whatever Socrates might have said at his trial was said in public, and a defense of the manner in which he had spoken there (such as Xenophon's) or even a defensible imitation of his actual speech (as supplied by Plato) remained almost as far removed from the man himself as the caricature in Aristophanes' *Clouds* had been. Whoever was to be πρῶτος with respect to Socratic dialogue would need to draw on personal experience of something more than his most public appearance. Plato and Xenophon were not the only Athenians who had had this experience. The turning point, then, was to reveal or disclose it: to make the public private. And of all the experiences that one might hesitate to reveal, the actual conversion—requiring the author to make a public statement of what could only have been a private confession of slavish ignorance—would be foremost. For reasons already given (chapter 3, section 3), there was nothing in the way of a long-overdue homecoming about such a confession from the pre-Socratic perspective, and Aristotle was able to revive μεγαλοψυχία only because it had never really died, except, that is, for the Socratics from whom Socrates had stripped theirs. But before Socrates, they had not only had it, but to an extreme degree: famous or not, Euthydemus shares this quality with Alcibiades, as did Glaucon and Callicles. To write believably about the Socratic reality would require a man to reveal his humiliation to an audience that saw nothing excellent in humility and nothing wrong with μεγαλοψυχία. This may explain why Xenophon was willing to present himself as rebuked by Socrates for holding a beautiful boy's kiss to be harmless: here, he remained a defensibly manly ἐραστής; the indirect rebuke of Euthydemus as a victimized ἐρώμενος made a pseudonym necessary. But so did the humiliation in 4.2; despite the pseudonym, anyone who had experienced Socratic conversion, as Plato also had, would know that the author of 4.2 could only be Euthydemus even if his acquaintance with Xenophon was exclusively literary. To depict Socrates telling a few good jokes is one thing; to depict oneself as refuted, ignorant, abased, and converted is entirely different. In a word, the inventor of Socratic dialogue needed to be both honest and brave.

To recreate a living Socrates thus required the death of an author's "proper pride," and a willingness to do so represented a revolution at once personal and literary. In his defense of joining 4.2 to the *Schutzschrift*, von Arnim works backward from the end of book 4, ably showing how its account of the trial modifies and replaces his earlier version in *Apology*. Moreover, since he takes Euthydemus to be Xenophon's source and not Xenophon himself, he overlooks the personal dimension that justifies Diogenes' πρῶτος. Only by making the private public could Xenophon have created the Socratic dialogue, and the comparison between Euthydemus and Plato's Alcibiades leaves no doubt as to which account of Socratic conversion was both prior and braver. Even if others didn't, Plato saw through Euthydemus, and thus fully realized the revolutionary nature of the step Xenophon had taken. The literary modifications he would subsequently introduce—e.g., turning a single moment in 4.2 into a direct dialogue such as *Second Alcibiades*—were characteristic but derivative, and derived not only from Xenophon's failure to discover the most persuasive manner in which to present a Socratic conversation, but even more so from Xenophon's courageous willingness to disclose the searing core of those conversations in public.

The tradition's rejection of both *Alcibiades Major* and *Second Alcibiades* may well render the foregoing nugatory, and the principal advantage of branding any of Plato's dialogues as inauthentic is that *in their case at least* it becomes possible to explain connections on the basis of Xenophon's priority. In other words, even if "the author" (or *der Verfasser*) of *Second Alcibiades* clearly was working from Xenophon's *Memorabilia*, that still leaves the modern Priority Axiom intact. It is therefore the third Platonic dialogue implicated by 4.2 that may provide more bite in defending Diogenes' πρῶτος. To begin with, there are respectable philologists who have regarded *Hippias Minor* as not only "early" but as having been written before Socrates' death;[28] since Xenophon's claim for priority depends on a necessarily post-399 date for *Memorabilia* I, this possibility, if provable, would put the matter to rest. There is also the anecdote about Socrates listening to Plato's *Lysis* that leads to the same place, and since Diogenes is this story's source, and since he distances himself from it in the usual way,[29] its countervailing weight can be ignored. But this is scarcely an adequate response to Ernst Heitsch's arguments for a pre-399 *Lesser Hippias*.

Unfortunately, anything resembling such a response must promptly open up not one but three cans of worms. Of these, the most important will require anticipating the subject of the next section, and given that this one is nearing its conclusion, that's not such a bad thing. In addition to upholding an early *Hippias Minor*, Heitsch rejects the authenticity of *Hippias Major*,[30] and from the perspective of Reading Order—the subject of the next section—these two moves hang together. Since *Hippias Minor* obviously follows *Hippias Major* in a dramatic sense, and since Heitsch's argument against the latter is that it is doctrinally "late," *Lesser Hippias* cannot be "early" if *Hippias Major* is genuine. Next, one would need to consider Heitsch's claim that it was *der Verfasser* of *Hippias Major* who made it merely *appear* to precede the already written *Hippias Minor*. Finally, one would need to address Heitsch's parallel arguments about *Ion*, another dialogue he regards as having been written before Socrates' death. It should be obvious that this is not the proper context to explore these issues, especially since the most important of them have been explored elsewhere.[31]

But it should already be obvious that Heitsch's case depends on de-authenticating *Hippias Major*, and the excellences of that dialogue may be allowed to plead on its behalf. More importantly, this brilliant dialogue scarcely stands alone: as already indicated, it mediates the distance between *Protagoras* and *Symposium*. It also stands in particularly close relation to Xenophon, and as likewise indicated previously, *Memorabilia* 3.8 is one of those "dialectical" passages to which it will be necessary to return at the end. Finally, *Hippias Major* is particularly well embedded in a Platonic Reading Order, connected to *Lovers* on one side and *Hippias Minor* on the other, with the latter in turn closely connected to *Ion*. In short, although the best argument against an early *Hippias Minor* is a delightfully Platonic *Hippias Major*, two other ways of responding to Heitsch are possible: a hardnosed philological approach that gets into the worms, and the foregoing indications based on the Reading Order hypothesis that *Hippias Minor* cannot be early because it is so closely connected to a series of dialogues whose principal purpose is to prepare for *Symposium*, and which therefore presuppose its composition. There is also Diogenes' πρῶτος to be considered in this context as well.

A principal purpose of this section has been to show how Xenophon laid the foundations for Plato's invention of the direct and thus entirely un-narrated Socratic dialogue, something Xenophon could only have done by inventing its narrated and indirect predecessor. Xenophon narrates *Memorabilia* I, concealing himself only by means of Euthydemus, a concealment that, as I have tried to show, was at once delightfully Xenophontic and perhaps also personally necessary. First in *Crito* and *Gorgias*, then in a long series of other direct dialogues spanning the whole of his literary career, Plato exploited the dramatic possibilities of this form to the fullest. But it was not the only form that he used, and it cannot be regarded as accidental that some of his most brilliant dialogues are indirect and narrated. In the remainder of this section, I want to show that Plato was indebted to Xenophon for the invention of this form as well.

To begin with, these two different debts arose in opposite ways. The invention of the direct dialogue arose from a dramatist's appreciation of the weakness of the form Xenophon had invented, and whatever way in which Plato may have eventually imitated Xenophon's indirectly narrated Socratic dialogues, he never resorted to depicting himself as their narrator. In that sense, both appropriations could be imagined equally as rejections. But this would be a mistake. Despite the fact that Plato himself would never narrate his narrated dialogues, he came to recognize the dramatic advantage Xenophon had created for himself by doing so, and he therefore modified what he found in his predecessor only by giving the narrator's role to men such as Apollodorus and Phaedo or, more directly, to Socrates as in *Republic*, *Lysis*, *Charmides*, *Lovers*, to which the hybrids *Protagoras* and *Euthydemus* should be added. And with respect to the latter, it would be easy to play the developmentalist game: the interpolation of a narrated dialogue within a direct frame—as in both *Euthydemus* and *Protagoras*—might be taken as evidence that they are both compositionally and above all doctrinally early in comparison with *Symposium*, *Phaedo*, and *Republic*.

Against those who have turned this game into dogma, there is the impact of Xenophon's *Symposium* to be considered, and its priority to Plato's is so crucial to this book's overall argument that the question will be revisited in greater detail in the last chapter. And that doesn't go far enough: one might imagine that this book's purpose has been to validate the priority of Xenophon's *Symposium* to Plato's. A digression on my position regarding contemporary scholarly composition techniques will provide a corrective. It has become standard practice for young academics in particular to stitch together as a book a number of previously published articles, and it may do the field no harm to observe that such books are rarely satisfactory. Although it is not irrelevant that this technique has certain affinities with the way I am suggesting Xenophon composed his books, the personal point that needs to be made is that my practice has been exactly the opposite: before even outlining the present book, I had written several articles on Xenophon, none of which will be found incorporated bodily into it. Among these, already cited in a note, is "The Priority of Xenophon's *Symposium* Revisited," a paper presented at the opening meeting of the Xenophon Society in 2021 and submitted for publication in a volume of those proceedings. There is no need to uphold that priority in detail here because it has already been upheld in greater detail elsewhere. But it is certainly true that its priority is foundational to this project, and thus was debated and defended before undertaking it.

In the context of the present section, the priority of Xenophon's *Symposium* to Plato's indicates that the latter's debts with respect to "the Socratic dialogue" are really twofold. Leaving aside the fact that the narrator of Xenophon's *Symposium* cannot possibly be Xenophon himself for chronological reasons, a chasm divides the way he uses the narrated dialogue form in it from the way he had used it in *Memorabilia* I. Xenophon has now embraced the "three unities" that had already marked Plato's great if also negatively derivative advance on his own invention, necessarily personal, of the Socratic dialogue. Thus far, the argument has emphasized only the comic alternative that Xenophon's *Symposium* offered to the grimly serious *Gorgias*, but it also represented Xenophon's acknowledgment of the superiority or at least the Platonic power of the isolated dialogue, depicting a single incident, time, and place. No matter how variegated the symposium genre allowed Xenophon to be,[32] embracing it as a vehicle for depicting Socrates illustrated Xenophon's surrender to Plato's methods even if the form still permitted its author to indulge his affection for conversational variety.

It also taught Plato to better appreciate the possibilities created by the narrative form his own dramatic genius had previously caused him to reject. Replacing the impossible chronology that might be thought to have vitiated Xenophon's narration with the comically tortured tale of the provenance of his own *Symposium*,[33] Plato learned the lesson of how much mimetic power can be gained by means of a narrator. It is narration that allows us to imagine that we are seeing the mime about Dionysus and Ariadne, just as it will later allow us both to see and to hear the drunken entrance of Alcibiades. The pattern has been repeated so many times as to become obvious: Plato repeatedly found a way to use Xenophon's methods to advance beyond him. As a result, Plato was indebted to his discovery of the Socratic dialogue not once but twice: no less than for the early direct dialogues than for the brilliant middle period narrated ones was Plato in Xenophon's debt. Please note that this progress has nothing to do with doctrine, but only with artistry. Plato will uphold as characteristically Socratic his hero's decision to face death in Athens all the way from *Crito* and *Gorgias* to *Laws*, and will depict that decision's ontological foundation indelibly in the Allegory of the Cave.

The Achilles heel of Plato's Priority is not that it strips Xenophon of originality but that it taxes him with the supreme folly of failing to recognize Plato's greatness. It is a profoundly uncharitable view, and one that likewise does no additional credit to Plato. With respect to the latter, we gain a greater appreciation for Plato's genius by seeing it in action, both dependent and revolutionary, building brilliantly but always humanly on the great achievements of others. But it is obviously Xenophon who is illuminated even more clearly by reversing the flow of influence or, rather, by making that interchange a mutual one. Instead of depicting Xenophon as the fool who thought he could surpass the unsurpassable, the alternative model allows him not only to appreciate Plato's genius but also, instead of hating his follower for surpassing him, grants him the solemn pride that must have been his for recognizing what so many have failed to see: that without him, Plato could not have done what he did. "You know what you did," says Tom Hanks to Francis Gary Powers in *The Bridge of Spies*. It is that quiet self-awareness, not the drive to be honored by others, celebrated as divine by the flattering Simonides (*Hier.* 7.3–4), that is the true mark of a man, regardless of gender. To give first without regard to any possible payback (*Mem.* 2.2.5) is the core of Xenophon's Socratic creed, and it is his abiding admiration for the giant that followed in his footsteps that proves that Xenophon was himself a giant.

The Reading Order

A brief notice of the elegance of the Reading Order of Plato's early dialogues was presented in chapter 3 in order to illustrate by contrast the lack of any such structure in the case of Xenophon's writings. This notice was confined to the first dialogues in that Reading Order, spanning the distance between an initial *Protagoras*—closely connected as it is to the elementary *Alcibiades Major*—and *Symposium*, the dialogue that marks the first clear sign that the larger structure that would eventually create a philosophical encyclopedia, still beginning with *Protagoras* but now ending with *Phaedo*, was already beginning to take hold in Plato's fecund literary imagination. Although I suggested that *Symposium* looked forward as well as back, it was only the backward look that was briefly explored. In the course of that exploration, the role of philosophy was emphasized, and this section will begin with that emphasis en route to giving an overview of "Plato's philosophical encyclopedia" as a whole. Only with that whole in place will it be possible to assess Plato's debts to Xenophon in creating it, not least of all because a previous discussion (chapter 3, section 1) has indicated that it was an Academic Editor, not Xenophon himself, who arranged Xenophon's writings in the same elegant manner that I am claiming Plato came to organize his.

Plato's *Lovers* is the first dialogue in the Reading Order in which Socrates raises the characteristic τί ἐστι question, and he will ask "What is it?" a second time in *Hippias Major* which directly follows it. In neither case is the object of this question one of the virtues or virtue itself, and further increasing the distance between what we find in Plato's dialogues and Aristotle's account of the historical Socrates—who allegedly sought to define the virtues while construing them as so many kinds of knowledge—is the fact that philosophy itself is not any form of knowledge but rather *between* wisdom and ignorance. Nor is it clear that Socrates' aim in either *Lovers* or *Greater Hippias* is to *define*, respectively, either philosophy or "the beautiful itself." It therefore makes sense that in *Symposium*, where both philosophy as μεταξύ or "between" and the Beautiful as transcendent come into view thanks to Diotima's lessons, the latter does not do so thanks to a merely verbal definition, while the former has been made constitutively propaedeutic to that beatific vision. And thus, when true virtue, as opposed to its shadow, is made dependent on that vision (*Smp.* 212a4–5), we have already been given some reason to doubt that virtue is more dependent on knowledge than it is on philosophy.

In preparation for the Idea of the Good, Socrates will refer to the Beautiful in *Republic* 5 to illustrate philosophy once again, having already defined four of the virtues in such a way as to encourage Aristotle to imagine that Plato had abandoned his earlier opposition to ἀκρασία as expressed in *Protagoras*. But between *Symposium* and *Republic*, Plato will give us some reason to believe that knowledge, and not the Idea of the Good, is the only good, and ignorance the only evil (*Euthd.* 281e3–5). This claim not only contradicts the account of the Good that we will subsequently encounter in *Republic*, but also tends to contradict what we have already learned about philosophy in *Symposium*. Philosophy as μεταξύ reappears in *Lysis* (*Ly.* 218a2–6), the dialogue that fits naturally between *Symposium* and *Euthydemus* in the (reconstructed) Platonic Reading Order, itself made visible because Socrates leaves Agathon's for the Lyceum (*Smp.* 223d10), describes himself as heading there at the beginning of *Lysis* (*Ly.* 203a1), and tells Crito what he did there yesterday in *Euthydemus* (*Euthd.* 271a1). *Charmides* likewise takes place in a gymnasium (*Chrm.* 153a3–4), as *Laches* probably does so as well (*La.* 178a1–2). What makes it easy to see that Plato is testing what we have learned about philosophy from *Symposium* and *Lysis* in *Euthydemus* is the trick question Euthydemus asks at the start (*Euthd.* 275d3–4): is it the wise or the ignorant that learn? It is in fact those who are philosophers who do so, and who will also recognize that wisdom is not the only good.

But let's not lose sight of Xenophon. To begin with, the need for both of the two so-called hybrid dialogues—*Euthydemus* and *Protagoras*—emerges from *Symposium*, while the Socratic narration that is still framed by direct dialogue in both becomes fully independent in *Lysis* and *Charmides*. Moreover, the presence of Laches in *Laches* and Potidaea in *Charmides* show that these two have emerged from *Symposium* as well. So much, then, for the huge indirect impact that Xenophon's *Symposium* may have had on the dialogues on either side of Plato's. But in the case of *Euthydemus*, the relationship touches on one of the central mysteries with which I continue to grapple: the problem of when and why Xenophon wrote *Memorabilia* 3.8–9. In fact, *Euthydemus* joins *Greater Hippias* as the Platonic epicenter of this mystery: just as the latter either echoes or anticipates 3.8, so too does the former either anticipate or echo 3.9.[34] The latter connection is particularly important because it implicates two passages in *Euthydemus*, both from the First Protreptic oration of Socrates that begins with the assertion that all human beings desire to εὖ πράττειν (*Euthd.* 278e3), and which appears to constitute the serious core of this comical and fallacy-rife dialogue. To be specific, Xenophon's Socrates seems to confirm what Plato's Socrates says about the importance of σοφία (*Mem.* 3.9.4–5) while rejecting what he says about the connection between σοφία and "good fortune" or εὐτυχία (*Mem.* 3.9.14–15). It will be necessary to return to this in the final chapter.

Both *Euthydemus* and *Meno* raise the general question, "What is virtue?" Between them, the proposed Reading Order places four dialogues dealing with the four individual virtues that will reappear in *Republic*: courage (*La.*), temperance (*Chrm.*), justice (*Grg.*), and wisdom (*Thg.*). The difficulties involved in construing *Gorgias* as the virtue-dialogue dealing with justice, and with upholding *Theages* as an authentic dialogue concerned with σοφία in a particularly pious form have been considered elsewhere.[35] But the increased attention to Order of Composition in this book suggests that part of what makes *Gorgias* anomalous among "the virtue dialogues" is that this is not how Plato originally conceived of it, and that the Reading Order structure in which he eventually embedded it followed not only Xenophon's *Symposium* but his *Oeconomicus* as well, understood as the inspiration for *Meno*. But the same applies to *Euthydemus* as well, the other bookend of the virtue dialogues. And *Meno* not only looks back to *Euthydemus*—thanks especially to what Vlastos called "its miniaturized doublet"[36]—but forward to *Republic*, and that primarily for the simple but profound reason that Plato will not tell those of us who are dissatisfied with the definitions of *Republic* 4 what justice truly is, forcing us to find it in the Cave on the basis of what we already know but have forgotten. *Clitophon* will help us to remember that what Socrates really needs to explain in *Republic* is what should we *do* next (*Clt.* 408e1–2).

Aulus Gellius only tells us how Xenophon responded to (almost) the first two books of "that famous work of Plato which has been written about the best constitution of a republic and of the administration of the state [*de optimo statu reipublicae civitatisque administrandae*],"[37] and not to the book as a whole. To begin with, Aulus Gellius is not offering us a hendiadys: a discourse concerning how it is necessary to administer a *civitas* is not simply a description of the best constitution of the *res publica*. As for Xenophon, *Memorabilia* 3 gives us some evidence that he did not read *Republic* only as Plato's account of "the best kind of state," and the first section of the first chapter of this book has already situated the conversations with Glaucon and Charmides (*Mem.* 3.6-7) in the context of a more civic reading of Plato's masterpiece, emphasizing their opposite messages *de administrandae civitatis*. A series of conversations about serving the state as a general (*Mem.* 3.1-2 and 3.4-5), a cavalry officer (*Mem.* 3.3), or a political advisor and politician speaking from the βῆμα in democratic Athens (*Mem.* 3.6-7) would already be consistent with a civic reading of Plato's *Republic* even without the allusion to Glaucon. But even if there is reason to regard *Memorabilia* 3.1-7 as "late," there remains the problem of 3.8-9.

To return to Plato, the four dialogues of Thrasyllus' eighth tetralogy—*Clitophon*, *Republic*, *Timaeus*, and *Critias*—illustrate the natural basis for Reading Order, and preserve it, as on my account so too does the seventh: *Hippias Major*, *Hippias Minor*, *Ion*, and *Menexenus*. It is not an arcane science. The character Clitophon joins *Clitophon* to *Republic* in much the same way that Ctesippus joins *Lysis* to *Euthydemus*. By following Socrates' classic account of the Idea of the Good and of the division between unchanging Being and the flux of Becoming with the observation-dependent discourse (*Ti.* 47a1-4) of the "most astronomical [ἀστρονομικώτατος]" Timaeus (*Ti.* 27a3-4), Plato preserved the Socratic response to pre-Socratic physics as described by Xenophon (*Mem.* 1.1.11-16), and if more readers had been guided by him rather than by Aristotle, many fewer would have believed themselves to be reading "Plato's Cosmology."[38] As for *Critias*, Xenophon's role in illuminating him for Plato's readers has already been noted.

But there is a notable falling off with respect to Xenophon's influence in the dialogues that follow *Critias* and *Phaedrus*: *Parmenides*, *Philebus*, *Cratylus*, and *Theaetetus*, and in tandem with the sense that Timaeus speaks for Plato, it is easy to see why so many would cease to regard Xenophon as a philosopher in the light of what these dialogues indicate that "serious philosophy" must look like. It is tempting to say that one of Plato's debts to Xenophon was that their shared concerns revealed the truth: Plato too was a Socratic, who—in Cicero's memorable phrase—found philosophy in the heavens and brought it down into the cities, making it speak about things good and bad.[39] Unfortunately, this truth was forgotten, and thus Xenophon failed to be of much help in this regard albeit through no fault of his own or of Plato's. As for *Phaedrus*, it is on the basis of its three speeches that it becomes possible to offer a new argument for the priority of Xenophon's *Symposium* to Plato's, and even a scholar intent on upholding Plato's Priority has noted the numerous parallels between those speeches and the attack of Xenophon's Socrates on sexualized pederasty.[40] Since Xenophon's Socrates argues that it would be equally misguided to gratify sexually—i.e., to χαρίζεσθαι (*Phdr.* 265a3; cf. 235e6–7)—either a lover or a non-lover, it is rather the misuse of his arguments that these parallels reveal, a pattern that begins with the speech of Pausanias in Plato's *Symposium* and reaches its apex in the Great Speech in *Phaedrus*.

Only with Socrates' departure for the King Archon's at the end of *Theaetetus* do we return to a world in which Xenophon would be at home, and it is here that Reading Order yields its most amazing results. Thanks to the hegemony of the Order of Composition paradigm, the unmistakable fact that *Euthyphro* immediately follows *Theaetetus* in a dramatic sense has been granted no significance. Adding to the obvious chronological connection, the ridiculous Euthyphro's justification for prosecuting his father for murder on the basis of what Zeus did to his father and what Cronos did to his (*Euthyp.* 5e5–6a3) should have made a long line of Platonists a bit less certain that "assimilation to god [ὁμοίωσις θεῷ]" (*Tht.* 176b1) was the last word in either Plato's ethics or his theology. And since the onus of killing Father Parmenides is what the Eleatic Stranger attempts to escape in *Sophist* (*Sph.* 241d1–3)—the dialogue that immediately follows *Euthyphro* in a dramatic sense—one might have thought that more readers would have applied Socrates' claim that the being or οὐσία of a thing cannot be explicated by what it passively undergoes (*Euthyp.* 11a6–b1) to the Eleatic Stranger's insistence that the unchanging οὐσία of the Friends of the Forms is changed by being known (*Sph.* 248d10–249a3). Finally, since Plato refused the Stranger the chance to describe the Philosopher as he already had the Sophist and the Statesman (*Sph.* 217a4), the single most amazing result of using Reading Order as opposed to Order of Composition is that now *Apology of Socrates* stands where *Philosopher* would have been but isn't.

By following *Republic* with *Timaeus*, *Sophist-Statesman* with *Apology of Socrates*, and *Crito* with *Laws-Epinomis*, Plato gave us all the clues we really need to greet Timaeus, the Eleatic, and the Athenian Strangers with acute suspicion. Instead, by ignoring Reading Order completely and thus construing *Timaeus*, *Sophist-Statesman*, and *Laws* as "late" dialogues—and therefore as containing the views Plato came to hold after outgrowing the Socratic inspiration of his "early" ones—it became possible to configure the greatest of the two greatest Socratics as ultimately post-Socratic, and it should surprise nobody that this configuration would turn him into a pre-Socratic. The result would be Aristotle's Pythagorean Plato, and it is no accident that the best textual evidence for attributing a neo-Pythagorean concern with Limit and the Unlimited is *Philebus*, where the entire absence of any chronological indications make it possible—for those who have read *Phaedo*, at least—to recognize Socrates himself in his pre-Socratic form.[41] Instead of finding an old Socrates, Order of Composition discovers in *Philebus* an old Plato, ignoring once again its close connection to *Parmenides*, where nobody can fail to find a young Socrates.

Once again, it is by reading Plato through Aristotle's eyes that all of this has become possible, and thus the chronological impossibility that Plato owed any debts to Aristotle deserves emphasis. It is, rather, to Xenophon that Plato owed multiple debts. But even if we ignore them, even if we simply recognize on the basis of their common concerns that both were true Socratics, and that both dedicated themselves to keeping Socrates alive through their writings, our ability to recognize Plato for who he was and is would be greatly increased. It is not, however, my intention to deny that Timaeus, the two Strangers, and even the Socrates of *Philebus appear* to speak for Plato; the fact that Plato intended them to do so must be emphasized. Beginning in *Phaedrus*, Plato has been actively and explicitly training us to recognize the use of deception in Socrates' speeches (*Phdr.* 261d10–262d2), but he had already been doing so informally since *Protagoras* (*Prt.* 343c6–7). One of the reasons that the "dialectical" sections of *Memorabilia* are so troublesome is that even though Xenophon's Socrates defends the use of salutary deception in the case of his friends (*Mem.* 4.2.17–21), it is nowhere entirely clear that he uses it on us himself, as Plato's repeatedly does. But if he does, then it was likewise in trying to make his followers "more dialectical" that he did so (*Mem.* 4.6.1).

Amazingly, *Lysis* is the only dialogue that mentions hemlock by name, and Plato does so in the context of the value of a jug of wine: since wine is its antidote, a father would pay most any price for it or even for the jug that contained it if his son had just imbibed some κώνειον (*Ly.* 219d5–220a1). Thanks to the mention of Crete and Sparta as possible destinations for Socrates in *Crito* (*Cri.* 52e6), Strauss suggested that the Athenian Stranger is who Socrates would have been if "he" had escaped drinking the hemlock.[42] Given the early composition of *Crito*, the difference on this point between the real Socrates who remains and the alternative "Socrates" who flees,[43] implicated Platonic bedrock: it was not a preference for death but rather for suffering an injustice as opposed to doing one that had marked the moral distance between Xenophon's clever but comparatively glib *Apology of Socrates* and Plato's already morally sublime *Crito*. But it will be the difference between hemlock and wine that connects *Laws* and *Phaedo* that will make the contrary-to-fact Reading Order unmistakable—i.e., the alternate "Socrates" who escapes Athens for Crete—especially when the Athenian Stranger denies that there is any drink that induces fear (see *Lg.* 647e1–648a6 on the φόβου φάρμακον) en route to justifying drinking wine, his otherwise curious obsession at the start of *Laws*.

Wine and hemlock can be distinguished with respect to confidence (θάρρος at *Lg.* 649c8; cf. *Phd.* 114d1–115a2) and fear (φόβος at *Lg.* 649a1–6; cf. *Phd.* 95d6–8). The Stranger's failure to recognize hemlock as the φόβου φάρμακον reveals that it is only Socrates, presiding as "symposiarch" over a drinking party in *Phaedo* (*Phd.* 117b6–7), who will master his own φόβος (*Phd.* 95d6–8), persuade others to demonstrate θάρρος and finally, after draining the "drink" or πῶμα (*Phd.* 117b6), once again become himself (*Phd.* 118a7–8). Joined together—as antidote is to poison—wine induces θάρρος, hemlock φόβος (cf. *Lg.* 644c9–d1). But this antithesis is only the first step: wine causes the drinker to overcome a *salutary* form of φόβος—a sense of shame (*Lg.* 646e10–647a2; cf. *Cri.* 53b6–c3)—while giving way to a *defective* θάρρος (*Lg.* 647a10) that leads to shamelessness (*Lg.* 649a8–b5). It is the double sense of both φόβος and θάρρος—θάρρος as confidence in the face of adversity as well as shamelessness φόβος as either cowardice or respectful awe (*Lg.* 647a8–b1)—that intellectually enlivens Plato's "tale of two drinking parties."

The most significant and satisfying revelation vouchsafed by this Reading Order connection is that just as Socrates demonstrates a praiseworthy θάρρος in the face of a life-threatening φόβος in *Phaedo*, the Stranger overcomes a salutary φόβος in order to give way to a shameless form of θάρρος in *Laws*. In other words: both Socrates and the Stranger are simultaneously "fearless and fearful" (*Lg.* 646b9–c1) but in diametrically opposite ways. The Stranger's fear of dying in Athens will lead him to a shameless "freedom of speech [παρρησία]" on Crete while Socrates, overawed by the Athenian laws in *Crito* (*Cri.* 52c8 and 54c2), acts in accordance with a philosopher's θάρρος in *Phaedo* (*Phd.* 95c1–4). Although both Socrates and the Stranger overcome φόβος while demonstrating θάρρος, they do so in opposite ways: in *Phaedo*, Socrates masters the evil form of φόβος with respect to death while demonstrating, for the benefit of others, the salutary form of θάρρος, whereas the Stranger, by giving way to his fear of death, as indicated by the counterfactual flight, simultaneously abandons a salutary form of φόβος in order to give voluble expression to an evil form of θάρρος throughout *Laws*.

Naturally, a full discussion is impossible here, but an example may suffice. Having passed the Stranger's wine test in the *Symposium* (*Smp.* 223c4–d12), Socrates passes the test of "the fear drug" in *Phaedo*; the Stranger not only fails the fear test by reversing the decision Socrates made in the *Crito* but will also *fail the test he himself institutes* in *Laws* (cf. βάσανος at *Lg.* 649d9 and 650b4), for Plato has endowed his law-giving protagonist with the relevant characteristics of a drunken man. Consider the Stranger's hesitation to reveal one of his proposals in book 7 (*Lg.* 810c4–811c2): given that he will be compelling the city's highest official (cf. *Lg.* 765d8–e2 and 811d5) to compel paid foreign teachers to indoctrinate the youth in his own discourses (*Lg.* 804c8–d1)—discourses he will praise immodestly (*Lg.* 811c9–d5)—this hesitation is perfectly natural. He must be brought to a state—and Clinias skillfully brings him there (*Lg.* 811c1–2)—where his natural inhibitions explicitly give way to θάρρος (*Lg.* 810e2) and παρρησία (*Lg.* 811a6).

Table 4.1. Reading Order of Plato's Dialogues

1. *Protagoras*	19. *Timaeus*
2. *Alcibiades Major*	20. *Critias*
3. *Alcibiades Minor*	21. *Phaedrus*
4. *Lovers*	22. *Parmenides*
5. *Hippias Major*	23. *Philebus*
6. *Hippias Minor*	24. *Cratylus*
7. *Ion*	25. *Theaetetus*
8. *Menexenus*	26. *Euthyphro*
9. *Symposium*	27. *Sophist*
10. *Lysis*	28. *Statesman*
11. *Euthydemus*	29. *Apology*
12. *Laches*	30. *Hipparchus*
13. *Charmides*	31. *Minos*
14. *Gorgias*	32. *Crito*
15. *Theages*	33. *Laws*
16. *Meno*	34. *Epinomis*
17. *Clitophon*	35. *Phaedo*
18. *Republic*	

A Reading Order connection between *Crito*, *Laws*, and *Phaedo* creates the sharpest possible contrast with the interpretation of Plato based on Order of Composition. In Reading Order, Plato has joined what are arguably the first and the last dialogues he wrote, with the composition of his immortal *Phaedo* famously located somewhere in the middle between these extremes. Just as Order of Composition must overlook the fact that, thanks to the end of *Theaetetus*, we can be sure that *Sophist-Statesman* belongs between *Euthyphro* and *Apology of Socrates*, so too it can be used to make nonsense out of any alleged connections between the "late" *Laws*, the "early" *Crito*, and the "middle period" *Phaedo*. Moreover, Reading Order can find a place for supposedly spurious dialogues such as *Minos*, *Hipparchus*, and *Epinomis*.

A reading of *Laws* that finds an anti-Socratic "Socrates" in the Athenian Stranger need not de-authenticate *Epinomis* for being radically anti-Platonic.[44] And once *Laws-Epinomis* are recognized as a pair that Plato placed between *Crito* and *Phaedo*, it not only joins *Sophist-Statesman* as a second pair of dialogues interpolated within the story of Socrates' trial and death, but also suggests the need for a third pair to be placed between *Apology* and *Crito*. Both because of its symmetrical relationship to *Sophist-Statesman* and the obvious connection, recognized in antiquity, between *Laws* and *Minos*, *Hipparchus-Minos* neatly fills this slot, with the unnamed comrade being Socrates' noble jailor who, having had some conversations with him, bursts into tears in *Phaedo* (*Phd.* 116d2–7).

In arguing for these Reading Order connections, there is no need to deny that *Crito* was written early and *Laws* late, nor to insist that the Athenian Stranger was already in Plato's mind when he wrote *Crito*. But there is likewise no justification for asserting that Plato's mind had changed on the crucial point in the interim: Socrates' decision to remain in Athens and die cheerfully there is καλόν, and Plato need never have wavered in maintaining that he was "most just of all" (*Phd.* 118a17). By making δικαιότατος the last word of *Phaedo*, Plato also made it the last word in his cycle of dialogues, and given Socrates' attack on the kind of "virtue" that measures pleasures and pains in *Phaedo* (*Phd.* 68e5–69c3), "cycle" is the right word, since this constitutes an explicit rejection of the view that the art of measurement might be "the salvation of our lives" (*Prt.* 356d3–4). Here again, there is no need to posit any change of mind, and any reader who came to the "early" *Protagoras* with Xenophon's *Cynegeticus* in mind was already well prepared to find Socrates hunting his prey there by fair means and foul. Without denying, then, that Plato wrote *Laws* late, there is no need to imagine that he died while writing it, especially since everything that makes it deliberately "unfinished" in a dramatic, geographical, and doctrinal sense is completed in *Epinomis*.[45] One would do better to imagine the octogenarian Plato working on his dialogues as whole, in accordance with the famous anecdote to that effect preserved by Dionysius of Halicarnassus, harmonizing and "braiding" them together.

The foregoing should be sufficient to indicate why it might not have been Plato's *Republic* that constitutes his crowning achievement but rather the whole of his philosophical encyclopedia, turning as it does around his central *Republic*. It was obviously a lifetime achievement, and a true *magnum opus*, this intertwined dialogue of dialogues. Growing gradually over the course of a long life, as it must have done, the final product is more accessible to analysis than a detailed reconstruction of how it came into being, and thus it was necessary, while attempting to reconstruct it, to take an agnostic approach to its composition and to the composition of its component parts. But by situating Plato in dialogue with Xenophon, some light can at last be shed on its genesis and growth, and in the remainder of this section, my purpose is to illustrate how indebted Plato was to Xenophon while imagining, constructing, and completing it.

It is unclear when Plato wrote *Phaedo*, but *Letters* indicates that he wanted us to believe that he had written it before he penned the earliest of them, placed last in the collection (*Ep*. 363a5–8). More relevant to present concerns is that Xenophon seems to have echoed or anticipated it while writing the death scene of Cyrus in *Cyropaedia*. As Cyrus's "arguments" for immortality indicate (*Cyr*. 8.7.18–22), Xenophon had little interest in their veracity: they are merely "functional" or "occasional" with respect to the homily on fraternal affection he offers his sons at the end (*Cyr*. 8.7.13–17 and 8.7.23–24) and in vain (*Cyr*. 8.8.1). But whatever may have been the true purpose of Xenophon's *Cyropaedia*, what made it original is that nobody else had ever written a cradle-to-grave fictional biography of a hero's life ending with his death. Despite the fact that such a work must now seem commonplace to us, it was for Xenophon's contemporaries anything but, and even if—thanks to the romantic elements and historical distortions in *Cyropaedia*—it is *Agesilaus* that is traditionally considered the first biography, the precedent for it had already been set. And even if one is inclined to place the completion of *Cyropaedia* I after *Phaedo*, and perhaps the completion of *Republic* as well, it is clearly not posterior to *Laws* (*Lg.* 693c5-8). In other words, even if he had already composed *Phaedo*, it is not certain that Plato had decided to end the cycle of his dialogues with Socrates' death before reading Xenophon's *Cyropaedia*.

The purpose of the following section is to document the impact of Xenophon's *Education of Cyrus* on Plato's *Laws* and also to suggest its parallel impact on other late dialogues as well. But for the same reason that it would be senseless to insist that *Laws* was already in Plato's mind when he wrote *Crito*, it is possible that he only decided to *end* his growing series of dialogues with *Crito* and *Phaedo* after deciding to interpolate *Laws* between them. In emphasizing the role of Plato's *Symposium* in leading Plato to conceive a series of dialogues that would both precede and follow it, no remarks were made regarding how he originally intended to end the series, and just as there must have been a time when he imagined that it could end with *Symposium*, there must also have been a time when he imagined that it would end with *Republic*. While it is possible that the mere composition of *Phaedo* would already have required him to imagine placing it last, the collective failure of the subsequent tradition to imagine it in anything like those terms—for *Parmenides* can scarcely supersede "the Theory of Forms" unless it was both written and is read later than *Phaedo*—makes this uncertain. But what the connection between *Laws* and *Phaedo* indicates is that there came a time when Plato realized the necessity of ending the series with *Phaedo*, and there is some reason to think that he was indebted to Xenophon's *Cyropaedia* for conceiving of what I take to be the final form of "the Reading Order." Although I will continue to attach "the" to "Reading Order," naturally I am only referring throughout to "the hypothetical reading order as I have attempted to reconstruct it in *Plato the Teacher*."

Placing *Phaedo* last is so central to the entire Reading Order conception that some further comment about Plato's "the middle period dialogues" is necessary before returning to Xenophon. Instead of joining *Symposium*, *Phaedo*, and *Republic* as a single and ultimately outgrown stage of "Plato's Development," the Reading Order places one of them at the end, the other in the middle, and the first, *Symposium*, between the beginning and the middle. Although the growth and genesis of the Reading Order played no part in *Plato the Teacher*, it has come into clearer focus here, and in *Symposium*, *Republic*, and *Phaedo* it is possible to see its growth in relation to three successive endpoints. Now, here's the point: whatever has made it seem to others that *Phaedo* is not the only natural conclusion or τέλος of the Platonic dialogues can now be enlisted in support of

Plato's debt to Xenophon's *Cyropaedia* in persuading him to make it so. In other words, those who find objectionable the view that *Phaedo* was always going to be Plato's last dialogue in both a dramatic and a doctrinal sense—and once again, their name is legion—are in a poor position to deny the possibility that if he ever did so, he was indebted to Xenophon for ultimately deciding to do so.

But even if Plato was not even partially indebted to Xenophon by choosing a final-*Phaedo* construction, he was entirely in his debt for the invention of "Reading Order" itself. And here a distinction is necessary. Even if Xenophon intended us to read *Oeconomicus* before *Cyropaedia* and both *Hiero* and *Agesilaus* after it, it is not with respect to the construction of an *interbook* Reading Order that he showed Plato the way. Rather, it was in the underlying conception of *Memorabilia* that Xenophon was the trailblazer. From the start, Xenophon was connecting a number of Socratic conversations into what seemed to him to be a coherent manner. For example, it was only after introducing Euthydemus in the context of Critias' swinish lust that he showed the manner in which Socrates dealt with the beautiful youngster. Since 4.2 began with Socrates stalking Euthydemus and speaking in his presence in such a manner as to capture his attention, Xenophon could easily have given the reader the wrong impression—as Plato does deliberately in the opening words of *Protagoras*—with respect to his own sexual attraction to his quarry. But unlike Plato, Xenophon has already clarified both Socrates' asexual regard for Euthydemus and his views on the sexualized ἐραστής before the hunt begins.

There are many such examples. *Memorabilia* 3.8, whenever it may have been added to the ever-growing collection, necessarily follows 2.1 since the narrator tells us that Aristodemus was "attempting to refute Socrates just as he himself was refuted at an earlier time [τὸ πρότερον] by him" (*Mem.* 3.8.1). The words τὸ πρότερον require the Reading Order concept, and even though any text necessarily unfolds in time such that, for instance, the death of Patroclus precedes the death of Hector and thus the conversation between Achilles and Priam, Xenophon was doing something nobody had done before him. It was not only that he deserves his πρῶτος with respect to the Socratic dialogue, he deserves it a second time for creating a *series* of such dialogues and arranging them in an artful *order*, deliberately designed to advance the argument of the overall work.[46] Consider Homer's mighty example once again: until he met an untimely demise in the late eighteenth century, it remained obvious that we should read the *Iliad* before the *Odyssey*,[47] and the oldest version of "the Homeric Question," preserved by Plato, was which of his two poems was more beautiful, and thus whether Odysseus or Achilles was the better man (*Hp. Mi.* 363b1-4). But even if there was a Homeric precedent for interbook Reading Order, Xenophon was still a literary innovator, and indeed doubly so.

At a certain point, the pattern might almost become tiresome, but since Plato's debt to Xenophon on Reading Order is the most important example, there is no alternative. Plato's initial response to both *Apology of Socrates* and *Memorabilia* I is to isolate and divide, extracting from the multitude of conversations Xenophon has seen fit to stitch together, and thereby introducing a revolutionary variation of the genre: the direct Socratic dialogue, introduced by no narrator and standing alone. But just as Xenophon's *Symposium* inspired him to reimagine the creative possibilities of a narrated indirect dialogue, so too he eventually came to see the advantages of following the example of *Memorabilia*, and taking it to yet greater heights. It begins to look as though Xenophon's *Symposium* was responsible for both of Plato's reconversions: one to the Reading Order structure embedded in *Memorabilia* from the start, and the other to the independent, indirect, and narrated dialogue. It is not simply that the symposium genre already implied a series of discrete speeches integrated into a coherent whole but rather that Plato reached a peak so towering in his *Symposium* that from its summit a much grander structure came into view for the first time, stretching back to *Protagoras* and forward to *Republic*.

The link between *Apology of Socrates* and *Crito* had been historical, and had owed more to Plato's decision to divide than to collect discrete bits into a larger whole; the link between *Crito* and *Gorgias* is thematic, not dramatic. But the moment Plato added the drunken Alcibiades to his *Symposium*, the backstory subsequently embodied in *Protagoras* and *Alcibiades Major* must have come into view, and of course that was only the beginning. The ongoing story of how Plato improved on the innovations of Xenophon is at the center of this book, but the debt with respect to Reading Order is the most important case, and that for two reasons: first, its construction was his crowning achievement, necessarily the culmination of his prodigious literary output, and thus the best example of his "late" literary activity. The second reason is that there was no literary precedent for this edifice other than Xenophon's *Memorabilia*. It is, of course, possible to dismiss the Reading Order conception entirely, imagining it as nothing more than the product of some later Platonist's overwrought imagination.

But if it is a conception worthy of consideration, then Xenophon's priority with respect to it is beyond question, for it was he who first arranged a series of Socratic dialogues in a logical and interconnected order. If only a small fraction of the charitable temper and methodological flexibility that allowed Erbse, Gray, and Dorion to validate a unitarian *Memorabilia* were to be applied to the Platonic Reading Order as I have reconstructed it, mine would not be a voice crying in the desert, for there is far greater evidence of coherent and integrated design in the one than in the other.

It should go without saying that Xenophon's ability to organize his Socratic conversations improved with time. The coherence of the Euthydemus conversations is less artful than "the temporality of virtue" theme that connects the various conversations in *Memorabilia* 2. And in defense of a late *Memorabilia* 3, his artistry here seems to be at its zenith. By placing the conversation with Glaucon between Socrates' advice to an elected general—and it deserves mention that young Pericles was one of the generals put to death in the aftermath of Arginusae (*Hell.* 1.7.34)—and his failed attempt to make the gifted Charmides an asset for the Athenians, Xenophon created unity of theme out of dissonance of detail: it was service to the city that united the three.[48] If the link between 3.7 and the dialectical 3.8 was considerably less obvious, perhaps that was because the series of 3.5-7 already had a dialectical coherence of its own. But thanks to the reappearance of Aristodemus, still smarting from 2.1, 3.8 also had its own deeper coherence in the structure of *Memorabilia* as a whole. After all, the earlier conversation turned on civic participation, as did the series of dialogues in 3.1-7, and since that series began by identifying those who sought civic honors—"those striving for beautiful things [τὰ καλά]" at 3.1.1—the relativity of τὸ καλόν in 3.8.4, one of the features that make this conversation in particular so interesting in the context of Xenophon's ongoing dialogue with Plato, might represent his response to the heights to which his follower, building once again on his foundations, had already taken the notion of Reading Order.

The Unreliable Hero

In his investigations of Xenophon's *Cyropaedia*, Christian Müller-Goldingen naturally attempts to establish when it was written, and he uses first Plato's *Statesman* and then his *Theaetetus* as the basis for establishing its earliest possible date.[49] The fact that Theaetetus is being carried back from

Corinth (*Tht.* 142a7) might tempt a reader of Xenophon's *Hellenica* to think that Plato is linking the frame to the Corinthian War, which ended with the King's Peace, but dating his death to 369 has become traditional even though it is debatable.[50] The more important matter is the Eleatic Stranger's claim in *Statesman*—closely connected to *Theaetetus* in a dramatic sense, and thus presumably composed, like it after 369—that until a ruler differs as much from the ruled in both body and soul as the queen bee does from the rest of the hive (*Plt.* 301d8–e4), written laws will remain necessary. Since Cyrus becomes what Xenophon calls "a seeing law" (*Cyr.* 8.1.22) and yet remains human in mind and form, scholars have split on the priorities involved. And not surprisingly, despite the fact that J. B. Skemp regarded Plato as responding to Xenophon,[51] Christian-Mueller regards Xenophon's idealized Cyrus as his response to Plato's presumably pessimistic position.[52]

The details are worth pursuing, especially since it is more typically Plato who receives the kind of detailed literary investigation that the relevant passages will prove that Xenophon deserves. Here is the relevant statement from the Eleatic Stranger:

> "STRANGER: But now however [νῦν δέ γε], at a time when there is not coming into being, as indeed we said, a king [βασιλεύς] in our cities like the one naturally implanted [ἐμφύεσθαι] in the hives, no single man [εἷς]—differing both with respect to body, and that straightway, and also soul—it is therefore necessary, having come together, to write written prescriptions, as it seems, chasing after the tracks of the truest polity [ἡ ἀληθεστάτη πολιτεία]" (*Plt.* 301d8–e4). The difficulties here are contextual: we need to recall the purpose of the Stranger's Cyclical Myth, which explains why true πολιτικός, who will rule men as a shepherd does her flocks, is not now—hence the emphatic νῦν δέ γε—being found among us, making it necessary to follow from behind the divine traces of ἡ ἀληθεστάτη πολιτεία, and in default of the ideal εἷς βασιλεύς, to rule our cities in an inferior manner with written laws. The larger context is that the Athenian Stranger will ultimately redeem this situation by speaking *ex cathedra* from the cave where Zeus instructed Minos.[53]

The parallel passage in Xenophon is more subtle, and requires appreciation for "the play of character" in the way that Plato's dialogues so often do:

But first, the one having once claimed to be the kinsman of Cyrus spoke: "But I, for my part," he said, "O king [ὦ βασιλεῦ]! For a king [βασιλεύς] you seem to have been by nature naturally formed [φύσει πεφυκέναι], in nothing less than the leader in the hive, arising naturally [participle from φύεσθαι] among the bees."[54]

Since Cyrus's father is still alive, this ὦ βασιλεῦ is premature, but the use of βασιλεύς, the emphasis on nature and the comparison with the bees are more than sufficient to make the relevant connection to *Statesman*. Skemp comments: "This may be a direct reference to Xenophon, *Cyropaedia* 5.1.24 where Artabazus is made to compare Cyrus to a leader of the bees, whom they will follow willingly because of his undoubted physical superiority."[55] Skemp is right: the name of "the one having once claimed to be the kinsman" is Artabazus, but he has not been named since 1.4.27, appearing there as Cyrus's ἐραστής—the narrator prefaces it with the words: "but if it is also necessary to recall a boy-friend story [παιδικὸς λόγος; 'a *love*-tale' in LSJ] (*Cyr.* 1.4.27)—to which the second reference to him, likewise without including his name, is: "the one having once claimed to be his kinsman and being kissed by him" (*Cyr.* 4.1.22). When Artabazus is named again in 6.1.9, he will appear in the familiar role of a planted speaker, advancing Cyrus's interests while apparently speaking only for himself: this technique is a *Leitmotiv* in *Cyropaedia*, and Artabazus will reappear in that role (*Cyr.* 7.5.48–54). In considering is suitability for that role, consider his address to ὦ βασιλεῦ:

"But I, king," he said, "for you seem to me to have been born a king by nature, no less than is the naturally born leader of the bees in the hive, for the bees obey him voluntarily. If he stays in a place, not one leaves it; and if he goes out somewhere, not one abandons him, so remarkably ardent is their innate love of being ruled by him. And human beings seem to me to be somewhat similarly disposed toward you, for even when you were going away from us to Persia, who among the Medes, whether young or old, failed to follow you [this was when Artabazus, pretending to be Cyrus's kinsman, was kissed by him], until Astyages turned us back? And when you set out from Persia to help us, we again saw nearly all your friends willingly following along. Further, when you desired this expedition, all Medes followed you here voluntarily. Now too we are so disposed that we are confident when with you, even though in enemy territory, but without you we are even afraid to go home. The others will say for themselves what they will do, but I, Cyrus, and those I control, will stay beside you: We will put up with seeing you and remain steadfast in the face of your benefactions."[56]

As emphasized at the conclusion of *Oeconomicus*, the kingly ruler secures voluntary obedience while the tyrant rules over the involuntary by force; we therefore naturally assume we are in the presence of a king by nature. On the other hand, Artabazus is a love-smitten flatterer and liar, for he merely *pretended* to be Cyrus's kinsman in order to receive a kiss from him. And the subtleties continue once we recognize the erotic subtext of this speech. Consider the rest of Skemp's note: "The Greeks spoke of the 'king' bee, not of the 'queen' bee, though Aristotle recognizes the existence of the view that the leader is a queen and Xenophon, *Oeconomicus* 7.32, exhorts his wife to emulate her."[57] Leaving aside the fact that it is Socrates' Ischomachus who does this, the sexual reversals do nothing to increase our confidence that the erotic flatteries of Artabazus should be identified with the political views of Xenophon.

But neither does the parallel increase our confidence in the Eleatic Stranger, who will reverse himself on the crucial question. In the immediate aftermath of the Myth, he uses the distinction between voluntary and involuntary obedience as the dividing line between tyrannical rule and that of the king or πολιτικός (*Plt.* 276d8–e14); afterward, the distinction becomes a matter of indifference to the scientific ruler—i.e., "the rulers truly knowing" (*Plt.* 293c7)—and is made so repeatedly (*Plt.* 293a2–c3 and 293c5–d1; cf. 291e1–5). Cyrus will rule over men as if they were sheep (he is a νομεύς at *Cyr.* 7.2.14), thus fulfilling the Stranger's dream of the good old days with its "divine herdsman [ὁ θεῖος νομεύς]" (*Plt.* 275c1), before the reversal of cosmic motion that has led us to νῦν δέ γε, where the kind of man Artabazus takes Cyrus to be can no longer be found among us.

Naturally, neither Skemp nor Christian-Mueller doubts either that Cyrus is Xenophon's ideal leader or that the Eleatic Stranger speaks for Plato. With the position of *Statesman* in the Platonic Reading Order having been described in the last section, the grounds for questioning this version of "the mouthpiece theory" have already been offered. And if the relationship between *Cyropaedia* and *Statesman* were this section's primary concern, it would not be the parallel between Cyrus and the Stranger's statesman or πολιτικός that would receive emphasis but rather the parallel between Cyrus and the Eleatic Stranger "himself," both of whom appear to embody their respective creator's ideals whether political or more broadly philosophical. The role of Socrates would figure prominently in such an investigation, present but silent (for the most part) in *Sophist-Statesman*, and completely absent in *Cyropaedia*, unless, that is, we bring him with us, or are prepared to find him in Cyrus's father Cambyses, the Greek-style teaching-man that Cambyses describes (*Cyr.* 1.6.31), or the murdered Armenian sophist (σοφιστής at *Cyr.* 3.1.14). This last shadowy incarnation would perhaps justify exploring further the relevant parallel, for the Eleatic Stranger likewise finds a way to construe Socrates as a σοφιστής in *Sophist* (*Sph.* 229c5–231b8 and 268a1–b6).

But in the case of Plato's *Laws*, there is no debate about priority like the one that divided Skemp from Müller-Goldingen with respect to *Statesman*. In *Laws* 3, the Athenian Stranger not only discusses Cyrus at length but criticizes him for paying no attention to οἰκονομία and for not having laid hold of a correct παιδεία in any way (*Lg.* 694c6–8), a remark directed not so much to the παιδεία he has received but rather to the kind of παιδεία he provided for his sons. Throughout, Plato's second Stranger emphasizes the terrible state into which Persia descended after Cyrus's death, proving, as it does, that he failed to educate them properly. In short, the παιδεία of Cyrus had disastrous results, and so too, the Stranger suggests, did his failure to give attention to οἰκονομία. The reference to Xenophon's *Cyropaedia* is obvious and, as already noted, it has been recognized as such by commentators on Plato's *Laws*. Moreover, all three of our ancient sources refer to Plato's criticism of Xenophon's *The Education of Cyrus*, a clear indication that the axiom of Plato's Priority had not yet taken hold in antiquity.[58]

But since Literary Rivalry was the order of the day, it became easy to imagine that Plato was *criticizing* Xenophon, the philosophical mouthpiece of one attacking the ideal ruler of the other. Writ largest in a chapter called "Plato's Debts to Xenophon," this book's purpose is to challenge both Literary Rivalry *and* Plato's Priority, but in this section, the challenge reaches its highpoint of complexity because, to begin with, even though the Athenian Stranger is attacking Cyrus's παιδεία, that does not mean that Plato is attacking Xenophon's *Cyropaedia* in his *Laws*. The reason this is only the beginning of the complexities involved is that since I will be claiming that the Athenian Stranger is no more Plato's ideal than Cyrus is Xenophon's, the basis of *his* criticism is not necessarily the same as Plato's. On the authorial level, once we understand that Xenophon is criticizing his own Cyrus, Plato's criticism of Cyrus is really praise for Xenophon: he has *divined* Xenophon's purpose (cf. μαντεύομαι at *Lg.* 694c5) and uses his Stranger to criticize Cyrus. But since Plato is criticizing the Athenian Stranger in the same way that Plato has divined that Xenophon is really criticizing his Cyrus—and his debt to him arises from the fact that it is from Xenophon's *Cyropaedia* that he learned how to do this—the Stranger's criticisms cannot reach the core of what makes Cyrus objectionable. This should serve to give some indication of the interpretive complexities involved when we are dealing not with one but rather with two "unreliable heroes."

Perhaps it is best to begin at the end. Although there were attempts to prove that Xenophon himself had not written the last chapter of Xenophon's *Cyropaedia*,[59] those attempts have been abandoned, and the result is an interpretive split: either the post-Cyrus collapse reveals Cyrus's flaws or it doesn't. For obvious reasons, this difference manifests itself in the difference between "dark" and "sunny" readings of *The Education of Cyrus*, and whether as symptom or cause, the interpretation of 8.8 is inseparable from the overall interpretation of the book. In the case of Plato's *Laws*, the situation is different: by a virtually unanimous consensus, *Epinomis* is regarded as inauthentic. Both *Epinomis* and 8.8 appear at the end of much longer works and both tend to undermine the reader's confidence that the main character of that longer work represents his creator's ideal. In the last sentence of *Epinomis* (*Epin.* 992d4–5), the Athenian Stranger begins legislating as if the "divine" Council (*Lg.* 968b2) had been duly constituted, which it has not been and indeed could not have been, thanks to the fact that only the Nocturnal Council can establish the membership criteria for its members (*Lg.* 968c3–7).[60] To put the thesis simply: Plato was indebted to Xenophon for having added 8.8 to *Cyropaedia* when he made the parallel decision to append *Epinomis* to *Laws*. In a word, both additions validate a "dark" reading of the texts to which they are added, and both should be regarded as equally authentic.

As the principal defender of the "sunny" reading of *The Education of Cyrus*, Vivienne Gray makes the crucial point about the origins of the "dark" alternative she rejects: "The driving force behind the attribution of the decline to a failure of education by Cyrus is Plato in *Laws* 693–5."[61] En route to suggesting in the attached note that it may not really have been Xenophon that Plato was criticizing, she nevertheless allows: "[P]erhaps

Plato was thinking of *Cyropaedia* and just misunderstood Xenophon's argument."[62] The first statement about "the driving force" is the clean one: Plato's *Laws* is the first text that attributes Persia's subsequent decline as described in 8.8 to Cyrus himself, and not to his absence.[63] But, *pace* Gray, it was not Plato who "misunderstood Xenophon's argument," and in criticizing Cyrus he once again paid Xenophon the highest compliment by imitating him. With its author's ongoing encouragement, we have been reading *Cyropaedia* with the assumption that its narrator is Xenophon and that its hero is Xenophon's ideal—if we were not, its last chapter would hardly come as a shock—much as Plato's readers, even in the absence of any trace of an authorial voice, have been encouraged to read *Laws* as if the Athenian Stranger was both *his* ideal and his spokesman. In *Laws* 3, Plato was the first to assimilate its shocking conclusion with the rest of Xenophon's book.

The way Xenophon reveals Cyrus to be an unreliable hero begins with Herodotus, and as is so often the case, the greater debt Plato owes to Xenophon's *Cyropaedia* begins with Xenophon's own debts. In this case, the relevant text is *Menexenus*, where Plato reveals Aspasia as unreliable by having her repeatedly distort historical facts as preserved by Thucydides in particular. Given his intimate knowledge of Thucydides, Xenophon was in the best possible position to get Plato's historical jokes quite apart from the claim that it was *Hellenica* II that had made the underlying unreliability of Aspasia's speech recognizable to everyone. Cyrus the Great is an important character in Herodotus' *History*, and indeed he ended his masterpiece with his prescient claim, for which Montesquieu was no doubt grateful:

> This Artayctes who was crucified was the grandson of that Artembares who instructed the Persians in a design which they took from him and laid before Cyrus; this was its purport: "Seeing that Zeus grants lordship to the Persian people, and to you, Cyrus, among them, let us, after reducing Astyages [κατελὼν Ἀστυάγην], depart from the little and rugged land which we possess and occupy one that is better. There are many such lands on our borders, and many further distant. If we take one of these, we will all have more reasons for renown. It is only reasonable that a ruling people should act in this way, for when will we have a better opportunity than now, when we are lords of so many men and of all Asia?" Cyrus heard them, and found nothing to marvel at in their design; "Go

ahead and do this," he said; "but if you do so, be prepared no longer to be rulers but rather subjects. Soft lands breed soft men; wondrous fruits of the earth and valiant warriors grow not from the same soil." The Persians now realized that Cyrus reasoned better than they, and they departed, choosing rather to be rulers on a barren mountain side than dwelling in tilled valleys to be slaves to others.[64]

Xenophon's three principal deviations from Herodotus are all visible in this concluding passage. The reference to Artembares reveals the truth about Cyrus's own education: son of Mandane the Medean princess and Cambyses though Cyrus might have been, he was raised as a Persian shepherd, with no tincture of Medean luxury.[65] The core of Herodotus' story is more closely connected and ignored. After the conquest of Babylon, Xenophon's Cyrus will reside there, and as Plato will emphasize, he will educate his sons in the midst of Medean luxury. Deborah Levine Gera has pointed out that it is only in *Cyropaedia* 7.5—when Cyrus describes his new housekeeping arrangements (*Cyr.* 7.5.56–58)—where indications begin to multiply that Cyrus is not as reliably heroic as we had been led to believe.[66] But the principal distortion is embodied in the words κατελὼν Ἀστυάγην: in Herodotus, Cyrus leads the Persians in a war of liberation against the ruling Medes; in Xenophon, he comes to the aid of his uncle Astyages against their common enemy. The result is the same in that Medea comes under Cyrus's control, but it is not by fighting an open enemy but by systematically outsmarting an apparent friend that Xenophon's Cyrus gains control. For reasons already indicated, it is the friends and enemies polarity that connects "almost" the first two books of Plato's *Republic* to *The Education of Cyrus* (chapter 2, section 4).

Readers of *Cyropaedia* will debate forever whether Cyrus actually wrongs Astyages, with proponents of a "dark" reading trying to find examples that prove he does. Xenophon makes such examples impossible to validate—finding them is easy—because the real crime is implicit in the contrast between his account and the historical truth as preserved by Herodotus. It would be nobler to conquer the Medes in a fair fight than to usurp their power under the guise of friendship, but it would defeat Xenophon's purpose if it were possible to find particular cases of obvious wrongdoing. Rather, the crime is structural, and implicates the problem Xenophon inherited from "almost the first two books" of Plato's *Republic*: What will prevent a skillful warrior, experienced in the ways of deception, and of "taking advantage [πλέον ἔχειν]" by using those skills on enemies, from *likewise* taking advantage and deceiving one's friends? Apart from the lie at the heart of the story—visible only in the context of Herodotus[67]—Cyrus's behavior is morally unimpeachable if always assiduously self-interested.[68] And the best evidence that the narrator, for whom Cyrus clearly remains a hero, is not Xenophon is that he treats as true what we know from Herodotus to be false. This isn't a merely a case of indulging in romantic fiction, it is Xenophon's invention of the unreliable hero.

In his discussion of Cyrus in *Laws*, it is precisely the conflation of Herodotus and Xenophon that the Athenian Stranger emphasizes: "*Athenian Stranger*: Let us listen then. For the Persians, when they preserved the due balance [τὸ μέτριον] under Cyrus more than both slavery [δουλεία] and freedom [ἐλευθερία], they became, first of all, free [ἐλεύθεροι], and, after that, masters [δεσπόται] of many others" (*Lg.* 694a3–5). This is clearly Herodotus' Cyrus, and the Stranger praises him for preserving the proper mixture of slavery and freedom. As a result, Plato is also using Herodotus to render his alleged hero—the Athenian Stranger in this case—equally unreliable: he introduced the δουλεία and ἐλευθερία in the properly Hellenic context of the Persian Wars, where Persia represents one and Athens the other (*Lg.* 692d1–693a5). But like the distinction between rule over the willing and over the unwilling that ultimately vanishes in *Statesman*, so too does this sharp distinction between Athenian freedom and Persian despotism collapse into τὸ μέτριον. Leaving Athens aside for a moment, it is this collapse in Persia's case that leads the Stranger to praise Cyrus before criticizing him:

> ATHENIAN STRANGER: For when the rulers [sc. of Persia] gave a share of freedom to the ruled [ἄρχοντες μεταδιδόντες ἀρχομένοις] and advanced them to a position of equality [καὶ ἐπὶ τὸ ἴσον ἄγοντες], the soldiers were more friendly towards their officers and showed their devotion in times of danger; and if there was any wise man [φρόνιμος] amongst them, able to give counsel, since the king was not jealous [οὐ φθονεροῦ τοῦ βασιλέως ὄντος] but allowed free speech [παρρησίαν] and respected those who could help at all by their counsel,—such a man had the opportunity of contributing to the common stock [εἰς τὸ μέσον] the fruit of his wisdom. Consequently, at that time all their affairs made progress, on account of freedom as well as friendship, and community of mind [δι' ἐλευθερίαν τε

καὶ φιλίαν καὶ νοῦ κοινωνίαν]. CLEINIAS: Probably that is pretty much the way in which the matters you speak of took place.[69]

Plato's account has here left Herodotus behind, just as Xenophon's book had already done. The Stranger is referring to the reorganization of the Persian army in *Cyropaedia* 2, where commoners are given the same weapons as Cyrus's noble officers. Leaving aside the fact that by making all of his followers equal to each other, Cyrus was also making them all equally inferior to him, the most interesting aspect of this passage points to those "planted" speeches to which reference was made above. In a public meeting of officers and men—to which the Stranger's τὸ μέσον (*Lg.* 694b5) refers here—first Chrysantas, an officer called "exemplary for φρόνησις" (*Cyr.* 2.3.5), and then Pheraulus (*Cyr.* 2.3.8–15) frame the debate that will persuade the commoners to vote against equality in the distribution of honors and rewards. The fact that Pheraulus is a commoner and is nevertheless empowered to give counsel validates not only the Stranger's claims about Cyrus's lack of envy and his encouragement of free speech, but provides the textual basis for the existence of freedom, egalitarian friendship, and common rationality in the Persian army. But the problem with this "sunny" account of 2.3 is that Cyrus has already endorsed in private (*Cyr.* 2.2.19–20) the same views that both Chrysantas and Pheraulus bring εἰς τὸ μέσον. In short, Plato is referring to a passage where Cyrus stages a public meeting as an apparently open and equal referendum on inequality, and the speeches of Chrysantas and Pheraulus are the means by which Cyrus persuades the army to grant him the exclusive ability to judge who deserves to be rewarded (*Cyr.* 2.3.16; cf. οἱ ἀπροφασίστως πειθόμενοι at 8.1.29).

Naturally, the more important passages will implicate the Stranger's criticism of Cyrus, and will therefore focus on παιδεία and οἰκονομία. As already indicated, the latter emerges in the context of Babylon, especially when Cyrus makes the decision to use eunuchs as his bodyguard in the palace (*Cyr.* 7.5.59–65), one of those troubling indications that Gera mentions. But the Stranger mentions eunuchs only in the context of the education Cyrus provided for his sons: "*Athenian:* [The consequences of] an education [παιδεία], the Medean kind—corrupted by so-called happiness—he overlooked; thus his own sons, having been educated [παιδευθέντας] by both women and eunuchs, were becoming as a result just as they were likely to become, having been reared up by a rearing without reproof" (*Lg.* 695a5–b2). In *Cyropaedia*, by contrast, we are not even made aware that Cyrus *has* sons until he is lying on his deathbed, admonishing them to do exactly the opposite of what they will do:

> ATHENIAN: And therefore, with Cyrus dead, and his sons having taken over—full of luxury and impunity—first, the one killed the other, chafing at their equality, and afterwards, made insane both by drink and through a lack of education [ἀπαιδευσία], he lost his rule [ἀρχή] through both the Medes and the then so-called "eunuch," the latter having come to despise the folly of Cambyses. CLEINIAS: That, certainly, is the story, and probably it is near to the truth.[70]

Here, Plato is using 8.8 as the basis for retrospectively criticizing Cyrus, the paradigmatic opening move of any "dark" reading, and it is a commonplace to observe that it is not Cyrus's own education that the Stranger is criticizing but only the one he provided for his sons.[71] But since Plato is also aware that Xenophon is distorting Herodotus, the way he praises Cyrus's own education necessarily criticizes the education that Xenophon's Cyrus received by blending Persian austerity with Medean luxury, softness, and self-indulgence:

> ATHENIAN STRANGER: And as for their father, then [sc. Cyrus]: even while acquiring flocks and cattle and herds [ἀγέλας]— many of them, both of men and of many other things—yet for those to whom he was intending to pass these things, he ignored their not being educated in the paternal craft, it being the Persian one—for the Persians are shepherds, children of a difficult environment [τραχεία χώρα]—rough and suitable to produce shepherds, extremely strong and able to camp out in the open and to keep watch and, if it should be necessary to campaign, to campaign as a warrior.[72]

In addition to confirming what Cyrus says at the end of Herodotus' *History*, this passage points to the way in which Xenophon's Cyrus will rule over herds of men, for what will make Xenophon's Cyrus so effective and dangerous is that he will place Persian austerity at the service of Medean self-indulgence. In short, Cyrus emerges straight out of a fascinating blend of Xenophon's Asian experiences, his lifelong concern with the essence of effective leadership, and his encounter with Glaucon's speech at the beginning of *Republic* 2: he is the perfectly unjust man who appears to be perfectly just.

In return for the favor, both the Eleatic and the Athenian Strangers emerged from Plato's encounter with Xenophon's *Cyropaedia*. The queen bee in *Statesman* and Socrates the noble sophist in *Sophist* point to the same place as *Laws* 3, and it was to acknowledge his debt to Xenophon that Plato called attention to the amazing dance of Herodotus and Xenophon in the Athenian Stranger's mixed-message account of Cyrus, allowing him to reveal, in the context of Darius and Xerxes, and as it were in passing, the essential truth of any "dark" reading of the *Cyropaedia*:

> ATHENIAN STRANGER: After Darius came Xerxes, and he again was educated with the luxurious and kingly education of a royal house: "O Darius"—for it is thus one may rightly address the father—"how is it that you have ignored the evil of Cyrus [τὸ Κύρου κακόν], and have reared up Xerxes in just the same habits of life in which Cyrus reared Cambyses?" And Xerxes, being the offspring of the same educations, ended by repeating almost exactly the misfortunes of Cambyses. Since then there has hardly ever been a single Persian king who was really, as well as nominally, "Great." And, as our argument asserts, the cause of this does not lie in luck, but in the evil life [ὁ κακὸς βίος] which the sons of the excessively rich and tyrants [οἱ τῶν διαφερόντως πλουσίων καὶ τυράννων παῖδες] for the most part live; for never from this upbringing can there come to be a boy or man or greybeard of surpassing goodness.[73]

And for the same reason that Xenophon will never number Cyrus among the τύραννοι, the closest Plato will come to unmasking his Stranger as such will be when he desiderates a tyrannical city in *Laws* 4 (*Lg.* 709e6) and a mindful, fast-learning, courageous, and impressive young tyrant to establish it (*Lg.* 709e6–7), although there are already signs in *Laws* 3, where he shows how easy it is for tyranny to develop in a young man (*Lg.* 692b4–6) shortly before mentioning Cyrus. But we should not expect Plato to reveal the Athenian Stranger as an unreliable hero unmistakably until the very end, for if he were to have done otherwise, he would have demonstrated his inferiority to Xenophon. On the other hand, the seeds have already been planted in *Laws* 3, quite apart from the defense of wine drinking in *Laws* 1.

What makes the Stranger's treatment of Cyrus Platonic is that its inaccuracies point the reader to the passages in Xenophon that really do demonstrate his tyrannical οἰκονομία and the equally tyrannical παιδεία that made him appear to be something other than what he is. And lest there be any doubt about that, he is the conqueror of Medea who masqueraded as its friend, and the erstwhile liberator of the Persians who enslaved them, voluntarily, to himself. Consider here another of those "planted" speeches, this one entrusted to Chrysantas:

> "Just as we [sc. Persians] deem ourselves worthy to lead those under us, then, so too let us ourselves perform obediently [πειθώμεθα] the things incumbent upon us. To this extent it is necessary to distinguish [ourselves] from slaves in that slaves involuntarily serve their masters, but we, if indeed we deem ourselves to be free, then it is necessary to do willingly what seems to be of greatest worth. And you will discover," he said, "that even where a city is arranged without monarchy, the one that most of all wishes to obey its rulers, that one will least of all be compelled to give way to its enemies. Let us therefore not only be present, as Cyrus commands, at this government center, but also let us practice those things through which we will most be able to maintain what is necessary, and let us provide ourselves for Cyrus to use however may be necessary."[74]

This passage points to what makes the Stranger's treatment of Cyrus consistent not with Plato's ends, but rather with his own, for it is the slavery-freedom dyad that governs *Laws* 3. Only if Plato can replicate in his Stranger what makes Cyrus *appear* to be Xenophon's hero—only if he can make us believe that the Athenian Stranger is Plato—will he have honored fully his debt to Xenophon: by helping us to understand *Cyropaedia* better, he will have discharged at best half of that debt.

Just as Persia was once free thanks to Cyrus the liberator, but subsequently degenerated into tyranny, so too the Stranger's account of Athens must follow a similar but opposite course. In her case, it is excessive freedom that will take the place of Persian tyranny, and thus must find a way to configure her undegenerated state as a salutary form of measured enslavement:

> ATHENIAN STRANGER: Therefore on account of these things [sc. freedom, amity, and rationality], having selected among political

arrangements both the most despotic [δεσποτικώτατον] and the freest [ἐλευθερικώτατον], we are now investigating which of those is rightly arranged politically. And having taken ahold in the case of each a certain measured mean [μετριότης] between the despotism [τὸ δεσπόζειν] of one of them and the freedom [τὸ ἐλευθεριάσαι] of the other, we discovered that wellbeing [εὐπραγία] came to be in them at that time especially, but that the extreme toward which each was tending—the slavery [δουλεία] of one of them, the opposite of the other—was no more advantageous to one of them than to the other.[75]

Plato has already helped us to detect the sophistry involved by introducing both Athens and Persia in the context of the Persian War (*Lg.* 692c5–693a5), where Athens, as already indicated, albeit unnamed in the preceding passage, is on the side of freedom. This means that the Stranger must argue that Athens was able to effectively resist Persian tyranny and thus preserve her freedom because she herself was enslaved in a righteous and salutary manner, and given the book's title and the Stranger's ongoing audition to be made the lawgiver of the new city in Crete, the kind of enslavement he is eager to praise should surprise nobody. It is therefore in the context of praising this older Athens that the Stranger first describes being voluntarily *enslaved to the laws* (*Lg.* 698b6, 698c1–2, 699c1–6, and 700a5), and it is only in the context of book 4 and the remainder of *Laws* that readers can reach a conclusion as to whether this is an ideal that they too are willing to embrace.[76] The important point for now is that although it is preceded by a discussion of young tyrants and the polarity of freedom and slavery originating in the Persian Wars, the parallel discussion of Persia and Athens that follows, although initially framed in terms of an amiable, rational, and freedom-preserving synthesis of monarchy and democracy, culminates in a much freer use of despotism and slavery, neither of which is rejected except in the most extreme of cases, and both of which are necessary if the desired "measured mean" is to be achieved.

The Eleatic and the Athenian Strangers are not Plato's only unreliable heroes, but since the tradition is content with placing the composition of *Timaeus* after the invention of at least one of them, one might be tempted to find Xenophon's influence there as well. That temptation should be resisted: Xenophon's impact on "Plato's Cosmology" was confined to his clear statement of Socrates' attitude toward physics in *Memorabilia* 1. But the Athenian Stranger echoes the same attitude in *Laws* 7, stating the true Socratic position as articulated by Xenophon, before proceeding to reject it:

STRANGER: "With regard to the greatest god [ὁ μέγιστος θεός] and the cosmos as a whole [ὁ κόσμος ὅλος], we say that it is neither necessary to investigate nor to busy oneself with trying to discover the causes [αἱ αἰτίαι], for it is not pious [ὅσιον] to do so." Yet it's likely that if entirely the opposite of this took place it would be correct. CLEINIAS: How are you speaking?[77]

First expressed by Xenophon, then confirmed in Aristotle, and finally given canonical treatment by Cicero, Socrates' distrust of cosmology constitutes another proof-text that the Athenian Stranger, like his Eleatic predecessor, is no reliable hero, nor should that surprise us, since only Socrates could be that for a Socratic.

By finding in Xenophon's *Cyrus* the origins of Plato's two Strangers, this section has illustrated how the two greatest Socratics paid tribute to Socratic irony, of which the pedagogical value of deliberate deception should be recognized as a species.[78] By creating a pseudo-Socratic speech for Pausanias, and then by making Critias and Meno appear less villainous than his readers knew they were, Plato built on Xenophon's foundations in an artistic sense. By creating his Cyrus, Xenophon would now build on Plato's foundation, fashioning in great detail and with no apparent irony—at least on first encounter—his own version of an attractive and pseudo-Socratic hero, inspired by the deceptive appearance of Glaucon's perfectly unjust man. With the creation of the Eleatic and Athenian Strangers, Plato would repay Xenophon once again, and in the characteristic manner. Now it was not the ability to craft artistically polished villains for which he had to thank Xenophon, but for illuminating the far more important pedagogical necessity of doing so, for it was only by recognizing the Socratic irony of presenting Cyrus and the Strangers as their author's ideals—after having first failed to recognize it, and having been accordingly led astray—that the reader of tomorrow could experience firsthand the sense of embarrassed shame that the living Socrates had long ago engendered in Xenophon and Plato.

The Elusive Author

In making originality claims about Greek literature, it is never safe to point to anyone other than Homer as the originator, and in his lengthy tale to the Phaeacians, Odysseus makes nonsense of the suggestion that Xenophon invented "the unreliable hero." And the same applies now to "the elusive author." How could the tradition have decided that Homer was blind if he had not told us that Demodocus was: he who famously sang of the quarrel between Odysseus and Achilles?[79] Even when they speak in the first person, authors can find and have found many ways to make themselves difficult to see, and even if, as here, the meaning of "elusive" is restricted to those authors who invite or even require us to search for them, any claims on Xenophon's behalf must reckon with blind Demodocus. Nevertheless, Xenophon's insistence on playing "Where's Waldo" is so pervasive that his claim to originality is entitled to serious consideration, Homer notwithstanding. In a word, Xenophon *required* his readers to search for him.

On the most primitive level, there is Euthydemus, himself an expanded version of Theopompus. This was Homer's trick, and when Phalinus praises Theopompus for his eloquence and philosophical proclivities, this is the rough equivalent of Homer praising Demodocus for possessing the "sweet-singing art." In both cases, there is a self-serving element, especially since his description of the way the audience treats Demodocus gives Homer's audience a gentle hint as to how they should treat him. But there is nothing self-serving about Xenophon's self-portrait, until, that is, we decide that Socrates was so great that anyone who knew him was boasting simply by claiming that they did. As already indicated, "Euthydemus" was not only an artful expedient but also perhaps a necessary one, for there was nothing praiseworthy about being humiliated and abased in Xenophon's cultural milieu. It is true that Euthydemus made a praiseworthy decision to return to Socrates, and some might even admire his desire to imitate him (*Mem.* 4.2.40), but here again this presupposes the success of Xenophon's defense. As long as Socrates remained controversial, Euthydemus was subject to criticism and contempt; once Socrates became an object of admiration, Euthydemus could no longer be Xenophon.

But Xenophon reached a whole new level of what might be called "elusivity" with Themistogenes. And here it is necessary to make a sharp distinction between publishing *Anabasis* I under an assumed name and referring to "him" as its author in *Hellenica*. Others had made themselves elusive with a pseudonym before Xenophon. What made Xenophon original was not the creation of "Themistogenes" but the creation of a narrator who gave every indication of believing that Themistogenes had written *Anabasis* I.[80] By allowing the narrator of *Hellenica* II to do this, Xenophon proved—to all who are willing to admit that he knew perfectly well who had really written *Anabasis* I—that he was not that narrator, or rather that the narrator of *Hellenica* II was not simply him. Here, then, we are in the presence of "an unreliable narrator," and Xenophon's willingness to make himself elusive in this way was revolutionary. It was also characteristic: it is still an unreliable narrator that Xenophon uses to tell Cyrus's post-truth story in *Cyropaedia*. In other words, the narrator of *The Education of Cyrus* writes as if he were entirely unfamiliar with Herodotus; Xenophon was not.

In certain circles, it has become a commonplace that nothing said by anyone in Plato's dialogues should or can be taken as simply representing what Plato thought. It is amazing how quickly this observation gets overlooked in practice, however. For example, in a comment attached to the last blocked quotation in the previous section (i.e., *Lg.* 821a2-5), E. B. England expressed amazement at Cicero's willingness to believe that the anti-cosmological view that the Athenian Stranger has just rejected might conceivably represent what Plato himself had thought. "Cicero (*De natura deorum* 1.12) seems incomprehensibly to regard this as Plato's real opinion, whereas it is quite clear that it is a 'popular notion' which he is combating with all his might."[81] There are two interesting things in England's comment, and the first is his use of "Cicero." Cicero's *De natura deorum* is a dialogue, and if it makes a difference that it is the Epicurean Cotta who is speaking at 1.[12.]30—as it surely must—then it also surely matters that it is the Athenian Stranger who is speaking at *Laws* 821a2-4 and, for that matter, that it is Timaeus who is speaking in another passage quoted by Cotta (*Ti.* 28c3-5).

More interesting is England's use of "he." If this pronoun applies to the Athenian Stranger, then England is correct: "[It] is quite clear that it is a 'popular notion' which he is combating with all his might." It would have been useful to point out, as W. K. C. Guthrie does, that this "popular notion" was in fact paradigmatically Socratic.[82] But it is England's certainty that "he" is Plato that remains remarkable. There must be something happening here that goes beyond one scholar's failure to grasp the authorial concealment that the dialogue form is affording both Plato and Cicero. Isn't England's certainty that he recognizes Plato and can see so clearly what "he is combatting with all his might" the proof that Plato is not in any way elusive? Has he not made himself obvious instead? Or is England proving precisely Plato's "elusivity" by misconstruing him so radically? This comes closer to the truth. But the truth must be deeper, and is somehow connected to what it means to be a Socratic. After all, Socrates himself was famously misunderstood, and appeared to many to be something other than he was. Perhaps there is something peculiarly Socratic and ironic about the way England is misunderstanding Plato here.

To push a bit farther, England must think that a simple-minded rejection of pre-Socratic physics, couched in terms of piety, the inscrutability of ὁ μέγιστος θεός, and the intellectual impermeability of ὁ κόσμος ὅλος could not possibly have been a position that Plato could have embraced, and this must be because England finds it infinitely easier to imagine Plato as Plato's Timaeus than as the follower of Xenophon's Socrates. To be sure, there is some intellectual superstructure that makes this certainty plausible, and it would hardly be strange if a scholar who devoted so many years to studying Plato's *Laws* would find it easy to believe that Plato had outgrown "the Socratic phase" that had been responsible for "the early dialogues." Aristotle's certainty that Socrates paid no attention to physics whatsoever, while Plato did, could only increase the certainty of later scholars that there was no basis for entertaining the possibility that Plato had in fact remained a Socratic. And this probably wasn't just because dialogues such as *Timaeus*, *Philebus*, and *Laws* seemed to indicate that Plato—or at any rate "the late Plato"—had himself become a keen student of ὁ κόσμος ὅλος,[83] and thus, far from finding cosmology as an impious response to ὁ μέγιστος θεός, he was validating the existence of one by his investigation of the other.

But it is unlikely that a difference with respect to "the investigation of nature" was sufficient to create the condition for the possibility of England's certainty that what is clearly true if "he" is the Athenian Stranger must likewise be true when "he" is Plato, and this must have something to do with "style." The etymological link between this word and "the art of writing" must not be ignored, but first there is the more common meaning to be considered. It must have become easier to imagine Plato as a pedant, creating complex discourses in a tone more hierophantic than aporetic, that would ultimately make a mistake such as England's possible. On that, there should be no doubt: even if Plato shares his Stranger's rejection of this "popular notion," the proof that he does so is not that one of his characters does, and the same applies with equal force—and no more than equal since it is a question of literary principle—to Cicero and his character Cotta the Epicurean. England clearly wants to imagine Plato as the expositor of an impressive, coherent, and systematic account of large and important subjects, and even though ὁ κόσμος ὅλος may well be the largest and most important of these, it is, rather, the apodictic *style* of Plato's late discussion-leaders that has come to seem more suitably

Platonic to so many. Plato, some of us have come to believe, must have been more like his Strangers and his Timaeus than he was like Socrates.

Above all, however, the tradition has arrived at the certainty that he was infinitely closer to them, and to Aristotle, than he was to Xenophon. In Xenophon's case, it has become easy to imagine that he misunderstood Socrates, oversimplified his teaching, had derived it not from the master but from other Socratics, and in general made him into a garrulous dispenser of insipid homilies instead of portraying him as the restlessly inquiring Socrates of Plato's early dialogues. But even though it is easy to doubt Xenophon's acumen or intellectual breadth—for it is equally in detail and in general that he has been found wanting—it is difficult to believe that he did not remain a loyal follower of Socrates to the best of his ability. We have come to believe that Plato can be nothing like that, and it is remarkable that the same dialogues that have proved to so many that Xenophon was incapable of understanding Socrates have nevertheless failed to persuade the tradition that the author of those dialogues could only have been a philosopher who *did* understand him, and who therefore might have just possibly seen no good reason to outgrow him.

Xenophon invites us to think that he's a horseman, a soldier, and a farmer, none of them being occupations that would seem to confer a towering intellect and infinite subtlety on those who engage in them; instead, words such as "sturdy," "reliable," "steady," and "competent" come to mind. Plato never gives us this impression, and between the ever-questioning Socrates of his early dialogues and the ever-explaining authorities of his later ones, we are always sure that Plato could be nothing like Xenophon. When Xenophon is teaching us to ride, we sense that this a competent teacher with something to teach even if we may regard equestrian enterprise as somehow lacking in intellectual dignity in comparison with "serious philosophy." Plato even exploits this prejudice in *Parmenides*, when he treats us to the spectacle of a man whose primary concern is now horses (*Prm.* 126c8) reciting a long and complicated discourse on what Plato's Parmenides calls "my hypothesis," that is to say, the One. Let's dig in there.

There is nothing in the fragments of the historical Parmenides that suggests that he ever gave independent consideration to "the One," and the words τὸ ἕν never appear in them. It may well be that in addition to calling Being or τὸ ἐόν—about which he famously speaks a great deal—unchanging or ἀκίνητον, he also calls it "one," but there is likewise no independent consideration of τὸ ἀκίνητον, and for good reason. Even *nothing* or οὐδέν might be said to be unmoving, and pending the resolution of whether or not nothing is itself ἕν—since if it were simply οὐδέν it could not even be singular or even named—there is ample reason to doubt that Parmenides could ever have referred to τὸ ἕν as "my hypothesis," especially since if he were really referring to τὸ ἐόν, he would never have called it a *hypothesis*. But this does not mean that Plato's use of "my hypothesis" is simply incorrect, it may only mean—and this is what I take it to mean—that τὸ ἕν is *Plato's* hypothesis, and that he was the first philosopher to recognize that "the One" is not that by virtue of which anything is, becomes, or can said to be "one"—for if it were, it would be a Platonic Idea—but rather is a strictly hypothetical abstraction that purchases its many-excluding and completely atomic unity at the expense of its existence (cf. *Prm.* 143a7-8, *R.* 510c3-d3 and *R.* 511c6-d5).

Now, all of this is obviously far removed from Xenophon's concerns, but it is not so clear that it is incompatible with the position that Socrates took up in response to what the Athenian Stranger called ὁ κόσμος ὅλος (*Lg.* 821a2). Already implicit in the noun κόσμος, and then reinforced by the adjective ὅλος, is the notion that we are dealing with "a One out of Many," namely, with a singular cosmological "whole" that includes the many things or indeed all of them. As already sketched, this kind of "whole" is incompatible with the kind of τὸ ἕν that cannot be many, and which just happens to be the exclusive focus of the investigation Socrates calls "arithmetic" in *Republic* 7 (*R.* 522c1-526c7). There, he insists that the One cannot be divided (*R.* 525d8-e3) and that our awareness of it emerges from the welter of contradictory sense-experiences (*R.* 524b3-c1), and that it is because of this that arithmetic, as well as geometry, is useful for turning us away from Becoming and toward Being (*R.* 523a1-3, 525c5-6, and 526e7-8), and that means away from cosmology and physics (*R.* 528e1-529c3) and toward the Idea of the Good (*R.* 534b7-d1). It should, therefore, come as no surprise that when the Athenian Stranger teaches arithmetic in *Laws* 7, he is perfectly happy to represent "ones" by physical things (*Lg.* 819b4-5) while in his discussion of the virtues in *Laws* 12 (*Lg.* 963c5-d7, 964a3-5, and 965b7-c4) and of celestial movement in *Epinomis* (*Epin.* 991d8-992a6 and 992b6-7) he repeatedly makes use of the phrase "One out of Many," which, no matter how patriotic it may sound to North American ears, has nothing to do with what Plato's Parmenides not altogether misleadingly calls "my hypothesis."

Here, then, is an example of Plato playing "Where's Wally," and there are many others. In *Lovers*, for example, Socrates asks the rivals to identify the man who knows how to plant in a measured way not literal seeds, like the farmer, but "concerning studies in the soul, both the sowing and growing, how many of them and of what kinds would be measured" (*Am.* 134e6-7). In *Timaeus*, Socrates uses the pronoun ἐγώ and the words "what I am even now saying [ἃ καὶ νῦν λέγω]" so uncannily and in a context so central to Plato's concerns—he wants to see his Guardians come to life— that one might almost imagine he is talking directly to us (*Ti.* 20b1-7), in much the same way that has just done in *Republic* 7 (*R.* 520b5-c5).[84] And Plato will reappear as the unnamed comrade who learns so much about his kinsman in *Charmides* (*Chrm.* 153b8 and 155d3) before introducing the man he would have become were it not for Socrates in *Gorgias*, for Callicles is best understood as Plato's version of Xenophon's Euthydemus.

It is customary to regard Callicles as intransigent, unrepentant, and indeed incurable (cf. *Grg.* 525c1-8), but there are a number of indications that this would be an error. To begin with, he stays until the end (*Grg.* 527e7). He also wavers (*Grg.* 513c4-6) in response to a particularly hard-hitting speech that proves that there is nothing noble about securing your own safety (see especially *Grg.* 512d2-e5). Then there is the amazing statement that Socrates makes to him: "If you should agree somehow with me, then that will already have been sufficiently tested both by me and by you, and no longer will it be necessary to apply to it any other test" (*Grg.* 487e1-3). As the foremost keeper and preserver of the Socratic flame, Plato *was* a "godsend [ἕρμαιον]" as Socrates tells Callicles that he is (*Grg.* 486e3), and when *Gorgias* is read in tandem with the criticism of Critias in *Charmides*, and when Callicles is identified as Plato, we can see that *Gorgias* is itself an example of the only proper use of rhetoric, for Plato is not defending himself, his relatives, and his city (*Grg.* 480b7-8) but accusing them of injustice.

Inspired by *Memorabilia* I, *Gorgias* marked Plato's debut as "an elusive author" but characteristically he made it all the more artful because he left the reader in suspense as to how Callicles would turn out. Xenophon, in turn, could see the advantages of leaving the choice to the reader: Callicles, not Socrates, would persuade some of them, and only as unresolved could *Gorgias* "try men's souls." It was in the silence that follows *Gorgias* that Xenophon would ultimately find the need for *The Education of Cyrus*, albeit with a great deal of help from Plato's Glaucon. In the meantime, by illustrating Euthydemus' conversion, Xenophon could only make his entrance into history—either as making it in *Anabasis* or as writing it in *Hellenica*—as the man he now was, although self-concealment would come to have a more practical purpose in the case of the sneak attack on the Piraeus. But even if Plato's *Gorgias* pushed Xenophon to discover the Socratic value of an unresolved literary challenge, it was his *Cyropaedia* that would ultimately push Plato to take this irresolution to the limit, for he never made himself more elusive than by creating his two Strangers, challenging all the rest of us, into eternity, to make England's error of thinking that "he" was Plato, and not merely his Athenian Stranger.

Chapter Five

A Socratic Relay Race

Aulus Gellius

Aulus Gellius, who was alive in AD 180, is responsible for both this book's and this chapter's title, and it is only proper that he should now receive some explicit gratitude for having preserved such valuable information about Plato and Xenophon in his *Noctes Atticae*. A useful, charming, sane, and above all largely unappreciated collection of anecdotes,[1] *Attic Nights* resembles Plato's *Symposium*—about which it also preserved useful information[2]—in being a blend of comedy and tragedy, the one written on the edge of an abyss, the other *set* on the edge of one. The wing beats of Hegel's Owl of Minerva are audible in both works; a charming and highly literate world is about to go from green to gray.

The third chapter of the fourteenth book of *Noctes Atticae* bears the traditional title: "Whether Xenophon and Plato were rivals [*aemuli*] and inimical to each other [*offensi inter sese*]."[3] In its first sentence, he refers to others who, in the course of writing about their lives and *mores*, have deduced from various indications in their works that there was a quiet and hidden hostility between them. Since Gellius cannot be referring to either Athenaeus or Diogenes Laertius—although quite possibly to their sources—the writings to which he refers are now lost, and one might think his response would have been: "good riddance." But this would be a mistake: the purpose of his chapter is to refute the view that they were *aemuli offensique inter sese*, and thus it would have been necessary for Gellius to invent such authors even if there were none. There was, of course, no need to do so, but by first stating the conjectural bases of their claims, Gellius anticipates the scholastic method, as in: "It would *seem* that Xenophon and Plato were *offensi inter sese*." Anticipating Thomas, then, Gellius lists the bases for these conjectures (*coniectatoria*), beginning with the facts that Xenophon is never mentioned in any of Plato's numerous books nor Plato in Xenophon's—this, of course, is false—even though both writers, and especially Plato, commemorate a great number of Socrates' followers or *sectatores*. The second has already been emphasized, and thus deserves to be quoted in full:

> They have believed this also to be no indication of an unmixed [*sincera*] and friendly intention [*amica voluntas*] that Xenophon—to that famous work of Plato which has been written about the best constitution of the republic and how the state should be administered—with almost two books from it having been read, which first had been made available to the public, then opposed it and described a different kind of royal administration which bears the title of "Cyrus's education [παιδεία Κύρου]."

The following section will be devoted to "*Republic, Cyropaedia,* and *Laws*" because, thanks to Gellius, there is ancient and external evidence for the back-and-forth influence—whether as hostile or friendly responses is of course a separate issue—in this case alone, clearly indicated by what he writes next:

> And by this having been done [sc. Xenophon's decision to write *Cyropaedia* in response to Plato, and in opposition to him] and by him having been written [sc. *Cyropaedia* itself], they claim that Plato was vexed to such an extent that in a certain book [sc. *Laws* 3], by including the mention of Cyrus's kingdom, and for the sake of pushing back and exonerating his own work [sc. *Republic*], though having allowed that Cyrus was bold and strong, said: "But not to have understood education correctly at all [παιδείας δὲ οὐκ ὀρθῶς ἧφθαι τὸ παράπαν]." For these are Plato's words about Cyrus.

As in the case of Xenophon's response to *Republic*, Gellius is not disputing *the facts* he is also preserving: it is rather the *coniectatoria* that others have drawn from them that he intends to dispute. In the process, he has been kind enough to allow room for me to supply what he has not: an explanation of how these specific facts can be consistent with his general conclusion, namely, that they are not an indication or *indicium* that what joined Xenophon and Plato must have been *non sincera neque amica voluntas*.

The third *indicium* is that Xenophon denies in *Memorabilia* that Socrates ever discoursed about the heavens and the rational causes of nature, and neither touched on nor approved the view that "those other studies, that the Greeks call μαθήματα, which do not pertain to living well and beautifully." It is interesting that these proponents of Literary Rivalry combine it here with Plato's Priority, for Xenophon is the agent when Gellius writes: "and therefore he says that they lie basely who attribute dissertations of this kind to Socrates." These critics claim that Xenophon must have had *Republic* 7 in view, and was therefore criticizing Plato since there, "Socrates discusses physics, music, and geometry." Although Socrates' rejection of empirical astronomy was merely cited in a parenthetical remark in the last section, it will be easier to recall that although he discusses arithmetic in *Republic* 7, it is not for the sake of, for instance, a neo-Pythagorean cosmology that will establish physics on a geometrical basis by means of "the harmony of the spheres." It is thus the invention of Timaeus, and the fact that he, and not Socrates, will offer Plato's readers a cosmology that shows that even if Xenophon had written *Memorabilia* I in response to Plato's *Republic*—which of course I'm claiming that he didn't—that still would not validate this final *indicium* of hostile criticism.

At this point, Gellius goes over to the scholastic "on the contrary," starting with a perfectly general observation. In dealing with such excellent and serious men as Plato and Xenophon were, we should generally be suspicious with the claim that they were engaged in a quarrel or *certio* whose cause was mutual vituperation, envy, or the acquisition of greater glory: "for these things are far removed from the *mores* of philosophy," then adding: "in which *mores* these two excelled in the judgment of all." Gellius then attempts to explain the cause of the error made by those who hold that Xenophon and Plato were *aemuli offensique inter sese*:

> What then is the reason [*ratio*] for that opinion? It is certainly this: it is their comparability itself [*aequiperatio ipsa*] along with their equality [*parilitas*]—and for the most part their virtues

are very similar to each other's—that creates this appearance of rivalry [*species aemulationis*] even if the zeal and will for competition is absent.

Here speaks the voice of *ratio* itself. As indicated by his proto-scholastic method, Gellius gives his opponents their say, and does not even bother to correct them for having falsely claimed that Xenophon never mentions Plato. And there is more. Those who will reject Gellius' use of *aequiperatio ipsa* and *parilitas* as absurd on the basis of their contempt for Xenophon will prove his point that it is their followers—he does not say the followers of Plato in particular in order to preserve *parilitas*—who are responsible for turning a *species aemulationis* into its reality:

> For when a certain kind of great inborn ability [*ingenia*] for the study of the same thing arises in two or more famous men of either equal or nearly equal reputation [*aut pari sunt fama, aut proxima*], strife [*contentio*] likewise arises among their various devotees [*fautores*] about the extent of their industry and fame. Afterwards, then, the contagion of competition spreads from this external competition to these men themselves, and the race of those pursuing the same finish-line of virtue [*cursus eorum ad eamdem virtutis calcem pergentium*], when the result is close or doubtful, descends into suspicions of rivalry not by their own, but rather by the zeal of their supporters [*faventes*].

Here then is the *ratio* for this book's title, borrowed from Gellius' brilliant image of Plato and Xenophon taking part in a race or *cursus*. To begin with, we would be wise to reconsider the letter and to revive the spirit of these generous remarks, paying due heed to the fact that it is not Plato who has won the day against his rival by demoting him to the rank of clumsy imitator. But the striking thing here is not simply that the two are considered "either equal in fame or nearly so," or the claim that they expended their respective talents (*ingenia*) "with eagerness for the same thing," but that Aulus Gellius has imagined them as being involved in a *cursus* (OLD 2b) without, however, being competitors. The image of a *cursus* would seem to defeat his purpose: for how can the two be racing *ad eandem calcem* (OLD on *calx*^{2}, 3: "the finishing line in a race-course, marked with chalk") without trying to defeat the other by getting there first? According to Aulus Gellius, the shared goal of Xenophon and Plato is *virtus*, and borrowing his image, I therefore suggest that the *cursus* in question is best understood as a relay race (cf. *R.* 328a3–4).

Meanwhile, Gellius will conclude his chapter in an appropriately beautiful manner, as one should by now have anticipated that he would:

> In the same way, then, both Xenophon and Plato, these two luminaries of Socratic charm [*Socraticae amoenitatis duo lumina*], have been judged to be quarreling and to be in competition with each other, because *concerning* them, among others, there *was* a quarrel about which of the two was superior, and because two pre-eminences [*duae eminentiae*], joined together [*simul iunctae*] in striving for the high ground [*in arduum nituntur*], brought forth a certain simulacrum of emulous rivalry [*simulacrum quoddam contentionis aemulae*].

This book is best understood as an explanatory commentary on and defense of this eminently human and perceptive—and of course beautifully written—account of these *Socraticae amoenitatis duo lumina*, with its title combining Gellius' use of *cursus, ad eandem virtutis calcem*, and *simul iunctae* to justify the image of a relay race.

It should therefore be obvious that no matter how improbable "Plato's debts to Xenophon" may have recently become, there is an ancient precedent for the cooperative model this book is attempting to provide. What is more, there is no ancient evidence for the substantial reality of the modern views that have come to seem unshakeable. The proposition that we are dealing with two *lumina* or *eminentiae*, and that in addition to a certain *aequiperatio* between them with regard to Socrates, their relationship is best understood in relation to *parilitas*,[4] this now seems laughable, but it was not always so. A charitable and sensitive guide to the past, Aulus Gellius also anticipates the future: it was thanks to Plato's *fautores* and *faventes*, Schleiermacher preeminent among them, that it has become virtually impossible to claim that they *aut pari sunt fama, aut proxima*; in short, Xenophon has been defamed. The irony is that this defamation has not worked to Plato's benefit. In addition to leading directly to Schleiermacher's contemporaneous excision of his most elementary and indeed Xenophontic dialogues—*Alcibiades Major* prominent among them—a way of reading Plato emerged in Schleiermacher's shadow that construed as intellectual development and changes of mind what were rather changes of style, themselves mediated by an ongoing dialogue between Plato and Xenophon.

This book attempts to bring that dialogue into view, and its last chapter will concentrate on three examples of it, corresponding with current certainty regarding Plato's early, middle, and late periods. The last of these, implicating the composition of the paradigmatically late *Laws*, has Gellius' support, and will be considered in the next section. A reexamination of Plato's *Symposium* in the context of the relay race metaphor will ensure that his "middle period" is also represented; this will be offered in this chapter's third section. As for the early period, remarks made in earlier chapters will need to suffice except in the problematic case of *Hippias Major* and *Memorabilia* 3.8, which will receive independent consideration if not resolution in the fourth section below. The necessity of examining *Memorabilia* as an evolving piece of work, thus requiring an unusually high degree of speculation from the analyst, will preclude further investigation in this final chapter; earlier remarks about the sequence of Xenophon's *Apology*, Plato's *Apology*, *Crito*, Xenophon's *Memorabilia* I, and *Gorgias* will therefore need to suffice.

But sufficient evidence has been presented to give the reader some sense of how the metaphorical "Relay Race" might have played itself out in practice. Quite apart from the weaknesses by which any attempt to establish Order of Composition is hampered, the evidence here is necessarily limited if only because the works of Xenophon that *could* have influenced Plato are so few in comparison with Platonic dialogues themselves: even by multiplying *Memorabilia* through the hypothesis of successive editions, this number remains low. Whether as likely or merely possible, the back-and-forth or stimulus-response model can only be applied effectively or plausibly to Xenophon's *Apology*, his *Symposium*, *Oeconomicus*, and *Cyropaedia*; as a result, nothing like a comprehensive reconstruction of Plato's literary history emerges from considering his dialogue with Xenophon. Although it should already be clear that creating this kind of reconstruction was never this study's goal, the results have been sufficiently comprehensive in scope to make the following statement necessary: it is the existence of the Relay Race that is central throughout. The metaphor is being proposed as a plausible alternative to the two equally speculative principles—although the term *axiom* has been applied to them, they are really prejudices—that have heretofore guided scholarly response to the relationship between Plato and Xenophon.

Gellius' eloquent words should therefore serve not only as ancient evidence for an alternative view but as a wise admonition regarding the state of mind in which we should approach these two luminaries in the future. Although modern scholarship must speak the language of objectivity, we necessarily arrive on the scene late, and therefore must recognize ourselves to have more in common with Gellius' *fautores* and *faventes* than with the *Socraticae amoenitatis duo lumina*. If the history of Xenophon's reception is not sufficient evidence that he has been the recent victim of scholarly prejudice, it is difficult to imagine what evidence could be clearer. At least the Literary Rivalry myth acknowledged Xenophon's excellence, and Diogenes Laertius explains Plato's antipathy in relation to the "Attic Muse." Moreover, it is not the case that Plato's *fautores* are presently dominating the reception of either Xenophon or Plato himself, and anyone who has read a page of G. E. L. Owen must recognize the significance of the fact that so many of his students have supervised so many dissertations at research institutions in the United States. Nor is it entirely clear that the Straussians, despite the appearance of being Xenophon's *faventes*, really are so, and if forced to choose between Owen's approach to *Sophist* and Strauss's to *Hiero*, an admirer of *both* Socratics will find herself in some considerable difficulties.

To speak personally, then, there cannot be any question about the extent of my admiration for Plato; if five volumes on the dialogues is not sufficient evidence, then a look at a page of any of one of them should make it obvious that its author is one of Plato's *fautores* and *faventes*. By privileging Reading Order over Order of Composition, the result is not only "Plato the Teacher" but also a genius whose "intellectual development" is of no consequence in comparison with the methods by which his dialogues were intended to contribute to the intellectual and philosophical development of his students. In repeated discussions with those who have been patient enough to read my work and kind enough to criticize it, an ongoing theme has been that my Plato is *too* brilliant and far-sighted, for it would have been impossible for *anyone* to see in advance where "the dialogues as whole" were going. In part, the present study is a response to this criticism, moving as it does beyond the resolute agnosticism with respect to chronology of composition. But it manifestly does so for the sake of both Xenophon and Plato, diminishing neither and glorifying both. Having given sufficient evidence of my unabashed admiration for Plato, then, it is therefore my hope that by showing the extent of his debts to Xenophon, I have achieved something resembling objectivity with respect to the alleged quarrel between them.

But however mutually fructifying their ongoing dialogue might have been, there is no escaping the fact that in the Relay Race as described here, it is Xenophon who runs the first leg and Plato the last one. Since Xenophon was almost certainly older than Plato, and in any case predeceased him, this might be thought obvious, but of course it has not been considered so. And thus, while, for instance, the priority of Xenophon's *Cyropaedia* to Plato's *Laws* also implicates the priority of Plato's *Republic* to it, it is necessary to explain and justify what Xenophon's Priority means within the Relay Race model. And the first of these has now been illustrated: imagined in the real time of the authors—and the self-contradiction should be recognized as intrinsic to any reconstruction of Order of Composition that doesn't depend on known publication dates—the priority of Xenophon's *Apology* to Plato's may stand as an example, and the next two sections will review others. While maintaining that this "real time" is a speculative construction, this study has indicated what Xenophon's Priority in the Socratic Relay Race could have looked like, albeit using no longer fashionable methods regarding the successive layers of ancient texts to do so. But there are three other senses of Xenophon's Priority that also deserve mention, and which are at least equally significant.

The first of these recalls the traditional order of Xenophon's writings, imagined on "the shelf" of the Academy's library, fitting snugly between the *History* of Thucydides and the dialogues of Plato. In any number of ways, Plato had good reason to regard the study of Xenophon as usefully propaedeutic to the study his own writings, and since he regarded the education of distant posterity that would stretch all the way into eternity as infinitely more important than the transient events of his own life, he had good reason to want us to read Xenophon first. The most important question facing any interpreter of Plato is what it is (see Preface and chapter 3, section 1), and the way I believe it should be answered—but of course need not be—is obvious. This study depends on a certain way of answering that question, and that is why the claim that Plato was writing exclusively for his contemporaries cannot simply be refuted but must rather be rejected in practice. But those who detect in the dialogues Plato's own attempt to create a κτῆμα that would remain "un-refuted into eternity"—a description that synthesizes the *History* and *Cynegeticus*—must regard the eternal priority of both Thucydides and Xenophon as vastly more important than the mere chronological priority of, for example, Xenophon's *Anabasis* to Plato's *Meno*.

In contrasting these two different conceptions of Xenophon's Priority, consider the ongoing problem of *Memorabilia* 3.8-9. In relation to chronology of composition, this is the knottiest problem under consideration here, and the fact that it is regarded as such explains not only why this book began with *Memorabilia* 3.6-7 but also why it will be receiving terminal attention below. But when considered in relation to the eternal priority of Xenophon's works in a pedagogical sense, there is no difficulty whatsoever: between the ruthless relativizing of the Good and the Beautiful in 3.8 and the glib intellectualism of 3.9, Plato expected his readers to find a useful dialectical friction with his own works, and with the *Hippias* dyad—along with the structures to which both *Hippias Major* and *Hippias Minor* were themselves propaedeutic—in particular. In relation to Plato's own pedagogical ends, which prominently include an equally ruthlessly *de*-relativized Beauty and the Idea of the Good, it scarcely matters whether 3.8-9 along with 4.6 were intended by their author to be "dialectical," and thus by no means as inconsistent with his own views as they appear to be: if not internally "dialectical" in the context of Xenophon's Socrates, they are more importantly and eternally "dialectical" in the context of his.

In general, then, Plato had good reason, indeed many good reasons, to think that students would better appreciate his dialogues if they came to them having already read Xenophon. Note that although this statement is consistent with Xenophon's "Eternal Priority" for the readers of the future, including us, it need not be restricted to it. As described above, Xenophon's Priority in the Relay Race is both chronological and author-centric, for Plato is being imagined as repeatedly responding to Xenophon's writings. But Xenophon's Eternal Priority is not author-centric except with regard to Plato's intentions: here, emphasis has shifted to the reader or student. As a result, an eternal and propaedeutic priority points to another kind, and could be at least equally applied to Plato's contemporary students as to us. It is another hybrid sense of priority, at once propaedeutic and chronologically *contemporary* with Plato and Xenophon, to which *The Letters of Chion* points the way.

Although it is a bedrock claim of this study that Plato was writing for us, he was also obviously writing for his contemporaries. More specifically, he was a schoolteacher who needed to attract students to the Academy, and whether as advertisements to the instruction offered there or as the curricular basis for that instruction itself, the dialogues needed to appeal to students. It is easy for us to see how they did so: they are appealing, indeed delightful. But Xenophon's Priority may have been responsible for making them so *to Plato's contemporaries* in ways that have now become invisible to us. On the most mundane level, if Plato's students were the adolescent boys that a curriculum based on the dialogues suggests that they were, they might have come to the Academy straight from hunting, just as the fourteen-year-old princes of Persia are said to have done in *Alcibiades Major* (*Alc.1* 121e1–122a1), and the many connections between *Protagoras* and *Cynegeticus* suggest that this was the case. The placement of *Cynegeticus* as last in *corpus Xenophonteum* along with a pre-*Alcibiades* placement of *Protagoras* in the Platonic Reading Order points to the same place even more forcefully.

But as the story of the Queen's Sash in *Alcibiades Major* indicates, Plato expected his students to be familiar not only with Xenophon the hunter but with the heroic soldier as well. It is clearly Xenophon the Soldier who persuades the fictionalized Chion to abandon his initial reluctance to study philosophy and guides him to the Academy (see Preface); this constitutes ancient evidence for Xenophon's contemporary and student-centered priority. But since the anonymous author of these apocryphal letters was obviously writing hundreds of years later, there is no need for restricting to the fourth century Xenophon's magnetic power. In order to be understood, *The Letters of Chion* presupposed not only knowledge of Xenophon but also an appreciation for his potential power to attract, for if contemporary readers had regarded this as unthinkable as we have come to do, the "suspension of disbelief" that "the letters" required would have been made impossible from the start. The beauty of this ancient evidence is that it allows us to reimagine Xenophon as "cool," and indeed such evidence is provided by Gellius as well, for whom "partisans of Xenophon" was by no means a null set. In short, this contemporary but noncompositional kind of priority based on the contemporary "coolness" of Xenophon the Soldier supports the hypothesis that the dialogues were the Academy's curriculum and that the Reading Order began with *Protagoras* and *Alcibiades Major*.

Supporting a conception of the Academy as a day school for boys fourteen to eighteen, another aspect of Xenophon's appeal might suggest the currently more fashionable model of a conservative think tank. Scholars such as Jean Luccioni may be right that the political message of Xenophon's *Anabasis*—supported by *Hellenica*, *Cyropaedia*, and *Agesilaus*—was that a pan-Hellenic conquest of the hopelessly corrupt Persian empire was an eminently practical solution to the problems of the day.[5] And if we are willing to imagine Xenophon as a political theorist as well as a charismatic soldier, a modern analogy suggests itself in the relationship between Martin Heidegger and Ernst Jünger. Although the diminutive Heidegger might privately have regarded Jünger as a mental midget, it was expedient for him to present himself as his fellow admirer,[6] for Jünger was wildly popular among the future warriors who flocked to Heidegger's abstruse lectures on the eve of World War II. Here again, it is a man of action who attracts students to an admittedly ghoulish inversion of the Academy. So much, then, for a conception of Xenophon's Priority based on imagining Plato's contemporary students.

A fourth sense of priority will complete the square, and here it is impossible to imagine Plato's foresight. For how could he have known that Attic Greek would one day become a dead language, only to be acquired "in states unborn, in accents yet unknown" by a course of arduous study? Plato knew, of course, that a great deal can happen in "eternity," and that unforeseen cataclysms might someday do to our legacy what they have already done in the past (*Ti.* 22c1–3). But could he have anticipated the day when some thoughtful Victorian schoolmasters—with Edgar Cardew Marchant as their culminating embodiment—would hit on the happy idea of introducing their students to Attic prose with Xenophon's *Anabasis*? One thing Plato knew for certain: he had written his dialogues to be read in Greek, and without a working knowledge of that language they could not be read intelligently, for he intended them to be studied and reread, with careful attention to every word. Xenophon's Priority would eventually make this look easy, even in the wake of a cataclysm, and I prefer "Xenophonic" to the traditional "Xenophontic" because it captures the acoustical sense of his writings, for a φωνή is what you hear, and a ξένος is your foreign friend who, depending on which of you is traveling abroad, is alternately your guest and host. Not the least of Plato's many debts to "the voice of a friendly stranger" is that the Ἀττικὴ Μοῦσα would offer the likes of us an introduction both economical and delightful to his brilliant dialogues, inspiring us with the hope that one day soon, we too would be able to read them with ease and pleasure.

Republic, Cyropaedia, and *Laws*

Aulus Gellius not only allows us to imagine the relationship between Plato and Xenophon as a Relay Race, but by preserving the evidence for placing the composition of *Cyropaedia* after *Republic*, he also provided a factual basis for recognizing it as such. But Gellius himself does not join the two in this way: the basis for the *metaphor* is his eloquent and humane conclusion, and the phrase *ad eandem calcem virtutis* in particular. The factual claims about the three books, on the other hand, are found in the "it would seem" section of the chapter, and are derived from the critics he is attempting to refute in his "on the contrary" response. He neither explains the interpretive basis that the proponents of Literary Rivalry must have had in mind when they drew attention to these facts nor does he offer any counterinterpretation that would explain them on the cooperative basis he is defending. But despite leaving these lacunae for someone else to fill, neither does he deny the factual basis of the relevant claim, that is, the one about Xenophon writing *Cyropaedia* in response to reading *almost* the first two books of Plato's *Republic*.

In short, the facts are not in dispute: the Athenian Stranger clearly did make the relevant remark about παιδεία—the difference between "to have grasped a correct education" and "to have grasped education correctly" hardly seems important. Assuming that "the παιδεία of Cyrus" is the subject of *Cyropaedia*, and that "the education of the guardians" in the *Republic* begins more than halfway through *Republic* 2 and continues at least through its fourth book, the book-division to which Aulus Gellius refers—although it is obviously his opponents who have really done so—must be different from ours. Leaving aside the possibility that this observation depends on what might well be a crude understanding of what "Cyrus's παιδεία" actually means in the context of all eight books of the *Cyropaedia*,[7] a brief review of the relevant facts is sufficient to settle this dispute on terms congenial to all ancient parties: Gellius, his opponents, Plato, and Xenophon.

Beginning with Polemarchus' citation of Simonides in *Republic* 1, the relationship between justice and the friends/enemies polarity has been a dominant theme; it reappears as the problem of "the education of the guardians" more than halfway through book 2 (cf. σκύλαξ at *R*. 375a2 and *Cyr.* 1.4.15). Xenophon had clearly given this problem a great deal of thought before Plato began his *Republic*, for it figured prominently in Euthydemus' initial conversation with Socrates in *Memorabilia* 4.2. But this polarity is also an important and indeed decisive element for any "dark" reading of *Cyropaedia*, beginning with the principal distortion of Herodotus whereby the Persian conquest of Medea is made to seem like "a friendly takeover" rather than a war of liberation against an enemy.

Also in book 1, Thrasymachus has used the metaphor of a self-interested shepherd to illustrate what might be called "the craftsman of injustice" (cf. *R.* 340e2–341a3) while at the beginning of *Republic* 2, Glaucon sculpts an image of this artist by imagining a perfectly unjust man who nevertheless appears to be just. In combination, all of these elements come together in Cyrus, or better: in a "dark" reading of *Cyropaedia*. Working his wiles equally effectively on friends and foes, Cyrus becomes the apparently pious "shepherd" of the human flock of his followers, never once failing to achieve his own good (cf. the truly good shepherd at *R.* 345c2–346a1) while avoiding successfully the appearance of injustice, and his success in this regard is persuasively confirmed by every proponent of a "sunny" reading of Xenophon's text.

In returning to Gellius' ancient proponents of Literary Rivalry, it is obvious that this axiom has influenced the way in which they interpreted the relevant facts. With regard to the text they quoted from *Laws*, the following is clear: (1) they assumed the Athenian Stranger speaks for Plato, (2) they considered "him" to have been critical of Xenophon's *Cyropaedia*, and (3) they themselves had given *Cyropaedia* a "sunny" ready, whereby any criticism of Cyrus's grasp of παιδεία could only be criticism of Xenophon himself. For reasons already given, none of these views is necessarily true, and indeed the reading on offer here makes all of them importantly false. If Xenophon intends the educated reader to recognize Cyrus as a man who not only neglected the παιδεία of his sons—as he quite obviously did—but abused his own, taking advantage of his sheep-like friends with methods appropriate to the treatment of enemies, then the Athenian Stranger's is friendly criticism at worst. Better, by allowing his Stranger to criticize Cyrus, Plato is praising Xenophon, helping their mutual friends—those educated readers again—to recognize the most dangerous kind of enemy, namely, one who appears to be your friend (cf. Meno at *An.* 2.6.24). And then there is the second fact cited by the proponents of Literary Rivalry: that since Xenophon wrote *Cyropaedia* in response to Plato's *Republic*, he must have been opposing a royal constitution to the kind of πολιτεία that Socrates has now begun to describe. Once again, this view presupposes a "sunny" reading of *The Education of Cyrus*, and ignores the way in which Xenophon's book might contribute to the reader's own παιδεία.

In using the sequence *Republic*, *Cyropaedia*, and *Laws* to illustrate the Socratic Relay Race, it may be useful to take a step back, and consider some indications of the Xenophontic origins of the kind of παιδεία Plato is offering us in his *Republic*. In an effort to convert Aristippus from an apolitical and thoroughly self-interested hedonism, Xenophon's Socrates used Prodicus' "Choice of Heracles" to show why he should reject "the most pleasant and easiest way" (*Mem.* 2.1.23), but by allowing Virtue to speak after Happiness (*Mem.* 2.1.30; cf. 2.1.26), Xenophon (or his source) seems to have made the crisis too easy. Plato built his *Republic* on a greatly expanded version of the choice of lives with its two ways, and even in its first two books, Xenophon saw an amazing task open before him. Consider by contrast the way Xenophon's Socrates undertakes the παιδεία of Glaucon in *Memorabilia* 3.6, proving to Plato's brother in great detail how ignorant he really is about essential aspects of the Athenian πολιτεία. A good argument for the priority of 3.6 to the "further education" Plato's Socrates will offer Glaucon in *Republic* is the way in which Xenophon responds to that παιδεία in *Cyropaedia*. Xenophon's Cyrus knows exactly the kinds of things of which Xenophon's Glaucon is ignorant in 3.6; does this make him a just ruler? If it was important for Plato to confront Glaucon with a further challenge regarding the choice of lives—an ethical challenge as opposed to an economical one—had he gone far enough? Apparently, Xenophon did not think so.

Xenophon's decision to create Glaucon's perfect statue of an unjust man who appeared to be just would lead Plato to create the most difficult tests in the *corpus Platonicum*, represented by the Eleatic and Athenian Strangers. All three—Plato's two Strangers and Cyrus—are highly skilled, and they would have passed the kind of test that Xenophon's Socrates administers to Glaucon in *Memorabilia* 3.6. Even if the Eleatic Stranger merely describes the πολιτικός, both Cyrus and the Athenian Stranger are political men and actively involved in politics, albeit hardly of a democratic kind. And despite the fact that both reveal some sympathy for pleasure, and especially for the political use of it in educating or training others (cf. *Lg.* 663a9–b6 and *Cyr.* 8.2.4), neither could be mistaken for an apolitical hedonist like Aristippus. More importantly, both are capable of giving the impression that they too have made the difficult choice of Heracles. In the context of the Relay Race, it is therefore the reader's παιδεία that is at stake in *Cyropaedia*, and this dimension should probably affect our way of understanding Xenophon's title. And here the distance between Plato and his Athenian Stranger comes into play: although Plato's character is only criticizing the kind of παιδεία offered his son, a more radically "dark" reading would locate the problem in Cyrus's own παιδεία.

But it is the reader's education that constitutes the τέλος of this Relay Race, for it is ultimately the παιδεία we gain as a result of our encounters with Cyrus and the two Strangers that will allow us too to reach *ad calcem virtutis*. Why it would be Cyrus and the Athenian Strangers in particular that Plato and Xenophon would use to test our education will be considered only in this chapter's fifth and final section, but for now it is enough to have recognized what they have in common. Although the Athenian Stranger will discuss Cyrus at some considerable length, thus making his Xenophontic literary lineage obvious, it is not on the basis of content but of style that Plato's Stranger emerges from Xenophon's *Cyropaedia*. But it is not from Cyrus that he does so, for it is very difficult to see what this garrulous old man might possibly have in common with a law-transcending king except a desire to rule over other men; rather, it is the apodictic and thoroughly misleading narrator of *The Education of Cyrus* that he more closely resembles, and he does so by persuading the overwhelming majority of those who hear his words that he speaks for Plato, just as most readers have assumed that the narrator does for Xenophon.

To recur to the typology of the previous chapter, it necessarily becomes difficult to distinguish "the elusive author" from "the unreliable hero," for they are kindred phenomena, united by the umbrella concept of "Socratic irony." But distinguished they must be, and perhaps the place to start is by identifying the way in which the Athenian Stranger does resemble Cyrus: he is extremely effective in taking advantage of his friends. Cyrus gains control of Medea through an amazing blend of cunning and amiability, while the Stranger maneuvers Cleinias into enlisting the aid of Megillus in order to compel him to do what he has been seeking from the start (*Lg.* 969d1–3): to be the new city's lawgiver. There are other similarities, and an ostentatious but completely self-serving piety is prominent among them, and deserves independent attention. But before receiving it, it can be left to Horace to spell out the master concept that binds all of the relevant material into the highest form of Socratic παιδεία: "We are deceived by the appearance of rectitude [*decipimur specie recti*]."[8] We must prove ourselves to be immune to deceptions of this kind, and this we can only be if we have been educated, step by step, to see through deception. Neither Xenophon nor Plato makes seeing through it impossible. If there were no *Epinomis*, we would not learn that the Athenian Stranger has achieved his goal; if there were no *Cyropaedia* 8.8, we could not see Cyrus as clearly either.

Unfortunately, we seem to have conspired to undermine our own Socratic education, first by eliminating *Epinomis*, then by elevating the

Eleatic Stranger to the level of Plato's *Philosopher* at the very moment that Socrates is facing his trial, and finally by dispensing with Xenophon's help almost entirely. A careful reading of Schleiermacher's illuminating Introduction to Plato's *Sophist*,[9] combined with the wrecking ball he took to the dialogues he was unable to appreciate, and the hatchet job he performed on Xenophon, may harmlessly be cited as the point of origin for these apparently disparate phenomena, but, in Shakespeare's phrase, "he were no lion were not the Romans hinds." Now it is *we* who are responsible, and recognizing Plato's debts to Xenophon is a good place to begin recovering the essence of Socratic παιδεία. Reserving further comment about the role of deception in making us impervious to it, this section will end with a few remarks about the role of piety in connecting *Cyropaedia* and *Laws*.

In a word, both Cyrus and the Athenian Stranger *appear* to be pious, and if they didn't, they couldn't deceive. They are not the only examples: Agesilaus might seem to be a "completely good man [τελέως ἀνὴρ ἀγαθός]" (*Ag.* 1.1), and Timaeus, like Spinoza, "a god-intoxicated" one.[10] In the end, the problem boils down to the Socratic question: "What is piety?" and each of us must hold ourselves responsible for answering it.[11] Socrates was famously put to death for impiety, and a true Socratic will be more inclined to regard his condemnation as a clearer sign that he was truly pious than the brilliant way in which both Cyrus (cf. *Cyr.* 1.6.2 and 8.3.24 with *Mem.* 1.3.1–4) and the Athenian Stranger (cf. *Lg.* 819b9–c3 and *Epin.* 992c3–d3) have learned to harness the appearance of piety for their own ends. After all, it was not only in the fictional world of Socratic literature that the perfectly just man appeared to be unjust, and the summit of impiety can only be attained by a man who appears to be pious.

"Know then thyself; presume not God to scan."[12] This is Socratic bedrock, and Xenophon began *Memorabilia* I with the earliest version of the Divided Line, carefully distinguishing what men could discover on their own from what only the gods know (*Mem.* 1.1.6–19). The question posed more and more insistently in Plato's late dialogues is how far are we willing to go in accepting the kind of man whose knowledge would make him capable of blurring this dividing line. Between the divine Demiurge of *Timaeus* who gives the cosmos a beginning in time to the Athenian Stranger who gives the Magnesia an extralegal beginning at the end of *Epinomis*, Plato beguiles us with the temptations of divine happiness (*Ti.* 90b6–c6), divine shepherds (*Criti.* 109b1–c4; cf. *Plt.* 275c1–4), "a divine man" (*Lg.* 818c3), and "a divine council" (*Lg.* 969b2); he also indicates the benefits of rejecting the kind of superhuman knowledge that creates such conceptions (*Prm.* 134d9-11). Mark McPherran therefore sounds the right note about Socrates while drawing the wrong conclusion about Plato:

> The *Sophist*, then, reminds us that Platonic piety developed in conscious contrast to Socratic piety. Where Socrates advises the traditional, sober Apollonian virtue of "knowing that we are all worth nothing with respect to {divine} wisdom" (*Ap.* 23b; cf. 20d-e), Platonic piety might fairly be said to storm the heavens with an erotically passionate, epistemic optimism that Socrates would have found intolerably hubristic and unrealistic (and reminiscent of the previous day's encounter with the amazing Euthyphro).[13]

If Plato had no intrinsic objection to the notion of a divine law (ὁ θεῖος νόμος at *Lg.* 716a3) to which everyone, including the city's rulers, should be slaves (*Lg.* 715d5), Socrates' persuasive Speech of the Laws in *Crito* proves nothing of the kind, and indeed constitutes an ironic counterpoint to such a view. And with respect to the Athenian Stranger's definition of law as ἡ τοῦ νοῦ διανομή (*Lg.* 714a1-2), it is useful to recall the last question that Socrates imagines someone (τις) asking him in *Minos*: "'Whatever then are those things that the good lawgiver [νομοθέτης] and apportioner [νομεύς] distributes [participle of διανέμειν; basis of διανομή] to the soul to make it better?'"[14] Philosophy, dialectic, and the dialogues of Plato—including of course his *Laws*—would be a good place to start; far better than what is on offer in *Laws* alone when regarded as Plato's "last word." The word νομεύς that Socrates uses here looks back to *Statesman* (*Plt.* 267e1-276d6; cf. *Lg.* 906b5 and 931d2), and the νομοθέτης will come forward in *Laws*: the myth has changed—for the longest day's destination is the cave in which Zeus taught Minos "the kingly art [ἡ βασιλικὴ τέχνη]" (*Min.* 320c1-2)—but its τέλος remains what it was in *Statesman*. Recovery of "the divine herdsman [ὁ θεῖος νομεύς]" and τροφή (*Plt.* 275c1-4) from the ancient Age of Kronos will be made possible by modern means: as an astronomical νομοθέτης, the Athenian Stranger will dispense (διανέμειν) cosmic νοῦς in the form of νόμος. Since his preferred μηχανή is the apparently pious claim that it is not he but rather ὁ λόγος that speaks through him, the Stranger will generally not call it "his" νόμος; he slips only once: in *Laws* 7 (ὁ ἐμὸς νόμος at *Lg.* 803a5).

Xenophon pointed the way to these further developments in *Cyropaedia* with his "good shepherd" (*Cyr.* 8.2.15), allowing Cyrus to resemble Socrates just enough to tempt us (*Mem.* 3.1). As for ἡ βασιλικὴ τέχνη,

272 | The Relay Race of Virtue

Xenophon's Socrates will point us toward that art without teaching it—for being intrinsically susceptible to abuse, it cannot be taught—with the Sweating Rowers in *Oeconomicus* (*Oec.* 21.3). It would be Plato and Xenophon who would reach their common destination, praising one another along with their coxswain, and being praised by Socrates in return.

Symposium, *Symposium*, *Oeconomicus*, and *Meno*

This section revisits the most interesting example of the Relay Race in action, imagined once again in terms of Order or Composition. Although the actual *cursus ad eandem calcem virtutis* involved far more baton passing, confining the sequence to four preserves the athletic aspect of the metaphor, and the assertion of Xenophon's Priority implicit in this particular back-and-forth quartet emphasizes one of its most controversial and characteristic claims. The advantage of revisiting this claim now is that the role of deception in Socratic παιδεία has come to the forefront in the previous section, and the central argument for the priority of Xenophon's *Symposium* to Plato's is that the connection between them most often cited to prove the opposite creates the basis for Plato's initial advance in deception-based παιδεία. This connection has, of course, already been mentioned, and it identifies the speech of Pausanias as the earliest example of what would become Plato's characteristic *modus operandi* with regard to Xenophontic priority, and more specifically with regard to the way Plato repeatedly and artfully depicts as apparently good a series of characters that Xenophon had already given Plato's intended audience good grounds for recognizing as thoroughly bad.

In some respects, Plato's Pausanias is the least skillfully realized of these dubious characters, at least in comparison with Meno, Critias, and Alcibiades. Although Plato will reach the summit of artistry only with Timaeus and his Strangers, he served his apprenticeship under the more direct influence of Xenophon, borrowing the raw materials he would then fashion into perfectly polished statues. By applying this metaphor to Plato, it becomes possible to see that Xenophon had once again received the baton from him before creating his Cyrus, although in that case, he borrows his villain from Herodotus and then washes him clean with Plato's tricks. But it makes sense that Plato reached his pre-*Cyropaedia* peak in *Meno*. Amid so many other felicities, the way Plato exploited the sexual dimension of Meno's character can be recognized as characteristic:

depicted by Xenophon as being at once the dominant ἐραστής and passive ἐρώμενος (*An.* 2.6.28), Plato captured beautifully his alternately peremptory (*Men.* 70a1–4) and coquettish elements (*Men.* 80c3–6), synthesized in the imperiousness of a spoiled and ignorant brat (*Men.* 86c6–e1). The sexual dimension is also evident in Plato's depiction of the intemperate Critias, where the pig-like lust for the beautiful Euthydemus Xenophon has already revealed should leave little doubt as to the nature of his feelings for the beautiful Charmides (*Chrm.* 162b8–e1; cf. πάντες at 154c2).

In turning to Plato's *Symposium*, the extent of Plato's debt to Xenophon in constructing the drunken speech of Alcibiades is difficult to assess, for there may well be none: there is nothing in Xenophon's *Symposium* that Plato could use in fashioning his Alcibiades apart from the need to find some way to incorporate the sexual element that his substitution for the sexy pantomime demanded. And even though Xenophon had provided indispensable information about Alcibiades in *Hellenica* I, none of that is really germane to the words and deeds of Plato's Alcibiades in *Symposium*, where the influence of Thucydides is sufficient to provide the requisite historical background. But was Thucydides' presentation sufficiently rich in depicting Alcibiades' psychological complexity? We have grown so dependent on Plutarch for making us believe that we know Alcibiades that it has become difficult to imagine how creative Plato must have been to capture the amazing blend of self-assurance and confessed weakness, of mastery and defeat, that makes the last speech of Plato's *Symposium* so memorable.

As already indicated, the only surviving evidence of any earlier attempt to capture the complexity of Alcibiades by replicating one of his speeches is Xenophon's *Constitution of the Athenians* when considered as a genuine Xenophontic work (see chapter 3, section 4). Some expressions used by Hartvig Frisch to describe the psychological complexity of the assumed author of this curious text—and, of course, Frisch regarded its author as neither Xenophon nor Alcibiades—were quoted there: "double tendency," "two souls," and "the wise reasoner and the traitor to his country." In Plato's *Symposium*, Alcibiades is at once the betrayer of Socrates and the one who usurps an exclusive prerogative to praise him, despite the logically and personally prior claims of both Aristodemus and Apollodorus. On the eve of his betrayal of Athens, Alcibiades presents himself as one of Socrates' victims, explaining the cause of his appeal while demonstrating his immunity to it. His speech is brilliant because it needed to be: Socrates' speech was "a tough act to follow," and only by praising his rival could he hope to surpass him. Ignoring the idealism in Diotima's speech—which of course he has not heard, either literally or figuratively—he materializes the vision of "the Beautiful itself" in the man Socrates, thereby confirming what Frisch found in pseudo-Xenophon, in a passage worth quoting again: "Thus two souls seem to be fighting in the author's breast, the one which is idealistic and ethical, is seated in his emotional life and finds vent in all the terms of abuse directed against the Athenians and the people, the other, seated in his reason, is realistic and materialistic, and from that all the arguments originate."[15]

Quite apart from the fact that an Alcibiades-based authenticity argument for *Constitution of the Athenians* is new and controversial on its face, the notion that Plato would have needed to depend on it in writing his *Symposium* will promptly meet the objection that there must have been a considerable body of lost literature about a character as remarkable as Alcibiades without relying on Xenophon. And this objection, generally deployed in a destructive manner, now creates a bridge between what Xenophon's Socrates says about Pausanias in his *Symposium* and the speeches of Pausanias and Phaedrus in Plato's. We need only to posit the existence of some lost source other than Plato's *Symposium* for what Xenophon's Socrates says here: "And indeed Pausanias, the lover [ἐραστής] of Agathon the poet, apologizing on behalf of those rolling about in incontinence [ἀκρασία], has also said that an army of boyfriends [παιδικά] and their lovers [ἐρασταί] would become most formidable" (*Smp.* 8.32).

The best argument for Plato's priority is that *his* Pausanias is tacitly defending the kind of ἀκρασία that Xenophon's Socrates places in a zero-sum opposition to his own thesis here; those who uphold the orthodoxy on this point must ignore the fact that Pausanias is doing so under the cover of ἀρετή (*Smp.* 184b6-c3, 184d5-e4, and 185b4-5). As Plato's reader, Xenophon would have needed to find a defense of ἀκρασία between the lines, and thus would have needed to prove himself to be an unusually astute reader of Plato's *Symposium* if he were to have realized the by no means obvious truth: that Plato's Pausanias is defending a sexualized pederasty under the cover provided by the merely apparent goal of praising ἔρως, by celebrating the influence of the heavenly Aphrodite, by linking sex to the pursuit of virtue—the word appears nine times in his speech—and by means of some false claims about the permanence of physical relationships.

But before turning to those permanence claims, it is worth restating the basic problem: by famously attributing to Pausanias what Plato's

Phaedrus has said about an army of lovers (*Smp.* 178e3–179a2), the same passage that reveals Xenophon to be an astute reader of Plato likewise serves "to simultaneously quench [συμαπομαραίνεσθαι]" (*Smp.* 8.14) that reputation by proving him to be a very careless one, and particularly careless with respect to reading the speech of Pausanias. As already indicated, what makes his speech so deceptive is that Plato's Pausanias echoes Xenophon's Socrates on matters both essential and corollary *and yet to a diametrically opposed effect.* The problem that defenders of Plato's priority have failed to face squarely is why Xenophon would have decided to model the speech of his Socrates on Plato's Pausanias.[16] This modeling is not only unlikely in itself—Diotima's is a much more plausible speech for Xenophon to have copied, for obvious reasons—but equally obvious reasons make a decision to copy Pausanias' speech particularly implausible: despite obvious similarities, the two speeches represent take opposite positions on matters both essential and corollary. If Xenophon's Socrates is more diffident as to the reality of the two versions of Aphrodite (*Smp.* 8.9), his repeated use of ἀνάγκη reveals the depth of his commitment to the difference that arises from those versions (*Smp.* 8.13, 8.14, and 8.18). But most problematic of all is that it is precisely *his hostility to Pausanias* that Xenophon's Socrates announces at 8.32—the single most important passage in Xenophon's *Symposium* for proving the priority of Plato's[17]—that makes it unlikely that Xenophon would choose to model the speech of his Socrates on the same Pausanias whose defense of sexualized pederasty that speech so famously attacks.

But Plato's *subsequent* decision to model the speech of Pausanias on that of Xenophon's Socrates makes perfect sense in the context of the higher education in the voluntary use of deception that will ultimately lead to the creation of Timaeus and his two Strangers, an education that is made explicit in *Phaedrus.*[18] Plato's complex *Phaedrus* is best and indeed has been frequently understood as mediating between *Symposium* and those later dialogues. As already indicated, both the speech of Lysias and the first speech of Socrates repeatedly allude to arguments made against sexualized pederasty in Xenophon's *Symposium* while, for exactly the same reason, Socrates' second speech must echo Plato's Pausanias, and it is indeed precisely these echoes that make the Great Speech a perfect introduction to the kind of deception that will eventually be entrusted to the Athenian Stranger. Consider in this context the claims Socrates (as "Stesichorus") makes about the inferior sexual pair of lovers at the end of the Great Speech:

If however they live a life less noble and without philosophy, but yet ruled by the love of honor, probably, when they have been drinking, or in some other moment of carelessness, the two unruly horses, taking the souls off their guard, will bring them together and seize upon and accomplish that which is by the many accounted blissful; and when this has once been done, they continue the practice, but infrequently, since what they are doing is not approved by the whole mind. Likewise are these two friends [φίλω μὲν οὖν καὶ τούτω], though not such friends as the others, both at the time of their love and afterwards, believing that they have exchanged the most binding pledges of love, and that they can never break them and fall into enmity. And at last, when they depart from the body, they are not winged, to be sure, but their wings have begun to grow, so that the madness of love brings them no small reward; for it is the law that those who have once begun their upward progress shall never again pass into darkness and the journey under the earth, but shall live a happy life in the light as they journey together [ἀλλὰ φανὸν βίον διάγοντας εὐδαιμονεῖν μετ' ἀλλήλων πορευομένους], and because of their love shall be alike in their plumage when they receive their wings.[19]

The second-best lovers whose weakness in the face of inner conflict leads them to have sex (cf. ἀκρασία at *Smp.* 8.32) are at the center of this passage *and the argumentative center of the Great Speech as whole.* What makes the passage consonant with the speaker's purpose is that despite their weakness and evident inferiority to the asexual pair, they too eventually secure a happy ending, replete with wings. Were they not to achieve this happy ending, the speaker could not persuade the youth to have sex with him; the youngster's choice to do so—to be persuaded to χαρίζεσθαι the ἐραστής—is made to seem both misguided *and ultimately innocuous*.[20] Invoking the poetic language of the myth, relying on the eternity of soul as such, and entirely dependent on the tripartite soul that both enlivens the myth and explains the mixed feelings of the sexual pair, the deceptiveness of the speech as a whole can be measured by the following considerations: (1) the reception's lack of attention to this passage,[21] (2) its elevation of a "new" conception of the soul's eternity—equally foreign to *Symposium* (*Smp.* 212a6-7), *Phaedo* (where there is no trace of *Phdr.* 245c5-246a2), and *Timaeus* (*Ti.* 35a1-b4)—as representing an advance in Plato's thought,[22] not as playing a necessary role in giving the sexual lovers the time they need to achieve what the sexless pair earns quickly, (3) the crucial role that the beautifully told chariot myth plays in the speaker's appealing description of this happy ending, and (4) the decisive importance that the tripartite soul plays in persuading the young man to have sex with the speaker, thus returning us to the ἀκρασία Xenophon's Socrates attached in Pausanias (*Smp.* 8.32). In simpler terms, this passage stands in a zero-sum opposition to Lysias, the first speech of Socrates, and above all Socrates' speech on ἔρως in Xenophon's *Symposium* in a manner *that confirms Plato's Pausanias*: the pair of corporeal lovers, despite giving way to ἀκρασία, end up as friends (hence the dual φίλω), and remain together, happy, and winged.

The priority of Xenophon's *Symposium* to Plato's depends first on the priority of Plato's *Symposium* to his *Phaedrus* (cf. *Phdr.* 276d5-8), and pending Schleiermacher's resuscitation, this is uncontroversial enough, whether that priority is based on Order of Composition or Reading Order. More controversially, it is based on a reading of Socrates' second speech in *Phaedrus* that emphasizes the importance of the lengthy passage just quoted. The basis for regarding the Great Speech as deliberately deceptive is something Socrates says in the second part of the dialogue, when he contrasts his two speeches:

> SOCRATES: The two [here he uses the dual form] were somehow [που] opposites; the one [ὁ μέν] was saying [dual form again] that it was necessary to gratify the one who loves, the other [ὁ δε], the one who doesn't [ἐναντίω που ἤστην: ὁ μὲν γὰρ ὡς τῷ ἐρῶντι, ὁ δ' ὡς τῷ μὴ δεῖ χαρίζεσθαι, ἐλεγέτην].[23]

The sexual purpose of "Stesichorus" has been generally overlooked, but this passage makes it plain; Socrates' diffidence about its veracity (*Phdr.* 265b6-8) has already been cited. What makes the passage about the pair who has sex so important is that it creates a happy ending—in the context of a lifelong and abiding φιλία—for the beloved who sexually gratifies the persuasive ἐραστής whose speech is expressly designed to secure such gratification. Not only is this exactly the point that separates the position of Xenophon's Socrates from both Pausanias in Plato's *Symposium* and "Stesichorus" here in *Phaedrus*, but it also replicates the technique Plato used in constructing the speech of Pausanias in the first place. Just as Pausanias argued that there was nothing wrong with a boy sexually gratifying even a deceptive ἐραστής (*Smp.* 184e5-185b1) by using the virtue-based language of Xenophon's Socrates as cover, so too does the deceptive Stesichorus use Diotima's language to achieve the same result.

It is only when Xenophon's *Symposium* is recognized as prior to Plato's that the full force and beauty of the Relay Race metaphor comes into its own, and enough has been said in earlier chapters to make it unnecessary to repeat here how the didactic Diotima passed the baton to Ischomachus before "Socrates schooled" could pass it on to Meno's slave. Although this quartet is particularly elegant and worthy of consideration in its own right, it has seemed more important to situate it in the midst of a much more complicated relay. In order to allow Xenophon to run the first leg, it was necessary to invoke later developments in *Phaedrus*, but in the context of a more complicated race, the emphasis on *Phaedrus* can also be justified because it stands between the kind of techniques that Plato used to make characters such as Pausanias, Alcibiades, Critias, and Meno appear less objectionable and more charming than Xenophon had done, and the new impetus emerging from *Cyropaedia* to create even more attractively deceptive characters, for without the capacity to recognize deception, a Socratic education remains incomplete.

The Origins of Platonism?

Plato's *Phaedrus* indicates that Socrates played a prominent role in teaching us how to recognize deception and that he did so by using it himself, particularly as "Stesichorus." There are ongoing indications in Xenophon that Plato did not invent this aspect of Socratic παιδεία and indeed the justice of using deception against enemies (*Mem.* 4.2.14-15) and friends (*Mem.* 4.2.16-19) played a prominent role in the first conversation with Euthydemus. But now, it is the last conversations with him that demand attention: the various arguments Socrates uses to make his followers "more dialectical" in *Memorabilia* 4.6. It is here that Xenophon's Socrates seems to come closest to "Stesichorus," for it is difficult to find anything that he says in 4.6 that is not open to obvious dialectical objections. Naturally the various claims in this chapter have generally been "read straight," and given that the Straussian school is disinclined to read anything in *Memorabilia* "straight," this rigid insistence on "the letter" is understandable. But the chapter's purpose indicates that Xenophon's Socrates is now doing something new, and since the previous section has highlighted the role of

Phaedrus, it can do no harm to suggest that 4.6 was added to *Memorabilia* after Xenophon had read that dialogue, which, thanks to its relation with his *Symposium*, he was in an ideal position to understand. The reference to division κατὰ γενή at the end of the chapter that precedes it (*Mem.* 4.5.11) might be considered as corroborating this suggestion.

But as already indicated, 4.6 does not stand alone as arguably being "dialectical," or rather deliberately deceptive. There are two other chapters in *Memorabilia* where the narrator insists that Socrates was answering "straight," and quite apart from "the lady doth protest too much" aspect—for why would we need to be told that Socrates was responding in a forthright manner when that is what we have been accustomed to think he is doing throughout—there is the objectionable character of what he then goes on to claim in each. Consider first the dialogue with Hippias in 4.4: here Socrates will defend the same legal positivism that will reappear in 4.6. At the start of 4.4, Xenophon tells us that Socrates "was not concealing what thought [γνώμη] he was having" about the Just (περὶ τοῦ δικαίου) and then proceeds to identify it with the lawful. At the start of 4.7, after the long series of objectionable claims just made in 4.6, Xenophon observes: "That Socrates was thus simply revealing his thought [γνώμη] to those consorting with him seems to me clear from these comments." It is difficult to take these words seriously, especially since Xenophon begins 4.6 with the words: "How he was also making his companions more dialectical, I will attempt to explain even this." As already indicated, it seems unlikely that Xenophon's Socrates could have made his companions more dialectical by offering them a series of bald pronouncements, including the identification of the legal and the just.[24]

Far more important in the context of Plato is the even more dubious identification of the beautiful and the useful, that is, of καλόν and χρήσιμον, in 3.8. Echoed verbatim in 4.6, this identification has already appeared in a comical context in Xenophon's *Symposium* (*Smp.* 5), where τὸ καλόν is defined "in relation to the functions on account of which we would acquire each of them." On this basis, Socrates claims to be more beautiful than Critobulus on the basis of his bulging eyes, thick lips, etc. This functional defense of beauty naturally falls flat, and Socrates loses the beauty contest. The question is: Did he expect to win it, or was he not only "in on the joke," but the joker? A similar problem arises in 3.8. The discussion of τὸ ἀγαθόν and τὸ καλόν arises from an attempt by Aristippus to trap Socrates seeking to avenge his earlier overthrow in 2.1; it is precisely the relativized versions of both that will allow Socrates to escape the trap. In other words, if Socrates had specified some across-the-board and in all circumstances "beautiful," it would have been Aristippus who could have been able to play the relativism card. But here's the passage that suggests the "dialectical" character of the chapter:

> When Aristippus attempted to cross-examine Socrates in the same fashion as he had been cross-examined by him in their previous encounter, Socrates, wishing to benefit his companions, was not replying like those guarding themselves [οἱ φυλαττόμενοι] lest somehow their account may be undone.[25]

The claim that Socrates did not respond guardedly simply does not ring true. Even if Xenophon had not denied it, I would have thought that Socrates *was* responding guardedly; the fact that he feels it necessary to deny it rather confirms than resolves my doubts.

And then there is *Memorabilia* 3.9, one-sided attention to which will be the inevitable consequence of the current revival of interest in Xenophon.[26] Linked to 3.8 by position and with both set off from 3.1–7 by the absence of the civic element, it is linked to 3.10 only by the list-like presentation of topics, including Socrates' responses to three questions posed by an unnamed interlocutor, beginning with "and again being asked" (*Mem.* 3.9.1; cf. 3.9.4 and 3.9.14).[27] Socrates' response to the last of these (3.9.14–15) looks like a response to the First Protreptic in Plato's *Euthydemus*; in addition to distinguishing εὐπραξία from εὐτυχία (cf. *Euthd.* 279d6–e2), he consistently supplies εὖ πράττειν with a direct object, thus disarming the equivocation, so often exploited by Plato's Socrates, with which the First Protreptic begins (*Euthd.* 278e3; cf. 280b6 and 282a1–2).[28] And since the same passage in Plato also includes the claim that σοφία is the only good and ἀμαθία the only evil (*Euthd.* 281e2–5; cf. *Hp. Ma.* 296a4–b2), Socrates' initial reduction of temperance and all the other virtues to σοφία (*Mem.* 3.9.4–5) looks like another reference to *Euthydemus*. As for the rest of the chapter, the introductory remarks on courage (*Mem.* 3.9.1–3) lead seamlessly into the reduction of the virtues to σοφία, while the discussion of madness that follows that reduction (3.9.6–7) likewise follows it in a logical sense. But the list of topics Socrates considers between 3.9.8 and 3.9.14—envy, leisure, kings, and tyrants—seems randomly chosen and with no obvious connection to *Euthydemus* or anything else in Plato.

Since we are about to experience an explosion of interest in 3.9.4–5 that will reveal young professors of Ancient Philosophy to have learned nothing from the widespread backlash against the decontextualized argument-analysis championed by Gregory Vlastos, the foregoing overview of 3.9 is offered as an alternative, but nothing can stem the tide. As already indicated, this passage contains a Socratist trifecta, synthesizing the unity of the virtues, virtue as knowledge, and the prudential version of the Socratic Paradox in a manner that makes the Socrates of Plato's *Protagoras* look vague and Aristotle's Socrates look like the genuine article. The passage's veridical status as indicating "the philosophy of Socrates" will be assumed—just as the First Protreptic's has been[29]—and we will therefore be entertained with scholarly discussion of a disembodied and decontextualized "Socrates" who "regards," "argues," and "would reply" in accordance with current conception of "Socratic intellectualism" while ignoring "Socratic ignorance." Here is the relevant passage, with brackets added to facilitate analysis:

> And he said also [I] that justice and every other virtue is wisdom. For [II] both just actions and all others that are done by means of virtue are actions both beautiful and good. [III] And neither will those knowing these things ever choose to do anything other than them [IV] nor are those who do not understand them able to do them, but even when they try, they fail. [V] Hence [οὕτω], while the wise do both beautiful and good actions [τὰ καλά τε καὶ ἀγαθά], those who are not wise are unable to do them, but if they try, they fail. [VI] Since then [ἐπεὶ οὖν], both the just actions and the other beautiful and just actions are done by means of virtue, [VII] it is clear [δῆλον εἶναι] that justice and all the rest of virtue is wisdom.[30]

Since [I] and [VII] are identical, we are dealing either with a "to prove"/Q. E. D. structure or with ring-composition, and the identity of [II] with [VI] makes it look more like the latter. And since [IV] and [V] are both identical and contiguous, the addition of οὕτω, along with the equally proof-like ἐπεὶ οὖν and δῆλον εἶναι, make the use of ring-composition look less like proof than circular reasoning. In any case, with these identities in view, [III] is the odd man out, and here is the Socratic Paradox; if this really is a proof, it depends on [III]. Supporting the importance of [III] is that the Socratic Paradox has just appeared at the end of 3.9.4 in a purely self-interested form: given alternatives, everyone—Socrates adds: "I think [οἴμαι]"—chooses "what they think to be most advantageous for them [συμφορώτατα αὐτοῖς], and these things they do." Insofar, then, as [III] has been proved, it depends on equating τὰ καλά τε καὶ ἀγαθά with συμφορώτατα αὐτοῖς. And this, of course, is the problem at the heart of the matter. If σοφία is that which allows us to recognize that doing τὰ καλά τε καὶ ἀγαθά is what is always most advantageous for us, and then never permits us to do anything else, all will be well. But if σοφία is morally neutral, permitting its misuse as well as its virtuous application (*Hp. Mi.* 368e5-369a3; cf. 375a9-376a1), if it is justice and the rest of virtue that must in fact guide σοφία (*Mx.* 246e7-247a2; cf. *Prt.* 329e5-6), if its only goal when isolated from the rest of virtue is success as εὐτυχία (*Euthd.* 280a6-8), or if in the end all men blamelessly follow what is συμφορώτατα αὐτοῖς (cf. *Ath. pol.* 2.20), they will be inclined to define τὰ καλά τε καὶ ἀγαθά on that basis. This is the problem at the center of *Cyropaedia.*

But it is more obviously the problem that unites 3.9 to 3.8. The problem of τὰ καλά τε καὶ ἀγαθά has already reached its most acute form in the previous chapter thanks to Socrates' apparently unguarded responses to Aristippus. There, he refuses to identify anything as "in itself" or absolutely beautiful or good, carefully insisting that things can only be good or beautiful in relation—signified in Greek with πρός τι and ἤ (*Mem.* 3.8.4-5)—to that *for which* they are beautiful and good. If what all men seek is happiness, if things are good and beautiful only in relation to it, and if σοφία is thus what allows us to discern and do such things, then it is clear (δῆλον εἶναι) that men always do the things that are συμφορώτατα αὐτοῖς. This argument has its appeal, but we must ask: To whom does it appeal most strongly? And as a first response, it may be useful to recall Socrates' diffidence about both σοφία and εὐδαιμονία in the initial conversation with Euthydemus (*Mem.* 4.2.33-36), the deceptiveness of Εὐδαιμονία in the Choice of Heracles (*Mem.* 2.1.26), and the de-equivocation of εὖ πράττειν (*Mem.* 3.9.14-15). But even if it is possible to indicate what makes 3.8-9 both attractive and problematic, there still remains the problem of how we are to understand this passage in relation to Plato.

There can be very little doubt that this is what we need to do, especially since it is not only *Euthydemus* that is repeatedly brought to mind in 3.9 but *Hippias Major* that is even more obviously implicated in 3.8.[31] In addition to the specific πρός τι examples of running and wrestling common to both (cf. *Mem.* 3.8.4 and *Hp. Ma.* 295c9), the connection is made even clearer when 4.6 will complete the relativizing of the beautiful and the good that begins in 3.8. In this ostentatiously dialectical context,

Xenophon's Socrates will identify the good with τὸ ὠφέλιμον (*Mem.* 4.6.8; cf. *Hp. Ma.* 296e5–297d11) and then the beautiful with τὸ χρήσιμον (*Mem.* 4.6.9; cf. *Hp. Ma.* 295d6–296d3), both of which are specifically rejected by Plato's Socrates in his search for αὐτὸ τὸ καλόν in *Hippias Major*. But let's not miss the forest for these trees even when they are mighty oaks: although there are also allusions to *Alcibiades Minor* in 3.8–9 (cf. *Alc.2* 139c1–d4 with *Mem.* 3.9.6; also 3.8.3 with *Alc.2* 139e1–140b6), nothing compares with the Protagorean indifference of Xenophon's Socrates to any notion of τὸ ἀγαθόν that is not explicitly and expressly good in relation to some specific purpose (cf. *Prt.* 334a3–b7).[32] As if the de-relativized Beautiful of Plato's *Symposium* were not sufficient to create a zero-sum contrast, the Idea of the Good in *Republic* certainly is. And here, finally, the significance of this section's title comes into view.

Considered in relation to the Academy's "Eternal Curriculum," it scarcely matters whether Xenophon regarded these passages as "dialectical" or not; in either case they create a pedagogically useful dialectical tension with Platonism. In other words, when a reader comes to the Platonic dialogues after reading *Memorabilia* as a whole, 3.8–9 in particular will reveal what looks like a—and perhaps even *the*—distinctively Platonic advance over Xenophon: "the emergence of Platonism." The difference between an absolute Beautiful and Good and the relativized account Xenophon offers us here is itself absolute, and this allows us to understand Platonism far more clearly than we could otherwise have done. This is especially true for those readers who will have been more inclined to find "the historical Socrates" in Xenophon and Aristotle than in Plato, since now the dividing line is the emergence of Platonism, not incontinence. And when coupled with a "straight" or "deadpan" reading of 4.6, the reader will emerge with a sharper but hardly flattering image of Xenophon as well. In a word, Xenophon has been made eternally *useful* to Plato quite apart from his own intentions.

But here, those intentions will not be ignored, and the problem of these "dialectical" chapters arises not in the context of eternity but in relation to the gradual composition of Xenophon's *Memorabilia* "in real time." When did he write them, and why? Was he referring to *Hippias Major* and *Euthydemus* or did Plato build those dialogues around what he could already find here? Although these are scarcely the most important questions relating to the relationship between Xenophon and Plato, I have not disguised the fact that they are questions that have principally vexed me from the start, and there has been nothing disingenuous about previous assertions of open-mindedness with regard to priority here. Having saved discussion of these problems for the end, I now feel able to offer some conclusions. To begin with, I have argued elsewhere that the First Protreptic in *Euthydemus* is "dialectical" in the operative sense:[33] Plato knows that σοφία is not the only good and that the way his Socrates uses εὖ πράττειν depends on deliberate equivocation. The first question, then, is: Did he learn this from Xenophon's 3.9? I consider this unlikely. But this does not prove that he was not responding to Xenophon.

Xenophon's Priority can help us to understand the mixed message of 3.9 with respect to *Euthydemus*: although 3.9.4–5 is consistent with a deadpan reading of the First Protreptic, thanks to the primacy of σοφία, 3.9.14–15 is inconsistent with such a reading thanks to εὖ πράττειν. This looks as though Plato built Socrates' First Protreptic on what he found in 3.9, using an equivocal εὖ πράττειν to justify the fraudulent equation of σοφία and εὐτυχία. This solution is consistent with a theme that has been discussed repeatedly in this book: Plato would once again be counting on Xenophon to have already unmasked his own subsequent use of deliberate deception. But can Xenophon's Priority help us in the case of *Hippias Major*? Here, it is not so clear, but if it can, it is certainly not in the same way. Plato's *Hippias Major*, whenever it may have been written, is propaedeutic to his *Symposium*, and not least of all by rejecting the identity of καλὸν and χρήσιμον, it is consistent with the de-relativized Beautiful Diotima reveals there. And at the very least, *Memorabilia* 3.8 and 4.6 *appear* to contradict this conception.

As already indicated, the easiest solution is that Plato was once again responding to Xenophon: he saw the limitations of the relativized position he found in 3.8 and 4.6 and constructed first *Hippias Major*, then *Symposium*, and finally *Republic* 6–7 in response. In short, Xenophon's compositional priority creates the basis for his eternal priority as well: in this model, Xenophon described Socrates as he understood or misunderstood him, then Plato recognized either the historical but more likely the philosophical limitations of this understanding, and responded with what we now know as Platonism. But this easy solution is incompatible with the way I am claiming that Plato responded to 3.9 in his *Euthydemus*. Moreover, this solution also ignores the possibility that Xenophon was being "dialectical" in 3.8 and 4.6 and that Plato knew it. I therefore propose a split decision: these chapters were added to the *Memorabilia* after Plato had written *Hippias Major* but before he wrote *Euthydemus*; it was the former that allowed him to be "dialectical"—this might also explain why he added the dialogue with Hippias in *Memorabilia* 4.4 at this time—while he in turn allowed Plato to be so in the First Protreptic. Once again, this makes Xenophon an innovator on whose innovations Plato would build, for by contradicting *Hippias Major* he was helping Plato to create the kind of Socrates he introduces in *Euthydemus*.

But this conception, while respectful of Xenophon, does not make him responsible, even in a dialectical sense, for what I have called "the emergence of Platonism." Once again, it is easy to see what makes that notion appealing—especially from the perspective of a Platonic κτῆμα εἰς ἀεί—and when the student reads Xenophon first, this appeal becomes virtually irresistible. But it ignores the ongoing Relay Race, unfolding in real time, at this book's center. This is not to say that it would be impossible to synthesize the two by deriving Platonism from the inner workings of that back-and-forth. At the New England Seminar on Ancient Philosophy, my dear friend Mitch Miller brilliantly suggested a more direct connection between "the emergence of Platonism" and the Relay Race on a literary level. Having made it possible for Plato to depict Pausanias, Critias, and Meno as apparently better but in reality worse, Xenophon was then able to use Cyrus to further elevate the ontological problem of appearance and reality, forcing the reader to look to something like the Forms in order to distinguish between the two (cf. *Hp. Ma.* 299d8–e2). In a follow-up conversation, Miller added a useful distinction by proposing that "in this *characterological* distinction there is the potential occasion for going on to draw the further *ontological* distinction of appearances from forms or Ideas," asking: "Isn't Xenophon's unwitting but on that account no less real contribution to have given Plato repeated occasion to ponder that ontological distinction and make it a core part of his thought?" As is often the case with Miller's insights, this one deserves more consideration than I can give it here.

With regard to Platonism, I continue to believe that the transcendent Idea was already implicit in Plato's appreciation for Socrates' *Heldentod*, and thus that Xenophon's contribution to Platonism was for the most part literary rather than philosophical. Socrates' decision in *Crito* to stay in Athens already implied a higher Good than one's personal happiness, a selfless desire to benefit others, and a de-relativized Beautiful in relation to which alone the real as opposed to the apparent value of all human action could be measured. In a word, the *message* of the Allegory of the Cave was in Plato's mind from the beginning, and for that he was beholden only to Socrates and θεία μοῖρα, not to Xenophon and the other giants upon whose shoulders he stood. It was therefore not Plato's Ideas that emerged from his dialogue with Xenophon. Rather, it was an ability that would gradually emerge, repeatedly progressing in response to the literary stimulation provided by his fellow Socratic, that allowed him to lead his students toward activity in accordance with those Ideas and, no less importantly, to test whether their lives had been reoriented by his dialogues in the same way that both his and Xenophon's had once had theirs tested and reoriented by Socrates.

The Lawgiver and the King

With his Budé edition of *Hiero* already in production,[34] Louis-André Dorion presented a portion of its introduction to the International Society for Socratic Studies with the title "Le *Hiéron* est-il un dialogue socratique?"[35] His answer was "yes," and his purpose in general was to minimize the significance of the differences between Simonides and Socrates. He did not deny that there were differences, and since he was responding critically to Stephan Schorn, he recognized that others might regard these differences as significant.[36] A telling indication of his response was the table he attached to the written version of the paper, a synoptic analysis of *Hiero* listing parallel passages in Xenophon's other works—including *Cyropaedia*—each item in the righthand column prefaced with "=" or "≠" to indicate consonance or divergence.[37] In the end, it was the preponderance of convergences that he regarded as compelling, especially since some of his arguments—e.g., that Socrates doesn't give Glaucon any more moral instruction in *Memorabilia* 3.6 than Simonides gives Hiero—seemed strangely deracinated from a perspective such as Schorn's. It was hardly surprising that Dorion would take this position, given his reading of *Cyropaedia*: for him, as for Vivienne Gray, it is on the basis of parallel passages in Xenophon's Socratic writings that his Cyrus is absolved from any suspicion of darkness.

It was while listening to Dorion's paper that I decided to begin this final section with the question I asked him in the Q&A that followed: after determining that he had taken no position on the testimony preserved by Aulus Gellius to the effect that Xenophon wrote *Cyropaedia* in response to the beginning of Plato's *Republic*, I invoked the distinction between appearance and reality to explain both the convergences and divergences he had tabulated and discussed. If there were no convergences, there could be no appearance that Simonides was Socratic, and there was no doubt that Xenophon had been at some pains to make Simonides *appear* to be. Naturally, there was insufficient time to discuss the devices that Xenophon uses to unmask Simonides as a flatterer—although I managed to quote the phrase πλούτιζε τοὺς φίλους—or the way in which it is in the interest of a praise-singer to make "love of honor" rather than "self-sufficiency" the most divine element in human beings. But Dorion's point was well made and well taken: the *preponderance of evidence* must always be on the side of Simonides and Cyrus—as also on the side of Timaeus and Plato's two Strangers—if they are to appear to be what they are not, and *Socratic* is as good a term as any for what they really aren't.

And Dorion is also right on the big question: like *Laws*, *Hiero* is "a Socratic dialogue," albeit not because either Simonides or the Athenian Stranger are Socratic. It is, rather, the ironic challenge to the reader that Plato and Xenophon used them to create that is Socratic through and through. Everyone recognizes that Plato's Socrates customarily reduces his interlocutors to ἀπορία, and not even the Xenophon-haters can deny that Xenophon's Socrates does the same to Euthydemus.[38] What critics and lovers of both have failed to consider is that the interpretive ἀπορίαι with which the works of Plato and Xenophon repeatedly confront their readers are the literary analogue of the Socratic ἔλεγχος,[39] that is, of test and refutation. It is not a failure to read well on either side that has created the conflict between "dark" and "sunny" readings of *Cyropaedia*; rather, it is Xenophon himself who has done so. He could not force the reader to discriminate between reality and appearance if it had not been his purpose to reduce us to ἀπορία. It is for this reason that critics who find an irremediable incoherence in, for instance, Plato's *Republic*, are closer to the truth than those who try to show why it is in the self-interest of the Guardians to return to the Cave.[40]

As this example is intended to illustrate, the relevant ἀπορίαι are not designed to be irresolvable nor the various deceptions to be impervious to detection. But even though the foregoing should have made clear that I regard the two as being the same in the case of *Cyropaedia* and *Laws*, the notion of a resolvable Socratic ἀπορία is closer to scholarly common sense than a deception deliberately designed to be detected. From the speech of Pausanias, the characterizations of Alcibiades, Critias, and Meno, the First Protreptic in *Euthydemus*, the Great Speech in *Phaedrus*, the creation of Timaeus, the Eleatic, and the Athenian Strangers, the *Leitmotiv* of "deliberate deception" runs through this book, and for some readers, this must vitiate its thesis. Until *Cyropaedia* and *Hiero*, Xenophon's deceptions are fewer, but if 3.8–9, 4.4, and 4.6 were really added to *Memorabilia* between *Hippias Major* and *Euthydemus*, he too was in on the game from an early date and not merely as Plato's enabler. It is one thing to suggest that Plato created deliberately deceptive arguments for the eristic brothers in *Euthydemus*; to claim the same for Socrates in that dialogue and in *Protagoras*, to find deliberate deception incarnate in "the late dialogues" is to court amusement or contempt. There may therefore be some value in returning at the end to where this book began: the *Letters of Chion of Heraclea* proves that there is ancient precedent for Plato having used this kind of deception.

In the collection's penultimate letter—the last is to Plato, where he defends his selfless act of tyrannicide as inspired by what he has learned in the Academy—Chion writes directly to Clearchus, the tyrant he will assassinate.[41] He assures Clearchus that the philosophy he has imbibed in Plato's Academy has rendered him entirely harmless. In the grand tradition of Diotima and the Athenian Laws in *Crito*, he includes in this letter a speech addressed to himself by the goddess "Tranquility [Ἡσυχία]," who reminds him: "[Y]ou practiced justice, acquired self-control, and learnt to know God." The stated reason that he poses no possible threat to Clearchus is that philosophy does in fact "soften the soul into quietude [ἥσυχον]," and the letter reaches a pinnacle of deception by falsely confirming exactly what Chion had initially feared was true before he met Xenophon (see Preface):

> When I was settled in Athens, I did not take part in hunting [κυνηγεῖν], nor did I go on shipboard to the Hellespont with the Athenians against the Spartans, nor did I imbibe such knowledge as makes men hate tyrants and kings, but I had intercourse with a man who is a lover of a quiet life and I was instructed in a most godlike doctrine. The very first precept of his was: seek stillness [ἡσυχίαν ποθεῖν].[42]

Having devoted himself to "contemplating the principles of nature," Chion includes an even more specific reference to the "assimilation to God [ὁμοίωσις θεῷ]" in the *Theaetetus* Digression (*Tht.* 176b1), asking: "What can be more beautiful [κάλλιον] than to devote one's leisure solely to one's immortal self and try to bring that part of oneself into closer contact with that which is akin?"[43] In this way, Chion's original misgivings about philosophy become the basis for his ability to deceive Clearchus and thus to attempt the liberation of Heraclea from tyranny:[44] what he had previously feared now becomes the spell by which he persuades the tyrant that he has nothing to fear from a student of Plato.

In the most recent edition of *The Letters of Chion* (2004), Pierre-Louis Malosse comments as follows:

> Curiously, it is in his deceptive letter to Clearchus that Chion reveals himself to be most Platonic; it is there that he discusses subjects of metaphysical order (the divine part of the human soul) and properly philosophical (the necessary conditions for study, the idea philosophy learns first how to search); it is there that he constructs his personification [*prosopopée*] of Ἡσυχία (serenity) modeled on the Laws who appear in *Crito*. But since the text is presented in the previous letter as intended to give the impression that it has been penned by "a mere windbag," is it necessary to grasp that the author does not care about Plato? This throws into doubt the sincerity of the Platonism in the work as a whole.[45]

Whether *The Letters of Chion* were written in the first or the fourth century AD, its unknown author has a far better understanding of Platonism than Malosse thinks. Throughout the five volumes of *Plato the Teacher*, I have tried to show that it is not in the political quietism of a Plotinus (see especially *Enneads* 1.2)—and above all not in the ὁμοίωσις θεῷ[46]— that we will rediscover the original purpose of Plato's Academy, but in the philosopher's return to the Cave.[47] In comparison with the aims of Neoplatonism, the active political involvement of Dion, Phocion, Demosthenes, Lycurgus, Hyperides, and Cicero may seem too down-to-earth to be genuinely Platonic, but Plato's ongoing dialogue with Xenophon points in the same direction, and that is why the unnamed author of *The Letters of Chion* made Xenophon responsible for leading the would-be liberator to the Academy. What causes Platonism to soar is not a self-deifying ascent to the ineffable majesty of the One but a self-transcending idealism in response to the Idea of the Good.

It is therefore not the so-called "noble lie" in *Republic* 3 that is our clearest indication of how Plato used deliberate deception: all the necessary evidence can already be found in *Lesser Hippias*, which puts the emphasis on Homer.[48] As already indicated, to attribute literary originality to any Greek author other than Homer is truly to court contempt, and when it comes to the use of deliberate deception, it should suffice to mention Odysseus. Does anyone believe that he really descended into the underworld? But if no one does so, then why have so many believed that Achilles really said that he'd prefer to be a slave to a poor man than to have died in Troy (*Odyssey* 11.489)? It is no accident that Plato first mentions a return to the Cave in the context of this lie of Odysseus (*R*. 516c4–e2; cf. 620c3–6), for Odysseus merely *appears* to speak the truth. It is because Odysseus habitually deceives that Plato built his dialogue on deliberate deception around Socrates' deliberately deceptive claim that Achilles, not Odysseus, is the deceiver (*Hp. Mi.* 369e2–371d7); thanks to Socrates' misinterpretation of Homer, *Hippias Minor* is the medium of its message. In addition to Plato's Socrates' admiration for Achilles (*Ap*. 28c1–29a2), there is the Xenophontic Socrates' sympathy for Palamedes to be considered (*Ap*. 26; cf. *Ap*. 41b2), and aside from the opening words of *Memorabilia* 4.7, the principal basis for regarding Socrates' claims in 4.6 as deliberately debatable is that he claims there that Homer set up Odysseus "to be a safely slip-free speaker [τὸ ἀσφαλῆ ῥήτορα εἶναι]" (*Mem*. 4.6.15; with διὰ τῶν δοκούντων τοῖς ἀνθρώποις, cf. *Phdr*. 262a2–3).

Quite apart from their philosophical value in the hands of true Socratics, deliberately deceptive discourses were clearly regarded as amusing, delightful, and worthy of admiration in Athens. Does this statement really require proof? If so, Attic Tragedy is no worse a place to start than Aristophanes' *Clouds*, and it is not for nothing that the influence of Gorgias can be found in both versions of the *Apology of Socrates*. Although there is a school of Platonic scholarship that regards the critique of writing in *Phaedrus* as if it were that brilliant dialogue's most important passage, it is the speech of Lysias that will allow Plato to pen those deliberately deceptive claims about writing, for thanks to its use of deliberate deception, a Platonic dialogue is *never* a lifeless text, speaking indiscriminately to all and sundry, and always saying the same thing each time we read it (cf. *Phdr*. 275d4–e5). Why does Phaedrus admire the speech of Lysias? Because his speaker merely appears to be a non-lover, and from the moment we see through this deliberate deception, we can find the speech delightfully amusing. And pre-Socratic deception is not confined to *jeux d'esprit* or the lies of Odysseus: Thucydides' Diodotus merely *pretends* that his advice is motivated only by self-interest, not by pity.[49]

We will be told, of course, that Plato despised poetry and deplored rhetoric; and thus the dance of Socratic irony goes on and will continue εἰς ἀεί. For what good would it do at this late date to use Plato's evident eloquence, his capacity to imitate, and the poetic beauty of his words and images to prove that his use of deliberate deception is not simply a matter of writing a speech or two or creating a few deceptive characters? I suppose Aristotle is responsible for the fact that we'd prefer our philosophers to be wrong than to grant them the intent to deceive us in a manner at once playful and pedagogically effective; we now expect them to tell us the truth—i.e., that which they regarded to be true at the time—and to tell it to us straight. And here it is necessary to recall Dorion's three-page chart, with its preponderance of evidence. For even if Plato was a poet, how could he have written twelve books of the *Laws* unless he believed that what his Stranger was saying is true? And how could Xenophon—a far more down-to-earth fellow than Plato—have thought it acceptable to write eight books about *The Education of Cyrus* if Cyrus did not embody his conception of an ideal leader?

To begin with, just imagine how many pages of parallel columns would be necessary to do for Plato's *Laws* and Xenophon's *Cyropaedia* what Dorion did for *Hiero*. His analytical table proceeds through *Hiero* chapter by chapter, and within those chapters, section by section; as a whole, the dialogue is shorter than any single book of *Cyropaedia* and *Laws*. But here's the important thing: I am willing to stipulate that in those longer tables as well, the symbol "=" would still appear more frequently than "≠" and would do so for exactly the same reason: only in this way could the Athenian Stranger *appear* to be Plato's ideal, or Cyrus appear to be Xenophon's. If Cyrus were not an avid hunter, if he were not a master strategist, if he did not sweat before eating, if he did not carefully consider economics and logistics, if he did not lead by example, if he did not speak eloquently, if he did not inspire his men with useful and warlike competitions, if he had not created the Persian cavalry and sung a beautiful hymn to the mounted man (*Cyr.* 4.3.15–20), and above all if he were not self-controlled,[50] how could he teach us anything about appearance and reality, or the essential substance of justice? Resolute defenders of a "sunny" *Cyropaedia* would do well to find some plausible grounds for rejecting Aulus Gellius' testimony, for the difference between appearance and reality is a dominant theme in *Republic* 1 and 2 (*R.* 334c1–3, 339c1–2, and 361a6–d3).

This book is going to end by revisiting the most important thing I learned while writing it: the convergence and divergence of Socratic and Christian conversion. An easy way to disarm the convergence is to cite "nobody sins voluntarily," the view Socrates claims that Simonides and every wise man shares (*Prt.* 345d9–e4): certainly, anyone would be insane to admit that one was unjust in public (*Prt.* 323b2–c2). The notions of ὕβρις and αἰδώς may likewise disarm the relevant divergence, to wit, that lacking any concept of humility—let alone that it was a virtue to be "broken in spirit"—Socratic conversion was actually more difficult. As for αἰδώς, it was the sense of reverence that prevented those who felt it from unjust action: it preceded, not followed injustice. Meanwhile ὕβρις did not include self-esteem or pride per se; it was, rather, an overestimation of one's abilities, not an accurate appreciation of one's excellences, that was in play. So that leaves οὐδεὶς ἑκὼν ἐξαμαρτάνει as the chief roadblock, and it is Aristotle—not the Socrates who introduces it in the context of his egregious misinterpretation of Simonides[51]—who has ensured that we will continue to regard it as Socratic bedrock. Meanwhile, there is more evidence that Gorgias invented this principle than that he believed it, and with the authority of Homer, Plato's Protagoras, Xenophon's Meno, and the common sense of mankind behind it, it is not difficult to see why a Socratic would insist on its truth, since a confession of voluntary wrong-doing is the most economical way to refute the paradox.[52]

Xenophon's *Memorabilia* 4.2 and Plato's *Gorgias* are the first pair of texts that give us a sense of what Socratic conversion was like, and the relevant passage from the former has been quoted and discussed above (on *Mem.* 4.2.39, see chapter 3, section 3). Briefly sketched at the end of chapter 4, the argument that Callicles is Plato—or rather who Plato would have been at the time of writing *Gorgias* had it not been for Socrates—has been made in detail elsewhere.[53] The traditional view is that Callicles is one of those "incurables [ἀνίατοι]" (*Grg.* 525c1–8); since Nietzsche, it is the "life-denying" Socrates who has been viewed in certain circles as the sick one. If οὐδεὶς ἑκὼν ἐξαμαρτάνει were true, there would be no legitimate use of rhetoric whatsoever, for self-accusation—in particular, with regard to one's injustice, not simply one's ignorance—is its central feature (*Grg.* 480c3–4). Both the convergence and divergence are visible here: only by a painful operation could a proud Athenian gentleman, schooled to regard himself with the "proper pride" that made μεγαλοψυχία a valuable character trait, confess himself to be worthless and no better than a slave: even if it were true that it was only ignorance that was to blame for any acts of injustice they might have done, confessing it was difficult enough for the bookish Xenophon who dreamed of being ἀξιόλογος (*Mem.* 4.2.40; cf. 4.2.1) or the brilliant young man who had discovered the oxymoronic "law of nature" (*Grg.* 483e3).

The other pair of texts is *Cyropaedia* and *Laws*. There are arguably farcical elements in the Eleatic Stranger and Simonides: the flatterer was a well-known type and if the bifurcating expert in fishing and weaving was less recognizable, he was perhaps even more ridiculous. But Cyrus and the Athenian Stranger operate on a higher level of the reader's imagination, and their authors have imbued them with a μεγαλοψυχία that seems so commensurate with their abilities—the one as a king, the other as a lawmaker—that whatever signs of ὕβρις either might display are more than overmatched by their ostentatious αἰδώς, particularly with respect to the gods. Their respective λόγοι may be long, but we are never encouraged to believe that either is anything but ἀξιόλογος. In a word, they have appeared to represent their authors' ideals because they were *intended* to do so. And in the remainder of this section, my purpose is to show that even though Xenophon and Plato also intended to deceive us with them, and that they were created to be deceptive, neither was invented out of whole cloth, but, rather, both represent what their creators had it within themselves—but for Socratic conversion—to have become.

Not literally, of course: Xenophon's father was no Cambyses and nobody offered Plato the chance to create the laws for a city on Crete. And since they were both designed to be seen through by those with Socratic eyes to see, there were structural elements that made any simple equation ridiculous: it was just as impossible to imagine Socrates running off to Crete to escape "the fear drink" as it was to imagine Xenophon wearing high-heeled shoes and eye makeup (*Cyr.* 8.1.40–41). But as the foregoing list of parallels between Xenophon and Cyrus indicates, the *preponderance of evidence* points to convergence rather than divergence, and if the man who sneezed had been planted by the speaker (*An.* 3.2.9; cf. 7.6.41 and *Cyr.* 1.6.19), it would not only be in ostentatiously unobjectionable ways that the author would resemble his king. As for Plato, the first thing Diogenes Laertius tells us about him is that his mother traced her descent back to Solon (cf. *Chrm.* 155a2-3).[54] It cannot be an accident that Plato tested us with a reasonable facsimile of Solon or that Xenophon did so with a successful general and leader. Both the Athenian Stranger and Cyrus were images of what two great pre-Socratics had once aspired to be.

"Twas I, but 'tis not I," says Shakespeare's Oliver in *As You Like It*, before explaining his confession perfectly: "I do not shame to tell you what I was, since my conversion so sweetly tastes, being the thing I am."[55] Thanks to the centrality of γνῶθι σεαυτόν in Socratic conversion (cf. *Mem.* 4.2.24-25 and *Alc.1* 124a7-b3), every true follower of Socrates was remade by the experience and yet did not lose touch with who they had been before. In *Alcibiades Major*, Plato suggests that Platonism was always already implicit in the transcendence of one's former self by means of αὐτὸ τὸ αὐτό (*Alc.1* 129b1-3, 130c9-d4, and 133b10-c23); perhaps Xenophon was too comfortable using a horse as his tool that he forgot his own body was nothing more. But perhaps not: there was already plenty of Platonic Love for Plato to discover in or remember through Xenophon's *Symposium*. Despite the preponderance of parallels, there was always a certain *je ne sais quoi* that separated both Cyrus and the Athenian Stranger from their creators, and Xenophon's Socrates explained it to his son as well as anyone (*Mem.* 2.2.5). Whatever it was, it had become visible to both as a result of self-knowledge, however painful, frightening, humbling, and isolating that acquisition really was. There was no cultural support for being unselfish in those days, and an Athenian's fall from pride was more precipitous as a result.

Although the last word must be reserved for Socrates, it is from Xenophon's unselfishness that I have learned the most. At every stage, he saw himself surpassed by the brilliant Plato—although it may be doubted that *Laws* is really a better book than *Cyropaedia*—and yet he never gave way to jealousy, anger, or shame. As for shame, he had acquired that through Socrates, and as for jealousy, no collector of Great Books could be in any doubt that Plato's would henceforth belong not in *his* library alone. He was more than content to be Xenophon the Athenian and had no need to dream of being Cyrus the Great King of Persia except insofar as reliving such dreams would contribute to making others less susceptible to nightmares. And in looking at Plato's achievements, Xenophon knew better than anyone that he had made them possible, and even his Cyrus realized that it was more advantageous to bestow gifts than to receive them (*Cyr.* 5.5.26; cf. 8.4.31). Xenophon and Plato shared the same goal, and through their Relay Race, Socrates would live forever through both. As for pride, it was enough that they—long since humbled—were proud of each other, and it was in their friendship that Plato and Xenophon were most pleasing to Socrates, for they were his boys.

Notes

Introduction

1. William H. F. Altman, "Division and Collection: A New Paradigm for the Relationship between Plato and Xenophon," in *Plato and Xenophon: Comparative Studies*, ed. Gabriel Danzig, David Johnson, and Donald Morrison, 99–114 (Leiden: Brill, 2018).

2. See the Epilogue of my *Ascent to the Beautiful: Plato the Teacher and the Pre-Republic Dialogues from Protagoras to Symposium* (Lanham, MD: Lexington Books, 2020).

3. See Patricia A. Rosenmeyer, *Ancient Epistolary Fictions: The Letter in Greek Literature* (Cambridge and New York: Cambridge University Press, 2001), 234.

4. I will be citing by letter and line numbers the text found in Ingemar Düring, ed., *Chion of Heraclea: A Novel in Letters* (Göteborg: Weitergren and Kerders, 1951), 43–79; this word is found at 17.6 and 17.18–19 (the letter to Plato); Chion's motives are explained in relation to freedom in 14.19–28, climaxing with (translation Düring): "For in order to save the freedom [ἐλευθερία] of my city I must sacrifice some of my own." So also 17.7–8, where his goal is to "destroy the tyranny [καταλύειν τὴν τυραννίδα]."

5. See Düring, *Chion of Heraclea*, 9–12 for the relevant *testimonia*. For further discussion see, in addition to Rosenmeyer, *Ancient Epistolary Fictions*, ch. 9, David Konstan and Phillip Mitsis, "Chion of Heraclea: A Philosophical Novel in Letters," *Apeiron* 23, no. 4 (Dec. 1990): 257–79, and J. L. Penwill, "Evolution of an Assassin: The Letters of Chion of Heraclea," *Ramus* 39, no. 1 (2010): 24–52, with up-to-date bibliography.

6. Most recently, see Pierre-Louis Malosse, *Lettres de Chion d'Héraclée* (Salerno: Helios, 2004), which favors the fourth century AD against the traditional first or second.

7. *Chion of Heraclea*, 3.1.

8. On the historical inaccuracies in letter 3, see Düring, *Chion of Heraclea*, 84, and Malosse, *Lettres de Chion d'Héraclée*, 78–80.

9. *Chion of Heraclea*, 3.3 (Düring). For ancient testimony concerning Xenophon's good looks, see chapter 1.

10. On ἐπὶ πόδ' ἀνάγειν as "[to] *retreat* [while] facing [the] enemy" (LSJ II.10), see Xenophon, *Cyropaedia*, 3.3; cf. *Chion of Heraclea*, 3.3.

11. Cf. Cicero, *Brutus*, 200 and 290: "so that a mere passer-by observing from a distance though quite ignorant of the case in question, will recognize that he is succeeding and that a Roscius is on the stage."

12. *Chion of Heraclea*, 3.3.

13. Cf. καὶ πράττειν καὶ λέγειν at Plato, *Protagoras*, 319a2, Xenophon, *Memorabilia*, 4.2.1–6, and λέγεις τε καὶ πράττεις at *Anabasis*, 3.1.45.

14. *Chion of Heraclea*, 3.4; cf. Düring's translation: "What I witnessed was a display of Xenophon's personality, his sound judgment and eloquence."

15. Cf. Xenophon, *Memorabilia*, 4.3.14.

16. *Chion of Heraclea*, 3.6: "And thus I was unaware that even toward courage [ἀνδρεία] those who have philosophized are better, and this, just now in fact, have I learned from Xenophon, not when he talked with me about it, but when he showed himself to be the kind of man he is [ὁποῖός ἐστι]. For having participated especially in the discussions of Socrates, he proved capable to save [σῴζειν] armies and cities, and in no respect has philosophy made him useless either to himself or to his friends."

17. *Chion of Heraclea*, 3.5–6: "For inactivity and tranquility, as you said to me, were the wondrous encomia of the philosophers. Therefore it seemed to me dreadful that if I, having become a philosopher, will be better in other things, but no longer bold, I will no longer be able to be either a soldier or a great man [ἀριστεύς] if it should be necessary." Chion's original misgivings about philosophy, subsequently and quietly dispelled first by Xenophon and then by Plato himself, eventually become the basis for his ability to deceive Clearchus and deliver his city from tyranny (see chapter 5, section 5).

18. *Chion of Heraclea*, 3.4 (Düring).

19. Ibid., 3.5.

20. I owe a tremendous debt of gratitude to Tony Preus, the first reader of what has now become this book, and to three anonymous readers who read it for the SUNY Press. I profited from a discussion at the New England Symposium on Ancient Philosophy organized by Jyl Gentler (January 27, 2022); the helpful insights of three of the symposium's participants will be acknowledged below. Thanks are also due to Mateo Duque, Michael Rinella, Eileen Nizer, and most of all to my dear sister Leslie Rescorla (née Altman) whose courage in combat with an implacable enemy inspired me while writing this book.

21. See [Longinus], *On the Sublime*, 13.2–14.3.

22. *La.* 193a3–b1. Abbreviations for Plato's dialogues and Xenophon's writings will be in accordance with LSJ. Citations will be based on E. C. Marchant, ed., *Xenophontis Opera*, five volumes (Oxford: Clarendon Press, 1900–1920), John

Burnet, ed., *Platonis Opera*, vol. 2-5 (Oxford: Clarendon Press, 1901-07), E. A. Duke et al., eds., *Platonis Opera*, vol. 1 (Oxford: Clarendon Press, 1995), and S. R. Slings, ed., *Platonis Rempublicam* (Oxford: Clarendon Press, 2003).

23. See *An.* 3.4.25-30, 3.4.49-50, and 4.2.10-26.

24. Thuc. 5.65.6 (J. M. Dent translation).

25. See Walter T. Schmid, *On Manly Courage: A Study of Plato's* Laches (Carbondale and Edwardsville: Southern Illinois University Press, 1992), 52-55 and 394n21.

26. Schmid, *On Manly Courage*, 38-47 deserves pride of place; cf. Gregory Vlastos, *Platonic Studies*, 2nd ed. (Princeton: Princeton University Press, 1981), 268. Representative are Robert G. Hoerber, "Plato's *Laches*," *Classical Philology* 63, no. 2 (April 1968): 95-105, on 100, Darrell Dobbs, "For Lack of Wisdom: Courage and Inquiry in Plato's *Laches*," *Journal of Politics* 48, no. 4 (Nov. 1986): 825-49, on 841n4, Linda R. Rabieh, *Plato and the Virtue of Courage* (Baltimore: Johns Hopkins University Press, 2006), 70, and Richard Foley, "The Better Part of Valor: The Role of Wisdom in Plato's *Laches*," *History of Philosophy Quarterly* 26, no. 3 (July 2009): 213-33, on 225.

27. For ignorance concerning the fifth century among even the fourth-century intelligentsia, see K. J. Maidment's "Introduction" to Andocides, *On the Peace* (494-95) in the Loeb *Minor Attic Orators*, vol. 1 (Cambridge: Harvard University Press, 1941).

Chapter One. Xenophon in Plato's Dialogues

1. Aristotle, *Poetics* 1447b1-3.

2. *Mem.* 3.6.1. Unless otherwise noted, all translations are mine, although generally in consultation with E. C. Marchant (as here) or H. G. Dakyns. In bracketing the relevant Greek, I will reproduce nouns in the nominative and verbs in the present infinitive form.

3. See Diogenes Laertius 2.57 and 3.34, Athenaeus 11.112-14, and Aulus Gellius 14.3. For Ammianus Marcellinus, see my "Xenophon and Plato's *Meno*." *Ancient Philosophy* 42, no. 1 (2022): 33-47, on 34.

4. Aside from this sentence, "Socrates" will never refer to the actual person Socrates except when preceded with a reasonably suitable adjective such as "real," "actual," or "historical." The context will determine whether the Socrates I am discussing is Xenophon's or Plato's.

5. Even here a distinction must be made; there is "a great gulf fixed" between the Straussian synthesis—visible in, e.g., Paul Vander Waerdt, "Socratic Justice and Self-Sufficiency: The Story of the Delphic Oracle in Xenophon's *Apology of Socrates*," *Oxford Studies in Ancient Philosophy* 11 (1993): 1-48, and now in Thomas L. Pangle, *The Socratic Way of Life: Xenophon's* Memorabilia (Chicago: University of Chicago

Press, 2018), 139, 215, 221n7, and 251n48—and the work of Louis-André Dorion, including "The Straussian Exegesis of Xenophon: The Paradigmatic Case of *Memorabilia* IV 4," in *Xenophon. Oxford Readings in Classical Studies*, ed. Vivienne Gray, 283–323 (Oxford: Oxford University Press, 2010). Nevertheless, despite a professed indifference to chronology, both axioms are visible in Louis-André Dorion and Michele Bandini, eds., *Xénophon, Mémorables*, two volumes (Paris: Belles Lettres, 2000 and 2011); cf. I.clvi and II.1.316–17 ("l'abîme"); but see also I.lxiv n. 2.

6. See my *Plato the Teacher: The Crisis of the Republic* (Lanham, MD: Lexington, 2012).

7. In addition to Chion's τυραννοκτονία, see Andrea Wörle, *Die politische Tätigkeit der Schüler Platons* (Darmstadt: Kümmerle, 1981).

8. See I. I. Hartman, *Analecta Xenophontea* (Leiden and Leipzig: Van Doesburgh and Harrassowitz, 1887), 1–11.

9. As per Leo Strauss, *The City and Man* (Chicago: University of Chicago Press, 1964), 65.

10. Dorion, *Mémorables*, II.1.322 n. 5.

11. Cf. Pangle, *Socratic Way of Life*, 138: "We conclude that Xenophon means to show here that Socrates seriously tried to reconcile the politically gifted Charmides with the democratic assembly—but failed in this attempt."

12. See Leo Strauss, *Xenophon's Socrates* (Ithaca: Cornell University Press, 1972), 73: "Socrates liberates Charmides from his native sense of shame and fear which hold him back from politics by debunking the democratic Assembly; he instills in him what he regards as a justified contempt for the *demos*." Cf. Dorion, *Mémorables*, II.1.322–24.

13. See *Mem.* 3.1.1, 3.2.1, 3.3.1, 3.4.12, 3.5.1, 3.6.18, and 3.7.9.

14. For Xenophon's attempt to influence an Athenian elite audience, and with special attention to *Mem.* 3.6 and 3.7 (43–51), see Matthew R. Christ, *Xenophon and the Athenian Democracy: The Education of an Elite Citizenry* (Cambridge: Cambridge University Press, 2020).

15. See my *Ascent to the Good: The Reading Order of Plato's Dialogues from Symposium to* Republic (Lanham, MD: Lexington Books, 2018), 109–11.

16. A preference for "Xenophonic" will be defended in chapter 5, section 1.

17. See, e.g., Steven B. Smith, "Philosophy as a Way of Life: The Case of Leo Strauss," *Review of Politics* 71, no. 1 (Winter 2009): 37–53, at 51.

18. Cf. Thomas L. Pangle, *Socrates Founding Political Philosophy in* Economist, Symposium, *and* Apology (Chicago: University of Chicago Press, 2020), 173–74.

19. Cf. Dorion, *Mémorables*, II.1.316–17.

20. See Michael Vickers, *Aristophanes and Alcibiades: Echoes of Contemporary History in Athenian Comedy* (Berlin: De Gruyter, 2015); also "Alcibiades on Stage: *Philoctetes* and *Cyclops*," *Historia* 36, no. 2 (2nd Quarter 1987): 171–97.

21. Since Critias took credit for authoring the decree that secured Alcibiades' return (Plutarch, *Life of Alcibiades* 33.1), it was not Plato who depended

on information that Xenophon would or had already supplied to the readers of future generations.

22. On "the historian from Oxyrhynchus" see the *Oxford Classical Dictionary*.

23. For this claim and for much else, I will be relying on Hans von Arnim, *Xenophons Memorabilien und Apologie des Sokrates* (Copenhagen: Høst and Son, 1923).

24. He comes closest with Isocrates in *Phdr.* and with Xenophon in *Lg.*

25. *Hell.* 3.1.2.

26. See Dorion, *Mémorables*, and I.ccxlviii–ix and II.1.294–95 n. 7. At the risk of overburdening the reader with these complexities at the start, the dramatic context of Socrates' conversation with young Pericles in 3.5 can be fully understood only by those who have already read *Hellenica* 1, or, to state the same thing from Xenophon's perspective, if he cared about readers like us in the generations to come, he had already made *Hellenica* I available to "a reader" before he did the same with 3.5.

27. See David M. Johnson, *Xenophon's Socratic Works* (Oxford and New York: Routledge, 2021), 25–26 n. 40.

28. See Ferdinand Dümmler, *Zur Komposition des platonischen Staates* (Basel: Reinhardt und Sohn, 1895), although the "separatist" approach to book 1 is older; see Charles H. Kahn, "Proleptic Composition in the *Republic*, or Why Book 1 Was Never a Separate Dialogue," *Classical Quarterly* (n.s.) 43, no. 1 (1993): 131–42, at 131–32.

29. See *Plato the Teacher*, 90–91, commenting on Kahn, "Proleptic Composition."

30. See ibid., 29–36, and *Ascent to the Good*, §16.

31. See Édouard Delebecque, *Essai sur la vie de Xénophon* (Paris: C. Klincksieck, 1957) for discussion of this and much else besides.

32. See Timothy Rood, *The sea! The sea!: The Shout of the Ten Thousand in the Modern Imagination* (London: Duckworth, 2004).

33. For the most valuable thing he entrusted to Megabyzus, see *An.* 5.3.6.

34. On the numerous connections between *Prt.* and *Cyn*, see *Ascent to the Beautiful*, §2.

35. See ibid., Preface.

36. Ibid., §15.

37. In support of his contention that Thucydides lived beyond the traditional date Ammianus suggests for his death, and that he wrote the *History* in 396–95 (323), Mark Munn, *The School of History: Athens in the Age of Socrates* (Berkeley: University of California Press, 2000) must regard the tradition concerning Xenophon's role in "the publication" of Thucydides (Diogenes Laertius 2.57) as "probably only a guess" (438 n. 91), while allowing that Xenophon was nevertheless "probably" the first to continue Thucydides (327). For the facts as we know them, see 347 n. 4: "Although the *Hellenica* as a whole was not completed until after 362, the date of composition of its earliest part, before 2.3.10, is a vexed question."

38. Cf. H. G. Dakyns, *The Works of Xenophon*, four volumes (London and New York: Macmillan, 1890–97), I.lviii–xiii, and John Dillery, *Xenophon and the History of his Times* (London and New York: Routledge, 1995), 13–15.

39. See Dillery, *History of his Times*, ch. 8 ("*Hellenica* Book 5 and the Crimes of Sparta"), 205–207, 209, 211–12, and 214: "As *Hell.* 5.4.1 makes clear, the central event of the history, the event that seems to help Xenophon trace a pattern of episodes that leads up to and away from a decisive moment, is the Spartans' illegal seizure of the Cadmea."

40. See Alice Swift Riginos, *The Anecdotes Concerning the Life and Writings of Plato* (Leiden: Brill, 1976), 184–85.

41. See chapter 2 ("The *Menexenus*: Plato's Critique of Political Rhetoric"), in Frances Anne Pownall, *Lessons from the Past: The Moral Use of History in Fourth-Century Prose*, 38–64 (Ann Arbor: University of Michigan Press, 2004).

42. See *Ascent to the Beautiful*, §13.

43. Cf. Quintilian, *Institutio Oratoria*, 12.10.23–24.

44. Demosthenes, *On the Crown*, 204.

45. See Porphyry, *Life of Plotinus* 7.32–47.

46. See Kai Trampedach, *Platon, die Akademie und die zeitgenössische Politik* (Stuttgart: Franz Steiner, 1994), 130–38; cf. 126–30 on Demosthenes.

47. See Anthony Francis Natoli, *The Letter of Speusippus to Philip II: Introduction, Text, Translation and Commentary* (Stuttgart: Franz Steiner, 2004). Much of the foregoing is based on my *Plato and Demosthenes: Recovering the Old Academy*, forthcoming from Lexington Books.

48. For modern acceptance of this claim, see E. B. England, ed., *The Laws of Plato: The Text Edited with Introduction, Notes, etc.*, 2 vol. (Manchester: University Press, and London: Longmans, Green, 1921), 1.394 (on 694c6); Klaus Schöpsdau, *Platon, Nomoi (Gesetze): Übersetzung und Kommentar*, 3 volumes (Göttingen: Vandenhoeck u. Ruprecht, 1994–2011), 1.458; Steven W. Hirsch, *The Friendship of the Barbarians: Xenophon and the Persian Empire* (Hanover, NH: University Press of New England, 1985), and Gabriel Danzig, "Did Plato Read Xenophon's *Cyropaedia*?" in *Plato's Laws: From Theory into Practice: Proceedings of the VI Symposium Platonicum Selected Papers*, ed. Samuel Scolnicov and Luc Brisson, 286–96 (Sankt Augustin: Academia, 2003).

49. Waterfield, "Xenophon's Socratic Mission," 104: "The emphasis on plain common sense [in *Oec.*] fits perfectly with Xenophon's mission. His Socrates has no need of hifalutin' theories of reincarnation and prenatal knowledge [in *Men.*]."

50. See Robert G. Hoerber, "Plato's *Meno*," *Phronesis* 5, no. 2 (1960): 78–102, 79n2.

51. See Max Pohlenz, *Aus Platos Werdezeit: philosophische Untersuchungen* (Berlin: Weidmann, 1913), 189n3; in the resulting confusion, Xenophon's use of τὰ χρήματα in this context (*Hell.* 3.5.2) has passed unnoticed.

52. J. S. Morrison (edited by H. T. W.-G.), "Meno of Pharsalus, Polycrates, and Ismenias," *Classical Quarterly* 36, no. 1/2 (Jan.-April 1942): 57-78.

53. Cf. Isocrates, *Busiris*, 4-5, and Libanius, *Apology of Socrates*. See Richardus Foerster, ed., *Libanii Opera*, vol. 5 (Leipzig: Teubner, 1909), 1-4.

54. W. K. C. Guthrie, *A History of Greek Philosophy*, 6 vol. (Cambridge: Cambridge University Press, 1967-1981), 3.346; the so-called *Schutzschrift* is a commonplace of the nineteenth-century reception of Xenophon. Even while denying it (32-36), Niall Livingstone, *A Commentary on Isocrates' Busiris* (Leiden: Brill, 2001), refers to it as "the orthodoxy" (33 n. 82).

55. Dominic Scott, *Plato's Meno* (Cambridge: Cambridge University Press, 2005).

56. See *Tht.* 210d3, *Euthyp.* 2a5, *Ap.* 19b1, and of course *Ap.* 24c4-28a9.

57. Arnim, *Xenophons Memorabilien und Apologie*, 21-23.

58. For a brilliant analysis of this passage, see Georg Wilhelm Friedrich Hegel, *Lectures on the History of Philosophy*, 3 vol., trans. E. S. Haldane (London: K. Paul, Trench, Trübner, 1892-96), 1.435-38.

59. As noted, albeit under the twin aegis of Literary Rivalry and Plato's Priority, by Delebecque, *La vie de Xénophon*, 218: "Il est notable que l'Anytus jugé competant, en matière de vertu, par le Socrate du *Ménon*, se trouve violemment attaqué par Xénophon dans l'*Apologie*, pour être un éducateur incapable."

60. For the latest possible date for *An.* (after 369), see Ewald Bruhn, "De Menone Larisaeo" in *XAPITEΣ; Friedrich Leo zum sechzigsten Geburtstag dargebracht*, 1-7 (Berlin: Weidmann, 1911), 7.

61. J. Mitscherling, "Xenophon and Plato," *Classical Quarterly* 32, no. 2 (1982): 468-69, explains the fact that both Xenophon and Plato misquote Theognis in the same way (Plato does so at *Men.* 95d6 and Xenophon in *Mem.* 1.2.20 and *Smp.* 2.4), because the latter uncritically repeated the former's *lapsus memoriae*.

62. See Ulrich von Wilamowitz-Moellendorff, *Platon*, 2d ed., 2 vols. (Berlin: Weidmann, 1920), 2.145.

63. See especially καὶ ἐθέλοι ἂν ἀδικεῖν at *An.* 2.6.27.

64. See Bruhn, "De Menone Larisaeo," and Pohlenz, 167n2 on "73c" (which must be 73d7-9).

65. See E. Seymour Thompson, *The Meno of Plato*, edited with Introduction, Notes, and Excurses (London: Macmillan, 1901), xix: "There is no real inconsistency between Plato's picture [sc. of Meno] and that of Xenophon."

66. See the judicious comments in R. S. Bluck, ed., *Plato, Meno; Edited with Introduction and Commentary* (Cambridge: Cambridge University Press, 1961), 124-25. By contrast, consider Delebecque, *La vie de Xénophon*, 205: "Or dans le Menon de Platon, le meme personnage [sc. Meno] est traité par Socrate comme un veritable ami, curieux d'apprendre, discourant sur la vertu, savant en géométrie, grand voyageur épris de philosophie." On *la vertu*, cf. Paul Friedländer, *Plato*,

vol. 2, trans. Hans Meyerhoff (New York: Bollingen, 1964), 274: "[W]e recognize how much sarcasm there is in making him [sc. Meno] the spokesman for *arete*."

67. *Men.* 77c2–7.

68. Cf. David Wolfsdorf, "Desire for Good in *Meno* 77B2–78B6," *Classical Quarterly* 56, no. 1 (May 2006): 77–92, at 82: "It is, of course, a question why Meno commits to (c) [sc. 'some people desire things that are bad and recognize that these things are bad']. The answer, simply, seems to be that at this point in the argument Meno fails to observe that desiring something bad *de re* implies desiring something harmful to oneself." This is at best *half* of the reason that Meno so commits.

69. *An.* 2.6.22 (Brownson): "Again, for the accomplishment of the objects upon which his heart was set, he imagined that the shortest route was by way of perjury and falsehood and deception, while he counted straightforwardness and truth the same thing as folly."

70. *Men.* 78a6–b2.

71. For further analysis, see *Ascent to the Good*, 399–404.

72. A welcome exception is Guthrie, *History of Greek Philosophy*, 3.337: "Socrates casts himself in the role of pupil but in reality, through narrating the conversation to one of his own young men, is acting as his guide to the method." Cf. Sarah B. Pomeroy, Xenophon, Oeconomicus: *A Social and Historical Commentary* (Oxford: Clarendon Press, 1994), 336–37 (at 19.15).

73. Following Leo Strauss, *Xenophon's Socratic Discourse: An Interpretation of the* Oeconomicus (originally published in 1970), preface by Allan Bloom, foreword by Christopher Bruell, with a new, literal translation of the *Oeconomicus* by Carnes Lord (South Bend: St. Augustine's Press, 1998), the Straussian tradition regards Socrates as critical of and superior to an independent Ischomachus; see also Leah Kronenberg, *Allegories of Farming from Greece and Rome: Philosophical Satire in Xenophon, Varro, and Virgil* (Cambridge: Cambridge University Press, 2009), 38 ("Socrates undermines"), and especially Gabriel Danzig, "Why Socrates was Not a Farmer: Xenophon's *Oeconomicus* as a Philosophical Dialogue," *Greece & Rome* 50, no. 1 (April 2003): 57–76, at 62–63: "The most serious theme of the *Oeconomicus* is not, in fact, Socrates' effort to turn Critobulus into an Ischomachus, but rather the investigation of the mutual antagonism between Socrates the philosopher and Ischomachus the respectable citizen of Athens"; cf. "the indictment of Ischomachus" on 71 and 73. For Socrates as schooled by and inferior to Ischomachus, see Carlo Natali, "Socrate dans L'*Économique* de Xénophon," trans. Sophie Van der Meeren, in *Socrate et les Socratiques*, dir. G. Romeyer Dherbey and ed. J.-B. Gourinat, 263–88 (Paris: J. Vrin, 2001); Louis-Andre Dorion, "Xénophon *oikonomicos*," in *Socrate et les Socratiques; Actes de colloque d'Aix-en-Provence (6–9 Novembre, 2003)*, ed. Michel Narcy and Alfonso Tordesillas, 253–81 (Paris: J. Vrin, 2008) completes the triad by arguing for the identity of their views, albeit not on the basis of the fact (see previous note) that one is the mere persona of the other; see Kronenberg, *Allegories*, 37n2, for additional bibliography.

74. The same location (cf. *Oec.* 7.1 with *Thg.* 121a6–7) where Socrates converses with Demodocus; cf. Jacques Bailly, *The Socratic Theages: Introduction, English Translation, Greek Text, and Commentary* (Zürich and New York: Georg Olms, 2004), 110–11. Making the intertextuality undeniable is that the setting is one of three allusions to *Oec.* in the opening words *Thg.*: Demodocus introduces his conundrum with a discussion of planting (*Thg.* 121b1–c5) while his tripled references to free time or σχολή (*Thg.* 121a1–5) echo *Oec.* 7.1. There are obviously far more significant issues at stake in *Thg.*, implicating in particular a friend-guiding account of Socrates' "divine sign" that confirms *Mem.* 1.1.4, on which see Gregory Vlastos, *Socrates: Ironist and Moral Philosopher* (Cambridge: Cambridge University Press, 1991), 282. But the important point is that it has become easy for scholars to find in an inauthentic *Thg.* what they have labored to ignore or conceal in Plato's legitimate dialogues: Xenophon's influence. The connection between Xenophon and [Plato] demands independent treatment.

75. Cf. Werner Jaeger, *Paideia: The Ideals of Greek Culture*, translated by Gilbert Highet, vol. 3 (Oxford: Blackwell, 1944), 175: "Ischomachus is of course the protagonist. Socrates only puts the questions which draw him out." Preferable is Thomas L. Pangle, "Socrates in the Context of Xenophon's Political Writings," in *The Socratic Movement*, ed. P. A. Vander Waerdt, 127–50 (Ithaca: Cornell University Press, 1995), at 138: "the conversation Socrates retold or invented in the *Oeconomicus*."

76. Cf. Fiona Hobden, "Xenophon's *Oeconomicus*," in *The Cambridge Companion to Xenophon*, ed. Michael A. Flower, 152–73 (Cambridge: Cambridge University Press, 2017), at 162: "For ironists, Socrates and Ischomachus stand in opposition."

77. Waterfield, "Xenophon's Socratic Mission," 93n50.

78. Ibid., 103; unfortunately a commonplace, see, e.g., Pierre Chantraine, ed. and trans., *Xénophon, Économique* (Paris: Les Belles Lettres, 1949), 15–16, 93n1 ("fausse maïeutique"), and 95n2 ("inattendue").

79. Waterfield, "Xenophon's Socratic Mission," 104: "The emphasis on plain commonsense fits perfectly with Xenophon's mission. His Socrates has no need of hifalutin' theories of reincarnation and prenatal knowledge, which would only serve to distance himself from all but a few readers. His Socrates (or in this case his Ischomachus, but Socrates is still the narrator) talks the kind of language that is readily accessible, and goes no further into abstruse theory than is minimally necessary."

80. Ibid., 103: "Ischomachus labors the point in chapter 18, repeatedly pointing out to Socrates how much he already knew about certain aspects of harvesting and threshing (18.1, 18.3, 18.5), until he concludes that Socrates could, as he had suggested at the start, teach someone else too."

81. Ibid., 104; the passage continues: "Whereas in his early dialogues Plato's Socrates had insisted that he only asked questions, and did no teaching, Xenophon claims that questions of this kind are a kind of teaching."

82. Ibid., quoted above.

83. Just as, in a play within a play, the actors watching the play are made to seem more real, so also the image, in this case Ischomachus, become more real not only by using images, but by being praised for using them by the actual image maker (Socrates).

84. Cf. Plato's *Smp.*, where Apollodorus tells Glaucon what he heard from Aristodemus about the speech in which Socrates explained to Agathon and the rest what Diotima had taught him.

85. See Strauss, *Xenophon's Socratic Discourse*, 189–90.

86. Note that Plato uses ἐρώτησις four times in *Meno* (79c4, 79c8, 79e1, and 86a7). The last is particularly important, where "true opinions, having been awakened by ἐρώτησις, become knowledges [ἐπιστῆμαι]."

87. See Hobden, "Xenophon's *Oeconomicus*," 166–68.

88. Used thirteen times in *Oec.*; see especially 16.2–6.

89. See William Chase Greene, ed., *Scholia Platonica* (Haverford, PA: American Philological Society, 1938), 171–73.

90. For the amiable claim that this parallel depends on the historical Socrates, see Robert R. Wellman, "Socratic Method in Xenophon," *Journal of the History of Ideas* 37 (1976): 307–18.

91. See Jacob Klein, *A Commentary on Plato's* Meno (Chicago and London: University of Chicago Press, 1965), 224–25, esp. 225n25.

92. See my "Xenophon and Plato's *Meno*."

93. This is the climax of Henrich Arbs, "De *Alcibiade I* qui fertur Platonis" (PhD dissertation: University of Kiel, 1906), 22–31.

94. See *Ascent to the Beautiful*, 219–20.

95. Briefly treated in my "Plato's Reception of Xenophon," forthcoming in Dustin Gish and Christopher Farrell, eds., *Brill's Companion to the Reception of Xenophon*.

96. Athenaeus, *Sophists at Dinner*, 11.114.

97. Friedrich Daniel Ernst Schleiermacher, *Über die Philosophie Platons*, ed. Peter M. Steiner, with contributions by Andreas Arndt and Jörg Jantzen (Hamburg: Felix Meiner, 1996), 321.

98. See Friedrich Ernst Daniel Schleiermacher, "Über den Werth des Sokrates als Philosophen" (originally published in 1818), in *Der Historische Sokrates*, ed. Andreas Patzer, 41–59 (Darmstadt: Wissenschaftliche Buchhandlung, 1987). For the effects of this essay on Xenophon's authority, see Louis-André Dorion, "A l'origine de la question socratique et de la critique di témoignage de Xénophon: l'étude de Schleiermacher sur Socrate (1815)," *Dionysius* 19 (Dec. 2001): 51–74.

99. Karl Joël, *Der echte und der Xenophontische Sokrates*, 2 vol. (Berlin: R. Gaertners, 1893–1901).

100. With respect to contempt for Xenophon, it would be difficult to surpass Andreas Patzer, "Der Xenophantische Sokrates als Dialektiker," in *Der*

fragende Sokrates, ed. Karl Pestalozzi, 50-78 (Stuttgart: Teubner, 1999), translated as "Xenophon's Socrates as Dialectician," in *Oxford Readings in Classical Studies: Xenophon*, ed. Vivienne J. Gray, 228-56 (Oxford: Oxford University Press, 2010).

101. See especially K. F. Hermann, *Geschichte und System der Platonischen Philosophie* (Heidelberg: C. F. Winter, 1839), 644.

102. Ibid., 523.

103. See *Ascent to the Good*, Introduction.

104. See Gunter Scholtz, "Schleiermacher und die platonische Ideenlehre," in *Internationaler Schleiermacher-Kongress (1984, Berlin, West)*, ed. Kurt-Victor Selde, 849-71 (Berlin: De Gruyter, 1985), esp. 867-68.

105. *Alc.1* 123b3-c3.

106. Nicholas Denyer, ed., *Alcibiades, Plato* (Cambridge and New York: Cambridge University Press, 2001), 187; he adds (on 123b7-c1; abbreviation expanded): "in *Anabasis* 1.4.9."

107. Ibid. (on 123b5).

108. See *Ascent to the Beautiful*, ch. 2, along with the Preface and the first two sections of ch. 1.

109. As per Delebecque, *Vie de Xénophon*, and others.

110. Note the mention of Cyrus the Great at *Alc.1*. 105c4-6.

111. Denyer, *Alcibiades*, 83, on 103a1.

112. Arbs, "De *Alcibiade I*," 23-28. Given the emphasis on 3.6.1 in section 1, see in particular 23 on 123d5-6, as well as the parallels based on 3.6.2 (105b4-6, 106c4-5, and 124b4-5).

113. *Alc.1* 106c4-9.

114. See David M. Johnson, "Xenophon at His Most Socratic (*Memorabilia* 4.2)," *Oxford Studies in Ancient Philosophy* 29 (2005): 39-73.

115. *Mem.* 4.2.1.

116. *Alc.1* 105c2-6.

117. Denyer, *Alcibiades*, 96 (on 105c5).

118. See Susan Prince, *Antisthenes of Athens; Texts, Translations, and Commentary* (Ann Arbor: University of Michigan Press, 2015), 254.

119. Denyer, *Alcibiades*, 96-97 (on 105c5); emphasis mine.

120. See ibid., 86 (on 104a6-b1) and, "for another allusion to this book," 174 (on 121a5-b1).

121. *Alc.1* 118c3-4.

122. *Mem.* 4.2.6.

123. This word appears four times between *Alc.1* 119c7 and 120b8, where it is coupled for the first time with the cognate verb ἀγωνίζεσθαι. Along with ἀντ-αγωνίζεσθαι, συν-αγωνίζεσθαι, and δι-αγωνίζεσθαι, this verb appears six times between 119e1 and 124a5.

124. Used fourteen times between *Alc.1* 127e1 and 128d11; ἐπιμέλεια appears in this passage only at 128b9, six other times in the dialogue as a whole.

125. Cf. *Prt.* 319a1-2.

126. On *Mem.* 4.2.24 and *Alc.1* 124b1, see Denyer, *Alcibiades*, 191.

127. Cf. Catherine H. Zuckert, *Plato's Philosophers: The Coherence of the Dialogues* (Chicago: University of Chicago Press, 2009), 231n28, and Laurence Lampert, *How Philosophy Became Socratic: A Study of Plato's* Protagoras, Charmides, *and* Republic (Chicago: University of Chicago Press, 2010), 143–44, with Christopher Bruell, *On the Socratic Education: An Introduction to the Shorter Platonic Dialogues* (Lanham, MD: Rowman and Littlefield, 1999), 48, Robert C. Bartlett, *Sophistry and Political Philosophy: Protagoras' Challenge to Socrates* (Chicago: University of Chicago Press, 2016), 226–27n4, and Ariel Helfer, *Socrates and Alcibiades: Plato's Drama of Political Ambition and Philosophy* (Philadelphia: University of Pennsylvania Press, 2017), 201n38.

128. As noted by Lampert, *How Philosophy Became Socratic*, 143–44.

129. See Nicholas Denyer, ed., *Plato,* Protagoras (Cambridge: Cambridge University Press, 2008), 65 (on 309a1); the parallel passage is *Mem.* 2.8.1.

130. *Alc.2* 142e1–143a5.

131. *Palatine Anthology*, 10.108.

132. *Mem.* 1.3.2. Cf. Harold Tarrant, *The Second Alcibiades: A Platonist Dialogue on Prayer and Ignorance* (Las Vegas: Parmenides Press, 2022), 136–37: "The one person that we do know of who adopted the same policy on prayer as does this passage of the *Alcibiades II* and the reported poet happens to be Socrates, who is said by Xenophon to have prayed only for what was good." Cf. Hubertus Neuhausen, *Der Zweite Alkibiades. Untersuchungen zu einem pseudo-platonischen Dialog* (Berlin and New York: De Gruyter, 2010), 152–67.

133. *Mem.* 4.2.17.

134. Dakyns, *Works of Xenophon*, III.1.139n1.

135. *An.* 3.2.1.

136. See J. K. Anderson, *Xenophon* (London: Duckworth, 1974), ch. 14; amazingly, Delebecque does not.

137. Delebecque, *Vie de Xénophon*, 17; he proceeds to add Ischomachus to the list.

138. Originating with Martin Handford, *Where's Wally* (London: Walker Books, 1987).

139. Francis Bacon, *The Proficience and Advancement of Learning Divine and Human*, book 1 (Robertson's edition, 71).

140. Hartman, *Analecta*, 2–3.

141. Dakyns, *Works of Xenophon*, III.1.xl–xlv.

142. See Barbara Tuchman, *The Guns of August* (New York: Macmillan, 1962), 191: "From eight in the morning until six in the evening his [sc. the Belgian General de Witte] steady volleys of rifle fire repelled repeated German charges with lance and saber. Slaughtered Uhlans of von Marwitz's finest squadrons covered the ground."

143. See Winston Churchill, *My Early Life: A Roving Commission* (London: Thornton Butterworth, 1930), esp. ch. 15.
144. Bodil Due, *The Cyropaedia: Xenophon's Aims and Methods* (Århus: Aarhus University Press, 1989), 11.
145. Dakyns, *Works of Xenophon*, III.1.xli.
146. Ibid., III.1.xlii–iv.
147. All quotations in this paragraph are from Dakyns, *Works of Xenophon*, III.1.xliv.
148. Charles G. Cobet, *Commentatio qua continetur prosopographia Xenophontea* (Leiden: J. Luchtman, 1836), 68.
149. See Hartmut Erbse "Die Architektonik im Aufbau von Xenophons *Memorabilien*," *Hermes* 89, no. 3 (1961): 257–87, at 274–75 n. 2, citing A. Döring, "Die Disposition von Xenophons *Memorabilien* als Hilfsmittel positiver Kritik," *Zeitschrift für Geschichte der Philosophie* 4 (1891): 34–60 at 56. Cf. Dorion, *Mémorables*, II.2.60–61 n. 2.
150. Dakyns, *Works of Xenophon*, III.1.xliv.
151. Recall here the connections between Euthydemus and Alcibiades noted by both Denyer and Arbs.
152. Leo Strauss, "The Spirit of Sparta or the Taste of Xenophon," *Social Research* 6, no. 4 (Nov. 1939): 502–36.
153. Strauss, *Xenophon's Socrates*, 94.
154. Cf. Pangle, *Socratic Way*, 167: "There is no sign that Euthydemus had actually read any of these books. Euthydemus comes to sight as a kind of caricature1 of the good natures." Cf. 257 n. 10 for "follow the leader."
155. See Pangle, *Socrates Founding*, 176; cf. *indoles* in Cobet, *Commentatio*, 68.
156. *Mem.* 4.2.39–40 (Marchant modified).
157. Strauss, *Xenophon's Socrates*, 100.
158. See Pierre Pontier, *Trouble et ordre chez Platon et Xénophon* (Paris: J. Vrin, 2006), 370–72.
159. *Smp.* 4.48 (Dakyns): "'Well then, my boast is that these gods, who know and can do all things, deign to be my friends; so that, by reason of their care for me, I can never escape from their sight, neither by night nor by day, whithersoever I essay to go, whatsoever I take in hand to do. But because they know beforehand the end and issue of each event, they give me signals, sending messengers, be it some voice, or vision of the night, with omens of the solitary bird [φῆμαι καὶ ἐνύπνια καὶ οἰωνοί], which tell me what I should and what I should not do. When I listen to their warnings all goes well with me, I have no reason to repent; but if, as ere now has been the case, I have been disobedient, chastisement has overtaken me.'"
160. Cf. "Philippus" in Leo Strauss to Jacob Klein, Wiccopee, N.Y., August 18, 1939 in Strauss, *Gesammelte Schriften*, vol. 3, ed. Heinrich and Wiebke Meier

(Stuttgart: J. B. Metzler, 2001), 580, and the last sentence of his *Symposium* chapter in *Xenophon's Socrates* (1972): now it was the Syracusan that Strauss darkly hinted was the hidden Xenophon (178): "As for Xenophon's choice of a Syracusan as the antagonist of Socrates, I fear that its explanation may depend on the explanation of 'Themistogenes of Syracuse,' the author of a book which is indistinguishable from Xenophon's *Anabasis* (*Hellenica* 3.1.2)."

161. Strauss, *Xenophon's Socrates*, 172–73; Strauss is referring to *Mem*. 3.5.24, where Young Pericles observes (Marchant): "'I can see, Socrates, that in saying this you don't really think I study these things, but you are trying to show me that one who is going to command an army must study all of them; and of course I admit that you are right.'" For what had been suggested before, see "indigent" (151), "grave" (155), "the serious, the very serious" (160), and "the still poorer" (161).

162. See Nails, *People of Plato*, on Glaucon (154–56) and on Euthydemus (151).

Chapter Two. Xenophon's Debts to Plato

1. Diogenes Laertius 2.48; translation from Pamela Mensch, trans., and James Miller, ed., *Diogenes Laertius, Lives of the Eminent Philosophers* (Oxford: Oxford University Press, 2018), 87–88.

2. Ibid., 3.37 (Mensch): "Some say that Philip of Opus transcribed Plato's *Laws*, which were preserved on wax tablets. They also maintain that Philip was the author of *Epinomis*." It is precisely because *Laws* is incomplete without *Epinomis* that it can be considered unfinished, and thus the dialogue Plato was writing when he died. The dating of Plato's dialogues by stylometric methods depends entirely on the hypothesis that *Laws* was his last and latest work.

3. Ibid., 2.48 (Mensch). It is difficult to decide whether this sentence might also be translated as "the first who wrote a history of philosophers," especially since Mensch's "first philosopher" is at best "first of philosophers."

4. Ibid., 2.57 (Mensch).

5. Ibid., 3.34 (Mensch).

6. Franz Hornstein, "Komposition und Herausgabe der Xenophontischen Memorabilien" (in two parts), *Wiener Studien* 36 (1915): 122–39, and 37 (1916): 63–87.

7. It is therefore revealing that Vivienne J. Gray, *The Framing of Socrates: The Literary Interpretation of Xenophon's Memorabilia* (Stuttgart: Franz Steiner, 1998) refers to (my emphasis): "*the turn against these theories* [sc. 'the idea of later additions'] in investigation of the *Anabasis* and *Hellenica* as well [i.e., as well as in post-Erbse scholarship on *Mem*.]" on 93.

8. Dorion, *Mémorables* upholds the one by rejecting the other (cf. I.clxxxiv n. 1 and clxxxix n. 1); this makes things too easy for him, especially at ccxl–li.

After first noting the crucial role of "le pamphlet de Polycrate" (clxxxiv) in distinguishing two parts of *Mem.*—cf. Gray, *Framing Socrates*, 9—he uses Heinrich Maier, *Sokrates: sein Werk und seine geschichtliche Stellung* (Tübingen: J. C. B. Mohr, 1913) as at once principal whipping boy and straw man; see clxxxviii n. 1 and clxxxix n. 1; "principal" is necessitated by the similar use of Anton-Hermann Chroust, "Socrates: A Source Problem," *New Scholasticism* 19 (1945): 48–72 in clxxxix n. 2, and of Charles H. Kahn, *Plato and the Socratic Dialogue: The Philosophical Use of a Literary Form* (Cambridge: Cambridge University Press, 1996), on ccxlix–cclii.

9. Building on Erbse, "Architektonik"—which cites Emma Edelstein, *Xenophontisches und Platonisches Bild des Sokrates* (Berlin: Emil Ebering, 1935) as pioneering (258 n. 1)—Breitenbach, "Xenophon von Athen," 1777, and Gray, *Framing Socrates*, Dorion, *Mémorables* is an ongoing defense of a unitarian *Mem.*; see especially "Unité et plan des *Mémorables*" (I.clxxxiii–ccxl). For Dorion on Erbse, cf. clxxxvii n. 2 with cxcii–vii. For a detailed introduction to and defense of a unitarian *Mem.*, see Gray, *The Framing of Socrates*, 1–16; for a succinct overview that takes unity for granted ("today there is a consensus), see Jaap Mansfeld, "Aristotle, Plato, and the Preplatonic Doxography and Chronography," in Mansfeld, *Studies in the Historiography of Greek Philosophy*, 22–83 (Assen: Van Gorcum, 1990), 59; see also 81 n. 194 on Breitenbach.

10. Dionysius of Halicarnassus, *De Compositione*, 3.16: "And Plato wasn't through with combing and curling his dialogues, and braiding [ἀναπλέκων] them in every which way, having reached his eightieth year."

11. See Benjamin McCloskey, "Xenophon the Philosopher: *E Pluribus Plura*," *American Journal of Philology* 138 (2017): 605–40.

12. See Adalbert Roquette, *De Xenophontis Vita* (Königsberg: Leopold, 1884), 46–52.

13. Although arguing throughout for the unity of *Mem.*, Dorion, *Mémorables* applies a correspondingly anti-unitarian approach to the Platonic dialogues; on the most basic level, discriminating "the Socratic dialogues of Plato" (i.e., "les dialogues de jeunesse," at I.cxxxvii) is necessary in order to sustain an opposition between a Plato's allegedly merely elenctic Socrates from Xenophon's didactic alternative; thus, Dorion's version of Plato's Socrates depends entirely on Gregory Vlastos, as noted by Pierre Destrée, "Review of Michele Bandini and Louis-André Dorion, *Mémorables*, tome I," *Revue philosophique de Louvain* 102, no. 1 (Feb. 2004): 150–56, at 154. It is by taking *Sophist* 230b-e as the definitive account of Plato's Socrates (cxxxviii–cxl n. 1), by denying the authenticity of *Clitophon* (cxxxiv–vi; see especially cxxxv n. 1), and by upholding Vlastos's ban on a hybrid *Meno* (cxxxii; see also II.2.114) that Dorion renews the case for Literary Rivalry, likewise arguing throughout for the opposition between Xenophon and Plato; see liv–ix, lxiii–v (note the references to Vander Waerdt, "Socratic Justice" at lxiv n. 2), II.1.317, and II.2.89–91. On Plato's Priority ("au premier rang desquels on peut compter Platon") see I.lvi n. 1; none of the three passages he cites are applicable to Plato.

14. "Plato the Writer" will be the subject of a forthcoming work by G. R. F. Ferrari.

15. See Breitenbach, "Xenophon," 1910–1921 following (1913) Ludwig Radermacher, "Ueber den Cynegeticus des Xenophon," *Rheinisches Museum für Philologie* (n.f.) 51 (1896): 596–629 and 52 (1897): 13–41. In response, see V. J. Gray, "Xenophon's *Cynegeticus*," *Hermes* 113, no. 2 (2nd quarter 1985): 156–72.

16. On this, see *Ascent to the Beautiful*, §8.

17. See Dakyns, *Works of Xenophon*, III.2.

18. For a similar case of Anglo-German division, see Hans von Arnim, *Xenophons Memorabilien und Apologie des Sokrates* (Copenhagen: Andr. Fred. Høst & Søn, 1923), 3: "Die für die griechische Philosophiegeschichte cardinal Frage, was der echte, geschichtliche Sokrates als Erzieher und Philosoph gewesen ist, kann trotz der reichen sie erörternden Litteratur noch nicht als entschieden gelten, solange die angesehensten Forscher sie in so verschiedenem, ja entgegengesetzten Sinne beantworten, wie H. Maier und U. v. Wilamowitz einerseits, John Burnet und A. E. Taylor andererseits thun."

19. *Times*, June 20, 1960.

20. Von Arnim's value is partially recognized by Dorion, *Mémorables*, II.2.54 n.3, and 246–50 but the flaws of his approach—the last resort to a posthumous editor (Arnim, *Xenophons Memorabilien*, 117) and a commitment to the historical accuracy of Xenophon's presentation of Socrates (II.1.295 and 308)—do not justify Dorion's failure to give him credit for joining *Mem.* 4 to 1.2.12–48 (see I.ccvi–xiii), which is his salient contribution; see *Xenophons Memorabilien*, 118–23, ending with: "das IV. Buch ein Bestandteil des ältesten Teils der *Memorabilien* ist, der gegen Polykrates gerichteten Schutzschrift, zu der auch der größte Teil des I. Buches (bis Kap. IV § 1 incl.) gehört."

21. See William M. Calder III, *Wilamowitz in Greifswald: Akten der Tagung zum 150. Geburtstag Ulrich von Wilamowitz-Moellendorffs in Greifswald, 19.–22. Dezember 1998* (Hildesheim, Zürich, and New York: Olms, 2000).

22. Hans v. Arnim, *Sprachliche Forschungen zur Chronologie der Platonischen Dialoge* (Vienna: Alfred Hölder, 1912).

23. See Hans v. Arnim, *Platos Jugenddialoge und die Entstehungszeit des Phaidros* (Leipzig and Berlin: B. G. Teubner, 1914); for the Pohlenz-von Arnim debate on *Ly.*, see *Ascent to the Good*, 19–20 and 53–54.

24. Arnim, *Xenophons Memorabilien*, 93–126.

25. See ibid., 9–93, especially 21–54.

26. Ibid., 54: "Aber auch außer der platonischen Apologie waren ihm inzwischen weitere Informationen zugekommen. Er beschloß daher, eine neue Schutzschrift für Sokrates zu verfassen und in dieser auch die kürzlich erschienene Anklageschrift des Polykrates gegen Sokrates zu widerlegen, die Apologie aber zu unterdrücken." Not surprisingly, Polycrates has already disappeared in Gray,

Framing Socrates, 61–66, even before reaching "the accuser now fades aporetically from the text."

27. The argument unfolds in two parts; for Xenophon's unfamiliarity with Plato's *Apology* while writing his *Apology*, see Arnim, *Xenophons Memorabilien*, 21; for its impact on 4.8, see 29–38, 43–44, and especially 54 (quoted below).

28. Ibid., 54.

29. See ibid., 66–68.

30. Attempts are often made to include Plato's *Ap.* among these; hence the need to ignore or palliate *Ap.* 40b6–c1; cf. Nicholas Denyer, ed., *Plato and Xenophon, Apologies of Socrates* (Cambridge: Cambridge University Press, 2019), 126 (on Xenophon *Ap.* 1.3 ("almost certainly include Plato") and on 1.5–6: "Plato's Socrates too suggests that death is preferable to life (Pl. 40b6–41d5)." The "but" explanation that follows must prove insufficient.

31. See Arnim, *Xenophons Memorabilien*, 118–22; cf. Hornstein, "Komposition," 123.

32. Arnim, *Xenophons Memorabilien*, 126.

33. But see Dorion, *Mémorables*, I.ccvii–ix; he uses πράττειν τε καὶ λέγειν (see II.2.116–18 n. 3) to connect *Mem.* 4.2 with 4.5 (via πράττειν) 4.6 (via λέγειν), and 4.7 (via αὐτάρκης) by means of 4.3.1.

34. Arnim, *Xenophons Memorabilien*, 113.

35. Ibid., 127–75.

36. See Louis-André Dorion, "The Rise and Fall of the Socrates Problem," in *The Cambridge Companion to Socrates*, ed. Donald R. Morrison, 1–23 (Cambridge: Cambridge University Press, 2011).

37. See Arnim, *Xenophons Memorabilien*, 129.

38. Ibid., 132: "Hätte Xenophon in den Papieren Euthydems genügendes Material gefunden, um die ganze Erziehung Euthydems in folgerichtigem Zusammenhang zu schildern, hätte ferner das hierbei sich ergebende Bild seiner apol. Absicht und seinem Geschmack entsprochen und wäre endlich er selbst fähig gewesen, aus dem Material ein zusammenhängendes Ganze zu machen, so wäre etwas für uns außerordentlich Wertvolles zustande gekommen."

39. For "Euthydemus the son of Diocles," in Plato's *Smp.*, see ibid., 130.

40. Ibid., 126; cf. Gray, *Framing Socrates*, 124–30 (on *Mem.* 1.4–2.1) and 130–42 (on 2.2–3.7).

41. Arnim, *Xenophons Memorabilien*, 117: "Ein Redactor aber, der nach Xenophons Tod unter Benützung aller drei vom Autor selbst besorgten Ausgaben und vielleicht auch einiger Paralipomma aus seinem Nachlaß (zu denen z. B. das Gespräch des Alkibiades mit Perikies I 2, 40–46 gehört haben dürfte) eine neue Ausgabe der Memorabilien veranstaltete, stellte den Satz, den er in der zweiten Ausgabe fand, thörichter Weise (für unsre Analyse: glücklicher Weise) wider her, in dem pietätvollen Bestreben, von seinem Autor nichts untergehen zu lassen."

42. Note that the parallels between the practical interrogation of Glaucon in *Mem.* 3.6 and Xenophon's last work indicate the latter; see Xenophon, *Poroi (Revenue-Sources)*, ed. David Whitehead, 91, 171, 187, and 228-29 (Oxford: Oxford University Press, 2019).

43. Dorion acknowledges the problem and struggles with it in *Mémorables*, I.ccxxiv-xi.

44. Dorion's solution is that they advance the case for the *utilité* of Socrates, starting with ὠφέλιμος ἦν at *Mem.* 3.10.1; this theme is *le fil d'Ariane* at *Mémorables*, I.ccxxxviii, an important passage that deserves careful consideration.

45. The latter likewise creates a problem to be struggled with at ibid., ccxxxi-vi.

46. For the connection between *Mem.* 1.2.40-46 and 4.4, see ibid., I.clxii; see also II.2.146-49 and 192 n.4, which extends the connection to 4.6.6.

47. Based on the fact that *Mem.* 4.6 reprises both the legal positivism that joins 4.4 to 1.2.40-46 (see previous note) and the relativism of 3.8.

48. First words of 4.6.1 (emphasis mine); in bracketing Greek words and phrases in quotations—as in discussion of those words or phrases in the text—I will convert oblique cases to the nominative, as here; in the text, one finds διαλεκτικωτέρους.

49. See my "Dialectic in Xenophon's *Memorabilia*: Responding to 4.6," *Guiaracá* 34 no. 2 (2018): 110-33.

50. For Polycrates, see especially Anton-Hermann Chroust, *Socrates, Man and Myth: The Two Socratic Apologies of Xenophon* (Notre Dame: University of Notre Dame Press, 1957), 69-100. Dorion does not doubt that Polycrates is "the accuser" introduced at *Mem.* 1.2.9—see *Mémorables*, I.79-81 n. 77, lxxxiii n. 2, ccxxxix—and he accepts the pamphlet's dating between 393 and 390 (I.80.n77; cf. Chroust, 69 and 139) but since his unitarian approach is incompatible with a preliminary *Schutzschrift*, he must maintain that Xenophon still found it necessary to reply to Polycrates more than twenty years later (cf. ccxlvi and ccxlviii-ix). On the basis of *Mem.* 3.5, he can therefore write: "Pour notre part, nous sommes prêt à accepter la date de 370 comme *terminus post quem*, mais nous nous empressons d'ajouter que cette date n'est pas d'une très grande utilité pour la comprehension des *Mémorables*" (ccxlix).

51. See especially Diskin Clay, "The Tragic and the Comic Poet of the *Symposium*," *Arion* (n.s.) 2, no. 2 (1975): 238-61.

52. For further discussion, see *Ascent to the Beautiful*, §15.

53. For a detailed defense of this approach, see Arnold Hug, "Ueber das gegenseitige verhältniss der symposien des Xenophon und Plato," *Philologus* 7, no. 4 (1852): 638-95.

54. For a praiseworthy attempt to do so, see Francesca Pentasuglio, "Duplice Afrodite, duplici *Eros*: Un caso di intertestualità nei *Simposi* socratici," *Elenchos* 33 (2012): 335-56.

55. For further discussion, see my conference paper "The Priority of Xenophon's *Symposium* Revisited" (2021), available at https://www.academia.edu/50124486; accessed Jan. 6, 2022.

56. Charles H. Kahn, *Plato and the Socratic Dialogue: The Philosophical Use of a Literary Form* (Cambridge: Cambridge University Press, 1996), 29–35, accords Xenophon no originality, insight, or accuracy whatsoever. For example, Kahn solved the knotty problem of *Mem.* 3.8's connection with *Hp. Ma.* by rejecting its authenticity—see Charles H. Kahn, "The Beautiful and the Genuine: A Discussion of Paul Woodruff's *Plato,* Hippias Major," *Oxford Studies in Ancient Philosophy* 2 (1985): 261–87—and thus, even if *its* author *was* indebted to Xenophon, Plato most certainly was not. But despite the crude effectiveness of this radical solution, it is Kahn's contempt for Xenophon that remains the moving force: he refuses to allow even Plato's imitator—the *Verfasser* of *Hippias Major*—to have been influenced by Xenophon (*Plato and the Socratic Dialogue*, 398n11).

57. See Charles H. Kahn, "On the Relative Date of the *Gorgias* and the *Protagoras,*" *Oxford Studies in Ancient Philosophy* 6 (1988): 69–102; he had called an early *Grg.* "my heresy" in Kahn, "Did Plato Write Socratic Dialogues?," 310.

58. As in Dominic Scott, "Platonic Pessimism and Moral Education," *Oxford Studies in Ancient Philosophy* 17 (1999): 15–36; Alessandra Fussi, "Why Is the *Gorgias* so Bitter?" *Philosophy & Rhetoric* 33, no. 1 (2000): 39–58, and Franco V. Trivigno, "Paratragedy in Plato's *Gorgias,*" *Oxford Studies in Ancient Philosophy* 36 (Summer 2009): 73–105. For an antidote, see Bernhard Kaiser, *Streit und Kampf: Die verbalen Angriffe gegen Sokrates in Platons* Gorgias (Stuttgart: Franz Steiner, 2021).

59. Arnim, *Platos Jugenddialoge*, 46.

60. Kahn, *Plato and the Socratic Dialogue*, 69; see also Kahn, "On the Relative Date."

61. See Ernst Kapp, "The Theory of Ideas in Plato's Earlier Dialogues (Nach 1942)," in Kapp, *Ausgewählte Schriften*, ed. Hans and Inez Diller, 61–150 (Berlin: de Gruyter, 1968), 81 n. 30: "[P]ractically everything depends on the question whether the *Gorgias* or the *Protagoras* preceded in order of time. Now, both of them are certainly earlier than the *Meno*, and, whereas the *Gorgias* simply has no reference to the problems of the *Protagoras*, this latter dialogue disregards the views of the *Gorgias* concerning 'good' and 'pleasant' only ostensibly, but cannot be understood and has not been understood by anyone, who does not take or has not taken just these views of the *Gorgias* as the real convictions of the author of the *Protagoras*."

62. For the hypothesis that Callicles is who Plato would have become without his Socratic conversion, see *Ascent to the Good*, §9.

63. See M. R. Engler, "Introduction," in Gorgias, *Elogio de Helena e Defesa de Palamedes. Tradução, introdução e notas* (São Paulo: Odysseus, 2022).

64. See (4) on Dorion, *Mémorables*, I.79.
65. Libanius, *Apology of Socrates*, 87.
66. See J. Humbert, "Le pamphlet de Polycratès et le *Gorgias* de Platon." *Revue de Philologie* 5 (1931): 20–77.
67. Cf. *Grg*. 484b7-8: "*Callicles*: He [sc. Pindar] says something like this—I don't know the poem [ᾷσμα]."
68. In addition to earlier proponents of a post-Polycrates *Grg*. who fail to make the case properly ("Pamphlet," 32–35), Humbert must refute the great Wilamowitz by showing, on the basis of *Lg*. (see 37–46), that Plato was fully aware of what Pindar had actually said or sung (cf. ᾷσμα in the previous note). Naturally, Livingstone must respond to Humbert (35) in his *Commentary on Isocrates'* Busiris.
69. See Kurt von Fritz, "Review of *Polycratès, l'accusation de Socrate et le Gorgias* by Jean Humbert," *Gnomon* 9, no. 2 (Feb. 1933): 88–95, at 92: "Ist dies aber richtig, dann kann gar kein Zweifel daran sein, daß Platons Gorgias auf die Anklageschrift des Polykrates Bezug nimmt und also später als diese verfaßt ist. Der Hauptgrund, der U. v. Wilamowitz zu seiner komplizierten Konstruktion veranlaßt hat, war denn auch zweifellos nicht die Schwierigkeit mit den Pindarversen an sich, sondern daß er von vornherein von der frühen Abfassung des Gorgias überzeugt war."
70. Humbert, "Pamphlet," 76. Cf. 65: "J'ai voulu seulement montrer qu'entre le Polycratès historique et le riche Calliclès du *Gorgias* il n'y a pas de fosse, et que tant de traits communs au sophiste et à l'hôte de Gorgias permettant de penser que Platon a, pour le moins, souvent songé à Polycratès quand il a imaginé son Calliclès." Although I will be claiming that Plato had no need to "imagine" his Callicles, the echoes of Polycrates do explain why he offers the most searing critique of Socrates in the dialogues.
71. Cf. Michael Stokes, "Three Defenses of Socrates: Relative Chronology, Politics and Religion," in Hobden and Tuplin, *Xenophon*, 243–67.
72. Albeit without citing von Arnim, Dorion, *Mémorables* uses the link between *Mem*.1.4.1 and 4.1–2 (I.ccxiii and ccvi) in order to dispense with an early *Schutzschrift* (I.clxxix-xxx) but in order to uphold his "unité et plan des *Mémorables*," he must have recourse to Polycrates to join *Mem*. 3.1–7 (I.cci-iv)— and indeed *Mem*. 2 and 3 as a whole (cciv-v)—to the resulting amalgam, despite the fact that ὁ κατήγορος appears only in 1.2. The Achilles Heel of Dorion's unitarian approach is this continued reliance on Polycrates, which he defends as follows on ccxlvi: "Si, comme nous le croyons fermement [as if that made it true!], les *Mémorables* constuent une œuvre unifiée et solidement charpentée [neither of which I deny], il n'y a aucune raison de supposer que sa redaction s'est échelonée sur quelques décennies [except for the references to ὁ κατήγορος in *Mem*. 1.2 that led to the *Schutzschrift* hypothesis in the first place, a hypothesis that dominated the field until Erbse 1961]. Il n'est pas nécessaire de supposer,

comme le font certains, que Xénophon a répondu à chaud au pamphlet de Polycrate, dont le *terminus post quem* est 393 [it's not necessary, but since the use of ὁ κατήγορος indicates Xenophon's reliance on his audience's familiarity with the pamphlet, it's likely]. Si l'influence de la de Polycrate s'est fait sentir pendant une grande partie de IVe siècle [this, by contrast, it is *nécessaire de supposer*], rien n'empêche d'imaginer [N.B.] que Xénophon a rédigé sa défense de Socrate pour refuter ceux qui colportaient encore [no evidence for their existence is cited] les accusations formulées naguère [twenty-three years is not recently; a response *à chaud* is more probable] par Polycrate." The attached note depends on a weak argument by analogy (ccxlvi n. 1)—see Mansfeld, "Preplatonic Doxography," 59: "The date of *Mem*. . . . does not really matter"—while the countervailing evidence, especially in *Mem*. 3.7, is lethal (II.1.332).

73. Note that Dorion cites Humbert and presumably accepts the view that Plato responded *à chaud* to Polycrates in *Grg*. (*Mémorables* II.1.80.).

74. Xenophon, *Ap*. 26; Marchant modified.

75. Josef Morr, "Das Gorgias *Palamedes* und Xenophons *Apology*," *Hermes* 61, no. 4 (1926): 467–70.

76. Xenophon, *Ap*. 27.

77. Diels-Kranz 82 B11a.1 (translation by Most and Laks, 32 D25.1).

78. Morr, "Gorgias *Palamedes*," 469n3.

79. Diogenes Laertius 2.44 (Mensch).

80. *Mem*. 4.2.33.

81. See Dorion, *Memorables*, II.2.99 n. 1: "En affirmant que la *sophia* est un bien incontestable (σοφία . . . ἀναμφισβητήτως ἀγαθόν ἐστι), Euthydème avance une position qui serait certainement endossée par Socrate^P." Dorion's certainty about Plato depends on *Euthd*. 278e–281e (106 n. 4), and it is importantly misplaced; by opening the famous First Protreptic with the claim that all men desire to εὖ πράττειν (*Euthd*. 278e3), Socrates offers an argument vitiated by equivocation, and which leads to the equation of σοφία with εὐτυχία at *Euthd*. 279d6–7); both moves are unmasked as fraudulent at *Mem*. 3.9.14–15. This is a perfect example of the difference between rivalry and cooperation (see chapter 5, section 4), and the former depends on Plato's Priority. In any case, there are sufficient internal reasons to question the commitment of Socrates^P to σοφία as the only good (and ignorance as the only evil at *Euthd*. 281e3–5) quite apart from philosophy as *between* wisdom and ignorance (*Smp*. 204a1–b2 and *Ly*. 218a2–b3) and *Alc.2* 143b6–c7 (note that Dorion's reading of this dialogue at II.1.354–55 depends on the view that Socrates is *denying* any intermediate state); the Protreptic is vitiated by two rival final goods: σοφία and the universal desire to εὖ πράττειν.

82. See *Ascent to the Good*, 72–73.

83. See ibid., §2.

84. DK 82 B11a.3 (Laks and Most; 32 D25 3); {}'s are those of Laks and Most; []'s will always be mine.

85. See Josef Morr, *Die Entstehung der Platonischen Apologie* (Reichenberg: Stiepel Brothers, 1929).

86. H. Gomperz, *Sophistik und Rhetorik: Das Bildungsideal des εὖ λέγειν in seinem Verhältnis zur Philosophie des V. Jahrhunderts* (Leipzig and Berlin: Teubner, 1912), 9–11.

87. James A. Coulter, "The Relation of the *Apology* of Socrates to Gorgias' *Defense of Palamedes* and Plato's Critique of Gorgianic Rhetoric," *Harvard Studies in Classical Philology* 68 (1964): 269–303; more recently, see Gerald J. Biesecker-Mast, "Forensic Rhetoric and the Constitution of the Subject: Innocence, Truth, and Wisdom in Gorgias' *Palamedes* and Plato's *Apology*," *Rhetoric Society Quarterly* 24, no. 3/4 (Summer-Autumn 1994): 148–66, and Maria Cecília de Miranda Nogueira Coelho, "Dispositivi dimostrativi utilizzati in tre modelli di difesa: Ippolito, Palamede e Socrate," in *Socratica III. Studies on Socrates, the Socratics, and the Ancient Socratic Literature*, ed. F. De Luise and A. Stavru, 213–20 (Sankt Augustin: Academia, 2013).

88. Cf. Humbert, "Pamphlet," 53–54.

89. In addition to *Ascent to the Good*, §9, see E. R. Dodds, *Plato: Gorgias: A Revised Text with Introduction and Commentary* (Oxford: Clarendon Press, 1959), 14.

90. Dodds, *Gorgias*, 28.

91. Arnim, *Xenophons Memorabilien*, 23.

92. Dodds, *Gorgias*, 29.

93. On Athenaeus, *Sophists at Dinner*, 11.505d-e, see Kahn, *Plato and the Socratic Dialogue*, 56n33, and Riginos, *Anecdotes*, 93–94.

94. Cf. Aulus Gellius, *Attic Nights*, 1.9, and *Ascent to the Beautiful*, 188–89, 396, and Epilogue.

95. Edith Hamilton, *The Greek Way* (New York: W. W. Norton, 1930), 125.

96. See Eduard Delebecque, "Sur la date et l'objet de l'*Économique*," *Revue des Études Grecques* 64, no. 299/301 (Jan.-June 1951): 21–58.

97. See *Ascent to the Good*, §3.

98. See *Vect.* 1.6 (translation by David Whitehead): "It would be no absurdity for anyone to think that Athens lies at the center of Hellas—indeed, of the whole inhabited world."

99. Delebecque, "L'*Économique*," 35–52.

100. See Anderson, *Xenophon*, ch. 14 ("Domestic Life").

101. Ibid., 172–73.

102. Diogenes Laertius 2.52.

103. Anderson, *Xenophon*, 174.

104. See ibid., chapter 1 ("Childhood and Youth"), especially 11–17, including 11n1.

105. See Hobden, "Xenophon's *Oeconomicus*," 168-73.
106. Anderson, *Xenophon*, 11.
107. Cf. Nicholas Smith, "A Problem in Plato's Hagiography of Socrates," *Athens Journal of Humanities and Arts* 5, no. 1 (Jan. 2018): 81-103, and Dorion, *Mémorables*, I.xciv. On my account, both Xenophon (see II.2.172) and Plato—in *Hp. Mi.* and *Ion*, and with special reference to philosophy as *between* wisdom and ignorance in *Smp.* and *Ly.*—emphasize the moral neutrality of knowledge, making it the weak link in Smith's triad.
108. On "the Εὖ Πράττειν Fallacy," see *Ascent to the Beautiful*, §5.
109. *Mem.* 3.9.14.
110. Ibid., 3.9.15.
111. *Grg.* 506b8-c5.
112. See Dorion, *Mémorables*, II.1.362-64 and II.2.94 on εὖ πράττειν.
113. *Mem.* 2.6.9-10. Both introduced and emphasized in *Memorabilia* 2, these φίλτρα will reappear at 3.11.16. For the applicability of the term to friendship, see Dorion, *Mémorables*, II.1.27 n. 1 and 201.
114. *Mem.* 4.1.1.
115. Ibid., 4.1.2.
116. Ibid., 2.2.5.
117. Its use forces us to consider Socrates' claim at *Mem.* 3.9.4 that everyone does "what they regard to be most advantageous for themselves [ἃ οἴονται συφορώτατα αὑτοῖς εἶναι]." Just as the Guardian's return to the Cave in Plato's *Republic* is the great exception to the ongoing argument that "justice pays," so too is the mother's willingness to benefit the child—at the expense of great pain, toil, and danger for herself—an exception to Socrates' self-benefiting φίλτρον. In order to neutralize the mother's selflessness, a modern version of what Diotima says at *Sym.* 207b6-d2 will become necessary.
118. On the lack of reciprocity in *Mem.* 2.2, see Dorion, *Mémorables*, II.2.174.
119. To begin with, *Mem.* 2.6 is also a dialogue with Critobulus. With 2.6.4, cf. *Oec.* 20.27-28 and 7.1; despite Socrates' insinuation that Ischomachus' father is motivated by the love of money—a critical element in separating Socrates from his son—his son has leisure to talk with Socrates. With the request to be taught at 2.6.32-33, cf. *Oec.* 15.3 and 15.9; for a similar request from Critobulus, see 6.11. With the reciprocity claim at 2.6.34, cf. *Oec.* 20.29. With οἰκονομικός at 2.6.38, cf. *Oec.* in general. Note also the echo of *Oec.* 21.3 at 2.7.9.
120. See my "Womanly Humanism in Cicero's Tusculan Disputations," *Transactions of the American Philological Association* 139 (2009): 411-45.
121. See *Ascent to the Beautiful*, §16.
122. For "X's liking for things in trios" see Whitehead, *Poroi*, 95.
123. Appian, *The Civil Wars*, 2.11.76.
124. For the Machiavellian side, see Christopher Nadon, *Xenophon's Prince: Republic and Empire in the* Cyropaedia (Berkeley: University of California Press,

2001), 13–25, guided as it is by the wrong question at 23–24: "What in Xenophon's understanding of the classical republic could have led him to give an apparently laudatory presentation of its destruction?" Only an emphasis on "apparently" redeems this *Fragestellung*. Note that *keine von beiden* is the answer to the questions Nadon poses on 19.

125. See my "Xenophon the Educator," in *A History of Western Philosophy of Education* (vol. 1), ed. Avi I. Mintz; *In Antiquity*, 75–95 (London: Bloomsbury, 2020).

126. *Oec.* 21.1–3.

127. See James Weldon Johnson, "O Black and Unknown Bards."

128. See "Xenophon the Educator."

129. Cf. Paul C. Diduch and Michael P. Harding, "Editors' Introduction: Why Clarifying Socrates' Motives Matter for Philosophy," in *Socrates in the Cave: On the Philosopher's Motive in Plato*, ed. Diduch and Harding, 1–10 (London: Palgrave Macmillan, Cham, 2019), at 4: "The passage [see below] is pivotal in the dialogue for several reasons, not least for its implications about the seeming lack of a genuine common good in even the 'best' or most just city. For our purposes, let it suffice to note that Socrates himself, in contrast to his portrait of the philosopher, is admitting implicitly that he does not owe a debt to his own regime and, thus, that there is no obvious civic or even moral necessity for him to 'go down' with Glaucon and help the brothers fend off the teachers of injustice. Modern readers are especially likely to balk at this suggestion [one imagines that Diduch and Harding have their (hapless) students in mind here since they do not cite any literature to this effect, least of all *Plato the Teacher*], given certain presumptions in favor of democratic enlightenment. On this view, one simply assumes that the philosopher, Socrates included, returns to the shadows to liberate others from their mental captivity—that this is somehow his duty or the moral responsibility [cf. καταβατέον at *R.* 520c1; note that 'the passage' which Diduch and Harding have just quoted is *R.* 519c–520b] of the genuinely wise."

130. For πολιτεία as "citizenship," see LSJ; cf. OLD on civitas and Anthony Preus, "The Citizenship of Socrates in the Light of Modern Citizenship Studies" (forthcoming).

131. Cicero, *De senectute*, 59.

132. Noticed most recently by Denyer, *Apologies of Socrates*, 7 n. 8.

133. *Oec.* 4.19.

134. *An.* 1.9.30–31.

135. In addition to Κῦρον τὸν ἀρχαῖον (*An.* 1.9.1) and ἐπαιδεύετο (1.9.2), cf. ἐπὶ ταῖς βασιλέως θύραις παιδεύονται at 1.9.3 with *Cyr.* 1.3.2; see also 8.1, φιλιππότατος at 1.9.5 with *Cyr.* 1.3.15, φιλιοκινδυνότατος at 1.9.6 with *Cyr.* 1.4.7–8 (where it is a boar, not an ἄρκτον), and κατεπέμφθη ὑπὸ τοῦ πατρός at 1.9.7 with *Cyr.* 1.4.9 (where it is Cyrus's uncle that scolds him).

136. *Oec.* 4.16.

137. See Benjamin Orion McCloskey, "Xenophon's *Kyrou Amathia*: Deceitful Narrative and the Birth of Tyranny" (PhD dissertation: Ohio State University, 2012).

138. See Nadon, *Xenophon's Prince*, 99–100, on, for instance, "Cyrus's willingness to deceive, to persuade his uncle to believe that his subjects' allegiance remains unaltered, and what he does to advance his own interests and ambition is in fact done for the common good."

139. Unfortunately, interest in this testimony has been confined to the hypothesis that it proves that the original version of Plato's *Republic* consisted of six books, not ten. Following Henri Alline, *Histoire du texte de Platon* (Paris: E. Champion, 1915), who states as a certainty on page 15 that "la Cyropédie est la contre-partie des quatres premiers livres actuel," and thus "il faut donc supposer qu' Aulu-Gelle se réfère à une autre division que celle de nos manuscrits," the theory of an earlier six-book version of *Republic* has recently been revived by Harold Tarrant, "The Origins and Shape of Plato's Six-Book *Republic*," *Antichthon* 46 (2012): 52–78 and David Sedley, "Socratic Intellectualism in the *Republic's* Central Digression," in *The Platonic Art of Philosophy*, ed. George Boys-Stones, Dimitri El Murr, and Christopher Gill, 70–89 (Cambridge and New York: Cambridge University Press, 2013).

140. With a bit more than twenty-six Stephanus pages in the book as a whole, Adeimantus replaces his brother at *R.* 376d4–5 with a bit less than seven pages in the book left to go.

141. See Nadon, *Xenophon's Prince*, 87–100, describing as "a masterpiece of political manipulation" the way Cyrus takes advantage of his uncle and ally Cyaxares.

142. "Rereading Xenophon's *Cyropaedia*," *Ancient Philosophy* 42, no. 2 (2022), 335–352.

143. See Gustav Eichler, "De *Cyrupaediae* capite extreme" (Grimma: C. Roessler, 1880), on which cf. James Tatum, *Xenophon's Imperial Fiction* (Princeton: Princeton University Press, 1989), 223–25.

144. See Deborah Levine Gera, *Xenophon's Cyropaedia: Style, Genre, and Literary Technique* (Oxford: Clarendon Press, 1993).

145. *R.* 361a2–b1.

146. For more sensitive readings, see Melina Tamiolaki, "Being or Appearing Virtuous? The Challenges of Leadership in Xenophon's *Cyropaedia*," in *Gaze, Vision, and Visuality in Ancient Greek Literature*, ed. Alexandros Kampakoglou and Anna Novokhatko, 308–30 (Berlin and Boston: de Gruyter, 2018), and Joseph R. Reisert, "Ambition and Corruption in Xenophon's *Education of Cyrus*," *Polis* 26, no. 2 (2009): 296–315, at 303.

147. But see Nadon, *Xenophon's Prince* (emphases mine): "to avoid *the appearance of any injustice* towards his uncle and commander" (96), "his [sc. Cyrus's] reasoning is that 'it does not seem to me more of a gain to take it [see *Cyr.* 4.2.38–47 for context; the quotation is from 4.2.42] than *to appear just* to them'" (103), and 103 n. 84: "Note the repeated stress Cyrus places on 'appearance'

when speaking to the peers" (4.2.38 φανῆναι, 4.2.42 φαινομένους; cf. 5.3.32 πᾶσι φαινοίμεθα).

148. See Vivienne J. Gray, *Xenophon's Mirror of Princes: Reading the Reflections* (Oxford and New York: Oxford University Press, 2011), 56; to "sunny," she prefers "innocent" (5). For Gray on Strauss, see 57.

149. See Altman, "Plato's *Laws* and Xenophon's *Cyropaedia*" (forthcoming).

150. See Altman, "The Straussian Reception of Xenophon's *Cyropaedia*." *Calíope* 38, no. 1 (2021): 4–40.

151. Cf. Laura K. Field, "Xenophon's *Cyropaedia*: Educating our Political Hopes," *Journal of Politics* 74, no. 3 (July 2012): 723–38, at 724: "a deliberate invitation to consider the book and its protagonist anew." See also Altman, "Rereading."

152. Cf. Dorion, *Mémorables*, I.lxxxix: "Faut-il croire, enfin, que Xeenophon a été à ce point profondément et duablement marqué par l'empreinte de Socrate qu'il a, en signe de reconnaissance, prêté à plusieurs de ses héros (Cyrus, Agésilas, Simonide) des vertus socratiques?" While the attached note suggests that by "Cyrus," Dorion is referring to "Cyrus the Young," see lxxxix on I.327.

153. *R*. 343b1–c1. On the connection between this passage and *Cyr.*, see Louis L'Allier, *Le bonheur des moutons; Étude sur l'homme et l'animal dans la hiérarchie de Xénophon* (Québec: Sphinx, 2004), 166; the book's title comes from *Cyr.* 8.2.14.

154. *Cyr.* 8.2.14 (Wayne Ambler translation).

155. At the New England Seminar on Ancient Philosophy, Ben McCloskey made the valuable observation that without 8.8, *Cyropaedia* might have encouraged readers such as Glaucon and Adeimantus to believe that "injustice pays" since Cyrus "gets off scot-free."

156. See Delebecque, *Vie de Xénophon*, ch. 10.

157. Due, *Cyropaedia*, 234–35.

158. See Denyer, *Apologies of Socrates*, 24.

159. See Altman, *Plato the Teacher*, §24.

160. See Leo Strauss, *On Tyranny* [first published in 1948]; *Revised and Expanded Edition; Including the Strauss-Kojève Correspondence*, ed. Victor Gourevitch and Michael S. Roth (Chicago: University of Chicago Press, 2000), 68: "Tyranny at its best, tyranny as corrected according to Simonides' suggestions, is no longer rule over unwilling subjects. It is most certainly rule over willing subjects." Cf. Strauss, *On Tyranny*, 24: "*The Education of Cyrus* may be said to be devoted to the perfect king in contradistinction to the tyrant, whereas the *Prince* is characterized by the deliberate disregard of the difference between king and tyrant."

161. See Eric Buzzetti, "A Guide to the Study of Leo Strauss's *On Tyranny*," in *Brill's Companion to Leo Strauss' Writings on Classical Political Thought*, ed. Timothy W. Burns, 227–57 (Leiden and Boston: Brill, 2015).

162. Stephan Schorn, "Die Vorstellung des xenophontischen Sokrates von Herrschaft und das Erziehungsprogramm des *Hieron*," in *Socratica 2005: Studi*

sulla letteratura socratica antica presentati alle Giornate di studio di Senigallia, ed. Livio Rossetti and Alessando Stavru, 177–203 (Bari: Levante Editori, 2008).

163. See Louis-André Dorion, ed., *Xénophon, Hiéron; texte établi par Michele Bandini, traduit et commenté par Louis-André Dorion* (Paris: Belles Lettres, 2021).

164. Schorn, *"Hieron,"* 178–79.

165. Ibid., 192.

166. *Hier.* 1.14.

167. Karen Margrethe Nielsen, "The Tyrant's Vice: *Pleonexia* and Lawlessness in Plato's *Republic*," *Philosophical Perspectives* 33 (2019): 146–69.

168. *Hier.* 1.15.

169. *Hier.* 7.3–4 (Marchant modified).

170. See Leo Strauss to Karl Löwith (Paris; June 23, 1935), in Strauss, *Gesammelte Schriften* 3, 648: "ich kann nur sagen, dass mich Nietzsche zwischen meinem 22. und 30. Jahr so beherrscht und bezaubert hat, dass ich ihm alles was von ihm verstand . . . aufs Wort glaubte."

171. See LSJ A.3.2 on ὑπολαμβάνω, citing *An.* 3.1.26 and *Cyr.* 5.5.35.

172. *Hier.* 9.10.

173. Schorn, *"Hieron,"* 178.

174. Aristotle, *Physics*, 4.2; 209b11–12; cf. Francis MacDonald Cornford, *Plato's Cosmology: The Timaeus of Plato* (London: Routledge and Kegan Paul, 1937).

175. See Patzer, "Xenophon's Socrates as Dialectician," 251–55.

176. *R.* 413b4–c7 (Paul Shorey translation).

177. Strauss, *On Tyranny*, 100; see 130n43 where the note attached to this claim invokes the distinction between "real men" and "human beings" to demonstrate the unpleasant character of justice.

178. Ibid.; note that this book was first published as Leo Strauss, *On Tyranny; An Interpretation of Xenophon's* Hiero, with a Foreword by Alvin Johnson (New York: Political Science Classics, 1948).

179. He comes closest at *Hier.* 8.6, where τὰ καλά refers to whatever attractive physical features Hiero might have.

Chapter Three. Ordering Xenophon's Writings

1. I have been unable to find any scholarly account of how, when, and where this order came into existence, and in proposing its Academic origin I will be exploiting that lacuna, although I suspect that rival speculation would gravitate toward second-century BC editors in Alexandria.

2. S. Montgomery Ewegen, *The Way of the Platonic Socrates* (Bloomington: Indiana University Press, 2020), 140: "What we know as the Platonic corpus, and the

typical ordering of the texts within it, is based on the editing efforts of Thrasyllus, a Greek astrologist who almost certainly had no access to Plato's originals."

3. Cf. Dorion, *Mémorables*, I.lxviii–ix: "The genius of Plato is to have proposed a defense of Socrates which is addressed, not so much to his accusers, as to generations to come . . . to defend his master in the eyes of posterity, before the court of history, whose judgment is the only one that can really secure the perennial value of a man and his doctrine. Xenophon's mistake is, on the contrary, to have tried to respond directly, with the help of his own arguments, to the accusers of Socrates." Note that this accurate assessment of Xenophon's *modus operandi* strengthens the case for a response *à chaud* to Polycrates.

4. Marchant, *Xenophontis opera omnia*, 5.219.

5. Gilbert Murray, *A History of Ancient Greek Literature* (London: Heinemann, 1897), 167.

6. See Diogenes Laertius, 2.57.

7. See Whitehead, *Poroi*.

8. Abram N. Shulsky, "Introduction to the *Ways and Means*," in *Xenophon: The Shorter Writings*, ed. Gregory A. McBrayer, 189–209 (Ithaca and London: Cornell University Press, 2018).

9. Ibid., 192; but see the comments on Eckart Schütrumpf in Whitehead, *Poroi*, 216–18 (on 4.33).

10. See especially Isocrates, *Areopagiticus* beginning at 19; for τὼ πόλη ("the two cities"), see *Panathenaicus* 262, *On the Peace*, 116, and *Panegyricus* 17 and 73.

11. See Delebecque, *Vie de Xénophon*, 173–81.

12. See *Ascent to the Beautiful*, ch. 1 and Epilogue; also *Ascent to the Good*, §11.

13. See *Ascent to the Beautiful*, §2.

14. See Glenn W. Most, "Simonides' Ode to Scopas in Contexts," in *Modern Critical Theory and Classical Literature*, ed. Irene J. F. de Jong and J. P. Sullivan, 127–52 (Leiden: E. J. Brill, 1994).

15. Cf. Guthrie, *History of Greek Philosophy*, 4.235: "If we look to the *Protagoras* for philosophical lessons, it may seem an irritating patchwork of niggling argument, irrelevant digressions, false starts and downright fallacy. Read as a play in which the most outstanding minds of a brilliant period meet and engage in a battle of wits, it will give a different impression. That is how it should be read."

16. See my "The Reading Order of Plato's Dialogues," *Phoenix* 64 (2010): 18–51.

17. The Reading Order of the first nine Platonic dialogues as reconstructed in *Plato the Teacher* is: *Prt.*, *Alc.1*, *Alc.2*, *Am.*, *Hp.Ma.*, *Hp.Mi.*, *Ion*, *Mx.*, and *Smp.*

18. This claim revolves around the comparative truthfulness of Achilles and Odysseus; since the latter is the paradigm of the deceptive speaker (*Odyssey*, 19.203), both Xenophon and Plato discover ways to speak deceptively about him (on *Mem.* 1.3.7, see Dorion, *Mémorables* I.128–29 n. 204; cf. *Hp. Mi.*, 369e5–370a1)

while preserving evidence of Socrates' enduring opposition to him, primarily in relation to Palamedes (cf. *Ap.* 41b1-c4 and *Ap.* 26).

19. See *Ascent to the Beautiful*, §11.

20. The "ambivalence of σοφία" figures prominently in Dorion's attempt to create an opposition between "Socrate^X" and "Socrate^P," as at *Mémorables* II.2.99 n. 1; see also Louis-André Dorion, "The Nature and Status of *sophia* in the *Memorabilia*," in *Xenophon: Ethical Principles and Historical Enquiry*, ed. Fiona Hobden and Christopher Tuplin, 455-75 (Leiden and Boston: Brill, 2012), at 457: "This major difference between Xenophon and Plato concerning *sophia* arises, perhaps—and this is the hypothesis I propose to explore—from the fact that Xenophon does not conceive of *sophia* right from the start as a moral knowledge but most often as a technical ability." Not surprisingly, his argument depends heavily on *Euthd.* and *La.* while *Hp. Mi.* is not mentioned. In addition to "the ambivalence premiss" in Terry Penner, "Socrates on Virtue and Motivation," in *Exegesis and Argument: Essays for Gregory Vlastos*, in *Phronesis*, ed. E. N. Lee, A. P. D. Mourelatos, and Richard Rorty, 133-51 (Assen: Van Gorcum, 1973), 139, see also Altman, *Ascent to the Beautiful*, §11.

21. See *Ascent to the Beautiful*, 321-23.

22. For the applicability of "its center," see *Ascent to the Beautiful*, §9.

23. The most detailed work on *Mem.* 3 is Armand Delatte, *Le troisième livre des Souvenirs Socratiques de Xénophon* (Paris: Droz, 1933); on 3.8, see especially 103-107.

24. See Ernst Heitsch, ed. and trans., *Platon, Grösserer Hippias; Übersetzung und Kommentar. Mit einem Beitrag von Franz von Kutschera* (Göttingen: Vandenhoeck u. Ruprecht, 2011); also his "Grenzen philologischer Echtheitskritik: Bemerkungen zum *Großen Hippias*," *Abhandlungen der Geistes- und Sozialwissenschaftlichen Klasse* 4 (1999): 1-40.

25. See Pomeroy, *Xenophon, Oeconomicus*, 93.

26. E. C. Marchant, "Introduction," in *Xenophon in Seven Volumes*, vol. 4, vii-xxix (Cambridge: Harvard University Press, 1923), xxiv.

27. See Marie-Pierre Noël, "Critobule dans les écrits socratiques de Xénophon: le portrait d'un mauvais élève," *Kentron* 31 (2015): 43-58.

28. See Nadon, *Xenophon's Prince*, 77-86.

29. See my "Review of Catherine Zuckert, *Plato's Philosophers*," *Polis* 27 (2010): 147-50.

30. He was long regarded as one; the first words of Eunapius (b. 346), *Lives of the Philosophers and Sophists*, are: "Xenophon the philosopher [Ξενοφῶν ὁ φιλόσοφος]."

31. On this passage, see Christopher Moore, *Calling Philosophers Names: On the Origin of a Discipline* (Princeton and London: Princeton University Press, 2020), 177-78; here Moore does not consider the use of φιλοσόφους at *Cyn.* 13.6, but cf. his "Xenophon on 'Philosophy' and Socrates," in Danzig, Johnson, and

Morrison, *Plato and Xenophon*, 128–64, at 134: "[H]e [sc. Xenophon] does not see the 'philosophers' as the only alternative to the 'sophists' (excluding a claim in the *Cynegeticus*, in a passage which Xenophon may not have written [in a 2015 draft of this piece, he had referred instead to 'the very dubious *Cynegeticus*'; cf. 159–60], and since he does not seek to define, or redefine, the term 'philosopher,' he does not go out of his way to suggest that Socrates would be better understood by that term." On the authenticity of *Cyn.*, see *Ascent to the Beautiful*, 68–71. For a further suggestion of another attempted erasure of Xenophon as a φιλόσοφος, see Christopher Moore, "Review of Stephen White, *Diogenes Laertius*," *Bryn Mawr Classical Review* (2022.01.04): "(The biography of Xenophon mentions no philosophy at all; it would seem he is there just as a Socratic.)"

32. Geoffrey Chaucer, General Prologue to *The Canterbury Tales*, 304–308: "Noght o word spak he more than was nede, And that was seyd in forme and reverence, And short and quik, and ful of hy sentence. Souninge in moral vertu was his speche, And gladly wolde he lerne, and gladly teche."

33. Cf. Pangle, *Socrates Founding*, 173.

34. For a sexualized Socrates, see Gabriel Danzig, *Apologizing for Socrates: How Plato and Xenophon Created Our Socrates* (Lanham, MD: Lexington Books, 2010), 164–65: "The emphasis on conspicuous behavior (φανερὸς ἦν) suggests that Socrates may have displayed great powers of self-restraint in public and still indulged in sexual relations in private." For Critias, Euthydemus, and Socrates, see 168.

35. See Michel Narcy, "La meilleure amie de Socrate; Xénophon, *Mémorables*, III.11," *Les Études philosophiques* 2 (May 2004): 213–34, and Michael Anton, "Socrates as Pickup Artist: An Interpretation of Xenophon's *Memorabilia* III.11," *Perspectives on Political Science* 44, no. 1 (2015): 40–54.

36. Cf. Clifford Hindley, "Xenophon on Male Love," *Classical Quarterly* 49, no. 1 (1999): 74–99.

37. Diogenes Laertius 2.54.

38. *Hell.* 7.5.27.

39. See Dorion, *Mémorables*, I.clviii–ix.

40. *Mem.* 4.2.29.

41. Cf. F. W. Nietzsche, *Götzen-Dämmerung*, "Das Problem des Sokrates," 12, and the "Preface" to *Beyond Good and Evil*. I am grateful to Pedro Baratieri for alerting me to this parallel, ironic in that Nietzsche is criticizing "Socratic conversion."

42. Richard Wilbur, trans., *Misanthrope*, Act III, scene 1.

43. Cf. Pangle, *Socrates Founding*, 173: "In Xenophon's oeuvre Socrates has a rival cynosure: Cyrus, the hero of a fictional saga (the *Education of Cyrus*) of the most successful ruler plausibly imaginable." Albeit largely by insinuation, Pangle's appendix ("Preliminary Observations on the Contrasts and Complementarities

between Xenophon's and Plato's Presentations of Socrates," 173–81) creates a neat counterpoint to the present work.

44. It is unfortunate that it was only during the revision process that I encountered Noreen Humble, *Xenophon the Athenian: A Socratic on Sparta* (Cambridge: Cambridge University Press, 2021), which develops this argument in detail. Of particular relevance to my larger project is this on 249 (emphasis mine): "[I]f we start instead by assuming that Xenophon actually was sufficiently intellectual for Plato and others to engage with, that similarities in their works might actually be the result of *mutually stimulating and beneficial dialogue* rather than plagiarism or antagonism, and that the lack of direct allusion to one another is of no consequence because they were well aware of when their ideas were being engaged with without the need for the type of signposting we wish they had provided, then a different picture emerges."

45. See Johannes Engels, "Die Ὑπομνήματα-Schriften und die Anfänge der politischen Biographie und Autobiographie in der griechischen Literatur," *Zeitschrift für Papyrologie und Epigraphik* 96 (1993): 19–36, at 25 n. 24: " 'Autobiographisches' findet sich bekanntlich auch in der 'Anabasis' des Themistogenes aus Syrakus (Xen. *An.* 3.1.2) alias Xenophon, in der wir einen Vorläufer der Autobiographie unter Pseudonym finden können."

46. Anderson, *Xenophon*, 48–60.

47. Ibid., 42: "Xenophon was certainly not the author [sc. of *The Constitution of the Athenians*], if for no other reason, because this work must have been composed in his childhood, before the Athenian power was ruined by the disasters in Sicily, the Spartans established a fixed base in Attica, and the Athenian confederation began to break up, when the revolts of the allies could no longer be contained. But Xenophon, like, it would seem, most of the young men of his age and social background, was brought up in the doctrines which the unknown author expresses."

48. Ibid., 55: "Xenophon does not expressly draw attention to his change in attitude since the election of the Thirty and the first killings which had been approved not only by the ambitious and greedy but by 'all those who were conscious' of their own moral superiority to the victims. But it would appear that he was among those who now voted under compulsion, and that he was thoroughly ashamed. One would gladly suppose that he found some means of changing sides, as 'about seventy' of the cavalry did shortly afterwards (*Hellenica* 2.4.25). But his story (*Hellenica* 2.4.10ff.) still contains details suggesting first-hand observation from the tyrants' side, and it seems likely that he stood by them to the end." Note the confessional element here.

49. Ibid., 54; cf. 56: "Xenophon's account [sc. at *Hell.* 2.4.13–17] reads as though he was watching, but we must regretfully suppose, from the wrong side." See previous note.

50. Ibid., 58.

51. Delebecque, *Vie de Xénophon*, 15: "Lire les sept livres d'ouvrage, n'est-ce pas suivre à la trace un Xénophon d'abord Athénien, puis exile en Péloponnèse, enfin rappelé d'exil et rentré au foyer national? Lire l'œuvre entire 'avec des yeux d'insect' [cf. the way one 'reads' *Where's Wally*] conduit, à condition de prendre enfin quelque essor, à disinguer nettement les grandes étapes de sa vie."

52. Ibid. With this last verb, cf. Dorion, *Mémorables*, II.2.117: "According to the illuminating statement of 4.3 [the text Dorion uses to connect *Mem*. 4.5–7 to 4.2], Socrates taught them the ability to speak [cf. 4.6.1], to act [4.5.1], and to get along [4.7.1]." Although the last of these is the weakest *à la lettre*, the second is weaker in content; only 4.6.15 seems relevant to teaching the first member of λέγειν τε καὶ πράττειν. But it deserves emphasis that by connecting 4.3 and 4.6–8 to 4.2, Dorion is upholding von Arnim's conception of the *Urmemorabilen*.

53. See ibid., 17–18.

54. Ibid., 19: "On peut meme discerner, dans les livres qui comportment une action, un certain nombre de signes, encore plus discrets, *par lequels, tout en évitant d'attirer la attention sur lui* [my emphasis; this is where Delebecque fails to find Xenophon], il rappelle sa présence à ceux des lecteurs contemporains qui sont de ses intimes."

55. Ibid., 18.

56. Ibid., 22.

57. See also Kronenberg, *Allegories of Farming*, 44–45.

58. See Paulo A. Tuci, " '*Apronoëtos Orgë*': The Role of Anger in Xenophon's Vision of History," in *Violence in Xenophon*, ed. Aggelos Kapellos, 25–44 (Berlin and Boston: De Gryuter, 2019).

59. *Hell*. 5.4.7.

60. Ibid., 5.1.4.

61. Ibid., 5.1.21 (Carleton L. Brownson translation).

62. Sallust, *Bellum Catilinae*, 20.

63. See McCloskey, "Xenophon's *Kyrou Amathia*," ii, 97–98, and 111–65.

64. *Hell*. 5.1.17.

65. Promptly and soundly rejected in Humble, *Xenophon the Athenian*, xxiii.

66. See Dillery, *History of his Times*, ch. 8; indeed, Teleutias (see especially 220) is thematic in his Conclusion (236): "Xenophon pays close attention to the activities and character of individuals in his history. Indeed, this accent on the individual permits him to enter his narrative as a commentator; it helps him to mobilize the tools of moral evaluation as well as historical explanation. For Xenophon, the critique of states is a critique of individuals: thus Phoebidas and Sphodrias, Teleutias and Agesilaus are all in their way representative of growing Spartan ambition and its failure."

67. Strauss, "Spirit of Sparta."

68. Used fifteen times in Strauss, *On Tyranny*, 68–75; for the link to *Cyr.*, see 120n46 and especially 117n66: "As for bewitching tricks to be used by absolute rulers, see *Cyropaedia* VIII 1.40–42; [8.]2.26; [8.]3.1. These less reserved remarks are those of a historian or a spectator rather than of an adviser. Compare Aristotle, *Politics* 1314a40: the tyrant ought to *play* the king."

69. Leo Strauss, "On Xenophon's *Education of Cyrus*" (1938), in *Toward Natural Right and History: Lectures and Essays by Leo Strauss, 1937–1946*, ed. J. A. Colen and S. Minkov, 138–46 (Chicago: University of Chicago Press, 2018), 143.

70. Leo Strauss to Jacob Klein (Nov. 27, 1938) in Strauss, *Gesammelte Schriften* 3, 559; cf. *Cyr.* as "προτρεπτικός zu παιδεία."

71. Leo Strauss, "Greek Historians," *Review of Metaphysics* 21, no. 4 (June 1968): 656–66; *Hell.* is the principal subject of this review. Unfortunately, this important piece is likewise not cited in Humble, *Xenophon the Athenian*, 352.

72. Strauss, "Spirit of Sparta," 533: "The *Constitution of the Lacedemonians* appears to be praise of an admirable constitution." For recent comment, see Humble, *Xenophon the Athenian*, 61–68.

73. Strauss, "Greek Historians," 665.

74. Ibbid., 665–66.

75. Robert C. Bartlett, "An Introduction to the *Agesilaus*," in McBrayer, *Xenophon: The Shorter Writings*, 79–105.

76. Ibid., 360n91.

77. See ibid., 81–82.

78. Ibid., 96.

79. Cf. Humble, *Xenophon the Athenian*, 287: "The only one of his [sc. Xenophon's] fourteen works which could be described as unabashedly pro-Spartan is the *Agesilaus*, but that is because it is an encomium, the very purpose of which is fulsome praise. To maintain that Agesilaus is Xenophon's hero against the clear evidence of the much more negative portrait presented in Xenophon's historical narrative of the period is, I think, as methodologically mistaken, as it is to focus on the *Agesilaus* to prove Xenophon's laconophilia."

80. See the last word of the translated version of Leo Strauss, "Anmerkungen zu Carl Schmitt, *Der Begriff des Politischen*," *Archiv für Sozialwissenschaft* 67 (1932): 732–49: "A radical critique of liberalism is thus possible only on the basis of an adequate understanding of Hobbes. To show what can be learned from Schmitt in order to achieve that urgent task was therefore the principal intention of our notes."

81. Strauss, "Spirit of Sparta," 530.

82. But see Leo Strauss, "Xenophon" (1963), session 7 at http://leostrauss-transcripts.uchicago.edu/navigate/8/8/; accessed Aug. 19, 2020.

83. Thucydides, 2.41.1.

84. See my "Xenophon the Educator," 79.

85. Diogenes Laertius, 2.57.

86. See Aggelos Kapellos, *Xenophon's Peloponnesian War* (Berlin and NewYork: De Gruyter, 2019). For a useful corrective, cf. Jacqueline de Romilly, *The Life of Alcibiades: Dangerous Ambition and the Betrayal of Athens*, translated by Elizabeth Trapnell Rawlings (Ithaca and London: Cornell University Press, 2019), 140: "For the most part, Xenophon does not appear eager to truly judge Alcibiades. His relationship to Socrates seems to have interested Xenophon less than his relationship to Plato [sic]. He is sometimes moved to present a version of the facts favorable to Alcibiades, but he never speaks of him with any warmth or interest. He was most likely inclined to reject a man who, brilliant though he was, represented, along with the oligarch Critias, the bad disciple. This point of view is still not as marked in the *Hellenica* as it will be later. It is clear, though, that between the virtuous military man Xenophon and the brilliant adventurer that Alcibiades always remained, there would not have been much sympathy."

87. Wolfgang Helbig, "Alkibiades als politischer Schriftsteller," *Rheinisches Museum* 16 (1861): 511–31.

88. Ibid., 519–20. What follows is based on my "Xenophon, the Old Oligarch, and Alcibiades." *Polis* 39, no. 2 (2022): 261–78.

89. Cf. Whitehead, *Poroi*, 12: "Whether Isocrates 8 was actually *written* in 355 can be debated, along with its literary and rhetorical sophistication, but it is incontrovertibly *set* then."

90. Helbig, "Alkibiades," 525: "Wenn es mir aber gelingt nachzuweißen, daß die Ansichten, welche Alkibiabes während seiner Verbannung über Staat und staatsliche Verhältnisse äuserte, vollständig mit denen der πολιτεία übereinstimmen, wenn ich ferner nachweiße, daß gewisse Schwierigkeiten in der Schrift ihre Erklärung finden, wenn mir Alkibiades als Verfasser annehmen, so darf ich wohl hoffen, meine Conjectur für mehr als bloße Hypothese gehalten zu sehen."

91. See Wilhelm Roscher, *Leben, Werke und Zeitalter des Thukydides. Mit einer Einleitung zur Aesthetik der historischen Kunst überhaupt* (Göttingen: Vandenhoeck u. Ruprecht, 1842); cf. Johann Gottlob Schneider, ΞΕΝΟΦΩΝΤΟΣ, ΤΑ ΣΩΖΟΜΕΝΑ; *Xenophontis, quae extant*, vol. 6 (Oxford: Clarendon Press, 1817), 64.

92. See Gregory A. McBrayer, "Introduction to the *Regime of the Athenians*," in McBrayer, Xenophon, *Shorter Writings*, 160–74, 163: "What appears on the surface to be an uncritical castigation of Athens, then, is in fact far more ambivalent."

93. Thucydides 6.89.6 (J. M. Dent translation).

94. For the single Spartan, see *Ath. pol.* 1.8 (σύ νομίζεις), 1.9 (ζητεῖς), σοι at 1.10, and σέ and σ' at 1.11.

95. Hartvig Frisch, *The Constitution of the Athenians; A Philological-Historical Analysis of Pseudo-Xenophon's Treatise De re publica Atheniensium* (Copenhagen: Gyldendalske Boghandel, 1942), 115–18.

96. Ibid., 127–29.

97. Cf. *Prt.* 327e1–328a1 and *Alc.1* 111a1–4.
98. Frisch, *The Constitution of the Athenians*, 104.
99. Ibid., 110.
100. Ibid., 109.
101. Ibid., 88–105.
102. Ibid., 89.
103. See Raphael Woolf, "Callicles and Socrates: Psychic (Dis)Harmony in the *Gorgias*," *Oxford Studies in Ancient Philosophy* 18: 1–40, especially the distinction between "Callicles I" and "Callicles II" (2–6). Cf. Kaiser, *Streit und Kampf*, on "cognitive dissonance."
104. Frisch, *The Constitution of the Athenians*, 100.
105. Ibid., 104.
106. As already indicated, by documenting the parallels between *Poroi* and *Mem.* 3.6—Socrates quizzes Glaucon on so many of the same issues that the connection is obvious (cf. Dorion, *Mémorables*, II.1.314–15)—Whitehead offers further evidence that 3.1–7, not the "dialectical" passages like 3.8–8, might constitute the latest additions to *Mem.* For "further," consider Dorion, II.1.267–68 n. 1 on the parallels between *Cyr.* 1.6 and *Mem.* 3.1, a revealing example of the author's improbable but ongoing insistence on a late *Mem.*, which must follow *Cyr.*
107. See Whitehead, *Poroi*, 129–30.
108. Ibid., 42–52.
109. [Plutarch], *Lives of the Ten Orators*, 841, in *Lives of the Attic Orators: Texts from pseudo-Plutarch, Photius, and the Suda*, ed. Joseph Roisman and Ian Worthington, trans. Robin Waterfield (Oxford: Oxford University Press, 2015). On Lycurgus and Demosthenes, see Wörle, *Die politische Tätigkeit der Schüler Platons*, 63–67 and 47–52.
110. Raphael Sealey, *Demosthenes and his Time: A Study in Defeat* (Oxford and New York: Oxford University Press, 1993) begins with the King's Peace ("The Crisis of 387/6").
111. At the New England Seminar on Ancient Philosophy, Sam Flores drew attention to the structural parallel between *Cyr.* 8.8 and *Lac.* 14; the otherwise unexplained reference to "*Constitution of the Spartans* II" in the following table reflects the possibility that Xenophon added the two destabilizing conclusions at approximately the same time.
112. Delebecque, *Vie de Xénophon*, 506–509; see also 527–32.
113. Aristotle, *Politics* 2.6 (1264b26–27).
114. Cf. Diodorus Siculus, 13.72, Maier, *Sokrates*, 34 n. 1, and David M. Johnson, "From Generals to Gluttony: *Memorabilia* Book 3," in *Socrates and the Socratic Dialogue*, ed. Alessandro Stavru and Christopher Moore, 481–99 (Leiden and Boston: Brill, 2018), 484 n. 3.
115. *Eq.* 1.1 (translation Amy L. Bonnette).

116. Delebecque, *Vie de Xénophon*, 246n36. See 195, 207–209, and 215–16.

117. For contempt, see Dorion, *Mémorables*, I.ccxlii–vi, ending with the sentence that begins: "Les élucubrations psycho-biographiques."

118. Guthrie, *History of Greek Philosophy*, 4.437.

119. See Reginald Hackforth, *The Authorship of the Platonic Epistles* (Manchester: At the University Press, 1913), 199.

120. W. D. Ross, ed., *Aristotelis Fragmenta Selecta* (Oxford: Clarendon Press, 1955), 7–8.

121. Sophocles, *Philoctetes*, 1213.

122. See *Ascent to the Good*, Introduction.

123. See Maier, *Sokrates*, 91–94.

124. Cf. K. J. Dover, "The Date of Plato's *Symposium*," *Phronesis* 10, no. 1 (1965): 2–20.

125. See Rood, *The Sea! The Sea!* 43–50.

126. See Herman Strasburger, *Caesars Eintritt in die Geschichte*, originally published in Munich, 1938 (Darmstadt: Wissenschaftliche Buchgesellschaft, 1966); cf. Ronald Syme, *The Roman Revolution* (Oxford: Oxford University Press, 1939), 25 n. 2.

127. Cf. Lily Ross Taylor, "Review of *Caesars Eintritt in die Geschichte*," *Classical Philology* 36 (1941): 413–14: "The thesis of this book that ancient and modern writers have exaggerated the part which Caesar played on the political stage before the year 59; that he was hardly noticed before his aedileship in 65, advanced into prominence when he was elected *pontifex maximus* in 63, but did not become a power to be reckoned with until the triumvirate was formed; that, in fact, only after his great victories in Gaul did many of his contemporaries recognize his importance."

128. Diogenes Laertius 2.57.

129. From Luciano Canfora, "Tucidide continuato e pubblicato," *Belfagor* 25, no. 2 (31 March 1970): 121–34, to "Biographical Obscurities and Problems of Composition," in *Brill's Companion to Thucydides*, ed. Antonios Rengakos and Antonios Tsakmakis, 3–32 (Leiden: Brill, 2006).

130. See B. G. Niebuhr, "Ueber Xenophons *Hellenika*," *Rheinisches Museum* 1 (1827): 194–98, at 196–97.

131. Patzer, "Xenophontische Sokrates als Dialektiker," 70–71.

132. *Mem.* 4.2.1 is quoted in chapter 1, section 5.

133. See Diogenes Laertius 3.4 both for both *Am.* and Plato as a wrestler. See Sandra Peterson, "Notes on *Lovers*," in Stavru and Moore, *Socrates and the Socratic Dialogue*, 412–31, on 416, 430n22, and 430: "Perhaps the wrestler wrote the narrative, to save the memory of an actual occasion."

134. For Xenophon and the fifth book of Thucydides, see Canfora, "Biographical Obscurities," 14–17.

Chapter Four. Plato's Debts to Xenophon

1. G. W. F. Hegel, *Philosophy of Right*, Preface: "Wenn die Philosophie ihr Grau in Grau malt, dann ist eine Gestalt des Lebens alt geworden, und mit Grau in Grau läßt sie sich nicht verjüngen, sondern nur erkennen; die Eule der Minerva beginnt erst mit der einbrechenden Dämmerung ihren Flug."
2. J. W. Goethe, *Faust*, part 1; in the study.
3. *Ap.* 32b1-7.
4. See John Burnet, ed., *Plato's* Euthyphro, Apology of Socrates, *and* Crito; *edited with Notes* (Oxford: Clarendon Press, 1924), 131 (on 32b1); see 131-33 for the other seven mentions.
5. See Altman, "Collection and Division," 104-105.
6. All of these are noted by Burnet, *Plato's Euthyphro*, 134-36.
7. Thucydides 2.41.1.
8. Terry Penner and Christopher Rowe, *Plato's* Lysis (Cambridge: Cambridge University Press, 2006), 74 n. 9.
9. Delebecque, *Vie de Xénophon*, 215.
10. Building on some perceptive comments by Denyer, *Alcibiades*, 22-24.
11. Thereby making possible a book such as Drew Hyland, *Finitude and Transcendence in the Platonic Dialogues* (Albany: State University of New York Press, 1995).
12. Plutarch, *Life of Alexander*, 1.
13. Cf. Mary Renault, *The Last of the Wine* (New York: Pantheon Books, 1956); she constructs her central fiction within the interstices of the Platonic dialogues, *Ly.* in particular.
14. See Robert B. Strassler, ed., *The Landmark Xenophon's Hellenika; A New Translation by John Marincola with Maps, Annotations, Appendices, and Encyclopedic Index*, intro. David Thomas (New York, Anchor Books, 2010), xliv-v and lx note; also Vivienne Gray, *The Character of Xenophon's* Hellenica (Baltimore: Johns Hopkins University Press, 1989), 83-91.
15. Cf. Dorion, *Mémorables*, II.2.66, on the "substitution" of Euthydemus for Alcibiades, another indication that Dorion's reading is more dependent on chronology of composition than he cares to admit.
16. Cf. μίμησις at [Longinus] *On the Sublime*, 13.2.
17. See Boris Hogenmüller, "The Influence of Plato's *Crito* and *Phaedo* on Xenophon's *Apology of Socrates*," *Kentron* 31 (2015): 127-38.
18. See ibid., 130-34.
19. Consider the structure of the *Ap.* 23: ἔπειτα τῶν ἑταίρων ἐκκλέψαι βουλομένων αὐτὸν οὐκ ἐφείπετο, ἀλλὰ καὶ ἐπισκῶψαι ἐδόκει ἐρόμενος εἴ που εἰδεῖέν τι χωρίον ἔξω τῆς Ἀττικῆς ἔνθα οὐ προσβατὸν θανάτῳ. Here, Xenophon prepares for the Socratic punch line—it is the first joke in the piece, and the setup

for the best one to come—by putting the reader on alert with ἐπισκῶψαι ἐδόκει. In *Ap*. 28, the high point of the piece as a whole, the "punch line structure" is even more evident: παρὼν δέ τις Ἀπολλόδωρος, ἐπιθυμητὴς μὲν ὢν ἰσχυρῶς αὐτοῦ, ἄλλως δ᾽ εὐήθης, εἶπεν ἄρα· ἀλλὰ τοῦτο ἔγωγε, ὦ Σώκρατες, χαλεπώτατα φέρω ὅτι ὁρῶ σε ἀδίκως ἀποθνῄσκοντα. τὸν δὲ λέγεται καταψήσαντα αὐτοῦ τὴν κεφαλὴν εἰπεῖν· σὺ δέ, ὦ φίλτατε Ἀπολλόδωρε, μᾶλλον ἐβούλου με ὁρᾶν δικαίως ἢ ἀδίκως ἀποθνῄσκοντα; καὶ ἅμα ἐπιγελάσαι. Here the last three words function as "the canned laughter" that follows a joke in televised sitcom.

20. Cf. Friedrich Nietzsche, *Die fröhliche Wissenschaft* 4.340 ("Der sterbende Sokrates"): "Sokrates hat *am Leben gelitten!*" and *Götzen-Dämmerung* ("Das Problem des Sokrates," §12): "Sagte er [sc. Socrates] sich das zuletzt [sc. in *Phaedo*], in der *Weisheit* seines Muthes zum Tod? . . . Sokrates *wollte* sterben."

21. Athenaeus 11.114.

22. The young Cicero echoes *Alc*.2 144d6 and 146e2 in *De inventione* 1 with *obesse plerumque prodesse numquam*.

23. See David M. Johnson, *Socrates and Alcibiades: Four Texts* (Newburyport, MA: Focus, 2003), xviii–xx, esp. xviii n. 9.

24. Preferable is the claim that Plato invented the direct or "dramatic dialogue," on which see the studies collected in Holger Thesleff, *Platonic Patterns: A Collection of Studies* (Las Vegas: Parmenides Press, 2009), especially 309–14 (from his 1982 *Studies in Platonic Chronology*).

25. For doubts about the relevant booklists, see Stephen White, *Diogenes Laertius. Lives of Eminent Philosophers: An Edited Translation* (Cambridge; New York: Cambridge University Press, 2021), at 2.121–25.

26. For criticism, see Adolf Busse, "Xenophons Schutzschrift und Apologie," *Rheinisches Museum* 79, no. 3 (1930): 215–29, especially 216, 226, and 228 (on Plato, *Ap*. 41b). More recently, see Gray, *Framing Socrates*, 91–92 n. 10.

27. Thucydides 1.71.3 and *Cyr*. 8.2.5–6.

28. See Ernst Heitsch, "Dialoge Platons vor 399 v.Chr.?" *Nachrichten der Akademie der Wissenschaften zu Göttingen* 6, no. 1 (2002): 303–45.

29. Note φασὶ δὲ καί at Diogenes Laertius, 3.35, noting also the context, especially the discussion of Xenophon in 3.34.

30. See especially Heitsch, "Grenzen."

31. See *Ascent to the Beautiful*, §8.

32. See V. J. Gray, "Xenophon's *Symposion*: The Display of Wisdom," *Hermes* 120, no. 1 (1992): 58–75. Emphasis on genre—"wisdom literature" in particular—is crucial for her unitarian *Mem*. In Gray, *Framing Socrates*, 24, 107, and 113–22.

33. See Hug, "Ueber das gegenseitige verhältniss," 654–56.

34. See my "Xenophon and Plato: Back and Forth with the Two Greatest Socratics." Paper delivered at APA-Central Division (February 24, 2021); accessible at academia.edu.

35. *Ascent to the Good*, §5.
36. Gregory Vlastos, "Happiness and Virtue in Socrates' Moral Theory," *Proceedings of the Cambridge Philological Society* 30 (1984): 181–213, at 199.
37. Aulus Gellius, *Attic Nights*, 14.3.
38. Cf. Cornford, *Plato's Cosmology*; for further discussion, see *The Guardians in Action: Plato the Teacher and the Post*-Republic *Dialogues from* Timaeus *to* Theaetetus (Lanham, MD: Lexington Books, 2016), §1.
39. Cicero, *Tusculan Disputations*, 5.10; with *rebusque bonis et malis quaerere*, cf. τὰ μὲν ἀγαθὰ προαιρεῖσθαι, τῶν δὲ κακῶν ἀπέχεσθαι at *Mem.* 4.5.11. The moral element is sufficient to show that this division κατὰ γένη owes nothing, *pace* Patzer, to the Eleatic Stranger.
40. See Bernard Huss, *Xenophons* Symposion. *Ein Kommentar* (Stuttgart and Leipzig: B. G. Teubner, 1999), 453–55.
41. See my "Socrates in Plato's *Philebus*," in *Socrates and the Socratic Philosophies: Selected Papers from SOCRATICA IV*, ed. Claudia Marsico, 143–51 (Sankt Augustin: Akademia, 2021).
42. See Leo Strauss to Jacob Klein; Feb. 16, 1939, in Strauss, *Gesammelte Schriften*, 3, 567: "*Laws* depends on the fiction that Socrates has escaped from prison, first to Thessaly and then to Crete—he escapes because he does not want to die—. *Laws* is, I believe, clear to me now."
43. Cf. Pangle, *Socrates Founding*, 173: "[I]n Plato's dialogues Socrates is the unrivaled, central figure (especially if we recognize that the Athenian Stranger in the *Laws* is a 'reincarnated' Socrates."
44. See my "Why Plato Wrote *Epinomis*; Leonardo Tarán and the Thirteenth Book of the *Laws*," *Polis* 29 (2012): 83–107.
45. See *The Guardians on Trial: The Reading Order of Plato's Dialogues from Euthyphro to Phaedo* (Lanham, MD: Lexington Books, 2016), §11.
46. Note that the hypothesis of a unitary *Mem.*, as defended by Erbse, Breitenbach, Gray, and Dorion, depends on a defense of the work's coherence and thus of the arrangement of its parts, exactly what must be denied in Olof Gigon, *Kommentar zum ersten Buch von Xenophons Memorabilien* (Basel: Reinhardt, 1953), and the same author's *Kommentar zum zweiten Buch von Xenophons Memorabilien* (Basel: Reinhardt, 1956). I am not denying the coherence of its final form, only that it was also its original form.
47. Cf. [Longinus] *On the Sublime*, 9.12. On Homer's "demise," see *Ascent to the Beautiful*, 333–36.
48. As an example of "methodological flexibility" for a unitarian end, see Gray, *Framing Socrates*, 138–42, where *Mem.* 3.1–7 are integrated as relating to "fellow-citizens" with book 2, described as concerning "family" and "friends, rich and poor."
49. See Mueller-Goldingen, *Untersuchungen*, 45–54.

50. Cf. Eva Sachs, *De Theaeteto atheniensi mathematico* (Berlin: G. Schade, 1914), 22–25, and Nails, *People of Plato*, 321 and 276–77 (note the reliance on *Hell.* for this challenge to the traditional dating).

51. See J. B. Skemp, *Plato's Statesman: A Translation of the Politicus of Plato with Introductory Essays and Footnotes* (London: Rouledge and Kegan Paul, 1952), 59–60.

52. See Mueller-Goldingen, *Untersuchungen*, 46–48.

53. Cf. Plotinus 6.9.7, 23–26; throughout the *Enneads*, Plotinus takes the authenticity of *Epin.* for granted, as *Min.* here.

54. *Cyr.* 5.1.24.

55. Skemp, *Plato's Statesman*, 212n1.

56. *Cyr.* 5.1.24–26 (trans. Wayne Ambler).

57. Skemp, *Plato's Statesman*, 212n1.

58. See Aulus Gellius, 14.3, Athenaeus 11.112, and Diogenes Laertius 3.34.

59. See Xenophon, *Cyropaedia*, trans. Walter Miller, 2 vol. (Cambridge: Harvard University Press, 1914), 2.438–39: "[T]he reader is recommended to close the book at this point [sc. after *Cyr.* 8.7] and read no further."

60. See Leonardo Tarán, *Academica: Plato, Philip of Opus, and the Pseudo-Platonic* Epinomis (Philadelphia: American Philosophical Society, 1975), 23.

61. Gray, *Xenophon's Mirror*, 260–61.

62. Ibid., 261n22.

63. As champions of the "sunny" reading would have it; in addition to Mueller-Goldingen, *Untersuchungen*, 262–71, see See Louis-André Dorion, "La responsibilité de Cyrus dans le déclin de l'empire perse selon Plato et Xénophon," in Dorion, *L'Autre Socrate. Études sur les écrits socratiques de Xénophon*, 393–412 (Paris: Les Belles Lettres, 2013).

64. Herodotus, 9.122 (A. D. Godley translation); see 1.114 on Artembares.

65. See ibid., 1.107–14.

66. See Gera, *Xenophon's Cyropaedia*, ch.r 5 ("Xenophon and his Hero"), especially 296: "Each of the less than ideal features of Cyrus' behavior as ruler of an empire, taken by itself, is perhaps no more than slightly disquieting; viewed cumulatively, they are disturbing and require some sort of explanation. The discrepancies and difficulties are too numerous and obtrusive not to have been deliberately included by Xenophon."

67. See McCloskey, "Xenophon's *Kyrou Amathia*," 112–15.

68. For a robust defense of the view that the ancients need not blush for equating self-interest with morality, see Gabriel Danzig, "Review of Vivienne Gray, *Xenophon's Mirror or Princes*," *Scripta Classica Israelica* 31 (2012): 196–99, at 199, and, in more detail, his "The Best of the Achaemenids: Benevolence, Self-Interest and the 'Ironic' Reading of *Cyropaedia*," in *Xenophon: Ethical Principles and Historical Enquiry*, ed. Fiona Hobden and Christopher Tuplin, 499–539 (Leiden and Boston: Brill, 2012), esp. 538.

69. *Lg.* 694a3–b7 (Bury translation modified).
70. Ibid., 695b2–c2 (Bury modified).
71. In addition to England and Schöpsdau, see Hirsch, *Friendship of the Barbarians*, 97–100.
72. *Lg.* 694e6–695a5 (Bury modified).
73. Ibid., 695d6–696a3 (Bury modified).
74. *Cyr.* 8.1.4–5.
75. *Lg.* 701e1–8.
76. If the Athenian Stranger is a fleeing version of Socrates, he is also a lawbreaking version of him, but even in his obedience to the laws of Athens, the real Socrates is not their slave in *Cri.*; he rather persuades himself to obey them.
77. *Lg.* 821a2–5 (Pangle modified). See *Guardians on Trial*, 302–307.
78. See Pedro Luz Baratieri, "*Hípias Menor*: pedagogia platônica, Homero e intelectualismo," *Hypnos* 42, no. 1 (2019): 89–113, at 103 n. 41 and 43.
79. Homer, *Odyssey*, 8.75–82; for his blindness, see 65.
80. See McCloskey, "Xenophon the Philosopher," 625: "The former [sc. Xenophon] knew that he wrote the *Anabasis*, knew that he commanded the Cyreans, and, at least according to Diogenes Laertius (2.54–5), was proud of his son's death; the latter [sc. The narrator of *Hell.*, i.e., 'N*Hell*'] believes Themistogenes wrote the *Anabasis*, is disinterested in the Cyreans' general, and is unaware of Gryllus. Based on the testimony of the N*Hell.*, the *Hellenika*'s narratorial and authorial levels are distinct."
81. England, *Laws of Plato*, 2.318.
82. See Guthrie, *History of Greek Philosophy*, 3.417–21, for the relevant texts and valuable comments.
83. See Charles H. Kahn, *Plato and the post-Socratic Dialogue: The Return to the Philosophy of Nature* (Cambridge: Cambridge University Press, 2013).
84. See *Guardians in Action*, Introduction.

Chapter Five. A Socratic Relay Race

1. See Joseph A. Howley, *Aulus Gellius and Roman Reading Culture: Text, Presence, and Imperial Knowledge in* Noctes Attica (Cambridge: Cambridge University Press, 2018). On Taurus, who taught Gellius how to read Plato (cf. following note), see John Dillon, *The Middle Platonists. A Study of Platonism 80 B.C. to A.D. 220*, revised edition (Ithaca: Cornell University Press, 1996), and Harold Tarrant, "Introduction: Early Imperial Reception of Plato," in *Brill's Companion to the Reception of Plato in Antiquity*, ed. Harold Tarrant, Danielle A. Layne, Dirk Baltzly, and François Renaud, 92–99 (Leiden and Boston: Brill, 2018), at 95.
2. See Aulus Gellius, *Attic Nights*, 1.9. (John C. Rolfe translation): "My friend Taurus continued: 'But nowadays these fellows who turn to philosophy on

a sudden with unwashed feet, not content with being wholly 'without purpose, without learning [ἄμουσοι], and without scientific training,' even lay down the law as to how they are to be taught philosophy. One says, 'first teach me this [*hoc me primum doce*];' another chimes in, 'I want to learn this, I don't want to learn that'; one is eager to begin [*incipere gestit*] with the *Symposium* of Plato because of the revel of Alcibiades, another with the *Phaedrus* on account of the speech of Lysias.'" Note that both of these texts excite sexual curiosity and, more importantly, that the students wanted to read them too early, that is, out of proper order.

3. Aulus Gellius, *Attic Nights*, 14.3; the next five blocked quotations translate the remainder of this chapter in serial order with no deletions.

4. Despite airing a number of disagreements with Louis-André Dorion, this book would be incomplete without a clear statement of gratitude to an amiable scholar who has done more than anyone else to set aside "the Socratic Question" in favor of an interpretive *parilitas* that demands respect for Xenophon's achievement independently of any difference between him and Plato with respect to "the historical Socrates."

5. See especially Jean Luccioni, *Les Idées politiques et sociales de Xénophon* (Athens: Ophrys, 1948).

6. See Martin Heidegger, *Zu Ernst Jünger, Gesamtausgabe* 90, ed. Peter Trawny (Frankfurt am Main: Vittorio Klostermann, 2004).

7. Cf. Robert C. Bartlett, "How to Rule the World: An Introduction to Xenophon's *The Education of Cyrus*," *American Political Science Review* 109, no. 1 (Feb. 2015): 143–54, at 154 (last word): "The 'education' of the title may include not only the education that Cyrus received but also the education that he makes possible for us, thanks to the artfulness of Xenophon."

8. Horace *Ars Poetica*, 25.

9. Schleiermacher, *Über die Philosophie Platons*, 244–60.

10. On Novalis's famous phrase, see Frederick C. Beiser, *German Idealism: The Struggle Against Subjectivism, 1781–1801* (Cambridge: Harvard University Press, 2002), 419.

11. On the Sign, see *Mem.* 1.1.2–5; cf. *Euthyp.* 2b5–6.

12. Pope's *An Essay on Man*, Epistle 2, 1.

13. Mark L. McPherran, *The Religion of Socrates* (University Park: Pennsylvania State University Press, 1996), 299.

14. *Min.* 321d1–3 (Malcolm Schofield translation).

15. Frisch, *The Constitution of the Athenians*, 110.

16. Exceptional in this regard is Francesca Pentassuglio, "Duplice Afrodite, duplici Eros: Un caso di intertestualità nei *Simposi* socratici." *Elenchos* 33 (2012): 335–56.

17. See Holger Thesleff, "The Interrelation and Date of the *Symposia* of Plato and Xenophon," *Bulletin of the Institute of Classical Studies* 25 (1978): 157–70, and

Gabriel Danzig, "Intra-Socratic Polemics: The *Symposia* of Plato and Xenophon," *Greek, Roman, and Byzantine Studies* 45 (2005): 331–57.
18. Se *Guardians in Action*, §2.
19. *Phdr.* 256b7–e2.
20. See *Guardian in Action*, §4.
21. See Ernst Heitsch, ed., Phaidros, *Platon; Übersetzung und Kommentar* (Göttingen: Vandenhoeck u. Ruprecht, 1993), 120, at 249d4–257a2.
22. Cf. Richard Bett, "Immortality and the Nature of the Soul in the *Phaedrus*," *Phronesis* 31, no. 1 (1986): 1–26, at 20–21.
23. *Phdr.* 265a2–3.
24. See Donald Morrison, "Xenophon's Socrates on the Just and the Lawful," *Ancient Philosophy* 15 (1995): 329–47, David M. Johnson, "Xenophon's Socrates on Law and Justice," *Ancient Philosophy* 23: 255–81, Gabriel Danzig, "Big Boys and Little Boys: Justice and Law in Xenophon's *Cyropaedia* and *Memorabilia*," *Polis* 26 (2009): 271–95, and especially Olga Chernyakhovskaya, *Sokrates bei Xenophon: Moral—Politik—Religion* (Tübingen: Narr, 2014), 198.
25. *Mem.* 3.8.1 (Marchant modified).
26. Cf. Russell E. Jones and Ravi Sharma, "Virtue and Self-Interest in Xenophon's *Memorabilia* 3.9.4–5," *Classical Quarterly* 68 n. 1 (2018): 79–90, and Joseph Bjelde, "Xenophon's Socrates on Wisdom and Action," *Classical Quarterly* 71, no. 2 (2021): 560–74.
27. See Delatte, *Le troisième livre*, ch. 9.
28. See Dodds, *Gorgias*, 335–36.
29. Cf. "The Importance of *Euthydemus*" (52), in Terence Irwin, *Plato's Ethics* (Oxford and New York: Oxford University Press, 1995).
30. *Mem.* 3.9.5.
31. In addition to Delatte, *Le triosième livre*, 103–105, see Peter Vrijlandt, *De Apologia Xenophontea cum Platonica comparata* (Leiden: A. W. Sijtoff's, 1919), 159–67.
32. See Delatte, *Le triosième livre*, 105–108; cf. Joël, *Sokrates*, 1.425–49.
33. See *Ascent to the Good*, §3.
34. Now published (2021) as Xénophon, *Hieron* in the prestigious Belles Lettres series; I am most grateful to Louis-André for giving me an exemplar of this work.
35. Louis-André Dorion, "Le *Hiéron* est-il un dialogue socratique?" (July 15, 2020).
36. See ibid., 8-9: "Le fait même que Simonide n'exhorte pas Hiéron à faire preuve de maîtrise de soi est l'une des principales raisons pour lesquelles certains interprètes refusent de considérer que le *Hiéron* expose une position socratique. La deuxième divergence concerne la tripartition animal/homme/dieu; selon Simonide, c'est l'aspiration aux honneurs qui distingue l'homme de l'animal

et qui le rapproche de la divinité (*Hier.* 7.3-4); quant à Socrate, il estime que c'est l'*enkrateia* qui distingue l'homme de l'animal (*Mem.* 2.1.4-5, 4.5.11) et que l'homme se rapproche de la divinité par la recherche de l'autosuffisance (*Mem.* 1.6.10)." On Schorn, see 21-25.

37. Dorion, *Hiéron*, 117-23.

38. Dorion is brilliant on "Du bon usage de l'*elenchus*: l'entretien entre Socrate et Euthydème (IV 2)" in *Mémorables*, I.clxix-xxxiii, and this section reaches its high point on clxxvii: "In Xenophon, the elenchus is a test that serves to select the interlocutors have the necessary dispositions to receive the teaching of Socrates." Unfortunately, Dorion is less brilliant on Plato (see following note).

39. The problem with Dorion's remarks on the ἔλεγχος is that he allows Vlastos's conceptions of "Plato's early dialogues" to guide his conception of the role of the ἔλεγχος in Plato, as is evident in what he writes next (see previous note) at *Mémorables* I.clxxvii: "The elenchus, in Plato, never plays this role, because Socrates has nothing to teach anyway. When Socrates subjects an interlocutor to successive refutations, it is not with a view to verifying whether he is possibly worthy of receiving his teaching, but to obtain from him an adequate definition of the virtue which is the subject of an examination." Note that it is by taking Aristotle's account of Socrates as definitive, then using it to segregate, as Vlastos did, the "Socratic" from the more didactic "Platonic" dialogues of the "transitional" or "middle period" that Dorion (cf. cxxxii n. 2) can make his case for a sharp distinction between Plato and Xenophon. For the ἔλεγχος as the principal evidence for this distinction, cf. xcii n. 1 and clvi-vii, beginning with: *Mémorables* I.clvi-vii, beginning with: "The contrast, or rather the opposition, between the Socrates of Xenophon and that of Plato is striking." Despite his wholesome rejection of "the Socratic question," Dorion fails to escape from its shadow in arguing for the opposition *between two different versions of Socrates*; it is rather *Plato*, speaking through *all* of his dialogues, who is no less didactic than Xenophon and his Socrates, not the "Socrates" of certain set of dialogues selected on the basis of a prior valorization of Aristotle at the expense of Xenophon, as in Vlastos, *Socrates*, chapter 3 ("The Evidence of Aristotle and Xenophon).

40. See *Plato the Teacher*, §19.

41. For an eloquent defense of τυραννοκτονία, see *Hell.* 7.3.6-12.

42. Düring, *Chion of Heraclea*, 75 (16.5); see also 104: "Our author speaks in general terms of expeditions to the Hellespont. He might have thought of the expeditions of Chabrias." Düring notes the connection to *Cyn.* on the same page; naturally *Hell.* is our source for "the expeditions of Chabrias."

43. *Chion of Heraclea*, 16.6 (Düring on 75); with the remark that follows— "(For I say that the divine things [τὰ θεῖα] are akin to the divine [τῷ θείῳ])"—cf. *Alc.1* 133c1-6 (without the disputed lines).

44. The attempt failed; see Justin 16.5.5: *Qua re factum est, ut tyrannus quidem occideretur, sed patria non liberaretur.*

45. Malosse, *Lettres de Chion d'Héraclée*, 89.
46. See *Guardians in Action*, §18.
47. This sentence constitutes the basis for a post-*Plato the Teacher* trilogy on Platonism consisting of (1) this book, (2) *Plato and Demosthenes: Recovering the Old Academy* (forthcoming from Lexington Books), and (3) a work in progress entitled "Plotinus the Master and the Apotheosis of Imperial Platonism."
48. Cf. Aristotle, *Poetics* 1460a18-19 (Bywater): "Homer more than any other has taught the others the art of framing lies in the right way." I am grateful to Pedro Baratieri for making this connection.
49. Cf. Thucydides 3.48.1 and 3.43.2.
50. A failure to acknowledge the morally neutral status of ἐγκράτεια vitiates the account of Socratic virtue in Dorion, *Mémorables*, I.ccxv-vi, beginning with: "For Xenophon—and this is an ethical position to the truth of which he is personally committed—the usefulness of man is rooted in the ἐνκράτεια, since it is this which allows him to be useful to himself." Self-control is a necessary but not a sufficient condition for Socratic excellence.
51. See *Ascent to the Beautiful*, 118-20.
52. See Guido Calogero, "Gorgias and the Socratic Principle *Nemo Sua Sponte Peccat*," *Journal of Hellenic Studies* 77, pt. 1 (1957): 12-17; for Homer, see *Iliad* 10.372, for Protagoras, see *Prt*. 323b3: καὶ εἰδῶσιν ὅτι ἄδικός ἐστιν; and for Meno, see *An*. 2.6.27: καὶ ἐθέλοι ἂν ἀδικεῖν.
53. See *Ascent to the Good*, §9.
54. Diogenes Laertius 3.1.
55. Act IV, scene 2, 161-63.

Bibliography

Alline, Henri. *Histoire du texte de Platon*. Paris: E. Champion, 1915.
Altman, William H. F. "Womanly Humanism in Cicero's *Tusculan Disputations.*" *Transactions of the American Philological Association* 139 (2009): 411–45.
———. "The Reading Order of Plato's Dialogues." *Phoenix* 64 (2010): 18–51.
———. "Review of Catherine Zuckert, *Plato's Philosophers.*" *Polis* 27 (2010): 147–50.
———. "A Tale of Two Drinking Parties: Plato's *Laws* in Context." *Polis* 27 (2010): 240–64.
———. "Why Plato Wrote *Epinomis*; Leonardo Tarán and the Thirteenth Book of the *Laws.*" *Polis* 29 (2012): 83–107.
———. *Plato the Teacher: The Crisis of the* Republic. Lanham, MD: Lexington Books, 2012.
———. *The Guardians in Action: Plato the Teacher and the Post-*Republic *Dialogues from* Timaeus *to* Theaetetus. Lanham, MD: Lexington Books, 2016.
———. *The Guardians on Trial: The Reading Order of Plato's Dialogues from* Euthyphro *to* Phaedo. Lanham, MD: Lexington Books, 2016.
———. "Division and Collection: A New Paradigm for the Relationship between Plato and Xenophon." In *Plato and Xenophon: Comparative Studies*, edited by Gabriel Danzig, David Johnson, and Donald Morrison, 99–114. Leiden: Brill, 2018.
———. "Dialectic in Xenophon's *Memorabilia*: Responding to 4.6." *Guiaracá* 34, no. 2 (2018): 110–33.
———. *Ascent to the Good: The Reading Order of Plato's Dialogues between* Symposium *and* Republic. Lanham, MD: Lexington Books, 2018.
———. *Ascent to the Beautiful: Plato the Teacher and the Pre-*Republic *Dialogues from* Protagoras *to* Symposium. Lanham, MD: Lexington Books, 2020.
———. "Xenophon the Educator." In *A History of Western Philosophy of Education* (volume 1); *In Antiquity*, edited by Avi I. Mintz, 75–95. London: Bloomsbury, 2020.
———. "The Straussian Reception of Xenophon's *Cyropaedia.*" *Calíope: Presença Clássica* 38, no. 1 (2021): 4–40.37.

———. "Socrates in Plato's *Philebus*." In *Socrates and the Socratic Philosophies: Selected Papers from SOCRATICA IV*, edited by Claudia Marsico, 143–151. Sankt Augustin: Akademia, 2021.
———. "Xenophon and Plato: Back and Forth with the Two Greatest Socratics." Paper delivered at APA-Central Division, February 24, 2021.
———. "Xenophon, the Old Oligarch, and Alcibiades." *Polis* 39, no. 2 (2022): 261–78.
———. "Xenophon and Plato's *Meno*." *Ancient Philosophy* 42, no. 1 (2022): 33–47.
———. "Rereading Xenophon's *Cyropaedia*." *Ancient Philosophy* 42, no. 2 (2022): 335–52.
———. "Xenophon's *Cyropaedia* and Plato's *Laws*." *Caliope* (Forthcoming 2022).
———. "The Priority of Xenophon's Symposium Revisited." https://www.academia.edu/50124486; accessed January 6, 2022.
Anderson, J. K. *Xenophon*. London: Duckworth, 1974.
Anton, Michael. "Socrates as Pickup Artist: An Interpretation of Xenophon's *Memorabilia* III.11." *Perspectives on Political Science* 44, no. 1 (2015): 40–54.
Arbs, Henrich. "De *Alcibiade I* qui fertur Platonis." PhD dissertation: University of Kiel, 1906.
Arnim, Hans von. *Sprachliche Forschungen zur Chronologie der Platonischen Dialoge*. Vienna: Alfred Hölder, 1912.
———. *Platos Jugenddialoge und die Entstehungszeit des Phaidros*. Leipzig and Berlin: B. G. Teubner, 1914.
———. *Xenophon's Memorabilien und Apologie des Sokrates*. Copenhagen: Høst and Son, 1923.
Baratieri, Pedro Luz. "*Hípias Menor*: pedagogia platônica, Homero e intelectualismo." *Hypnos* 42, no. 1 (2019): 89–113.
Bartlett, Robert C. "How to Rule the World: An Introduction to Xenophon's *The Education of Cyrus*." *American Political Science Review* 109, no. 1 (February 2015): 143–54.
———. *Sophistry and Political Philosophy: Protagoras' Challenge to Socrates*. Chicago: University of Chicago Press, 2016.
———. "An Introduction to the *Agesilaus*." In *Xenophon: The Shorter Writings*, edited by Gregory A. McBrayer, 79–105. Ithaca and London: Cornell University Press, 2018.
Beiser, Frederick C. *German Idealism: The Struggle against Subjectivism, 1781–1801*. Cambridge: Harvard University Press, 2002.
Bett, Richard. "Immortality and the Nature of the Soul in the *Phaedrus*." *Phronesis* 31, no. 1 (1986): 1–26.
Biesecker-Mast, Gerald J. "Forensic Rhetoric and the Constitution of the Subject: Innocence, Truth, and Wisdom in Gorgias' *Palamedes* and Plato's *Apology*." *Rhetoric Society Quarterly* 24, no. 3/4 (Summer-Autumn, 1994): 148–66.

Bjelde, Joseph. "Xenophon's Socrates on Wisdom and Action." *Classical Quarterly* 71, no. 2 (2021): 560–74.
Bluck, R. S., ed. *Plato, Meno; Edited with Introduction and Commentary*. Cambridge: Cambridge University Press, 1961.
Breitenbach, H. R. "Xenophon von Athen." *Paulys Realencyclopädie der classischen Altertumswissenschaft* 9 A.2 (1967): 1569–1928.
Bruell, Christopher. *On the Socratic Education: An Introduction to the Shorter Platonic Dialogues*. Lanham, MD: Rowman and Littlefield, 1999.
Bruhn, Ewald. "De Menone Larisaeo." In *ΧΑΡΙΤΕΣ; Friedrich Leo zum sechzigsten Geburtstag dargebracht*, 1–7. Berlin: Weidmann, 1911.
Burnet, John, ed. *Platonis Opera*, volumes 2–5. Oxford: Clarendon Press, 1901–07.
———. *Plato's* Euthyphro, Apology of Socrates, *and* Crito; *Edited with Notes*. Oxford: Clarendon Press, 1924.
Busse, Adolf. "Xenophons Schutzschrift und Apologie." *Rheinisches Museum* 79, no. 3 (1930): 215–29.
Buzzetti, Eric. "A Guide to the Study of Leo Strauss's On Tyranny." In *Brill's Companion to Leo Strauss' Writings on Classical Political Thought*, edited by Timothy W. Burns, 227–57. Leiden and Boston: Brill, 2015.
Calder, William M. III. *Wilamowitz in Greifswald: Akten der Tagung zum 150. Geburtstag Ulrich von Wilamowitz-Moellendorffs in Greifswald, 19.–22. Dezember 1998*. Hildesheim, Zürich, and New York: Olms, 2000.
Calogero, Guido. "Gorgias and the Socratic Principle *Nemo Sua Sponte Peccat*." *Journal of Hellenic Studies* 77, pt. 1 (1957): 12–17.
Canfora, Luciano. "Tucidide continuato e pubblicato." *Belfagor* 25, no. 2 (31 March 1970): 121–34.
———. "Biographical Obscurities and Problems of Composition." In *Brill's Companion to Thucydides*, edited by Antonios Rengakos and Antonios Tsakmakis, 3–32. Leiden: Brill, 2006.
Chantraine, Pierre, ed. and trans. *Xénophon, Économique*. Paris: Les Belles Lettres, 1949.
Chernyakhovskaya, Olga. *Sokrates bei Xenophon: Moral—Politik—Religion*. Tübingen: Narr, 2014.
Christ, Matthew R. *Xenophon and the Athenian Democracy: The Education of an Elite Citizenry*. Cambridge: Cambridge University Press, 2020.
Chroust, Anton-Hermann. "Socrates: A Source Problem." *New Scholasticism* 19 (1945): 48–72.
———. *Socrates, Man and Myth: The Two Socratic Apologies of Xenophon*. Notre Dame: University of Notre Dame Press, 1957.
Churchill, Winston. *My Early Life: A Roving Commission*. London: Thornton Butterworth, 1930.
Cobet, Charles G. *Commentatio qua continetur prosopographia Xenophontea*. Leiden: J. Luchtman, 1836.

Coelho, Maria Cecília de Miranda Nogueira. "Dispositivi dimostrativi utilizzati in tre modelli di difesa: Ippolito, Palamede e Socrate." In *Socratica III. Studies on Socrates, the Socratics, and the Ancient Socratic Literature*, edited by F. De Luise and A. Stavru, 213–20. Sankt Augustin: Academia, 2013.

Cornford, Francis MacDonald. *Plato's Cosmology: The Timaeus of Plato*. London: Routledge and Kegan Paul, 1937.

Coulter, James A. "The Relation of the *Apology* of Socrates to Gorgias' *Defense of Palamedes* and Plato's Critique of Gorgianic Rhetoric." *Harvard Studies in Classical Philology* 68 (1964): 269–303.

Dakyns, H. G. *The Works of Xenophon*, four volumes. London and New York: Macmillan, 1890–1897.

Danzig, Gabriel. "Why Socrates Was Not a Farmer: Xenophon's *Oeconomicus* as a Philosophical Dialogue." *Greece & Rome* 50, no. 1 (April 2003): 57–76.

———. "Did Plato Read Xenophon's *Cyropaedia*?" In *Plato's Laws: From Theory into Practice: Proceedings of the VI Symposium Platonicum Selected Papers*, edited by Samuel Scolnicov and Luc Brisson, 286–96. Sankt Augustin: Academia, 2003.

———. "Intra-Socratic Polemics: The *Symposia* of Plato and Xenophon." *Greek, Roman, and Byzantine Studies* 45 (2005): 331–57.

———. "Big Boys and Little Boys: Justice and Law in Xenophon's *Cyropaedia* and *Memorabilia*." *Polis* 26 (2009): 271–95.

———. *Apologizing for Socrates: How Plato and Xenophon Created Our Socrates*. Lanham, MD: Lexington Books, 2010.

———. "Review of Vivienne Gray, *Xenophon's Mirror or Princes*." *Scripta Classica Israelica* 31 (2012): 196–99.

———. "The Best of the Achaemenids: Benevolence, Self-Interest, and the 'Ironic' Reading of *Cyropaedia*." In *Xenophon: Ethical Principles and Historical Enquiry*, edited by Fiona Hobden and Christopher Tuplin, 499–539. Leiden and Boston: Brill, 2012.

Delatte, Armand. *Le troisième livre des Souvenirs Socratiques de Xénophon*. Paris: Droz, 1933.

Delebecque, Édouard. "Sur la date et l'objet de l'*Économique*." *Revue des Études Grecques* 64, no. 299/301 (January-June 1951): 21–58.

———. *Essai sur la vie de Xénophon*. Paris: C. Klincksieck, 1957.

Denyer, Nicholas, ed. *Alcibiades, Plato*. Cambridge and New York: Cambridge University Press, 2001.

———. *Plato, Protagoras*. Cambridge: Cambridge University Press, 2008.

———. *Plato and Xenophon, Apologies of Socrates*. Cambridge: Cambridge University Press, 2019.

Destrée, Pierre. "Review of Michele Bandini and Louis-André Dorion, *Mémorables*, tome I." *Revue philosophique de Louvain* 102, no. 1 (February 2004): 150–56.

Diduch, Paul C., and Michael P. Harding, "Editors' Introduction: Why Clarifying Socrates' Motives Matter for Philosophy." In *Socrates in the Cave: On the*

Philosopher's Motive in Plato, edited by Diduch and Harding, 1-10. Cham: Palgrave Macmillan, 2019.
Dillery, John. *Xenophon and the History of his Times*. London and New York: Routledge, 1995.
Dillon, John. *The Middle Platonists. A Study of Platonism 80 B.C. to A.D. 220*, revised edition. Ithaca: Cornell University Press, 1996.
Diogenes Laertius, *Lives of the Eminent Philosophers*. Translated by Pamela Mensch and Edited by James Miller. Oxford: Oxford University Press, 2018.
Dobbs, Darrell. "For Lack of Wisdom: Courage and Inquiry in Plato's *Laches*." *Journal of Politics* 48, no. 4 (November 1986): 825-49.
Dodds, E. R. *Plato: Gorgias: A Revised Text with Introduction and Commentary*. Oxford: Clarendon Press, 1959.
Döring, A. "Die Disposition von Xenophons *Memorabilien* als Hilfsmittel positiver Kritik." *Zeitschrift für Geschichte der Philosophie* 4 (1891): 34-60.
Dorion, Louis-André. "À l'origine de la question socratique et de la critique di témoignage de Xénophon: l'étude de Schleiermacher sur Socrate (1815)." *Dionysius* 19 (December 2001): 51-74.
———. "Xénophon *oikonomicos*." In *Socrate et les Socratiques; Actes de colloque d'Aix-en-Provence (6-9 Novembre, 2003)*, edited by Michel Narcy and Alfonso Tordesillas, 253-81. Paris: J. Vrin, 2008.
———. "The Straussian Exegesis of Xenophon: The Paradigmatic Case of *Memorabilia* IV 4." In *Xenophon. Oxford Readings in Classical Studies*, edited by Vivienne Gray, 283-323. Oxford: Oxford University Press, 2010.
———. "The Rise and Fall of the Socrates Problem." In *The Cambridge Companion to Socrates*, edited by Donald R. Morrison, 1-23. Cambridge: Cambridge University Press, 2011.
———. "The Nature and Status of *sophia* in the *Memorabilia*." In *Xenophon: Ethical Principles and Historical Enquiry*, edited by Fiona Hobden and Christopher Tuplin, 455-75. Leiden and Boston: Brill, 2012.
———. "La responsibilité de Cyrus dans le déclin de l'empire perse selon Plato et Xénophon." In *L'Autre Socrate. Études sur les écrits socratiques de Xénophon*, 393-412. Paris: Les Belles Lettres, 2013.
———. "Le *Hiéron* est-il un dialogue socratique?" Paper delivered to the International Society for Socratic Studies, July 15, 2020.
———, and Michele Bandini, eds. *Xénophon, Mémorables*, two volumes. Paris: Belles Lettres, 2000 and 2011.
———. *Xénophon, Hiéron*. Paris: Belles Lettres, 2021.
Dover, K. J. "The Date of Plato's *Symposium*." *Phronesis* 10, no. 1 (1965): 2-20.
Due, Bodil. *The Cyropaedia: Xenophon's Aims and Methods*. Århus: Aarhus University Press, 1989.
Duke, E. A. et al., eds. *Platonis Opera*, volume 1. Oxford: Clarendon Press, 1995.
Dümmler, Ferdinand. *Zur Komposition des platonischen Staates*. Basel: Reinhardt und Sohn, 1895.

Düring, Ingemar, ed. *Chion of Heraclea: A Novel in Letters*. Göteborg: Weitergren u. Kerders, 1951.
Edelstein, Emma. *Xenophontisches und Platonisches Bild des Sokrates*. Berlin: Emil Ebering, 1935.
Eichler, Gustav. "De *Cyrupaediae* capite extreme." Grimma: C. Roessler, 1880.
Engels, Johannes. "Die Ὑπομνήματα-Schriften und die Anfänge der politischen Biographie und Autobiographie in der griechischen Literatur." *Zeitschrift für Papyrologie und Epigraphik* 96 (1993): 19–36.
England, E. B., ed. *The Laws of Plato: The Text Edited with Introduction, Notes, etc.*, two volumes. Manchester: University Press, and London: Longmans, Green, 1921.
Engler, M. R., "Introduction." In Gorgias, *Elogio de Helena e Defesa de Palamedes. Tradução, introdução e notas*. São Paulo: Odysseus, 2022.
Erbse, Hartmut. "Die Architektonik im Aufbau von Xenophons *Memorabilien*." *Hermes* 89 no. 3 (1961): 257–87.
Ewegen, S. Montgomery. *The Way of the Platonic Socrates*. Bloomington: Indiana University Press, 2020.
Field, Laura K. "Xenophon's *Cyropaedia*: Educating our Political Hopes." *Journal of Politics* 74, no. 3 (July 2012): 723–38.
Foerster, Richardus, ed. *Libanii Opera*, volume 5. Leipzig: Teubner, 1909.
Foley, Richard. "The Better Part of Valor: The Role of Wisdom in Plato's *Laches*." *History of Philosophy Quarterly* 26, no. 3 (July 2009): 213–33.
Friedländer, Paul. *Plato*, volume two. Translated by Hans Meyerhoff. New York: Bollingen, 1964.
Frisch, Hartvig. *The Constitution of the Athenians; A Philological-Historical Analysis of Pseudo-Xenophon's Treatise* De re publica Atheniensium. Copenhagen: Gyldendalske Boghandel, 1942.
Fritz, Kurt von. "Review of *Polycratès, l'accusation de Socrate et le Gorgias* by Jean Humbert." *Gnomon* 9, no. 2 (February 1933): 88–95.
Fussi, Alessandra. "Why Is the *Gorgias* so Bitter?" *Philosophy & Rhetoric* 33, no. 1 (2000): 39–58.
Gera, Deborah Levine. *Xenophon's* Cyropaedia: *Style, Genre, and Literary Technique*. Oxford: Clarendon Press, 1993.
Gigon, Olof. *Kommentar zum ersten Buch von Xenophons Memorabilien*. Basel: Reinhardt, 1953.
———. *Kommentar zum zweiten Buch von Xenophons Memorabilien*. Basel: Reinhardt, 1956.
Gomperz, H. *Sophistik und Rhetorik: Das Bildungsideal des εὖ λέγειν in seinem Verhältnis zur Philosophie des V. Jahrhunderts*. Leipzig and Berlin: Teubner, 1912.
Gray, Vivienne J. "Xenophon's *Cynegeticus*." *Hermes* 113, no. 2 (2nd Quarter 1985): 156–72.

---. *The Character of Xenophon's Hellenica*. Baltimore: Johns Hopkins University Press, 1989.
---. "Xenophon's *Symposion*: The Display of Wisdom." *Hermes* 120, no. 1 (1992): 58-75.
---. *The Framing of Socrates: The Literary Interpretation of Xenophon's Memorabilia*. Stuttgart: Franz Steiner, 1998.
---. *Xenophon's Mirror of Princes: Reading the Reflections*. Oxford and New York: Oxford University Press, 2011.
Greene, William Chase, ed. *Scholia Platonica*. Haverford, PA: American Philological Society, 1938.
Guthrie, W. K. C. *A History of Greek Philosophy*, six volumes. Cambridge: Cambridge University Press, 1967-1981.
Hackforth, Reginald. *The Authorship of the Platonic Epistles*. Manchester: At the University Press, 1913.
Hamilton, Edith. *The Greek Way*. New York: W. W. Norton, 1930.
Handford, Martin. *Where's Wally*. London: Walker Books, 1987.
Hartman, I. I. *Analecta Xenophontea*. Leiden and Leipzig: Van Doesburgh and Harrassowitz, 1887.
Hegel, Georg Wilhelm Friedrich. *Lectures on the History of Philosophy*, three volumes. Translated by E. S. Haldane. London: K. Paul, Trench, Trübner, 1892-96.
Heidegger, Martin. *Zu Ernst Jünger, Gesamtausgabe* 90. Edited by Peter Trawny. Frankfurt am Main: Vittorio Klostermann, 2004.
Heitsch, Ernst, ed. *Phaidros, Platon; Übersetzung und Kommentar*. Göttingen: Vandenhoeck u. Ruprecht, 1993.
---. "Grenzen philologischer Echtheitskritik: Bemerkungen zum *Großen Hippias*." *Abhandlungen der Geistes- und Sozialwissenschaftlichen Klasse* 4 (1999): 1-40.
---. "Dialoge Platons vor 399 v.Chr.?" *Nachrichten der Akademie der Wissenschaften zu Göttingen* 6, no. 1 (2002): 303-45.
---. *Platon, Grösserer Hippias; Übersetzung und Kommentar. Mit einem Beitrag von Franz von Kutschera*. Göttingen: Vandenhoeck u. Ruprecht, 2011.
Helbig, Wolfgang. "Alkibiades als politischer Schriftsteller." *Rheinisches Museum* 16 (1861): 511-31.
Helfer, Ariel. *Socrates and Alcibiades: Plato's Drama of Political Ambition and Philosophy*. Philadelphia: University of Pennsylvania Press, 2017.
Hermann, K. F. *Geschichte und System der Platonischen Philosophie*. Heidelberg: C. F. Winter, 1839.
Hindley, Clifford. "Xenophon on Male Love." *Classical Quarterly* 49, no. 1 (1999): 74-99.
Hirsch, Steven W. *The Friendship of the Barbarians: Xenophon and the Persian Empire*. Hanover NH: University Press of New England, 1985.

Hobden, Fiona. "Xenophon's *Oeconomicus*." In *The Cambridge Companion to Xenophon*, edited by Michael A. Flower, 152–73. Cambridge: Cambridge University Press, 2017.
Hoerber, Robert G. "Plato's *Meno*." *Phronesis* 5, no. 2 (1960): 78–102.
———. "Plato's *Laches*." *Classical Philology* 63, no. 2 (April 1968): 95–105.
Hogenmüller, Boris. "The Influence of Plato's *Crito* and *Phaedo* on Xenophon's *Apology of Socrates*." *Kentron* 31 (2015): 127–38.
Hornstein, Franz. "Komposition und Herausgabe der Xenophontischen Memorabilien" (in two parts). *Wiener Studien* 36 (1915): 122–39, and 37 (1916): 63–87.
Howley, Joseph A. *Aulus Gellius and Roman Reading Culture: Text, Presence, and Imperial Knowledge in* Noctes Attica. Cambridge: Cambridge University Press, 2018.
Hug, Arnold. "Ueber das gegenseitige verhältniss der symposien des Xenophon und Plato." *Philologus* 7, no. 4 (1852): 638–95.
Humbert, J. "Le pamphlet de Polycratès et le *Gorgias* de Platon." *Revue de Philologie* 5 (1931): 20–77.
Humble, Noreen. *Xenophon the Athenian: A Socratic on Sparta*. Cambridge: Cambridge University Press, 2021.
Huss, Bernard. *Xenophons* Symposion. *Ein Kommentar*. Stuttgart and Leipzig: B. G. Teubner, 1999.
Hyland, Drew. *Finitude and Transcendence in the Platonic Dialogues*. Albany: State University of New York Press, 1995.
Irwin, Terence. *Plato's Ethics*. Oxford and New York: Oxford University Press, 1995.
Jaeger, Werner. *Paideia: The Ideals of Greek Culture*. Translated by Gilbert Highet. Vol. three. Oxford: Blackwell, 1944.
Joël, Karl. *Der echte und der Xenophontische Sokrates*, two volumes. Berlin: R. Gaertners, 1893–1901.
Johnson, David M. *Socrates and Alcibiades: Four Texts*. Newburyport, MA: Focus, 2003.
———. "Xenophon's Socrates on Law and Justice." *Ancient Philosophy* 23, no. 2 (2003): 255–81.
———. "Xenophon at his most Socratic (*Memorabilia* 4.2)." *Oxford Studies in Ancient Philosophy* 29 (2005): 39–73.
———. "From Generals to Gluttony: *Memorabilia* Book 3." In *Socrates and the Socratic Dialogue*, edited by Alessandro Stavru and Christopher Moore, 481–99. Leiden and Boston: Brill, 2018.
———. *Xenophon's Socratic Works*. Oxford and New York: Routledge, 2021.
Jones H. S., ed. *Thucydidis Historiae*. Oxford: Clarendon Press, 1900.
Jones, Russell E., and Ravi Sharma. "Virtue and Self-Interest in Xenophon's *Memorabilia* 3.9.4–5." *Classical Quarterly* 68, no. 1 (2018): 79–90.
Kahn, Charles H. "Did Plato Write Socratic Dialogues?" *Classical Quarterly* 31 (1981): 305–20.

———. "The Beautiful and the Genuine: A Discussion of Paul Woodruff's *Plato, Hippias Major*." *Oxford Studies in Ancient Philosophy* 2 (1985): 261–87.
———. "Plato's *Charmides* and the Proleptic Reading of Socratic Dialogues." *Journal of Philosophy* 85 (1988): 541–49.
———. "On the Relative Date of the *Gorgias* and the *Protagoras*." *Oxford Studies in Ancient Philosophy* 6 (1988): 69–102.
———. *Plato and the Socratic Dialogue: The Philosophical Use of a Literary Form*. Cambridge: Cambridge University Press, 1996.
———. *Plato and the post-Socratic Dialogue: The Return to the Philosophy of Nature*. Cambridge: Cambridge University Press, 2013.
Kaiser, Bernhard. *Streit und Kampf: Die verbalen Angriffe gegen Sokrates in Platons Gorgias*. Stuttgart: Franz Steiner, 2021.
Kapellos, Aggelos. *Xenophon's Peloponnesian War*. Berlin and New York: De Gruyter, 2019.
Kapp, Ernst. "The Theory of Ideas in Plato's Earlier Dialogues (Nach 1942)." In *Ausgewählte Schriften*, edited by Hans and Inez Diller, 61–150. Berlin: de Gruyter, 1968.
Klein, Jacob. *A Commentary on Plato's* Meno. Chicago and London: University of Chicago Press, 1965.
Konstan, David, and Phillip Mitsis, "Chion of Heraclea: A Philosophical Novel in Letters." *Apeiron* 23, no. 4 (December 1990): 257–79.
Kronenberg, Leah. *Allegories of Farming from Greece and Rome: Philosophical Satire in Xenophon, Varro, and Virgil*. Cambridge: Cambridge University Press, 2009.
L'Allier, Louis. *Le bonheur des moutons; Étude sur l'homme et l'animal dans la hiérarchie de Xénophon*. Québec: Sphinx, 2004.
Lampert, Laurence. *How Philosophy Became Socratic: A Study of Plato's* Protagoras, Charmides, *and* Republic. Chicago: University of Chicago Press, 2010.
Luccioni, Jean. *Les Idées politiques et sociales de Xénophon*. Athens: Ophrys, 1948.
Maidment, K. J. "Introduction" to Andocides' *On the Peace* in *Minor Attic Orators*, volume 1. Cambridge: Harvard University Press, 1941.
Maier, Heinrich. *Sokrates: sein Werk und seine geschichtliche Stellung*. Tübingen: J. C. B. Mohr, 1913.
Malosse, Pierre-Louis. *Lettres de Chion d'Héraclée*. Salerno: Helios, 2004.
Mansfeld, Jaap. "Aristotle, Plato, and the Preplatonic Doxography and Chronography." In *Studies in the Historiography of Greek Philosophy*, 22–83. Assen: Van Gorcum, 1990.
Marchant, E. C., ed. *Xenophontis opera omnia*, five volumes. Oxford: Clarendon Press, 1900–1920.
———. "Introduction." In *Xenophon in Seven Volumes*, volume 4, vii–xxix. Cambridge: Harvard University Press, 1923.

McBrayer, Gregory A. "Introduction to the *Regime of the Athenians*." In *Xenophon: The Shorter Writings*, 160–74. Ithaca and London: Cornell University Press, 2018.
McCloskey, Benjamin. "Xenophon's *Kyrou Amathia*: Deceitful Narrative and the Birth of Tyranny." PhD diss., Ohio State University; 2012.
———. "Xenophon the Philosopher: *E Pluribus Plura*." *American Journal of Philology* 138 (2017): 605–40.
McPherran, Mark L. *The Religion of Socrates*. University Park: Pennsylvania State University Press, 1996.
Mitscherling, J. "Xenophon and Plato." *Classical Quarterly* 32, no. 2 (1982): 468–69.
Moore, Christopher. "Xenophon on 'Philosophy' and Socrates." In *Plato and Xenophon: Comparative Studies*, edited by Gabriel Danzig, David Johnson, and Donald Morrison, 128–64. Leiden: Brill, 2018.
———. *Calling Philosophers Names: On the Origin of a Discipline*. Princeton and London: Princeton University Press, 2020.
———. "Review of Stephen White, *Diogenes Laertius*." *Bryn Mawr Classical Review* (2022.01.04).
Morr, Josef. "Das Gorgias *Palamedes* und Xenophons *Apology*." *Hermes* 61, no. 4 (1926): 467–70.
———. *Die Entstehung der Platonischen Apologie*. Reichenberg: Stiepel Brothers, 1929.
Morrison, Donald. "Xenophon's Socrates on the Just and the Lawful." *Ancient Philosophy* 15 (1995): 329–47.
Morrison, J. S. "Meno of Pharsalus, Polycrates, and Ismenias." Edited by H. T. W.-G. *Classical Quarterly* 36, no. 1/2 (January-April 1942): 57–78.
Most, Glenn W. "Simonides' Ode to Scopas in Contexts." In *Modern Critical Theory and Classical Literature*, edited by Irene J. F. de Jong and J. P. Sullivan, 127–52. Leiden: E. J. Brill, 1994.
Mueller-Goldingen, Christian. *Untersuchungen zu Xenophons Kyrupädie*. Stuttgart and Leipzig: Teubner, 1995.
Munn, Mark. *The School of History: Athens in the Age of Socrates*. Berkeley: University of California Press, 2000.
Murray, Gilbert. *A History of Ancient Greek Literature*. London: Heinemann, 1897.
Nadon, Christopher. *Xenophon's Prince: Republic and Empire in the* Cyropaedia. Berkeley: University of California Press, 2001.
Nails, Debra. *The People of Plato: A Prosopography of Plato and Other Socratics*, Indianapolis: Hackett, 2002.
Narcy, Michel. "La meilleure amie de Socrate; Xénophon, *Mémorables*, III.11." *Les Études philosophiques* 2 (May 2004): 213–34.
Natali, Carlo. "Socrate dans *L'Économique* de Xénophon." Translated by Sophie Van der Meeren. In *Socrate et les Socratiques*, under the direction of G. Romeyer Dherbey and edited by J.-B. Gourinat, 263–88. Paris: J. Vrin, 2001.

Natoli, Anthony Francis. *The Letter of Speusippus to Philip II: Introduction, Text, Translation and Commentary*. Stuttgart: Franz Steiner, 2004.
Niebuhr, B. G. "Ueber Xenophons *Hellenika*." *Rheinisches Museum* 1 (1827): 194–98.
Nielsen, Karen Margrethe. "The Tyrant's Vice: Pleonexia and Lawlessness in Plato's *Republic*." *Philosophical Perspectives* 33 (2019): 146–69.
Neuhausen, Hubertus. *Der Zweite Alkibiades. Untersuchungen zu einem pseudo-platonischen Dialog*. Berlin and New York: De Gruyter, 2010.
Noël, Marie-Pierre. "Critobule dans les écrits socratiques de Xénophon: le portrait d'un mauvais élève." *Kentron* 31 (2015): 43–58.
Pangle, Thomas L. "Socrates in the Context of Xenophon's Political Writings." In *The Socratic Movement*, edited by P. A. Vander Waerdt, 127–50. Ithaca: Cornell University Press, 1995.
———. *The Socratic Way of Life: Xenophon's* Memorabilia. Chicago: University of Chicago Press, 2018.
———. *Socrates Founding Political Philosophy in* Economist, Symposium, *and* Apology. Chicago: University of Chicago Press, 2020.
Patzer, Andreas. "Der Xenophantische Sokrates als Dialektiker." In *Der fragende Sokrates*, edited by Karl Pestalozzi, 50–78. Stuttgart: Teubner, 1999.
———. "Xenophon's Socrates as Dialectician." In *Oxford Readings in Classical Studies: Xenophon*, edited by Vivienne J. Gray, 228–56. Oxford: Oxford University Press, 2010.
Penner, Terry. "Socrates on Virtue and Motivation." In *Exegesis and Argument: Essays for Gregory Vlastos*, in *Phronesis*, edited by E. N. Lee, A. P. D. Mourelatos, and Richard Rorty, 133–51. Assen: Van Gorcum, 1973.
———, and Christopher Rowe, *Plato's* Lysis. Cambridge: Cambridge University Press, 2006.
Pentassuglio, Francesca. "Duplice Afrodite, duplici Eros: Un caso di intertestualità nei *Simposi* socratici." *Elenchos* 33 (2012): 335–56.
Penwill, J. L. "Evolution of an Assassin: The Letters of Chion of Heraclea." *Ramus* 39, no. 1 (2010): 24–52.
Peterson, Sandra. "Notes on *Lovers*." In *Socrates and the Socratic Dialogue*, edited by Alessandro Stavru and Christopher Moore, 412–31. Leiden and Boston: Brill, 2018.
Planeaux, Chr. "Socrates, Alcibiades, and Plato's TA ΠΟΤΕΙΔΕΑΤΙΚΑ. Does the *Charmides* Have an Historical Setting?" *Mnemosyne* 52 (fourth series), no. 1 (February 1999): 72–77.
Pohlenz, Max. *Aus Platos Werdezeit: philosophische Untersuchungen*. Berlin: Weidmann, 1913.
Pomeroy, Sarah B. Xenophon, Oeconomicus: *A Social and Historical Commentary*. Oxford: Clarendon Press, 1994.
Pontier, Pierre. *Trouble et ordre chez Platon et Xénophon*. Paris: J. Vrin, 2006.

Pownall, Frances Anne. *Lessons from the Past: The Moral Use of History in Fourth-Century Prose.* Ann Arbor: University of Michigan Press, 2004.
Preus, Anthony. "The Citizenship of Socrates in the Light of Modern Citizenship Studies" (forthcoming).
Prince, Susan. *Antisthenes of Athens; Texts, Translations, and Commentary.* Ann Arbor: University of Michigan Press, 2015.
Rabieh, Linda R. *Plato and the Virtue of Courage.* Baltimore: Johns Hopkins University Press, 2006.
Radermacher, Ludwig. "Ueber den Cynegeticus des Xenophon." *Rheinisches Museum für Philologie* (n.f.) 51 (1896): 596–629 and 52 (1897): 13–41.
Reisert, Joseph R. "Ambition and Corruption in Xenophon's *Education of Cyrus*." *Polis* 26, no. 2 (2009): 296–315.
———. "Xenophon on Gentlemanliness and Friendship." In *The Arts of Rule: Essays in Honor of Harvey C. Mansfield,* edited by Sharon R. Krause and Mary Ann McGrail, 23–41. Lanham, MD: Lexington Books, 2009.
Renault, Mary. *The Last of the Wine.* New York: Pantheon Books, 1956.
Riginos, Alice Swift. *The Anecdotes Concerning the Life and Writings of Plato.* Leiden: Brill, 1976.
Roisman, Joseph, and Ian Worthington, eds., and Robin Waterfield, trans. *Lives of the Attic Orators: Texts from pseudo-Plutarch, Photius, and the Suda.* Oxford: Oxford University Press, 2015.
Rood, Timothy. *The sea! The sea!: The Shout of the Ten Thousand in the Modern Imagination.* London: Duckworth, 2004.
Romilly, Jacqueline de. *The Life of Alcibiades: Dangerous Ambition and the Betrayal of Athens.* Translated by Elizabeth Trapnell Rawlings. Ithaca and London: Cornell University Press, 2019.
Roquette, Adalbert. *De Xenophontis Vita.* Königsberg: Leopold, 1884.
Roscher, Wilhelm. *Leben, Werke und Zeitalter des Thukydides. Mit einer Einleitung zur Aesthetik der historischen Kunst überhaupt.* Göttingen: Vandenhoeck u. Ruprecht, 1842.
Rosenmeyer, Patricia A. *Ancient Epistolary Fictions: The Letter in Greek Literature.* Cambridge and New York: Cambridge University Press, 2001.
Ross, W. D., ed. *Aristotelis Fragmenta Selecta.* Oxford: Clarendon Press, 1955.
Sachs, Eva. *De Theaeteto atheniensi mathematico.* Berlin: G. Schade, 1914.
Schleiermacher, Friedrich Ernst Daniel. "Über den Werth des Sokrates als Philosophen" (originally published in 1818). In *Der Historische Sokrates,* edited by Andreas Patzer, 41–59. Darmstadt: Wissenschaftliche Buchhandlung, 1987.
———. *Über die Philosophie Platons.* Edited by Peter M. Steiner with contributions by Andreas Arndt and Jörg Jantzen. Hamburg: Felix Meiner, 1996.
Scholtz, Gunter. "Schleiermacher und die platonische Ideenlehre." In *Internationaler Schleiermacher-Kongress (1984, Berlin, West),* edited by Kurt-Victor Selde, 849–71. Berlin: De Gruyter, 1985.

Schmid, Walter T. *On Manly Courage: A Study of Plato's Laches*. Carbondale and Edwardsville: Southern Illinois University Press, 1992.
Schneider, Johann Gottlob. ΞΕΝΟΦΩΝΤΟΣ, ΤΑ ΣΩΖΟΜΕΝΑ; *Xenophontis, quae extant*, volume 6. Oxford: Clarendon Press, 1817.
Schöpsdau, Klaus. *Platon, Nomoi (Gesetze): Übersetzung und Kommentar*, 3 volumes. Göttingen: Vandenhoeck u. Ruprecht, 1994–2011.
Schorn, Stephan. "Die Vorstellung des xenophontischen Sokrates von Herrschaft und das Erziehungsprogramm des *Hieron*." In *Socratica 2005: Studi sulla letteratura socratica antica presentati alle Giornate di studio di Senigallia*, edited by Livio Rossetti and Alessandro Stavru, 177–203. Bari: Levante Editori, 2008.
Scott, Dominic. "Platonic Pessimism and Moral Education." *Oxford Studies in Ancient Philosophy* 17 (1999): 15–36.
———. *Plato's Meno*. Cambridge: Cambridge University Press, 2005.
Sealey, Raphael. *Demosthenes and his Time: A Study in Defeat*. Oxford and New York: Oxford University Press, 1993.
Sedley, David. "Socratic Intellectualism in the *Republic*'s Central Digression." In *The Platonic Art of Philosophy*, edited by George Boys-Stones, Dimitri El Murr, and Christopher Gill, 70–89. Cambridge and New York: Cambridge University Press, 2013.
Shulsky, Abram N. "Introduction to the *Ways and Means*." In *Xenophon: The Shorter Writings*, edited by Gregory A. McBrayer, 189–209. Ithaca and London: Cornell University Press, 2018.
Skemp, J. B. *Plato's Statesman: A Translation of the* Politicus *of Plato with Introductory Essays and Footnotes*. London: Rouledge and Kegan Paul, 1952.
Slings, S. R., ed. *Platonis Rempublicam*. Oxford: Clarendon Press, 2003.
Smith, Nicholas. "A Problem in Plato's Hagiography of Socrates." *Athens Journal of Humanities and Arts* 5, no. 1 (January 2018): 81–103.
Smith, Steven B. "Philosophy as a Way of Life: The Case of Leo Strauss." *Review of Politics* 71, no. 1 (Winter 2009): 37–53.
Stokes, Michael. "Three Defenses of Socrates: Relative Chronology, Politics and Religion." In *Xenophon: Ethical Principles and Historical Enquiry*, edited by Fiona Hobden and Christopher Tuplin, 243–67. Leiden and Boston: Brill, 2012.
Strasburger, Herman. *Caesars Eintritt in die Geschichte*, originally published in Munich, 1938. Darmstadt: Wissenschaftliche Buchgesellschaft, 1966.
Strassler, Robert B., ed. *The Landmark Xenophon's* Hellenika; *A New Translation by John Marincola with Maps, Annotations, Appendices, and Encyclopedic Index*. Introduction by David Thomas. New York, Anchor Books, 2010.
Strauss, Leo. "Anmerkungen zu Carl Schmitt, Der Begriff des Politischen." *Archiv für Sozialwissenschaft* 67 (1932): 732–49.
———. "On Xenophon's *Education of Cyrus*" (1938). In *Toward Natural Right and History: Lectures and Essays by Leo Strauss, 1937–1946*, edited by J.

A. Colen and S. Minkov, 138–46. Chicago: University of Chicago Press, 2018.

———. "The Spirit of Sparta or the Taste of Xenophon." *Social Research* 6 no. 4 (November 1939): 502–36.

———. *On Tyranny; An Interpretation of Xenophon's* Hiero, with a Foreword by Alvin Johnson. New York: Political Science Classics, 1948.

———. "Xenophon" (1963), session 7; http://leostrausstranscripts.uchicago.edu/navigate/8/8/; accessed August 19, 2020.

———. *The City and Man*. Chicago: University of Chicago Press, 1964.

———. "Greek Historians." *Review of Metaphysics* 21, no. 4 (June 1968): 656–66.

———. *Xenophon's Socrates*. Ithaca: Cornell University Press, 1972.

———. *Xenophon's Socratic Discourse: An Interpretation of the* Oeconomicus (originally published in 1970). Preface by Allan Bloom, Foreword by Christopher Bruell, with a new, literal translation of the *Oeconomicus* by Carnes Lord. South Bend: St. Augustine's Press, 1998.

———. *On Tyranny; Revised and Expanded Edition; Including the Strauss-Kojève Correspondence*. Edited by Victor Gourevitch and Michael S. Roth. Chicago: University of Chicago Press, 2000.

———. *Gesammelte Schriften*, volume 3; *Hobbes' politische Wissenschaft und zugehörige Schriften—Briefe*. Edited by Heinrich Meier, with the editorial assistance of Wiebke Meier. Stuttgart and Weimar: J. B. Metzler, 2002.

Syme, Ronald. *The Roman Revolution*. Oxford: Oxford University Press, 1939.

Tamiolaki, Melina. "Being or Appearing Virtuous? The Challenges of Leadership in Xenophon's *Cyropaedia*." In *Gaze, Vision, and Visuality in Ancient Greek Literature*, edited by Alexandros Kampakoglou and Anna Novokhatko, 308–30. Berlin and Boston: de Gruyter, 2018.

Tarán, Leonardo. *Academica: Plato, Philip of Opus, and the Pseudo-Platonic* Epinomis. Philadelphia: American Philosophical Society, 1975.

Tarrant, Harold. "The Origins and Shape of Plato's Six-Book *Republic*." *Antichthon* 46 (2012): 52–78.

———. "Introduction: Early Imperial Reception of Plato." In *Brill's Companion to the Reception of Plato in Antiquity*, edited by Tarrant, Danielle A. Layne, Dirk Baltzly, and François Renaud, 92–99. Leiden and Boston: Brill, 2018.

———. *The Second Alcibiades: A Platonist Dialogue on Prayer and Ignorance*. Las Vegas: Parmenides Press, 2022.

Tatum, James. *Xenophon's Imperial Fiction*. Princeton: Princeton University Press, 1989.

Taylor, Lily Ross. "Review of *Caesars Eintritt in die Geschichte*." *Classical Philology* 36 (1941): 413–14.

Thesleff, Holger. "The Interrelation and Date of the *Symposia* of Plato and Xenophon." *Bulletin of the Institute of Classical Studies* 25 (1978): 157–70.

———. *Platonic Patterns: A Collection of Studies*. Las Vegas: Parmenides Press, 2009.

Thompson, E. Seymour. *The Meno of Plato, edited with Introduction, Notes, and Excurses*. London: Macmillan, 1901.
Trampedach, Kai. *Platon, die Akademie und die zeitgenössische Politik*. Stuttgart: Franz Steiner, 1994.
Trivigno, Franco V. "Paratragedy in Plato's *Gorgias*." *Oxford Studies in Ancient Philosophy* 36 (Summer 2009): 73-105.
Tuchmann, Barbara. *The Guns of August*. New York: Macmillan, 1962.
Tuci, Paulo A. "'*Apronoētos Orgē*': The Role of Anger in Xenophon's Vision of History." In *Violence in Xenophon*, edited by Aggelos Kapellos, 25-44. Berlin and Boston: De Gryuter, 2019.
Vander Waerdt, Paul. "Socratic Justice and Self-Sufficiency: The Story of the Delphic Oracle in Xenophon's *Apology of Socrates*." *Oxford Studies in Ancient Philosophy* 11 (1993): 1-48.
Vickers, Michael. "Alcibiades on Stage: *Philoctetes* and *Cyclops*." *Historia* 36, no. 2 (2nd Quarter 1987): 171-97.
———. *Aristophanes and Alcibiades: Echoes of Contemporary History in Athenian Comedy*. Berlin: De Gruyter, 2015.
Vlastos, Gregory. "Happiness and Virtue in Socrates' Moral Theory." *Proceedings of the Cambridge Philological Society* 30 (1984): 181-213.
———. *Socrates: Ironist and Moral Philosopher*. Cambridge: Cambridge University Press, 1991.
Vrijlandt, Peter. *De Apologia Xenophontea cum Platonica comparata*. Leiden: A. W. Sijtoff's, 1919.
Waterfield, Robin. "Xenophon's Socratic Mission." In *Xenophon and his World: Papers from a Conference Held in Liverpool in July 1999*, edited by Vincent Azoulay, 79-113. Stuttgart: Franz Steiner, 2004.
Wellman, Robert R. "Socratic Method in Xenophon." *Journal of the History of Ideas* 37 (1976): 307-18.
White, Stephen. *Diogenes Laertius. Lives of Eminent Philosophers: An Edited Translation*. Cambridge and New York: Cambridge University Press, 2021.
Whitehead, David, ed. Xenophon, *Poroi (Revenue-Sources)*. Oxford: Oxford University Press, 2019.
Wilamowitz-Moellendorff, Ulrich von. *Platon*, 2nd edition, two volumes. Berlin: Weidmann, 1920.
Wolfsdorf, David. "Desire for Good in *Meno* 77B2-78B6." *Classical Quarterly* 56, no. 1 (May 2006): 77-92.
Woolf, Raphael. "Callicles and Socrates: Psychic (Dis)Harmony in the *Gorgias*." *Oxford Studies in Ancient Philosophy* 18 (2000): 1-40.
Wörle, Andrea. *Die politische Tätigkeit der Schüler Platons*. Darmstadt: Kümmerle, 1981.
Xenophon, *Cyropaedia*. Translated by Walter Miller, two volumes. Cambridge: Harvard University Press, 1914.

———. *Hiéron*. Texte établi par Michele Bandini; traduit et commenté par Louis-André Dorion. Paris: Belles Lettres, 2021.

Zuckert, Catherine H. *Plato's Philosophers: The Coherence of the Dialogues*. Chicago: University of Chicago Press, 2009.

Index

Academic editor of Xenophon's writings, hypothesis of, 138–41, 145, 150, 193, 220
Academy, ix, xi–xii, 1, 10, 24–25, 27–29, 46–47, 88, 131–33, 139, 144, 153, 179, 181, 188, 200–202, 262–65, 283, 288–89, 339n47; and "Academic ordering," 132; see also Academic editor of Xenophon's writings, hypothesis of; and Allegory of the Cave, 289; and Aristotle, 31, 179, 181; and Chion of Heraclea, xi–xii, 288; and Cynegeticus, 264; and Lycurgus, 179, 181; and Protagoras, 143–44, 264; and Xenophon, 46; as day school for boys, 264; curriculum of, 25, 202, 264, "eternal curriculum" of, 283; library of, 69, 132, 139, 262; original purpose of, 10, 289; transformation of, 31, 179
Achilles, 158, 231–32, 248, 290, 322n18
Adeimantus, 112–13, 319n140, 320n155
Aeschines Socraticus, 4, 133, 212
Aeschylus, 50
Agesilaus and Agesilaus, 50, 55, 134, 136, 162, 165, 171–72, 180, 182, 193, 229, 231, 264, 270, 326n66, 327n79; Leo Strauss on, 171
Alcestis, 103
Alcibiades, 2–3, 16–18, 30, 33, 42–55, 64–65, 76–79, 88–89, 105, 118–19, 142–46, 160, 173–79, 193, 204–206, 209, 214–15, 219, 232, 272–74, 278, 298, 307, 328, 331, 336; and Plato's artistry, 203–204, 278, as power-drunk, 4
Alcibiades Major, 16, 43, 48–53, 60, 64, 68, 87, 105, 118, 143–46, 148, 150, 161, 181, 201–204, 209–10, 214–15, 220, 227, 232, 259, 264, 294, 305–306, 322, 329, 338; and *Memorabilia* 4.2, 203–204; and Queen's Sash, 46, 50, 68, 201, 204, 264; as masterpiece of elementary pedagogy, 201; as *Xenophontisch*, 43–44, 46–47, 52, 259
Alcibiades Minor, 16, 54–55, 81, 144–46, 148, 150, 208–11, 214–16, 227, 283, 308, 315, 322, 332; attributed to Xenophon, 43
Anabasis, xii, 11, 14, 20–25, 28, 34, 36–38, 45–50, 55–58, 60, 63, 68–70, 78, 89, 93, 98, 105, 108–10, 118, 120, 133–34, 152–54, 156, 158–59, 162, 180–81, 186–91, 201, 206, 213,

357

Anabasis (continued)
248, 253, 262–65, 267, 273, 293, 296–97, 299, 301–302, 305–306, 308, 318, 321, 325, 335, 339; and *Anabasis* I, 46–47, 78, 89, 93, 109, 162, 181, 187, 190, 201, 206, 248; and *Anabasis* II, 93, 105, 110, 181, 187–88; and *Anabasis* III, 181; and Themistogenes; *see* Themistogenes the Syracusan; as introduction to Greek, 58, 265; as two-part, 21–22, 25, 70; as unitary, 20, 23, 36, 46, 201, 301, 333n46; dream in, 11, 14; memoranda for, 22, 68, 181; Parabasis of, 21–22, 36, 46–47, 93, 152; "publication" of, 22; Skillus in, *see* Skillus

Anderson, J. K., 92–95, 159, 163–64, 169, 306, 316–17, 325, 342

Andocides, 93–94

Antiphon, 4, 133, 210

Anytus, 19, 23, 34–36, 38, 42, 83–84, 88, 190–91

Aphrodite; 80, 274–75; see also *Symposia*, priority of Xenophon's, arguments for:, (4) Parallels between Socrates's Speech in Xenophon's *Symposium* and Pausanias' Speech in Plato's

Apollodorus, 64, 103, 147, 207, 217, 273, 304n84, 332n19

Apollodorus of Cyzicus, 205

Apology of Socrates (Libanius), 301, 314

Apology of Socrates (Plato), 1, 8–9, 32, 70, 75, 78, 86, 120, 127, 155, 196, 198, 201, 204–205, 224, 228, 232, 271, 290, 301n56, 311, 316, 323, 331–32; Plato's artistry in, 204–205; Plato's intention in, 198

Apology of Socrates (Xenophon), 8–9, 15, 19, 35–36, 38, 42, 74–75, 78, 83, 120, 133–34, 151–52, 186, 189, 198, 207–208, 212, 226, 232, 290, 311, 315, 323, 331–32; and *Crito*, 82, 84, 88, 208

ἀπορία, literary, 287

Arginusae, 32, 196–99, 201, 204, 212, 233; as illustration of Plato's debts to Xenophon, 196–98

Aristippus, 59, 129–30, 133, 190, 210, 212, 267–68, 279–80

Aristodemus, 103, 231, 233, 273, 304n84

Aristophanes, 1–2, 174, 214, 290, 298

Aristotle, xiii, 7, 14, 31, 57, 128, 168, 179, 181, 183, 188–89, 202, 214, 221, 223, 225, 236, 247, 251, 283, 291–92, 297, 321, 327, 329, 338–39; acumen, audacity, and poor taste of, 188; and defeat of Athens, 179; and Xenophon, 189; as better example than the Athenian orators and statesmen and of what it meant to be Plato's student, 31

Arnim, Hans von, 74–77, 82, 88, 151, 186, 189, 212–13, 215, 299, 301, 310–11, 313–14, 316

Aspasia, 17–19, 24, 29–32, 147, 239

Athena, 1, 195–96

Athens, xii–xiii, 1, 7, 11–12, 15, 17–19, 25, 27, 29–32, 35, 46, 50, 71, 76, 87–90, 93, 132, 136–39, 144, 162–63, 167–69, 172–81, 185–87, 190, 195–96, 199–207, 219, 223, 226, 241, 245–46, 273, 285, 288, 290, 316n98, 328n92; and deceptive discourse, 290; as "center of Hellas," 316n98; as rejuvenated, 196, 200; as "long gone," 87; as "School of Hellas," 199–200; tragedy of, 82, 84

Athenaeus, 8, 33, 36, 43, 208, 210, 255, 297, 304, 316, 332, 334

Athenian Stranger, 71, 120, 225–26, 228, 234, 237–54, 266–71, 275, 287,

291, 293–94, as fleeing version of
Socrates, 225–26, 228, 335n76; as
Plato's ideal, 237–38, 291, 293
Attic Muse, *see* Xenophon
Attic orators, 31
Attic Tragedy, 290
Augustine, 161
Augustus, 106
Aulus Gellius, 8, 33, 111–12, 115,
188, 222, 255–65, 316, 333–36; and
my title, 255, 258; and the voice
of reason, 258; and this book, 259;
as antidote to the three following
axioms, 111–12; as charitable and
sensitive, 259
axiom, ancient (Literary Rivalry
[between Xenophon and Plato]),
8–10, 33, 36, 39, 67, 78 91–92,
111–12, 120, 163, 186, 201, 208,
237, 257, 260–61, 266–67, 309n13;
as myth, 186; as prejudice, 33,
260; author's challenge to, 237;
explanation of, 8–9
axiom, modern (Plato's
[compositional] Priority), 9–10, 15,
18, 20, 24, 36, 38–39, 52, 54–55,
67, 70, 78–79, 91, 149, 198, 216,
219, 224, 237, 257, 274–75, 301n59,
309n13; 315n81; Achilles Heel
of, 78, 219; as prejudice, 79, 260,
author's challenge to, 237; problem
defenders of Plato's Priority have
failed to face, 80, 275
axiom, ultramodern (ancient and
modern axioms combined), 10,
91, 163, 257; as poisonous fruit,
163; author's polemical stance to,
10

Bacon, Francis, 306n139
Baratieri, Pedro, 324n41, 335n78,
339n48

Breitenbach, H. R., 309n9, 310n15,
333n46
Bridge of Spies, 219
Bryan, William Jennings, 106

Caesar, 106, 191, 206, 330n127
Cavalry Officer, 55, 59, 107, 111,
137–40, 148, 153, 182, 184–85
Chaeronea, 30–31, 179, 195
charity, hermeneutic, 23, 33, 78, 91,
219, 233
Charmides, 5, 8, 11–16, 33, 57, 64,
152, 223, 233, 273, 298n11,
298n12
Charmides, 12–16, 18, 20, 23, 82, 151,
207, 209, 217, 221–22, 227, 253,
273, 293; Plato in, 253
Chaucer, 324n32
Chion of Heraclea, xi–xiii, 30, 46,
207, 263–64, 288–89, 296n16
Churchill, Winston, 22, 59
Cicero, xii, 105–106, 109, 135, 223,
247, 249–50, 289, 296n11; and
Oeconomicus, 106
Clitophon, 21, 43, 151, 211, 222–23,
227, 309n13
Cobet, C. G., 60, 307n155
confession, repentance, conversion,
160–62, 291–94; and Plato, 160–61,
203, 214–15, 292; and Xenophon,
158, 160–62, 169, 179, 203, 214–15,
253, 292; as Socratic, 160–62,
292–94; comparison of Socratic and
Judeo-Christian, 160, 162; greater
difficulty of Socratic, 161–62, 214,
248, 291–92, 294
Constitution of the Athenians, 135–37,
146, 174–76, 178–79, 181, 206,
273–74, 325n47; authenticity of,
174–76, 273–74
Constitution of the Spartans, 134–37,
146, 170–72, 182, 186, 329n111

conversion; *see* confession, repentance, and conversion
Cratylus, 211, 223, 227
Critias, 5, 12–18, 21, 23–24, 33, 49, 52, 61, 64, 81, 90, 157–58, 193, 206, 209, 214, 231, 247, 253, 272–73, 278, 285, 287, 298n21; and Plato's artistry, 81, 247, 278
Critias, 127, 130, 155, 211, 223, 227, 270
Crito, 221
Crito, 82–84, 88–89, 127, 181, 190–91, 198–99, 201, 207–209, 211, 213, 217, 219, 224–28, 230, 232, 260, 271, 285, 288–89
Critobulus, 38–40, 94, 98, 103–105, 107–108, 111, 122, 127, 151–52, 157, 279, 302n73, 317n119
Cynegeticus, 24, 72–73, 89, 93, 107, 112, 138–39, 141–43, 152, 181, 184, 186, 189, 192–93, 199, 228, 262, 264, 324n31; as Xenophon's earliest work, 72, 189
Cyropaedia, xii, 27, 33, 50–51, 55, 69–70, 95, 105–20, 125–28, 134, 135, 137, 139, 152–54, 156, 167–70, 180–83, 187, 229–31, 233–39, 240, 242, 244–45, 249, 254, 256, 260, 262, 264–71, 278, 282, 286–87, 291, 293–94; and *Cyropaedia* I, 119, 181, 187; and *Cyropaedia* II, 126–27, 181; and *Cyropaedia* III, 119, 126–27, 182; and *Epinomis*, 239, 269; and Herodotus, 193; *see also* Herodotus; and *Laws*, 33, 237–39, 262, 265, 268–69, 271, 293–94; and Plato's limits, 254; and *Republic*, 27, 111–18, 256, 262, 265–68; and silence that follows *Gorgias*, 253; and *Sophist*, 237; and *Statesman*, 236, 244, 271; contested reading of, 115, 287; hero of, 245, 247;

last chapter (8.8) of, 114, 118–19, 238–39, 243, 329n111; *Leitmotiv* in, 51, 85; narrator of, 169, 193, 249, 269; Panthea in, 156, 158; "sunny" (vs. "dark") reading of, 115, 121, 238, 242, 267, 287, 291, 320n148, 334n63; title of, 336n7
Cyrus the Great, 50, 69, 105–106, 111, 113–21, 125–28, 133, 154, 156, 158, 169–71, 180, 193, 229, 234–47, 249, 256, 266–72, 285–87, 291, 293–94, 318n135, 319, 320n155; and Alcibiades, 50, 119, 305n110; and piety, 270; and Simonides, 287; and Socrates, 271, 324n43; and the Athenian Stranger, 237; and Thrasymachus, 118, 267; and Xerxes, 50; as Glaucon's perfectly unjust man, 115–16; as Xenophon's hero, 113–16, 162, 239, 245, 320n152, 324n43, generosity of, 111, 115, 126; "less than ideal features of," 334n66
Cyrus the Younger, 20, 89, 105, 109–10, 154, 158, 165, 169, 180–81, 320n152; and Ariaeus, 109–10, obituary of, 154, 180–81

Dakyns, H. G., 26, 55, 58–61, 64, 73–74, 87
Danzig, Gabriel, 295n1, 300n48, 302n73, 323n31, 324n34, 334n68, 337n17, 337n24
deception, deliberate, 247, 284, 287–91; and Chion of Heraclea, 289; and critique of writing in *Phaedrus*, 290; and *Cyropaedia*, 118, 247, 278; and deception-based παιδεία, 272, 275, 278; and "dialectical" sections of *Memorabilia*, 279, 322n18; and εὖ πράττειν, 98; and Odysseus, 289–90, 322n18; and Socratic irony,

247, 290-91; and Simonides, 126; and speech of Lysias in *Phaedrus*, 290; and speech of Socrates in *Phaedrus*, 277-78; and "the noble lie," 289; and Thucydides, 290; as *Leitmotiv* in this book, 287; as pervious, 287; Athenian admiration for, 290; how Xenophon unmasks Plato's artistic use of, 284; how Xenophon unmasks use of it with Meno, 23-24, 206; with Critias, 23-24, 206; with Pausanias, 80-81, 275; immunity from, 269; pedagogical value of, 247; Plato's use of in *Euthydemus*, 288; Plato's use of in *Hippias Major*, 144; Plato's use of in *Hippias Minor*, 289; Plato's use of in late dialogues, 247, 288; Plato's use of in *Menexenus*, 29; Plato's use of in *Protagoras*, 82; Xenophon's use of, 101-102, 110-11
Delebecque, Édouard, 56-57, 60, 63, 90, 92-93, 104, 138, 156, 159, 164, 182, 186-87, 189-90, 201, 301n59, 301n66; and *Where's Wally*, 326n51
Demetrius of Magnesia, 135
Democritus, 7, 131
Demosthenes, 30-31, 179, 181, 289, 329n109, 339n47
"dialectical" defined, 77
Diés, Auguste, 188
Dillery, John, 25-26, 71, 170, 300n39, 326n66
Diodorus Siculus, 29, 329n114
Diodotus, 290
Diogenes Laertius, 8, 68-70, 72, 75-76, 78, 83, 85, 93-94, 132, 135, 158, 183, 185, 190-92, 211-13, 215-17, 255, 261, 293, 334n58
Dion, 289
Dionysius of Halicarnassus, 183, 229, 309n10

Dionysus and Ariadne, 79, 219
Diotima, 18, 38, 94, 100, 102-104, 146-47, 149, 278, 284, 288, 304n84, 317n117
Dorion, Louis-André, xiii, 121, 233, 286-87, 291, 298n5, 308n8, 309n9, 309n13, 310n20, 311n33, 312n43, 312n50, 314n72, 315n81, 317n113, 317n118, 320n152, 321n163, 322n3, 322n18, 323n20, 326n52, 329n106, 330n117, 331n15, 333n46, 334n63, 336n4, 337n38, 337n39, 339n50; and a unitarian *Memorabilia*, 309n9, 309n13, 333n46; and chronology of composition, 331n15; and Literary Rivalry, 309n13; and Plato, 309n13, 322n3, 323n20, 337n39; and Polycrates, 312n50, 314n72, 315n73, 322n3; and *Schutzschrift*, 314n72; and Socrates, 315n81, 339n50; assessment of, 336n4

Eleatic Stranger, 128, 192, 224, 234, 236-37, 254, 268, 270, 293, 333n39
Engler, M. R., 313n63
Epinomis, 68, 153, 182, 211, 227-29, 238, 252, 270, 308n2; and *Cyropaedia* 8.8, 238, 269
Erbse, Hartmut, 60, 233, 307n49, 309n9, 314n72; 333n46, and *Schutzschrift*, 314n72
Eunapius, 323n30
εὖ πράττειν, 86, 96-98, 102, 222, 280, 284, 315n81, 317n108; de-equivocation of, 282; equivocation explained, 96-97
Euripides, 74, 85-86
Euryptolemos, 206
Euthydemus (Xenophon's); 30, 47-65, 68-69, 76, 78, 83-90, 92, 142-44, 155-58, 160-61, 190,

Euthydemus *(continued)*
192, 201, 203–204, 206, 209–10,
214–15, 217, 231, 233, 248, 253,
266, 273, 278, 282, 287, 307n151,
308n162, 324n34, 331n15; and
Alcibiades in *Alcibiades Major*,
47–54, 60, 64, 203–204, 206, 215,
307n151, 331n15; and Alcibiades in
Alcibiades Minor, 54; and Callicles,
83, 87, 253; and Leo Strauss, 61–63;
and sex, 157–58; and Straussians,
307n154; and Theopompus, 248;
as *indoles*, 307n155; as Xenophon,
57–62, 76, 86, 157; conversion
of, 160–61, 253; goals of, 30, 49;
library of, 48–49, 51, 144, 192, 294
Euthydemus (in Plato's *Symposium*),
64–65, 92, 190, 311n39
Euthydemus, 77, 81, 86, 96, 151, 217,
218, 221–23, 227, 280, 282–85,
287–88, 315n81, 323n20, 337n29
Euthyphro, 53, 155, 211, 224, 227–28,
271, 301n56

"fare well"/"do well," see εὖ πράττειν
Ferrari, G. R. F., 310n14
Frisch, Hartvig, 176–78, 273–74

Galen, 151
Gibbon, 191
Gilbert, W. S., 251
Glaucon, 7–16, 29–30, 32–33, 64, 77,
92, 108, 112, 114–16, 147, 152, 215,
223, 233, 243, 247, 253, 267–68,
286, 304n84, 308n64, 312n42,
318n129, 320n155, 329n106
Gorgias, 83, 85–88, 292; and Plato,
86–87; and Xenophon, 85–87
Gorgias, 27–28, 30, 36, 82–84, 87–92,
97, 129, 148, 151, 160–61, 181,
190–91, 198–99, 211, 213, 217–19,
222, 227, 232, 253–54, 260, 290,
292; and Callicles, 253; *see also*
Callicles; and *Crito*, 83–84, 217,
232; and Kapp-Kahn hypothesis, 82,
313n57, 313n61; and *Memorabilia*
I, 253; and Polycrates, 190; *see
also* Polycrates; and the claim that
turned the world upside down,
213; as virtue-dialogue, 22; early
composition of, 83–90; explosive
energy of, 90, 211; Plato in, 87–88,
253; silence that follows, 253
Grand Illusion, 58
Gray, V. J., 121, 233, 238–39, 286,
298n5, 305n100, 308n7, 309n8,
309n9, 310n15, 310n26, 311n40,
320n148, 331n14, 332n26, 332n32,
333n46, 333n48, 334n61, 334n68
Great War (1914–18), 58–59, 63,
73–74, 106, 109, 170, 306n142; as
personal disaster for Xenophon, 58
Gryllus, son of Xenophon, 32, 94–95,
119, 136–37, 158, 181, 185–86, 188,
335n80
Gryllus (Aristotle), 188
Guthrie, W. K. C., 188, 249, 301n54,
302n72, 322n30, 330n118, 335n82;
as judicious, 188
Gyges, 116

Hamilton, Edith, 89–90
Handford, Martin, 57
Hartman, J. J., 11, 58, 298n8
Hegel, G. W. F., 195–96, 301n58
Heidegger, Martin, 265, 336n6
Helbig, Wolfgang, 174–75, 177,
328n87, 328n90
Hellenica, 1, 5, 12–16, 24, 32–34, 46,
55, 57, 68–70, 88, 109, 133–35,
137, 150, 154, 165–69, 174, 176,
179, 193, 197–98, 206, 213, 233,
253, 264; and *Agesilaus*, 172; and
Alcibiades, 17–18, 149, 174, 176,

Index | 363

206, 273, 328n86; and *Alcibiades Major*, 201–202; and *Anabasis*, 20–21, 152–53; and *Apology of Socrates* (Plato's), 197–201; and Chabrias, 338n43; and *Charmides*, 12–16, 20; and *Constitution of the Athenians*, 176; and Critias, 5, 12–18, 21, 49; and Gryllus, 137; and *Hellenica* I, 25–27, 89, 109, 139, 181, 198, 200, 202, 273, 299n26; and *Hellenica* II, 26, 28, 31, 109, 139, 181, 186–87, 191, 202, 239, 248–49; and *Hellenica* III, 26–27, 71, 139, 170, 180, 182, 300n39; and King's Peace, 1, 17, 19, 21–23, 26, 28–32; and *Memorabilia* 3.5, 299n26; and *Menexenus*, 1, 5, 12, 23, 14, 17–33, 150; and *Meno*, 24–25, 33–35, 38; and Plato's anachronisms, 35; and *Protagoras*, 17; and *Symposium* (Plato's), 25; and *Theaetetus*, 234, 334n50; and Themistogenes, 20, 137, 248; *see also* Themistogenes the Syracusan; and the Thirty, 12–13, 18, 20, 163, 175, 325n48; and Thucydides, 16–19, 25, 89, 139, 153, 197; and tyranny, 338n41; and "Where's Xenophon," 156–69, 206, 248, 325n48, 325n49; as a whole, 25, 27, 32, 299n37, 308n7; composition of, 26; confession in, 162, 167–69; first in traditional order, 133–39, 153; narrator of, 248, 335n80; three parts of, 25–27, 70; two parts of, 25
Herippidas, 165, 168
Hermogenes, 15, 19, 57, 59, 63, 68, 75, 81, 83, 89, 92, 152, 190, 205; as Xenophon, 68, 152
Herodotus, 17, 19, 24, 29, 32, 50, 115, 154, 170, 193, 202, 239–44, 249, 266, 272, and Cyrus the Great, 239–41, 272; and Cyrus the Great in *Cyropaedia*, 115, 154, 193, 239, 243, 266; and Cyrus the Great in *Laws*, 241–42, 244, and narrator of *Cyropaedia*, 249; as eighth Wise Man, 193
Hesiod, 8
Hiero, 118–30, 134, 136, 138–39, 152, 170, 180, 182, 231, 261, 286–87, 291, 321n179, 337n36
Hipparchus, 211, 227–28
Hippias Major, 76–77, 81, 103, 127, 144, 146–51, 155, 182, 210–11, 216–17, 220, 223, 227, 260, 282–85, 313n56; and *Memorabilia* 3.8, 76, 149–50, 260, 282, 284–85
Hippias Minor, 57, 127, 146, 148, 199, 210–11, 216–17, 223, 227, 263, 290; and *Memorabilia* 4.2, 57
Hogenmüller, Boris, 207–208, 213, 331n17
Homer, 1, 72, 146–47, 247–48, 289–90, 292, 335n79, 339n48, 339n52; and "the elusive author," 248; Demodocus as, 248; originality of, 247, 289, 339n48
Horace, 200, 269
Horsemanship, On, 19, 107, 137–39, 153, 182, 185–86, 193
Hug, Arnold, 312n53, 332n33
Humbert, Jean, 83, 314n66
Humble, Noreen, 325n44, 326n65, 327n72, 327n79
Hyperides, 30–31, 289

intent, authorial, 2, 61, 184, 283, denial of as deadly, 2
Ion, 127, 145, 148, 205, 211, 223, 317n107, 322n17; and Xenophon, 205
Ischomachus, 38–42, 56, 90, 93–95, 99–108, 111, 120, 150, 186, 236,

Ischomachus *(continued)*
278, 302n73, 303, 304n83, 306n137, 317n119; and Diotima, 94, 103–104
Isocrates, 4, 188, 299n24, 301n53, 322n10, 328n89
Ismenius the Theban, 23–24, 34–36, 42, 45, 315n52

Jażdżewska, Katarzyna, xi, 207
Jefferson, Thomas, 105–106
Jesus, 98, 161
Joël, Karl, 44, 304n99, 337n32
Johnson, D. M., 295n1, 299n27, 305n114, 323n31, 329n114, 332n23, 337n24
Johnson, James Weldon, 318n127
Judenfrei ("Jew-free"), 160
Jünger, Ernst, 265

Kahn, C. H., 82–83, 87, 129, 141, 148, 190, 199, 299n28, 299n29, 309n8, 313, 316n93, 335n; and Kapp-Kahn hypothesis, 82, 129, 190, 199
Kapp, Ernst, 82; *see previous entry*

Laches, 3–5, 12, 221
Laches, 2–5, 12, 82, 151, 211, 221, 227, 297n26
Laws, 120, 211, 219, 224–30, 234, 237–39, 241–42, 244–47, 249–50, 252, 254, 256, 260, 262, 265, 267–71, 275, 287, 291, 293–94, 299n24, 314n68, 335; and Athens, 241, 245–46; and *Cyropaedia*, 237, 294; as "Socratic dialogue," 287; *see also Cyropaedia*, and *Laws*
Lesser Hippias; *see Hippias Minor*
Letters (Plato's), 119, 229
Letters of Chion; *see* Chion of Heraclea
Lincoln, 137, 219

Literary Rivalry; *see* axiom, ancient
Lombardi, Vince, 98
Longinus, 296n21, 331n16, 333n47
Lovers, 81, 144–46, 148–50, 192, 217, 220, 227, 252–53; Plato in, 252–53
Lycurgus (of Athens), 30, 179, 188, 289, 329n109
Lycurgus (of Sparta), 173
Lysander, 109
Lysis, 74, 81–82, 151, 216–17, 221, 223, 225, 227

Machiavelli, 105–107, 136; two faces of, 106
Malosse, Pierre-Louis, 289, 295n6, 295n8, 339n45
Marcellinus Ammianus, 8, 299n37
Marchant, E. C., v, 73–74, 135, 151–52, 265
McBrayer, G. A., 322n8, 328n92
McCloskey, Benjamin, 309n11, 319n137, 320n155, 326n63, 334n67, 335n80
Memorabilia, v, 5, 7–21, 38, 48, 54, 58, 67–83, 95–96, 99, 102, 122, 127, 130, 133, 152–56, 180, 210–11, 216, 231–32; 1.1, 35, 59, 197, 270; 1.2, v, 16–17, 19, 23, 33–35, 49, 75–76, 90, 92, 157–58, 176, 209; 1.3, 55, 57, 152, 157–58, 270; 1.4, 76, 78; 1.6, 210; 2, 76, 78, 96, 98, 100, 188, 233; 2.1, 18, 49, 59, 76, 114, 129–30, 210, 231, 268, 282; 2.2, 92, 96–105, 129, 156, 220, 294; 2.2–10, 96; 2.3, 96, 98; 2.4, 98; 2.5, 98; 2.6, 91, 98, 122, 127, 317n113; 2.10, 98; 3, 76–77, 107, 149, 180, 222–23, 233; 3.1, 13–14, 271; 3.1–7, 12–15, 77–78, 280; 3.1–2, 223; 3.3, 94, 223; 3.4–5, 223; 3.5, 20, 31–32, 111, 211–12; 3.6, 7–15, 18,

29, 64, 69, 108–109, 223, 263, 268, 286; 3.7, 11, 14–15, 18, 64, 152, 223, 263; 3.8, 59, 76–77, 149–50, 210, 216, 218, 231, 260, 263, 280, 282–85, 288; 3.9, 77, 86, 96, 149, 168, 189, 218, 222, 263, 280–85, 288, 337n26; 3.10–12, 77–78; 3.11, 158, 317n113, 324n35; 4, 30, 47, 57, 59, 64, 68, 74–75, 151, 210, 212; 4.1, 99, 158; 4.2, 47–49, 55, 57, 59, 68–69, 75–76, 83, 86–87, 90, 142, 145, 148, 150, 157, 160, 190, 192–93, 201–203, 209–10, 212–14, 225, 248, 266, 278, 282, 292, 294, 296n13; 4.3, 59; 4.4, 77, 88, 197, 285, 288; 4.5, 59, 279; 4.6, 59, 77, 149, 225, 278–80, 288–90; 4.7, 290; 4.8, 15, 75; and Hans von Arnim, 74; *see also* Arnim, Hans von; and Henry Graham Dakyns, 58–59; *see also* Dakyns, H. G.; and *Memorabilia* I, 88–91, 181, 189–91, 198, 201, 216–18, 232, 246, 253, 257, 270; apologetic purpose of, 209; and *Memorabilia* II, 114, 181, 187–88; and *Memorabilia* III, 182; and Polycrates, 35, 75; *see also* Polycrates; as innovative, 127, 231; as unitary, 70, 72, 233, 309n9; composition of, 48, 70, 151, 211–12; "dialectical" stage of, 78, 128, 148–49, 216, 225, 288; dead center of, 99; "editor" of, 70, 310n18; oldest part of, 70, 75, 78, 84, 189; "publication" of, 70; *Schutzschrift* in, 75–76, 83–84, 88, 213, 215, 301n54, 312n50, 314n72; Temporality of Virtue in, 98–101, 129, 233; "three phases" of, 78; *Urmemorablien* in, 76, 78, 82–83, 99; written in installments, 72, 151

Menexenus, 1, 5, 12, 14, 17–34, 81, 127, 145, 147–48, 150, 181, 183, 223, 227, 239, 282, 322n17; *see also Hellenica*, and *Menexenus*
Meno the Thessalian, 23–24, 34–36, 38, 42, 81, 160, 206, 267, 272, 285, 287, 292; and Plato's artistry, 81, 247, 278, in Plato and Xenophon, 301n65
Meno, 20, 22–25, 33–43, 95, 103, 120, 128, 151, 181, 183, 192, 207, 222, 227, 262, 272–73, 278, 300n49, 301n61; as *tombeau de Xénophon*, 34, 42, 128
Miller, Mitch, 285
Miller, Walter, 334n59
Milton, 24
Minos, 211, 227–28, 271
Molière, 161
Morr, Josef, 85–87, 315n75, 316n85

Nicias, 3, 12, Peace of, 79
Niebuhr, 192
Nietzsche, 126, 160–61, 208, 292, 321n170, 324n21, 332n20, disciples of, 160, 321n170
Nuremburg Trials, 164

Odysseus, 84, 86, 173, 232, 247–48, 290, 322n18, as Xenophon, 173: as "the unreliable hero," 247
Oeconomicus, 38–43, 56, 90, 92–96, 99, 102–10, 115, 120, 123, 125–29, 133, 149–52, 154, 156, 163, 165, 181, 186–88, 222, 231, 236, 260, 272, 302n72, 303; and *Meno*, 39, 41; and *Symposium* (Plato's), 38, 94, 100, 102–104, 278; and Xenophon's Socrates, 96; as Xenophon's Socratic masterpiece, 38, 95–96, 100; Sweating Rowers in, 108, 110, 163, 272

366 | Index

Owen, G. E. L., 261
Oxyrhynchus historian, 299n22

Paine, Thomas, 253
Palamedes, 83–87, 290, 323n18
Palamedes (Euripides), 85–86
Palamedes, Defense of (Gorgias), 83, 85–87, 313n67
Pangle, T. L., 297n5, 298n11, 298n18, 303n75, 307n154, 307n155, 324n33, 324n43, 333n43
Parmenides, 131, 224, 251–52
Parmenides, 155, 223, 225, 227, 230, 251; and "my hypothesis," 251–52
Pausanias, 79–81, 91, 224, 247, 272, 274–75, 277–78, 287; and Phaedrus, 79–80, 274–75; and Plato's artistry, 81, 278, 285
Pentateuch, 72
Pericles, 48, 51, 76–77, 147, 176; Funeral Oration of, 147, 173, 193, 199
Pericles the younger, 20, 31–33, 233, 299n26, 308n161
Phaedo, 207–208, 212–13, 218, 220, 225–31, 276, 331n17, 332n20
Phaedrus, 18, 74, 91, 211, 223–25, 227, 275–79, 287, 290, 299n24, 336n2
Philebus, 211, 223, 225, 227, 250, 333n41
Philesia, 93, 101–102, 119, 157–58, 187
Philip of Macedon, 31, 179
Philip of Opus, 308n2
Philo of Alexandria, 74
philology, nineteenth-century, 30, 34, 71–74, 211, 301n54; tools of better applied to Xenophon than Plato, 71–72, 144–45
Phocion, 30, 289
Pindar, 83, 87, 314n67, 314n68

Plato, *passim*; and Allegory of the Cave, 202–203, 219, 285, 318n129; and Aristotle, 189, 223, 225, 251; and Athens, 87–88; and chronology of composition, 72; and pedagogical deception, 91; *see also* deception, deliberate, and poetry, 147, 290–91; and rhetoric, 30, 147, 160, 253, 290–91; and the historical novel, 204; and Socratic Irony, 247; and "Socratic phase," 250; and *Timaeus*, 128, 223, 249–51, 257, ; and Xenophon, 251; and Xenophon's courage, 215; and Xenophon's tools/methods, 205, 219, 272, 284; and Xenophon's villains, 206; artistry of, 23, 81, 196, 206, 208, 211, 219, 272; as artist, 206, 213, 272; as master of Attic prose, 185; as dramatist, 71, 209–10, 217; as genius, 261; as giant, 4, 27, 43, 220; as great thinker, 185; as Pythagorean, 225; as Socratic; *see* Socratic, Plato as; as philosopher, 27, 71, 185; as philosopher of unchanging Idea, 71; as standing on shoulders of giants, 23, 190, 286; as teacher, 27, 71, 201–202; as writer, 43; as writing in the Athenian twilight, 195; audience of (ancient), 2–3, 103, 197, 201–202, 263–64, 272; audience of (eternal), 2, 4, 32, 196–97, 202, 205, 263, 272; debts to Xenophon, 55, 81, 232, 261, 270; hypothesis of, 252; most important question facing interpreters of, 2, 132–33, 262–63; paradox of the preserved past in, 203; rejuvenated Athens, 196
[Plato] and Xenophon, 43, 64, 215–16, 303n74, 304n95
Platonic Love, 80, 294; as Socratic 80
Platonism, 9–10, 30, 46, 202, 278, 283–85, 289, 294, 339n47; and

Xenophon, 10, 202, 283, 285; emergence of, 283, 285; later apolitical forms of, 30; outer reaches of, 9
Plato's Priority, *see* axiom, modern
Plotinus, 30, 289, 300n45, 334n54, 339n47
Plutarch, 171, 179, 204, 273, 298n21, 329n109, 331n12
Pohlenz, Max, 74, 300n51, 301n64, 310n23
Polycrates, 19, 34–35, 75, 78, 83–84, 87–88, 181, 189–91, 201, 310n26, 312n50, 314n70, 314n72, 315n73, 322n3
Pope, Alexander, 270
"possession into eternity" (κτῆμα εἰς ἀεί), 2, 4–5, 29, 132–33, 198–200, 203, 262, 285; *see also* Plato, most important question facing interpreters of
Poroi; *see Ways and Means* or *Poroi*;
Procles of Phlion, 57
Prodicus, 18, 49, 78, 130, 268
Protagoras, 9, 16–18, 23–24, 37, 52–54, 77, 81–82, 84, 89, 120, 129, 133, 140–46, 148–51, 155, 181, 189, 191, 199, 209, 213, 216–17, 220–21, 225, 227–28, 231–32, 264, 281, 288, 292, 313n61, 322n15; and *Cynegeticus*, 141–43, 228, 264; as post-apologetic, 209; Protagoras overcome by pleasure in, 143; sympathetic portrait of Protagoras in, 142

Quintilian, 300n43
Quixote, 130

"Reading Order of Plato's dialogues, the," 140
Relay Race, 190, 259–60, 262–63, 265, 267–68, 272, 278, 285, 294

repentance; *see* confession, repentance, and conversion
republics, 105–107; a harmless Caesar as dangerous to, 191; Florentine, 107, 136; North American, 106; Roman, 105–106, 191
Republic, 1, 9–11, 14–15, 18, 20–21, 27, 29–30, 40, 57, 69, 72, 77–78, 81, 108–109, 111–19, 122, 128–30, 142, 151, 155, 172, 181, 183, 187–88, 191, 213, 217–18, 221–22, 227, 229–30, 232, 240, 244, 252–53, 256–57, 262, 265–68, 283–84, 286–87, 289–91, 298n6; and "Choice of Heracles," 78, 114; and *Clitophon*, 21; and *Memorabilia* 3.6, 10; and *Cyropaedia*, 27, 69, 111–18, 187, 244; and Prodicus, 78; and *Thrasymachus*, 21; six-book version, 319n139

Sallust, 168
Satan, 24
Schleiermacher, F. E. D., 43–45, 52, 156, 259; on Xenophon, 304n98
Schorn, Stephan, 121–23, 127–28, 130, 152, 286
Schutzschrift; *see Memorabilia*, and *Schutzschrift*
Schwartz, Eduard, 82
Second Alcibiades; *see Alcibiades Minor*
Shakespeare, 24, 68, 120–21, 123, 125, 133, 143, 170, 206–207, 265, 270, 279, 293
Skemp, J. B., 234–37
Skillus, 22–23, 47, 56, 78, 89, 93–96, 110, 119, 168, 180–82, 184, 186–89, 201; reward of, 168
Socrates, *passim*; and self-knowledge, 52; as boring pedant, 58; as down-to-earth and Idea-less, 44;

Socrates *(continued)*
as garrulous dispenser of insipid homilies, 251; as Plato's hero, 23, 219; as preachy know-it-all, 96; as Xenophon's hero, 78, 84, 114; boys of, 294, son of, 100; Funeral Oration for, 33; kept alive in all his dialectical and ironic complexity, 184, 201
"Socrates schooled," 40–42, 103, 278, 302n73
Socratic, *passim*; and μεγαλοψυχία, 214–15; and pseudo- or non-Socratics, 122, 130 (Simonides), 206 (Meno and Critias), 247 (Cyrus and Pausanias), 287 (Simonides, Cyrus, Timaeus, and the two Strangers); and Socratic παιδεία, 270; method, 95; Plato as, xiii, 8–9, 82, 213, 223, 249–50; what it means to be a, 249–50; Xenophon as, xiii, 4, 9, 44, 58, 61, 95, 220, 251, 324n31; 325n44; Xenophon and Plato as, xiii, 9, 15, 19, 27, 72, 92, 249, 286; Xenophon and Plato as two greatest Socratics, 33, 183, 224, 247, 332n34
Socratic ignorance, 95–96, 281, and the confession of ignorance, 160–61
Socratic intellectualism, 86, 263, 281, 323n20
Socratic Irony, 247, 269, and "elusive author," 269; and "unreliable hero," 269; eternal dance of, 290
Socratic Paradox, 37–38, 281, 291–92
"Socratic Question," xiii, 76, 336n4, 338n39
Solon, 293
Sophist, 53, 128, 155, 182, 211, 224–25, 227, 237, 244, 247, 254, 261, 268–71, 275, 287, 309n13
Sophocles, 330n121
Sophron, 7, 211
Spinoza, 270

Statesman, 118, 155, 182, 211, 224–25, 227, 233–37, 241, 244, 247, 254, 268–69, 271, 275, 287
Strauss, Leo, 61–63, 115, 121, 130, 170–72, 225, 298n9, 298n12, 298n17, 302n73, 304n85, 307n152, 307n153, 307n157, 307n160, 308n161, 320n148, 320n160, 321n170, 321n178, 326n67, 327, 333n42; and Athenian Stranger, 225, 333n42; and Charmides, 298n12; and Euthydemus, *see* Euthydemus (Xenophon's), and Leo Strauss; and Nietzsche, 321n170; and *Oeconomicus*, 302n73; and Simonides, 121, 130; and Sparta, 170–72; as unreliable interpreter of Xenophon, 62
Symposia, 8–9, 43, 69, 78, 90–91, 93, 218, 223–24, 272–78; priority of Xenophon's, 78–81, 90–92, 218, 272–78; arguments for: (1) Plato's addition of tragic element, 79; (2) Plato's Priority convicts Xenophon of poor taste, 79, 91; (3) Plato's Priority convicts Xenophon of careless reading/copying, 80, 91, 274; (4) Parallels between Socrates' Speech in Xenophon's *Symposium* and Pausanias' Speech in Plato's, 80, 224, 272, 274, 277; (5) Plato's use of deliberate deception, 81, 272; (6) Great Speech in *Phaedrus*, 223–24, 274–77; (7) deceptive Pausanias characteristic of Plato's artistry, 272; (8) Priority of Plato's *Symposium* to *Phaedrus*, 277; (9) Relay Race metaphor, 278; (10) sexy substitution, 79, 273; importance of the question, 218, 313n55
Symposium (Plato's), 1–3, 8, 16, 24–25, 40, 43, 69, 78–81, 88–95, 103–104, 127, 142, 144–51, 177, 181, 190–91,

199, 213, 216–22, 227, 230, 232, 255, 260, 272–74, 276, 278, 283–84; and *Hellenica*, 24; and *Menexenus*, 25; and *Oeconomicus*, 103–104; and *Phaedrus*, 277; and Thucydides, 2, and Xenophon, 40, 94; as both comic and tragic, 79, 88; as τέλος, 81; sexualized pederasty in, 80, 274–75, substitution of Alcibiades' drunken speech for sexy pantomime in, 79, 273

Symposium (Xenophon's), 8–9, 16, 38, 40, 57, 63, 68–69, 78–82, 84, 89–93, 100, 102, 133, 148–49, 151–52, 158, 181, 187, 218–19, 222, 224, 232, 272–74, 277–79, 294; and *Gorgias*, 82, 84, 91, 191, 218; as comic, 79, 81, 88, 218; as delightful and productive, 82, 92, 232; Hermogenes in, 63, 68, 152; Pausanias in, 274; sexualized pederasty in, 80, 89, 158, 275; sexy pantomime in, 79, 273

Syracuse, disaster in the Great Harbor of, 2, 79, 174

Taurus, 335
Teleutias, 165–69, 326n66
teshuvah, 161
Theaetetus, 18, 53, 155, 223–24, 227–28, 233–34, 288, 301n56
Theages, 43, 151, 211, 222, 227, 303n74, and *Oeconomicus*, 303n77
Themistocles, 137
Themistogenes the Syracusan, 20, 22, 24, 45, 56, 109, 137, 152, 158–59, 248, 308n160, 325n45, 335n80
Theognis, 301n61
Theopompus, as Xenophon, 57–58, 156, 248
Thomas Aquinas, 256
Thrasyllus, 53, 132–33, 135, 140, 150–51, 153, 211, 223, 322n2

Thrasymachus, 116–18, 188, 267
Thucydides, 2–5, 7, 12, 16–19, 24–26, 28–29, 32, 71, 87, 89–90, 133, 139, 147, 153, 155, 159, 170, 178–79, 181, 184, 192, 197–200, 202–207, 239, 262, 273, 290, 330n134; and "a possession into eternity," 2, 200; and *Constitution of the Athenians*, 174–75, 192–93; and *Hellenica*; see *Hellenica*; and Thucydides; and Melian Dialogue, 87; and Plato, 3–5, 7, 139, 202, 262; and *Symposium* (Plato's), 273; and Xenophon, 173, 192–93, 200; see also *Hellenica*; and Thucydides; composition of, 299n37
Timaeus, 7, 128, 155, 211, 223–27, 246, 249–51, 253, 257, 265, 270, 272, 275–76, 287; Plato in, 253

Verfasser meaning, 43
Vergil, 105–106
virtue, *passim*; as instrumental, 130; as knowledge, 96; see also Socratic intellectualism, as utilitarian, 96, 98, 100–101, speaks, 130; temporality of, see *Memorabilia*, Temporality of Virtue in
Vlastos, Gregory, 222, 281, 297n26, 303n74, 309n13, 338n39
voilà la course de relais, 198, 247

Ways and Means or *Poroi*, 107, 111, 135–37, 139, 146, 148, 171–72, 179–80, 182, 185, 329n106
Whitman, 94
"who is?," 43
Wilamowitz-Moellendorff, Ulrich von, 74, 82, 310n18, 314n68, 314n69
womanly humanism, 102, 317n20

Xanthippe, 100, 102

Xenophon, *passim*; and Aristotle, 31, 179; and Athens, 92, 104, 136–37, 167, 172–79, 207, 233; and bestowing benefits, 91, 294; and eternity, 184–85; and Funeral Oration of Pericles, 173, 193; and "philosopher," 323n31; and Plato, 185, 207, 219, 294; and Plato's tricks, 272; and sex, 156–58; and Socratic Irony, 247; and the horse, 77, 137–38, 294; and the preserved past, 202–203; and "the Socratic dialogue," 204, 215; and Thucydides, 192–93; and Xenophon-haters, 60; artistry of, 115, 177–78, 233; as able to lead and to follow, 91; as artist, 61, 115; as Athenian, 193; as "Attic Muse," 69, 261, 265; as boring pedant, 58; as "careless copyist," 79, 91; as "cool," 264; as critic of Platonic Idealism, 91; 300n49, 303n79; as eloquent, xii; as εὐτράπηλος, 101, 193; as general, 55–56, 58; as handsome, xii, 67–68; as human being, 92; as incompetent defender of a morally bankrupt pragmatism, 102; as indispensable, 23, 43; as innovator, 90–91, 185, 191, 232, 285; as intellect, 251; as first (πρῶτος), 67–70, 75, 78, 83, 190–91, 211–17, 231, 262; as giant, 190; as Procles, 57; as proto-Machiavellian, 93, 106; as "school of Hellas," 173; as Socratic, 58, 95, 193; *see also* Socratic, Xenophon as; as "subtle Socratic," 61, as surpassed by Plato, 78, 185; as trail blazer, 72, 90–91, 127–28, 231; as tyrant-friendly, 13, 15; as "unreliable narrator," 249; as "voice of a friendly stranger," 265; as writer, 43, 55, 58; character of, 84, 91–92; characterized, 92; confession of, 165; contempt for, 304n100; courage of, xii, 296n16; moral greatness of, 192; πολυμαθία of, 193; Socratic method of, 95; unselfishness of, 101, 294

"Xenophonic," 265

Xenophon's Priority, xi, 37, 48, 54–55, 68–70, 78, 213–14, 216, 233, 262–65, 272, 284; traditional defense of, 213; as "Eternal Priority," 262–63, 284; as pedagogical, xi–xii

Xenophon's works (*see individual titles*); traditional order of, *see* Academic editor

Xerxes, 50, 244

www.ingramcontent.com/pod-product-compliance
Lightning Source LLC
Chambersburg PA
CBHW031417230426
43668CB00007B/335